'013

Roger J A Wilson

A Guide to the
ROMAN REMAINS
IN BRITAIN

With a foreword by
the late Professor J M C Toynbee

and with an Appendix by
Matthew Symonds

Fourth edition

Constable • London

To the memory of my Mother and my Father

who first encouraged my love
of Roman archaeology and
who tolerated countless
detours in search of Roman Britain

The author and publisher would like to record with gratitude and sorrow the contribution made to this book by Joanne Thompson, who was largely responsible for typesetting this fourth edition, but who unexpectedly and tragically died at the age of 30 on February 25th 2002.

This fourth edition published in the UK in 2002 by Constable,
an Imprint of Constable & Robinson Ltd
3 The Lanchesters
162 Fulham Palace Road
London W6 9ER

www.constablerobinson.com

913. 42

1403664

First edition 1975
Second edition 1980
Third edition 1988 (reprinted 1996)
Copyright © 1974, 1980, 1988, 2002 Roger J A Wilson

British Library Cataloguing in Publication Data
Wilson, Roger John Antony
A guide to the Roman Remains in Britain - 4th ed
1 Great Britain - Antiquities, Roman
1 Title
936.1'04 DA145

ISBN 1 84119 318 6

Printed in the EU

Cover illustrations: (front) Castle Nick milecastle and Hadrian's Wall, looking east; (back) Rockbourne Roman villa, detail of baths in north wing; (spine) tombstone of Ahteha daughter of Nobilis, who died aged five, in Corbridge Museum
(all photographs © R J A Wilson)

Opposite: 1   Dorchester Museum, shale table-leg

Contents

List of Illustrations

Maps

Photographs, plans and line-drawings

Illustration credits

Photographs
Colchester and Essex Museum: 45; Crown Copyright Reserved: 16, 104, 118; *Illustrated London News*: 137; Newcastle upon Tyne Museum of Antiquities: 2; National Museum of Wales: 64; Otto Fein, Warburg Institute: 1, 21, 28, 139; Trustees of the British Museum: 140; University of Cambridge (J K St Joseph): 17, 86; Verulamium Museum: 48

The following photographs were taken by the author, by courtesy of the following museums and organizations: Corinium Museum, Cirencester: 36; Leicester Museums: 61; National Museum of Wales: 67; Yorkshire Museum: 81; Trustees of the Senhouse Collection: 89; Hull Museums: 93; Museum of Antiquities, Newcastle upon Tyne: 123, 124; The (former) National Museum of Antiquities, Edinburgh (now the Museum of Scotland): 127; Hunterian Museum, University of Glasgow: 129; Historic Scotland: 135 (drawing by Mike Moore, courtesy of David Breeze); Trustees of the British Museum: 141–4.

Also taken by the author: 3, 6–8, 12–13, 18, 20, 22, 24, 29, 33, 38, 40–1, 43, 46, 49–55, 57, 60, 62, 65–6, 69, 71–2, 75–6, 78–9, 83–4, 88, 90–2, 96, 98–9, 103, 105–8, 110–11, 113–17, 119, 121–3, 130–2, 138

Line drawings
4: after J Ward, *Romano-British buildings and earthworks* (1911), fig. 83 opposite p. 274; **5** after J S Johnson, *Richborough and Reculver* (1987), 7; **9** after A Harmsworth, *Roman Canterbury* (1994), 32; **11** after J E Bogaers, *Britannia* 10 (1979), 245, fig. 2 (by courtesy of the Society for the Promotion for Roman Studies); **12** after B Cunliffe, *Fishbourne Roman Palace: a guide to the site* (1994), 30; **14** after *Sussex Archaeological Collections* 133 (1995), 182, fig. 62; **15** after D S Neal, *Lullingstone Roman villa* (1991), 6–7; **19** after G C Boon, *The Roman town at Calleva Atrebatum at Silchester, Hampshire: a new guide* (1963), back cover; **22** after *Littlecote Roman villa: illustrated guide* (1994), 9; **26** after *RIB* I, 2233; **27** after *House for all seasons; a guide to the Roman villa at Brading* (1988), 17; **30** after K Branigan and P J Fowler (eds.), *The Roman West Country* (1976), 185, fig. 46; **31** after B Cunliffe and P Davenport, *The temple of Sulis Minerva at Bath* I (1988), 177, fig. 99; **37** P Leach, *Great Witcombe Roman Villa, Gloucestershire. A report on excavations by Ernest Greenfield, 1960–1973* (1998), 4, fig. 4; **39** after R Goodburn, *The Roman Villa at Chedworth* (1972), fig. 3 facing p. 59; **42** after D R Wilson and D Sherlock, *North Leigh Roman villa, Oxfordshire* (1980), folding plan at back, and *Britannia*

Foreword

by the late Professor J M C Toynbee

Archaeology, the study of the material, as contrasted with the written, evidence for history, is now firmly entrenched as an important element in a liberal education. It can be studied at school and as part, or even as the whole, of a degree course in most universities; whilst the television, the radio and adult education classes have placed it within the reach of anyone who has not been confronted with it at the normal student stage. The majority of people would seem to be particularly impressed by the relics of the earliest periods, in this country by the monuments that ante-date the Norman Conquest. And of such series of early monuments none is more rewarding or exciting to investigate than those of Romano-British times, of the 400 years during which this island was a province of a highly civilized world, at once unified and intensely diversified, that stretched from the Euphrates to the Tyne and Solway, from the Sahara to the Rhine and Danube.

In our present age, with its passion for reality and urge to be ever on the move, no one who is interested in Romano-British archaeology can be content to look at photographs and read descriptions in books. He must be up and out to see the actual monuments, whether in town or country or within museum walls. He must have first-hand knowledge of the things he has heard about; and it is the purpose of the present work to help him (particularly if he is a 'layman') to find out how that knowledge may be gained. No Romano-British earthwork or building or collection of objects has escaped the author's net: those most worthy of the reader's attention are given full descriptions in the text, and the rest can be pursued with the help of information given in the appendices. Nearly every site he has personally visited and checked in 1971 or 1972. These journeys he has done by car – a possession now so almost universal that probably most of the users of this guide will follow him on wheels. But his minute and crystal-clear instructions as to how to find a given site will be just as valuable to the humbler, but no less energetic, non-car-owner, travelling by train, bus, and finally on foot. The present book is, in fact, unique for the comprehensiveness of its contents and for the detail contained in its directions. Quite a number of items little known even to specialists are noted in its pages. If the Introduction covers ground with which some will already be familiar, it will usefully draw the threads of their knowledge together and provide the neophyte with the basic information, succinctly set out, for appreciating what he sees. The numerous illustrations are a very welcome and conspicuous feature.

As the author states, the substance of this guide is primarily factual. But his always lucid and unpedantic and often vivid style of writing brings all the facts to life. He will certainly succeed in kindling his readers' interest and enthusiasm by his personal approach – an approach in which a living scholarship and a controlled imagination are happily blended.

JMCT

From the Preface to the First Edition

In writing this book I have received help from many people. They include Graham Tingay, Elizabeth Dwiar, Stephen Johnson, Sheppard Frere, Cecilia and Roy Dyckhoff, my brother Donald, Patricia Drummond and Kevin Shaughnessy. I am equally grateful to those who gave me access to land, answered queries and contributed, usually unwittingly, to the contents of this book. Several museums have given permission to reproduce copyright material: this is acknowledged in the list of illustrations above.

My greatest debt is to the two people who have read the typescript in full. Firstly, my friend John Crawshaw, who spent countless hours ironing out the inconsistencies and aberrations of my English style, always with alarmingly keen perceptiveness. Secondly, Professor Jocelyn Toynbee, who made many useful comments on my manuscript and has kindly contributed a generous foreword. But my debt to her is also a much wider one: from the time I went up to Oxford as an undergraduate she has always taken a warm interest in my studies, and encouraged and helped me in numerous ways. To all these, and many others, I am deeply grateful.

A book of this kind is unfortunately doomed to be out of date in some respect even before it appears in print; to the best of my knowledge everything is correct at the time of going to press. In case the book should have a second edition, I shall be very grateful to receive any information about omissions and mistakes.

RJAW, *Palmero, March 1973*

Preface to the Second Edition

In the seven years which have elapsed since the preparation of the first edition, Romano-British archaeology has expanded as never before. The sheer volume of excavation work has been enormous, and there have been corresponding advances in knowledge. Most sites have been dug in advance of destruction and do not therefore feature in this book, but the pace of modern development, particularly construction of new roads, together with archaeological changes, made it evident that a second edition could not be prepared from the armchair. At a time when my research interests have been wholly directed overseas, I am grateful to a number of friends and colleagues who have kept me abreast of recent developments and checked over a dozen sites: they include Roger Goodburn, Stephen Johnson, Christina Hooi, Brian and Elizabeth Merriman, Kenneth Milne and Peter Wiseman. But of the remaining 217 places selected for the first edition, 183 were visited by myself over a period of twenty-five days in September 1978 and March 1979. Six sites in the first edition have been removed or relegated to Appendix One, but thirteen make an appearance for the first time. Few of the other entries have been left unaltered, and sometimes the changes have been substantial. This is, therefore, I hope, as fully revised an edition as circumstances will allow. I should like to thank all those who have taken the trouble to write to me with information about changes, omissions and mistakes, and I would be grateful to readers for further information in case the book should ever go into a third edition.

RJAW, *Trinity College Dublin, 1st July 1979*

Preface to the Third Edition

The past nine years have not seen quite the same amount of
hectic archaeological activity which marked the heady days of
the 1970s, but excavation and research have of course
continued to make major advances in our knowledge of
Roman Britain, necessitating substantial alterations in this
book. To keep the price within bounds the publishers have
allowed me to make text changes provided that the pagination
was not affected, and to include a section of supplementary
material at the end of the book. The signal to turn to this
section is a double asterisk (**) in the margin of the main text
at the appropriate places. Sixteen new sites are included for
the first time, but five places mentioned in the second edition
can now be excluded, three because they are no longer
regarded as Roman (Carisbrooke, Blackpool Bridge,
Blackstone Edge), two because they have been backfilled
(Kingscote, Combley). If the main text of this edition looks
superficially similar to that of the second edition, appearances
are deceptive: more than 60 per cent of the pages have received
some alteration, and in many cases this has been substantial.
Opening hours have also been revised in accordance with the
latest available information, and the select bibliography has
been thoroughly updated. My debts as usual are many;
warmest thanks go especially to Sally Stow, Heather Goodhue,
Roger Ling, Tim Potter and above all Max White, most
enthusiastic and regular of correspondents. The finishing
touches were put, and the proofs read, in the congenial
surroundings of the Archäologisches Institut in Bonn, where
I owe much to the hospitality of Professor Nikolaus
Himmelmann and the generosity of the Alexander von
Humboldt Stiftung.

RJAW, *Bonn, October 1987*

Preface to the Fourth Edition

This year marks the thirtieth anniversary of my receiving the contract to write the first edition of this book, and I am gratified that the continuing demand for it has encouraged the publishers to issue a fourth edition. Much has changed since the third edition of 1988, both archaeologically and in terms of access, and the text has been expanded and considerably rewritten, making this by far the most substantial revision since the original edition of 1975 – a comparison of this book with the third edition will reveal major changes on virtually every page. I have also taken the opportunity of adding 21 new sites, some of them (like the bridge abutment at Swainshill, or the villa at Orpington) fresh discoveries, others (like the camps at Troutbeck) promoted to the main text from Appendix 1. Nevertheless the total number of new sites in Britain preserved on permanent display in the decade (and more) since the last edition is disappointing: of the numerous Roman excavations in Britain each year, the political will and the appropriate funding for permanent preservation are rarely forthcoming. It is significant that both the important additions in recent years to the small number of permanently accessible Roman villas in Britain, those of Littlecote and Crofton Road Orpington, were the outcome of purely private initiatives, and that the outstanding Segedunum project at Wallsend was the result of local enterprise backed up by regional, European and lottery funding. The contrast with the policies pursued by our European partners, where the *mise en valeur* and presentation of new Roman sites to the public have accelerated significantly in countries like Germany, France and Italy during recent years, could not be starker.

A handbook of this kind cannot be satisfactorily revised from the study, and between October 2000 and October 2001, therefore, virtually every site in this book was personally visited and checked by me, a process necessarily interrupted by the outbreak of Foot and Mouth disease in February 2001: indeed at the time of writing a very few sites are still closed and inaccessible to me. I was fortunate to be accompanied on many of these visits by my pupil Matthew Symonds: his sharp eye and shrewd reading of monuments on the ground have materially enriched this book, and I am most grateful to him for his stimulating company and his very real practical help. He has also kindly compiled Appendix 2. My debts to others are, as usual, many. Several friends and colleagues opened up sites for me at irregular times and supplied helpful information and offprints: they include David Breeze (Edinburgh), Tony Butler (Newport, IOW), Michael Jones (Lincoln), Sylvia Jones (Lydney), Richard Keen (Dolaucothi), Lawrence Keppie (Glasgow), Brian Philp (Dover), Steve Wallis (Dorchester), Hedley Swain and Jenny Hall (London), and Robin and Andrew Birley (Vindolanda). I am grateful too to Mandy Suheimat (Bideford), who very kindly verified details of access to the Roman fortlet at Martinhoe; to Krystyna Matyjaszkiewicz for sending me details about a recent change of access at Canterbury; to Janet and Jonathan Slack for spending part of their holiday checking Cornish sites for me; and to my brother Donald, who assisted in tracking down some of the more scattered relics of Roman Lincoln as well as updating a site in Appendix 1. Ian Roberts (Rochester, Northumberland) generously and enthusiastically shared his unrivalled knowledge of Redesdale with me, and performed many other kindnesses. Janet and Jonathan Slack (Bradford-on-Avon), Zosia and Ian Archibald (Chester), Lawrence Keppie (Glasgow), James Megoran (Pitney, Somerset), John Serrati (St Andrews), and Malcolm and Linda Symonds (Ashtead) provided warm and very welcome hospitality; an especial debt of gratitude, however, is due to Jonathan and Maíre West (Horsley, Northumberland), most generous of hosts, for putting up with my frequent invasions of their wonderful home. Pete Duncan at Constable & Robinson has been the most patient, understanding and accommodating of publishers. My wife Charlotte has as ever been tolerant of my continual comings and goings; this and many other of my projects would never have reached fruition without her constant and loving support. To Martin Turner (East

Grinstead), most regular of correspondents, I am also most grateful for alerting me to inaccuracies and to other necessary alterations. Inevitably, however, a work of this nature is likely to be out of date even before it is published, and I urge readers to let me know of changes, in case this handbook should ever reach a fifth edition.*

RJAW, *Rome, British School at Rome, November 2001*

* In the interim I intend to help readers with access to the Internet by posting substantial changes which come to my notice on www.roman-remains.info
E-mail address for notification of changes:
roger.wilson@nottingham.ac.uk

Introduction

Purpose

This book is intended to be a guide to the visible remains of Roman Britain. It does not pretend to give a balanced or complete picture of Britain under the Roman Empire; for that the reader must turn to one of the books listed at the beginning of Appendix 3. It is designed primarily for the ordinary individual who has an interest in his Roman past but no prior specialized knowledge (some background information has therefore been provided in the second half of this introduction); but I also hope that the book may be found useful by those who have been confronted with Roman Britain in the classroom or lecture-hall and who want to know precisely how much of the places they have learnt about remains permanently accessible.

I have also tried to make this guide a comprehensive survey of *all* the antiquities of Roman Britain which are visible *in situ*, with the following exceptions:

(a) Roman linear works, e.g. roads, frontiers, canals. It has been impossible to describe *every* visible portion of these. On Hadrian's Wall, for example, there are long lengths of unconsolidated Wall, including milecastles and turrets, which are not described, and earthworks in the near vicinity, such as the numerous well preserved temporary camps, are not mentioned at all. Visitors anxious to track all these extra antiquities down will need to resort to J Collingwood Bruce, *Handbook to the Roman Wall* in its latest edition (currently the 13th, 1978), and also the *Ordnance Survey Historical Map and Guide to Hadrian's Wall*. Readers interested in Roman roads will find a complete record in I D Margary, *Roman Roads in Britain* (Baker, rev. edn 1973), and only a few outstanding stretches have been included in this book. Further details about visiting Roman roads can be found in the works listed in the relevant sections of Appendix 3, where I have tried to include all recent regional monograph titles known to me which deal with the tracing of Roman roads on the ground.

(b) The vast majority of native settlements inhabited during the Roman period, as there are many thousands of these. A handful of them has been included (in Chapters 2, 6 and 7), in order to give a slightly more balanced picture of the countryside in Roman times.

(c) Sites such as mines and quarries which were used in Roman times but also later, and where it is not certain which, if any, of the workings visible today are Roman.

(d) Antiquities claimed as Roman but of which the Roman date is unlikely or unproven.

Ground-plans of Roman buildings marked out in modern materials, and Roman remains removed from their original positions, are not normally included. Nor have I attempted to cover the topic of the re-use of Roman building materials in later structures (although I mention examples of these incidentally): this is now admirably covered in T Eaton, *Plundering the Past: Roman stonework in medieval Britain* (Stroud: Tempus 2000) (and for Hadrian's Wall, refer to A M Whitworth's *Hadrian's Wall: some aspects of its post-Roman influence on the landscape* [British Archaeological Reports, British Series 296] [Oxford: Archaeopress 2000]). Some museums are described, others merely mentioned in passing: although I have discussed many collections in more depth in this edition than in previous ones, few have received the space they deserve. Most of the important collections are listed in Appendix 2.

For each site I have tried to give answers to the questions that I think will be asked by the visitor, i.e. when was it built, why was it built, and what was the purpose of x and y. This means that nearly all my account is factual, and I have rarely had the space to provide 'atmospheric colouring'. This I hope readers will supply for themselves at each individual site. For imagination *is* required when visiting Romano-British remains: if you treat knobbly little bits of wall as knobbly little bits of wall you are going to be disappointed. There are no Roman monuments in this country which can compare with the Pont du Gard in Provence, the aqueduct at Segovia in Spain, the temples at Baalbeck in the Lebanon or the amphitheatre at El Djem in Tunisia; Roman buildings in Britain are generally reduced to little more than their foundations. The reason is partly that few such colossal structures were ever built here, partly that our country has been intensively inhabited and cultivated since Roman times, robbing or destroying Roman structures in the process, and partly that the British climate deals unkindly with ancient structures. I hope, therefore, that with the knowledge of a little background history, and with some idea of their original appearance, you will be able to picture these places when they were not dead relics but thronging with people and alive with activity.

How to Use this Book

The main text. I have found from experience that to link all the sites in a given area with a single itinerary is impractical. It is infuriating if you happen to be doing the route in the reverse order; and often you will want to see places other than Roman sites, and so the itinerary carefully provided by the author becomes useless. In each chapter of this book, therefore (with the exceptions mentioned below), I have paid little attention to the geographical proximity of one site to another, but have grouped them according to the character of the remains, i.e. forts, towns, villas. When you wish to visit some Roman sites, first look at the map on p. 1 which will show you which chapter covers the area you are interested in. Then turn to the beginning of that chapter, where a map is given showing all the sites discussed in the section, and work out your own itinerary from there. In some cases it has proved impossible to treat each site in isolation, especially where several exist very close together. This applies in particular to the Stainmore Pass (Chapter 7), Dere Street from Corbridge to the Scottish border (Chapter 9, §1), and to Hadrian's Wall (Chapter 8) and the Antonine Wall (Chapter 9, §2). Here I have had to link sites together to form a coherent itinerary, and I can only apologize to those who have to visit these places in the reverse order. I hope that some, at least, of my directions will still be helpful after they have been 'translated' (i.e. for 'left' read 'right' etc.).

Particular stress has been laid on giving directions to monuments. The only map I assume you will have is a decent large-scale Road Atlas of which many are widely available. I do *not* expect readers to have any 1:50,000 Ordnance Survey maps, except in a few instances where I have explicitly said so. You will, of course, find them helpful if you do have them, and a six-figure National Grid reference is therefore included in brackets after the name of every place. At each site I have talked about 'left' and 'right' wherever practicable, but this is often not possible and indicating the points of the compass are the inevitable alternative.

Outstanding remains which I consider deserve a special effort to see have been given a double asterisk (**). Other sites which are particularly interesting and instructive of their type have been given a single asterisk (*). The standard, however, is only set in relation to the other sites *in the same chapter*, and not to the book as a whole. Thus, High Rochester (p. 540) would have no chance of a double asterisk if it were situated on Hadrian's Wall; it receives one because it preserves stone remains, in contrast to most of the other sites of Chapter 9, which are earthworks.

Inevitably, technical expressions keep recurring in a book of this nature. Rather than waste space explaining these each time they occur, I have grouped them together in a Glossary following this Introduction (p. 30). Roman names of forts and towns are usually given where they are known: note that in Latin V is used both as a consonant and as the vowel U.

Plans and photographs. I have only included a plan of a site when I think that it is impossible to understand the remains without one. This means that unimportant sites, often earthworks, sometimes receive a plan when major monuments do not. For monuments situated in towns, if I have not supplied a plan, I have assumed that you will have access to town-plans in a road handbook such as that published by the AA; if you do not, you can at least ask directions locally. The caption of each illustration is necessarily brief: further details are given in the list on pp. vi–x.

Appendix 1. All the visible Roman antiquities in Britain which are not described in the text are listed in Appendix 1, usually referred to as App. 1 (pp. 653–64). These cannot be found without the help of 1:50,000 OS maps, and the grid

reference and the map number are therefore given in the first
two columns. (s) or (e) is added after the type of antiquity has
been noted (column 5). In the case of (s), which means that
stone remains are visible, it may be assumed that these are so
fragmentary as to be of interest only to the most avid
enthusiast. This is not always so in the case of earthworks (e).
In the north of England, Scotland and Wales many fort-
platforms and other military antiquities are still prominently
visible, and it has been impossible to include details of all of
them in the text. The term 'earthwork' (e), incidentally, only
describes the present state of the site and is no indication of its
original condition: in forts, for example, most rampart-
mounds cover stone defensive walls which are not now
visible. What constitutes 'visible' is sometimes a delicate
matter of judgement, and obviously some will think that there
is nothing to see at some of the sites that I have listed,
whereas other sites that are faintly visible I may have omitted.
My guideline has normally been the relevant symbol on the
old, now long superseded, 7th series 1" OS maps (which
showed far more antiquities than the 1:50,000 series),
although occasionally some places have been included that the
OS considered 'site of' (i.e. nothing visible), and vice versa.

Access

Some of the most important monuments of Roman Britain in
England are in the care of 'English Heritage' (EH), *alias* the
Historic Buildings and Monuments Commission (HBMC).
The equivalent in Wales is 'Cadw, Heritage in Wales', in
Scotland 'Heritage Scotland'. All monuments in the care of
these bodies are indicated by the letters AM (for 'Ancient
Monument') in square brackets after the name of the site,
followed by their opening hours. If these monuments are
accessible at any time, [A] appears as well. Other sites which
have no opening hours given and no [A] can also be assumed
to be accessible at any reasonable time (but are in other
ownership). Many sites run by English Heritage have standard
opening hours which are currently: daily, April–September
1000–1800; October 1000–1700; November–March
1000–1600. Rather than repeat this for every site, the letter
[S], for 'standard', is given to denote such opening times.

These and other opening hours as far as possible are correct at
the time of going to press in December 2001.

The vast majority of the places described in this book, or
listed in Appendix 1, are on private land. In cases where I
know from whom permission to visit can be obtained, I give
this information. But in places where I do not, you must NOT
assume that you are free to wander: the much vaunted 'Right
to Roam' legislation, passed in 2001, does not give walkers
the freedom which many think it does. Most landowners are
proud of their ancient monuments and are happy to let
interested visitors see them, but *only* if the latter make the
effort to enquire first, and *only* if they shut gates, keep dogs
on a lead, do not trample down standing crops, and do not
damage fences or dry-stone walls. A little courtesy will go a
long way, and will make things easier for yourself and the
other would-be visitors who will come after you.

The Roman Army in Britain

Under the Empire, the Roman army consisted of two distinct
forces, the legions and the *auxilia*. A **legion**, with a strength
of about 5,300 men, was originally recruited only from men
with full Roman citizenship (i.e. Italians and men from
Roman colonies during much of the first century AD), but the
rule was relaxed in the second century, and in the early third
century all free-born provincials were given Roman
citizenship. The main body of fighting men was organized
into *centuriae*, 'centuries', of 80 men under the command of a
centurion. Six centuries formed a *cohort* (about 480 men), and
ten cohorts made up a legion, but the first cohort was bigger
(about 800 men). The legionary soldier would normally serve
25 years before being discharged as a *veteran*. The
commander of the legion, the *legatus*, or 'legate', was a
Roman senator, and under him were six *tribunes*, or junior
officers, also of senatorial rank. Like the legate, they were not
full-time professional soldiers, but held the post as part of
their public career, which included both civilian and military
jobs.

The **auxilia**, or auxiliary troops, were not Roman citizens,
but were recruited from the provinces of the Roman Empire.
They usually took their names from the areas in which they

were originally levied (e.g. the First Cohort of Thracians from what is now Bulgaria), and I have often given these areas when naming auxiliary garrisons. Do not, however, be misled into thinking that British forts were all manned by foreigners from many lands; for each unit, while retaining its original native name, would have received fresh recruits from the area in which it was stationed, i.e. from the local British population.

The auxiliaries were organized into *cohorts* if they were infantry, or *alae* ('wings') if they were cavalry. Both generally had a nominal strength of 500, but units of 1,000 men are also known. A cohort could either be composed entirely of infantry or contain a contingent of 120 (or 240) men on horseback. The *auxilia* were generally commanded by Romans of the equestrian rank (i.e. below that of senator), who had the title of 'prefect' (*praefectus*) if the cohort was 500 strong, or 'tribune' (*tribunus*) if 1,000 strong; *alae* were commanded by prefects.

Auxilia were placed in forts and were expected to bear the brunt of fighting and frontier-duty. Legions were placed in fortresses behind the main frontier areas, and were the crack troops used only in emergency. In addition to being a soldier, the legionary was also a considerable technician, and he was often away from his fortress for long periods constructing auxiliary forts or frontier-works.

The original *auxilia* had come from what at the time were the fringes of the Roman-controlled world, but by the third century they were an integral part of the Roman army. In the later Empire, the tribes on the fringes were also organized into military units, but to distinguish them from the *auxilia* they were called **numeri**. Not attested in Britain before the third century, these forces were composed of light-armed infantry (the cavalry equivalents were called **cunei**). They always served away from their place of drafting. An example of a *numerus* was that stationed at South Shields in the fourth century, of Tigris boatmen from Mesopotamia.

Roman Remains in Britain

Military Sites
Marching-camps
The words 'camp' and 'fort' must be carefully distinguished: the former is used only of temporary earthworks, the latter

applies to permanent posts, whether constructed in turf and timber or in stone.

An army on the march always defended itself when it stopped for the night by erecting a camp. These are called *marching-camps* or *temporary camps*. Their plans are often irregular, to suit the terrain. They consist of an earth rampart, originally perhaps 1.50–1.80 m (5–6 ft) high, and crowned with some sort of timber obstacle. The examples of the poles for this which have survived (e.g. the example in Newcastle Museum) are sharpened at both ends, and have a narrower 'waist' in the middle for tying together. They cannot therefore have been set vertically in the rampart, as hammering them in would have damaged the sharp ends. It seems therefore that sets of three or four were tied together at angles and placed on the rampart as giant 'caltrops' (what the Roman military writer Vegetus calls *tribuli*), and each of these would also no doubt have been tied with its neighbour. Tangling with such an obstacle in attack would have caused chaos: they are the Roman equivalent of barbed wire. The tents which housed the men inside the ramparts were carried by mules. Outside the defences was a single ditch (rarely two). The entrances of temporary camps are of two types: those defended by *tituli* (or *titula* – the precise Latin word is uncertain; I have here opted for the former), which are short pieces of rampart and ditch set a few metres in front of the gap in the main rampart (in theory they would break the charge of an enemy); and those defended by *claviculae*, which are curved extensions of the rampart (and sometimes its ditch), usually inside the area of the camp, although external and double *claviculae* are also known. Dating evidence from these camps is slight: both types of gateway are found in the first century, but from the second century onwards *claviculae* seem no longer to have been used (Chew Green IV and Cawthorn A, both probably not later than *c.* 120, are the latest known; plan, Fig. 125). Very occasionally *tituli* are found protecting the gates of forts (Hod Hill, Bar Hill) and fortlets (Durisdeer). The best examples of marching-camps are at Rey Cross (*tituli*, Fig. 85) and Y Pigwn (*claviculae*, Figs. 70–1). Calculating the number of troops each would have housed is fraught with difficulties, but as a rule of thumb it is usually thought that a full legion (5,300 men) could be accommodated under leather in about

30 acres (12 ha) (compare 50 acres [20 ha] for an average, fully-built, permanent fortress).

Practice camps

Troops also built earthworks as part of their training, but these were never meant to be occupied. The rounded corners and the entrances are the most difficult features of a camp to build, and practice camps are often, therefore, very small, avoiding the need for unnecessary lengths of straight rampart. Today these earthworks are rarely more than 30 cm (1 ft) high, such as examples near Castell Collen and Tomen-y-Mur. Others are of normal size and may be built as part of a mock-siege (as for example at Burnswark).

Legionary fortresses

These are larger versions of the fort (see below), and contain similar buildings similarly arranged. They hold a legion and normally cover about 50 acres (20 ha). There were several short-term legionary fortresses, with turf ramparts and timber buildings, but the three permanent bases, later rebuilt in stone, were at Caerleon, Chester and York.

Vexillation fortresses

These were short-term store-bases and quarters for both legionaries and auxiliaries during the conquest period in the first century. Nineteen examples are known, all between 20 and 30 acres (8–12 ha); only Clyro (App. 1) has ramparts which are still partly visible.

Forts

These were the permanent bases of the auxiliary units, and except as a temporary measure rarely housed even a detachment of legionaries. Their size varies according to the type of garrison, but most forts in the first and second centuries cover between $2\frac{1}{2}$ and 8 acres (1–3.25 ha). Their shape from the 70s onwards is almost universally like that of a playing-card, with straight sides and rounded corners.

Defences. The earliest forts in Britain had a rampart of turf, earth or clay (revetted in turf if not wholly composed of turves), on average about 5.50 m (18 ft) wide at base, which was crowned with a breastwork and wall-walk of timber. Gateways and towers at intervals around this rampart were also of timber. The best examples of first-century forts in Britain are Hod Hill (Fig. 17) and the restored Baginton (see Figs. 53–5), but neither represent typical types.

From early in the second century onwards, the front of the rampart was usually cut back and a stone wall was inserted in front of it. Henceforth all new forts were usually, but by no means always, built with a stone wall from the beginning, although an earth rampart nearly always accompanied it behind. This stone wall was originally about 4.25 m (14 ft high), to which was added a parapet about 1.25 m (4 ft) high at the top, making a total height of 5.50 m (18 ft). Today the facing-stones have usually been robbed away, revealing the irregular core of the wall; and in many places the stone wall is now buried beneath a broad mound which marks the line of the defences. There were normally four gateways, consisting of either one or two arched carriageways, often flanked by guardrooms. Internal towers, perhaps with open crenellations (Fig. 2) rather than with sloping roofs (Fig. 64), were placed at the four rounded corners, and at intervals between the latter and the gateways.

Outside the ramparts there were one or more ditches, usually V-shaped. Each had a narrow drainage-channel in the bottom and was never meant to be filled with water like a medieval moat.

Internal buildings. These conform to a standard pattern. In the earliest forts they were timber-framed with walls of wattle-and-daub, but all visible examples are understandably of stone. In some forts, only the central buildings were made of stone, while the barracks were entirely of timber. Stone foundations need not always imply stone superstructures: half-timbering on a stone footing, especially for barracks, may have been common.

In the centre of each fort is the *principia*, or headquarters building (1 on Fig. 2). The front part consists of a large courtyard, usually surrounded on three sides by a colonnade. It leads to the covered *cross-hall* which stretches the full width of the building. This was capable of holding the complete contingent standing shoulder to shoulder; here it

would have assembled for an address by the commanding
officer, who spoke from the raised platform, or *tribunal*, at
one end. At the back of the building are some smaller rooms,
often five in number. The central one is the *sacellum* or *aedes*,
the shrine where the regimental standards and the statue of the
emperor stood (see Fig. 104). Below its floor the pay-chest
was kept, sometimes (from the mid-second century onwards)
in an underground strong-room. The rooms on either side
were used for administrative purposes.

On one side of the *principia* is the *praetorium*, or
commandant's house, usually consisting of a range of rooms
round a central courtyard (2). Private bath-suites seem to have
been a luxury installed only in the late Empire. On the other
side stand two or more *horrea*, granaries (3). These are always
buttressed and have raised floors to keep their contents dry.
A *fabrica*, workshop (4), and sometimes a *valetudinarium*,
hospital (5), also occupy the central area of a fort.

The rest of the area is taken up by *barrack-blocks* (6). A
single barrack-block in an infantry fort was designed to hold a
centuria of 80 men. The main part of the building is divided
up into approximately ten portions. Each is further subdivided

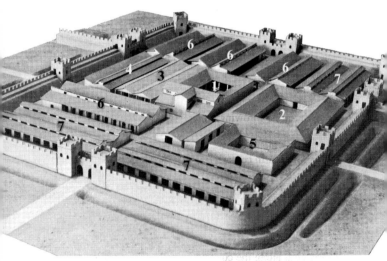

2   *Model of a Roman fort*

into two (not always by stone partitions): in one cubicle the men ate and slept, and in the other they kept their weapons and other equipment. There was a veranda running down one side of the building. The centurion and his junior officer(s) lived in the more spacious accommodation provided at one end. The most instructive infantry barrack-block in Britain is the legionary example at Caerleon. If the regiment was cavalry or part-mounted, separate *cavalry barracks* (7) were provided, in which men and their mounts lived together, the men in one cubicle and their mounts in the adjacent one: the most instructive example in Britain is at Wallsend.

The road running from the front of the HQ to the front gate is called the *via praetoria*; from the back to the back gate, the *via decumana*. The road joining the gates in the long sides and running along the front of the HQ is known as the *via principalis*. There was also a road going all round the fort in the *intervallum*, or the space between the back of the rampart and the internal buildings. Outside the ramparts lay the garrison bath-house, and usually a civilian settlement (*vicus*).

The best examples of Roman forts in Britain are Chesters, Housesteads, Wallsend, Vindolanda and South Shields on or near Hadrian's Wall, Hardknott in the Lake District, and Caernarfon in north Wales.

Tactics. Early forts are meant to house garrisons trained to fight in the open: they would sally forth from their gates and meet the enemy outside. Later, there is a trend towards making the fort more of a stronghold impregnable to attack, when ditches increase in number, and the artillery machines, such as the stone-throwing *onagri*, became more powerful so that an attacker could potentially be bombarded. The final move towards the medieval appearance of a 'castle' came in the third and fourth centuries with the Saxon Shore forts.

Saxon Shore forts. These abandon the conventional (playing-card) shape and layout. They have massive stone walls, up to 9 m (30 ft) high, usually without an earth bank behind. Most are defended by projecting towers, to have maximum view of and control over an attacker. Gateways are narrow. These are the forts built along the coastline from the Wash to Southampton, lining the *mare Saxonicum*, the 'sea facing

Saxony'; but it is probably also the case that Saxon pirate raids (although not attested in the written sources until much later) were on the increase, judging from the sudden rise in the number of hoards in the late 260s, and the decision also to fortify a town like Canterbury *c.* 270, hitherto not thought necessary. Curiously, Saxon Shore forts have little sign of substantial interior buildings, and they seem therefore to have been principally fortified bases, protecting harbours, for the official trans-shipment of supplies and bullion (see further p. 43); they seem unduly massive if dealing with Saxon raiders was their prime function. The remains of Richborough, Pevensey and Portchester are among the most spectacular monuments of Roman Britain. Similar late forts were built in the west, and the restored example at Cardiff gives an excellent idea of the formidable nature of these strongholds (see Fig. 75).

Fortlets

These are small guard-posts, often filling gaps between forts, and seem to have had a variety of functions. Some have twin barracks only and are clearly small troop stations; others are reduced forts and have other buildings within; a third type may have had special customs and tax duties on main roads. Their size varies: each probably held between 50 and 150 men. Defences usually consist of a rampart broken by a single gate, and surrounded by one or two ditches. Some (e.g. Maiden Castle, Cumbria) had stone walls, but most were earthworks (e.g. Castle Greg). The fortlet at Castleshaw, where the ramparts have been partly reconstituted, has been completely excavated.

Signal stations

Simple beacon fire, combination of torch signals to send coded messages, and flag semaphore (the last only usable over very short distances, probably not much more than a mile), were all employed by the Romans in transmitting messages. Most of the known signal stations in Britain consist of a timber tower, surrounded by an earth rampart and ditch (e.g. Bowes Moor), but some first-century towers (e.g. most of those on the Gask Ridge) have no rampart. Stone towers are also known (e.g. Pike Hill and Walltown, both later

incorporated into Hadrian's Wall). In the late fourth century, a
row of strongly defended stone signal stations was built along
the Yorkshire coast, of which the plan of that at Scarborough
has been marked out.

Civilian Remains
Towns
The Romans were the first to build towns in Britain, with
streets laid out in a regular chess-board pattern (street-grid).
Most of the sites they chose are still flourishing cities today,
but by modern standards Roman towns were small (the
population of the whole of Britain at the end of the second
century is unlikely to have much exceeded 3 million people).
Very little is visible of minor settlements or villages (*vici*),
such as those which formed around forts in the military zone:
by far the most instructive example is that at Vindolanda.
More important were the small market-centres and roadside
settlements, but these too have not left many visible remains
(Chapter 5, pp. 287–99, for the best examples). Most of the
towns described in this book, therefore, belong to one of the
following three categories:

(i) *Coloniae.* These were special foundations for veterans,
retired Roman legionaries, and were automatically therefore
composed of Roman citizens: in Britain, Colchester, Lincoln
and Gloucester were founded in this way. The title later
became an honorary one, conferred on a prosperous town
already in existence. We know that York's civilian settlement
received this honour, and it is a fair guess that at least London
(Chapter 10) did so too. *Coloniae* were self-governing
communities, with a city council (*ordo*) and a system of
magistrates modelled on that of Rome.

(ii) *Civitas capitals.* The pre-Roman tribal organization
was not obliterated by the invaders, although the boundaries
were modified and some new artificial administrative units
were created, such as the Regini and the Belgae, if the original
geographical and political unit was too large. Towns were
founded, either on (in a few cases, such as Canterbury and
Silchester) or close to Iron Age centres of power, to serve as
the new market and administrative focus of each *civitas* or
tribal unit; in many cases the sites chosen had started as
military forts in the conquest period. *Civitas* capitals, too,

were self-governing communities, and their magistrates would
have been elected from among the local aristocracy. The size
of Romano-British *civitas* capitals varies: areas enclosed by
defences range from Cirencester, 240 acres (97 ha), to
Carmarthen, 31 acres (13 ha). Inhabitants of tribal capitals
were not awarded the privilege of Roman citizenship,
although individuals could be so rewarded for outstanding
service at any time, such as Tiberius Claudius Togidubnus at
Chichester, and Tiberius Claudius Catuarus at Fishbourne.

(iii) *Municipia.* This is a legal term (our word
'municipality' comes from it) to refer to those communities
which had been awarded a grant of *ius Latii*, 'Latin rights'. By
the normal version of this, the two chief magistrates in a town,
and their families, were automatically awarded Roman
citizenship at the end of their year of office, thus (in theory)
encouraging a pool of pro-Roman-thinking leading individuals
in a city community. The only example from Britain known to
us is Verulamium (St Albans), the *civitas* capital of the
Catuvellauni, if we take Tacitus at face value (for he is our
only testimony). It would be astounding, by analogy with
other provinces, if London had not become a *municipium* by
early in the second century, and York must have gained
municipal status before being promoted to the honorary rank
of *colonia* in the late second or early third century (for such is
the normal process). Some other *civitas* capitals may well
have been granted a municipal charter as well as Verulamium,
but the evidence eludes us. Winchester, for example, has
precociously early defences for a *civitas* capital (*c.* AD 70),
and may have erected them as a mark of municipal status.

Public buildings. The centre of a *colonia* or a tribal capital
was occupied by the administrative unit, the forum and
basilica. The *forum* was the civic centre and market-place, and
consisted of a large courtyard surrounded by a colonnade. The
basilica was a long hall, sometimes with apsidal ends, where
justice was dispensed. It lay along one end of the forum.
Adjoining it were administrative offices. The plan of the
forum and basilica is derived from the military *principia*, as
early (Augustan) examples on the Continent make clear. The
only forum and basilica in Britain partially accessible today is

at Caerwent, although the colonnade on the entrance façade of
the forum at Wroxeter is also visible.

The *bath-house* was an indispensable part of Roman life,
and examples are found in every town and villa of any note,
and also outside every fort. They varied enormously in
elaboration. The system was close to the present-day Turkish
baths, and consisted of a series of rooms heated to different
temperatures. The bather first took his or her clothes off in the
apodyterium (undressing room), proceeded to the *frigidarium*
(cold room), started sweating in the moderately heated
tepidarium (warm room), and perspired profusely in the
caldarium, the room of intense sticky heat. Here he or she
would scrape the body, to remove dirt from the skin, with an
oiled metal instrument called a *strigil*, a sort of blunt
'cut-throat' razor. A small hot-water bath was usually also
available adjoining the *caldarium*. The bather would then go
through the rooms in reverse order, taking a dip in the cold
immersion-bath in the *frigidarium* to close the pores and so
avoid catching cold. This was the most common system, and
depended for its effect on moist heat: steam was created by
sprinkling water on the floor, which was heated by a
hypocaust (see Glossary, p. 32). A more rigorous experience
was sweating in dry heat, when the hot room was known as
the *laconicum* (Spartan room) or the *sudatorium* (sweating
room). A complete bath-house contained both systems, and
the public establishments also had *palaestrae*, exercise-courts:
although the early baths at Silchester (not visible) had an
open-air one on the Mediterranean model, most in Britain
were covered, as at Wroxeter and Leicester. Open-air
swimming-baths as we know them were rare: there are visible
examples at Wroxeter and Caerleon. The best example of a
Roman public bath-house in Britain is at Wroxeter, and of a
military one at Chesters and Vindolanda (which has two);
Wallsend has a reconstructed one. The Caerleon legionary
baths are also instructive. The thermal establishment at Bath is
exceptionally grand, and without parallel in Britain.

Other public buildings within a town included *temples*
(below, p. 21), a *mansio*, or inn (partly for the use of officials
travelling on public business), and (sometimes) *theatres*. The
only completely excavated and visible example of the last, at
St Albans, is described in its proper place (p. 235). The

theatre was a D-shaped building and must be distinguished from the *amphitheatre*. The latter, nearly always outside the built-up area, consisted of an elliptical arena surrounded by tiers of wooden seats erected on earth banks. These banks were usually revetted in stone or timber, but no monumental structures built entirely of stone, like the amphitheatres of Arles or Nîmes or the Colosseum, have yet been found in Britain. Gladiatorial combats and animal sports were staged here. Today, civilian amphitheatres survive usually as earth banks (e.g. at Silchester, where the stone revetment bordering the arena is also visible). The military amphitheatres at the legionary fortresses of Chester and Caerleon have been more extensively exposed, but here weapon-training came before gladiatorial entertainment, and the arenas were consequently rather larger in relation to the seating space than in their civilian counterparts.

Water supply. Aqueducts raised in part on arches (e.g. Lincoln), were rare in Britain and none is now visible. Where water was brought from a distance it was usually conducted in an open channel, following natural contours. Dorchester has the best preserved example. Aqueduct leats also occur in industrial contexts, most notably at Dolaucothi. Examples of substantially built *drains* and *sewers* have been found at Lincoln, Bath, St Albans and York, but only that at Bath is accessible. *Latrines* are common: the public lavatory at Wroxeter can be seen, but more instructive are the military ones such as that at Housesteads (Fig. 111). Wooden or stone seats were mounted over a deep sewer, and running water in a gutter was provided in front of the seats. For those privileged enough to own them, this was where sponges, the Roman equivalent of toilet-paper, could be washed; but it is very possible that other alternatives, such as water simply applied by hand (as in many parts of the world today), were more commonly employed.

Private houses. The simplest dwelling was a long, narrow building, with one end fronting the street (often a shop, with living-quarters behind). This type was sometimes expanded and had a wing or wings added at the back. The largest houses consisted of a series of rooms ranged about a courtyard; a few might have their own bath-suites. The most elaborate were decorated with mosaics and painted wall-plaster, and had heated living-rooms for winter use. Few town-houses have been preserved in Britain: Dorchester and Caerwent have the most instructive examples.

Defences. All the large towns, and many smaller settlements, were equipped with defences at some time before the end of the Roman occupation. Some, such as St Albans, received an earth bank and ditch soon after AD 61 (probably a sign of its municipal rank), and the *coloniae* were given stone walls, undoubtedly a symbol of their privileged status, soon after their foundation (Colchester before AD 80, Gloucester in the 90s, and Lincoln early in the second century). At the other extreme, some very small towns did not receive ramparts until the fourth century. The defences of most other Romano-British towns show three distinct phases: an earth bank, a stone wall inserted in front of it, and projecting towers added to that. Excavation at different sites has produced different dates for each of these phases, as will be noticed by comparing my account of one town wall with another. It is most unlikely, however, that such diversity in dates is real, at any rate for the first phase of earthen-bank defences. Most towns were given these, with a wooden stockade or breastwork, at the end of the second century. These must have been erected on the command of a central authority, probably in response to, rather than in anticipation of, a crisis, either that of *c.* 180, or, more likely, that of 196–7 (see p. 26). In most places the stone wall was inserted in front of the earth bank at a later period, probably at various times in the third century. The third phase, the addition of projecting towers, is given various dates in the fourth century, but it too may be the product of a single policy. A date nearer to 350 rather than in the late 360s (Theodosian) now seems probable, at least for some. Projecting towers gave more complete control over an attacker, and although there is no certain evidence that they were provided with artillery machines, it is hard to explain otherwise the new broad ditches (to keep an attacker at artillery range?) which frequently accompany such defences. The best examples of urban stone defences in Britain can be seen at Caerwent and Silchester.

Villas

These are the most popular and familiar monuments of Roman
Britain because of the spectacular mosaics which often adorn
their floors. Nearly all the mosaics, however, belong only to
the last phase of a (usually) complicated development. The
simplest houses of just a few rooms have not generally been
preserved, although Lullingstone in its final form is a
luxurious, expanded example of a very compact house,
without projecting wings or spacious courtyards. Most of the
villas visible in Britain belong either to the 'winged corridor-
type', in which several rooms open off a long corridor and are
often flanked by short 'wings', often no more than projecting
rooms, on either side (e.g. Newport and the main residential
block at Littlecote), or the extensive 'courtyard-type', in
which blocks of rooms forming separate wings are grouped
around one or more courtyards (best appreciated at Chedworth
and North Leigh). Most villas were not pleasure-palaces but
the centres of agricultural estates, and farm buildings are
usually found on the outskirts of the main living-area (or in
the outer courtyard of some courtyard villas). The courtyard-
type, usually a development from simpler dwellings, belongs
(in the visible examples) to the fourth century, except for the
first-century palace at Fishbourne, which is quite exceptional.
Even the smallest villas had by the fourth century hypocausts,
mosaics or plain tessellated floors, and painted wall-plaster.
A bath-house or one or more bath-suites was also normal.

Native settlements

A high proportion of the population of the countryside,
especially in Wales and northern and SW England, remained
largely uninfluenced by Roman civilization. They used Roman
pottery and coins and sometimes even had refinements such as
painted wall-plaster, but the settlements they inhabited
belonged mainly to the pre-Roman tradition. The dwelling-
place was usually a circular hut, although in the Roman period
rectangular huts often replaced or co-existed with those of a
circular plan. Some of the very few native settlements
mentioned in this book are built of stone (Chysauster, Tre'r
Ceiri), and are therefore substantial monuments, but most
survive only as earth ridges (e.g. Ewe Close). It is always best
to visit the latter if possible on a sunny evening, when long

shadows pick out the surviving banks and make the remains more intelligible.

Temples

The true classical-style temple was built on a lofty platform (*podium*), and was approached by a flight of steps. The shrine (*cella*) had a front porch of freestanding columns supporting a triangular pediment. This type is rare in Britain: Colchester has one (its substructures are preserved), and the steps leading up to a classical temple at Bath are also visible.

The most common type of temple is called Romano-Celtic. The ground-plan of the visible examples consists of two squares, one inside the other. The inner wall enclosed the *cella*, and there was an ambulatory between it and the outer wall. They are often reconstructed on paper with an outer wall supporting dwarf stone columns, but only seven excavated examples have actually provided evidence for columns. The

3 *Suggested appearance of a Romano-Celtic temple (Beaune, France)*

two alternative possibilities are that the supports were of timber (see Fig. 3), or that the outer ambulatory was entirely enclosed by a solid wall, pierced only by windows. This would have made for a darker temple but would have increased the air of religious mystery. The best visible examples are at Maiden Castle, Caerwent and Vindolanda.

Other temples were of the 'basilican' type, an early forerunner of the Christian church. The outer walls of these are solid, and the interior may be divided into a nave and side-aisles. Lydney and the London Temple of Mithras are examples. The Carrawburgh Mithraeum is a smaller and simpler version of the same basic type. Undisputed Roman churches are rare, but two examples which I accept as churches are now visible, at Colchester and Vindolanda; there is also an early Christian baptismal font at Richborough.

Roads

Most Roman trunk-roads were built in a series of straight stretches, usually changing direction on hill-tops, but straightness was not always possible and in mountainous terrain a Roman road can wind as much as a modern one. The composition of each road varied a great deal: generally there was a foundation of large slabs or stones, and the final surface consisted of rammed gravel. The latter has washed away, leaving the foundation-slabs exposed (e.g. Wheeldale Moor, Fig. 83). Sometimes iron cinder was used for surfacing (e.g. Ashdown Forest), but a paving of stone blocks was apparently not used in Britain (I no longer accept the road on Blackstone Edge as Roman). To ensure good drainage (a vital element when roads lacked the cohesion afforded by modern macadamized surfaces), Roman highways were often built on raised embankments (*aggeres*), and were sometimes accompanied by ditches on either side. The Ackling Dyke is a fine example of a raised *agger* of this type.

Burials

By Roman law burial was prohibited inside a city, except for infants; in cases which appear to contradict this, e.g. at Canterbury, the burial must have preceded urban expansion. Both cremation and inhumation were practised in Roman Britain: the former was predominant in the first and second centuries, the latter in the fourth. Most burial-places were simple graves marked by tombstones (of wood, no doubt, for the less affluent), and many such stones are on display in museums. Roman cemeteries do not normally leave permanent surface traces in Britain: the remarkable cemetery of low earthen mounds covering cremations at High Rochester is wholly exceptional. Larger, monumental tombs are by contrast sometimes visible *in situ*, and these fall broadly into two categories:

(i) *The earth barrow*, or *tumulus*, which has a steep, high, conical profile. These are particularly frequent in SE Britain, and are a direct descendant of pre-Roman burial-mounds. Most date from the first and second centuries. The burials, usually cremations and often associated with grave goods, were placed in a receptacle in the middle of the barrow. *Tumuli* often occur in groups, such as the Bartlow Hills.

(ii) *Stone-built tombs*. The circular structures at Keston and High Rochester were probably retaining-walls for a central mound of earth, perhaps with a conical top. Those at Stone-by-Faversham and Harpenden, however, have internal chambers and were freestanding.

Historical Outline

55–54 BC   Caesar raids Britain.

AD 43   Invasion of Britain under Aulus Plautius with four legions, Second Augusta, Ninth Hispana, Fourteenth Gemina and Twentieth Valeria, and auxiliaries (about 40,000 men in all). Landing at Richborough (alternative theories about a landing near Chichester fail to convince). Battle on the Medway. Native chieftain Caratacus flees to Wales. Plautius pauses to await the Emperor Claudius before advancing to Colchester.

44–60   Division of the invading army: the Second Legion advances SW, the Ninth towards Lincoln, the Fourteenth and part of the Twentieth through the Midlands, initially via the Oxford region (fortress at Alchester, late 44). Rest of *Legio XX* is kept in a base-fortress at Colchester. Early

frontier-line marked by the Fosse Way, the
Roman road from Exeter to Lincoln, with forts
along it.

47–52   Ostorius Scapula governor. Campaigns against
the Silures (south Wales) and the Ordovices (mid
and north Wales), who are inspired by Caratacus.
Beaten in battle in AD 51, he flees to northern
Britain, where Queen Cartimandua of the
Brigantes betrays him and hands him over to the
Romans.

52–7   Aulus Didius governor. Further campaigns in
Wales. Civil war among the Brigantes and
Roman intervention there.

61   King Prasutagus of the Iceni (East Anglia) dies.
Rapacity of Roman administrators causes revolt
of Boudica (Boadicea). Petillius Cerialis,
commander of the Ninth, with part of his legion,
is ambushed by Boudica – his infantry massacred,
but he himself escapes. Suetonius Paullinus,
governor, rushes back from Anglesey but not
soon enough to save Colchester, London and St
Albans from going up in flames. Seventy
thousand inhabitants massacred. Poenius
Postumus, acting commander of the Second
Legion, probably in Exeter, refuses Suetonius'
call for assistance and falls on his sword after
hearing news of the final battle, when 80,000
Britons are killed. Julius Alpinus Classicianus, a
Gaul, comes to Britain as the new chief financial
administrator of the province (*procurator*).
Disagreement over policy leads to the recall of
Suetonius.

66   Fourteenth Gemina withdrawn from Britain for
service in the East.

71–4   Petillius Cerialis, now governor, arrives with a
new legion, the Second Adiutrix, and campaigns
against the Brigantes. Base for Ninth Legion
established at York *c*. 71.

74–8   Julius Frontinus, governor, finally pacifies the
Silures. Legionary fortresses established for the
Second Augusta at Caerleon near Newport

c. 74–5, and for the Second Adiutrix at Chester *c.* 77–9.

Late 78 Arrival in Britain of Cnaeus Julius Agricola, most famous of the governors of Britain, because of the surviving biography written by his son-in-law, Tacitus. Final mopping-up in Wales. The chronology of Agricola's governorship is not absolutely certain: I have adopted here (below) 78–84/5, but some think it was held 77–83/4.

79 Advance to the Tyne–Solway isthmus.

80 Advance to the Forth–Clyde isthmus, and reconnaissance as far as the Tay.

81 Consolidation, building of forts and roads.

82 Invasion of SW Scotland.

83–4 Agricola pushes up to the Spey, building forts behind him, including a legionary fortress for the Twentieth at Inchtuthil. Battle of Mons Graupius, in which 30,000 Caledonians under their leader Calgacus are crushed. Roman fleet circumnavigates Britain.

84 Recall of Agricola.

c. 87 Withdrawal from Scotland north of the Forth–Clyde isthmus, including the abandonment of Inchtuthil: its garrison, the Twentieth Legion, moves to Chester; Second Adiutrix withdrawn from Britain.

c. 105 Complete withdrawal from southern Scotland, perhaps after a disaster. Frontier now the Stanegate, the road across the Tyne–Solway isthmus between Corbridge and Carlisle built by Agricola or a successor. New forts built along it, and its line probably extended westwards and eastwards now.

118 Revolt in Britain, perhaps among the Brigantes. Suppressed by 119 (coins).

122 Emperor Hadrian visits Britain. Hadrian's Wall and its attendant works begun, under the supervision of the new governor, Aulus Platorius Nepos, who brings another legion to Britain, the Sixth Victrix. Disappearance of the Ninth Legion, last recorded in 107/8 – probably withdrawn from

Britain *c.* 121–2, eventually to perish in a disaster in the East, possibly in 161.

139–42   Antoninus Pius, Emperor, orders a new advance in Britain, under Lollius Urbicus. Reoccupation and refortification of southern Scotland. Building of the Antonine Wall.

c. 155   Serious revolt, possibly of Brigantes, in northern Britain with heavy Roman casualties. Cnaeus Julius Verus arrives as governor with legionary reinforcements, and rebuilding of Pennine forts burnt in the revolt is begun. Antonine Wall held.

c. 161/3   Abandonment of the Antonine Wall and of southern Scotland, probably on the death of Antoninus (new foreign policy under his joint successors Marcus Aurelius and Lucius Verus). Hadrian's Wall fully recommissioned. More rebuilding of forts in northern Britain under Calpurnius Agricola (governor *c.* 162–6).

c. 180   The historian Dio records a war in Britain, with the death in battle of a Roman general (probably the governor), and the invasion of tribes across 'The Wall'. This must mean Hadrian's Wall, and the forts at Corbridge and in the adjacent sector of the Wall (Rudchester, Halton) were probably destroyed now. Ulpius Marcellus, known to have been governor *c.* 177–80, is sent back to Britain, and victory is achieved by 184–5 (coins).

193–7   Clodius Albinus (governor of Britain from *c.* 191) claims the imperial throne in 193 and is recognized as Deputy Emperor (with the title 'Caesar') by Septimius Severus, Emperor from 193. Growing tension between the two. In 196 Albinus strips Britain of its troops and crosses to France. Was defeated and killed by Severus near Lyon in February 197. Many forts in north Britain burnt, probably by Brigantes, but it is far from certain that Hadrian's Wall was destroyed now; if so, reconstruction was delayed ten years. Probably as a reaction to the Albinus crisis, most of Britain's towns were equipped with defences *c.* 193–7.

197–201/2	Virius Lupus sent to Britain to restore the situation. Many Pennine forts rebuilt now. Britain divided into two provinces (*Superior* and *Inferior*, Upper and Lower).
205–8	L. Alfenus Senecio, energetic governor, restores Hadrian's Wall and its forts, sometimes from foundations, after a long period of neglect. Further rebuilding of Pennine forts, where reconstruction had begun earlier (in 197).
208–9	Emperor Severus and his sons Caracalla and Geta campaign in northern Scotland.
210	Caracalla conducts campaigning because Severus is too ill.
211	Severus dies in York, 4 February. Complete withdrawal from Scotland, but probably not before 213.
c. 213–65	Period of peace. Rebuilding and reorganization of forts in northern Britain continues (until *c.* 230). Towns given stone walls at various stages during the third century. From 259 Britain part of a Gallic separatist Empire.
c. 268–75	Signs of increasing insecurity in SE Britain: coin hoards increase, and Canterbury and St Albans get full defences now for the first time. Fort at Burgh Castle built.
286–7	Carausius, commander of the British fleet, declares himself Emperor of Britain and North Gaul, but loses control of latter in 293. More of the Saxon Shore forts built, either now (Portchester) or under Allectus (Pevensey).
Late 293	Carausius is murdered by his finance minister, Allectus.
296	Constantius (the Emperor Maximian's 'Caesar') recovers Britain, and Allectus is killed in battle in southern Britain. Constantius sets in hand a lot of rebuilding on Hadrian's Wall (where late third-century destruction at a number of sites is attested), in the Pennine forts, and at the legionary fortresses of Chester and York. Perhaps natural decay was mainly the reason for the reconstruction, at least in most places. Britain

divided into four provinces. Office established about now of *Dux Britanniarum*, commander-in-chief of all land forces in Britain.

306   Constantius returns to Britain, now as Emperor, and campaigns in Scotland (but little archaeological trace). Dies at York, 25 July: Constantine ('the Great') proclaimed Emperor there.

313   Christianity tolerated by the Edict of Milan, and three British bishops attend the Council of Arles in 314.

300–42   Peace and prosperity in many parts of Roman Britain, but some towns already in decline.

342–3   Trouble north of Hadrian's Wall. Emperor Constans comes to Britain and pacifies Scottish tribes. Projecting towers on some town walls.

360   More trouble with the tribes north of the Wall, the Picts of Scotland and also with the Scots of Ireland. Peace settled by Lupicinus.

367–8   Britain is overwhelmed by a great barbarian conspiracy: concerted attacks by Picts (Scotland) and Scots (Ireland) according to Ammianus Marcellinus. Nectaridius, Count of the Saxon Shore, is killed, and Fullofaudes, *Dux Britanniarum*, is besieged or captured. Much of the countryside of lowland Britain probably unaffected, although some villas are deserted around this time.

369   Theodosius comes to Britain to restore the situation. A fifth province, Valentia (NW Britain?), is established. Hadrian's Wall is restored and its forts patched up. Some forts in northern Britain rebuilt, others abandoned. Theodosian restoration is evidently effective, as some towns and villas continue to show signs of prosperity until the late fourth century (mosaics still being laid in some places as late as *c.* 380).

383   Magnus Maximus, perhaps *Dux Britanniarum*, revolts, removes troops from Wales and northern Britain, and crosses to the Continent. Irish raids in northern Wales probably prompts the building

of a fort at Holyhead and associated signal
stations soon after; those on the Yorkshire coast
probably also belong now. Hadrian's Wall
probably still intact.

395   Stilicho, general of the Emperor Honorius, orders
an expedition against Scots (in Ireland), Picts and
Saxons. Coins no longer reach Wales, where all
garrisons were probably withdrawn by
Argobastes during the revolt of Eugenius, 392–5.

c. 400   Final end of Hadrian's Wall.

402   Troops withdrawn from Britain to defend Italy.

407   Constantine III, a usurper, removes the remaining
garrisons from Britain, and crosses to the
Continent.

410   The Emperor Honorius tells the British cities to
look to their own defence.

Some Roman Emperors

The dates of some Roman Emperors mentioned in this book:

Claudius	41–54	Severus	193–211
Nero	54–68	Caracalla	211–17
Vespasian	69–79	Geta	211–12
Domitian	81–96	Gordian III	238–44
Nerva	96–8	(Carausius	287–93)
Trajan	98–117	Constantius	293–306
Hadrian	117–38	Constantine I	306–37
Antoninus Pius	138–61	Constans	333–50

The frequently-used adjective *Flavian* refers to the period
when Vespasian and his sons Titus and Domitian (Flavius is
their family name) were Emperors (69–96). The adjectives
Hadrianic, *Severan* and *Constantian* refer of course to the
years when Hadrian, Septimius Severus and Constantius were
Emperors. *Antonine* refers to the period AD 138–92. *Agricolan*
refers to the years when Cnaeus Julius Agricola was governor
of Britain (either 77–83 or 78–84), and Theodosian to 369–70.

Glossary

A page number in brackets gives a reference to the Introduction, where a fuller explanation of the relevant term may be found.

abutment: masonry platform or earth embankment on a river bank, serving to support the central structure of a bridge

acrostic: a word-square in which the lines can be read in more than one direction (e.g. across or down)

adit: horizontal mining tunnel into the hillside

agger: cambered embankment-mound carrying a Roman road

ala: unit of cavalry in the Roman auxiliary army (p. 8)

ambulatory: covered portico, e.g. surrounding the inner shrine of a temple (p. 21)

apodyterium: undressing room in a bath-suite or bath-house (p. 17)

apotropaic: bringing good luck, designed to ward off evil (used of, e.g., sculptured phalluses and mosaic Medusas)

architrave: the horizontal member above two columns (or piers, etc.), spanning the interval between them

bailey: fortified enclosure in a medieval castle

ballista: artillery weapon mounted on a stand, capable of shooting catapult bolts; other types were stone throwers, supplemented in the late Empire by the *onager* (q.v.)

basilica: hall for civic purposes and the dispensation of justice, usually adjacent to or an integral part of the forum (q.v.) (p. 16)

berm: in military defences, the level space between two features (e.g. ditch and rampart)

bonding-course: bands of brickwork (or occasionally of stone slabs) which alternate with wider sections of regular stonework; they sometimes but by no means always run through the entire thickness of the wall, presumably to give cohesion and stability to the mortared rubble-core; but they were also used merely as levelling courses during construction

breastwork: the vertical timber-work built on top of the earth rampart of a fort to provide screening for the sentry; see Fig. 53

caldarium: hot room (of moist heat) in a bath-house or bath-suite (p. 17)

cam-driven: in mill-machinery, referring to the use of cogged wheels to impart motion to another mechanical part with which it makes contact as it rotates

cantharus: an elaborate vase with scroll handles on either side, often depicted in schematic form on mosaics

capstone: flat slab, usually with a projecting edge, which sits on top of a jamb (q.v.), and from which an arch springs

cella: the inner shrine of a temple (p. 21)

centuria: military unit comprising 80 men (100 during the Roman Republic, hence its name) (p. 7)

chamfered: the way of treating a projecting course (usually a base plinth, q.v.), with a rounded or oblique moulding, to highlight or to make more elegant an offset (q.v.)

chi-rho: Christian symbol composed of the first two letters of the Greek name for Christ (Χριστός); see Fig. 143

civitas: tribal unit, as organized for adminstrative purposes under Roman rule (p. 15)

clavicula: in a Roman camp, curved extension of rampart (and ditch) protecting a gateway (p. 9)

cohort: unit of infantry soldiers, legionary or auxiliary (pp. 7–8)

colonia: settlement of retired legionary soldiers (and therefore of Roman citizens) with a constitution modelled on that of Rome; for York (and no doubt other places in Britain, such as London), a honorific title bestowing the same privileges (p. 15)

crop-mark: colour differentiation in ripening crops or vegetation (best seen from the air), indicating the presence of buried ancient features

cross-hall: covered assembly area in the headquarters building of a fort (p. 11)

culvert: drainage-channel

curtain: wall of fortification

dado: continuous border round the lower part of a wall decorated with painted plaster

dendrochronology: the science of dating timbers from the annual growth rings that trees form during their life, the width of each ring varying according to climatic conditions (temperature and rainfall). The resulting pattern (like a bar code) can then be matched against a master sequence to provide an exact 'fit', but the precise year of the felling of a tree can only be established when the outer part (the bark and/or the sap) is preserved in the finished timber

duoviri: literally 'two men': the chief magistrates in self-governing towns

field-system: regular pattern of rectangular fields attached to an ancient farming settlement

flue-arch: underfloor arch in a hypocaust (q.v.), allowing hot air to pass from furnace to room, or from one heated room to another

flue-tiles: open-ended, box-shaped tiles built in the thickness of the walls of a room heated by a hypocaust (q.v.), to allow hot air to rise vertically through the walls

frieze: horizontal band above an architrave (q.v.), sometimes carved with sculpture

frigidarium: cold room in a bath-suite or bath-house (p. 17)

geophysics: a method of prospecting using a resistivity meter (which measures relative soil humidity) or a fluxgate gradiometer (which charts magnetic data) which enables features to be traced below ground without excavation

graffito: writing scratched on tile, pottery, plaster, etc.

guilloche: in mosaics, decorative feature consisting of two or more intertwining bands

herringbone: descriptive of a style of construction in which stonework or floor tiles are laid in zig-zag pattern

hypocaust: Roman method of central heating: see Fig. 4. The floor was raised, usually on *pilae* (q.v.), and flue-tiles (q.v.) were built in the thickness of the walls. The draught created by these flues enabled hot air to be drawn from the stoke-hole (q.v.; on the right in Fig. 4), where brushwood or other fuel was burnt, to circulate under the floor, and to escape up the wall-flues to the air outside. In the channelled type of hypocaust, the hot air circulated not around *pilae* but

through narrow channels built under the floor
(a combination of both types is also possible)

imbrex: semicircular roofing-tile (plural: *imbrices*), linking
two flat tiles (*tegulae*)

impost: the flat slab on top of a pier from which an arch
springs

in situ: Latin for 'in its original position'

insula: square or rectangular unit of buildings in a Roman
town, bordered on all four sides by streets, usually at
right-angles to one another

intervallum: the perimeter space round the interior of a fort or
fortress, between the rampart (*vallum*) and the interior
buildings, usually occupied by a road

jamb: upright slab on either side of a doorway or window

keep: central stronghold of a medieval castle

laconicum: hot room (of intense dry heat) in a bath-suite or
bath-house (p. 17), so called because the people of Sparta in
Greece (Laconians) had a reputation for enduring pain

latrine: lavatory (p. 18)

4   *The working of a hypocaust*

leat: aqueduct-channel

lewis holes: holes cut in large blocks to take crowbars or, in elaborate cases, iron scissor-like grippers, to assist moving and lifting the blocks during construction

ligatured: used of inscriptions, when two letters are joined together to save space

lilia: systematic rows of small pits dug in the ground (usually on the berm, q.v.), in which sharpened stakes were placed, and then concealed by a covering of bracken and heather; the idea, described by Julius Caesar (who so names them), was to deceive an enemy into thinking that the ground was solid. They are attested in Britain on Hadrian's Wall (pp. 464 and 465) and on the Antonine Wall (pp. 572 and 574) as well as at Piercebridge (p. 398), the last over 300 years after Caesar was writing (so they must have worked)

lintel: wooden beam or stone slab lying horizontally above a doorway (or window)

lozenge: a diamond shape

lunate: a sub-semicircular compartment, with one straight side, usually used of a panel of such a shape containing decorative motifs in a mosaic pavement

maenad: a female companion of Bacchus, often disporting herself in frenzied fashion

mansio: an inn, especially for government officials

monogram: set of letters combined into one (used of a chi-rho, q.v.)

mosaic: floor composed of pieces of coloured *tesserae* (q.v.), to form geometric or figured designs

motte: earth mound marking the site of a small medieval castle, generally of timber

municipium: chartered town in which its chief magistrates automatically received Roman citizenship on leaving office (p. 16)

narthex: a vestibule to a temple or church, usually the full width of the building, and so with its long axis at right-angles to the main room beyond

nemeseum: shrine to Nemesis, goddess of Fate

nereid: a female sea-nymph or sea-creature, normally mostly human in form (e.g. in Fig. 144)

offset: point at which the thickness of a wall is reduced, forming a 'step' in the structure *onager*: a large artillery machine capable of hurling stone balls, first so named in the fourth century because of its vicious kick-back after firing (*onager* means 'wild ass' in Latin)

opus sectile: the name given to a floor composed of pieces of cut marble or other coloured stones, to form a pattern; literally 'cut work'

opus signinum: a distinctive waterproof Roman pink mortar, made of lime with an admixture of crushed brick or tile, which is commonly found in floors and lining pools in bath-suites; named after the town of Segni (Signia) in Italy, although its origins lie in Carthaginian north Africa

opus spicatum: a floor made up of rows of small bricks in herringbone fashion, i.e. with each alternate row laid at an oblique angle to that adjacent

ordo: the senate of a provincial town

palaestra: exercise-yard of a public bath-house, in Britain sometimes covered

palindrome: a phrase or word which reads the same backwards and forwards, such as 'was it a cat I saw?'

parapet: top of a Roman fortification consisting of a wall-walk (q.v.) and battlements

pediment: triangular gabled end of a roof (usually used of temples)

pelta: a decorative device popular in mosaics, defined by a semicircular outer edge on one side, and two smaller semicircles (with the arc facing in the same direction) on the inner side; the shape is that of the light shield carried by Amazons in Greek art

pilae: pillars of brick (or stone) supporting the floor of a room with a hypocaust (q.v.)

pilaster: column or pillar incorporated in, but projecting from, a wall

piscina: swimming-bath in a public bath-house

pisé: a type of wall construction in which stiff clay or mud is poured between shuttering boards and then left to harden

plinth: projecting course at the foot of a wall; also used of a base, e.g. for an altar

podium: raised platform (especially used of temples); also the vertical wall running round the arena of an amphitheatre

portal: doorway or carriageway, especially of a fort-gateway *postern*: minor gate or door in a fort or in a late Roman town wall

post-hole: hole dug to receive a wooden upright

posting-station: small town on a main road where officials could find an inn (*mansio*, q.v.)

principia: headquarters building, normally applied to one in a fort or fortress (p. 11)

procurator: financial administrator in the provincial government (or of an imperial estate)

putlog holes: row(s) of square or rectangular holes in a masonry wall which held horizontal scaffolding timbers during construction; on completion of the work they were plugged with loose material, since fallen out, to enable scaffolding to be inserted again during repairs

relieving arch: arch built as part of a solid wall to take the weight of the construction above, and to alleviate the downward thrust on weak points such as doors and windows lower down, by diverting it laterally

revetment: facing of one material given to a structure of a different material (e.g. a stone wall given to an earth bank), usually to retain it, i.e. to keep it from collapsing or slumping

roundel: circular panel containing a design (e.g. on mosaics)

rusticated: a style of masonry in which the outer face of each block is left deliberately rough for aesthetic effect, to suggest robustness

sacellum: shrine in a fort's headquarters building (p. 12)

saltire: composition-pattern of a mosaic pavement, particularly favoured in Britain by mosaicists based in fourth-century Cirencester, in which the central element consists of a panel in the form of an equal-armed cross (see centre of Fig. 43)

samian: high-quality, red-slipped pottery, manufactured in a wide number of centres in Gaul and Germany; misleadingly so-called because it was once thought by antiquaries (from a reference in Pliny) that the pottery was made on the Greek island of Samos

sarcophagus: coffin of stone or lead

Saxon Shore: coast of SE England exposed to Saxon pirate raids (p. 13) *sleeper wall*: low wall supporting a raised floor, especially in a granary

springer: the first voussoir (q.v.) which rests on the capstone (q.v.) above a jamb (q.v.), and which marks the beginning of an arch

stoke-hole: furnace area for a hypocaust (q.v.)

street-grid: regular pattern of streets crossing at right-angles

stylobate: the base of a classical-style temple or paved colonnade (e.g. lining a forum) on which columns were placed

sudatorium: hot room (of dry heat) in a bath-suite or bath-house (p. 17)

tegula: a flat roof-tile (plural: *tegulae*) with flanged edges along the long sides, used in conjunction with *imbrices* to form a roof (see *imbrex*)

tepidarium: warm room (of moist heat) in a bath-suite or bath-house (p. 17)

tessellated: composed of *tesserae* (q.v.), usually used of a floor without decoration

tesserae: small cubes of coloured stone, glass or tile, of which a mosaic (q.v.) or tessellated (q.v.) floor is composed

tholos: any small circular structure, generally with a colonnaded exterior

thyrsus: sacred wand carried by the god Bacchus and his attendants

titulus: short detached stretch of rampart (and ditch) protecting the entrance of a marching-camp (p. 9); there is dispute whether the correct Latin form is *titulus* or *titulum*, but either is preferable to the lame English word 'traverse'

tondo: roundel (q.v.), especially one occurring in fresco

tribunal: platform for the commanding officer in a *principia* (q.v.) (p. 12), or on a parade-ground

triclinium: dining-room

triton: a mythical male sea-creature, normally mostly human in form, often shown holding or blowing a conch-shell

tumulus: burial-mound (p. 23)

vexillatio: detachment of a legion (normally 1,000 men)

vexillation fortress: campaign base for legionaries and auxiliaries (p. 10)

via decumana: road in a fort running from the back of *principia* (q.v.) to the back gate

via principalis: road in a fort linking the gate in the long sides
    and passing in front of the *principia* (q.v.)

vicus: small civilian settlement, especially one outside a fort

voussoir: wedge-shaped stone forming one of the units of an
    arch

wall-walk: level platform for the sentry on top of a
    fortification (see parapet)

wattle-and-daub: wall-construction consisting of wickerwork
    plastered with mud

Chapter 1

South-East England

Kent and Sussex

(Appendix 1 only – Surrey)

In 55 and 54 BC, Gaius Julius Caesar made his famous invasions of Britain. On the second expedition he crossed the Thames and penetrated into what is now Hertfordshire; the great ditch known as Devil's Dyke on the east side of Wheathampstead is sometimes claimed (on insufficient evidence) as part of the fortress of the native king Cassivellaunus, which Caesar successfully assaulted. There was, however, no permanent Roman occupation, and none of the marching-camps which Caesar must have built has ever been found.

We have, therefore, to turn to **Richborough**** (TR 325602) [AM; April–September, daily 1000–1800; October, daily 1000–1700; November and March, Wednesday–Sunday 1000–1600; December–February, Saturday–Sunday 1000–1600; closed 1300–1400] for the earliest visible traces of Roman Britain. The site lies 1½ miles (2.4 km) NW of Sandwich in Kent, and is reached by taking a minor road (signposted) to the right just before the level-crossing on the Canterbury road (A257) out of Sandwich. It is difficult to imagine this place as it was in AD 43, the year of the Roman invasion under Aulus Plautius, as the coastline is much

changed: the whole of the NE corner of Kent, the Isle of
Thanet, was indeed an island, and Richborough itself lay on a
small peninsula attached to the mainland. In particular, the
steep escarpment on the east, where the railway-line and river
Stour now lie, has carried away the east wall of the later stone
fort, and in AD 43 the ground must have extended flat for
some considerable distance beyond this.

On arrival, walk round the exterior of the massive walls to
the west gate, and then go straight into the interior. Almost at
once you will see (1 on plan, Fig. 5) a line of double ditches
interrupted by a causeway. These ditches have been traced in
both directions for a total length of 690 m (2,700 ft), but only
this short portion has been dug out and left visible. Everything
that is described in this book – all the villas, towns and forts
of the Roman occupation – are later than these ditches, dug by
the Roman invading army in AD 43 to accompany a now-
vanished rampart which defended their beach-head.

These ditches were soon filled up once the progress of the
invasion had ensured that a defended base was no longer
necessary at RVTVPIAE (as the Romans called Richborough; the
meaning of the name is uncertain). The area then became a
supply-base; several buildings, all of timber, are known, and
the plans of three of them have been marked out in concrete
on the site. One of them, marked 2 on Fig. 5, is immediately
adjacent to the early ditches: it had a row of posts (now
concrete circles) forming a veranda on its east side, which
continued also on the south. To reach the other two, walk
across the causeway between the triple ditches towards the
centre of the site (4): the outlines of two of the ten storehouses
or granaries known in this part of the invasion-period supply-
base are marked out to your right (3).

By about AD 85, the area of the store-base had been cleared
for the erection of a great marble-faced monument, of which
all that remains is the great cruciform mass of concreted
rubble and part of a surrounding wall (4). What you have to
imagine here is a magnificent four-way arch, towering 25 m
(85 ft) high, and sumptuously adorned with bronze statuary
and marble imported from Italy. A model in the museum (see
below) gives an idea of its original appearance. The concrete
cross was the platform for the passageway between the arches,
reached by four flights of steps (now gone); but all trace of the

massive masonry of the arch itself, which formed a rectangle
around the passageway, has been completely removed by
subsequent stone-robbing. Richborough was the chief port of
Roman Britain, at least during the first century, and the
monument was evidently a piece of propaganda, probably
celebrating the completion of the conquest of the province,
and designed to impress the many visitors passing through. It
was placed here because it was at Richborough that the
invading forces had first landed, and where the initial steps
were taken towards the acquisition of a new province,
Britannia, for the Roman Empire.

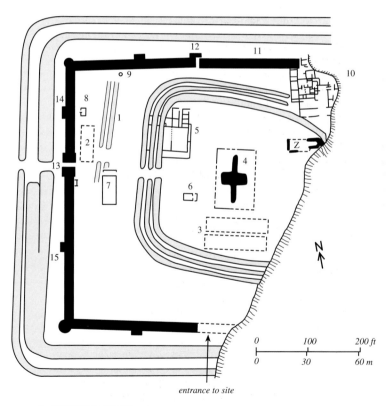

5   *Richborough, site plan*

About the middle of the third century, the grandiose monument was stripped of all its ornament, and apparently served as a signal tower. At any rate it was surrounded by an earth rampart (not visible) and the prominent triple ditches which surround it on three sides, although what exactly this earthwork was designed to contain in the third century is by no means clear. Shortly afterwards, the monument was totally levelled, the earth bank slighted, and the triple ditches were filled in, when the walls of the Saxon Shore fort were built in the late third century.

The other buildings immediately adjacent to 4 can be dealt with briefly. Building 6 belongs to the fourth century but its function is uncertain (it bears some resemblance to certain temple plans). Note the differences in surface-level: this and the top of the monument's platform represent the ground-level of the Saxon Shore fort. Building 5 was interpreted as a block of shops built in the early second century, but it looks more likely to have been a substantial dwelling rather than shops; part of an earlier building is marked out below. The block consisted of three large rooms, with a corridor in front and smaller rooms for living-quarters or storage behind. Half of it was removed when the triple ditches were dug in the third century (two substantial brick piers were left isolated by the triple ditches), and the rest was demolished and buried beneath the now-vanished earth rampart of the fortlet. Z is the ground-plan of a Saxon church. The substantial stone building in the NE corner (10) had a long history. The earliest building of *c*. AD 85 (plan marked by brown concrete-dressing) was rebuilt on a larger scale in the second century (white concrete marking, and the surviving walls at the lower of the two levels). It was clearly an official building, perhaps a *mansio* or inn, since it was respected by the ditches of the third-century earth fortlet which stopped short of it. It remained in use until the construction of the Saxon Shore fort, when a small military bath building was built on the site: its remains, which include a hypocaust, a brick stoke-hole arch, and a plunge-bath in the shape of an elongated octagon, are at the higher level. In a late phase the plunge-bath was filled in and covered with tiles, of which about a third has been left in place.

From here you can reach the outside of the walls of the Saxon Shore fort on the north side. RVTVPIAE was one of a series of forts, built at different periods, which run from the Wash to Portsmouth. The term 'Saxon Shore' only occurs in a single late source (*c.* 395), and although its name has been taken as meaning 'the shore exposed to Saxon pirate raids', the term may be purely geographical ('the sea facing Saxony'). It was once believed that the fort at Richborough was put up by Carausius (287–93), who revolted from Rome and made himself master of an independent empire of Britain and parts of Gaul, but it seems more likely that it belongs a decade or so before him, *c.* 275/80. Certainly the whole system took time to evolve, and there are good grounds for attributing at least some of the series to Carausius and his successor Allectus (such as Portchester and Pevensey).

The absence of substantial buildings within these forts, both at Richborough and elsewhere, is puzzling; they may have been principally used as secure bases for temporary troop postings and for supplies and bullion rather than as fully manned forts in the conventional manner, in which case we would expect a full complement of interior buildings. Although there is evidence for growing insecurity around SE England at this time, the scale of any sea-borne attack is hardly by itself likely to have been on a scale as to warrant such powerful defences: so these impregnable bases probably had additional security functions in late Roman strategy. Nevertheless, whatever their true function, their construction represents a huge outlay of money, manpower and materials, curious if they were intended to be no more than in transient and occasional use. The Saxon Shore forts, among the most impressive surviving monuments of Roman Britain, remain therefore an enigma.

The massive walls of Richborough, probably 9 m (30 ft) high, were faced, as can be seen, with rows of squared stones separated at intervals by bonding-courses of bricks. This facing is best preserved here on the north side, which presents other noteworthy features. The wall was built in sections by different construction gangs, and the join between two of the sections is very clear to the east of the north postern (11): note how the rows of patterning in chalk and ironstone blocks are not on the same level in each section. Next you reach the first tower (12), which has an opening for a postern gate; its outer face contains a large re-used stone, now much worn, thought to have represented a recumbent lion (if so, it was presumably robbed from a grave monument). Just beyond the postern the sharp eye will detect another anomaly: note how the lower of the two brick courses in the right-hand stretch corresponds to the upper of the two brick courses to the left, and the colour of the bricks is also different for each building gang in this sector (maroon red to the right; yellow or orange bricks to the left).

Now go back inside the fort through the postern gate (12) and follow the inside of the wall to the NW corner, passing a hexagonal structure of brick on the way (9). Of fourth-century date, it was interpreted by its excavator as a water-tank, but Continental parallels make it certain that it was a baptismal font, and must have stood inside a timber building. The Christian church to which it was attached lay to its west in this NW corner of the fort: it was of timber panelling between a stone framework, and part of the latter is visible in some excavation photographs, but the stones were entirely removed in the 1920s without being understood and without proper record. This of course was a church of Roman date, not to be confused with the Saxon church already noted. Together with the visible Roman churches at Colchester and (probably) Vindolanda, the baptismal font at Richborough is one of the oldest Christian structures in Britain.

Further on you will pass no. 8, an early second-century cellar, the only surviving part of an otherwise timber building. Then make your way to the west gate, noting to the left the outline of building 7, a fourth-century structure of unknown purpose like no. 6. Their plans both suggest that they were small shrines fronted by a portico, but one does not normally expect to find freestanding temples inside even late Roman forts, and an alternative suggestion is that they may have been meeting-rooms for military clubs (if so they are very small). The other buildings belonging to the Saxon Shore fort, apart from the small bath-house already noted, must have been of timber, if indeed there were any. The boundary wall round the cruciform platform also dates to this period.

Now pass to the outside of the fort, through the west gate (13): this had a single passageway defended by a guard-chamber on either side, of which one is visible. Here began the Roman road later called Watling Street, which ran through London and the Midlands to Chester. Turning right as far as the foundations of the first projecting tower (14), you can see in the corner, between it and the fort wall, the remains of a tile chute, possibly the discharge from a latrine at a higher level. Retracing your steps past the west gate, walk along the berm, keeping the fort ditches to your right (their curious appearance here is due to a Roman error in cutting them, but this would not have been visible in the way it is today on completion). At the first tower you reach (15), two rows of putlog holes for timber scaffolding are clearly visible, as are also four much larger holes, at the level of the lower putlog holes: the holes mark the position of timber floor joists, visible here because the front half of the tower has fallen away. Rounding the SW corner tower, you arrive back at the entrance to the site and the small museum. The model of the four-way arch and fragments of its marble architectural decoration and bronze statuary occupy the central case; another slab taken from the arch, in the case under the window, was re-used later as a gaming board. Copies of important items now in the British Museum are also here, such as the elegant goose-neck ornament, possibly from a boat. The amphora in the corner brought fish-sauce from southern Spain.

Beyond the fort walls, no surface features are visible except for the amphitheatre. After leaving the main site, park in the lay-by just beyond the brick piers of a disused railway-bridge. Cross the stile to your right, and head across the field for a short distance until you are on the bank marking the line of the former railway. Keeping the house to your right, make for the break in the hedge in front of you, and then go up the slope to the metal gate and so into the field beyond. The amphitheatre [AM; A] is visible as an unimpressive hollow in the middle of this field: no stonework is exposed. Geophysical prospection in 2001 revealed details of its plan, suggesting that it was a more complex building than hinted at by antiquarian digging in 1849. The geophysical research has also provided information for the first time about the considerable civilian settlement which occupied the land between here and the fort: trial excavations are planned.

Richborough is only one of four Saxon Shore forts in Kent; others were at Reculver, Dover and Lympne. **Reculver** (TR 227693) [AH; A], the Roman REGVLBIVM or 'great headland', lies 3 miles (4.8 km) east of Herne Bay, and is signposted

from the dual carriageway of the Canterbury–Ramsgate road
(A299). Here too the coastline has changed dramatically, but
whereas Richborough is now some way inland, the fort at
Reculver has been eroded by the sea, and only the southern
half of the original 8-acre (3.3 ha) enclosure remains. A fortlet
connected with the Roman invasion in AD 43 was built here,
but the surviving walls belong to the first half of the third
century. This was confirmed by the finding in 1960 of a
fragmentary but important inscription referring to the building
of the *principia* and cross-hall under a certain Rufinus,
perhaps the Q. Aradius Rufinus who was governor of Upper
Britain *c.* 240. The fort is certainly on archaeological grounds
earlier than that at Richborough, and the absence of towers
and tile bonding-courses at Reculver confirms this.
Excavations since 1952 have shown that it was furnished with
the customary buildings of a Roman fort, but these were much
robbed and are not now visible. Coin evidence shows that
occupation ceased in the 360s. The garrison, as indicated by
numerous tiles stamped C(ohors) I B(aetasiorum), was the
First Cohort of Baetasians, originally raised from what is now
Belgium and south-west Holland. The unit is known to have
been in Maryport (p. 418) and on the Antonine Wall (p. 580)
in the second century, and was later transferred here when the
decision was taken to build the fort at Reculver.

To see what remains of the defences (and if you have just
come from Richborough be prepared for disappointment), take
the path from the seashore car-park (opposite the King
Ethelbert pub), which leads up to the twin towers of the Saxon
and medieval church. Passing this, you reach the east gate,
excavated in 1967, with a single guardroom on its north side.
Turning right, the path follows a stretch of wall, about 2.5 m
(8 ft) high, but only rubble-core remains, as nearly all the
facing-stones have been robbed (some are visible near
ground-level south of the east gate). About 40 m (130 ft) from
the SE angle a rough piece of projecting masonry indicates a
repair to the wall in late Roman times. The south side of the
wall is, at the time of writing (2000), almost completely
obscured with trees and shrubbery (a disgrace for a national
monument), and the position of the south gate, excavated in
1964, is therefore invisible from the path: to see what little
remains of it, you need to climb up on to the fort platform

near the SW corner. The blocks of one gate-pier remain, but the plan of the rest, and the position of the timber gate-posts, have been marked out in concrete. It consisted of a single passageway, 3 m (9 ft 10 in) wide, with a guardroom on the west side only. From here you can follow the path round to the car-park again.

The village of **Lympne** (TR 117342) lies on the B2067, 3 miles (4.8 km) west of Hythe. To find the remains of the Saxon Shore fort, known today as Stutfall Castle but as PORTVS LEMANIS under the Romans, take the turning in the village to Lympne Castle; where the road turns 90° to the left, by a building called 'The Cottage' (also known as 'Smugglers' End'), walk down the public footpath which leads straight on. As soon as this emerges from the wood on to the escarpment, you can see the forlorn Roman walls in the middle distance below you. For a closer look, continue along the path for two minutes until just after the fence on your left turns a corner, and descend the escarpment by the narrow grass path. After a further ten minutes, this passes close to the west side of the fort, but direct access to the field in which the walls lie (which is private land in the possession of Lympne Castle) is not now possible, except by prior written appointment with the owner. The walls have been much tossed around by landslides, and the sea has now retreated far away, but the overgrown ruins have an air of impressive, almost romantic, solitude. Some fragments are still about 7.50 m (25 ft) high and 4.25 m (14 ft) thick, even though fallen from their original positions. The walls originally formed an irregular pentagon enclosing about 10 acres (4 ha). Tile-courses and projecting towers (one good example survives on the NW) make it likely that the fort is contemporary with Richborough (perhaps the late 270s), although pottery indicates the presence here of a naval base already in the second century. The garrison in the final period is recorded as the *numeri Turnacensium*, recruited in the Tournai region of Belgium, but no interior buildings are known apart from a small bath-house and what may have been part of a headquarters building; both were explored in the nineteenth century but are not now visible. The fort at Lympne was abandoned c. AD 340/50. Excavations in 1976–8 revealed some further details of the fort, but these have been backfilled.

Part of the east gate has, however, been left exposed, including the large flagstones of the entrance passage and the more southerly of the two solid semicircular towers which flanked it (now about 0.60 m [2 ft] high and lying at a 45° angle because of subsidence and landslips), but this is not now accessible.

The fourth of the Kentish Saxon Shore forts was at **Dover**** (TR 319414), the Roman DVBRIS (which means 'waters' or 'streams', the name also of the river Dour). Until rescue excavations in 1970–1 along the path of the inner relief road, the exact position of the Saxon Shore fort was uncertain. Now, however, the south and west walls of the fort are known, together with the position of five projecting towers – a later addition and not, as at Richborough, of one bond with the wall. Totally unexpected was the discovery of another fort, built for a garrison of about 700 men on a slightly different site in the second century. The evidence of numerous tiles stamped CL BR makes it certain that this was one of the headquarters of the British fleet, the *classis Britannica*; excavations have shown that the first fort of *c.* 117/20, never finished, was replaced by a new fort *c.* AD 130, occupied with interruptions and rebuildings until *c.* 210. A sister fort is known in Boulogne.

The most spectacular discovery of 1971, however, was part of a building in the extensive civilian settlement which grew up in the second and third centuries north of the *classis Britannica* fort. Parts of five rooms, all with hypocausts, together with a corridor, were salvaged. It was built *c.* AD 200 over an earlier building of *c.* 150, of which part of one room is also visible. The walls, still standing 3 m (10 ft) high in places, are covered with brightly coloured painted plaster, exceptionally well preserved in one room and in part of a second. Substantial finds of painted wall-plaster *in situ* are extremely rare in this country: Dover can in fact boast of the only large area in Britain of Roman wall-plaster (over 37.2 sq m or 400 sq ft) which is still in place on the walls where it was painted 1,800 years ago. Thanks to the energy and initiative of its excavator, Brian Philp, this exceptional discovery was saved for the nation, and the so-called 'Roman Painted House' was opened to the public in 1977. It is clearly signposted from York Street on the inner relief road (daily except Mondays, April and September, 1000–1700; May–August, 1000–1800 [and open Mondays, July–August]; closed October–March).

After passing the ticket-office, you look down on the Saxon Shore fort defences, well preserved to your left, but robbed on your right. Beyond are the remains of the 'Painted House': its astonishing state of preservation is due to the burial of these rooms under the earth bank behind the wall of the Roman fort, the construction of which (c. AD 270) removed most of the rest of the earlier building. Room 3 is in the foreground, and room 2 beyond; the latter is very well preserved apart from a breach in the far wall. You will note a blocked doorway, lacking fresco treatment, to the right. The floors in both rooms are of good quality *opus signinum* (mortar with a crushed brick admixture), and are virtually intact apart from a couple of medieval pits, one of which reveals details of the hypocaust below. Box flue-tiles are visible in the walls of both rooms. But it is the extraordinary survival of the frescoed walls up to 2 m (6 ft 6 in) high which will have caught your eye in these two rooms: above a dado of red or green is a series of white panels framed predominantly in yellow and red, and flanked by elegant columns in perspective, of which the lower parts and bases are visible. Such a framework reflects developments in painting in Italy during the second century, and ultimately reflects the taste for this kind of wall decoration so prevalent at Pompeii and Herculaneum in the first centuries BC and AD. This is evidence for classical Mediterranean taste in interior decor being displayed in cosmopolitan Dover in the years around AD 200.

Yet even more intriguing are the objects on the perspective 'shelf' in front of these panels: they include a torch, a vine tendril, a basket, and a Bacchic wand (*thyrsus*), repeated several times round the walls of rooms 2, 3 and 4 (to your right). Fallen fragments from room 3, displayed in a case on the upper level (far side), show that here the white panels were occupied by human figures, including probably Bacchus and his female companions, the maenads. While having one room of your private house occupied by Bacchic murals would occasion no surprise, having three of the rooms so decorated would be surprising. Yet all four of the major rooms discovered here have hypocausts, and such a number in a private house at this date, even in the wealthiest of towns, would be exceptional. It seems therefore more likely that the structure is part of a public building – not a bath-house (there are no immersion baths anywhere), but perhaps, as the excavator suggested, a *mansio* or official inn for travellers of high rank, such as we might expect in a major port such as Dover. Viewed in this light, the uniform decorative scheme repeated in several rooms seems more plausible.

Moving to your left, past the diorama of Roman Dover with its forts and twin lighthouses, and then down the stairs, you come to a display case of some unusual finds (including a bronze hand holding an imperial eagle). Facing you are the remains of room 1, with a channelled hypocaust built of blocks of limestone capped by flat tiles. There are further flue-tiles in the walls but no surviving frescoes in this room, where the neat coursed masonry of its walls, with tile bonding-courses, contrasts strikingly with the irregularity of the doorway blocking.

Moving round, you come to the three impressively preserved brick flue-arches, of which only the left one shows evidence of substantial use. The walling here stands 3 m (10 ft) high, and even part of the external rendering, painted red, is still intact. The lower walls in front of you clearly belong to an earlier structure: one is actually incorporated into the walling of the Painted House. The room to the left here seems to be a later addition, because it masks the flue at this point. In the case behind you, note especially the tile scratched with what looks more like an antelope than a bull, despite the graffito TAVRI – which may mean 'belonging to Taurus' rather than 'of the bull' or 'bulls'. Pause at the corner to observe the fresco in room 4, and the foundation trench of the Saxon Shore fort which sliced through it. Now walk round to the other side of the projecting tower and note how it rests on the demolished remains of room 5 of the Painted House; the room had a channelled hypocaust of the same type as in room 1. Massive building blocks were thrown on the floor of this room to provide an adequate foundation for the third-century defences. Finally here, you can observe the well preserved facing of the Roman fort wall, here nine courses or so high, and 2.5 m (8 ft 2 in) thick. The tower is not bonded with the curtain wall and was therefore a later addition; how much later is uncertain.

Adjacent to the Roman Painted House along York Street is a huge building erected to house the White Cliffs Experience, which opened in 1991 but which closed its doors for the last time in 2000. At the time of writing (late 2001), the future of the building is still uncertain: one possibility under discussion is that it will become Dover's new public library. Just outside the building's façade are the remains of the north part of the east gate of the *classis Britannica* fort of *c.* AD 130, and a projecting tower added to the Saxon Shore fort of *c.* 270 adjacent to it at a higher level: for this spot marks one of the points where the defences of the two forts intersected (Fig. 6). The semicircular front of the *classis Britannica* gate-tower, projecting forward from the line of the walls, is a feature highly unusual at this date (cf. Castell Collen in Wales for a

6 *Dover, gate-tower of* classis Britannica *fort (foreground), with tower of late Roman fort*

slightly later example: p. 329). The Dover fort was clearly a
prestige monument, designed to impress: the whole gate was
originally some 12.5 m (41 ft) wide. These Roman structures
can be comfortably viewed by looking over the low wall on
York Street at the SW corner of the modern building which
formerly housed the White Cliffs Experience.

When access to this building is possible again, a further
portion of the *classis Britannica* fort, with a stretch of the
north defensive wall and part of a barrack-block within it, will
be able to be seen in the basement, where some pottery finds
are also displayed. The barrack belongs to the fort of *c.* 130,
which was partly rebuilt *c.* 150 and more fundamentally
refurbished *c.* 200; but ten years or so later the fleet seems to
have given up its base completely. In the 1970–1 excavations,
nine barracks (out of a likely total of ten) were located as well
as two granaries and a latrine, and in 1990 part of another
building within the fort, with painted plaster of some
distinction (the commandant's house?) was located in the SW
quadrant, but these are not now visible. Long-term plans to
uncover and consolidate another of the buildings excavated in
the 1970s, a well preserved extramural military bath-house,
have not so far come to fruition.

In addition to these important post-war discoveries, Dover
possesses another monument unique in Britain which, by
contrast, has always been known. This is the Roman *pharos*,
or lighthouse, which adjoins the church of St Mary close to
the car-park in the grounds of Dover Castle [AM; S]; it is
reached from the old Dover–Deal road on the east side of the
town – avoid the A2 eastern ring road, Jubilee Way. The top
6 m (19 ft) are entirely medieval, the result of alterations by
Humphrey Duke of Gloucester between 1415 and 1437, but
the lower 13 m (43 ft) are good Roman work: it is built of
flint-rubble, originally faced in ashlar blocks, with external
brick bonding-courses (Fig. 7). The outer face, octagonal in
plan, is now much battered by decay and by medieval refacing
(especially on the NW); in Roman times it rose in a series of
eight vertical stages, with an offset of 30 cm (1 ft) at each
stage. It was probably about 25 m (80 ft) high, or 6 m (20 ft)
higher than the whole monument is today; and from the top a
beacon of fire would have risen by day and night, to guide
ships using the Channel. The Roman entrance survives on the

7 Dover, the Roman lighthouse

south, and some of the upper windows retain their stone voussoirs interlaced with brick. The square interior, now a roosting-place for pigeons, is equally impressive. The lighthouse was probably built in the second century, but this is general inference (on the basis of growing cross-Channel traffic then) rather than derived from secure archaeological evidence; a first-century date is not impossible. The church, which is late Saxon (*c*. 1000) in origin and was accompanied by a contemporary cemetery excavated in the 1960s, not surprisingly incorporates Roman material in its walls.

A second lighthouse was also built at Dover, on the Western Heights. Paintings show that it was still standing at the end of the seventeenth century, but a drawing of 1760

depicts a mere shapeless chunk of masonry, known variously
as 'The Bredenstone' and as 'The Devil's Drop', and what
was left was mutilated when the Western Heights
fortifications [AM; A] were built in 1805–6. All that survives
today is a long stretch of flints and tile-course encased in
stonework of 1861, and, on the surface above, three displaced
chunks of concrete propped up against one another. Re-used
material, including stamped tiles, indicates that this lighthouse
probably belongs to the later Roman period. The Western
Heights have partially re-opened to visitors in recent years,
but the paltry remains of this Roman lighthouse are not
currently accessible.

One more Saxon Shore fort belongs to this chapter, and it is
even more impressive than the examples in Kent – the site at
Pevensey** (TQ 644048) [AM; A]; it lies between
Eastbourne and Hastings, just south of the A27 which
bypasses it. This fort, too, now lies inland; in Roman times
the walls were built on a peninsula, with the sea coming right
up to the south wall and the harbour, assumed to have been
situated to the east in the area of the present car-park. The
Roman walls enclose an oval area of about 9 acres (3.65 ha).
That on the south has almost entirely vanished except for two
projecting towers, incorporated into the keep and the outer
walls of the medieval castle which lies at the SE angle. The
Roman name for Pevensey was ANDERITVM (or possibly
ANDERITV), meaning 'the great ford'; this is more likely than
the variant reading ANDERIDA.

Although earlier occupation of the site cannot be ruled out,
the fort as we see it today was built *c.* AD 295, either during
the period of the pretender Carausius' break-away 'empire'
(consisting of Britain and parts of Gaul), or more probably
during that of his successor, Allectus (AD 293–6). The date is
reasonably certain: it derives partly from the tree-ring dating
of wooden piles, found in excavations in 1994 underpinning
the stone foundations of the walls on the SE side, but also on
coin evidence from building debris left at the time of
construction. An estimate based on the quantities of the
different materials required, the distance they needed to be
conveyed from source, and the transport options, has
suggested that the fort required 160,000 man days to complete
– in other words, that a team of 285 men could have finished

it in two years, or a team of 115 in five years. A coin of
AD 330/5 found under a tower in the 1930s, if its find-spot is
correctly recorded, might suggest a later, major repair of that
date. The appearance of the 'Pevensey fleet' (*classis
Anderetianorum*) stationed in Gaul in a late Roman document
of *c.* 395 (the *Notitia Dignitatum*) may imply that ANDERITVM
was already given up by then; for two brick stamps,
previously taken as evidence for further reconstruction at
Pevensey under the Emperor Honorius (AD 395–423), have
now been shown to be fakes – they were hoaxes probably
'planted' during excavation work by a well-known forger, Mr
Charles Dawson, who exhibited them to the Society of
Antiquaries in London in 1907. The Anglo-Saxon Chronicle
relates how a vain defence of the fort was made in 491,
ending in a terrible massacre. The site then lay derelict until
the Normans used the walls as an outer bailey for their castle.

Starting at The Royal Oak and Castle pub, you should first
go through the east postern. Putlog holes for Roman
scaffolding are clearly visible in the upper part of the exterior
masonry on either side of the gate. The present opening is
medieval. Whether there was also a Roman postern gate here
is uncertain: the Roman east gate may, for example, have been
located further south, and was destroyed during the building
of the medieval castle. The interior of the fort was partially
excavated in the early years of the twentieth century, when
only a few traces of timber buildings and hearths were found.
On the right, near the trees just before the gap where the wall
has fallen away, the internal face has been cleared down
below present-day ground-level. Here you can see that the
thickness of the wall is reduced by offsets; note, too, how the
lowest 2.50 m (8 ft) retain their facing-stones, as this part of
the wall was covered by earth in the post-Roman period and
so escaped the later stone-robbing and weathering which have
ravaged the top part. You will also see, from the 1930s
excavation photograph which is displayed here, that a further
nine courses of faced Roman masonry lie buried below the
present level of the grass.

Now return to the path and go on towards the west gate. A
short isolated stretch of south wall, its outer facing still well
preserved, can be seen among trees to the left of the path. The
west gate consisted of a central arched entrance 2.75 m (9 ft)

wide, with two guardrooms on either side, of which only the
lowest courses of one survive; the whole was then flanked by
the two gigantic towers (the existing gate jamb is medieval).
Putlog holes are particularly visible above the first layer of
bonding-courses, less so in the row immediately above the
second bonding-course. In the more southerly tower, note that
much of the surface is covered by flintwork which represents
medieval refacing; only in fact at the rounded front face of the
tower are original Roman facing-stones still preserved. In
front of this west entrance a ditch was dug across the isthmus
joining the peninsula on which the fort stood to the mainland,
and part of it too is visible.

From here mount the fence to follow the walls closely, back
towards the east gate again: they are about 3.65 m (12 ft) thick
and stand virtually to their original height except for the
parapet. Facing-stones and bonding-courses are well
preserved, and the few patches of flintwork used in the facing
(where the parapet survives, for example) show how little
repair the Roman walls needed during medieval times. From
the west gate you first reach three towers; here, as elsewhere,
they are bonded into the wall and therefore must have been
built at the same time. Putlog holes are again particularly
visible between the second and third towers. Then comes a
magnificent stretch of wall (Fig. 8) where section-joins
between building-parties can easily be detected (note how the
rows of green sandstone or brick bonding-courses do not tally
with those of adjacent sections). A drainage culvert will be
spotted in the lowest course at the point where the first
vertical fissure in the wall occurs. Next, immediately before
the fallen sector, was a small postern gate, a simple curved
passage in the wall, now obscured by a 1939–45 gun turret.
Follow the path through the collapsed remains and out on to
the grass in front of the next standing stretch. The highest
tower here includes a blocked Roman window in its west side.
Now pass through the gap in the hedge and cross the road, to
follow the walls back to the east gate. The herringbone
patchwork representing Norman repair-work is especially
clear on the last tower before the gate.

The military antiquities of Kent and Sussex predominantly
belong, as we have seen, to a late phase in the Roman
occupation of Britain, when the peace and security of SE

8   Pevensey, late Roman fort, the north wall

England was threatened for the first time since AD 43. Now it is time to turn to the civilian life of the towns and villas in this part of the province. Two trunk-roads, both built in the early years of the occupation, served SE England. One was Watling Street, which started at Richborough and reached London by way of Canterbury and Rochester: the A2 follows the Roman line for much of its course. The other was Stane Street, which linked London and Chichester (for the posting-stations en route at Alfoldean and Hardham, see App. 1). From Canterbury there were roads to Reculver, Dover and Lympne, the last one surviving as the B2068 (Stone Street); and another road branched off Watling Street near London and headed for the south coast near Lewes, enabling swift transport to the Thames of corn from the Downs and iron from the Wealden mines. The road is unusual in being metalled for many miles with iron slag. Earlier editions of this book took readers to a stretch exposed by the Sussex Archaeological Society at Holtye, reached by a footpath on the south side of the A264,

100 m east of the White Horse Inn (sign). Since, however, that
fragment is now overgrown and unimpressive, a more easily
accessible stretch of it can be seen on Camp Hill in **Ashdown
Forest** (TQ 471290) a little further south. This lies on the
B2026, ½ mile (800 m) south of its junction with the B2188,
about 5 miles (8 km) north of Uckfield: watch out for a small
car-park on the west side of the road, opposite a tall radio
mast. Next to the car-park is a short stretch of the London–
Lewes Roman road, with the mound of the *agger* prominent
here; unusually, the ditch lining the Roman road is still
partially preserved on the far side (provision of ditches on
either side of a Roman road was standard practice). The near
side of the *agger*, however, has been partly disfigured by a
stream which has eroded it. As at Holtye, the road here was
surfaced with iron slag, but this has been protected by a cover
of heather and is not visible. The road is here in a fine
position, with extensive views westwards over Ashdown
Forest.

Large parts of the London–Lewes Roman road were
metalled with iron slag for convenience, because of the
proximity of major Roman iron works in the Sussex Weald.
Three dozen sites have been identified between the East
Grinstead area on the west and the Battle–Sedlescombe area
on the east. Iron working and smelting was already in
operation at many of these by the end of the first century, but
the real boom for the industry came in the second century.
Decline and abandonment had set in by the mid third century,
possibly because of over-exploitation or because deforestation
had made fuel for the furnaces more expensive and more
difficult to obtain: in both cases working will have become
uneconomic. The largest of these sites was that at **Beauport
Park** (TQ 786140), 3 miles (4.8 km) east of Battle. Much of
the huge iron slag-heap here was taken away for road
metalling in the nineteenth century, but what remains is still
quite impressive; it has been estimated that there were
originally about 100,000 tons of it, representing an iron
production of some 50,000 tons. Even more impressive is a
small but excellently preserved bath-house, excavated in
1970–5 on the slope above the slag bank. Its carefully
constructed walls stand over 2.15 m (7 ft) high in places, and
the lower part of a window also survives. Five rooms had

hypocausts, two with *pilae*, three of the channelled variety.
The bath-house was built in the second quarter of the second
century and was repaired and extended in the early third,
before being abandoned and systematically stripped *c*. 250, at
a time of general decline in the whole Wealden iron industry.
The discovery of over 1,300 tiles stamped CL BR here (as
well as on other Wealden sites) demonstrates the direct
involvement of the British fleet, the *classis Britannica*, in the
operation of the iron workings. It must be stressed that at
present (2001) the bath-house is covered, and its walls
sand-bagged; there is nothing whatever to see at the site. That
this has been the case for many years because of a shortage of
funds is nothing short of a national disgrace; one hopes that
the long-term project conceived by the man who discovered
the bath-house, the late Gerald Brodribb, to conserve it and
present it to the public, can be brought to fruition in the near
future with funding from the National Heritage Lottery Fund.

At Beauport Park a settlement of some 8 acres (3.25 ha) is
indicated by surface finds across the stream from the
bath-house. This of course was only a small mining village;
the major settlements of the south-east were at Chichester,
Rochester and Canterbury, but none of them has much left of
their Roman past to see.

Canterbury* (TR 151578) was DVROVERNVM
CANTIACORVM, the 'town by the marshes' which was the tribal
capital of the Cantiaci. Excavation since 1945 has revealed
many features of the Roman town, but little is now visible.
The medieval walls follow the line of their Roman
predecessors, enclosing an area of 130 acres (53 ha), but little
Roman masonry is now exposed. One fragment of a gateway
(the 'Quenin Gate') can be seen embedded in the medieval
wall about 1.20 m (4 ft) from the ground, at the most
northerly (right-hand) end of the car-park in Broad Street,
very close to the last square tower in this NE sector of city
wall (1 on Fig. 9). It consists of two large Kentish ragstone
blocks and a dozen brick courses marking the turn of an arch;
the two further large blocks at the same level, 2.60 m
(8 ft 6 in) to the left, are also Roman work *in situ*, and formed
part of the eastern jamb of the same gateway. This was a
single-passageway gate; by contrast the SE gate (Riding
Gate), the entry into the city which travellers on Watling

Street from Dover would have first reached, had a double-carriageway. Excavation at the latter in 1986–7 demonstrated, however, that the more southerly passageway was blocked up before *c.* AD 325, and its former roadway used for bronze-

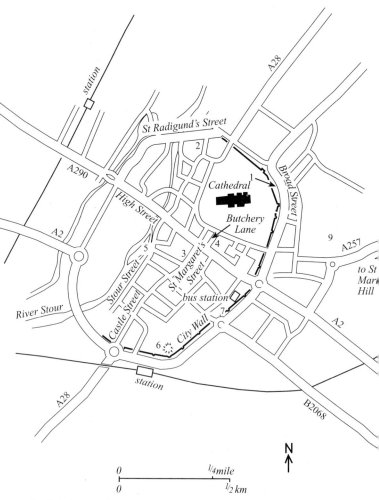

9   *Canterbury, location map*

working. There was no evidence of an early gateway below, so the gates of Canterbury are contemporary with the building of the defences, *c*. AD 270/90. The plan of this gate is marked out in red in the pavement at the roundabout west of the bus station (7 on Fig. 9), but no Roman masonry is visible.

On the north side of the walled circuit, in St Radigund's Street (2), the removal of plasterwork on the north wall of the church of St Mary Northgate has revealed that the city wall, incorporated in it, stood to its full height of nearly 9 m (29 ft). A very sharp eye may detect faint traces of corner stones marking the position of the crenellations, now blocked, on a level immediately below a small round-headed window. The latter belongs to the twelfth century and so the city wall below is earlier: it has been suggested that much of the visible facing is even of Roman date, but the use of flintwork at all periods in this part of England makes it very difficult to be certain that this is indeed Roman work rather than Saxon or Norman. Excavations in 1977 on the base of the city wall immediately adjacent showed that the Roman flint core, still visible in part, had been refaced and rebuilt in the fourteenth century. Work here has also confirmed the results from elsewhere, that the Roman walls and a contemporary earth bank behind them were not built until *c*. 270/90, later than their counterparts in most other Romano-British towns.

Of public buildings, we know most about the theatre which lay at the junction of St Margaret's Street and Watling Street. This was of two main periods: about AD 80/90, when the first building was erected with timber seats on banks of gravel; and about 210/20, when the whole theatre was rebuilt in stone on a larger scale. To the later period belongs the one accessible fragment of the theatre which are the most easily accessible: a portion of the back wall is visible in Alberry's wine and food bar at 38, St Margaret's Street. An imposing fragment, 1.20 m (4 ft) high, of the curving outer wall of the auditorium exists in the basement of the property opposite, the 'Ha! Ha! Bar and Canteen' (3 on Fig. 9), but after redevelopment in 2001 the Roman structure has been hidden below floor level and is now accessible only with difficulty (by prior written arrangement) via trap-door and ladder. Other fragments are visible on private property in the cellars of 23, Watling Street and 5 and 6, St. Margaret's Street, but these are also not accessible without prior written permission from the owners.

At the heart of Canterbury, in Butchery Lane just off High Street (4 on Fig. 9), is the Roman Museum (Monday–Saturday, 1000–1700, all year round; Sunday, June–October only 1330–1700). Opened in 1994, the Museum contains important and unusual finds in a rather cramped setting, and in a display which regrettably often ignores the precise provenance and dating of objects. Among the large number of mock-ups dedicated to aspects of Roman life, note in the first room the unusual survival of a Roman wooden spade with iron outer edges (similar to the one from Stonea in the British Museum: p. 643), and, in the same case, a builder's bronze 'try and mitre' square inscribed with the name of its owner, G(aius) Cu(. . .) Valenus, found in 1978. In the next section, the case on fabric has a rare example of a triangular bone tablet used for the weaving of braid. The following room houses some of the principal finds from Roman Canterbury: in the case on the left, note a second-century samian ware dish from St Martin's cemetery with the Christian monogram, the chi-rho, scratched on its base (and PIA, 'pious', on the side), but both the form of the chi-rho and the early date of the pot raise doubts about the authenticity of this piece. Also here are a face-pot unusually decorated with the tools of a blacksmith (hammer, anvil, wedge, tongs etc.), presumably custom-made for the cremation burial it contained; and a pair of fine Roman swords, found in 1977 in the second-century burial of two men whose bodies had been hastily thrown in on top of each other (a Roman murder?). The case opposite, illustrating the Roman baths, contains a rare terracotta wall-spacer, together with the iron staple designed to create a cavity for hot air between the masonry wall and the plastered surface next to the bather (an alternative method to the more normal box flue-tile). Also here is a piece of the lead sheeting from a bathing pool, with outflow pipe and three lead staples, the position of which indicates that the lead would have been lined internally with stone veneer. Another case contains fragments of stone decoration (rudimentary acanthus leaves) from a classical-style temple believed to lie in a precinct next to the Roman theatre. Note in particular the fragment of green marble wall veneer (left panel, second row), which comes all the way from the Sparta region of Greece – a luxury item rare in Britain. An important hoard of late fourth-century silver-ware, deposited in the early fifth century (the latest coin is of AD 411/17), follows in the next section. Found in 1962, it includes four silver ingots, stamped with the names of the various workshops (*ex off*[*icina*]) which made them, and 11 silver spoons. One of the spoons bears the chi-rho Christian monogram, and another is inscribed VIRIBONIS(u)M (= 'I belong to a good man'); the curious silver implement, decorated with another chi-rho and ending in a curved prong, is currently interpreted, somewhat prosaically, and perhaps erroneously, as a toothpick.

The final part of the Museum contains the remains of part of a town-house preserved here *in situ*. First comes a room with a hypocaust, of which only the *pilae* supporting the vanished floor remain. The skeleton of a baby and a small hoard of bronze coins (*c*. AD 270) were found here. Beyond is a corridor paved with a tessellated floor containing two decorative mosaic panels with leaf- and flower-motifs, and fragments of a third. Unlike the earlier display before the current Museum was built, when the mosaics could be seen from above, this floor can now only be viewed from an oblique angle which makes real appreciation of it difficult. Excavation in 1946 showed that the corridor itself was a second-century addition to a late first-century stone house, but that the mosaic was added later, probably in the third century. The Canterbury Heritage Centre in Stour Street (5 on Fig. 9; same hours as the Roman Museum) also displays a small selection of finds in its first room, notably a silvered bronze brooch with a cupid astride a dolphin (mid-first century AD).

Two other Roman relics in Canterbury deserve a brief mention. One is the Dane John, probably a Roman burial-mound of the first or second century, much obscured and altered by landscape-gardening (6 on Fig. 9). This and an attendant cremation cemetery originally lay outside the Roman town but were later incorporated within the third-century defences. The other is St Martin's church, which lies on a hill to the east of the city on the Sandwich road, in an area of Roman cemeteries (A257: 8 on Fig. 9). Inside, a wall of Roman brickwork, still 5 m (16 ft 6 in) high, is clearly visible on the right-hand side of the chancel, pierced by a Saxon doorway. The rear wall of the nave, though much repaired, contains unmistakable Roman tile bonding-courses:

re-used Roman brick is, however a commonplace in early
medieval buildings in Canterbury (a good example is the
church of St Pancras, next to St Augustine's Abbey [AM; S]
on the Sandwich road: 9 on Fig. 9). Bede, writing in 731,
mentions 'a church built in honour of St Martin while the
Romans still lived in Britain'. The presence of Christianity in
Roman Canterbury is confirmed by the silver hoard mentioned
above; it is uncertain whether the Roman wall at St Martin's
is part of a Roman cemetery church, or of a Roman pagan
mausoleum only later converted to Christian worship. It is
often assumed that there was a Roman church under the
cathedral, but although a massive stone-built late Saxon
cathedral and traces of two predecessors were found in 1993
during reflooring of the present nave, no certain evidence for a
Roman church has been discovered there.

The remains of DVROBRIVAE ('the fort at the bridge') at
Rochester (TQ 738695) need not detain us long. The town,
23 acres (9.3 ha) in size, controlled the important crossing of
the Medway by Watling Street; there may well have been a
short-lived fort of the conquest period here. The urban
defences consisted, as so often, of an earth rampart and ditch
of the late second century fronted, at some time in the third
century, by a stone wall. Park in a car-park just off the inner
ring road which swings round the north side of the town
(marked *i* for 'Information'). On the south side of this
car-park is High Street with the Eagle Tavern (public house).
Go down the narrow footpath to the left of this pub, and
follow the path round to the seat. Straight ahead of you stands
the fine SW corner of the Roman town wall, faced with
Kentish ragstone but without tile-courses, an impressive 3 m
(10 ft) high; all its facing-stones are intact. Note that just after
the Roman wall begins to turn the corner, the medieval wall to
the left, carrying straight on, abuts on to it. If you follow the
path round, a further stretch of Roman facing is visible
beyond the metal gate. Another fragment is incarcerated in the
adjacent property to the west of Eagle Tavern (a wine bar),
and the rear of the Roman wall just viewed, including the
SW corner, is traceable in the small public garden behind the
wine bar. The first neat stretch has been over-restored and
stops abruptly, but the untampered Roman core is visible
beyond, although partly obscured by shrubbery.

Now cross High Street and follow the medieval walls along the ring road. After turning the corner you will see, under a stretch of modern brickwork, the core of the Roman stone defences at the west end of the car-park. Other fragments of core, unimpressive and difficult to reach, are visible in the Deanery Garden and elsewhere in the cathedral precinct. Another forms the foundations of the bailey-wall (built in 1087/9) of the Norman castle on its west side, fronting the Medway [AM; S]: remains of Roman work can be detected at the broken north end of this stretch, revealed by subsidence. From the Esplanade below, Roman rubble-core and two or three courses of Roman foundations, underpinned by the nineteenth-century revetment of the cliff, can be spotted below the Norman wall.

Of Roman **Chichester** (SU 861047), the NOVIOMAGVS REGINORVM ('new place of the Regini'), even less is visible. Fragmentary remains of timber buildings below the heart of the modern city, parts of military ditches near the east gate, and legionary belt-buckles, a sword and other armour, all point to Chichester's military origin. It may possibly have been a short-lived fortress for the Second Legion (c. AD 44–55?) during its thrust to the west, but more probably it served as a stores- and supply-base, especially if this area was a client-kingdom (see below) which did not need military control in the form of a fortress or fort. A further phase of timber building with associated industrial activity (c. 55–70) is civilian rather than military, indicating early urban development, but the fledgling town did not receive a regular street-grid until c. 75–85. From then onwards Chichester seems to have developed into a flourishing town, although little is known in detail of its buildings. Substantial parts of houses have been excavated from time to time, and the bath-house between Tower Street and West Street is known to have covered an area of some 95 m by 70 m (310 ft by 230 ft). None of this is now visible, and a plan in 1990 to re-excavate part of the baths for public display has regrettably not so far been realized.

The Museum at 29, Little London, contains the best of the small finds (Tuesdays–Saturdays, 1000–1730, all year round; 1 on Fig. 10): note in particular finds from the first-century military installations at Chichester, including the belt-plate

with the unusual engraved decoration of a running deer;
a huge marble head of an emperor from Bosham, probably
first-century (perhaps documenting further exceptional
patronage from Togidubnus? – see below, p. 68); an
extramural inscription in Purbeck marble dedicated to mother
goddesses (*matres domesticae*) by a treasurer, an *arc(arius)*;
two fragments of fourth-century polychrome geometric
mosaic from East Street; and a fragment of rare engraved

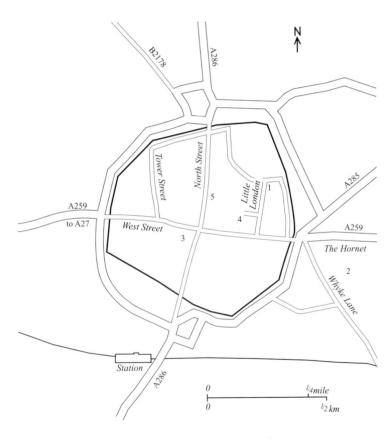

10   Chichester, location map

glass from the Chilgrove villa, showing Silenus (a companion of Bacchus) with a donkey.

The site of the amphitheatre (2 on Fig. 10) is visible as a hollow surrounded by a low elliptical bank in a recreation area on the east side of the city, reached from the south end of a passage called Whyke Lane from the A259/A286 (The Hornet); turn left along the path into the recreation ground. A metal plaque beside the path draws attention to the amphitheatre, which the path bisects. Its overall dimensions are about 55 m by 45 m (185 ft by 150 ft). According to its excavator in 1934, it was built about AD 80 and abandoned at the end of the second century, although the latter date in particular needs verifying in future work. The city walls follow their Roman course but no Roman masonry is visible, although the earth bank behind the walls is often well preserved: their line, together with information boards at intervals, can now be easily followed with the help of a leaflet, 'Chichester Walls Walk', obtainable at the Museum or at the Tourist Information Office, South Street. These defences, erected originally in the late second century as an earth bank and timber palisade and only later revetted in stone, enclose about 99 acres (40 ha). The projecting towers came still later, presumably in the fourth century. There is a portion of polychrome geometric mosaic on show *in situ* in the south aisle of the cathedral's retrochoir (3 on Fig. 10); found in 1966, it dates to the second century. For the sake of completeness, mention may be made also of a fourth-century fragment of coarse tessellation, in buff, set into the wall on the left of the opening leading into Little London Mews; this is at the entrance to the Little London car-park (4). And, for the record, The Army and Navy store in West Street has a fragment of black and white mosaic which decorated a room in the bath-house; and part of a massive flint foundation is visible in the cellars of the Dolphin and Anchor Hotel (perhaps belonging to a colonnade which lay on the south side of the forum).

Much more significant than any of these scattered relics is an inscription (5) found in 1723 and now placed in the wall under the portico of the Assembly Rooms in North Street (Fig. 11). This records a temple to Neptune and Minerva erected by a guild of artisans (*collegium fabrorum*) on the

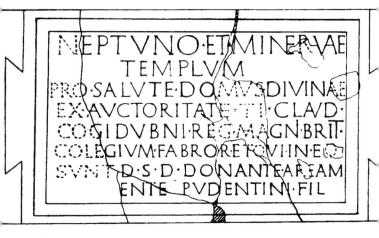

11   Chichester, North Street, the Togidubnus inscription

authority of Tiberius Claudius [. . .]dubnus, who is described
as *rex magnus Augusti in Britannia*, 'great king of the emperor
in Britain'; the title is paralleled on inscriptions elsewhere in
the Empire. This must refer to the man whom the historian
Tacitus calls Cogidubnus, described as one 'who maintained
his unswerving loyalty down to our own times'. Recent
research has suggested that the more correct form of the name
is likely on linguistic grounds to have been Togidubnus
(a variant reading, in fact, in one of the manuscripts of
Tacitus). Togidubnus or Cogidubnus established his kingdom
in the former kingdom of the Atrebates, which included the
Chichester region on its eastern flank, and did his best to
foster pro-Roman attitudes in the early years of the conquest;
it seems most likely that he was made a client-king in AD 43
or 44, presumably when still a very young man, rather than
later. In return, the Romans respected his authority as a native
client-king and only after his death was the area formally
assimilated into the Roman province. It was almost certainly
by this loyal subject of Rome that the next site, Fishbourne,
was erected.

  Fishbourne** (SU 841047) is one of the outstanding sites
of Roman Britain. It was discovered accidentally in 1960 and

excavations continued annually from 1961 until the site opened to the public in 1968. Thanks to the generosity of the late Donald Margary, the area was saved from housing development and an impressive modern cover-building was erected. The site is signposted from a roundabout on the A259 ring road on the west side of Chichester, and can be visited every day from 1000 between early February and mid-December, closing at 1600 in February, November and December, at 1700 between March and July and in September and October, and at 1800 in August. From mid-December to February the site is open only on Saturdays and Sundays 1000–1600.

The first occupation at Fishbourne was military: the remains of two timber store-buildings excavated under the east wing of the later palace belong to what is clearly a military supply-depot dating to the early years of the conquest. The depot was soon cleared away, and some time in the late 40s or early 50s a timber house with a separate building (perhaps a servants' range) was constructed. It had clay or mortar floors, and there were traces of painted plaster, so a man of some status must have lived here.

Then, in the 60s, the first masonry building was erected at Fishbourne. Its site lies astride the main road and so could not be completely excavated, but trenching was able to show that it comprised a large colonnaded garden, a bath-suite, a set of living-rooms and servants' quarters. The whole was elaborately decorated with stucco and painted plaster; its floors were paved in mosaic or marble. It was no ordinary building; yet its magnificence was to be far outstripped by what was to come.

Some time after 75/80, a start was made on the building of the great palace which has made Fishbourne famous. Only half of the palace itself is visible today: originally it consisted of four wings arranged around a formal garden. The main living-rooms of the owner lay on the south, and are now largely under the houses and a modern road; this wing had a colonnade on both sides, overlooking the formal garden on one side and a natural garden stretching down to the sea on the other. The official wing was on the west; its chief room, in the centre, was an apsed audience-chamber where the owner would have received official visitors. The east wing contained an entrance-hall designed to impress (as, indeed, was the whole palace), and suites of rooms arranged around courtyards, probably for visitors of lower rank as the standard of comfort was less than that of the north wing. The latter, protected in its entirety by the modern cover-building, had a sumptuous series of mosaic-paved guest-rooms ranged about two private courtyards. Servants' quarters must lie elsewhere, still to be uncovered.

We have here, then, a palace of some 10 acres (4 ha) – a staggering complex of colonnades, halls and rooms magnificently adorned with painted plaster, stucco and mosaic, built by an army of skilled craftsmen from the Continent (either from southern Gaul or possibly from northern Italy, to judge from the closest parallels for the mosaics). The estimated cost for the entire project in modern-day terms stands at about £2.5 million. It is true that some British villas approached the size of Fishbourne, but that was not until the fourth century. For the first century AD the Fishbourne Palace is entirely without parallel, not only in Britain but in the whole of Europe outside Italy: it is a piece of Italy transplanted into a distant, newly conquered province. Who, then, could be the owner of such a palace – a high-ranking Roman official, or a local landowner of great distinction? This is where Tiberius Claudius Togidubnus (above, p. 68) fits into the picture. For a Roman official residence to be built so close to one of the capitals of a loyal ally would have been an intolerable snub; and it is therefore more likely (although we shall never know for certain) that the palace was the home of King Togidubnus in his old age, and that the earlier structures at Fishbourne (the timber house and the first masonry building) represent the earlier stages of his rise to luxury.

One striking piece of evidence found in 1995 goes some way to supporting this hypothesis: a gold ring of mid-first-century date (itself a rarity in Roman Britain at this time) was found east of the Roman palace inscribed with the name TI(berii) CLAVDI CATVARI, 'I belong to Tiberius Claudius Catuarus'. Catuarus is a British, not a Roman name, and 'Tiberius Claudius' indicates that, like Togidubnus, he had earned the Roman citizenship from the Emperor Claudius, either in his own right, or as part of the family of Togidubnus.

It is surely not coincidence that this ring was found so close to the palace which has very good claim to be considered as the home of another Briton of high birth who was also a Roman citizen – King Tiberius Claudius Togidubnus himself.

Excavations east of the main site in 1983–6, in advance of the building of the bypass, found a gravelled road leading straight to the east entrance, and that the whole of this area east of the palace was laid out as a semi-formal garden with trees, shrubs and paths. More recently, in 1995–9, immediately east of the east wing, an enigmatic stone courtyard building was excavated; it has now been backfilled. It was erected as early as the proto-palace (AD 50/60), and was still in use in the second century. A contemporary timber aqueduct supplying water for both proto-palace and palace was also found. The function of the courtyard building is uncertain: superficial similarity with early military *principia* is probably misleading, so perhaps this was the administrative office of the steward who ran the estate, at any rate during the palace period and after, complete with sump (for a strong-box?) under the floor of one of the rooms. Another possibility, that favoured by the excavators, is to see it as a security- and control-point for those entering and leaving the palace, policed by the client king's military bodyguard. A third suggestion, that it is a shrine, lacks credibility.

Drastic changes in the palace itself occurred *c*. AD 90/100, no doubt soon after the death of Togidubnus or of his immediate heir. A bath-suite was inserted into the north wing, and another into the east, suggesting the splitting up of the palace into separate units (the palace baths lay at the SE corner – convenient for the owner, but a long way for his guests in the north wing). Various other modifications to the north wing, including the laying of more mosaics, will be noted in turn below: the villa, though lacking its former grandeur, still maintained a level of affluence markedly higher than elsewhere in the contemporary Romano-British countryside. Finally, at the end of the third century, a disastrous fire brought the life of Fishbourne to a close until its resurrection in 1960, the year of the laying of a water-main which caused its discovery.

On arriving at the site (note the massive square oven, presumably part of the palace kitchens, beside the path to the

ticket-office), first pay a visit to the Museum where all the
phases described above are imaginatively set out and
illustrated with photographs, models and plans. Here too are
the principal small finds. Watch out in particular for the fresco
decoration and *opus sectile* floor patterns from the proto-
palace in case 12; massive Corinthian and Tuscan capitals
nearby (demonstrating that the full language of classical
architecture was presented in the palace); and in case 24 *opus
sectile* decoration, a fragment of impressionistically painted
wall-plaster, and a moulded stucco cornice, all from the
palace. Opposite 27 is the head of a boy in expensive white
marble, a material rarely used at any time for Romano-British
portraiture, while at the exit make sure you do not miss the
replica of the Catuarus ring (p. 70). A lathe-turned wooden
bowl and a hipposandal for a horse's hoof, uniquely made of
lead (a votive?), are also displayed here. In the main
concourse is a model of the palace as it may have appeared in
about AD 80. Just beyond it, to your right, is part of a simple
corridor mosaic in red and grey laid *c.* AD 100. From here you
begin your tour of the north wing.

The first room which you see on the left of the viewing-
platform (labelled 1, also on Fig. 12) was also one of the last
additions to the palace: this hypocaust was still being
constructed when fire destroyed the whole building at the end
of the third century. The diagonal flues are built with flat roof-
tiles (*tegulae*), their flanges still visible; so is the brickwork in
the central part of the hypocaust, which is made up of *tegulae*
placed upside-down (the *pilae* themselves are, however, of

12   Fishbourne, Roman palace, plan of the north wing

purpose-made bricks). No trace of the floor above was found, and it had probably never been laid. The floor-level here was in the process of being raised: fragments of the mosaic laid when the palace was first built can be seen, with traces of fire on those and below the hypocaust wall in front of you. Of the floor in 2, of second-century date, little remains, but the adjoining room (5) has preserved its polychrome floor (also second-century): it can be viewed either as a pair of scallop-shells, or as the splayed tail of a peacock, with the main body of the bird destroyed but the feet (?) surviving. On the other side of the catwalk (rooms 3 and 4) are two simple geometric mosaics and a solid dividing wall which do belong to the original palace; these floors seem to have survived later use without the need for replacement. The masonry in the corner of room 4 represents the flue of a second-century oven.

Moving on, you reach a courtyard of the palace-phase, originally open to the sky. Its stone gutter, poorly preserved, has been totally replaced in modern materials. The tiles seen here are part of the collapsed superstructure. Opposite (behind you) is the best-preserved mosaic at Fishbourne (7), dating to the second half of the second century and again, therefore, laid when the palace had ceased to operate as a single unit: remember that only half of the visible mosaics at Fishbourne belong to the original palace. The central roundel depicts a winged cupid riding a dolphin, with sea-panthers and sea-horses in the surrounding semicircles. Compare the two sea-horses: that nearer the catwalk is much more skilfully executed. Note, too, how the guilloche border which surrounds the mosaic changes its colour-composition: several craftsmen must have been at work on the same mosaic. At the same time as the laying of this floor, the little rooms on either side (6 and 6a) were given hypocausts; only the impressions of *pilae* remain, the heating proving so ineffective that they were destroyed in the third century. The charred wooden door threshold to 6a is still *in situ*, testimony to the fire which destroyed the villa in the later third century. The little mosaic in a room to your right (8), a simple knot-motif and a guilloche circle surrounded by dolphins, was laid in the early third century.

At the top of the steps, note another burnt door-sill at the entrance to the red tessellated corridor (27). Now come down the steps and examine room 12, which contains the best preserved of the first-century palace mosaics – a pleasing geometric design – as it was never refloored even when a partition (perhaps of pisé rather than of timber) chopped it in two. Remains of its wall-plaster have been reassembled on the wall in front of you, while more of it lies fallen to the right. The success of the floor design is shown by the poor imitation of it which was laid in the mid second century in the room beyond (14). Return to the catwalk now, which skirts rooms 9–11. In room 9 the white mortar floor replaced an earlier palace-period mosaic, a fragment of which still survives in one corner. The skeleton here was buried in the ruins of the building some time after its final destruction. Rooms 10–11 have plain or simple mosaic floors laid in the second or third century, except that in 11 a small fragment of first-century black and white mosaic may be seen, contrasting with the much larger and coarser tesserae of the pavement above it.

Now turn around and examine the fine but fragmentary mosaic in room 16. This is a first-century palace-phase pavement of c. AD 80, but unlike the rest at Fishbourne it is not in its original place, since it was discovered below the cupid mosaic when the latter was raised for conservation in 1979. Inevitably most of the original floor, transferred to this room in 1980, had been destroyed when the cupid mosaic was laid, but much of two sides of its border and parts of seven of the 16 square panels it contained survive. The stylized town wall depicted in the border, with towers at the corners and a single- or double-portal gateway in the middle of each side, is a design comparatively common in Italy and elsewhere in the western Empire, but rare in Britain.

Next retrace your steps a little, passing on your right the mosaic already mentioned (14), to examine the floors in the room beyond (13): this displays two superimposed mosaics, the original geometric pavement being replaced about AD 100, probably when the palace first changed hands. The centre of the new mosaic depicted a head of Medusa, of which part of her right eye and eyebrow and some of her snaky hair can be made out (upside-down from this viewpoint). The floor has been much damaged by ploughing, but enough remains to show its poor technical standard, and it is perhaps the work of a local, not a foreign, mosaicist – if so, one of the earliest such practitioners in Britain. Note, for example, of the two eight-sided panels in front of you, how that on the left has a double octagonal frame in black, but that the one on your right is different: both the size of the central rosette and the squashed shape of the octagon have left no room for the inclusion of the inner frame. Such incompetence arose from the fact that too many chequer-boards had already been laid further to the right, when of course this easier background part of the floor should have been set in place after the more intricate floral designs had been completed.

Behind you is the site of another of the open courtyards of the original palace. Here are displayed some fragments of black and white geometric mosaics lifted from the west wing, with signs of the heavy burning from the third-century conflagration on the largest. Note also that two other fragments here have coarse red tesserae, patching wear in their door thresholds.

Of the north wing beyond this point very little remains, as before the mid second century the whole of it, including a newly inserted bath-suite, was demolished because of serious subsidence. Parts of three mosaics, however, which belonged to the original palace, still survive. The first mosaic (21) is simple but quite effective. The small white diamond on its border is clearly not part of the design and may be the mosaicist's signature. The next room (20) has a fine, if fragmentary, polychrome mosaic (Fig. 13). The central portion is destroyed, but enough remains of the surrounding rosettes and ivy-leaves, the band of guilloche, and the corner vases, to show the skill of the mosaicist both in his mastery of composition and in his use of colour. Little is left of the third mosaic (19), partially destroyed by the water-main trench of 1960.

After the mock-up of a Roman dining-room are some mosaic pavements from other sites – a fragmentary fourth-century geometric mosaic from Chichester, and a well preserved mosaic of *c.* 300 from a villa at Chilgrove, 6 miles (9.6 km) north of Chichester. It is a product of the so-called Central Southern Group of mosaicists who later worked at Bignor: the interlaced square is one of their favourite compositions, and motifs such as the chalice from which a flower grows (bottom left-hand corner), lotus flowers (bottom

13   Fishbourne, Roman palace, first-century polychrome mosaic

right), and the guilloche knot with additions (the lozenge at
centre bottom) also recur in their work. All these motifs, in a
slightly more developed form, recur at Bignor (p. 81). A few
fragments of the early second-century bath-suite survive at the
far end of the cover-building: best preserved is the small
hot-water bath (28), with remains of its quarter-moulding
mortar sealing round the bottom, and square tiles with
concentric circles marked on them.

Now you should go out into the garden, flanked by parts of
the east and west wings. The plan of the former is marked out
in modern materials (note especially the entrance-hall with its

central pool, which lies on the main east-west axis of the palace at the centre of the east wing). Near here a 'Roman garden' has been planted: note in the covered building here the small display of garden finds, especially a Roman bedding pot with holes in it for plants to take root.

Next retrace your steps and make your way along the central path towards the west wing. What you see here is not guesswork: excavation revealed the pattern of the bedding-trenches, and these have been followed in the reconstruction. Although pollen analysis could not determine what shrub was used, box is the most likely and that is what has been planted. At the west end of the central path (remember that only half the formal garden is visible today), there is a square construction made of tiles, probably the base for a statue.

Ahead are steps leading up to the site of the audience-chamber, a square room with a semicircular apse, where the owner would have welcomed official guests, heard petitions, etc. This is architecturally a most unusual shape of room to find in a provincial setting as early as the first century AD: its closest parallels are in the imperial palace on the Palatine in Rome, and in the palaces of hellenistic kings such as Herod the Great. It underlines the exceptional nature of the Fishbourne building, and strengthens the case that a king did indeed own and live in the palace. The site of this and that part of the west wing still accessible is still grassed over: early plans to expose its masonry have been shelved, but at least it deserves to have its plan marked out, as with the east wing. Finally, going back towards the modern entrance along the outside wall of the west wing, you reach the NW corner, where the gutter, column-bases, and the projecting corner of the stone foundation for a water-tank (to feed the fountains which adorned the garden), can be seen. Here your visit to this extraordinary site ends. Nowhere else in Britain will you see a Roman garden laid out in its original bedding, nowhere else will you see *in situ* mosaics laid as early as some of those in the north wing. Fishbourne is an exceptional site, without parallel at such an early date, as noted above, in the European provinces of the Roman world.

Another villa-site can easily be reached from Chichester: it is near **Bignor**** (SU 987146), a village situated about 14 miles (22.4 km) to the NE, mid-way between the A285 and the A29, but more conveniently approached from the latter (minor road via West Burton, leaving the A29 near the inn at the foot of Bury Hill). It is open from 1 March to 31 October, daily except Monday 1000–1700, except that between June and September it is open every day and closes at 1800. The villa at Bignor, found in 1811, was excavated and published in superb folio volumes by the antiquary Samuel Lysons in the following years. But it was not until partial re-excavation in the late 1950s and early 60s that anything of its historical sequence was revealed, and this information has been supplemented by a series of important research excavations, conducted annually from 1985 to 2000. There is increasing evidence for occupation on the site in the first century, including a substantial ditched enclosure, but as yet no associated structures. A number of both timber-framed and stone foundation walls, together with associated pits and gullies, dates to the second century AD (Phase I). The first coherent residential building with stone footings, however, a simple five-roomed rectangular villa (rooms 27–30 and 40 on Fig. 14), subsequently incorporated in the later west wing, was not erected before about AD 225 (Phase IIA). It was given a corridor and small 'wings' (rooms 33–4 and 41) later in the third century (Phase IIE), so becoming an example of the 'winged corridor' villa so widespread in the Romano-British countryside. Only in the early fourth century did the villa expand to enclose a courtyard, at first around three sides (Phase IIIA), with barn 1 and shed 1 as outbuildings. Slightly later in the fourth century, the villa reached its maximum extent: the barn and shed were demolished and replaced by a new extension of rooms at the NE corner (rooms 11 and 16–24, added in two separate stages); the courtyard was enclosed on the east by a fourth corridor (60–3, also in two stages); new rooms were built on the NW and sumptuous mosaics laid (3, 5, 6 and 7); an additional wing was erected on the SW (43–4, 78–80); and fresh outbuildings, replacing earlier ones demolished by the expansion of the villa eastwards (shed 2 and barn 2), were put up, as well as an enclosing farmyard wall.

To get some idea of the Bignor villa's size in this last phase, stand with your back to the huts at the modern entrance and face the driveway up to the villa. On your right, the west wing has been marked out: in front of you, part of the corridor serving the south wing is exposed. The south wing ended at the point where a modern hut covers the Medusa mosaic (far left), and another corridor then turned to join up with the north wing, less than half of which is represented by the huts behind you. The farm buildings lay further still to the left. A model of the villa, together with some of the finds, can be seen in a room (8 on the plan, Fig. 14), still floored with its Roman mosaic, to the right of the present entrance.

The glory of Bignor is its splendid series of mosaic pavements laid in the first half of the fourth century, probably c. 325/50. The mosaic in the first room (7, to the left of the entrance), which may have been the principal dining-room, is divided into two parts. One represents a large well-drawn eagle carrying off the shepherd Ganymede to serve as Jupiter's cup-bearer on Mount Olympus; Ganymede, naked except for boots, a red cap and a red cloak, carries his shepherd's crook. Note the form of the chalice in the four corners: the identical type occurs also, as we shall see, in room 3. The rest of the room contains six hexagonal panels of dancing girls, now much destroyed, with an ornamental stone water-basin in the centre. A model of the villa's baths is displayed here, and also a substantial portion of frescoed wall of c. AD 300 from the west wing, where the colour scheme is intended to imitate imported marbles: the green border with flecking in the circular panel, for example, imitates green porphyry (*serpentino*) from near Sparta (cf. p. 62 for the real marble in Canterbury Roman Museum); the yellow copies Chemtou marble from Tunisia, and the red probably porphyry from Egypt. These exotica are comparatively rare in Roman Britain, and such frescoes are the 'poor man's' substitute for the real thing.

Moving to your left from the room with the mosaic of the dancers, you come to a 25-m (80-ft) length of well preserved geometric mosaic, uncovered in 1975 (10). This is the western part of the villa's north corridor, which was 67 m (220 ft) long in all. The lead water-pipe here carried excess water from the basin in the previous room. At the far end of the corridor, on the left, is a very naive mosaic representing a head of Medusa in the centre and busts of the Seasons in the corners (33). This, the earliest visible mosaic at Bignor, was

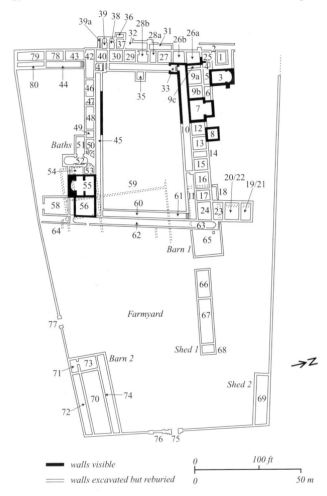

14 Bignor, Roman villa, site plan

laid *c.* 300. The curious border of the central roundel
alternates meander with distinctive motifs, including lozenges
and snails. Two steps inadequately bridge the difference in
level between the north wing's corridor and the beginning of

the west wing represented by the Medusa room; the steps are clearly later than the mosaic and destroyed part of it.

Next, on the right, comes a fragment of pavement depicting a dolphin and the letters TER (with the E ligatured and reversed): this is too insignificant to refer to the owner, and so is almost certainly the signature of the mosaicist, whose name must have been Terentius, Tertullus, Tertius or something similar; but it is the only one to survive of eight such triangular panels which this floor contained, and absolute certainty is impossible. A recent suggestion, that it might stand for Ter(psichore), and refer to a Muse depicted in an adjacent (lost) panel, is unlikely, since such labels, when they occur (as at Aldborough: p. 429), are normally placed alongside the figures they identify, and not in a detached frame. Further on, another mosaic depicts a powerful head of Winter, heavily muffled in cloak and hood, with a bare twig over her left shoulder. Lysons' reconstruction-drawing of 1817, displayed on the wall here, shows the original size and form of the single large pavement to which these panels belonged (26). The use of interlaced squares of guilloche to frame Winter and the other Seasons is one of the most favoured compositions of the Central Southern Group of mosaicists who worked at Bignor (cf. also Chilgrove, p. 75). One of the roundels with guilloche at the far end of this mosaic (to your right) shows evidence of burning.

Now come out of the hut and go right round the back of it. Laid out on the grass here is the plan of the west wing, with a long connecting corridor (34), a room projecting off it (35), and a bath-suite at the far end (the two apsidal rooms, 38 and 39, were the *tepidarium* and the *caldarium*, added *c.* 300). As noted above, this wing incorporates the rooms which comprised the earliest coherent stone-built villa on the site, a modest structure of *c.* AD 225 (p. 78). Retracing your steps, you next reach the hut containing the best preserved pavement (3), restored in the nineteenth century and again in 1929. The central portion of the floor is destroyed, exposing the hypocaust *pilae*; hollow flue-tiles for carrying the heat upwards can be seen in the right-hand wall and the apse. Of the main mosaic here only parts of three dancing cupids survive, two carrying shields, the third a Bacchic wand (the *thyrsus*). Delicately executed floral and geometric designs surround the figured panels. The apse contains a superb, delicate rendering of a goddess, usually thought to represent Venus, with head-dress and halo, flanked by a pair of peacocks and festoons. The top of her halo, incorporating a strange pelta design, represents a modern restoration (here and elsewhere the repairs of 1929 are indicated by the brighter coloured tesserae). The chalice immediately below the bust is identical to those noted on the Ganymede mosaic above. Below that again is a charming panel showing winged cupids engaged in various forms of gladiatorial combat; trainers or umpires each with a stick can be seen between them. The function of the room is uncertain, but the arrangement of the mosaic design seems to preclude its use in dining: at any rate the apse is unlikely to have received a semicircular dining couch (*stibadium*), because the head of the Venus and the accompanying gladiators panel would then be facing the wrong way. A battered water-tank stands outside this hut near the fence. After this, the final door leads you to a room with a pleasing geometric mosaic once in excellent condition but now in danger of 'blistering'; conservation is urgently needed (6). There was no opening between this room and the Ganymede room (7) in antiquity.

Finally, do not forget to cross the area of the courtyard diagonally to the far side to see the cold immersion-bath (55), and beyond it, the floor of the undressing room (*apodyterium*: 56). These rooms were part of a separate and larger bath-suite from that already noted in the west wing. The *apodyterium* has a central panel depicting the snaky head of Medusa, often used on floors as a charm to ward off evil: according to myth, a single gaze on it would turn you into stone, and the naked body was supposed to be in need of protection from such apotropaic emblems. Again the use of interlaced squares, characteristic of the Central Southern Group of mosaicists, will be noted.

The third outstanding villa-site in SE England is at **Lullingstone**** in Kent (TQ 529651) [AM; S], reached by a road (signposted) off the A225 in Eynsford. Covered by an ugly hangar, the villa lies in a delightful spot beside the river Darent. That a Roman building stood here had been known from the eighteenth century, but systematic excavation began only in 1949 and continued for 12 years. The first stone house was built *c*. AD 125: it consisted of a front corridor flanked by wing rooms and a simple range of rooms behind, and it was linked also by a transverse back corridor. It was enlarged between *c*. AD 150 and *c*. 180, when a new owner added a series of cult-rooms at one end of the villa and a bath-suite at the other, possibly replacing an earlier, smaller set of baths. He was a man of some distinction and wealth, his rooms being adorned with two portrait-busts of his ancestors, finely executed in Greek marble. About AD 275 the villa was apparently deserted: the owner either did not return one day or was forced to leave without collecting his personal possessions, for even the busts were left behind. It was soon reoccupied by a new family, however, who partly demolished the cult-rooms, sealed off the room with the busts, and planned a heated room adjacent to it; the baths were also refurbished. In the fourth century a large granary (no longer visible) was built between the house and the river, and mosaic floors were laid *c*. AD 350 in a new apsidal dining-room added then, as well as in the adjacent living-room. Then, about 360/70, the owner became a Christian, and part of the villa was converted to Christian use. At the same time the baths were filled in, and a little later the granary was pulled down. Finally, in the early fifth century, a fire destroyed the villa, whether deliberate or accidental is unknown.

Passing the ticket-office and moving to your left, turn the corner and pause in front of the Deep Room, labelled 4 (Fig. 15). It was probably first used for storing grain, but in the late second century a pit containing ritual water was sunk into the centre of the room and a niche built in the left-hand wall. The latter was decorated with a fine painting of originally three water-nymphs; the head of one is still in good condition, with green leaves in her hair and water falling from her breasts. The room was presumably dedicated to the worship of these water-goddesses, and was connected on the right to another cult-room, surrounded by a corridor on all four sides (one side of the corridor is marked out in the pink gravel visible in rooms 1–2, but the rest is now under the modern concrete concourse and is not shown on Fig. 15). All this was swept away in later alteration, and only the tiled stairway which served the cult-rooms is clearly visible now (to the right of and behind the Deep Room).

In the late third century the Deep Room was blocked off
and the niche containing the water-nymphs covered up: the
right-hand figure of the trio was totally destroyed, and the
central portion of what remained of the fresco was marred by
the erection of a shelf, as can be seen from the plain plaster
(restored) in the middle of the painting. The busts belonging
to the previous owner were also placed here, on the steps at
the back; the originals are now displayed in the British
Museum, but casts of the busts may be seen in a showcase on
the upper level at Lullingstone.

Meanwhile, a new long heated room (1–2) was constructed
to the right of the Deep Room, concealing the second-century
staircase and cult-rooms. Its floor was apparently of timber
supported on wooden rafters, and therefore, of course, no
longer visible: all we can see now is the area below the floor
where the hot air circulated, passing from one compartment to
another through the flue-arch prominently visible here. Flue-
tiles built in the thickness of the walls can be seen in the
farther room (3). This is the conventional explanation of these
features, but it poses several problems, not least the
susceptibility of a timber hypocaust to catching fire. Perhaps

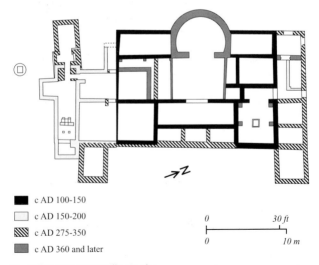

■ c AD 100-150

□ c AD 150-200

▨ c AD 275-350

▨ c AD 360 and later

0 ————— 30 ft
0 ————— 10 m

15   Lullingstone, Roman villa, site plan

more probably the area marked 1 and 2 was intended as a
stoking yard and fuel store: there are no wall flues, so the arch
here was not an interconnecting flue but a stoke-hole. The
intended floor-level of the room beyond is marked by the shelf
in its far wall, but it may be questioned whether the intended
installation of the hypocaust here (indicated also by wall flue-
tiles, inserted, perhaps significantly, in only half the room)
could ever have been completed without the removal of the
earlier staircase to create a level basement. The absence of
any sign of scorching on the stoke-hole arch strengthens the
hypothesis that the intended hypocaust was never completed
and never fired.

In the second half of the fourth century, as we know from
the painstaking reconstruction of the painted plaster found in
tiny fragments among fallen debris in the Deep Room (4), the
room on the first floor above the latter was converted into a
Christian house-chapel. Although no specific ritual or other
object was found to prove the use of the rooms for Christian
worship, the subject matter of the paintings makes it clear:
along the end-wall facing you were painted six human figures
in elaborate robes, with arms outstretched (the 'orans'
attitude, the way early Christians prayed), separated by ornate
columns resting on a dado. Next to the figures, on the left-
hand wall, was a large painted representation of the Christian
chi-rho monogram (the first two letters of Christ's name in
Greek) within a wreath. If there was also an altar table on the
wooden floor, no sign of it was found in the collapsed debris:
it was probably of wood. The chapel was approached by an
anteroom (27), which had another chi-rho, and a vestibule (26,
at the top right-hand corner of the villa from where you are
standing). This house-chapel, and a number of probable
churches at Silchester, Colchester, Richborough and
elsewhere, constitute the earliest known Christian shrines in
Britain. The original wall-plaster is now in the British
Museum (Fig. 143), but a modern painting showing part of it
is displayed at Lullingstone on the far side of the villa
opposite you.

Moving on, you pass the reconstruction-drawing displayed
in what had been the front corridor of the house (6) in the
original stone villa of the first half of the second century. As
noted above, Lullingstone started life as a compact example of

the 'winged corridor' type of villa, with room 7 to your left comprising one projecting 'wing', and the Deep Room to your right (4) the other. You can see by their straight joints that the walls immediately in front of you are later additions which masked the original arrangement. Next you reach the bath-suite at the far end, built towards the end of the second century. The various rooms – hot, tepid and cold – are labelled, and there are two cold-water pools at one end (16 and 18, underneath the walkway), the larger being a third-century addition. The hot room (11) had a pool for hot water in the apse on the left (13). The fixtures of the baths (only a few *pilae* are visible) are not well preserved, having been largely demolished in the late fourth century. Why this happened is uncertain (because the house was no longer used as a residential villa?), but the suggested connection between their demolition and the owner's espousal of Christianity is unlikely, since the Church's disapproval of bathing was largely directed against the supposedly lax morals of public bathing and not at private facilities.

Turning the corner, pause at the well which supplied the house with water (19). Note how at the foot of the stairway into the baths (20) is a higher piece of mosaic with a box flue-tile in the wall opposite. This indicates that the vestibule to the baths was itself heated in a late phase, by which time the bottom two steps of the original staircase had been covered. From here you are also able to see away to your right the larger cold plunge-bath (18) in its entirety: observe how its floor had two phases, an upper mortar one originally covered with stone flags of which only impressions remain, and the original mortar floor of the bath visible at the lower level in the far corner.

Passing the reconstructed portion of roofing, you go up to the balcony and look down on the whole building from above. In one room a large fourth-century pot, made at Farnham in Surrey, marks the site of a possible kitchen (8), but the L-shaped wall here cannot be contemporary with the outer wall which encloses it. The most striking feature is, of course, the splendid mosaic flooring laid in the mid-fourth century. The part nearer you is the dining-room for the master and his guests (23): the couches would have been arranged on the semicircular border so that diners could look down on the

16   Lullingstone, Roman villa, mosaic of Europa and the bull

main mosaic panel. The apsed shape of the room reflects the taste for semicircular dining couches (*stibadia*) in the late Empire, replacing the straight couches of an earlier tradition. Common elsewhere in the late Empire, the semicircular apsed dining-room occurs infrequently in Britain: the only other visible example in the province is the more elaborate triple-apsed *triclinium* at Littlecote in Wiltshire (p. 126).

The mosaic here depicts Europa being abducted by the lascivious Jupiter in the guise of a bull, accompanied by winged cupids on either side (Fig. 16). The smiling bull, evidently delighted with his prize, leaps over the sea (the dark blue portion of mosaic) with lively charm. Above is a Latin couplet alluding to an episode (the storm suffered by Aeneas) in the first book of Virgil's *Aeneid*, and can be translated: 'if jealous Juno had seen the swimming of the bull, she might have more justly gone to the halls of Aeolus'. Juno was the wife of Jupiter; Aeolus was ruler of the winds and therefore capable of producing a tempest to upset Jupiter's amorous adventure. The Latin composition, in tolerable verse, provides a vivid reflection of the owner's literary knowledge; one wonders how many of his dinner guests were also sufficiently steeped in classical literature to recognize the allusion. Yet a recent attempt to instil even greater sophistication into this couplet, and to see it as the starting point for elaborate word games based on acrostics (with which the owner might have entertained or bored his guests), strains credulity: this misguided sophistry has even extracted the name of the villa owner from the Latin couplet, a certain Avitus, not to mention references to Isis and Iesus (Jesus) – interpreted as the owner's declaration of his abandonment of paganism and his embrace of Christianity. Part of the mosaic here has been disfigured by burning rafters in the final conflagration.

The mosaic in the principal room (22), a reception-room and additional dining-hall for a big party, has a skilfully executed central panel. It depicts the hero Bellerophon, seated on the winged horse Pegasus, killing the Chimaera, which is a monster with a lion's head and serpent's tail. Surrounding this and much less realistically drawn are four dolphins and two opened-out mussel-shells, perhaps representing the sea journey which Bellerophon had to make in order to carry out his task. Heads of the Seasons fill out the four corners – Winter, an old woman with a hooded cloak (top left); Spring, a girl with a bird on her shoulder (top right); and Summer, a middle-aged woman with corn in her hair (upside-down). Autumn was destroyed when a fence was being put up in the eighteenth century. The rest of the mosaic is composed of a medley of geometric patterns, poorly designed and laid, and clearly the work of the craftsman's assistants. The finding of these pagan mosaics so close to the almost contemporary Christian rooms may suggest a symbolic meaning for them. It is significant, for example, that Bellerophon also appears on a Christian mosaic from Hinton St Mary in the British Museum: his killing of the Chimaera represents the triumph of life over death and good over evil – the Roman equivalent of Saint George and the Dragon.

Showcases at Lullingstone contain *inter alia* a flat casting, made up of copper and lead, found together with four ingots under the floor of one of the rooms. Also here (next to the ticket-office) is a male skeleton in a decorated lead sarcophagus, from the mausoleum constructed in the early fourth century on the terrace behind the villa. On leaving the villa, turn left and follow the path up the slope. A small circular temple erected *c*. AD 80/90 has been marked out in modern materials on the intermediate terrace, but the site of the adjacent mausoleum has now been backfilled.

The three villas so far mentioned are among the most luxurious of their type known in Britain. A more typical building of the Romano-British countryside is represented by the more modest structure uncovered at **Crofton Road, Orpington*** (April–October only, Wednesday, Friday and Bank Holiday Mondays, 1000–1300 and 1400–1700; Sundays, 1400–1700), immediately opposite Orpington station; it is best to park in York Rise just south of the villa. The north end was destroyed during the building of the railway in the nineteenth century, and more was bulldozed in 1926. What remained was excavated by Brian Philp in 1988 under the threat of a new car-park. Thanks once again to his sheer determination and energy, he persuaded Bromley Council to change their mind, and so saved the remains of the villa for the nation. It opened in 1993. Excavation has showed that there was a small winged corridor villa here, with five rooms, around the middle of the second century (*c*. 140/70), but that this was later doubled in size *c*. AD 200/25, when a new corridor was built along the back (east) side, and additional rooms were added on the south. In the late third century, the northern part of the villa was apparently abandoned, and the southern part remodelled to provide a suite of five heated rooms, an unusual degree of comfort even for a larger villa. Occupation seems to have continued throughout much of the fourth century. If there were outbuildings and/or a detached bath-house, they have not been located, and were presumably swept away in the nineteenth- and twentieth-century development of Orpington.

Parts of ten rooms at the southern end of the villa have been preserved under the cover-building, largely dating in their visible form to the late third-century alterations. To your right is a room (6) rather oddly heated by a hypocaust with two parallel underfloor channels; to the far left (room 13) is part of another with a more conventional channelled hypocaust, with diagonal flues leading to the corners. In between is a portion of red tessellated floor from the corridor built round the back

and on one side of the villa *c.* AD 200. Moving round to the
other side of the walkway, you will see that the white mortar
floor of room 9 was cut away *c.* 270/300 to insert the stoke-
hole for firing a new hypocaust in the adjacent room, 10: its
flue is unusual in being splayed at an angle through the wall,
and two voussoirs of its flue arch are visible. Note how to
your left (room 8) the roof-tiles have been left as they fell
over the wall of this room, indicating that its walls had
already been demolished when the roof fell in: 8 was one of
those rooms in the northern half of the villa which were no
longer used in the fourth century. To your right, most of the
bricks in the *pilae* of the hypocaust in room 10 (all but six)
are modern. Beyond room 16 (a modern reconstructed
hypocaust), there is a fine example (in room 14) of a
channelled hypocaust, with all the tiles covering the X-shaped
underfloor flues intact and original. The thin concrete wall
running through this room is a modern house-drain. On
completion of your visit, turn left out of the cover-building
and round its side: in the verge to the right are the scanty
remains of some of the rooms in the northern part of the villa,
all that is left between the twin destruction of the railway
cutting and the 1926 drive.

Another Roman structure is visible nearby, in the district of
Fordcroft, Orpington (TQ 467676), 1½ miles (2.4 km) (as the
crow flies) NE of the Crofton Road villa. The building at
Fordcroft, excavated in 1972–8 and again in 1993, measures
approximately 12.80 m by 6.40 m (42 ft by 21 ft), and its
walls still stand up to 1.20 m (4 ft) high. It consists of a small,
probably detached, bath-house, standing on a slight slope
above the river Cray: there are rectangular and apsed
immersion-baths and two heated rooms, but the floors and
pilae of these have been completely robbed. The building
probably dates to the third century, but coins and pottery
indicate occupation on the site from the late first to the fourth
century. It is not clear if the structure was part of a villa or
whether there was a small settlement here: other excavations
in the vicinity have found a metalled, east-west Roman road
which ran past the bath-house, parallel to Poverest road, and a
corn-drying oven and cremation burials are known not far
away. Later the area was used as an Anglo-Saxon burial-
ground, of which 75 graves were uncovered nearby in the

1960s and more during recent work in the immediate vicinity of the Roman building. To reach the site from the centre of Orpington, go north from High Street and follow the one-way system, turning right at Perry Hall Road, then left, and left at the traffic-lights. Turn left at the next traffic-lights (Poverest Road), and you will see the cover-building set at the back of a piece of greensward, on the left immediately after a turning (Bridge Road). The site is not, however, ever open on a regular basis, and intending visitors should make prior arrangements with the Bromley Museum, Church Hill, Orpington (01689–873826), which contains a selection of local finds (daily, Sunday–Friday 1300–1700; Saturday 1000–1700; closed Sundays, November–March).

Another villa, much larger, is known 5 miles (8 km) to the south-west at **Keston** (TQ 415634); an early farmstead of *c*. AD 50–160 was superseded by a timber house *c*. 160–200, and then replaced by a more substantial stone-built villa (with timber outbuildings) *c*. 200. Although nothing of it is now visible part of a Roman cemetery is, adjacent to the site of the villa on its north side. The remains are situated on the west side of the A233, the Bromley Common to Westerham road, on a sharp bend just south of its junction with the B-road from Hayes Common (take care parking). A pair of Roman mausolea lies in the grounds of a private house called Brambletye. Although the monuments themselves are owned by Bromley Council, access to them is private; guard-dogs do not permit entry. This ludicrous situation is all the more regrettable because substantial stone-built Roman mausolea are a rarity among the visible remains of Roman Britain. The tombs can be viewed from a distance from the gate to the property. Alternatively, walk a few metres further south and take the footpath to Nash: the mausolea can be seen at closer quarters from the first field to the right of the path after you emerge from the wood. Practice in recent years (1999, 2000) has been to open the site to the public on one Sunday a year, generally in late September (phone Bromley Museum on 01689–873826 for details).

The site has been known for over 150 years and sporadically dug on a number of occasions, but proper excavation and consolidation was not carried out until 1967–8. The main feature is a large circular mausoleum,

8.85 m (29 ft) in diameter, strengthened by six buttresses
which are integral to it; the exterior wall, originally rendered
with red plaster, was perhaps up to 6 m (20 ft) high. It was
clearly a monumental tomb, built in the third century for the
family who owned the villa, which was situated on the lower
part of the hill. Adjoining it is a rectangular tomb with a large
buttress on one side, and from it came the stone coffin set up
nearby on the perimeter of the site. This coffin has quite a
history of its own: it was found about 1800 and performed a
variety of tasks in the district, including that of a garden-box
and a horse-trough; in 1941 it was smashed by a German
bomb and only in 1968 was it restored and brought back to
the site. A third tomb had eluded all the earlier excavators as
it lay between two buttresses of the large circular tomb. It
consists of a small chamber covered by a vault made of tiles
set in mortar; a lead casket with the remains of an adult
cremation was found inside. A dozen or so simple graves
were also found in the area but are not now visible. One
adolescent inhumation had two congenitally missing bones in
the sacrum, indicating that he/she suffered from spina bifida.

Another burial site is at **Stone-by-Faversham** (TQ 992614)
[AM; A], which lies by a group of trees in a field 100 m north
of the A2 opposite a minor road leading to Newnham; this is
at the foot of Judd's Hill, $\frac{1}{2}$ mile (800 m) west of Ospringe
village and $1\frac{1}{4}$ miles (2 km) west of Faversham. Most of the
masonry here belongs to a medieval church, but it
incorporates a square Roman building into the western part of
its chancel. The Roman work is unmistakable, consisting of
regularly tooled stones separated after each layer by tile
bonding-courses. This is especially clear on the exterior south
face (that nearest the road), where the break between the neat
Roman work and the medieval masonry without the tile-
courses is obvious. The Roman building is entered on the west
by a massive stone sill, and the pivot-hole for the door is still
visible. It was built in the middle of the fourth century and is
most probably an isolated mausoleum, presumably on a villa-
estate. No trace of a burial, however, was found in the
excavations of 1967–8 (it may have been robbed in medieval
times or later), and no other burials are known in the
immediate vicinity. Nevertheless its interpretation as a
mausoleum is certain, and it is in fact a very rare, certain

example in Britain of a pagan mausoleum being incorporated into a later (post-Roman) Christian church. The suggestion that the Stone-by-Faversham building was already functioning as a church in Roman times is unsubstantiated: there is no additional apse, nor any evidence for liturgical use, and the Christian use of a freestanding, square building as a church without alteration would be unparalleled.

Finds from many other burials in and around Ospringe are displayed in the Maison Dieu Museum (open 1400–1700, Saturday, Sunday and Bank Holidays only, mid-April to end of October), $\frac{3}{4}$ mile (1 km) to the east (at the junction of the A2 with Water Lane). The Roman settlement of DVROLEVVM ('the town on the smooth-flowing river') has been sought hereabouts, but the earthworks on Judd's Hill (overlooking the Stone-by-Faversham mausoleum, a little to its SE), which have sometimes been claimed to be the site, are very probably due to comparatively recent landscape-gardening. Thus the low 'rampart' on the brow of the hill to your right, immediately after leaving the A2 to enter the grounds of the Syndale Motel, is probably modern; it has, however, recently been claimed as belonging to a Roman fort of the Claudian period, on the basis of inconclusive trenches cut through it in 1999–2000. Excavation in 1977 near the Maison Dieu in Ospringe village revealed no trace of a Roman settlement. By contrast, excavations since 1995 have found substantial buildings in the outskirts of Faversham itself, on an inlet, and this seems a more likely candidate for DVROLEVVM, with Ospringe one of its outlying cemeteries.

Chapter 2

Wessex and the South-West

Hampshire, Wiltshire, Dorset, southern Somerset, Devon and Cornwall

(Appendix 1 only – Berkshire)

In AD 44, with SE England reasonably secure, the invading army split up into separate units to attempt the subjugation of the rest of Britain. The division chosen to advance south-westwards was the Second Augustan Legion, then commanded by the man who was later to become the emperor Vespasian. His biographer Suetonius has left us the bare information that he fought 30 battles, overcame two powerful tribes and more than 20 hill-forts, and reduced the Isle of

Wight to surrender. Archaeology, however, has been able to
shed light on the nature of the opposition offered by the two
tribes mentioned, the Durotriges of Dorset and south
Somerset, and the Dumnonii of Devon and Cornwall; and this
opposition resulted in the building of a series of forts which
held the area in check during the early years of the Roman
occupation. Few of these have left any features traceable on

the ground today. The principal base of the Second Legion in
these early years was probably the 29-acre (11.7-ha) fortress
at Lake Farm near Wimborne Minister in Dorset (of which
nothing is visible). The fact that it is below full legionary size
suggests the permanent brigading of some legionary cohorts
and even vexillations elsewhere: military dispositions were
fluid in the conquest period. By about AD 55, however, the
Second Legion was already in Exeter, where excavations have
revealed its fortress.

Ramparts of the smaller forts, designed for auxiliary forces
with perhaps a small contingent of legionaries, are visible,

unimpressively, at Waddon Hill in Dorset, at Wiveliscombe in
Somerset, at North Tawton, Clayhanger and Bury Barton in
Devon, and at Nanstallon in Cornwall (for details, see App.
1). Excavation at the last has indicated an occupation of
c. AD 55–80. For better preserved earthworks associated with
the Roman occupying army of the conquest years, we have to
turn to Hod Hill (see below), and to two fortlets on the north
Devon coast, at **Old Burrow*** (SS 788493) and **Martinhoe**
(SS 663493). The earth defences of both of these are clearly
visible on the ground: they consist in both cases of an outer,
roughly circular rampart and ditch with an entrance on the
south, and an inner square rampart and ditch or ditches with
an entrance on the north. The position of the entrances
ensured (in theory) that an attacker who had stormed the outer
gate on the south would have to traverse half the circuit of the
outer compound before attempting the gate to the fortlet
proper. The earthworks at Old Burrow are very well
preserved, better than those of Martinhoe, where the northern
part of the outer rampart has slipped over the cliff. Excavation
in the early 1960s found a pair of timber barracks (perhaps for
about 80 soldiers) inside the Martinhoe fortlet, but little
survived in the interior at Old Burrow. The excavators
claimed that one fortlet succeeded the other, Old Burrow
being allegedly the earlier, with occupation there beginning
perhaps about AD 48 and lasting only a short time. The
slightly less exposed fortlet at Martinhoe was built, it was
thought, about AD 60 and evacuated c. AD 78 on the final
subjugation of the Silures in south Wales. However, as my
pupil Matthew Symonds has pointed out (in a forthcoming
publication), the scanty pottery finds are not susceptible to
such close dating, and in any case the identical and unusual
layout of the earthworks, with both inner and outer enclosures,
strongly suggests that they are contemporary. Indeed he points
out that they make much better sense as a pair, each with a
different part of the coastline to watch, especially since the
two fortlets are not visible from one another. These posts were
probably designed to keep an eye on irregular activity in the
Bristol Channel, including possible incursion from south
Wales, and were probably created in the early 50s when the
Roman attempts to subjugate the Silures were at their height;

but whether they formed part of a larger, integrated chain of fortlets guarding this coast is unknown.

The Old Burrow fortlet is reached from a track on the north side of the A39 (Minehead–Lynmouth), $\frac{1}{2}$ mile (800 m) after crossing the Somerset–Devon border at County Gate if you are coming from the east, or $\frac{3}{4}$ mile (1.2 km) after the turning to Brendon if you are coming from the west. There is a lay-by on the south side of the road at this point, and the track you need is labelled 'Glenthorne Estate' (post-box and cattle-grid). Here you will see the earthworks of the fortlet ahead of you on the skyline: a stile on the left of the track gives access to the field where the fortlet lies.

The less well preserved fortlet of Martinhoe is reached from a cliff path which passes the fortlet. Leave the A39 at Martinhoe Cross, 4 miles (6.4 km) west of Lynton; go straight across at the crossroads, and then right at the next T-junction, signposted Slattenside and Woody Bay. Follow the road down to the left in the direction of Woody Bay, and at $\frac{1}{2}$ mile (800 m) from the T-junction, on a hairpin bend, you will see a gate on the left which marks the start of the footpath to Hunter's Inn (wooden signpost). After walking for approximately 1 mile (1.6 km), having crossed the Hollow Brook and climbed the hill beyond called The Beacon, there is a signpost to the left announcing 'Roman signal station: viewpoint only', and a few steps in the stone wall lead you up to the earthworks of the Roman fortlet in grassland at the summit of the hill.

One of the unusual features about Roman forts in the conquest period in Britain is that they were sometimes situated not on virgin sites on low-lying ground, but inside pre-existing Iron Age hill-forts. That at Hod Hill (p. 98) remains the best known example of this phenomenon, but another, a supply-depot rather than a fort proper, has been excavated at Brandon Camp (in Herefordshire [Chapter 3]: nothing of Roman date is visible there); a third is suspected at Ham Hill (Somerset), quarried away without record in the nineteenth century (finds of Roman armour and weapons from here are displayed in Taunton Castle Museum); and a fourth example is known at **Hembury** (ST 113031) in Devon. This is one of the finest Iron Age hill-forts in south-west Britain, which alone is well worth a visit; but you must be warned that the visible Roman earthwork here is very slight. The site lies on the Honiton to Tiverton road (A373) about 16 miles (25.6 km) NE of Exeter: take the turning to Dunkeswell on the north side of this road, 4 miles (6.4 km) west of Honiton (and 2 miles [3.2 km] west of Awliscombe), or 7 miles (11 km) east of Cullompton. After $\frac{1}{2}$ mile (800 m), park on the left at a lay-by near a wooden gate. Cross the road and take the path southwards through the woods; it soon joins a broad track which leads you to the NE gate of the hill-fort, where the Iron Age ramparts survive impressively. Follow now the path across the interior of the hill-fort until it turns left and follows the inner face of the west rampart. Stop where the path swings slightly to the right down a slope: here excavation found remains of the stout timber posts of a Roman gateway, inserted into the Iron Age west entrance. At this point you can see a slight bank to your left which is probably of comparatively recent origin; but immediately beyond it and running parallel to it is a broader mound, with a ditch on its far (south) side. This earthwork is almost certainly of Roman date. Partial excavation in 1980–3 inside the NE sector of the hill-fort revealed the undoubted presence of Roman military timber buildings (one was of courtyard type, with evidence of iron-working – probably a *fabrica* or workshop), and it is clear that the northern half of the hill-fort, comprising a conveniently rectangular area of 6 acres (2.5 ha), was requisitioned by the Roman army to serve as a short-lived military post. On the basis of the scanty finds, occupation lasted no more than a decade, *c.* AD 50–60, and probably for less. The Iron Age ramparts served for protection on three sides, but on the fourth (south) side a new defensive earthwork, much slighter of course (in line with Roman practice), was erected across the width of the hill-fort. The site is best visited in winter or spring before bracken growth impairs the visibility of the Roman features.

By far the most impressive of the early Roman military works in the area covered by this chapter, however, is the fort built inside the NW corner of the ramparts of the Iron Age hill-fort of **Hod Hill**** in Dorset (ST 857106). Take the Warminster road (A350) for 4 miles (6.4 km) out of Blandford Forum, and about 1 mile (1.6 km) after leaving Stourpaine, turn left along the minor road signposted Child Okeford. After

$\frac{1}{2}$ mile (800 m) there is space for parking on both sides of the road as it enters a wood. Park here and take the track on your left which leads steeply up after 15 minutes to a metal gate. Climb the stile on your right here, and you come immediately to the Roman causeway across the Iron Age ditches, and the Roman breach in the ramparts (defended by a single-portal timber gateway), which leads directly into the NW corner of the Roman fort.

The Roman garrison-fort at Hod Hill is unusual, but not as we have seen unique, in being set inside the corner of a pre-existing hill-fort rather than on virgin territory: the Iron Age ramparts were used to form its north and west sides, but new Roman defences were built on the south and east. The latter have been damaged by ploughing over the centuries, but are still impressively preserved. The Roman rampart consisted of packed chalk, faced with turf back and front, and was originally 3 m (10 ft) high to rampart-walk; it still stands to about 1.50 m (5 ft) near the NE angle. Outside the rampart were three ditches, all only about 1.50 m (5 ft) deep but skilfully designed. The innermost two each had a nasty ankle-breaking channel at the bottom. Then came a flat platform 16.75 m (55 ft) wide before the outer ditch, which was so shaped as to be easy to cross in attack but deceptively difficult in retreat (called 'Punic' in Roman military terminology, a label synonymous with 'treacherous' in Latin vocabulary – so bad had Roman experience been of the Carthaginians [='Poeni']). These ditches are interrupted by causeways leading to the south and east gates, which are slightly wedge-shaped: this was in theory to jostle an attacking enemy by giving it less breadth of space as it approached the gate – surely an unnecessary elaboration which can scarcely if ever have worked in practice. Both gates are defended by *tituli* (visible in Fig. 17), a feature more appropriate to temporary earthworks such as marching-camps than in a semi-permanent fort: the ditches of the *tituli* are prominent, but not much survives of the accompanying upcast mounds. Note also the large projecting mound on the inside of the rampart immediately east of the south gate (there was another just north of the east gate, although this is less visible on the ground): these probably contained *ascensus*, the bases of staircases up to the rampart-walk (although they seem unduly

17   Hod Hill, Roman fort from the air, looking south

large for the purpose), but Richmond interpreted them also as
the base for artillery machines (*ballistae*), taking them as
proof that legionaries as well as auxiliaries garrisoned Hod
Hill (since artillery was not given to auxiliaries in the Roman
army of the first and second centuries). This however is most
uncertain, not least because the kick-back of Roman artillery
machines before the late Empire was not sufficient to justify
large, specially prepared platforms of this nature. The NW
gate by which you have entered the fort was made to provide
the garrison with convenient access to water from the river
Stour below.

   The entire plan of the interior of this fort was recovered in
excavations by the late Sir Ian Richmond between 1951 and
1958. These revealed the foundation-slots cut in the chalk to
receive the timber-framed buildings of which the fort was
composed. The layout of these indicates that the garrison
consisted of about 600 legionaries supplemented by an
auxiliary cavalry-unit 250 strong. It was evacuated after a fire

had destroyed some of the buildings, probably by accident, and coins and pottery show that this cannot have happened more than about eight years after the original building of the fort in AD 44 or 45.

Now leave the Roman defences and strike diagonally across the Iron Age hill-fort towards its SE corner. The breach there is of medieval or modern origin (and the gap in the middle of the east rampart is Roman); the main Iron Age entrances to the hill-fort were at the NE and SW. Before reaching the SE corner, however, note the mass of circular platforms and depressions which mark the sites of the huts occupied by Iron Age peoples immediately prior to the Roman invasion, miraculously spared by the ploughing which has removed evidence elsewhere inside the interior of the hill-fort. Excavation has shown that one of them, surrounded by a hexagonal enclosure, was a particular target for Roman artillery-fire during the assault on Hod Hill in AD 44. It is assumed, therefore, that this was a chieftain's hut and, as no evidence was found of fighting at the gates or of massacre within, this bombardment alone may have been sufficient to secure the surrender of the hill-fort's inhabitants.

Hod Hill can therefore be included among the 20 hill-forts which Suetonius records as having been captured under Vespasian's command. Much more dramatic evidence, however, appears to have been found in excavations in 1934–7 by Sir Mortimer Wheeler at the most famous and impressive of all British hill-forts, **Maiden Castle*** (SY 669884) [AM; A]. It is reached by the signposted road to the right off the Weymouth road (B3147) in the southern outskirts of Dorchester, before you get as far as the southern bypass. The massive triple ramparts which surround the site were erected in the early first century BC, and the defences are even more intricate at the two entrances. The west gate (that nearer the car-park) is the more strongly defended and has not been excavated. It is not, therefore, known if the Romans attacked it, but it seems more likely that Vespasian concentrated his assault at the less complex east gate.

Wheeler reconstructed a vivid picture of that attack on the basis of his interpretation of the archaeological evidence. In contrast to Hod Hill, the Romans apparently met with tough resistance. According to Wheeler, their artillery first fired

some rounds of *ballista* bolts, one of which landed in a
defender's spine; the skeleton with the bolt-tip embedded in a
vertebra is now displayed in a case in the Dorchester
Museum. Then an advance party gained access to the interior
and set some huts on fire, and the resulting smokescreen,
claimed Wheeler, enabled the gate to be stormed by the rest of
the troops. It cannot have been easy: try running up and down
the slopes at the east gate today, then imagine determined
natives raining sling-stones down on you, and you will
appreciate that even for tough, well-disciplined Roman
soldiers the battle was not a walk-over. This, Wheeler
suggested, was confirmed by the fury they showed on gaining
entrance: the inhabitants, regardless of age or sex, were
brutally hacked down before a halt to the slaughter was called.
The natives were left to give a hasty burial to their dead. The
evidence for all this can be read in Wheeler's report, and
some of it is displayed in Dorchester Museum. It makes a
gripping story – but is it true?

Re-excavation at Maiden Castle in 1985–6, and subsequent
re-interpretation of Wheeler's evidence, suggest a rather
different account. Some of the burning that Wheeler saw can
now be viewed as evidence for Iron Age iron-working rather
than Roman pillage. The so-called *ballista* bolt is more
probably a small javelin head, and the cemetery, so far from
being hastily arranged, as Wheeler claimed, seems to have
grown up over two centuries, with a large number of rich
grave-groups and the careful positioning of the bodies in
conformity with Durotrigan burial practice. Yet 14 out of 52
skeletons excavated by Wheeler show evidence of violent
death, and although it has been claimed that some of the
smashed skulls might be connected with Iron Age ritual and
violence rather than with Roman brutality, the spear-head
alone betokens in this cemetery at least one British casualty at
the hands of Romans, and it is perverse not to see the
hack-marks on the skulls of at least the majority as the result
of impacts from Roman weaponry. Wheeler may have been
wrong on some details and over-colourful on others, but it is
still certain that Maiden Castle was one of the hill-forts
attacked by Vespasian's troops. No trace of the battle can, of
course, be seen at the site today.

There are, however, Roman remains visible at Maiden

Castle, although they date from nearly 350 years later than the assault of AD 44. In the closing years of the fourth century, at a time when Christianity was the official religion but paganism still apparently flourished, a new temple was built in the NE part of the hill-fort (the opposite end to the car-park). It is one of the best examples of the typical Romano-Celtic temple to be seen in Britain, and consists of the normal central shrine and surrounding ambulatory (Fig. 18). It was dated to after AD 367 by a hoard of coins sealed under its plain mosaic floor. Outside the east wall of the ambulatory was found what Wheeler thought was a section of 'paved approach', 5 m (17 ft) across; but it is more likely to be the temple's collapsed outer wall, so suggesting that the latter was solid, and not made up of dwarf columns on a low wall as is often imagined (see p. 21). Next to the Romano-Celtic temple is a tiny two-roomed construction interpreted as the priest's dwelling. A second temple, a circular hut-shrine 12 m (40 ft) to the south, is no longer visible. The deity (or deities)

18   *Maiden Castle, the Roman temple*

worshipped here are not known, but the most extraordinary
find was a unique bronze representation of a triple-horned bull
with three female figures on its back; it may be related to the
obscure Gaulish cult of Tarvostrigaranus, the 'three-horned
bull with the three cranes'. The figurine is now in Dorset
County Museum, Dorchester.

The very slight remains of another Roman temple can be
seen a short distance away, on **Jordon Hill** (SY 698821)
[AM; A], dug in 1843 and 1931–2. Here, however, the outer
wall is not visible and has not in fact been found: it seems
likely that the stonework had been completely robbed and its
traces escaped the notice of the excavators. Coins indicate that
the shrine flourished, like the one at Maiden Castle, in the
second half of the fourth century. There may well have been
other buildings around the temple: note, just before reaching
the wicket gate, the fragmentary foundations of another wall
in the path, and further pieces are visible in a dry summer to
the left and on the other side of the fence. To reach it, follow
the A353 out of Weymouth (for Wimborne and Wareham),
and turn right where the A-road swings inland, with a brown
signpost indicating the Roman temple. The temple lies on the
brow of the hill, to the left of the drive, after $\frac{1}{4}$ mile (400 m)
(signposted 'Public Footpath').

The native occupation of Maiden Castle did not cease
immediately after the battle of 44, but it did not continue
beyond the end of the first century. Its inhabitants gradually
drifted elsewhere, some no doubt to rural farmsteads, others to
the new town which the Romans founded in the valley below,
at **Dorchester*** (SY 694900). Finds and topography make a
military origin certain here, but no structural remains of a fort
have yet been identified, unless a defensive ditch located in
1972, allegedly of late first-century date, belonged to it. The
town which took its place was known as DVRNOVARIA (its
meaning is uncertain), and served as a tribal capital for the
Durotriges, although in the fourth century it may have shared
this role with Ilchester in Somerset (App. 1). At any rate it
was then that both towns reached the height of their
prosperity, and the many mosaics found in and around
Dorchester indicate the existence of a flourishing school of
mosaicists in the town at that date.

To the fourth century, too, belongs the Roman town-house

in Colliton Park, situated behind County Hall in the extreme
NW corner of the Roman walled area. Go up the ramp just
north of the Hardy Statue on the west side of the town centre,
and park near the library in the visitors' car-park in the
County Hall complex. Walk north from here to find the
Roman site in the far NW corner of the enclosure. The Roman
building was excavated in 1937–9, and part of it and a single
mosaic has been accessible ever since; but an imaginative new
scheme for its presentation to the public, opened in 1999, saw
the re-excavation of the mosaics and other floor levels of this
house, together with the creation of an attractive and sensitive
cover-building designed to make the Roman remains visible
from the outside at all times (the interior is open at irregular
hours during the summer which fluctuate from year to year;
telephone the County Council main switchboard on
01305–251000 for current details). The County Council and
the then County Archaeologist, Lawrence Keen, deserve much
credit for this initiative, which has turned the Colliton Park
house into the most impressive visible Roman *domus*
(town-house) in Britain.

The house consists in its final form of two separate ranges.
The south range was the earlier, and probably started life as a
simple three-roomed stone house in the third century,
replacing earlier timber structures on the site. It was enlarged
in the early fourth century, when the west wing (under cover)
was started; that in turn was enlarged *c*. 340. Coins cease
c. 375, but squatter occupation went on, perhaps into the fifth
century. In the south range (on your left as you enter the site),
it is probably the central three rooms which constituted the
original house (one of the rooms has a niche for a statue or
shrine against the back wall). In the alterations the large room
(the furthest to your left), the corridor, and the heated room at
the west end were built. A dwarf column, found amongst
rubbish in the adjacent well (which was 10 m [33 ft] deep),
has been re-erected on the corridor wall. The heated room is
an excellent example of a channelled hypocaust. Some of the
paving-flags of the floor are in position, and the hollows once
containing flue-tiles for the rising hot air can be seen in the
surrounding walls.

Inside the cover-building, note the well preserved geometric
mosaic in the room to the left, and the splayed opening for a

window (a rare survival from Roman Britain), found collapsed
into the room below and now reconstructed. The well in front
of you is surely late, dug through the floor when the house
was no longer a rich person's home; it partly hinders access to
the mosaic-paved room beyond. The latter, as the house's
largest room, and the only one to show even the tiniest scrap
of figural mosaic, was probably the dining-room (*triclinium*).
In the surviving strip of mosaic along the left-hand side, note
the lower part of the head of Spring at the centre. The whole
head survived when first uncovered in 1937, but it had sadly
suffered, presumably from worm action, in the 60 years after
its initial reburial. This and the other mosaics were laid
c. AD 340 by local Durnovarian mosaicists, then at the height
of their popularity. There is a drain visible in the room with
the well, and also in the wall of the corridor leading to the
western part of the house. Here on the left is another excellent
example of a channelled hypocaust, with recesses in the walls
to take hollow flue-tiles. Two stoke-holes to heat it are visible
in the grass outside. The mosaic in the facing room is almost
entirely lost, but note the patch of burning near the right-hand
wall: this may date from the period of squatter occupation.
This room, too, has a drain in one wall, and all three in the
house (designed to make easier the process of washing the
floors) drain into the sump visible outside. The Kimmeridge
shale table-leg (Fig. 1, on the Contents page) was found at
Colliton Park, but in a pit which was sealed just before the
visible stone *domus* was constructed.

Elsewhere in Dorchester, a partially preserved geometric
mosaic, with similarities in style to those in the Colliton Park
house, was found along with fragments of two others during
building work on the site of the former Dorset County
Hospital at Somerleigh Court in 2001 (in the SW sector of the
Roman walled area). This is due to be displayed under glass
in an open courtyard, accessible to all, within the new
development of sheltered housing (68 flatlets). Another
mosaic panel, found in 1967, has been preserved *in situ* in
premises at 26, Trinity Street, and can be viewed on request to
the management. But little is known in detail about these or
other houses in Roman Dorchester, and the only public
building extensively excavated is the public baths, found in
1977 in the grounds of Wollaston House. These, however,

have not been consolidated and left on display, although recently (2000) ambitious plans to do just that have been aired once again in Dorchester.

The course of the defences of Roman Dorchester is not precisely known over their entire circuit, but they enclosed an area of between 80 and 90 acres (32–6 ha). An earth bank and ditch came first, towards the end of the second century, and this was fronted with a stone wall at some later date, probably just before AD 300. A rather wretched fragment of this, penned behind railings and capped by a modern brick wall, is visible in West Walk, a short distance south of the Hardy Statue. Only the core of the wall is left, at most 2.50 m (8 ft) high, and displaying a double course of limestone bonding-slabs near the top. Nearby, in High West Street, is the Dorset County Museum's important archaeological collection (Monday–Saturday, 1000–1700; Sunday, May–October only, also 1000–1700). The most interesting items to note are the finds from Maiden Castle, the coin-hoard from South Street, the table-legs (Fig. 1) and other products from the Kimmeridge shale industry, and several mosaic floors which reflect the opulence of fourth-century Dorchester.

The rest of the Roman remains in the Dorchester neighbourhood lie outside the walled area of DVRNOVARIA. The most impressive is the amphitheatre, known as Maumbury Rings, which lies on the left (east) side of Weymouth Avenue just before the railway bridge in the southern outskirts of the town. The earthworks started life as a Neolithic monument *c*. 2000 BC, when the banks were about 3.35 m (11 ft) high. The Romans converted it into an amphitheatre by lowering the ground-level to create an arena floor and raising the banks to their present 9 m or so (30 ft). There was a timbered gangway round the arena, which had its principal entrance on the north, less wide than the present gap, and a lesser entrance on the south. It appears to have been built during the second half of the first century, surely *c*. AD 70–80 rather than earlier, and allegedly had an active life of no more than 80, and possibly as little as 50, years (although this is hard to believe). Later ages employed it in other ways. In the seventeenth century it was used as a gun-emplacement, and the internal terraces on the banks belong to this period. In the eighteenth century it was used as a place of public execution, and in 1952 the people of Dorset assembled here to greet HM the Queen.

The second Roman feature outside the walls is interesting rather than spectacular. It is the aqueduct which carried water to the town over a winding course nearly 7 miles (11 km) long. Its source, immediately south of Frampton village, was a dammed lake, evidence for which was established by excavation in 1997. This and other investigation of the aqueduct has revealed that, after an abortive start on a first leat (period 1a), a terrace was carved out of the hillside, in the bottom of which, in the chalk, was cut a channel 1.5 m (5 ft) wide and 30 cm (1 ft) deep. Into this last was set a timber box-framed water-leat, packed with turf on either side and probably covered with a single layer of turf on top to protect it and to ease maintenance (period 1b). We do not know for certain when this aqueduct was built or for how long it functioned; attempts to ascribe it to the Claudian period and as the work of the Roman army, on the basis of an undated enclosure (allegedly a Roman fortlet) close to the dam, seem to me implausible. Pottery in the silt at the bottom of a section of leat excavated near Poundbury is datable to the late first or early second century, so perhaps the aqueduct is not later than the Flavian period, or at any rate not by much. At some stage, however, perhaps in the second or third century rather than later, a decision was taken to replace the aqueduct with a larger construction, probably of terracotta pipes in a concrete bed, to replace the timber water-channel. A larger terrace, sometimes up to 3 m (10 ft) wide and 1.50 m (5 ft) deep, was prepared to take the new aqueduct, but the project was still-born, and no water was ever flowed along it. Presumably thereafter Dorchester had to rely for its water on the springs and wells which are plentiful in the town. Not all Roman water engineering had successful outcomes.

It is this abortive final terrace which is now visible (in part) as an embanked shelf following the contours of the hillside. Take the Honiton road at the roundabout by the Hardy Statue and then turn immediately right at the castle along Poundbury Road. After crossing the railway, go on for $\frac{1}{2}$ mile (800 m), past a first lay-by on the right (with an information panel), to a second lay-by almost at the brow of the hill. A stile here leads you to the SW corner of the ramparts of the Iron Age

Poundbury Camp. Walk to its NW corner, and just outside, near the entrance to the railway-tunnel, you will see the shelf of the aqueduct – not the one immediately below the Iron Age rampart, but the terracing below that. Walk westwards from here as far as a stile: the aqueduct is particularly prominent from here straight ahead of you at eye-level, curving round the hillside by the river. Now return to your car and continue on past the hill-fort (following the alignment, incidentally, of a Roman road). Just after crossing over the Dorchester bypass you can see a further stretch of aqueduct on a low shelf, below the line of trees in the hillside to your left. About 300 m further on, as the road climbs steeply again, the aqueduct is once more visible on a shelf in the hillside to your left, but these traces of the aqueduct (the best is in Fordington Bottom) are on private land and are inaccessible.

Finally, mention may be made of two other relics in the neighbourhood of Dorchester, both to the east. One is a finely carved marble tombstone which was erected to a certain Carinus in the mid-second century, by his wife and three children. It is now inside St George's church at Fordington, a suburb of Dorchester. The other is a Roman milestone, nearly 1.80 m (6 ft) high, which can be seen 1 mile (1.6 km) NE of the town, on the south side of the road for Dorchester immediately after leaving the Stinsford roundabout. It is situated on the bank (in summer somewhat choked by undergrowth) immediately after you pass a 'Clearway' sign on leaving the roundabout. The milestone, no longer inscribed, was moved a short distance from its original find-spot in the nineteenth century, and a further time in 1956; its most recent move was in 1986 when the roundabout was built. It stood beside the Roman road heading for the hill-fort of Badbury Rings near Wimborne, where there was a small roadside settlement.

Three other tribal capitals were founded by the Romans in Wessex and the south-west, at Exeter, Winchester and Silchester. The military origin of **Exeter** (SX 923925), long suspected, was confirmed first by the discovery of a military ditch near the south gate in 1964, and then of military buildings in the centre of the city in 1971/3. These included barracks, a workshop and a granary of timber and a fine stone bath-house, and it is now clear that a 41-acre (16.5-ha) legionary fortress was built at Exeter during the 50s, presumably by and for the Second Legion. A military store-base of contemporary date has also been identified outside the south angle of the fortress. At some stage, probably *c*. 75, the soldiery moved on, and before the end of the first century the place was laid out as a *civitas* capital for the Dumnonii, ISCA DVMNONIORVM, with a street-grid and the usual public buildings. The name ISCA means 'water' or 'river' in Celtic, and still survives in the modern river name (the Exe). At this time the legionary baths were converted into the basilica: the hypocausts were demolished and stripped, the floor-levels raised, and a range of steps provided to enter the basilica from the forum. This and the baths it replaced lie buried under the greensward immediately west of the cathedral. Plans to re-expose these structures and to erect a subterranean cover-building over them are aired from time to time, but have not so far been carried through to fruition.

For the present, therefore, the only visible remains of ISCA are the defences, which enclosed some 93 acres (38 ha), an average size for a Romano-British tribal capital. As usual, a clay bank and ditch came first, in the late second century, and in the early third the bank was faced in stone. The walls have been much repaired and altered in medieval and later times, and consequently the Roman masonry is not everywhere apparent. To identify Roman work, therefore, look out for regularly coursed blocks of purple-grey volcanic stone, with a projecting plinth at the base.

The best place to start is in Northernhay Gardens, entered from Queen Street opposite Northernhay Street. Take the path immediately striking off to your right, and you will see the base-plinth and up to two courses of Roman work clearly visible; the contrast with medieval and modern patching elsewhere is obvious. The rubble walling below the plinth represents Roman foundations, faced and further underpinned by medieval masons when the ground-level was lowered. Following the path uphill towards the war memorial, you will see another portion of the plinth beyond the Acland Statue; it is here 1.20 m (4 ft) above the present ground-level. Now take the narrow path leading up to the castle, and you can see on your right at the first tree a good stretch of the Roman town wall with base plinth and up to 12 further courses above.

Follow the castle walls round to the garden exit, turn left at
the end of the street, first right, and then first right at the
traffic lights into High Street. Turn first left at Eastgate House
into the pedestrianized precinct, at the end of which the wall
again becomes visible. Pass it on the left (its outer face). The
wall facing here is a heterogeneous amalgam of facing blocks,
re-using in part Roman stones: the most authentically Roman
work is that standing just beyond the second breach here,
some 4.50 m (15 ft) high, with plinth and 20 courses of
masonry above it.

Now turn left, then first right into Southernhay West, and
then right into Cathedral Close. In the car-park on your right
just before the metal bridge is a long stretch of wall, but none
of the facing is original except for a short piece of base-plinth
at the car-park entrance. Now retrace your steps and turn right
at the public footpath, following the line of the wall (largely
repatched here). Cross South Street and you will see marked
out in modern materials the foundations of the west
guard-tower of the Roman south gate. First excavated in
1964–5, it was further investigated in 1989 and 1993, when
the plan of the gate was established as consisting of a single
carriageway flanked by towers. It was built *c.* 200, replacing a
timber gate of *c.* AD 160/80. Immediately beyond, the wall is
mostly medieval in its present form, although a small section
of Roman plinth is visible below the footbridge. Finally, on
the other side of the inner bypass, there is at first a superb
20 m (65 ft) stretch of wall, with Roman facing-stones
impressively visible up to 19 courses. As elsewhere at Exeter,
the base-plinth marking Roman ground-level stands above the
modern pavement: the Roman foundations have been faced in
medieval and later times with blocks of poor-quality red
sandstone, which contrasts with the purplish-grey volcanic
'trap' stone from nearby Rougemont Hill which the Romans
used. Roman finds from Exeter are displayed in the Royal
Albert Memorial Museum (Monday–Saturday 1000–1700).

Of Roman **Winchester** (SU 480295) virtually nothing is
visible. It was VENTA BELGARVM, the 'market' and
administrative capital of the 'Belgae'. Their tribal area
covered much of what is now Hampshire and part of
Wiltshire; but this was one of the few instances where
pre-Roman tribal boundaries were ignored by Rome for

administrative convenience, the 'Belgae' being a new and
artificial *civitas* carved out of the former, vast territory of the
Atrebates. There was an important Iron Age settlement here,
and an earthwork called Oram's Arbour partly underlying the
NW sector of the later town is dated to this period (second/
first centuries BC); abandoned well before AD 43, it was
succeeded by another Iron Age settlement immediately
outside it to the south. A Roman fort in the conquest period
has been conjectured, but if the Winchester area remained part
of the client kingdom of Togidubnus (p. 68) in the early years
of the Roman occupation, it is likely that no military presence
was thought necessary. Several early phases of timber
buildings are known before the town was properly laid out
with a street-grid about AD 90. Earlier than this, probably
c. AD 70, the town had received its first earth defences with
timber gateways, a phenomenon appearing at Winchester so
much earlier than usual that the place must have enjoyed
privileged status – possibly after promotion to the rank of
municipium. It is the clearest evidence, in fact, that the
settlement belonged to a pro-Roman client-kingdom.

The forum, situated immediately north of the cathedral, was
built about AD 100 and enlarged 50 years later, and other
public buildings, including a small temple, also appeared in
stone *c*. 100. Private houses on the other hand were built of
timber until the mid-second century. Towards the end of the
second century new earth defences were erected to enclose an
enlarged urban area of 144 acres (60 ha), making it the fifth
largest town in Roman Britain. These defences were
refurbished in stone in the early third century. Decline set in,
however, in the mid-fourth century, when part of the forum
fell into disuse and several houses were demolished without
being rebuilt.

The only readily accessible relic of Roman Winchester *in
situ* is a fragment of the third-century town wall visible behind
a metal grille immediately south of the river-bridge at the east
end of High Street; it is reached via a footpath called the
Weirs, beside The Old Monk public house. Note that the river
Itchen here still follows the course dug for it by Roman
engineers in the late first or early second century AD:
previously it had flowed further west through the middle of
the area later occupied by the Roman (and medieval) town,

but the river was then deliberately diverted into a newly-dug, artificial channel, and the land thus reclaimed to the west was earmarked for urban expansion. Nevertheless problems remained: there is archaeological evidence to suggest that the whole of this low-lying eastern side of the town was liable to flood in Roman times.

Elsewhere in Winchester there is also a portion of the core of the Roman wall in the private grounds of St Bartholomew's Maternity Home, Hyde Street, and a piece of mosaic has been relaid on the floor beneath the entrance to the Deanery, south of the cathedral. More rewarding is the Brooks Experience, opened in 1996 in the Brooks Shopping Centre at the heart of the town (opt for 'Parking, Lower Level'). This has a little Roman material on display, as well as a life-size reconstruction of a room in a Roman town-house, based on one excavated here in 1987–8: parts of seven Roman houses were recorded in all on this extensive site in advance of the construction of the shopping centre. The display (entry free) is open 0900–1730, Monday–Saturday, throughout the year.

The remains of VENTA BELGARVM are, however, best understood through a visit to the City Museum, at the NW corner of the Cathedral Green, where finds from the city and nearby are superbly displayed (April–October, weekdays 1000–1700, Sunday 1400–1700; November–March, Tuesday–Saturday 1000–1600, Sunday 1400–1600). The Roman room at the top of the stairs is a model of modern museum presentation. A near-intact geometric mosaic of c. AD 300 from a villa at Sparsholt forms the central exhibit, and also outstanding are frescoes from the same site, including an over-restored female bust in a tondo, perhaps a portrait of the mistress of the house (*domina*). From Sparsholt, too, comes a painted version of guilloche, a framing device familiar from its ubiquitous use in mosaic; but in fresco it is extremely rare, occurring at three other villa sites in southern Britain (a fad of a single workshop?), but not apparently anywhere else in the Roman world. Watch out too for other exceptional finds in this gallery: a graffito on a roof-tile with the exclamation 'Good luck to the man who made this tile [*imbrex*]!'; a fragmentary inscription from a public building in Winchester mentioning an emperor with the name A]nto[ninus, carved in letters one Roman foot high (29.2 cm or $11\frac{1}{2}$ in) – the tallest of any inscription in Roman Britain; and a wooden statuette, itself a rare survival in Britain, of a cloaked figure, probably (from the hairstyle) female. She holds a key and a napkin (*mappa*), and it has also been claimed that she wears a torc, the Celtic neck-ring which was a symbol of status, prestige and power; but there is no apparent gap in the centre, and it seems more likely that this was intended as no more than a rolled top to her cloak. She may be the Romano-Celtic horse goddess Epona, who is usually shown riding side-saddle on her mount; but parallels from near Strasbourg and elsewhere in Gaul sometimes show her in the same guise as the Winchester figure, the napkin perhaps alluding obliquely to horses (chariot races were started with the wave of a *mappa*), and the key to opening the stable door. Whether there is deeper symbolism here – unlocking the 'gate of life', the key to prosperity and happiness, or indeed to the gates of the underworld for a safe passage to the hereafter – is a matter for speculation, as so often when we attempt today to interpret these silent manifestations of ancient spirituality.

To attempt to give coherent directions to the most famous of all Romano-British towns, **Silchester**** (SU 640625) [AM; A], is virtually impossible, for it lies in the middle of a maze of minor roads in the extreme north of Hampshire, inside a triangle formed by Newbury, Reading and Basingstoke. Curiously (and quite scandalously), English Heritage has erected not a single sign to lead visitors to this remarkable site, even though the entire circuit of the Roman city walls is in its care. The site is, however, marked on most maps, and I will leave readers to make their own way there. It is a charming place, peacefully set in deep countryside far from the bustle of the twenty-first century. It truly is a 'dead' city, since whereas most Roman towns in Britain continue in occupation to this day, Silchester did not find favour with later town-planners, and it remains deserted, with only a medieval church and a farm within its ancient walls. Yet, paradoxically, the fact that it is dead makes CALLEVA ATREBATVM, which means 'the town in the woods of the Atrebates', very much alive with the spirit of the past, and most people find a visit to the spot, whatever the season and whatever the weather, a moving and uncanny experience.

The reason for Silchester's fame is that the area within the walls was totally excavated in 1864–78 and, more especially, in 1890–1909. Techniques employed were not very scientific, even by the standards of the day, and so the chronological development of the town was not revealed – a deficiency only remedied by the work of excavation and re-excavation carried out on the defences, the amphitheatre, the basilica and a residential *insula* over the past 30 years. But the Victorian and Edwardian excavations did produce not only a wealth of objects but the more or less complete ground-plan of a Romano-British town, even if many timber buildings were undoubtedly missed – one of the most complete town-plans indeed from anywhere in the Roman Empire. The forum and basilica lay as usual at the centre, and the baths were discovered to the SE where the ground slopes down to a stream; several temples, an inn (near the south gate) and, of course, many houses were also uncovered. A tiny building, 12.80 m by 10 m (42 ft by 33 ft), found near the forum in 1892 and re-excavated in 1961, was almost certainly a church, although no specific objects conclusively proved its use for Christian worship. All these buildings, however, now lie under a blanket of soil; and apart from the forum, which was visible from 1875 to 1909, and the amphitheatre, where the excavated stonework has been consolidated and left exposed, no attempt has been made to leave the remains open in an accessible form. Today the cost of conserving anything but a tiny area would be prohibitive.

Despite the lack of visible remains within the walls there is still plenty to see at Silchester today. Apart from the town walls a series of late Iron Age earthworks once encircled the site, although the precise dating of these is not clear. The outer earthwork (5 and 10 on Fig. 19) has two distinct phases, but was not continuous, and may never have been completed: it is known only to the west of the later Roman town. The 'inner earthwork', not marked on the plan (Fig. 19), was erected at the very end of the first century BC (after 20/10 BC) around the pre-Roman settlement of the Atrebates, and enclosed only a slightly smaller area (about 80 acres [32.5 ha]) than that of the later town walls. The outer earthwork is not dated but is usually reckoned to be earlier, although probably not by much; there is very little occupation

at any kind in the centre of the site before *c.* 20 BC.
Excavations there in 1980–6, under the basilica of the Roman
town, found that a phase of Iron Age settlement with round
houses had been superseded in the early first century AD by
elements of proto-urban planning, with two streets laid out
approximately at right angles.

All this (except the outer earthwork) was levelled when
Silchester was re-founded along Roman lines in the 40s. The
Roman town was not slow to develop, and the fact that the
pro-Roman client king Togidubnus (p. 68) was an Atrebatan
must have stimulated early development: indeed the first
phase of the forum, in timber, as early as AD 45/50, is the
earliest forum in Britain (preferable to the military
interpretation once advanced for it); the first phase of the
baths is probably Neronian (*c.* 65); and the amphitheatre, too,
is another precociously early building, possibly as early as
55/65, in its first form. The forum and basilica were rebuilt,
again in timber, during the Flavian period (*c.* AD 80/90), but
the first stone forum was not constructed until the second

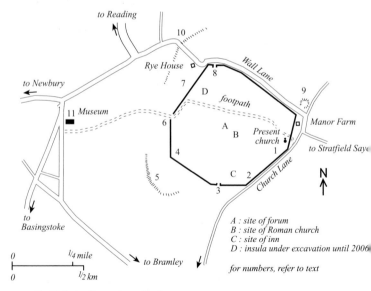

19   Silchester, Roman town, site plan

quarter of the second century (*c.* AD 130/50). The formal street-grid belongs to the end of the first century or even a little later (the baths, for example, are not quite aligned with it), but its planning was over-ambitious: the earth defences of the late second century enclose a smaller area than that envisaged by the original street-grid. A time-and-motion study has suggested that the earth rampart could have been built by 300 men in as little as 100 days. Finally, some time between about AD 260 and 280, the front of the earth bank was cut back and the visible stone defensive wall was erected.

The church provides a small car-park and a good starting point for a tour of the visible remains (1 on Fig. 19). By the path behind the church is a sun-dial (missing in 2000), supported on part of a Roman column which comes from a temple precinct underlying the churchyard. Walking south from the car-park here you will soon see the wall preserved to a good height. Further on it becomes more impressive, even though, as usual at Silchester, almost all the facing-stones have been robbed, leaving visible only the mortared flint-rubble core, separated at intervals by bonding-courses of large flat slabs. It is a spectacular sight here, still standing 4.50 m (15 ft) high, probably close to its original height apart from the patrol-walk (Fig. 20). Just before the wall changes direction (2) is a postern gate for pedestrians, erroneously interpreted as a sluice-gate in 1893 but re-excavated in 1976. It consists of a narrow inturned entrance, largely destroyed at the front, but with the brick piers of its single archway well preserved at the back. At some uncertain date (either in the late Roman period or after 410) the gate was blocked, and part of the blocking-wall is still in position. Then the wall turns the corner and makes for the south gate (3). Its single arch rose from the mortared flint piers with brick facing at front and back that can be seen at the rear of the passage. Excavation here in 1975 showed that the stone gateway was contemporary with the earth rampart of the late second century, and that the outer part of the passage was formed in the third century by inturning the new curtain walls. A similar sequence occurred at the SE postern, but there an earlier timber gate is also known. The south gate became increasingly rubbish-strewn after the mid-fourth century, a possible pointer to late Roman urban decline detected also in the basilica and elsewhere.

20   Silchester, Roman town wall, SE sector

From the rampart beside the south gate you have a fine
view of the interior of CALLEVA. Close to the walls on your
right you have to imagine a large inn (C on Fig. 19) with
rooms ranged round a courtyard; in the middle distance a
polygonal temple; and beyond, in the centre of the town, close
to the footpath on the skyline, the forum (A) with, along its
western side, a basilica rising some 21 m (70 ft) above the
ground. Part of one *insula* of private housing in the NW sector
is currently (2001) being re-excavated in July and August
each year, a project likely to continue until 2006 (D). Three
stone houses partially uncovered by the Edwardian excavators
of Silchester are being re-examined, one of them very
substantial (40 m [130 ft] long) and at a curiously oblique
angle to the *insula*'s orientation; it was demolished in the mid-
or late third century. In the period AD 250–400, the NE corner
of the *insula* had five properties lining the street, two entirely
timber-framed, and three with stone foundations. Only two of
these five appear on the 1909 plan of Silchester, underlining

(as noted above) how misleading an impression the published plan is likely to give us of the true urban population density of CALLEVA. A pit here in 1893 produced a stone, possibly a boundary marker, written in Ogham script in the late fourth or fifth century on a re-used Roman column (it is now in Reading Museum): it records an Irish settler, Tebicatus, and gives us a fascinating glimpse into the last years of the Roman town. Later still, part of the *insula* was dug into by a series of enormous pits which contained very little, and which the current excavators think might be a deliberate, post-Roman, ritualized 'pollution' of the site. Future years will investigate the early Roman and Iron Age levels below these late Roman and sub-Roman deposits.

Visitors pressed for time should now return to the car-park, and walk straight past it to the amphitheatre (9: p. 120). Others may like to continue following the walls at least as far as the west gate. At first the stretch of defences is much less impressive than elsewhere on the south side of the town, but the ditch accompanying the wall is visible here. At the SW corner (4) a detour can be made to Rampier Copse, where the outer earthwork survives to an impressive height of 6 m (20 ft) (5); but access is difficult. After the wall changes direction again and heads for the west gate, a short stretch of wall-facing can be seen, a rarity at Silchester. It is about 1 m (3 ft) high, with neat rows of flints separated by bonding-slabs. At the west gate (6), now a simple breach, but originally a twin-portalled gate with guard-chambers, you should go inside the wall: you have the choice now of either following the drove road back across the buried city (and past the 1997–2006 excavation site to your left: D on Fig. 19) to the churchyard and car-park, or of completing your circuit of the town walls, initially along the inside of the defences.

A short distance north of the west gate, a sector of the inner face of the wall, projecting above the earth rampart which backs it, shows an offset, part of a rectangular projection, 3.65 m (12 ft) long, found at regular intervals on the Silchester walled circuit. These are sections where the full thickness of the wall at base (2.90 m or 9 ft 6 in) is carried up the full height rather than, as elsewhere, being reduced in width by an offset to 2.30 m (7 ft 6 in). The purpose of such projections (which are found also at Caerwent: p. 360) is unclear: the suggestion that timber staircases joined the projections at either end and so provided access to the wall-walk is plausible but unproven. A little further on, opposite the private grounds of Rye House, the ditch is conspicuous (7): this is a late third-century ditch dug to replace two smaller ditches which accompanied the late second-century earth defences. Although it is impossible to see from the top of the wall, this section of the defences displays a long sag at this point, because of partial subsidence into the ditch of the inner earthwork, now invisible, which passed obliquely under the line of the wall here (this feature can only be viewed, with permission arranged with the owner in advance, from the gardens of Rye House).

Soon after, you come to the remains of the north gate (8), identical in type to the south gate but less well preserved. First investigated in the 1870s and again in 1909, it was totally re-excavated in 1991. There was some evidence for thinking that a short-lived timber gate, contemporary with the late second-century earth defences, preceded the stone gate of a few years later (a sequence not noted at the south gate, where the stone gate and earth defences appeared to be contemporary). Only part of the west brick pier marking the position of the gate itself survives. The kerb-stone showing the outer line of the wall curving round to meet the north face of the defences is especially clear on the west side. An information board here suggests that skulls were displayed as trophies either on or near the gate, but recent radio-carbon dating of two of the human fragments has ascribed one to the Iron Age and the other to the sub-Roman period; they therefore have no direct association with the Roman defences.

Proceeding eastwards from the north gate, you soon come to a stretch where the wall has largely fallen away: here you should cross its line to follow the path next to the fence along the outer face of the walls. Further on, a 15 m (45 ft) stretch of wall facing has been preserved, up to six courses high. Further on again, where three trees stand close together next to the wall, the large base slabs at the foot of the wall are preserved for a long stretch, at times with a few courses above of the mortared flintwork facing as well. The path leads past Manor Farm and so back to the road.

From here the amphitheatre (9: AM; A) is only a short

distance away. Turn left for 100 m along the road, as far
as the bend: the monument is reached through a wicket-gate
(no sign), next to the sign marking Wall Lane. Its tree-grown
elliptical banks still stand 5.50 m (18 ft) above the level of the
arena. In the south entrance, which you come to first, note the
substantial brick-built drains close to the arena wall. The latter
is visible in its entirety; inverted V-shaped drains, made up of
pieces of tile, which were designed to drain the seating banks
and make them as stable as possible, will be noticed at regular
intervals around the arena wall. On the amphitheatre's short
axis are two small semicircular recesses (that on the east still
stands 2.45 m [8 ft] high), which are probably shrines,
perhaps to Nemesis (cf. Chester, p. 319) and Fortuna. The
amphitheatre was not examined during the Victorian and
Edwardian explorations, but extensive excavation in 1979–85
showed that the visible stonework belongs most probably to
the third century, whether under Septimius Severus (193–211)
or later is unclear, but that it was preceded by two earlier
amphitheatres with arena walls and entrances of timber. The
earliest was erected *c.* AD 55/75, precociously early (one
would have thought) for a *civitas* capital, and perhaps
therefore built at the instigation of a pro-Roman client-king
like Togidubnus: possession of an amphitheatre, that most
quintessentially Roman of buildings, was a clear signal by the
city fathers of staking a claim to the *Romanitas* of their
community. The original amphitheatre received refurbishment
and slight modification, also carried out in timber, at some
time after the middle of the second century. Unlike the
military amphitheatres of Caerleon and Chester, the stone
revetment when it came in the third century was limited to the
arena area: the exterior of the earth seating bank was by
contrast revetted in cut turves. The seating was wooden
throughout the life of the amphitheatre, which probably
continued well into the fourth century.

Now return to your car and take the road along the north
defences and on to the Museum (11), passing through a well
preserved section of the outer earthwork (10) on your way.
The tiny Museum contains a few objects but mostly plans and
photographs of the excavations, as well as a model of the
Christian church; open daily, it is refreshingly (in today's
security-conscious age) without a custodian, and visitors are

free to come and go as they please. The main collections from
Silchester are excellently displayed in Reading Museum
(Tuesday–Saturday, 1000–1700, Sunday, 1400–1700);
scrutiny of its Roman gallery, refurbished in 1995, forms an
essential complement to a visit to CALLEVA itself. The objects
in the showcases there speak for themselves; many of them,
especially the iron tools (such as the carpenter's plane), look
remarkably similar to their modern counterparts. The
inscriptions, too, are fascinating: one, part of a monumental
inscription on stone, contains the word CALLEVA, a
confirmation of the Roman name for the town; others
scrawled on tile, such as 'Clementinus made this box-tile', or
'enough' (because the tile-maker was being worked too
hard?), show a high standard of literacy among the ordinary
inhabitants of the town. Another *graffito*, reading *conticuere
omnes* (the opening words of *Aeneid*, Book II), indicates that
Virgil was known to at least some people in the towns of
Roman Britain.

Turning now from the towns to the countryside, we find a
complex pattern of settlement. Romanized villas are absent
west of Exeter and on the downs of Wiltshire and Dorset.
Instead, they stick to the more cultivable and better-watered
valleys, especially around Ilchester in south Somerset (App.
1), Winchester and, to a lesser extent, Dorchester. Apart,
however, from the examples in the Isle of Wight, described
below (pp. 140–9), only the villas at Littlecote in Wiltshire
and Rockbourne in Hampshire preserve permanently
accessible remains, although an outstanding mosaic from
another site deserves a mention here. It was uncovered in
1946 in the cold room of a villa's bath-house at Low Ham
near Langport (Somerset), and is now in **Taunton** Castle, the
home of the Somerset County Museum (Tuesday–Saturday
1000–1730). Unfortunately it has been displayed on the wall,
and only one of the five scenes can be viewed in comfort. The
mosaic, of *c.* AD 340, tells the story of Dido and Aeneas as
recounted in Virgil's *Aeneid*, a vivid reflection of the literary
tastes of its owner. As displayed, the panel on the left shows
Aeneas' ships arriving at Carthage, with one of the Trojans
bearing a diadem for Queen Dido; at the bottom, a topless
Dido displays obvious interest in Aeneas on the left, with
Ascanius (Aeneas' son) and Venus between (Fig. 21); the

21   Low Ham mosaic (detail), Aeneas, Ascanius, Venus and Dido (Taunton Museum)

panel on the right shows Dido and Aeneas out hunting with Ascanius in the lead; at the top is the embrace of a fully clothed Aeneas and a scantily clad Dido, in a cave (according to Virgil) but here shown between two stylized trees. On the central panel stands Venus between two cupids, one with torch raised symbolizing life (Aeneas, who set sail to found Rome), the other with torch reversed standing for death and darkness (referring to Dido's suicide on Aeneas' departure). Also displayed here is a fragmentary mosaic from East Coker showing a pair of huntsmen with a deer upside down on a pole, a floor chiefly of interest because this composition ultimately derives from mosaic copybooks in north Africa (where the animal is a boar). Other finds on display in Taunton Museum include lead pigs from Charterhouse and nearby, including the latest dated example known (AD 164/9; p. 155); early military finds found during quarrying on Ham Hill, where there was almost certainly a fort, now destroyed;

and the hoard of 9,238 silver *denarii*, the latest dated to AD 224, which was found in 1998 at a Roman villa at Shapwick. Apart from the Hoxne hoard (which also contained gold and bronze coins; p. 648), it is the largest ever recorded hoard of Roman silver coinage from anywhere in Britain.

The villa in **Littlecote Park**** (SU 297708), excavated between 1978 and 1991, is situated in the grounds of the sixteenth-century Littlecote House; the latter is signposted from the B4192 2½ miles (4 km) NW of Hungerford. The house is now a luxury country hotel owned by Warner Holidays, but the Roman villa is accessible in parkland at any time. When inside the grounds, ignore the turning to the hotel itself but keep straight, and then turn right at the crossroads at the end of the row of trees, 200 m beyond Littlecote House. This leads down to the river and the elegant cover over the mosaic (1 on Fig. 22), erected in 2000 to allow patrons year-round access.

A spectacular mosaic, described as 'the finest pavement that sun ever shone upon in England', was uncovered in 1728 and

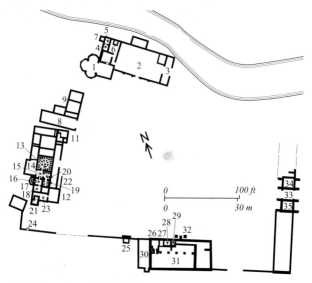

22   *Littlecote, Roman villa, site plan*

recorded in both an embroidered tapestry, and also on an
engraving now in the Ashmolean Museum, Oxford. The
mosaic, presumed lost, was laid bare anew in 1978, but
although there is every reason to think that it had originally
been found intact (it lay beneath over 2 m [7 ft] of soil),
neglect, building work and rodent activity in the intervening
two and a half centuries had destroyed over half the original
floor. The mosaic which you see today, therefore (Fig. 23),
has been largely recreated from the tapestry design, and
although overall it makes a striking impression, it is a pity that
the portions of Roman original have not been more clearly
distinguished from the modern work. It is true that the parts
entirely in modern materials are detectable by the use of
cream rather than white background tesserae, but the full
extent of the repair can only be worked out by studying
excavation photographs of 1978. The floor, a work of
undistinguished draughtmanship, is in two parts. One is a
rectangular area containing geometric designs, which are

23   Littlecote, Roman villa, mosaic in three-apsed dining-room

flanked by two strips depicting sea-beasts and panthers
respectively, arranged either side of centrally placed chalices.
The other, principal part has figured scenes in the central
square and, around it, three semicircular apses floored with
scallop-shell motifs. The figured scenes feature a female
figure on the back of an animal in each of the quadrants,
probably the Seasons, and a male figure with a lyre in the
central roundel. His Phrygian cap suggests that he is Orpheus,
but the animals which invariably accompany him, charmed by
his music, are missing, while the Seasons are more
appropriate to another lyre-bearing god, Apollo: such
conflation of two divine or semi-divine figures is not
uncommon in Romano-British iconography.

The three-apsed room (*triconchos*) containing the mosaic
is an ambitious architectural conception. It first appears in
town-houses in north Africa in the late third century and is
then found soon afterwards in Italian and Sicilian country
villas. It soon became fashionable elsewhere in the late
Empire, not least because by then the preferred dining couch
was semicircular in shape, replacing the straight couches of an
earlier age. The apse of Lullingstone villa's dining-room
(p. 87) also reflects this fashion, but a triple-apsed room is
unique in Britain. This may provide a clue that either the
owner or the architect had close links with the central
Mediterranean world, or at least was aware of contemporary
architectural thinking there. It also points very firmly to the
room's function as a dining-room for use in the summer (it is
unheated), in a very pleasant location overlooking a charming
river. I remain totally unconvinced by the excavators'
preferred interpretation that the room was a meeting-hall for
an Orphic cult.

The building to which the mosaic belonged consists of a
large open yard (2) preceded by a vestibule with the main
entrance (3), down by the river (although this is a later
addition to the original yard, as straight joints make clear);
there is a lesser entrance in the long wall of the yard. That
wall contains recesses in it presumably to take timber posts
(rather than the stone columns shown in site reconstructions).
Also here is a small bath complex with two heated rooms
(4–5), a small cold immersion-bath (with white mortar floor,
6), and a hot-water bath with its own hypocaust (7). The

stoke-hole for firing these rooms is visible in the wall nearest the river. That the bath-suite is later than the original yard can be seen from the straight joints between the original structure and the added hot and cold pools, and also by the fact that the original yard's outer wall was hacked through to insert a brick flue leading to the hot room.

On the other side of the mosaic room (1) you first come to a workshop (8) with adjacent domestic quarters (9, for a farm worker or slave?); the visible layout dates from the late third century. Bronze-working furnaces were found in the largest room (8) here. It is separated by a narrow alley from the main residential block, which was originally laid out about AD 170 but was substantially remodelled in the closing years of the third century. This is the clearest visible example in Britain of what is called a 'winged corridor villa', a type very widespread as well in France and Germany (Fig. 24). A

24   Littlecote, Roman villa, 'winged corridor' residence (west range)

corridor (10) runs along the front of the house giving access to
the principal rooms, and is flanked at either end by projecting
L-shaped rooms, which in the late alterations were converted
into square chambers: added masonry can be detected by the
straight joints with earlier walls (11–12). The central room of
this house, presumably the principal winter dining-room (13),
is that heated by an unusual radial hypocaust (installed
c. 270); it combines both dwarf supporting walls and
conventional brick *pilae* to support the floor. Behind this room
is a kitchen with its oven (14), and also the original bath-suite
of the villa. The stoke-hole for these baths was in the passage
between them and the large heated dining-room (15); of its
two flues leading into the tiny adjacent *caldarium* (16) one
was later blocked, the blocking-wall being still *in situ*. The
channelled hypocaust in the apse of the *caldarium* (17) would
have heated water in a hot bath above; the box-tile used as its
outflow drain can be seen. The next room to the south (18)
was the *tepidarium*. Many of the brick *pilae* have for
conservation reasons been replaced in modern materials. In
the room closest to the front corridor (19) is what has been
viewed as another small hypocaust, interpreted by the
excavators as perhaps a dry-heat *laconicum*; but it is not clear
where it was fired, and its structure looks much more likely to
have been a pottery- or tile-kiln, inserted in the ruins at a late
period when the villa was no longer used for elegant living.
The adjacent rooms to the north also received hypocausts: the
four pairs of piers here in 20 are supports for brick arches
(still extant is the impression in the mortar for a brick
voussoir), which served to support the floor above. The use of
flat tiles (*tegulae*) on top of one another to create walling here
and in the adjacent room is unusual. At the far southern end of
this wing (21) is a cold-water bath and steps down to it. Not
all the visible walls here are contemporary: for example, in
front of the projecting 'wing' on this side are the foundations
of an earlier projecting room and associated corridor wall
(22), which look like the remains of an earlier winged corridor
villa, demolished and rebuilt at a later date. The wall footing
next to the cold bath, just inside the villa's outer wall, also
belongs to this earlier phase.

   The excavations established that the bath-suite was entirely
demolished in the late alterations of *c.* 290, when the main

radial hypocaust was also filled in; the only heating thenceforth seems to have been in the square room (12) at the south end of the front corridor (only its brick flue is visible; the *pilae* have gone), stoked from what had formerly been the *frigidarium* (23). At least five of the rooms had tessellated or mosaic floors (only scraps survived), including at least one added after demolition of both baths and main hypocaust. The block was certainly a much less comfortable residence then, perhaps for summer occupation only. Final decay did not set in until the late fourth or early fifth century.

Beyond the residential block is a well (24), earlier than the courtyard wall (*c*. 280) which incorporates it. Also earlier (it was built about 270) is another square well (25) which the boundary wall apparently makes a detour to avoid. The principal feature in the south range was another bath-suite, built *c*. AD 280, with two heated rooms (26–27) and a hot pool in the apse closest to the stoke-hole. Several of the brick fragments built into its cheeks have comb marks and even a dog's paw-print. A small cold room (28) and cold pool (29, with *opus signinum* floor) lie beyond. The adjacent large room on the other side of the baths (30) has a small apse with box flue-tiles, clearly designed to be a heated pool in another bathing-suite, which was started (*c*. 360) but never finished.

The completed set of baths overlies a large rectangular building of *c*. 250 (31) which must have been largely demolished when the baths were built: walls below and beyond the cold room belonged to it. These in turn overlie four square piers which can be seen adjacent to the line of the later wall. These and the other four square freestanding piers belonged to the rectangular building in its original mid-third-century phase, when there was a row of columns along one side (for a lean-to?). The two further piers outside this wing to the north (32) were interpreted by the excavators as part of a grandiose entrance into the south wing, which seems unlikely in view of its otherwise comparatively humble nature. Presumably the small baths here were used by a farm manager (*vilicus*) and/or estate workers.

Finally you come to the east wing, added in the later third century when an imposing entrance to the villa (33, under the tree) was constructed, flanked by gatemen's lodges (34, 35). The massiveness of the projecting piers here suggests a

gateway intended to impress. The projecting masonry inside
the passage presumably marks the position of the imposts for
hanging the gates, of which there were two pairs.

The **Rockbourne*** villa (SU 120170) (early April to early
October, Monday–Friday 1400–1800, Saturday, Sunday and
Bank Holidays 1030–1800; July and August, daily
1030–1800), is signposted from the A354 5 miles (8 km) SW
of Salisbury, and it can also be reached by turning north off
the B3078 at Sandleheath, 2 miles (3.2 km) west of
Fordingbridge. Its late owner and excavator (A T Morley-
Hewitt), a retired architect, kept the villa open to the public
during excavation, which continued each year from 1956 to
1974. The villa has now been largely backfilled for its own
preservation, although some parts have been consolidated and
left exposed; the rest has been marked out in modern
materials. The earliest structure, in the courtyard of the later
villa, was a circular late Iron Age hut, replaced by a three-
room cottage in the later first century. This was demolished
and replaced by a new house in the second century, later
incorporated into the west wing. A bath-suite was added to it
perhaps *c*. 150/200. The north wing was added in the third
century and had its own tiny baths, replaced by a new and
larger bath-suite *c*. 300. The south side of the yard contained
farm buildings. Occupation continued here down to *c*. 400,
but by the final phase the villa (which contained 40 or so
rooms in its heyday) had fallen on hard times and the
residential rooms and baths were no longer in use.

First visit the small but rewarding museum, with some
unusual finds. Look out especially for two well preserved
colour-coated bowls from the New Forest kilns (active
c. 260/370); the carved stone roof finial of Chilmark stone
(quarried 14 miles [22.4 km] to the NW), and a decorated
table-top in the same material; and the two third-century
inscribed milestones, found re-used in the villa – a rare (and
highly irregular?) find for a rural site. On leaving the Museum
and turning left, you first come to the north wing of *c*. AD 200,
including one square room with a simple mosaic of *c*. 300.
Note the contrast in the size of the tesserae between the
meander pattern in the centre and its surround; the
asymmetrical arrangement of the pattern suggest that this was
a small dining-room, with the couches placed on the

undecorated parts of the floor. Further on towards the trees is a set of baths, of two separate phases of *c*. 200 and 300. At first the long corridor was the cold room, the room in the middle of its south side (facing the courtyard) serving as its cold-water immersion-bath. Later, in the fourth century, this became the *tepidarium* and a new octagonal cold bath, with tiled steps leading into it, was added on the other side of the *frigidarium*. The mosaic in the corridor (see back cover photograph), laid *c*. 300, is partly restored (the bright white tesserae and the associated pattern are modern); by contrast the stone flagging represents ancient repair. This room has an outflow drain towards its east end, close to the similar drain for the cold-water bath (also visible in its east wall). The other room with tessellated work here is the undressing room, preceded by the entrance lobby. The latter is clearly a secondary addition, built of ironstone and not flint, and forming a straight joint with the walling of the undressing room. The baths remained in use until *c*. 350, when the hypocausts were dismantled and new floors laid.

Now go over to the far side of the courtyard to the south wing. The tree trunks mark the posts of part of a second-century aisled barn (only its western half has been excavated), but the only ancient features visible here are a well and a late third-century T-shaped 'corn-drying oven' (on the function of these structures, see p. 147 below). Another corn-drier is schematically marked out in brown stones further west in the south wing. Finds suggest that the room adjacent to it was a smithy. Moving back towards the Museum you follow the line of the west wing, with the main gateway to the villa marked by the wooden posts. Of the baths added to this wing *c*. 150/200, one highly unusual heated room has been left exposed, in which the *pilae* consist of re-used semicircular roofing-tiles (*imbrices*) (Fig. 25). The plan of both the Iron Age circular hut (grey stones) and the first farm of *c*. AD 75, forerunners in turn of the later and much enlarged villa, are marked out in the NW corner of the courtyard.

In addition to Romanized villas, however, there are hundreds of native settlements which could be mentioned in this book, ranging in size from single homesteads to large villages, each displaying varying degrees of cultural contact

25   Rockbourne, Roman villa, hypocaust using roof-tiles (imbrices)

with Rome. Their economy was based on small-scale mixed
farming, consisting of both corn-growing and sheep- or
cattle-raising. In Cranbourne Chase, immediately west of
Rockbourne, however, a change seems to have been
introduced in the late third century, if not before, when the
area may have been appropriated as an imperial estate. At this
time several of the settlements became deserted, field-systems
fell into disuse, and new cattle-enclosures were erected. It
looks, therefore, as if government-controlled sheep- and
cattle-farming replaced arable farming – a theory supported
by the record that there was an imperial weaving-mill in the
fourth century listed in an official document at 'VENTA',
probably Winchester rather than Caistor in Norfolk or
Caerwent in south Wales. One such cattle-enclosure, known
as **Soldier's Ring** (SU 082176), is close to the Rockbourne
villa. To reach it from the latter, take the road towards the
village of Rockbourne, and turn first left; then in the village of

Damerham turn first right (signposted Martin and Cranborne).
Continue straight along this road for $1\frac{1}{4}$ miles (2 km) (ignoring
the turning to Cranborne), and take the first turning on the left
after South Allenford Farm. The polygonal enclosure's slight
earthworks, somewhat overgrown with nettles, are visible at
the end of this track behind the wire fence on your left. It can
be better seen, crowned with trees, a little further on to the
right of the track. It surrounded an enclosure of 26 acres (10.5
ha).

Several other Roman sites can be visited in close proximity
on Cranbourne Chase, and so I will describe them in
geographical, not chronological, order. Continue along the
minor road at Soldier's Ring through the village of Martin to
the A354. Turn left at this junction and keep going for
$1\frac{1}{4}$ miles (2 km) until you cross the Hampshire-Dorset border,
where there is a lay-by on the right. Running alongside the
left of the road here for 100 m, before it changes direction, is
a bush-covered stretch of the impressive barrier known as the
Bokerley Dyke (SU 035198). Earlier editions of this book
had considered part of this multi-phase earthwork to be late
Roman in date, on the basis of trenches cut by General Pitt-
Rivers in the nineteenth century as re-assessed by Professor
Hawkes in the twentieth. That dating now seems implausible.
The Bokerley Dyke is basically a late Bronze Age or early
Iron Age boundary line with later Iron Age and post-Roman
additions. The Roman highway broke through it at this point,
and its *agger*, heading northwards towards Old Sarum, is
visible on the right (west) of the modern road (take the path
leading away from the lay-by at its widest point: 25 m (75 ft)
along this, at a metal field-gate, the *agger* is clearly visible
straight ahead of you). Its alignment touches the A354 at this
point and then joins it at the village of Woodyates for 1 mile
(1.6 km), before the modern highway swings away towards
Blandford and leaves the Roman line altogether.

The best place to examine the Roman road, however, is a
little further south. Continue along the A354 for another mile
(1.6 km) and turn left at the roundabout for Ringwood along
the B3081. The *agger* of the Roman road, known here as the
Ackling Dyke* (SU 015163), crosses the B-road at the crest
of the slope after $\frac{1}{4}$ mile (400 km) (first field-boundary on the
left; pull in on the left just after passing it). To the left (north)

it forms a striking sight, as far as the A354 which joins the
Roman alignment. Southwards it also strides magnificently
over the downland, dead straight and visible for miles, aiming
for the hill-fort of Badbury Rings, over 8 miles (12 km) away.
The whole of this stretch is a right-of-way and it provides a
wonderful walk. Here the *agger* is at its best, 12.20 m (40 ft)
wide and 1.50 to 1.80 m (5 or 6 ft) high. Such an embankment
is unnecessary on this dry ground, and it has been suggested
that the road was deliberately built in this fashion to impress
the native population.

Return now along the B3081 and go straight across at the
roundabout for Sixpenny Handley. Two miles (3.2 km)
beyond this village is a turning to the left, signposted
Cashmoor and Dean, and immediately after this, on the right
by a telephone booth (opposite 'Chase Cottage'), is a grass
track. This leads, after 12 minutes' walk (keep straight), to a
metal gate at the point where the track veers left. Go through
the gate into the first field, where there is a tree-filled hollow
to the right (a well?), and a prominent semicircular earthwork
to the left. Beyond the second, smaller metal gate and disused
electric fence there is a smaller semicircular earthwork to your
left, and two small mounds straight ahead. Strike left here for
the main enclosure, which forms part of the classic native
settlement of **Woodcuts** (ST 964182). Excavated in 1884 by
General Pitt-Rivers, the pioneer of scientific archaeology, and
later re-interpreted by Professor Christopher Hawkes, the site
is now known to have had three separate phases. The first
lasted from the early first century AD, before the Roman
invasion, to the third quarter of the second century, and was
entirely native in character. The homestead was surrounded by
a circular bank and ditch within which were 80 storage pits
for grain, although only a few were dug at a time. From the
late second century Roman influence had certainly made an
impact in the form of wall-plaster, two stone-built wells, and
corn-driers. There was further remodelling of the enclosure-
banks at the end of the third century, but by the later fourth
century the place was deserted. The visible earthworks,
restored by Pitt-Rivers, belong to all periods, but still give
some idea of the level of native occupation under Roman rule.
The main enclosure is thistle-filled in summer; a Victorian
inscription marks the hollow where a 'Roman well 4 feet in

diameter and the same deep' was excavated. Further
enclosures were tacked on to the left-hand side (the smaller)
and the far side of the principal one; a second well is marked
by a now illegible inscription in the one furthest away. The
corn-driers (not visible) were also found there.

Of the many hundreds of similar settlements in which
Wessex is so rich, I will mention just three more – sites
generally reckoned to be among the best preserved of their
kind. Giving directions to these is not easy and readers will
find it better to locate them with the help of the 1:50,000
series OS maps. At none of them is there anything to see
beyond some often confusing ridges, mounds and building-
platforms, but they deserve to be visited to remind ourselves
that it was only a minority of the inhabitants of Roman Britain
who enjoyed the plush luxury of the stone-built villas, with
their hypocausts and mosaics, that are so popularly associated
with the countryside. Very close to Woodcuts, and reached
from the bridleway leading due north from Tollard Royal on
the B3081 (turn right at the pillar-box and telephone booth,
and then on foot bear right up the hill – signposted 'By-way to
Win Green') is the native settlement on **Berwick Down**
(ST 941197). It adjoins the right-hand side of the track
$1\frac{1}{4}$ miles (2 km) from Tollard, at the point where the electricity
power lines cross over it from left to right. Apart from the
stunning views the site is not worth visiting in summer, when
the earthworks are obscured by long nettles. There are three
separate areas here: behind the beech trees is a U-shaped bank
enclosing an oblong hut-enclosure which has yielded finds of
the first century AD; 100 m to the north, where the trees end, is
a circular enclosure over 2 acres (0.8 ha) in extent, with a
mass of rectangular building-platforms, certainly of Romano-
British date; and north again is a concentration of pits and a
large circular hut which belongs to pre-Roman times. Half a
mile (800 m) due east, across the other side of the valley and
on the edge of another wood, is **Rotherley** (ST 948196),
which is very remote and best reached by another path from
Tollard Royal (see OS map). It was excavated by Pitt-Rivers
in 1885–6 and, like Woodcuts, restored by him. The main
layout of the earthworks must be dated to the immediate
pre-Roman period, but occupation continued with few
changes, except for the introduction of Roman coins and

pottery, until about AD 300. The main features are a large
circular enclosure where the principal house was situated, a
smaller enclosure to the NE, where there was a granary, and
other hollows, working-areas and gullies to the east. The
settlement never seems to have been more than a single
community with at most two or three dwelling-huts.

Finally in Wessex the settlement on **Meriden Down**
(ST 802049) is worth a mention, as visitors are welcome even
though the land is private, and there is a plan of the
earthworks displayed on the site. There is very little of interest
to see, but it is set in some of the most peaceful and delightful
countryside in Dorset, and the walk alone should make the
visit worth while. Take the minor road signposted Milton
Abbas in Winterbourne Whitchurch on the A354, 5 miles
(8 km) SW of Blandford Forum. Keep straight on without
going into Milton, and then turn left at the fork (signposted
Bulbarrow). Go on for $1\frac{1}{4}$ miles (2 km) until you see a gate
marked 'Delcombe Manor'. Two hundred metres (220 yds)
further on, on the right, a track goes off through the woods
(wooden bar). Follow this immediately round to the left, and
after five minutes take the left fork (ignore the right-hand one
leading to a field-gate). Shortly after passing through a gate on
this track, and then keeping straight, you come to a large
exercise-ground for horses. The site lies at the far end of this
field and a plan, now somewhat battered, is displayed in a
fenced enclosure near the trees on the right. Behind you as
you face the sign is the low straight bank of an ancient field-
boundary, but the main part of the settlement lies to your left,
honeycombed with banks and level platforms indicating the
site of working-areas and building-structures; the earthworks
are no more than 0.45–0.60 m (18 in–2 ft) high. Four roads
(a–d on the site plan) lead to open spaces outside the nucleus;
one of the western roads (f) is accompanied by four small
mounds of unknown purpose. Now go through the gap in the
trees to your right immediately beyond the plan, and follow
the bushes round to your left. Three looped enclosures,
probably the compounds for three large buildings, are clearly
visible here. To the south is a large area of perfectly
preserved contemporary fields, tilled by the Romano-British
inhabitants of the settlement.

An interesting sidelight on (probably) Romano-British

Wessex is shed by the **Cerne Giant** (ST 667016), a chalk figure cut into the hillside above the village of Cerne Abbas on the A352, a few miles north of Dorchester. He is a powerfully muscular figure, 55 m (180 ft) high, emphatically displaying his potency with prominent erect phallus, and wielding a knotted club above his head. Nipples and six ribs, as well as a simple belt, are also rather crudely shown; it has also been claimed that he once wore a cloak over one arm, now overgrown. The club clearly indicates that the figure is meant to represent the god Hercules, albeit in iconographically unique form, and it was presumably carved by the local population to promote fertility. The question is: precisely when? We know that the figure is earlier than 1694, the date of the first documentary record of it, and the club with its clear allusion to Hercules surely rules out a pre-Roman date, although that chronology too has its adherents. A sketch of 1763, the earliest to survive, shows that it once had a separate navel and a phallus not quite so long; subsequent judicious removal of grass has lengthened the latter. Its Romano-British origin has been widely accepted, and the failure of any reference to it by sixteenth- and early seventeenth-century antiquarians, perhaps through prudery, cannot be used as an argument to deny its earlier existence. On balance it is probably more likely to be Roman than not; but scientific tests of the type which have recently been used to clarify the date of another chalk figure, the Uffington White Horse in Oxfordshire, are needed to clear up the chronological uncertainty over the Cerne Abbas giant.

In the Cornish peninsula, Roman influence was virtually non-existent, and only a single example of a Romanized house is known in Cornwall, at Magor, Camborne (not now visible). For the vast majority life must have been little changed by the Roman conquest. The classic native settlement in this part of Britain is **Chysauster*** (SW 472350) [AM; April–September, daily 1000–1800; October, daily 1000–1700; November–March 1000–1600] on the Land's End peninsula, 4 miles (6.4 km) north of Penzance. It is signposted from the B3311 (Penzance–St Ives) at Badger's Cross and from the Penzance to Gurnard's Head road at New Mill. The well preserved remains (reached across a field) consist of eight oval stone-built houses arranged in pairs (two rows of four dwellings),

with another to the right of the path near the entrance-stile.
Pass this and go to the next two houses, no. 3 on the left and
no. 5 on the right. It is best to study house 5 first, since its
plan is simple and characteristic of the 'courtyard-house' of
which this and other similar villages are composed. The
entrance-passage leads into a courtyard, open to the sky, in the
centre of the enclosure. On the left is a recessed portion,
perhaps covered by a lean-to for cattle, and on the right is a
long narrow room, possibly used as a workshop or for storage.
The living-room was the round or oval hut at the far side of
the courtyard opposite the entrance, and its roof was
supported by a central beam in a stone socket (here *in situ*).
There are sometimes other small rooms or recesses opening
off the central courtyard, but the other houses all display these
same basic features. No. 3, however, is more complicated as it
is 'semi-detached': there are two entrances, two round rooms
and two recesses on the left, all enclosed in the single unit.
Many of the houses have terraced areas (?gardens) adjacent.
Pottery indicates that the Chysauster village goes back to the
first century BC, but the main occupation occurred in the first
and second centuries AD until peaceful abandonment
c. AD 300. The inhabitants existed on small-scale mixed
farming; there are remains of the accompanying field-system
in the near vicinity.

Another peculiar feature of some Cornish settlements is a
subterranean chamber known as a *fogou*, apparently used as a
cellar for keeping food cool and dry. There is a very ruinous
example at Chysauster, reached from the main area by a
separate footpath (to the right of the ticket-office), but the best
fogou is at a nearby village, **Carn Euny** (SW 403288)
[AM; A], 4 miles (6.4 km) west of Penzance and signposted
from the A30 at Lower Drift. It is approached from one of the
houses by a roofless stone-lined passage, which leads to the
main curving gallery, 1.50 m (5 ft) wide and 1.80 m (6 ft)
deep, still roofed with massive stone slabs. Opening off it at
its south end is a tiny tunnel leading to a circular chamber
which probably originally had a timber and turf roof; at its
north end is a large entrance to a beehive, vaulted chamber
4 m (13 ft) across and 3.50 m (11 ft 6 in) high. It is believed
that the *fogous*, like the villages themselves, are of pre-Roman
origin, but continued in use during the Roman period. Carn

Euny also has four stone 'courtyard-houses' and four smaller stone dwellings. Excavations between 1964 and 1972 showed that these replaced earlier timber huts from the first century BC onwards; the farming settlement was peacefully abandoned at the end of the fourth century.

Analogous round houses occupied during Romano-British times can be seen in the Scilly Isles, most notably at Halangy Down on St Mary's (SW 908118) and, if you can arrange for a boat to take you there, on the uninhabited island of **Nornour** (SV 944148). The last, exposed by a storm in 1962 and excavated in 1968–70, has produced an extraordinary wealth of objects. There are 11 round houses here, up to 5.5 m (18 ft) in diameter, with walls up to 1.2 m (4 ft) high. It was suggested by the excavators that the most westerly hut had become a shrine in Roman times. The evidence found for cereal cultivation and stock-raising suggests that there was more cultivable land here in antiquity than today. The small finds from this settlement, some quite exotic, include Roman rings, over 280 brooches, some 25 rings, 83 coins and 22 glass beads as well as 13 good-quality Romano-Gaulish clay figurines showing Venus and a mother goddess. The finds date mostly *c*. AD 80–220 (although the coins go later), but with a preponderance belonging to the second century. Such a range of finds would be exceptional even on a rural site much closer to the heartlands of Roman Britain than Nornour, and while they appear to throw fascinating light on the penetration of Roman artefacts into an area remote from mainstream Roman influence and culture, the suspicion persists that the second-century material is not primary but was washed up on shore from a nearby shipwreck.

Apart from the early invasion period, official Roman interest in the far west was confined to the exploitation of the tin-streams of central Cornwall in the third and fourth centuries AD, after the Spanish tin-mines, Rome's previous major source, were exhausted. The workings themselves have been largely destroyed by later activity, but five crudely cut Roman milestones, all of them just a few metres from their original find-spots, bear witness to road-building or repair in Cornwall, although actual traces of these roads have not been found. Two milestones imply a short stretch of road on the north coast. One, 1.6 m (4 ft 5 in) high and dated to AD 251/3

(the joint reign of Gallus and Volusianus), is in the private
garden of 'St Piran's', **Trethevy** (SX 076892), a village
1½ miles (3 km) NE of Tintagel on the B3263. 'St Piran's' is a
small nursery opposite the church. The other, which is
dedicated to Licinius, emperor between 308 and 324, is in the
south transept of **Tintagel** church (SX 051884); it was spotted
built into the lychgate of the church in 1899. Further west is a
better example, found by ploughing in 1940 and now erected
in the private garden of Mynheer Farm at **Gwennap Pit** (SW
720421), a hamlet 2 miles (3.2 km) due east of Redruth (ask
permission to view). Take the minor road west towards
Redruth in the outskirts of St Day, and then take the left fork
signposted Gwennap Pit opposite the Star Inn: Mynheer Farm
lies on the left of this road after ⅓ mile (500 m). The earliest of
the Cornish milestones, it is dedicated to the emperor Caesar
Antonius Gordianus Pius Felix (AD 238–44), and belongs
either to a road running down the spine of Cornwall or to a
cross-road linking the north and south coasts, to assist in the
transport of tin from the mines to the ports. In south Cornwall
two more milestones are known: one erected to Postumus,
emperor 258–68, is now inside the church at **Breage** (SW
618285), a village north of the A394, 4 miles (6.4 km) west of
Helston; and the best preserved of all the Cornish milestones
is now cemented into the floor of the south aisle of the church
at **St Hilary** (SW 550313), which lies north of the B3280, 1¾
miles (about 3 km) east of its junction with the A394 near
Marazion. It was set up in AD 306/8: 'To the Emperor
Caesar Flavius Valerius Constantinus Pius, most noble
Caesar, son of the deified Constantius Pius Felix Augustus'
(Fig. 26).

I have stayed long enough on the fringes of Roman Britain
and it is time to return and deal with a more familiar
monument of the Romano-British countryside, the villa. The
Rockbourne and Littlecote villas have been noted above; two
more are visible in the region covered by this chapter, both of
them on the Isle of Wight (VECTIS to the Romans). The Roman
villa at **Brading**** (SZ 599863), open from April to the end
of October (daily, 1000–1730, Sunday, 1030–1730), is
signposted from the A3055 in the southern outskirts of the
town. The excavations, conducted in 1880–5, paid little
attention to chronology, but pottery finds indicate that the site

26   *St Hilary, Roman milestone of Constantine's reign (AD 306/8)*

was occupied from the later first century AD onwards, and there are traces of Iron Age occupation where the car-park now is (Fig. 27). In its final form, in the fourth century, the villa consisted of a main residential block of 12 rooms and two subsidiary wings ranged around a courtyard. Sea came up to the foot of the slope where the villa lies until drainage works in the 1880s; the area is still prone to flooding. The main block, which in plan is a compact example of the 'winged corridor' villa so widespread in Britain, is completely accessible under its cover-building, and is chiefly notable for the remarkable mid-fourth-century figured mosaics in four of its rooms. There is a scheme afoot (2001) to replace the existing cover-building with a new one in the next few years.

The first mosaic seen on entering lies in the middle of a long corridor (6) and represents Orpheus charming the animals with his lyre: on the left is a monkey with a bird below, on the right another bird and a fox. Eight other British examples of this scene are known, but only the Brading

mosaic puts charmer and charmed within the same circle. To
the right, a corn-drier has been inserted into the floor,
presumably at a time when this part of the villa no longer
mattered as a residence, even if the site continued in use as an
agricultural centre. The red and white chequer-board
tessellation, to the left of the Orpheus mosaic, used sawn-up
pieces of terracotta box flue-tiles for some of the red tesserae:
the combed patterning characteristic of these (for better
adherence of the wall-plaster, in its original function) can be
seen on several. Note also how the white limestone panels
have a heavily water-eroded surface and so are not level with
the indestructible terracotta of the adjacent red panels; those
white panels which are flush with the red ones represent
modern repair.

Moving now to the left, you come to the second mosaic (3),
which is badly damaged; its relaying in 1982 has
unfortunately dulled the colours of the tesserae. The central
roundel has a bust of Bacchus, identifiable by the god's wand
(*thyrsus*) over his right shoulder; and there is a bust of a
member of his entourage (a maenad?) in the one surviving

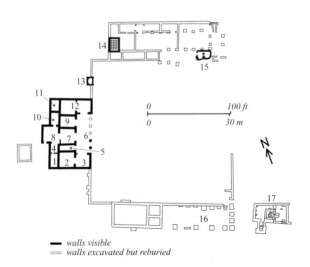

■ *walls visible*
═ *walls excavated but reburied*

27   Brading, Roman villa, site plan

corner, also carrying a *thyrsus*. Of the side-panels only one is
substantially complete (with signs of burning on the right-
hand side). On the left is an enigmatic cock-headed man
dressed in a tunic, in the centre is a small hut approached by a
ladder, and on the right are two griffins (Fig. 28). It used to be
thought that the cock-headed man had connections with
Gnosticism, a philosophical sect which believed that through
knowledge (*gnosis*) man could gain everlasting life. In
particular he was identified with Abraxas, depicted in gnostic
art with a cock's head and serpent's tail; but the absence of
the latter feature makes this interpretation of the Brading
figure highly unlikely. Rather the panel echoes elements of
spectacles in the amphitheatre: the griffins, emblems of
Nemesis (goddess of Fate), are found on mosaics associated
with this theme in north Africa and Sicily, and the connection
is strengthened if the 'sticks' in yellow and red tesserae
running diagonally across and above the griffins are millet
stalks, as has been suggested: millet was the symbol of some

28   Brading, Roman villa, mosaic with the cock-headed man

of the factions of animal-fighters (*venatores*) in north African
amphitheatres (another, the crescent on the stick, occurs in
Britain at Rudston: p. 430). The little building has been
interpreted as a temple or as an animal cage; I see it rather as
one of the huts placed around the arena out of which
venatores sprang to give an element of surprise during the
shows. That leaves the cock-headed man unexplained (he is
unique in the whole of Roman art), but he may be a
misunderstood representation of one of the exotic but
fantastical animals believed by the ancients to have lived in
Somalia and the Sudan, and which occasionally turn up on
mosaics, such as a dog-headed man on a floor at Rimini. The
alternative explanation, that the figure is a pun on the name
gallus, 'cock', and refers to a well-known *venator* of that
name, seems to me much less likely (still less that the mosaic
is poking fun at Gallus, short-lived deputy emperor of the East
between 351 and 354). The fragmentary panel opposite, with a
chasing dog and another hut, this time domed, may be a
further snapshot from the amphitheatre; and the adjacent panel
depicting a gladiatorial combat, of which a man with a trident
and sword survives, certainly is. Furthermore, in north African
mosaics Bacchus is frequently portrayed as a patron of
amphitheatre spectacles. Whether the villa's owner who
commissioned the floor, or the mosaicist who laid it, were
aware of these north African echoes seems highly unlikely;
the source was probably a pattern book where well-known
themes and scenes used elsewhere in mosaic composition in
the Roman world were transmitted in increasingly simplified
or at least altered form. It is also fascinating to speculate
whether the villa owner chose this floor because of a specific
animal show he had put on locally (in Chichester?), or merely
because he liked the look of it in the copybook.

Other rooms nearby have little of note except for a neatly
displayed selection of finds. There are some interesting metal
objects, including ploughshares, a fine bronze linch-pin from a
wheeled vehicle, a bronze key-plate, and a square brick with
combed decoration overlain by a human hand-print. Note also
the painted plaster with a peacock and a bowl of fruit, found
in the corridor and presented to the British Museum on
discovery, but now returned to the site; and also the almost
complete dish of Kimmeridge shale from Dorset (cf. p. 106

and Fig. 1), found with a more fragmentary one, also displayed, in the villa's north wing. A section of roofing-slabs of local Bembridge stone has also been reassembled here: this was an important export commodity for the Isle of Wight in Roman times, and the stone has been identified at the Fishbourne Palace near Chichester (p. 68) and in Roman buildings as far away as Essex.

Nearby is a room projecting out the back of the villa (8), and two rooms to its left (south) with hypocausts in the final phase (1, 4), now stripped out (there are modern *pilae* in one). Fragmentary remains of an 'oven' in room 8, still visible, made the original excavators interpret this room as a kitchen, but its size and position makes it likely that it was the principal dining-room; indeed a fragmentary mosaic was found in room 8 in 1881 but has not survived. The crucible and metal slag discovered during more recent investigations (on display in one of the cases) may indicate that the oven is rather a furnace and that the industrial activity belongs, like the corn-drier, to a period when the block no longer functioned as the landowner's residence.

Now mount the wooden catwalk again, and pass on the right a simple geometric mosaic (9) much damaged by fire (by squatters in the final phase?). On the left, are a couple of small rooms, the first of which (10), paved with roof-tiles, has a masonry bench round two walls. But it is the fascinating mosaics of the remaining pair of rooms (12) which will claim your attention: their function is uncertain but it seems more likely that they were used as living- and reception-rooms rather than for dining. The floor of the larger has mostly disappeared, but one side-panel is nearly complete. It represents Andromeda (on the left) being rescued from the rock to which she was chained (to be a sacrifice to a local sea-monster): the rescuer is the hero Perseus, who holds aloft the head of the newly-slain Medusa (with which he has turned the sea-monster to stone). To the right of this panel is the bust of Summer with poppies in her hair, and of the other seasons Winter (diagonally opposite) and Spring also survive. Note the curious T-bar decoration of the border, with an additional swastika of uncertain significance nearest the panel with Perseus and Andromeda.

Go now to the far end of the shed to admire the superbly

preserved mosaics of the remaining room. In the foreground is a lively strip showing tritons and nereids, the Roman equivalent of mermaids. The central roundel of the main section contains a sad-looking, snaky head of Medusa. Four oblong panels which surround it depict mythological scenes. Starting with left-foreground, they show in clockwise order: (i) Lycurgus, carrying his two-headed axe, pursues the nymph Ambrosia, who in response to her cry for help (to Bacchus) is being swallowed up by the earth, while Lycurgus is entwined by a vine-tendril and throttled; (ii) Attis (Phrygian cap, crook, pipes) chats up the water-nymph, Sagaritis (reeds in hair, upturned vase), prior to making love to her (after which the goddess Cybele causes her death in a fit of jealousy, and Attis, driven mad, castrates himself); (iii) Ceres, goddess of the crops, gives seed to Triptolemus, the inventor of the plough; (iv) nymph pursued or seized by a man. Three of these four panels allude to mystery religions popular in the late Roman world, those of Bacchus, Cybele/Attis and the Eleusinian mystery cult of Demeter-Ceres; the significance of the fourth panel is now lost to us. In the triangles between these scenes are busts of the Four Winds, each blowing a conch.

In the panel separating the two parts of the room is the figure of a seated, half-draped man pointing at a globe, above which is a pillar surmounted by a sun-dial. A panel from a mosaic of *c.* AD 300 in Trier, Germany, depicting a man in identical pose conveniently labelled with a name, allows us to identify the Brading figure as Aratus, a Greek astronomer of the third century BC who wrote a book about the constellations (the *Phaenomena*) which still survives. Although the overall standard of figure-drawing at Brading is far from masterly, it is the unusual subject matter which puts these fourth-century mosaics in a class of their own, and indicates a cultured Romano-British owner with wide-ranging classical tastes in philosophy, mythology and religion.

Outside, the only visible elements are an isolated pool (13: a fountain or a water shrine?) and two separate elements of the north wing, a well (15), and a hypocaust (14: note the steps leading upwards near the stoke-hole arch, probably to a boiler mounted above). The plan of this building recovered by the Victorian excavators suggests that it started life as an aisled barn, and was then progressively subdivided to provide living quarters, perhaps for an estate steward; by the fourth century this included a heated living-room, painted plaster and a tiny bath-suite (next to the well). The position of the south wing (16), of largely agricultural character, and the adjacent bath-house (17), have been marked out in the grass.

The second villa on the Isle of Wight, at **Newport***
(SZ 500880), discovered and excavated in 1926, deserves to be better known. It is open from April to the end of October, Monday–Saturday 1000–1630, and on Sundays in July and August only (same times). Avoid the ring road round the east side of Newport, but follow signs for town centre; as you approach the latter, the villa is signposted (entrance from Cypress Road). The fourth-century corn-drying oven from Newchurch Undercover, rebuilt outside the villa, is one of the best preserved examples still visible in Britain of a type of structure which occurred very frequently on rural sites, especially in the late Empire. They have not, however, normally been consolidated and left exposed: one is preserved *in situ* at Rockbourne (p. 131), and another is marked out at the same site; a third can be seen at Brading (p. 142). Finds of charred grain (in particular wheat and oats) in several of these structures show that they were definitely used for heating and drying corn, to prevent it sprouting during the wet winter; but others again were certainly used for warming barley as the first stage of the process for brewing beer, and so are better described as malting ovens. Without specific archaeological evidence of charred grains (which only occurred, of course, if the heating process got out of control), it is impossible to say whether any individual structure was a corn-drying oven or one used for malting.

The Newport villa, refurbished with a new display in 1992, is an excellent example of the 'winged corridor' type of villa, the corridor itself and four of the rooms which led from it lying outside the modern cover-building. A model of the villa as it may have appeared is at the entrance. The villa was built towards the end of the second century and seems to have had an active life of little more than 100 years. You first come to the bath-suite of the villa: the *frigidarium* (cold room) preserves a portion of its geometric mosaic floor, as well as its cold-water immersion-bath with a lead drainpipe *in situ*. A section of stone roofing-slates with nail holes to fasten them is

mounted on the wall alongside. The three rooms of varying
heat beyond still have hypocaust *pilae* standing to a good
height; the floors they once supported are missing but have
been partly reconstituted in modern materials. At the far end
is a semicircular hot immersion-bath, with box flue-tiles still
jacketed in the thickness of the walls; its intact floor has been
cut through to reveal details of the hypocaust beneath. The
furnace for the baths lies beyond: as you turn the corner and
mount the stairway, the stoke-hole arch is visible below you.
By contrast the flue interconnecting the two heated rooms
beyond does not have a true arch but is made up of flat bricks
each slightly overlapping with its neighbour below, with a flat
tile bridging the gap at the top.

   Then follow three rooms with tessellated floors, of which
the largest has the very unusual feature of a fireplace, built of
tiles, projecting from the far wall (apart from Beadlam
[p. 434] no other example is visible *in situ* in Britain). It is
built on top of the simple chequer-board mosaic floor here,
and is clearly therefore a later feature. Since the chequer-
board design of the mosaic is off-centre, this must have been
the dining-room, with the couches arranged on the plain parts
of the pavement. The modern painted walls here are derived
from known Roman decorative wall schemes attested at this
and other Isle of Wight villas. An imaginative reconstruction
of the kitchen follows, although whether the delicacy of
dormouse (a fattening pot is shown on the table) would
have been enjoyed by the occupants of the comparatively
modest Newport villa is open to debate. The construction
technique of half-timbering, the wooden framework
and the wattle-and-daub panels being set on original
Roman dwarf stone walls, is excellently illustrated by this
life-size mock-up. Note also the reconstructed glazed
window: Romano-British window glass was generally not
transparent.

   Now go outside to the remaining rooms of the villa. That at
the SE corner was heated (you pass through the foundations of
a brick flue arch): hypocaust *pilae* found here when the villa
was excavated in 1926 have long since disappeared. On the
floor of this room is a rectangular base of unknown purpose;
curiously it seems to have blocked access to the room next
door and is presumably secondary. You then pass into the

corridor along the front of the building, from which it can be appreciated that the house faced left (south). The walls of the villa are here preserved to their full height, ready for the half-timbered superstructure above; only the bath-suite was probably entirely of stone. A simulated 'Roman garden' lies beyond, with a beehive of the type described by the Roman agricultural writer Varro (the one made in 1992 had rotted by 2000; a replacement was due!). Five showcases in the final section contain a selection of finds from various Isle of Wight sites. The disembodied skull of a woman in her thirties, found in one of the now-outdoor rooms at the Newport villa, will be noted; what happened to the rest of her (eaten by dogs? Ritual decapitation?) is unknown.

Other villa-sites are known on the island at Combley, Rock and Carisbrooke, but none is worth visiting now. At Carisbrooke Castle (SZ 487878) [AM; S], a defensive wall 1.50 m (5 ft) high together with a small round tower used to be considered Roman: go out into the castle-bailey by the small gate below the keep on the east side and you will see it embedded in the lower banks of the later castle-ramparts. In this east side there is also a gateway, 6.70 m (22 ft) wide, visible to the right where the wall curves inwards. These walls are also exposed along the whole of the west side of the castle, both in the grounds of the tea-rooms and on the other side of the gatehouse. A Saxon date now seems likely for these fortifications, for neither the gate type nor the small tower can be paralleled in late Roman fortification. A small collection of Roman material is displayed in the Carisbrooke Castle Museum.

There is no uncertainty, however, about another of the forts in this series, **Portchester**** (SU 625046) [AM; A], which is one of the most impressive Roman structures anywhere in Britain, even if in most places medieval refacing has covered or obscured the original Roman facing. Unlike many of the Saxon Shore forts, the topography has changed little here over 1,700 years, and on the east the water still laps up to the walls as it did in Roman times. Unlike the majority of Roman sites in this country, it needs little imagination to visualize the fort in its heyday (Fig. 29). The Roman name is uncertain, but it is probably the PORTVS ADVRNI listed in the late Roman

29   Portchester, late Roman fort, the south wall

document called the *Notitia Dignitatum*, although the
particular form of the name recorded there may be corrupt.

Portchester Castle is signposted from the A27 between
Fareham and Portsmouth. The entire defensive wall of this
fort, 3 m (10 ft) thick and over 6 m (20 ft) high, together with
14 of the original 20 towers, still survives, except at the NW
corner where the Normans built their keep [AM; S]. The
towers were originally floored with timber at the top, probably
to mount artillery. The inner face of the walls has been largely
cut back in medieval times, but the original Roman width can
be seen in the places where the walls have been excavated
down to Roman ground-level, as for example south of the
Landgate. The surviving battlements are entirely Norman.

The Roman work is best studied in the tower you reach
immediately after crossing the wooden bridge over the moat
from the car-park: it consists of a dozen or so rows of coursed
flintwork at the bottom, and thereafter two or three courses of
flints, each separated by a single or double bonding-course of
tiles. Each tower was hollow and was provided with a tiled
drain at the bottom to allow water to escape: an example of
such a drain, a terracotta pipe, can be seen in this tower on its
east (left-hand) side, in the bottom course (it is sometimes
obscured by grass in summer). Now that you can identify

Roman facing, turn seawards and watch out for it elsewhere
on the circuit – it is easy to spot because of the distinctive tile-
courses, but it does not survive very often. The first tower
south of the Watergate has a small portion of Roman work –
two courses of double tile bonding-courses separating four
courses of flintwork; and three double tile bonding-courses
will be spotted high up on the east side of the first tower you
come to after rounding the SE corner. There is a single course
of tiles surviving in the west side of the same tower, and the
horizontal levelling course of stone slabs in the adjacent
stretch of fort wall is also Roman work, with traces of a
second course lower down. By now your eye should be 'in':
another short length of double stone-slab coursing is visible in
the curtain wall immediately beyond the second tower on the
south side; and there are four double bonding-courses
separating three or four courses of flintwork in the third tower,
as well as a double bonding-course in the curtain wall beyond
that. Further stretches of tile or stone levelling courses will be
spotted elsewhere in the south wall and in the southern part of
the west wall – they are particularly prominent, for example,
in the last tower before the Landgate.

Go inside the walls here to examine what remains of the
Roman west gate. The fort was defended by four gates: in the
north and south walls there were simple posterns, now
blocked up, but the main gates in the middle of the west and
east sides were formed by inturning the curtain walls to form
a forecourt 13.75 m (45 ft) wide and 11 m (36 ft) deep, and
closing the inner end of this passage with a gate 3 m (10 ft)
wide flanked by two square guard-chambers. The idea of this
arrangement is that an enemy attacking the gate would be
surrounded on three sides by defenders on the battlements
above. The east gate is entirely buried beneath the medieval
Watergate, but part of the lower courses of the west gate are
traceable immediately south of the Landgate. The lowest
courses of the inner face of the Roman defences are visible in
the cutting here, a witness to how drastically they were
narrowed in medieval times (and also, incidentally, a
demonstration that Roman ground level was some 0.75 m
[2 ft] below the present one). The double Roman gate-sill is
also visible here.

Inside the walls excavation has revealed some traces of

timber barracks and pits, but the Roman levels have been
much disturbed by later occupation. First-century finds have
been made, but the walls belong to the end of the third
century. Portchester was disused for a time in the early fourth
century but reoccupied on a large scale again *c.* AD 340. It was
finally abandoned *c.* 370. It used to be thought that a different
site with a better harbour, a few miles away, could be
considered its successor. This is Bitterne, probably the Roman
CLAVSENTVM, where a promontory jutting into the river Itchen,
the site of a small settlement in the first and second centuries,
was later fortified with a stone defensive wall. The dating
given to this by the excavators, however, of *c.* 370, has now
been shown emphatically to be wrong, and the late Roman
walls here were probably erected *c.* 280/90, at approximately
the same time as Portchester. Virtually nothing is visible at
the site today, which is a suburb of Southampton, except for
the fragmentary remains of a tiny second-century bath-house,
and a fragment of the walls adjacent (App. 1).

Chapter 3

Mendips and Cotswolds

Avon, Gloucestershire, Herefordshire, Oxfordshire, North Somerset

The tribe that inhabited the area of the Cotswolds and the Upper Thames in the pre-Roman period was known as the Dobunni. They appear to have caused little or no trouble to Roman armies in the early years of the invasion, but forts were established in their territory to protect them and the province behind from the aggressive Silures of south Wales: excavation in 2000 of a vexillation fortress at Alchester north of Oxford showed that it was being built as early as the autumn of AD 44, the felling date (provided by

dendrochronology) of the timbers used in its west gate.
Further west, a few years later, there were forts at Cirencester
and probably another at Bath, both places on the great Roman
trunk-road, the Fosse Way, which ran from Lincoln to Exeter.
Much of its course in the area covered by this chapter is
followed by modern A-roads, but, for a 3-mile (4.8-km)
stretch going north from Shepton Mallet over Beacon Hill, the
Roman highway has become no more than a track, and traces
of the original metalling survive. Other forts were established
in advance of the road itself, notably at Gloucester and Sea
Mills, but hardly any trace of this military phase is visible
anywhere now.

The Romans did not waste much time in exploiting the
Mendip lead-mines around **Charterhouse** (ST 500565),
which were in operation at least by AD 49, just six years after
the conquest. Lead was important not only in itself (to make
water-pipes, tanks and coffins, to create tie-fastenings for
building blocks, to make weights and anchors), but also for
the manufacture of pewter, and especially for the extraction of
silver by a process known as cupellation. The lead remaining
after the silver had been removed was cast in the form of
ingots, often inscribed with the emperor's name, the date, and
the authority in control of the mines. These ingots, therefore,
furnish valuable historical information: one, now lost, is dated
by Claudius' titulature to AD 49, giving us the evidence for
early working mentioned above; one was found near
Southampton and another two in northern France, so we know
that the lead was being exported to the Continent.
Metallurgical tests have even claimed that a cistern in
Pompeii, buried by the eruption of Vesuvius in 79, was made
of British lead, probably from Charterhouse. One French ingot
also records that the Second Augustan Legion was in control
of the mines in Nero's reign (AD 54–68), but another dated to
AD 60 from near Stockbridge (Hampshire), now in the British
Museum, is marked 'from the lead-silver works of Gaius
Nipius Ascanius', making it clear that initial military control
soon passed to private lessees. The full Roman name of
Charterhouse is unknown, but the first three letters of it are
tantalizingly recorded on a group of ingots from Vespasian's
reign reading BRIT.EX.ARG.VEB., 'British lead from the
Veb . . . lead-silver mines' (four of these, found together, are

on display in Wells Museum). The last securely datable ingot
(in Taunton Museum) was made between 164 and 169, but
another from Lillebonne (Normandy) of AD 195/211 is
probably also of Mendip lead. Coin finds at Charterhouse,
however, indicate that occupation of the settlement (and
presumably also the working of the mines) continued into the
fourth century.

Very little of the Roman mines or the associated settlement
can be seen today; the former have been worked for a long
time, especially in the nineteenth century, and the latter has
never been adequately explored. A few earthworks, some of
uncertain date and purpose, are the main features. The site is
most conveniently approached from Cheddar. Take the road
through the famous gorge (B3135), and then fork left along
the B3371. One mile (1.6 km) after the fork, turn left at the
crossroads, signposted Charterhouse. After another $\frac{3}{4}$ mile
(1.2 km), as the road bends to dip into the valley bottom, you
will see both to left and to right of the road extensive evidence
of deep trenching and pitting, which represent areas of
mineral extraction of Roman and later date (1 on Fig. 30).

Just beyond the church is a crossroads where you should
turn right. After 200 m, on the left-hand side of the road just
beyond a group of trees, are the faint traces of a small
earthwork about 65 m (210 ft) square (2 on Fig. 30); the south
and east sides are largely destroyed. This is the ploughed-out
remains of a Roman fortlet, measuring 55 m by 50 m (180 ft
by 165 ft) within its rampart, which was created in the mid
first century to guard the lead-mines. Excavation in 1993–4
showed that its single ditch was 1.6 m (5 ft 4 in) deep, and
that it was of 'Punic' type with a steep outer profile (p. 99).
Pottery of c. AD 50/65 was found in the primary silt of this
ditch, with late first/early second century material higher up,
so the fortlet had a short life. An earlier fortlet, with a rock-
cut ditch 1.2 m (3 ft 11 in) deep, was found below; the
abundant rubbish in it, including samian ware and amphorae,
indicates that this first-phase fortlet is Claudian, c. 45/55. It is
worth noting that the small size of the post indicates that a full
auxiliary unit was not considered necessary to watch over the
lead-mining operations; the excavator of the fortlet has
suggested that its primary purpose was not so much to shelter

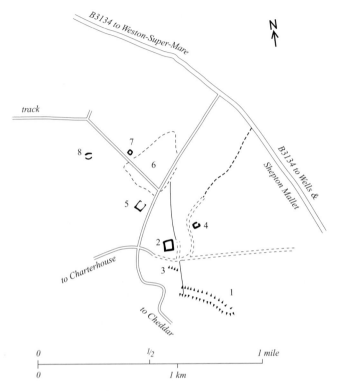

30   Charterhouse, site plan

troops as to provide safe-keeping for metal bullion before its transportation and shipment elsewhere.

The pitting and trenching hereabouts is mostly of post-medieval and especially nineteenth-century date, but a trial excavation in 1994, due south of the fortlet on the other side of the track (3), found clear evidence of Roman mining for the first time at Charterhouse. In contrast to 20 circular medieval shafts and the more irregular post-medieval extraction holes hereabouts, the Roman activity is marked (as in other lead-mining sites in Europe) by a number of well-defined grooves or 'rakes'. The Roman miners had pecked out the lead ore along natural, very narrow fissures and veins (there was no sign of fire-setting or pick-marks), opening up into a complex, narrow and deep, natural cave system. Discarded pieces of lead ore were found, all associated with plentiful Roman pottery of the first century AD, mostly fine wares. The mining fissures excavated in 1994 had been deliberately filled with material, no doubt from other explorations (to avoid clogging the site with unnecessary waste), before the end of the first century AD. Five Roman-period 'rakes' are visible on the surface here, but the rest in this area have been destroyed by later extraction.

Continue on, and when the track forks take the left one. About 110 m (360 ft) along it from the fork, watch out for the point where the fence close to the track turns away from you. Strike up the grassy slope here and aim slightly left: you will come immediately to the traces of a small earthwork, which lies in rough ground to the left of the pasture field (4 on Fig. 30). It is an odd enclosure, consisting of a rectangular bank with a ditch *inside* it, quite unlike Roman military earthworks. Limited excavation here suggested that it is medieval, probably after 1300; a lead-working hearth was found within.

Now return to the crossroads and turn right. On the left of the minor road at the bottom of the dip is another small earthwork (5), usually reckoned to be medieval. Immediately after this take the track which goes off to the left. The site of the Roman town (6) lay mostly on the right of the track at its junction with the road, in 'Town Field', but nothing is traceable now, although aerial photography has revealed something of the street-plan. Trial excavation between 1960 and 1967 found pottery of mid first to late third-century date as well as lead waste, charcoal, slag and other indications of industrial activity, but the investigations were too limited to reveal the plans of buildings or yield any detailed information about the settlement. A small square banked enclosure (7) can just be traced on the ground immediately beyond an iron stile on the right of the track, where the stone wall stops. Limited excavation seemed to indicate a medieval date for it, a chronology supported by the apparent lack of an accompanying ditch.

Continue on for another $\frac{1}{4}$ mile (400 m), and park at the top;

take the gate on the left, opposite the first radio transmitter. In this field lies the most conspicuous of the Roman earthworks at Charterhouse, those of a small amphitheatre (8). It was inconclusively excavated in 1908, when more Neolithic and early Bronze Age material was found than Roman: it is not impossible, therefore, as at Dorchester (p. 107), that a small prehistoric henge was adapted and enlarged to form the amphitheatre. That it is, however, a Roman amphitheatre in its present form is not in doubt: the banks are still about 4.50 m (15 ft) above the arena floor, and the entrances at either end are clear. Finds from here and other sites in Charterhouse can be found in the Bristol and Taunton Museums.

Charterhouse was not a normal Roman settlement, in that its position and *raison d'être* were determined by the nearby lead-mines. Another Roman town which owes its existence to a natural phenomenon, the extraordinary hot springs emerging from the ground at 00°C (120°F), is **Bath**** (ST 751647). Here the thermal establishment (daily, April–October, 0900–1800 [also 2000–2200 in August]; November–February 0900–1700 [winter Sundays, 1000–1700]) is Rome's most famous witness in Britain after Hadrian's Wall. And rightly so, for this was no ordinary bathing-station: it was a spa designed on the most elegant and ambitious scale.

The deity of the natural spring had very probably been worshipped before the Roman period. Although no pre-Roman structures have ever been found (flint tools are, however, among the finds from the spring), the name of the place, AQVAE SVLIS, indicates that the waters were sacred to a native goddess, Sulis, whom the Romans identified with Minerva. There was probably a fort here in the period of the Roman conquest, as the spacing of military posts along the Fosse Way demands it, but of this, too, not a trace has been found. Towards the end of the first century, the centre was laid out with an outstanding series of monumental buildings (Fig. 31). The focus of the whole complex was clearly the sacred spring itself, contained within its reservoir (2). It lies under the eighteenth-century King's Bath, but details of its construction and part of the deposit of votive offerings thrown into it was excavated in 1979–80 when the waters of the spring had to be diverted. The spring was viewed from a hall in the baths (where the Circular Bath now is: 15), and beyond it, on the same axis, the bather would have caught a glimpse of a great altar, its corners richly carved with figures of deities (4; see below).

While the altar lay on a north-south axis from a bather's viewpoint, it also lay on an east-west axis in front of a splendid temple dedicated to Sulis Minerva (3). Part of the plan of this temple was plotted in 1867–8 on the west side of Stall Street, but the precise dimensions, including the position of the bottom steps leading to the temple-platform (*podium*), were only established in 1964–5; much more was learnt during the extensive work of 1981–3. This was not the usual Romano-Celtic temple with central *cella* and lean-to ambulatory: rather it was a full-scale classical-style temple on a lofty *podium*, approached by a flight of steps, and fronted by a porch four columns wide which supported an architrave, frieze and pediment. The centre of the pediment was formed by the striking head of Medusa, found in 1790 and now in the

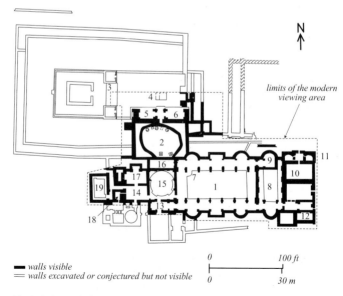

■ *walls visible*
= *walls excavated or conjectured but not visible*

0   100 ft

0   30 m

31   Bath, Roman baths, simplified site plan

Museum. The temple and altar were set in a large paved
courtyard enclosed by a colonnade. The temple is Flavian,
some time in the last third of the first century, but the
benefactor is unknown; one intriguing possibility, however, is
that it was none other than the pro-Roman client king Tiberius
Claudius Togidubnus, probable builder of the Fishbourne
Palace (p. 68). This hypothesis can be advanced on the basis
of a fragment of monumental inscription reading TI CL T[. . .
which was found in the 1980s excavations. Of this
magnificent temple complex a good deal, as we shall see, has
been made accessible to visitors since 1984.

The baths themselves were at first quite simple, although on
a monumental scale. From the central hall (*frigidarium*), with
its vista of the spring and the altar, the bather could either turn
right to the Great Bath and to the two smaller swimming-baths
at its east end, or he/she could turn left to the west end and
indulge in the artificial heat of the conventional Roman baths,
which at this stage were very simple in layout. This set of
baths with damp heat ('Turkish' baths) was found insufficient,
for in the second phase (probably early second-century) they
were modified by the addition of a circular *laconicum* of the
dry-heat (sauna) variety (not visible), and a large circular
plunge-bath was inserted in the former *frigidarium*. At the
same time, the further of the two swimming-pools at the east
end was replaced by a second set of moist-heat baths. In
Period III, around AD 200, the Great Bath was re-roofed with
a grandiose barrel-vault which covered also the plunge- and
swimming-pools at either end of it. Some years later (Period
IV) extensive reorganization occurred: the eastern baths were
rebuilt on a much larger scale; the alcove north of the tepid
plunge-bath at this end was converted into an immersion-bath;
and at the west end the heating systems were rearranged, and
a new heated chamber as well as a cold swimming-bath were
added. Later still, in Period V, minor modifications were
made, including the insertion of some small immersion-baths
at the west end. Finally, before the end of the Roman period,
there was trouble with the drainage, and in the late fourth or
early fifth century the flooding became serious: the baths were
abandoned, the area became a marsh, and the vault of the
Great Bath eventually collapsed. Not until the eighteenth

century was something of Bath's former grandeur and popularity to be regained.

Nearly the whole of this elaborate and complicated sequence of baths is now laid open on permanent show: of the Roman establishment as so far known, only a few rooms on the west and SW side are inaccessible below modern buildings. Your visit starts with a walk along the esplanade at first-floor level, looking down at the central feature of the Roman baths at all periods, the Great Bath (1 on Fig. 31; see below). Notice at the far end the diagram showing that the height of the vaulted roof of the bath in its second phase was twice the height at which you now are – which by Romano-British standards constitutes an unusually impressive piece of Roman structural engineering.

Now descend the stairs to the first room of the superbly displayed Museum, containing a wooden model of the baths and life-size mock-ups of a priest at sacrifice and of a bather leaving the changing-room. The latter's loin cloth is an unlikely feature of ancient bathing (modern prudery at work?); and leaving his sandals under the bench would have given him problems on the heated rooms' floors (bathers generally wore sandals at all times except when in the pools). Excellent computer simulations here and elsewhere in the Museum give visitors a vivid idea of the original appearance of the complex. The reconstruction painting of Roman Bath as it may have appeared (next to the window overlooking the Great Bath) shows how the grandiose bathing establishment and the temple precinct dominated the whole settlement; but recent attempts to interpret the entire area within the walls as a sacred complex and not as a 'normal' town fail to convince.

Now come down the steps to the famous Medusa head (Fig. 32), and the other surviving elements of the temple's pediment. The wings in the hair and the snakes tied beneath the chin put the identification absolutely beyond doubt; recent attempts to interpret the head as either Neptune or Oceanus or the obscure earth monster Typheus (associated with volcanic activity under Mount Etna) are to be discarded. The snaky-headed Medusa appeared on Minerva's shield and so is an appropriate subject for the temple, but the native sculptor has turned her into a male, with craggy face, penetrating gaze and luxuriant moustache. In particular a Celtic love of patterning

32   *Bath, Temple of Sulis Minerva, the Medusa head from the pediment*

for its own sake can be seen in the arrangement of the hair and the lines etched in the Gorgon's forehead. It is an odd synthesis, but the effect is striking: 'it represents,' as J M C Toynbee put it, 'the perfect marriage of classical standards and traditions with Celtic taste and native inventiveness.' The iconography of the whole composition is eclectic, but the classical allusions are clear: notice the owl, bird of Minerva, for example, below Victory's hand holding up the central wreath, to the right of the Gorgon head. The star at the top (damaged) is probably a generalized celestial and possibly also apotropaic symbol (it frequently occurs in antiquity above depictions of divinities such as Fortuna, and is closely associated with astrological symbolism). It is unlikely to be a reference either to a deified emperor or to the imperial house in general, as has been claimed (in my view wrongly) to support the notion that the temple was dedicated by a king (which it might have been on other grounds: p. 160). The massive column and Corinthian capital tucked away in the corner here provide further witness to the striking impact that this temple must have had on AQVAE SVLIS as a whole when first built *c.* AD 70/90.

The walkway beyond has three sculptured pieces from a round building, some 8 m (26 ft) in diameter, the precise position of which is unknown. Its decoration, of rosettes in an acanthus spiral separated by palmettes, is a provincial version of a very Mediterranean form of architectural ornament, the origins of which go back to the fourth century BC. The fact that the ornament occurs on both sides shows that this circular building (*tholos*) was highly decorated both inside and out. Whether the work is by the hands of Gaulish sculptors, as the display panel claims, or could have been done by British sculptors (the *tholos* need not be earlier than the second century), is uncertain.

You now enter a corridor with a view down to the King's Bath which overlies the Roman reservoir (2 on Fig. 31; note the reconstruction-drawings of its possible original appearance). Excavation in 1880 and 1979–80, when the spring was temporarily diverted, revealed an astonishing array of votive offerings, including gemstones, brooches, silver and pewter vessels, 12,000 coins and over 100 lead 'curse-tablets' in which Sulis' help was invoked to bring disaster to an enemy – the texts of some of them are translated on the board above your head. Two showcases here display a selection of these and other votive offerings from the reservoir: exceptional finds include the bronze washer of a Roman military artillery machine (*ballista*), and the bronze openwork decoration with lotus and ivy leaves believed to come from a priest's regalia. The excavations of 1979–80 also revealed the remarkable engineering skill needed for the reservoir's construction: massive stone blocks, laid on a foundation of rammed oak piles and held firm by iron clamps, were covered with lead sheets sealed at the bottom by thick waterproof mortar. All this must have been built while a coffer dam temporarily diverted the spring waters elsewhere. It was a remarkable achievement by any standards, presumably the work of army engineers or specialists called in from the Continent, because British expertise capable of achieving this technological triumph as early as the Flavian period was most assuredly lacking.

Next you reach the area of the temple precinct, with the open paved area to your right, and the site of the temple to your left. To the right of the catwalk, the substantial wall here (with brick bonding-courses, and still partially covered by its *opus signinum* mortar rendering) was constructed when the sacred spring was enclosed for the first time and given a vaulted roof *c*. AD 200 (5). Later, however, gradual subsidence led to the erection (in the later third century) of a raised portico-like arrangement, reached by two steps from the main piazza: the two massive stone buttresses were built later to prevent the wall from further settling. Note how the later floor-level covered the original pavement, part of which together with a side gutter is exposed at the lower level; it also partly obscured the worn steps leading up through the doorway in the middle of this wall to the reservoir.

Next you come to the remarkable survival of a gilt-bronze head of Minerva, found in 1727. Now lacking the helmet she would once have worn, it is executed in a competent if provincial classical style in striking contrast to the sculptured pediment. The head may have come from the cult image (if so, it is rather small for such a massive temple); alternatively it belonged to a subsidiary statue in the temple. Either way, in the absence of a pre-Roman iconography for Sulis, it is more

or less certain that Sulis would have adopted the appearance
of the Roman goddess Minerva. Go up behind the head to see
the temple steps themselves, worn by the tread of Sulis'
devotees; the rest of the temple lies buried beyond (3).

You now descend to the paved precinct in front of the
temple. On the left of the catwalk is a dedication to Sulis from
L. Marcius Memor, a *haruspex* (an inspector of sacred
entrails). The letters VSP have clearly been added later to the
centrally placed HAR (thereby ruining the symmetrical
layout), presumably because nobody could understand the
original abbreviation. Beyond are two of the corner slabs of
the great altar mentioned above (p. 159) now reset in their
original positions (4). The first you come to, found in 1790,
depicts Jupiter with sceptre on one face and, on the other,
Hercules with his club and lion skin. The second slab,
discovered in 1965, shows on one side Bacchus with a *thyrsus*
and on the other an unidentified female figure. A third corner
slab, much weathered, used to be built into a buttress of the
church at Compton Dando, 7 miles (11.3 km) to the west of
Bath, but although the original was brought back to the
Museum in 1997, it is not yet at the time of writing (2001) on
public display. A cul-de-sac on the left leads to a further
section of precinct floor and the entrance threshold over which
visitors gained access to the religious precinct.

Particularly striking in the next section, to the right of the
walkway, are the massive stone blocks forming a buttress at
one corner of the reservoir enclosure (6). Lewis holes on some
stones were designed to provide purchase when levering the
blocks into position, and also visible are the horizontal slots
between blocks. Some of these still have fragments of iron
and lead *in situ*, which were intended to tie the stones firmly
together (an unnecessary precaution with such huge stones).
On the other side of the walkway are some perfunctory reliefs
of gods and goddesses – a reminder that, for all the
sophistication of the classical architecture displayed at Bath,
the standard of carving in many of the private dedications was
often abysmally low.

The next room contains sculptural fragments of the façade
of the Four Seasons and a pediment with Luna, goddess of the
Moon (perhaps belonging with it); they decorated some other
part of the temple precinct (its unexcavated north side?).

Finally comes a selection of the altars and tombstones of
others who 'took the waters', which emphasizes the Empire-
wide reputation of AQVAE SVLIS. From left to right, note
especially the tombstone of Vitalis of the Twentieth Legion,
who originally came from Gallia Belgica (NE France and
Luxembourg); the damaged tombstone of a retired soldier
from Nic(opolis) – whether the place of that name in Greece
or Bulgaria or Turkey is unknown; a stonemason, Priscus son
of Toutius, who came from the Chartres area of northern
France; Peregrinus, a citizen of the Treveri centred on Trier in
what is now Germany; and L. Vitellius Tancinus from
Caurium in western Spain.

Now come down the steps and turn right to the huge
outflow-arch and vaulted drain which took excess water from
the reservoir. From here you reach the most impressive
feature of the Roman remains at Bath, the Great Bath, which
until 1880–1 was still covered by houses of the Georgian city
(1). It belonged to the original scheme of the Roman bathing
establishment in the first century and remained its most
important feature throughout. It is one of the rare Romano-
British structures which need no detailed description and
explanation, for its appeal is immediate and obvious – a great
rectangular swimming-bath, still lined with its Roman lead
sheeting (Fig. 33), and still fed by the constant flow of water
from the sacred spring. But although the bath is still intact, the
hall that enclosed it is not, and the present open-air effect is
misleading. From the beginning it was roofed over, at first
with a timbered ceiling supported by 12 simple piers lining
the bath and the exterior walls. In the third period, some time
around the end of the second century, the whole area was re-
roofed with an enormous barrel-vault, over 15 m (50 ft) high.
It was made of hollow box-tiles, to lessen the weight, and was
left open at either end to allow steam to escape. At the same
time, the piers lining the bath had to be strengthened to take
the extra thrust of the vault. Close inspection of the piers will
reveal that the middle (original) portion of each was cut back
at this period, and extra masonry added both in front of and
behind it. Additional piers also strengthened the inner and
outer corners of the alcoves which face on to the ambulatory.
Other details are also worth noticing: in front of you a
fountain rested on the block projecting over the Great Slab; a

33   Bath, the Great Bath empty (1979)

semicircular, shrine-like structure lay on the slab at the NW
corner (7: to your right), where the water enters the bath; and,
between the two, a water-pipe of Charterhouse lead inserted
into the badly cracked paving of Period IV (third/fourth
centuries) was designed to take water from the spring direct to
a new immersion-bath (see below). A section of the fallen
vault near the lead pipe still bears its pink mortar rendering
adhering to the hollow box-tiles, which as commonly are
scored to improve the adhesion ('keying') of the mortar.
Similar *opus signinum* mortar rendering with its brick
inclusions can be seen on the wall of the adjacent recess.

Now retrace your steps to the Museum exit and go past it to
the far end (the East Baths), where a smaller swimming-bath
and a series of rooms with a complicated history are reached.
You first come to a rectangular tepid bath (Period I) to your
right: lean over the railings to see the steps leading into it (8).
Later the floor of this pool was raised because of flooding

problems, and pieces of the infill (which bore a stone-flagged floor, of which impressions remain) are also visible. On your left is a semicircular immersion-bath (9), added to the previously empty apse in Period IV (the lead pipe noted above was heading for here). The original Phase I pier, together with its Phase II strengthening (when the Great Bath was vaulted), stand on the very edge of the floor of the new pool, the original pavement having been hacked back to make room for the new arrangement. On the far side of this area, a small pool built in Period I was demolished and replaced by a set of moist-heat baths in Period II, and this in turn was then rebuilt on a much larger scale in Period IV (10): note how the *caldarium* with its semicircular apse, for example, was demolished and stripped, and the floor-level raised by some 0.45 m (18 in). Parts of the new hypocausts, clearly themselves much repaired over time, are visible at the higher level, together with a portion of mosaic in the far left-hand corner (reflected in a mirror), which floored another semicircular immersion-bath here (11). At the far right-hand end of this section are three further rooms with hypocausts, one with its *pilae* entirely robbed out (12). To their left, at the lowest level in front of you, note part of the stone flagging of the Phase I pool, and a substantial Phase II outfall drain, which runs obliquely across it and slices through the perimeter wall of the earlier (first-century) swimming-bath.

Now go out to the other side of the Great Bath and down to the opposite end. Part of the huge vault, with its hollow box-tiles and its neat brick facing, is displayed here, to the right: this represents part of one of the finished ends of the barrel-vault where steam was allowed to escape. Keep straight on and enter a double arcade (13), on the south side of the Circular Bath. The Roman masonry here is very well preserved: the inner arcade, to your right, is now filled up with modern concrete, but to your left an entire pier and two voussoirs at the start of a pair of arches still survive. Through the window at the far end can be viewed a drain and two stoke-holes: you will see the *tepidarium* which they heated presently. The *pilae* of this *tepidarium* can be seen through the second window (14), next to the circular pool (where you are standing on a Roman threshold). Note the two doorways in the far wall with worn thresholds, and, in the right-hand wall, a massive threshold block (immediately below the modern plaster) with a straight joint on either side. This represents a doorway into this room at an earlier phase, before it took on its present shape.

Now pass from the corridor to the Circular Bath itself (15), which served as a cold plunge for the dry-heat sauna baths added in the early second century; before that, the room was a simple *frigidarium*. In the re-roofing phase of the later second century, it was provided with a vault springing from new piers fitted between the bath and the side walls.

From the Circular Bath retrace your steps to the Great Bath, turn left past the fallen vault, and then mount the steps which lead up to a viewing point over the King's Bath. As you duck your head to look at this, you are leaning under one of the most substantial pieces of Roman architecture in Britain (16): the rounded arch above and the square-headed arch to the right, both now partially blocked (for safety) with modern stonework, still display superbly jointed, massive cut masonry in the same position as it was when built in the later first century AD. They form two of originally three vast windows belonging to the original *frigidarium* (the room now occupied by the Circular Bath), designed to give an impressive view over the sacred spring and through to the altar of the temple complex beyond.

From here move to your left and through the doors beyond. This part of the baths, first uncovered in 1885–7, was re-excavated in 1969–70. On the right is an oblong swimming-bath of cold water, with rounded ends (17). This was inserted only in Period V (probably fourth-century) into a rectangular room (with recesses), which in all preceding periods from the very beginning of the baths had served as a hot room (*caldarium*) in the moist-heat suite here. The adjacent *tepidarium* to your left (14), however, survived in use throughout the life of the baths, although it went through numerous modifications, including a rebuilding of the hypocaust and alteration of the furnace-flues. Most of its *pilae* are still *in situ* (three were replaced by re-used columns in a repair), and two flues are visible in the far wall, as well as another in the right-hand wall, blocked in a subsequent alteration. It was the furnace area to this room which you saw earlier through the glass window.

Finally, beyond the *tepidarium*, a small room on the left which had a hypocaust in Periods III and IV was demolished in Period V (only the impressions of *pilae* remain) and the area was used as a new furnace-room for the adjacent *tepidarium* (18). The last structure is a cold pool (19) added to the baths in the fourth century (Period IV). Thus ends your visit to one of the most remarkable witnesses of the presence of Rome in Britain. Here is an establishment which was not conceived along the normal lines of Romano-British provincial architecture, but was an offspring of the mainstream classical tradition which would have been readily acceptable in Italy itself.

Of the rest of Roman Bath nothing is visible except an unimpressive black and white mosaic in the basement of the Royal Mineral Water Hospital (enquire at the entrance). There may have been a theatre under the abbey; there was another bathing-establishment SW of the main baths; and there was certainly a Roman town wall on the line of its medieval successor. But whether Bath was an administrative centre is uncertain – no trace of a forum has ever been found – and the town's precise status remains obscure. That it was in fact a 'town' seems, however, intrinsically more probable than the alternative view, that the whole site was a vast sacred precinct, and that the 'town wall' merely defined the religious zone (*temenos*). Only further excavation and the discovery of fresh buildings within the walled area – difficult in a sensitive conservation city like Bath – will settle the matter.

The status of the two remaining towns in this region is not, however, in doubt: Gloucester was a *colonia*, a settlement of retired Roman legionaries and their families, whereas Cirencester was the tribal capital of the Dobunni. **Gloucester** (SO 830180), the Roman GLEVVM ('bright place'), was the scene of important rescue excavations during the 1970s, but very little has been preserved *in situ*. Much is now known about the early history of the site. An early legionary fortress covering at least 56 acres (22 ha) lay at Kingsholm, 1 mile (1.6 km) north of Gloucester, close to a large Iron Age settlement. The fortress was probably established from *c.* AD 49 (although the earliest base may not have been of full legionary size); it was occupied until the mid 60s AD (the latest coin is of AD 64/8). It may have had a mixed garrison of both legionaries and auxiliaries: a bronze cheek-piece found in 1972, decorated with a seated Jupiter holding a thunderbolt, has been claimed as part of an auxiliary cavalryman's helmet. This, however, is far from certain, as the distinction between legionary and auxiliary armour is not as clear-cut as was once believed. More significantly Rufus Sita, whose tombstone is in the Museum, belonged to an auxiliary cohort of Thracians (originally from Bulgaria). If he was not attached to the Kingsholm fortress, one has to postulate the existence of a standard auxiliary fort, presumably one which preceded the arrival of a legion and the building of the Kingsholm fortress.

For reasons that we do not fully understand, but probably because of problems associated with flooding, the Kingsholm fortress was abandoned, and a new fortress of 43 acres (17 ha) was built in the mid or late 60s AD under what is now the heart of modern Gloucester. Parts of its turf and timber defences and some of its internal wooden buildings have been identified since the 1970s. The fortress was refurbished in the late 80s (coin evidence suggests that it cannot have been earlier than AD 87/8), with some barrack-blocks being rebuilt in stone and the defences being given a new facing in the form of a dry-stone wall. Military occupation seems to have ceased during the 90s, when the formal urban settlement of the site as a *colonia* was made under the emperor Nerva (AD 96–8), as we know from an inscription (from Rome) giving its full title as *Colonia Nervia Glevensium*; yet there is some evidence that the earliest civilians still lived in the military buildings before the site was properly cleared and rebuilt during the second century.

This interpretation of the sequence of events is, however, disputed: the alternative view is to see the military phase as coming to an end in the 80s rather than the 90s, and to interpret the 'refurbishment' in stone, both of internal buildings and of the defences, as the first actions of the newly-established urban settlers. In that case, the formal grant of a charter as a *colonia* would have been issued somewhat after the town's physical start (or perhaps it was reissued by Nerva, if the original charter had been handed down by the subsequently disgraced Domitian). It is unlikely that this disagreement can be resolved without further large-scale excavation within the heart of modern Gloucester.

The peak of the town's prosperity seems to have been during the second century; in the later fourth century, by contrast, civic decline was setting in, if the rubbish deposits accumulating in the forum then are an accurate indicator. There was considerable occupation, including monumental buildings, outside the 43 acres (17 ha) enclosed by the defences: in all the built-up area of Roman Gloucester in its prime covered about 120 acres (50 ha). The old view, therefore, that Gloucester was a 'failed town', stunted by the proximity of flourishing Cirencester, is no longer credible.

The visible remains of Roman Gloucester are not plentiful: medieval and modern development has dealt with them unkindly (Fig. 34). The main layout of the legionary fortress and the later Roman *colonia* is clear in the modern street-plan,

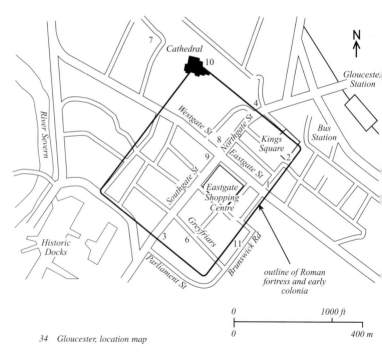

34   *Gloucester, location map*

Northgate, Southgate and part of Eastgate Streets all running on the lines of Roman predecessors. The only substantial remains are the stretches of Roman city wall which have been preserved. Of these the most accessible is that visible in the City Museum (see below), but a clearer understanding of the sequence of defences from Roman to medieval can be appreciated in the chamber containing part of the East Gate, in front of Boots' store at 38–44, Eastgate Street (1 on Fig. 34). The medieval phase (in particular a large circular tower belonging to the thirteenth century) is partly visible through a window at street-level, but the chamber itself, which used to be open at regular hours during the summer, can now only be viewed by joining a tour which leaves the City Museum in Brunswick Road, between May and September only, at 1015, 1115, 1415, 1515 and 1615.

Excavation on the Eastgate site in 1974 revealed three distinct Roman phases: fragments of the timber gate-tower of the legionary fortress of c. AD 64/6; the stone gate-tower (1.85 m or 6 ft high) and the first stone defensive wall, built in the late first century, which was of dry-stone construction, and was partly re-used in the later wall; and the base-plinth of the late third-century city wall, above which rose the conspicuous large limestone blocks of the final Roman rebuilding which replaced the earlier wall. The first stone defensive wall was at the time of its discovery interpreted as belonging to the *colonia*, but it has more recently been claimed to be part of the refurbishments to the legionary fortress made in the late 80s, and later retained as the defensive wall of the new town which replaced the military fortress. As noted above (p. 171), this disagreement is incapable at present of being satisfactorily resolved. At the bottom of the stairs inside the inspection-chamber, turn sharply left to reach the fine ashlar masonry of the Roman gate-tower of c. AD 90. The position of one of the wooden posts of the legionary fortress gate is indicated in the linoleum floor, and an actual oak post, from an interval tower, is displayed nearby. The masonry foundation for the late Roman wall of c. 270–90 is also impressive; note the lewis holes in many of the stones, to facilitate lifting. The blocks above this belonged to the Roman wall erected on this foundation, but were reset in their present position during a medieval repair. The black line marked in the floor near the entrance indicates the course of a third-century water-pipe; a black area beyond marks the position of the wide, shallow Roman defensive ditch of the fourth century, dug as elsewhere in Roman Britain to replace the V-shaped ditches of earlier centuries (cf. p. 295). Projecting towers apparently belonged to the *c.* 270–90 reconstruction, rather than later as was more customary in Romano-British towns (indicating perhaps a quasi-military role for Gloucester at this period), but none is now visible.

Other portions of the defences are preserved on the east and south sides: one in King's Walk is not at present (2001) accessible because of a lack of electricity (enquire at the City Museum if the situation has changed), and a second nearby (2), consisting of two short fragments viewed from above through glass covers, exists in the basement of a store called Poundland, in the corner of King's Square at the entrance to King's Walk (the manager may be able to show them to you if the store is not busy, but frankly they are not worth the trouble). By contrast the stretch of large-block defences of *c.* 270/90 belonging to the south wall can be viewed with ease on the left-hand side of the Gloucester Furniture Exhibition Centre (3) at 71–3 Southgate Street (on the corner with Parliament Street). A quaint sign wrongly informing visitors that the wall was built by Vespasian in the first century may be removed during cleaning and refurbishment planned for 2002. Massive blocks in a store at 45, Northgate Street, currently (2001) being used to prop up the reception counter and a table-top in a hairdresser's salon called Number Forty-Five, are the last displaced remnants of the gate which stood adjacent to this site (4).

Other scraps of Roman Gloucester are hardly worth tracking down. A fragment of fourth-century mosaic featuring an ivy-leaf tendril, from a Roman town-house, is displayed on the wall on your right as you enter the Eastgate Market Hall, reached from within the Eastgate Shopping Centre (5). It formed part of a fragmentary mosaic over 4 m (13 ft) square which depicted Bacchus with a leopard in the central roundel. A rectangular panel composed only of grey tesserae has been relaid at the entrance to the Friends' Meeting House (6) in Greyfriars (visible from the street at any time). Another Roman mosaic excavated in 1978–9 is visible through a trap-

door in the nave of St Mary-de-Lode, the church which lies
immediately outside the west gate to the cathedral precinct;
but the church is generally closed except for services (7).
Other mosaics, presumably belonging to the same Roman
house (built in the second century and occupied until the
fourth), were found during the earlier repair work in the
church, in 1825. At 4, Westgate Street, the premises of HSBC
on the corner with Northgate Street (8), is displayed behind a
gloomy glass panel on the street a stone base found in 1971,
on which once stood the substantial column now in the
entrance of the City Museum (see below). At 1, Westgate
Street, The Royal Bank of Scotland has a small display of
Roman material (9). Finally, a small building inscription is
built upside-down in the outer (south) face of the blocking-
wall of the second arch from the west in the triforium of the
cathedral (10). It refers to the century of Cornelius Crescens
of the Twentieth Legion, Valeria Victrix (a title it received for
valiant service, perhaps but not certainly that against Boudica
in 61). The stone confirms the presence of this legion at
Gloucester (and probably also at Kingsholm) in the first
century. The inscription may have come from the legionary
baths, at first the only stone building in the otherwise timber
fortress; but if the rebuilding in stone during the late 80s was
military rather than civilian (see above), other buildings
within the fortress are a possible source for the stone.

Much more rewarding than any of these *disiecta membra* is
a visit to the archaeology galleries of the City Museum (11),
Brunswick Street (Monday–Saturday, 1000–1700; Sunday,
July–September only 1000–1600). The column in the entrance
hall from Westgate Street (see above), still 2 m (6 ft 6 in)
high, would originally have stood to an impressive height of 9
m (30 ft); it formed part of a massive colonnade, of uncertain
purpose (defining a temple precinct or enclosing baths?),
known to have extended for at least 100 m (328 ft) along
Westgate Street. A geometric mosaic from Northgate Street
leads into the prehistoric gallery, at the end of which note the
case with the finds from the Birdlip burial of *c.* AD 50. This
contains remains of both a man and a woman (an attempted
simulation of the appearance of the lady, based on her skull
structure, is displayed in the adjacent case), together with
accompanying grave goods. The Birdlip mirror, one of these,

is a superb example of late La Tène decoration, with its graceful flowing lines, a style which still continued to be used in Romano-British metalwork until at least the very end of the second century.

The first Roman room displays military finds from the two fortresses, including a substantial timber from the eastern defences in King's Square belonging to the 60s legionary fortress, and a decorated helmet cheek-piece (p. 171) from the earlier Kingsholm site. Here too are displayed the fine tombstone of the auxiliary cavalryman Rufus Sita, mentioned above (p. 171), riding down his barbarian foe; the more fragmentary one of L. Valerius Aurelius, veteran of the Twentieth Legion, which belongs to the later second century and so records a man who had served in the legion at Chester and who presumably had retired to Gloucester; and that of Philus, standing rather mournfully in his hooded cloak under a very classical-looking pediment. Note too, in the last case in this room, a stamped brick of the second century from the municipal tileworks, starting with the letters RPG (which stand for *res publica Glevensium*, the 'community of the people of Gloucester'), and followed by the names of two chief magistrates who held the post of *duumvir quinquennalis* (QQ on the tile), leaders of the city council elected every fifth year to conduct a community-wide census; their names are Jul(ius) Flor(us?) and Cor(nelius) S(i)m(plex?). Gloucester is the only city in Britain known to have possessed municipal tileworks, which lay under St Oswald's Priory just outside the north corner of the walls of the *colonia*.

The second Roman gallery contains an important collection of Romano-British stone sculpture, mostly of divinities; but the 'Bon Marché' head with huge bulging eyes is much more probably of medieval date and does not belong here. Of particular interest is the fascinating altar of Romulus, shown in the guise of Mars, of which both dedicator (Gulioepius) and sculptor (Iuventinus) are recorded; it is not well displayed, being set high up on a shelf and not therefore easily visible from the ground. Gulioepius is clearly from his name a Celt (i.e. a native Briton), yet the dedication (in Latin) to the mythical founder of Rome, and the rudimentary classical pediment under which the divinized hero is standing, display a familiarity with both the symbolism and the architectural language of the classical world. Other cases in this gallery include a notable display of pottery and amphorae (note especially the complete Rhodian wine amphora from the Kingsholm fortress) and some finds from the Frocester villa (of which the long-handled iron 'peel', for removing bread from an oven, is the most unusual artefact). The room also contains *in situ* a well preserved stretch of the defences of Roman Gloucester, displaying the base-plinth and large-block construction characteristic of the late third-century rebuilding. There are plans afoot to move the Museum to a new location nearby and to use the present building for the city library, in which case public access to this stretch of the Roman defences will be maintained.

Cirencester** (SP 020020), CORINIVM DOBVNNORVM, has the distinction of being the second largest town of Roman Britain after London (237 acres [96 ha] within the walls), but its medieval and modern successor is considerably smaller, and so large areas within the walls remain free from buildings. Very little, however, of the Roman town is visible, although rescue excavations in the 1970s and 1980s contributed an enormous amount to our knowledge. Once again, the place had a military origin: a first fort (or possibly a 30-acre [12.5-ha] fortress – its exact size is unknown), which was established in the area of the Watermoor Hospital, was found to be too close to marshy land, and so another fort was built, about AD 49, on better-drained soil, on a site bounded approximately by The Avenue, Chester Street, Watermoor Road and St Michael's Fields.

By the late 70s, when the military moved on, the civilian settlement which had grown up around this fort became the new administrative centre for the *civitas* of the Dobunni. It was laid out on an ambitious scale, with an impressive stone forum and basilica (only London's was larger) not earlier than the very end of the first century; whether there was a timber predecessor is unknown. Other public buildings followed soon after, including a possible market-hall, a theatre, and an amphitheatre too. The basilica had to be completely reconstructed in the Hadrianic or early Antonine period: the first building, erected over the filled-in ditches of the early fort, had badly subsided. At the end of the second century CORINIVM received its first earth defences, and these were faced in stone in the third century (not before *c.* AD 240), at first with a narrow wall, and later with one double the width over much of the circuit. The prosperity of CORINIVM did not (unlike in some Romano-British towns) slacken off in the fourth century: then it was the capital of Britannia Prima, one of the four British provinces after Diocletian's reorganization of provincial administration.

Cirencester's wealth during the fourth century is manifestly demonstrated by the splendid mosaic pavements laid by mosaicists centred in the town. Decline set in only in the last quarter of the fourth century, and when it came was rapid: of the numerous excavated examples of town-houses in Cirencester (many of course only very partially known), it has been estimated that 23 were in use *c.* AD 375, ten *c.* AD 400, four *c.* AD 425, and none thereafter. In the fifth century discipline broke down and the time came when unburied bodies were left rotting in the street gutters.

The Corinium Museum in Park Street (1 on Fig. 35) contains a splendid display of material which vividly demonstrates the prosperity of the Roman town (daily throughout the year, Monday–Saturday, 1000–1700; Sunday, 1400–1700). The first three sections have been recently refurbished, but the rest of the Museum is due to be reorganized over the next few years in an ambitious and exciting new display, if funding is forthcoming; so the order in which the key exhibits are mentioned below may change. The first Roman room contains some of the evidence for the military origins of the town, including an impressive full-scale mock-up of a Roman cavalryman and the tombstones of two cavalry troopers, belonging to different regiments (the *ala Indiana* and the *ala Thraecum*). Like Rufus Sita at Gloucester (p. 176), they are shown trampling their foe. After sections on the founding of Corinium and a reconstruction of a butcher's shop, you reach the hall with the fourth-century mosaic of the hare, discovered in a compact and well-equipped town-house in Beeches Road in 1971. In the next room, after the fragmentary Corinthian capital which impresses by its sheer size (it must have surmounted a column some 12 m [40 ft] high), come the spectacular remains of Roman town-houses – a reconstructed section of Roman plaster and three more

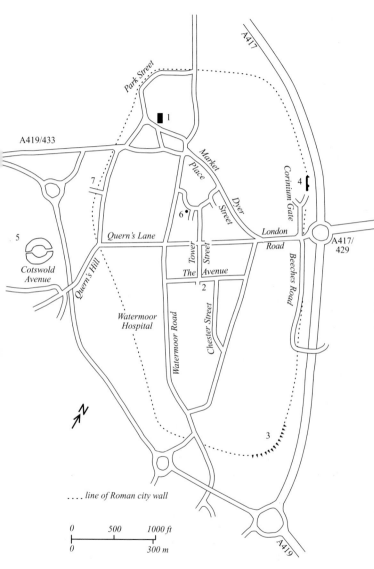

35   Cirencester, location map

mosaic pavements – which amply display both the taste and
the wealth of the inhabitants of CORINIVM.

The first mosaic depicts hunting-dogs chasing a (lost) prey
in the central roundel, with sea-beasts, and heads of Medusa
and Oceanus, in the surround. The second floor is part of an
elaborate composition of which five roundels survive
complete. Three contain Seasons (Winter is missing) and the
other two portray mythological events – Actaeon being torn to
pieces by his dogs (for seeing the goddess Diana at her bath)
(Fig. 36), and Silenus, one of Dionysus' attendants, riding on
a donkey. Both these mosaics were probably laid in the late
second century, and are, technically speaking, among the most
accomplished examples of mosaic art from the entire
province. The imaginative reconstruction around the second
mosaic gives an excellent impression of what a Romano-
British interior in a wealthy house may have looked like.

The third mosaic was laid in the early fourth century and
comes not from Cirencester itself but from a suburban villa
found immediately outside the walls. It depicts Orpheus with

36   Cirencester, Roman town, mosaic of Actaeon (Corinium Museum)

his lyre, charming the birds and animals which proceed in
stately fashion around him. The idea of putting the animals
and birds in concentric circles around the central figure of
Orpheus is an original one, found nowhere else in the Roman
Empire, emanating from a mosaic workshop operating at
Corinium itself. The subject appears on several mosaics
known from the neighbourhood, all now covered up or lost:
Woodchester (p. 197) is one of them. Also displayed here is
another fourth-century mosaic with a central roundel figuring
a bust of Venus, identified by her mirror over one shoulder;
there are ungainly, bulbous dolphins on the threshold panel.
The floor, excavated in 1975 at a Roman estate centre at
Kingscote, 14 miles (22 km) west of Cirencester, is again the
work of mosaicists based in CORINIVM: the outer border and
the *cantharus* in one corner are virtually identical with those
at the Chedworth villa (room 10: p. 194), and the Z-border
next to the dolphins can be paralleled on the Bancroft mosaic
(p. 251), also laid by Cirencester mosaicists.

   This end of the museum is dominated by a huge and
striking Corinthian capital of *c.* AD 200, adorned with the
heads of Bacchus (bearing the grapes) and his companions – a
maenad (with tambourine) and the bald and drunken Silenus
(with drinking horn); but it is surprising to find also in the
same company a depiction of one of Bacchus' victims, the
bearded king Lycurgus (identifiable by his double axe), who
for chasing the nymph Ambrosia was throttled to death by a
vine miraculously sent by Bacchus. Perhaps the commissioner
of the capital chose images from a copybook without being
too well informed about the niceties of Bacchic mythology.
Next to it is a dedication to Jupiter by Septimius, governor of
Britannia Prima (PRIMAE PROVINCIAE RECTOR), one of four
newly-created provinces when Britannia, already two
provinces, was further subdivided at the end of the third
century. CORINIVM was almost certainly its capital. The
mention of the word 'column' ([*col*]*umnam*) on the left-hand
panel has given rise to the suggestion that the inscription
served as the base of a 'Jupiter Column' on the Continental
model (they are common in eastern France and Germany), in
which the statue of Jupiter, generally on horseback and
brandishing a thunderbolt, is placed on top of a lofty column;
but the European examples are not demonstrably later than

c. AD 260, whereas the Cirencester inscription cannot be earlier than the 290s. Models of the Chedworth villa and its bath suites are also displayed here.

In the next section on religion, be sure not to miss the word-square scratched on a piece of wall-plaster. It reads ROTAS OPERA TENET AREPO SATOR, 'Arepo the sower holds the wheels with care'. The words are set out one above the other, so that, most ingeniously, the line reads the same from left to right, right to left, bottom to top and top to bottom. The first words of the Lord's Prayer, *Pater Noster*, are contained twice over in the formula (with two As and Os, alpha and omega, the first and last letters of the Greek alphabet, left to spare; cf. Jesus' saying, 'I am alpha and omega, the beginning and the end': *Revelations* 1.8). This is surely too extraordinary to be coincidental, and it seems likely, therefore, that the *graffito* attests to the presence of Christians in CORINIVM. The date of the Cirencester plaster is not known, but the first three words of another example, found in Manchester in 1978, were scratched on a broken amphora datable *c.* AD 175/85, claimed as the earliest archaeological evidence for Christianity in Britain. Others, however, are more doubtful, and think that this and other first- and second-century examples of the palindrome (such as at Pompeii and Budapest) occur in contexts too early to be considered Christian, and result purely from a delight in palindromes.

The final Roman section contains tombstones and several sculptures illustrating the diversity of deities honoured in the town: a strange little relief showing three hooded divinities, and the pair of triple Matres (mother goddesses) reliefs, underline the importance of triplism in the pre-Roman native religious tradition, one which was maintained well into the Roman period.

Apart from the objects in the Museum, Cirencester does not have much of its Roman past on display. The apse of the basilica (2 on Fig. 35) is marked out in modern materials in a cul-de-sac which opens off The Avenue. The defences survive as a prominent bank on the south-east side of the town, in Watermoor recreation-ground (3 on Fig. 35), and north of London Road a stretch has been fully excavated and conserved (4). It is reached from the housing-estate of Corinium Gate (off London Road), and is signposted from the footbridge on the right. The stretch of walls here had two projecting towers. One is square, the other polygonal, but the superstructure of both was probably polygonal; the square one has recently been backfilled for its protection. These towers belong to the latest phase of the defences and were probably added about AD 330. Now climb the bank and study the defences from above. There was a floodbank here in the late first century (not now visible), but the first proper defences were erected towards the end of the second century. These consisted of an earth bank, and a square internal tower of stone, which is visible roughly half-way along the bank. The major gateways were also built in stone at the same time. The earth defences themselves, however, were not given a stone front until *c.* 240 at the earliest. It was only about 1.20 m (4 ft) wide, as can be seen from the section of it still standing, south of, and adjacent to, the tower. That the tower precedes the curtain wall can be seen from the straight joint with the later masonry on the north side of the tower (best viewed from the exterior of the wall). But you will also notice that elsewhere the wall is much thicker, between 2.15 m and 2.75 m (7–9 ft) wide: such parts of the original wall which were in danger of collapse were rebuilt as occasion demanded.

Also well worth a visit is the amphitheatre (5). Turn left at the end of Querns Lane, sharp right immediately after crossing the bypass, and then right at the fork, along Cotswold Avenue (EH signpost). The footpath to the amphitheatre [AM; A] is opposite Martin Close. It is now a large grassy depression, with entrance gaps at either end and banks still standing to an impressive height of about 8 m (27 ft) above the arena floor. Excavation has shown that the earliest building, erected in an earlier quarry early in the second century on alignment with the town's street-grid, had entrance walls of timber posts with dry-stone walling, and this was rebuilt in mortared masonry, together with the arena wall, before the middle of the second century. There were several other rebuildings and alterations (one of the stone passageways was demolished and replaced in timber in the mid fourth century, for example), and the amphitheatre remained in use into the beginning of the fifth century. The seats throughout were of timber, but shallow stone terracing walls in the banks provided some stability. No stonework has been left exposed. The amphitheatre is surrounded by large quarry pits from which both building stone and the spoil constituting the amphitheatre's seating banks were taken: the large hollow you cross on the way to the amphitheatre represents one of these quarries. It has been estimated that the total area of the quarry, covering some 25 acres (10 ha), represents some 800,000 tons of extracted stone, used over the second, third and fourth centuries to construct the buildings of Roman Cirencester.

For the assiduous student of Roman Cirencester, two additional Roman antiquities may be of interest, although neither is *in situ*. There is a Roman column-base at the corner of West Way and South Way, just to the left of the police station as one faces it (6; South Way, not marked as such on Fig. 35, p. 179, is the northward continuation of Tower Street); and a fourth-century Roman coffin from a cemetery of 450 burials excavated prior to the building of the western bypass is exhibited in the forecourt of the premises of Messrs Brann, Phoenix Way (7: turn right at the west end of Quern's Lane and first left into Phoenix Way: you need the building straight ahead of you after turning into the latter).

The prosperity of Cirencester must have been largely due to the wealth of the surrounding countryside. The town formed the market-centre for the agricultural products of the many villas which are known in the Cotswold region. Much is still to be learnt about them, especially the chronology of their development and the details of their farming economy: most were excavated at a time when mosaics and hypocausts were of greater interest than the less spectacular evidence of farmbuildings or industrial activity.

Bristol itself was not a Roman town, although the City Museum (daily, 1000–1700) has a good collection of local finds. There was, however, a settlement in the suburb of **Sea Mills** (ST 551758), the Roman ABONA – which means 'river' in Celtic, a name which still survives in the modern river, the Avon. The settlement probably developed out of an early Roman fort of *c.* 55–65: an extensive area of timber buildings (shops and houses) is known for the second century, rebuilt in stone in the third and fourth centuries. The foundations of one stone building excavated in 1934, probably a house, are visible on the north side of Portway (A4) at its

junction with Roman Way, opposite a bus-shelter about
3 miles (5 km) south of Avonmouth. This consists of a small
courtyard with rooms surrounding it.

About $2\frac{3}{4}$ miles (4.4 km) NW of Sea Mills is the Roman
villa of **King's Weston** (ST 534776). From the more southerly
of the two roundabouts on the A4 in Avonmouth (motorway-
spur with M5), take the B4054 for $\frac{1}{2}$ mile (800 m), then turn
left at the traffic-lights along King's Weston Avenue. The
Roman villa lies on the right after another $\frac{1}{2}$ mile. The key can
be obtained on payment of a deposit from the Blaise Castle
House Museum in Henbury (April–October only, Saturday–
Wednesday 1000–1700 [tel: 0117–950–6789]; from the villa
continue straight on as far as you can, then turn left for the
centre of Henbury). In winter the key is held by the Bristol
City Museum (daily, 1000–1700), but arrangements have to
be made in advance (tel: 0117–922–3571). The part of the
villa still accessible was built at some time between AD 270
and 300, and saw various alterations before its abandonment
towards the end of the fourth century. It was excavated in
1948–50. The entrance leads immediately to the four rooms of
the east wing, of which the largest had a hypocaust inserted
into the floor some time later than the original building;
fragments of its mosaic floor were also found. The offset in
the walls of all four rooms here probably marks original floor-
level; if so the floor was raised in the room with the hypocaust
when that was inserted, and its north wall with the stoke-hole
was totally rebuilt at the time. This room's entrance threshold
(now covered over for its protection) leads to a long corridor
which gave access through columns (a few bases are visible)
to a gravelled court on the right – a type of villa more
common in Germany than in Britain. The building was
entered by a small porch which projects from the south (left-
hand) wall of the corridor.

The west wing is covered by a wooden shed. The room on
the left has an unusual geometric mosaic, with a large
cantharus on one side flanked by tendrils. Judging from its
size this room was surely the dining-room (*triclinium*). The
floor of the adjacent room had largely perished, and the
present mosaic comes from another Bristol villa (at
Brislington) which was found in 1900. Beyond are the
remains of a small bath-suite. The apsidal heated room has a

few fragments of its *pilae*: the floor would have been level with the top of the surviving walls, as the height of the flue opening to the right makes clear. The apsed bath and the adjoining room to the right, now destroyed, belonged to the original building, but the other two compartments – on the left, an undressing room, and, in the centre, a room with steps leading down to a cold bath – are of later date. The vestibule to the cold bath has a fragmentary guilloche mosaic panel.

Of the villas situated around Cirencester, the least worth visiting is that at **Wadfield** (SP 023260). It lies on the left of the Winchcombe to Andoversford minor road, 2 miles (3.2 km) south of the former: park at the turning signposted Cotswold Way, 500 m (550 yd) south of the EH sign for Belas Knap Long Barrow. Walk down the drive as far as the first house and then walk into the field on your left, following its edge if there is a standing crop. The villa is situated in the small wooded enclosure of trees in the middle of a field, and is reached by a gate in its east (valley) side. The villa was first discovered and partly explored in 1863 and again in 1894–5. Some of the walls, now overgrown, are still traceable (one contains a moulded, half-octagonal stone base), but the overall ground-plan, consisting of two wings ranged about a courtyard, is not now distinguishable; that on your left (south) contained the bath-suite. The main reception-room, covered by a wooden hut, has a partly restored geometric mosaic, of which half is in position: the restorations (especially to the right of centre) are clearly distinguishable by the more brightly coloured tesserae. The rest of the pavement was presumably lost soon after discovery, for of some mosaic it was written that 'its speedy removal was found to be absolutely necessary in order to preserve it from the Winchcombe public, who in the space of one Sunday afternoon carried off a large portion, in small pieces, as souvenirs'. The mosaic may belong to the second century, in contrast to the other visible villa-mosaics of this region, which are of the fourth century. Another villa is situated in Spoonley Wood, only 1 mile (1.6 km) away across the valley, but it is in a totally ruined state now and not worth a visit (App. 1).

Much better preserved is the **Great Witcombe*** villa (SO 899142) [AM; A]. It is situated like so many villas in a beautiful position close to a source of water; but here the water is a little *too* near, for the whole hillside is riddled with springs, and the owners had some difficulty in preventing these from undermining the whole house and carrying it away down the slope. The first stone villa (the walls shown in black on Fig. 37), built in the first half of the third century, follows an unusual plan consisting of two ranges either side of an open courtyard, linked by a long gallery; the contemporary bath-block was a small detached suite to the south of the SW wing (7 and 8 on Fig. 37). Enlargements and alterations occurred, probably on more than one occasion, in the late third and fourth centuries, especially in the bath-suite and in the NE wing (white on Fig. 37). Scanty traces have also been found of earlier occupation on the site, dating to the second century. The villa continued to be occupied until *c.* AD 380, with some squatter occupation thereafter.

To reach the villa, turn off the A46 in the village of Brockworth (roundabout at The Crossed Hands) in the direction of Birdlip, and turn right almost immediately. A mile-long (1.6-km) road leads to a car-park: the villa is then ten minutes' walk further on. If you wish to get inside one of the locked rooms to see the mosaics in the bath-suite, you

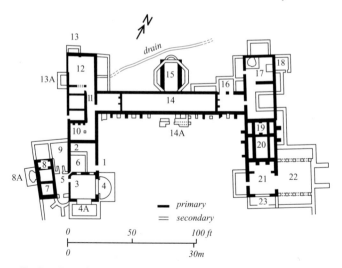

37 *Great Witcombe, Roman villa, site plan*

need to make arrangements in advance and collect the key
from the Corinium Museum in Cirencester (tel:
01285–655611). Ignore the painting of the 'typical villa' at
the entrance which is nothing of the sort – as at North Leigh
(p. 200), a reconstruction of the *mansio* at Wall (p. 293) is
misleadingly displayed here. The next painting by contrast
does indeed show the Great Witcombe villa.

First walk over to the far corner of the site to visit the
remains of the bath-house, most of which belongs to the
secondary phase, although its development was more
complicated than shown on the plan (Fig. 37). You first pass
two cold pools (4, 4a; not all of the latter is exposed), and
then make your way to the further of the two huts. Under it is
a hot immersion-bath (8; there is another at 8a), with a lead
pipe in one corner and evidence for successive refloorings:
large tiles were used in the first phase, smaller square tiles in
the second, and stone flags in the third. These features are
invisible in winter when the windows of the shed are blocked.
Associated with this hot-water bath was the room of intense,
sticky, damp heat (the *caldarium*, 7), under the square cover.
The wooden bridge passes over the hypocausted *tepidarium*
(5), with apse to the right and stoking area to the left (9). Note
the two slabs immured on the left of the entrance to the
second hut: this was a doorway, built on the skew, to link the
tepidarium to the *sudatorium* of dry heat (6). The latter has a
fragmentary geometric floor mosaic, and there are box flue-
tiles preserved in its walls. Another well preserved doorway
links this room with the *frigidarium* (3), which is floored with
a crude but lively marine mosaic, with naïvely drawn, outsize
fish and a variety of sea-creatures executed in limited
polychrome. You have now gone through the baths in the
reverse order to that used by the Roman bather, who would
have entered the suite from the courtyard (1), changed in 3,
moved into 5 with its tepid heat, and then either chosen the
moist heat of 7 or the more rigorous dry heat of 6 before
returning to 3 for a dip in the cold bath in 4 or 4a. Room 2
was almost certainly a latrine.

The next room on the uphill side (10) has a central basin
and three niches in the walls (Fig. 38). It is believed to have
had a religious function, perhaps the worship of the local
water-nymphs, who no doubt needed appeasing to prevent

landslides (cf. the Deep Room at Lullingstone, p. 83). The end
of this wing, at the top of the slope, was at first occupied by
another set of baths; 12 once had a hypocaust and 13/13a are
the foundations of immersion-baths. The latter were probably
demolished when the more spacious bath-suite was built
further south, but 12 may have been retained as a heated
living-room. Turn right along the long corridor (14) and note,
away to the left in the grass, a drain and, on the right, a series
of buttresses designed to prevent the foundations from
settling. The substantial base built at the centre (14a) is
probably the foundation of a grand entrance staircase, by
means of which the floor of the corridor (higher than the
present level) could be reached. Opening off the corridor,
facing this entrance, is an octagonal construction, added in the
second period to replace the original rectangular room, also
visible beneath (15); it may have been the principal dining-
room, especially as it was laid with an intricate and no doubt
expensive pavement of cut stone which formed a pattern in
contrasting colours (*opus sectile*) – a rare example of the use

38   *Great Witcombe, Roman villa, shrine*

of this floor technique in Britain, and the only one where the overall decorative scheme was recoverable (not now visible).

The rest of the villa, first uncovered by Samuel Lysons in 1818–19, contains little of interest. The rooms grouped around 16 seem to have been a subsidiary entrance area; 17 was the kitchen in the secondary phase, with an oven in the west corner and a hearth against the NE wall, and a possible latrine (18) lies beyond. Rooms 19 and 20 are massive substructures for what are presumed to have been living-quarters above; if they were not here, it is hard to see where else they were in the villa, unless the SW wing also had an upper storey. Room 21 was found to contain a couple of ovens and three hearths: this may have been the kitchen in the primary third-century building, before being replaced by that in 17. Room 22 contained a couple of lead-smelting hearths, but what remains of a drain is the only visible feature. Room 23 contained a corn-drying oven (also no longer visible), so this part of the villa in the secondary phase apparently housed agricultural and metal-working activities – curiously close to the presumed living area above, and possessing an architectural solidity uncharacteristic of such structures. Alternatively, some or all of these features may belong rather to the final phase at the end of the fourth century, when the villa was no longer functioning as an elegant and sophisticated dwelling.

The outstanding Cotswold villa site, however, is at **Chedworth**** (SP 053134), which used to be regarded by some as the finest preserved villa in the country. It is certainly one of the most beautiful, lying at the head of the peaceful wooded valley of the Coln in an utterly charming position. There have been considerable problems with damp and frost damage in recent years, however, and a long-term conservation programme has hindered access to some parts of the site. At the time of writing, the National Trust is considering plans for a major new cover-building over the west wing, which if they come to fruition should considerably improve the presentation of this site by 2004. The villa is open as follows: May–September, Tuesday–Sunday (and Bank Holiday Mondays) 1100–1700; March–April and October–late November, Wednesday–Sunday 1100–1600. It is closed on Good Friday and from late November to the end of February.

The villa is best approached from the Fosse Way (A429) 1 mile (1.6 km) south of the crossroads with the A40: take the road to Yanworth (*not* Chedworth village) and then to the site (signposted). The other approach is from the north: take the turning to Withington from the A436, $\frac{1}{2}$ mile (800 m) west of Andoversford, and then follow signposts to the villa. It was discovered accidentally in 1864 by a gamekeeper digging for a lost ferret, and has been National Trust property since 1924. Only excavations since the 1960s, however, have clarified the history of the site, and four major phases are now known. In the first, dated to the first half of the second century, the house consisted of two separate buildings on the west and south and a detached bath-suite to the north. In the early third century (Phase II), the west and south wings were rebuilt after a fire, the baths were enlarged, and a few rooms were added on their east side. In the early fourth century (Phase III) the villa took on its present appearance (Fig. 39): the existing elements were united with a covered veranda, and an inner garden and outer courtyard were created. At the same time the dining-room received its mosaics and the north half of the west wing was converted to take a second set of baths (damp heat); soon after (Phase IIIA) the existing baths in the north wing were substantially rebuilt and modified as dry-heat sauna-baths. Finally, in Phase IV (in the late fourth century), the north wing was further extended by the addition of a new dining-room. Occupation continued to the very end of the fourth century and even into the fifth.

The path first leads on your right to the latrine (labelled 4) with its usual sewer (now gravel-filled) and channel for running water. This and the nearby 'estate office' (2), so-called because a large number of coins were found here, were added in the fourth century to the original south wing, which once began just before the steps. The rest of the south wing is largely unexplored, but excavations in 2000 have revealed a room with a hypocaust, and shown that even the corridor was heated (an extreme rarity); so this part of the villa was also designed for comfortable living. The insertion of a corn-drier into the corridor in the fifth century also sheds light on the decline of the villa in the sub-Roman period. These excavations have not currently been left exposed.

Now retrace your steps, passing through the kitchen (3),

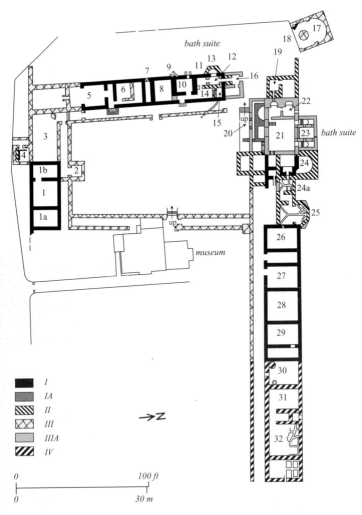

39   Chedworth, Roman villa, site plan

with an oven-base marked out in modern materials. The kitchen served the dining-room (*triclinium*) with channelled hypocaust below (5), which is reached by turning right along the corridor of the west wing. In its present form it dates to the first half of the fourth century. The most striking feature is its mosaic floor, laid by craftsmen based in Cirencester. The main portion is partially destroyed, but originally it contained a central octagon (perhaps with a representation of Bacchus) surrounded by eight main panels. Some of these were filled with figures of nymphs and satyrs, but one pair of the three that remain probably shows Bacchus (with his wand, the *thyrsus*, and long curls) and Ariadne, his consort. Perfectly preserved, however, are three of the Seasons, represented as charming little boys: Spring wears only a scarf and holds a bird and flower-basket (Fig. 40); Summer, who is completely naked and also winged, holds a garland and flower-basket; and Winter, wearing a hood, cloak and leggings, holds a twig and a dead hare. This part of the room probably formed an

40   Chedworth, Roman villa, mosaic of Spring in dining-room of west wing

antechamber; the dining-room proper lies beyond the projecting piers and has an ordinary geometric floor bordered on two sides by superb floral scrolls springing from vases. A drain in the far left-hand corner, to remove surface water when washing the floors, is not visible under current viewing arrangements (2001). Fragmentary mosaics in the corridor and in room 5b, re-excavated in 2000 but temporarily reburied, may be exposed if the new cover-building mentioned above (p. 190) goes ahead.

The next three rooms (6, 7, 8) have nothing of interest and were probably ordinary day-rooms or possibly bedrooms; 6 had a geometric mosaic and a hypocaust (note recesses for the wall-flues). Next we enter the baths of damp heat, which also belong to the fourth-century expansion of Chedworth. They constitute a well preserved example of their type and give an excellent idea of the Roman bathing system; but access is currently restricted, and many details mentioned below are impossible to see from the entrance to the present cover-building, to which visitors are currently restricted. First (10) is the undressing room with a mosaic floor relaid in 1978; it has a hypocaust underneath and box-shaped flue-tiles in the walls. The tree-stump here was deliberately retained to show the ground-level in 1864 when the villa was found. The composition here, with a central roundel at the heart of a cross-shaped area with pointed ends in the corners (what is termed a saltire), is an original creation of mosaicists working at Cirencester in the fourth century; the *peltae* in the arms of the cross, with two concentric circles framed by tendrils attached, is also typical of this workshop (a very similar floor is visible at North Leigh: Fig. 43). Next (11) is the little *tepidarium*, with flue-tiles and hypocaust *pilae* clearly visible and a mosaic floor in position; the door jambs are also well preserved. The floor of the *caldarium* (12) has vanished, leaving just the *pilae*. A semicircular hot bath opens off it (13). Then the bather would have returned to the mosaic-floored *frigidarium* (14), to cool off before taking a dip in the cold bath (15), still complete with its steps and drainage-pipe. The bather would then go back to 10 to dress again. The heavy wear on the door-sill of 11 shows the popularity of these baths with the owners and their guests. The furnace for heating the baths (16) can be studied outside (turn left and left again); you cross the drainage-pipe from 15 en route.

Now go up to the far left corner to the shrine of the water-nymphs (*nymphaeum*: 17), with curved back and octagonal pool; this was the villa's natural source of spring water. The full 2 m (6 ft 6 in) height of this represents Roman work, not Victorian restoration; the re-use of architectural fragments suggests that it is a late structure (mid-fourth century?). Its prominence has partly prompted a theory, completely unfounded, that the site is not a villa at all but a religious cult-centre. A Christian monogram scratched on the rim of the pool attests to the presence of Christians at Chedworth, presumably in the fourth century; it is now in the site Museum (see below).

The first part of the north wing contains another bath-suite, the original baths of the villa. These were originally quite simple, but were extended in Phase II, and then partly demolished. The plan of the demolished rooms is marked out

41   Chedworth villa, the north wing looking east

in modern concrete. The final, fourth-century alterations included the building of the colonnade, of which the column-stumps are visible (Fig. 41), and the conversion of the baths to the dry-heat variety to supplement those in the west wing. Mount the steps into room 21, which was the undressing room of the final baths (previously the *tepidarium*). On your left you can look through the glass to see two small hot rooms, originally with apsidal immersion-baths, later disused (22). Straight ahead (23) is a large cold immersion-bath and two flanking immersion-baths, all added in the fourth century. Now come down the steps (a blocked doorway can be seen on your left) and note on your left (24) an apsed room with a hypocaust of which only a few *pilae* remain intact. Two rooms with channelled hypocausts (24A, 25) follow, the larger probably being a reception- or living-room.

The rest of the north wing can be dealt with briefly. Don't, incidentally, be misled by the tiresome modern 'roofs' which the walls have been given here, as elsewhere: they are solely designed to protect the ancient structure from rain and frost. They are, however, being gradually replaced with a more acceptable, alternative capping of flat slabs. Rooms 26–9 belong to the early third-century extension of the north wing. Room 26 displays its stone hypocaust *pilae* but the floor has gone: a cover-building is planned too for this room. Room 28 contained a fragmentary geometric mosaic and may have been a summer dining-room. The north corridor here is also floored with a geometric mosaic, uncovered in 1990 but reburied for its protection: if a cover-building over 26 materializes, it may be possible to display part of the corridor mosaic as well.

The rest of the north wing (30–2) was apparently constructed in the villa's closing years at the end of the fourth century. The very last room, the largest in the villa, was probably another dining-room, heated by a channelled hypocaust. It used to be thought that the hypocaust on a higher level at the far end indicated a raised dais for the owner's 'top table'; but renewed excavation in 2000 has cast doubt on this interpretation, which is probably the result of Victorian 're-arrangement' of the remains. Recent geophysical research behind the north wing has revealed further structures there which might represent the servants' quarters; they are so far unexcavated. Trial excavation in the garden courtyard in

2000 found no evidence for trees or bedding plants; as now it was probably lawned. In the last third of the fourth century it was roughly paved with stone flags and turned into a yard, presumably when the villa was no longer being used as a place of gracious and elegant living.

A visit to the little Museum completes your tour of this lovely site. Watch out especially, in the case to the right of the door, for the relief of a hunter god from the temple found 170 m (185 yd) west of the villa (not visible); a crude relief of Mars Lenus, a variant normally attested only in the Trier region of Germany; and the large slab from the *nymphaeum* incised with the chi-rho Christian symbol, in the lower part of the case to the left of the door.

Brief mention must also be made of another villa, one of the largest and most luxurious found in Britain, although, as in all cases except Fishbourne, the summit of prosperity was not reached until the fourth century. It lies at **Woodchester** (ST 840030), a village 2 miles (3.2 km) south of Stroud off the A46 (EH signpost): either follow the EH sign, parking in Southfield Road, and approaching on foot across a field, or take the first turning to the right ('No Through Road'), at the end of which, on the left, you will find the Old Churchyard and a display board recording the villa. No fewer than 64 rooms grouped around two courtyards were found in the eighteenth century, lovingly recorded and lavishly published by the great antiquary Samuel Lysons (1763–1819), who deserves recognition as the founding father of Romano-British archaeology. There is nothing whatever visible at the site today, but such is the fame of this site that English Heritage has recently erected 'Roman villa' signposts, leading the unsuspecting visitor to think that there is more to see than there in fact is. The chief mosaic, 14.95 m (49 ft) square and one of largest known north of the Alps, built on a hypocaust 1.20 m (4 ft) high, used to be exposed every 12 years or so (the last time in 1973), but access problems from ever-greater visitor numbers have sadly prevented re-exposure since. It is a magnificent portrayal of Orpheus charming the birds and animals, a larger version of the mosaic with the same theme in the Corinium Museum and, like that one, laid by Cirencester mosaicists in the first half of the fourth century AD. A replica of the Woodchester mosaic, made in modern materials and

transportable in sections, was made many years ago and is
occasionally displayed at venues in the west of England; it is
greatly to be hoped that a permanent home can be found for it
soon in Gloucestershire. The square depression close to the
stile where you enter the churchyard marks the site of the
great mosaic. Roman brick will be detected re-used in the
walls of the ruined church, and the beautiful setting of the
villa will be appreciated.

Excavations at the villa when the Orpheus mosaic was last
exposed in 1973 added significantly to our knowledge of the
site. As so often, the final plan as recovered in the eighteenth-
century excavations represents only the culmination of a long
period of development, beginning perhaps c. AD 100. Its water
supply was provided by a stone-built conduit leading from a
spring 550 m (600 yds) to the west, found during the
construction of houses (Lawn Field). Thirteen rooms in the
villa are known to have had mosaics, most of them
contemporary with the laying of the Orpheus pavement
(probably c. 325/50 rather than earlier), but more no doubt
await discovery: the main bath-suite, for example, has not yet
been located. Imported marble veneers and statuary
(fragments of 11 sculptures are known) further emphasize the
impression of a high-status, luxury dwelling: indeed no other
known fourth-century villa in Britain can match its degree of
lavish interior decor.

Further away from the area so far dealt with, but still in the
Cotswolds, is the villa at **North Leigh*** (SP 397154) [AH; A]
in Oxfordshire. It was first discovered and excavated in
1813–16 and again before the First World War; further
examination and consolidation were undertaken in the 1970s.
In its final fourth-century form, North Leigh is an excellent
example of the courtyard type of villa, with wings on three
sides and an entrance-gate on the fourth (Fig. 42). This was,
however, only the last stage in a long and complicated
development. Slight traces were found under the south wing
of an Iron Age farm, but the earliest stone-built villa, built in
the early second century AD, consisted of a small main house
(under the centre of the later west wing), another structure
immediately to the south, and a detached bath-house at the
NW corner. These were gradually extended and amalgamated,
and other structures added, until the whole was united by

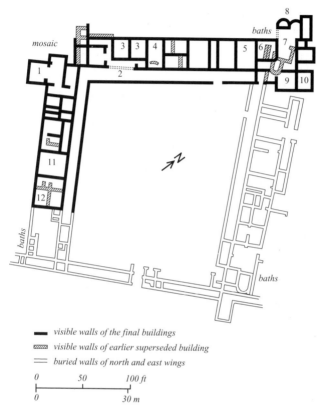

42   *North Leigh, Roman villa, site plan*

continuous corridors linking the three wings in the early
fourth century. Most of the mosaics in the west wing were
probably laid in the second quarter of the fourth century, and
there were further improvements to the NW baths in the mid-
fourth century. The nineteenth-century excavators record that
16 rooms were furnished with mosaics, all but two in the west
range, quite apart from rooms with plain tessellated floors;
with the exception of the visible mosaic all of these have
sadly now perished. Further buildings, discovered by aerial

photography but as yet unexcavated, lie to the south of the
main villa: they very probably include the agricultural
buildings of the villa-estate.

The site is signposted from the A4095, 3 miles (4.8 km) NE
of Witney (East End; ignore directions to North Leigh
village); from the lay-by there is a 15-minute walk to the site.
Ignore the reconstruction painting of the alleged 'typical villa'
disgracefully displayed at the entrance (it represents the
mansio at Wall [p. 293] which is not a villa at all; the two-
storeyed appearance is also misleading, since North Leigh was
almost certainly a single-storeyed house). Follow the path
round to the cover-building, which preserves one of the villa's
principal dining-rooms. It is floored with a geometric mosaic
laid by Cirencester mosaicists in the second quarter of the
fourth century, as is known from both the overall arrangement
of the floor (the saltire pattern) and the individual motifs used
(such as the *peltae* with tendrils), which are closely
comparable with those of other mosaics in the Cirencester
district (Fig. 43) – for example that in the undressing room of

43   North Leigh, mosaic in dining-room (room 1)

the baths in the west wing of the Chedworth villa (p. 194). The hypocaust is still in perfect condition, and from the large window you can see the box flue-tiles in the walls which carried the heat upwards (for example, in the spur walls which divided the room into two). You can also see, with difficulty, that part of the floor has been cut away to reveal the *pilae* beneath. Unfortunately, while these details are observable from the exterior at any time, the cover-building is now rarely open to visitors (phone 01483–304869 for details), a retrograde step by comparison with earlier years. From the smaller windows of the cover-shed you can see a Tuscan capital (upside-down) and some column-bases, which give a hint of the architectural elegance of the courtyard colonnade.

Now walk along the corridor (2) of the west wing, the main living-quarters, towards the modern cottage at the NW corner. On your left is another heated room (3), this time with a channelled hypocaust, as distinct from the pillared type in the mosaic room; it was fired by two stoke-holes, visible in the far wall. Beyond room 3 the walls of some more living-rooms have been consolidated, but not all the visible remains belong to the same period. Thus the curved wall in room 4 and the wall built of stones pitched at an angle both belong to earlier (second-century) phases in the villa's history, and would have been buried below the floors of the final building. Room 5 has another channelled hypocaust, after which begins the main bath-suite of the NW angle.

The rooms here have a complicated structural history, elucidated during consolidation work in 1975–7. The earliest structures are the apsed room underneath 7 and the two parallel walls under room 6: the more northerly of these, the later addition, was interpreted as a bench added along the inside of the wall. They were part of a bath-house built in the second century, which originally stood detached from a much smaller west wing. The west wing (as far as 5) was itself substantially rebuilt at a later period (perhaps towards the end of the third century), and extended some years afterwards by the addition of the unheated living-rooms 6 and 7. Finally rooms were created around these in the early fourth century to form a new bath-suite, with a pair of semicircular immersion-baths at 8, one better preserved than the other. The pair of rooms with channelled hypocausts (9 and 10), heated by stoke-holes on their south side, represent a mid-fourth-century improvement and enlargement of these baths. The rectangular dry-stone structure adjacent to 8 is modern, but represents the outline of a heated room in the original, late third-century baths. A hoard of 163 counterfeit coins of *c*. 360/70, together with evidence for their manufacture (waste, pellets), was found dumped in the by then disused room 6.

Now walk down towards the river, following the site of the north wing, which contained another set of baths. Turning right, past the site of the gateway leading to the courtyard, you reach the foundations of the south wing, perhaps the servants' quarters. Again not all the walls visible here belong to the same period: for example, the construction of a new west wall to room 12 clearly sliced through two now-truncated earlier walls, which would have been buried below the floor in the final rebuilding. Room 11 once had four ovens in it, at least one used for smelting. Just beyond, two gate-posts projecting out slightly into the courtyard, later blocked, mark the site of an entrance into the corridor; another entrance is visible in the west wing near 5.

It will have been noted that nearly all the villas mentioned above reached the height of their prosperity during the fourth century. Their owners must clearly have been very wealthy to be able to afford the sumptuous mosaics of which such impressive vestiges remain to this day. An equally rich patronage, presumably by the owners of these same villas, is implied by the building of an elegant temple complex at **Lydney***(SO 616027), probably towards the end of the third century. The site has long been known, having been first explored in 1805; it was then extensively excavated by Sir Mortimer Wheeler in 1928–9, while work in 1980–1 has clarified aspects of its chronology. The temple itself was dedicated to Nodens, a Celtic divinity who was probably the same as the Nuadu of Irish legend. Nodens appears at Lydney to be connected above all with healing, and the discovery of votive figures of dogs (both as freestanding stone sculptures and as miniature figurines) supports this interpretation, as dogs are often associated with healing sanctuaries in the ancient world. In addition, finds such as a miniature bronze hand (a votive to render thanks for the mended part of the body), and an oculist's stamp for eye salve, also point clearly to a healing role for the sanctuary. The Mars, therefore, with which Nodens is assimilated on inscriptions, is likely to be that god in his healing capacity (attested elsewhere in the Celtic versions of the Mars cult), rather than his warlike one. There were however other aspects of multi-faceted Nodens which the Lydney finds demonstrate: he was also a hunting god, or at least a god of the wooded glades, as one inscription addresses the deity as 'Nodens Silvanus'; and a link with Neptune, perhaps as god of the nearby Severn estuary, also seems possible.

Apart from the temple, the precinct was furnished with other buildings – a guest-house, a set of baths and a long 'dormitory' structure consisting of 11 individual cells. The sanctuary was clearly built by and for worshippers of some standing, for both the elaboration of the structures and the quality of the finds suggest high-status devotees. Wheeler thought on numismatic evidence that the whole complex was built after *c.* 365, but limited re-excavation has shown that earlier floors lie below the ones that Wheeler found, one of them (in the baths) associated with a coin of Gallienus (of 258–68); and re-examination of the older coin finds supports a starting date for construction of the sanctuary in the second half of the third century rather than later. The cult was still popular in the second half of the fourth century when Christianity was growing in popularity at the expense of paganism; but only a single brooch belongs to the fifth century, and by then the cult's attraction had faded.

The Lydney sanctuary constitutes the best visible example of a Romano-British pagan cult-centre, of which many other examples are known through fieldwork or excavation. The remains lie in a beautiful setting within an Iron Age hill-fort amidst the luxuriant foliage of a private deer-park. The park is only open (1100–1800) on Sundays, Wednesdays and Bank Holidays during a restricted season between late March and early June, and every day for the last week in April. Precise dates however vary from year to year, and so you are advised to check when the park is open by telephoning 01594–842844 or 842027 in advance (on a weekday in office hours). Visits at other times, for groups only, may be possible, but only if arrangements have been made in advance with the Lydney Estate Office (at the numbers given above). Lydney Park is reached by a drive on the west side of Lydney, between the village and the roundabout for the Lydney bypass (gate-piers). The drive leads up to the back of the house in which a small Museum containing the principal finds (including many of those mentioned above) can be seen. Notice especially the little bronze votive inscription to M(ars) Nodens vowed by Flavius Blandinus, a drill-instructor (*armatura*); the stamp with dispensing instructions for eye salve made by one Julius Jucundus; and the exquisite bronze statuette of a reclining dog (represented by a copy), alert and realistic, yet combining classically inspired naturalism with somewhat stylized eyes and coat – and with the extraordinary addition of a circular motif repeated four times, each consisting of a central point from which start individual, curved lines. The whole device is suggestive of movement, and is almost certainly a Celtic magical symbol representing the sun, added to the votive figurine presumably for good luck.

From the house, a 15-minute walk, down into the valley and up to the ridge facing you, leads you to the Roman site. The Roman entrance to the sanctuary is marked by a gap in the rampart on your right at the point where the track makes a sharp 90° bend to the right, just before the summit: the modern track leads you not to the front of the temple but to its back. On reaching the temple, therefore, it is best to walk round to its far side, in order to enter it from the staircase in the middle of its front façade.

The temple is of unusual plan, being neither strictly classical nor Romano-Celtic: it consisted of a rectangular outer wall with bays or recesses, and an inner shrine with three small sanctuaries at the far end. The reason for the three shrines is not clear: either Nodens had associated godlings about which nothing is known, or else the god was represented in triplicate, as commonly in the world of Celtic religion (cf. Coventina, p. 484). In the first period, the roof was supported on six freestanding piers, but when one of these subsided, some time in the mid fourth century, with the consequent collapse of the temple, the spaces between the piers were blocked up in the rebuilding to make a continuous wall. The juxtaposition of an originally freestanding pier and the added walls on either side is particularly clear at the pier on the right, inside the main *cella*. A mosaic was added to the *cella* at the same time. It is now lost, but the part which survived until the nineteenth century depicted dolphins and fish, and was dedicated by Titus Flavius Senilis, the cult superintendent, and Victorinus, his 'interpreter' (of dreams?). Also in this secondary period, L-shaped walls were built adjacent to three of the bays in the ambulatory. Their purpose is unknown, but they presumably were connected with some temple rite: were some worshippers permitted to sleep here in the temple, by rotation, in the hope of greater efficacy for their cure? The outer ambulatory of the temple could once be reached from the rear end of the building through doorways in the back wall, but these were blocked at some later period: the blocking in the right-hand door is particularly obvious.

Immediately behind the temple, on the far side of the track, there was a long building of 11 mosaic-paved rooms opening, at least in part, on to a veranda: this was probably for patients to spend the night in the hope of a visitation from the god – a type of structure common in Mediterranean healing sanctuaries – rather than shops, for which floor mosaics in this context would be inappropriate (the mosaics are, however, secondary, the rooms being originally stone-paved). The building is not visible, however, apart from a short section of its rear wall close to the bath-house (and at an oblique angle to it). The remains of the guest-house, with numerous rooms ranged about a courtyard, lie to the right of the track, opposite the bath-house, but are also filled in; the baths are by contrast partly visible. This was a large and elaborate structure, with half a dozen heated rooms, presumably for both dry-heat (sauna) and the standard moist-heat bathing. From the display board you look down on the furnace area serving the double-apsed *caldarium*, one apse of which still stands up to 1.80 m (6 ft) high; its *pilae* have however gone. The metal cover here closes off the entrance to an exploratory iron-mine, of which another example will be noted presently. Just beyond, the Roman floor-level between *tepidarium* and *caldarium* is marked by a massive door-sill still in position. A further set of three small heated rooms lies to the right, two with their own furnaces; the furthest has a hypocaust with, unusually, underfloor channels (only one is now visible) set at an oblique angle to its containing walls, rather than the brick *pilae* which are visible in some of the other heated rooms. Note that the foundations of the *tepidarium* and *caldarium* on the ravine side are heavily buttressed by offsets to ensure greater stability so close to the cliff edge. Beyond it, also on this outer edge of the building, a cold pool and a latrine have now been backfilled. So too has the suite of cold rooms and the changing-room, which stretched across the width of the bath building; they lie under the grass beyond the last visible heated rooms.

Continue along the track a little further, and after it bends to the left you will see immediately on the left the grass-covered foundations of the square tank which supplied water to the baths. It has been interpreted as a cistern, but how it was supplied is not clear; more probably it was the catchment basin for a natural spring here which has now dried up. The line of the channel which carried water to the baths is clear; a portion of its stonework was visible in 2001 close to the basin.

Now retrace your steps and walk over to the ramparts of the Iron Age hill-fort on your left. Excavation in 1980–1 has demonstrated that these, originally erected some time in the first century BC or early first century AD, were heightened in the Roman period to serve as the precinct's enclosure wall; they are at their most impressive here. A high square metal fence here marks the entrance to another iron-mine, once accessible but now too dangerous: the steps lead down to the walls of a narrow passage cut in the rock which still bear the pick-marks of its miners. The mine was never fully operational: this passage was only a test-dig in the hope of finding a body of iron ore rich enough to be worth extracting. Backfill in one of these mining entrances produced a late third-century coin, but there is no independent dating evidence for when the iron extraction started. It seems however more likely to be Roman than pre-Roman.

A number of other temples are known in the Forest of Dean. One structure at Littledean, included in the third edition of this book with misgivings, may not be a temple at all, and may not even be Roman; I have therefore relegated it to Appendix 1. Another was found during the building of an industrial estate at Coleford in 1985 (in Musket Industrial Park, Crucible Close), but is no longer visible. The Forest of Dean was more noted in Roman times, however, for its extensive iron workings, such as at The Scowles just south of

Coleford (App. 1), and the centre of the industry was the
small town of ARICONIVM, now Weston-under-Penyard near
Ross-on-Wye (where nothing is visible). The road which
linked Weston with Lydney has long been thought of as
Roman, and the first and second editions of this book directed
readers to the preserved stretch of it at Blackpool Bridge
(SO 653087), reached by taking the Coleford road in the
western outskirts of Blakeney on the A48 and turning right
after 2 miles (3.2 km) (no signpost); the ancient road is on the
left after the railway-bridge. Questions had been raised from
time to time about whether it was really Roman, and neither
the kerb-stones, nor the paved surface, nor its exceptionally
narrow width (2.45 m or 8 ft), conformed to the behaviour of
Roman roads elsewhere in Britain. In 1985 a section cut
across the road at Soudley found that the paving rested on a
foundation of charcoal, samples of which were sent for radio-
carbon dating. The conclusion from the laboratory results is
that the road is not earlier than the seventeenth century.

The loss from the roll of visible Roman monuments of the
Blackpool Bridge road has been partly offset by the recent
discovery of a Roman bridge abutment near Hereford, in the
Weir Garden at **Swainshill** (SO 435421); this National Trust
property is clearly signposted 5 miles (8 km) west of Hereford
on the Brecon Road, A438 (mid-February–end of October,
Wednesday–Sunday and Bank Holiday Mondays 1100–1800).
Take the lower of the two paths immediately past the ticket-
office at the car-park, and you pass first on your left an
octagonal well, an eighteenth-century feature but undoubtedly
fashioned from large Roman blocks taken from the bridge
abutment. The abutment itself lies a few metres further on,
where a wooden fence prevents visitors from falling over the
cliff above the river Wye. It is in fact too dangerous to climb
down here to water-level, and the surviving Roman masonry
(the main face of the abutment) is in fact better viewed from
private land on the opposite bank of the river. From the fence,
however, you can clearly see the east side of the abutment
with large-block masonry at the foundations and neat stone
coursework above. Excavation at one point has revealed a
portion of rendering still surviving: all the masonry was
covered in white stucco on to which lines had been painted, to
give the impression that the whole bridge was made of large

ashlar blocks – a practice widely attested elsewhere in the
Roman world. A further section of large blocks is visible at
the water's edge to your left: whether this forms part of a
different abutment for a bridge on a separate alignment, or
was a Roman attempt to revet the river bank here and prevent
scouring, is not clear. The modern stones in the water were
placed here in 1995 to prevent erosion of the Roman work; in
the course of this operation over 240 blocks were recovered
from the river bed, many with lewis holes and clamp sockets,
and some clearly deriving from cutwater piers. The bridge
which crossed the Wye at this point carried the Roman road
from the small town of Kenchester (MAGNA), 1 mile (1.6 km)
to the north (of which very little is now visible: App. 1), in the
direction of the fort and later civilian settlement at
Abergavenny (GOBANNIVM), but the course of the road over its
entire length is not yet known.

Chapter 4

East Anglia

Buckinghamshire, Cambridgeshire (part of), Essex,
Hertfordshire, Norfolk and Suffolk

In about AD 10 Cunobelinus, better known as the Cymbeline
of Shakespeare's play, and a king of the Catuvellauni, became
king also of the Trinovantes, the tribe occupying the area of
modern Essex. Very rapidly his influence extended over the
whole of SE England, and his new capital at Colchester
replaced Verlamion (St Albans) as the most important centre
of pre-Roman Britain. It was defended by a complicated series
of dykes still traceable to the west and south of the modern
town. It is not surprising, therefore, that the Roman invading
army under Aulus Plautius in AD 43, three years or so after
Cunobelinus' death, made first for Colchester after crossing

the Thames. Before advancing on the capital, however, Plautius sent for Claudius, and the triumph over Camulodunon, 'the fortress of Camulos' (a war god), was duly completed in the company of the emperor – along, it seems, with elephants, to provide both intimidation and an appropriate level of pomp.

The first Roman occupation of **Colchester**** (TL 995253) took the form of a legionary fortress for the Twentieth Legion situated under the western half of the later town. A military origin, first suggested in 1965, was confirmed in the excavations of 1971–5, when part of the eastern legionary defences, as well as fragments of barrack-blocks, were found under a shopping precinct (Lion Walk) on the south side of High Street. At the same time, the legionary ditch was identified on the west side near the Balkerne Gate, and additional excavations in the 1980s added further details of the legionary fortress. Then, in AD 49–50, when the military moved on, the first town was founded at CAMVLODVNVM. It was, as the historian Tacitus tells us, 'a strong *colonia* of ex-soldiers established on conquered territory, to provide a protection against rebels and a centre for instructing the provincials in the procedures of the law'. Its official title was COLONIA CLAVDIA VICTRICENSIS, 'the Claudian colony of Victory' (in commemoration of the military triumph of AD 43). The town did not spring up overnight. Excavations in the 1970s and 1980s have shown that, as perhaps at Gloucester (p. 171), the earliest settlers were initially housed in the legionary barracks, which were hardly altered to accommodate them. Meanwhile the authorities, no doubt assisted by army specialists and craftsmen imported from the Continent, busied themselves with erecting public buildings, mostly a little to the east of the former fortress.

Chief among these, from 54/5 onwards, was a vast classical-style temple raised on a lofty *podium* and approached by a flight of steps. Dedicated to the deified Emperor Claudius, who had died in 54, it was viewed, in British eyes, as the *arx aeternae dominationis*, 'the stronghold of everlasting domination', according to Tacitus. The presence of this symbol and the alleged rapacity of the imperial financial administrator, Catus Decianus, were enough to spark off the famous revolt of the Iceni under their queen Boudica

(Boadicea) in AD 60 or 61. The portents in Colchester immediately before the revolt are described by Tacitus in graphic detail: 'the statue of Victory fell down, its back turned as though in retreat from the enemy. Women roused into frenzy chanted of approaching destruction, and declared that the cries of barbarians had been heard in the council-chamber, that the theatre had re-echoed with shrieks, that a reflection of the *colonia*, overthrown, had been seen in the Thames estuary. The sea appeared blood-red, and spectres of human corpses were left behind as the tide went out.' The passage incidentally provides evidence that the town of Colchester was already equipped, in the first dozen years of its existence, with a forum (where the council-chamber or *curia* was normally situated) and a theatre (perhaps built of timber rather than stone).

When the revolt broke, there was no hope for the Roman inhabitants of the *colonia*. Tacitus reports that the settlement was undefended: how the colonists must have rued the slighting of the legionary defences, a demolition demonstrated by excavations in 1972–3. 'In the attack,' says Tacitus, 'everything was broken down and burnt. The temple where the soldiers had congregated was besieged for two days and then sacked.' Archaeological evidence of Boudica's attack has been encountered mostly in the area west of the Temple of Claudius, suggesting that the earliest *colonia* was indeed confined to this western half of the later town, on the site of the earlier fortress. The evidence for the Boudican sack is generally a thick layer of ash and burnt wattle-and-daub; blackened *terra sigillata* pottery, stacked together waiting to be sold, which was found in 1927 together with molten fragments of the glass vessels which had fused into them, provides an even more vivid illustration of Tacitus' words. The Boudican fire also uniquely preserved part of a bed or couch, the weave of its cloth mattress still visible in carbonized form.

Recovery after the Boudican fire seems initially to have been slow, but by the beginning of the second century occupation had spread into most of the 108 acres (45 ha) enclosed by the town walls. Excavations have shown that the latter were built remarkably early, perhaps soon after the Boudican fire and certainly by *c.* AD 80, and were at first

freestanding; the bank behind was only added *c.* 175/200.
Colchester was thus provided with city walls at least a century
and a half earlier than most other Romano-British towns, a
proud witness of its prestigious rank as *colonia* (cf. also
Gloucester, p. 171, and Lincoln, p. 265).

The best starting-place for a tour of Roman Colchester is
the Museum (1 on Fig. 44), situated in the castle which the
Normans built on the foundations of the Temple of Claudius
(Monday–Saturday, 1000–1700; Sunday [March–November
only], 1100–1700). This is without a doubt the finest collection
of Roman artefacts, and the best presented, to be seen in any
museum in the country outside London. The displays are
attractive and informative (there is none of the 'dumbing
down' which has afflicted some museums elsewhere in recent
years), and the artefacts impress both by their quality and by
their sheer quantity. So many splendid objects are on display
that only a few can be singled out here for brief comment.

On the right of the entrance-passageway is the Beryfield
pavement of *c.* AD 180/200, the best-preserved of the more
than 50 mosaics so far known from the Roman town. Inside
the main hall, on the left, are fragments of a fourth-century
mosaic from Lion Walk, followed by showcases with three of
the Museum's star attractions: the figure of Mercury from the
Gosbecks sanctuary, one of the finest bronze statuettes to
survive from Roman Britain, assumed (from its quality) to
have been imported from the Continent about AD 200; the
Colchester Sphinx, a powerful funerary monument vigorously
rendered in British stone, with a man's head (no doubt
representing the deceased) between her paws; and the
Colchester Vase, produced by a local workshop about AD 200,
depicting a combat between Memnon and Valentinus, as the
inscription round the top informs us. They belonged to the
Thirtieth Legion stationed at Vetera near Xanten on the Rhine,
and presumably therefore this vase was made in Colchester to
commemorate a particularly famous group of visiting
gladiators, perhaps a rare event for the town. The vase also
provides a reminder that Colchester's amphitheatre awaits
discovery, presumably (as with most other Romano-British
amphitheatres) outside the walls.

The fine second-century geometric mosaic from North Hill
is followed by the prehistory section, at the end of which are

44   Colchester, location map

several cases illustrating the contacts before AD 43 between
the late Iron Age aristocracy and the Roman world on the
Continent. Watch out, for example, on your left (all in one
case), for a wine flagon in a white fabric from a grave in
Lexden of *c.* AD 5/40, imported from NE Gaul; a red arretine
dish, rare in Britain, from Sheepen, which was imported from
north Italy; and also a local imitation of *c.* AD 25 of the same
shape and style in a (comparatively) unattractive brown fabric.
Next to it are displayed two Dressel 1 wine amphorae, which
brought wine from Italy to SE Britain in the second half of the
first century BC. At the foot of the stairs are finds from the
Lexden *tumulus* in Fitzwalter Road (p. 224), once thought to
be the resting place of Cunobelinus himself. Re-examination
of the finds, however, has shown that its date is 40 years too
early for Cunobelinus, the tomb having been sealed *c.* 10 BC.
A suggested new candidate is Addedomaros, a shadowy king
of the Trinovantes of about the right date, but we do not really
know – beyond that the grave is clearly that of a wealthy
leading aristocrat. Note in particular the fragments of Dressel
1 wine amphorae, and other imports from the Continent, such
as the bronze figurines, and the silver medallion imitating a
coin of Augustus.

Upstairs starts understandably with the Claudian invasion,
with copies of the head of Claudius now in the British
Museum (p. 644) and of a gold coin showing his arch in
Rome which commemorated the British triumph. The case
with military finds includes a dagger with decorated scabbard-
plate from North Hill, found in 1965 and the first real clue
that the early legionary fortress lay buried below the later
town. Also in this case is the fragment of the tombstone of an
auxiliary from the First Cohort of Vardulli from Spain, from
Balkerne Hill. This is of interest not only for providing
evidence (as does the Longinus tombstone mentioned below)
that a mixed garrison of both legionaries and some auxiliaries
was likely to have manned the fortress, but also because it is
of Purbeck marble: it implies that these important quarries on
the south coast of England were already being exploited
before AD 49 (when the military presence at Colchester was
withdrawn and the civilian *colonia* established).

The pre-Boudican life of the fledgling *colonia* is illustrated
in the next section. Moulds demonstrate the production of

lamps at Colchester in these early days, and in a facing case is
an astonishing group of charming objects from a grave of
c. AD 55/60, found in 1866, including terracottas in the shape
of a boar, a bull and other animals, and caricatures of
reclining and reciting figures. Most of these were imported
from Gaul, as were also the lead-glazed flagons and the very
thin ('eggshell') ware from Lyon. This was a high-status
burial, possibly of a wealthy legionary: well suited to a
military context, for example, are the lamps and the lamp
filler. The latter was erroneously taken in the past to be a
'feeding bottle', and the figurines as 'toys', leading to the
misinterpretation of this burial as that of a child. The next
case illustrates the dramatic results of Boudica's violent
sacking of Colchester in AD 60/1, especially the molten glass,
burnt *terra sigillata* pottery, and pieces of scorched daub.
Fragments of stone building veneers in this case hint at the
sophistication of some buildings in Colchester from the very
beginning of the city's life: there is even a fragment (no. 326)
of prized *giallo antico* ('ancient yellow') marble, all the way
from Chemtou in Tunisia.

Next, magnificently displayed, are two famous military
tombstones from the early days of Roman Colchester. One is
that of Marcus Favonius Facilis, centurion of the Twentieth
Legion, with a superb full-length portrait of the dead man
(Fig. 45). Great attention has been paid to the details of his
uniform and weapons, including his sword, his dagger and the
vine-staff, the symbol of his rank, which he holds in his right
hand. The other tombstone depicts an auxiliary cavalryman
from Sardi(ca), modern Sofia in Bulgaria, wearing a metal-
plated jerkin; he was enrolled in the First Thracian troop (*ala*).
He is called Longinus Sdapeze (a neat conjunction of both a
native and a Roman name), and he was son of Matycus. The
fact that both tombstones were found broken deliberately in
two, and the relatively unworn state of the sculptures
indicating that they had not long been exposed to the
inclement British climate, make it reasonable to assume that
both were damaged by Boudica's followers in the sack of
Colchester in AD 60/1. Earlier claims that Sdapeze's portrait
had been vandalized by them, however, can now be
discounted: re-excavation of the tombstone's find-spot in 1996
found the sculptured face, which had splintered off when the

45   *Colchester, tombstone of the centurion Marcus Favonius Facilis*

grave marker fell, and it has now been restored to its rightful place on the tombstone.

To the left of these memorials is a much larger fragment of wattle-and daub-wall (from Lion Walk), a further dramatic witness to the destruction of AD 60/1: note how the impressions of the wattle have been left in the burnt daub. A striking model of the Temple of Claudius comes next. Certainly some details of it (such as the text of the inscription) are conjectural, but Roman temples of classical type, rare in Britain, are sufficiently stereotyped to allow a high degree of confidence in its reconstruction. In the case below it are displayed fragments of the precious imported coloured marbles that are known to have been used in the temple or its precinct, including red porphyry from Egypt and a further piece of yellow Chemtou marble.

An attractive mosaic found in 1979 in an extramural house just outside the NW corner of the walls can be seen from here. The central panel depicts wrestling cupids, and there are sea-horses in the surrounding lunates. The floor, datable to c. 150/75, is one of the earliest products of a workshop later responsible for the mosaics from North Hill and Beryfield already noted, as well as for other floors at both Colchester and Verulamium. The sea-horses on both the cupid and the (later) Beryfield floors, for example, share details which suggest that they derive from a common pattern. Daily life is imaginatively reconstructed in the next section with full-scale mock-ups of a kitchen and a living-room, together with cases of glassware, jewellery, etc. Turning left from the model of Duncan's Gate (p. 221), you come next to a display on the countryside: note in particular the lead container and the glass cinerary urn found in the burial-chamber under the Mersea *tumulus* (p. 255). The penultimate section contains a very fine collection of Roman pottery, both wares produced locally and the full range of imports reaching Colchester – a model display of its kind. Finally comes a fascinating section illustrating burial customs, where long-known finds such as the face-pot burial have been joined by more recent discoveries, including those from the Butt Road cemetery (see p. 222). The skeletal remains on display here each have their own personal story to tell: one man had severe arthritis in a hip joint, another had distorted bones in his left foot, while the skull of an unfortunate woman had been smashed on the top by a hammer blow.

When you have finished looking at the Museum, it is worth joining one of the guided tours which at set hours take you down into the vaults forming part of the substructures of the massive Temple of Claudius. Construction work began probably in 54 or 55, soon after Claudius' death and deification (rather than before), and was still unfinished at the time of the Boudican rebellion; but the concrete of the substructures must surely belong to the initial building period of *c.* AD 55/60. The structure is therefore not only one of the more impressive monuments of Roman Britain; it is also the earliest substantial stone building of Roman date visible in this country (although the fragments of first-phase stonework still preserved at the Balkerne Gate [p. 220] are likely to be earlier still, by half a dozen years). The superstructure was entirely swept away by the Normans when they built their castle at the end of the eleventh century. The vaults still visible were designed purely to support the weight of the temple above; there was no access to them in Roman times, and they were filled with rammed sand until the seventeenth century, although the Roman date of the work was not recognized until 1919. The plan consists of two parallel vaults with one cross-wall off-centre.

A few other Roman remnants can be traced in the castle grounds. On leaving the Museum turn right and follow the path running alongside the castle wall, which here, as elsewhere, displays plentiful re-use of Roman tile. Near the NW corner, the path slopes down and, at the point where the flowerbeds end, cuts through a rubble wall capped by modern slabs (2 on Fig. 44). This wall is a miserable surviving fragment of the north boundary wall of the temple's precinct, which was added as part of a formal monumentalization of the sanctuary *c.* AD 80/100. Excavation in 1950 near its NE corner, under the impressive Norman earth rampart away to your right, found the Roman precinct wall still standing an astonishing 3 m (10 ft) high – it had been deliberately left unrobbed by the Norman castle-builders to lend stability to their new earth bank. Nearby, over in the shrubbery to the left of the path, near the fence, a section of Roman drain is preserved behind railings. West of the bandstand, a little further on, are some red tessellated pavements (3) belonging to a town-house excavated by a young Sir Mortimer Wheeler in 1920, still in their original position (the foundation walls separating them are protected by modern slabs). Finally, two further portions of Roman drain are visible with difficulty (much overgrown with ferns in 2000) through grilles in the grass east of the castle, near the children's playground (4).

Now leave Upper Castle Park near the small gate on its west side (near the fragment of precinct wall just noted) and go through the short alley opposite you into Maidenbugh Street. Immediately on your left here is St Helen's Chapel, the north wall of which rests on Roman foundations, visible projecting at its base. This formed part of the NE corner of the Roman theatre (5), a building of classical D-shaped plan, about 70 m (230 ft) in diameter. Turn left here and you come almost immediately to the massive curved wall and part of the adjacent passage's mortar floor, displayed inside a modern building on your right: it is clearly visible through windows (and also lit at night), together with explanatory plans and a reconstruction-painting of the theatre in its heyday. For those keen to have a closer look, the key to gain entry can be obtained from the Colchester and Essex Museum, provided that prior booking has been made in advance (telephone 01206–282928). In the street between here and the chapel the outer wall of the theatre, first exposed in 1891 (when its significance was not understood) and again in 1984, has been marked out with differently coloured bricks. Dating evidence for the theatre recovered by excavation was negligible, but the visible walls probably belong to a second-century rebuilding. Whether the early theatre mentioned by Tacitus, completed before the Boudican rebellion in AD 60/1, stood on the same site (as certainly seems logical), rather than elsewhere, cannot at present be verified.

Nothing else of Roman Colchester is visible within the walls, but the latter survive for much of their original course; a walk round them takes approximately an hour and a half. The Roman work is at its best on the west side of the town near the mighty Balkerne Gate (6). This is reached from the Museum by turning right along High Street and going down the narrow lane at the end (Balkerne Passage) by the Waggon and Horses. In the grounds of Mercury Theatre beyond the water-tower, the (secondary) earth bank behind the Roman wall is clearly visible, and next to it the ruins of the gateway, though much mutilated, are still impressive. Its position, wholly in front of the line of the adjacent wall, and its massive size (32.65 m or 107 ft wide), set it quite apart from other city gates in Roman Britain, an anomaly which requires explanation. Careful examination of the structure revealed that a freestanding monumental arch with two passageways was first erected here, perhaps *c.* AD 50, and that this was incorporated into the stone defences when these were built a few years later (*c.* AD 65/80) by the addition of narrower pedestrian passageways and D-shaped guard-chambers on either side. The guard-chamber on the south side and the passageway (with its original pitched-brick vaulting still mostly intact and unrestored) are well preserved, but the middle portion of the gate is almost entirely invisible. The footings of the central pier, however, and the positions of the north carriageway and the north pedestrian passage, are clearly marked in the display area on the outer side of the gateway. The earliest masonry, belonging to the freestanding arch, is represented by the small fragment of walling (four courses) at the right-hand end of the display area, and the nine courses of similar neat blocks further to the left; these contrast strikingly with the later masonry abutting it, which makes substantial use of brickwork absent in the earliest walling. Also visible is a rough wall which blocked the entire gateway, probably in the Saxon period, thus causing the permanent shift southward of the main road to London which had until then passed through the Balkerne Gate.

To the left of the pub, the north gate-tower still stands 6 m (20 ft) high, and from here the Roman wall can be followed down Balkerne Hill. Only rubble-core is visible, but immediately left of the Balkerne Gate is a fine stretch standing at nearly its full original height, with prominent use of brick bonding-courses. Nowhere else at Colchester does pure Roman work stand to such a height. Further on, however, part of the wall down to the foot of Balkerne Hill has a modern protective facing to the Roman core, although after the gap another well preserved section of Roman work is visible.

From the foot of Balkerne Hill to the traffic-lights the wall is largely repatched with later material, but the tile bonding-

courses which occasionally appear make it easy to spot the
little Roman work that still remains visible here. Cross
straight over at the traffic-lights and walk along St Peter's
Street, where the wall is not visible. At the end of this is the
entrance to Castle Park: the path following the wall divides
the park into two and is accessible even when the rest of the
park is closed. Again here the original Roman core, first
exposed in the nineteenth century, has been obscured by
modern stonework designed to protect the Roman rubble.
After a while you come to the railed-in enclosure containing
the well preserved remains of Duncan's Gate (7), named after
its discoverer in 1853 (plans being discussed in 2000 to 'open'
the gate once more to pedestrians after 1,500 years may lead
to the removal of the railings). It consists of a single
passageway set back a little from the line of the wall, which
turns in to meet it. You can appreciate here from the inturned
wall footings near the railings how much of the front of the
Roman defences has been removed. The fallen masonry here
is from the superstructure of the gate; it includes part of the
arches of two windows. The wall can now be followed round
the NE corner and for much of the north part of the east side.
Towards the end of this stretch the Roman core, though at
present (2000) very overgrown, survives unaffected by later
protective patching.

Now leave the park and follow the alley towards East Hill.
Turn right, cross the road and then go immediately left down
the alley bordering the church. Note the arched brick drain (8)
high up at the beginning of this portion of the Roman wall.
Bonding-courses are also clearly visible at the far end of this
stretch (which is on private property), but sight of it is denied
if the high wooden gate is closed. The site of the east gate,
demolished in 1675, lies near here under East Hill. Retrace
your steps down this and turn right into Priory Street. The
wall again becomes visible rounding the SE corner and
running along the car-park on the south side. After a breach
filled with seventeenth-century brickwork, the Roman tile
bonding-courses are again visible near the top of the wall. The
towers here are all medieval, though incorporating Roman
materials. The tower near the end of the car-park, for
example, uses Roman tiles in coursed rows at its top; a
blocked opening, its archway turned entirely in Roman brick,

is also visible here. There is no evidence at present that the Roman wall had external towers, but it had the usual internal turrets at intervals, some of which have been excavated.

On the left at the end of Priory Street is the eleventh-century St Botolph's Priory, built largely of Roman stones and tiles [AM; A]. Cross now into Vineyard Street, where the wall is again visible, much mutilated, first at the back of an alley, and then along another car-park. Another well preserved Roman arched drain (9) can be seen issuing from the wall at ground-level, 30 m (33 yds) east of the staircase at the west end of the car-park. Several putlog holes, usually with a tile bonding-course above or below the opening (or both), are visible in this stretch, especially at the far end. After the recently made breach for a service-road (supplying the Lion Walk complex), the wall reappears for a short stretch in another car-park. From here a path leads you immediately into St John Street. Some 150 m (165 yds) along this, just past the steps called St John's Wynd, is the goods entrance for another shopping precinct, Culver Square. A stretch of the north (i.e. inner) face of the Roman wall has been rebuilt here (in 1987) on the right of the entrance tunnel, at right-angles to its original alignment (10). The actual core of the wall *in situ* can be seen on the right of the tunnel entrance, high up (visible through the grilles of the doors if the latter are closed), and the original thickness of the Roman defences is marked out in white on the modern wall both here and on the other side of the service road.

From here turn left at the traffic-lights (Headgate) and cross the dual carriageway, making for the police station in front of you. In the grass at its west end, facing the roundabout, is a remarkable Roman extramural monument, not well preserved but of exceptional interest (Fig. 46). In the 1970s and 1980s, in advance of the building of the police station, excavations revealed a substantial part of the late Roman inhumation cemetery of Butt Road, over 700 burials in all. The fourth-century burials were aligned east-west in keeping with Christian practice (third-century inhumations by contrast were aligned north-south): bodies were mostly laid in wooden coffins or occasionally in ones of lead. Some had accompanying pottery, glass or jewellery, but most lacked grave goods – again as appropriate in a Christian context,

irrespective of the wealth of the deceased. In this cemetery
a masonry structure 25 m (82 ft) long was constructed
c. AD 320/40, with an eastern apse possibly added later,
c. AD 380 (11). Two pits at the east end (one found with two
skeletons) looked like the resting places of influential persons.
Wooden posts show that the interior was divided up into a
'nave' and two aisles with an extensive narthex (without the
posts) beyond; excavation apparently showed that in a
secondary period (c. 400?), the nave and aisles were extended
to fill the whole building (although it might be argued that
structurally these would have been desirable here too from the
start). No specific evidence of ritual use was found (although
bones of chicken and pig suggest that memorial feasts or
'wakes' were held here), but there seems no reason to doubt
that this structure was a Roman funerary church; an
alternative view, that it was a funerary banqueting-hall
without Christian associations, does not convince.
Consolidated in 1989, the church is built of neatly coursed
masonry with brick bonding-courses, strengthened by the

46   Colchester, Roman town, Romano-Christian church (Butt Road)

additional use of brickwork at the SE corner, where the
masonry stands ten courses high.

Now cross to the other side of the roundabout and resume
your tour of the Roman walls on Balkerne Hill, for the final
part of the circuit leading back to the Balkerne Gate. Here is
another magnificently preserved stretch, some 4.50 m (15 ft)
high. Broken at first by the stairs for the church, and then
marred by patching, the walls become very fine nearer the
Balkerne Gate. Four rows of quadruple tile bonding-courses
are clearly visible, and even (unusually at Colchester) many of
the facing-stones in neatly coursed rows. Note how the
brickwork now stands proud of the rows of limestone facing-
stones between: the latter have suffered from exposure to the
British climate over 1,900 years, whereas Roman kiln-fired
brick has proved resilient.

Four other monuments to the west and SW of the modern
town may be mentioned in conclusion, one pre-Roman, one
probably pre-Roman and two Roman. From the Maldon Road
roundabout in front of the Roman church, take the A1124
signposted Lexden (there was, however, no sign on the
roundabout itself in 2000: it is the turning after the Maldon
Road). After $1\frac{1}{4}$ miles (2 km) (opposite a pillar box), turn left
down Fitzwalter Road. The low mound behind the hedge
beyond no. 30 was excavated in 1924 and found to contain an
exceptionally rich group of grave goods, datable to the end of
the first century BC and now displayed in Colchester Museum.
Clearly a native royal prince was buried here, but an earlier
theory that it may have been Cunobelinus himself has been
ruled out on grounds of chronology by a fresh study of the
material, and the suggested occupant of the tomb is now
Addedomaros, a little known king of the Trinovantes (see
further p. 214).

More impressive structurally, but lacking any speculative
historical connection, is another *tumulus* a short distance
away. Continue along the A1124 to the village of Lexden, and
turn left along Church Lane. Then take the first turning on the
right (Shakespeare Road) and right again down Thomson
Avenue, then first left (Masefield Drive) and right
(Wordsworth Road). The burial-mound lies in the back garden
of the first house on the left beyond Marlowe Way, but is now
very overgrown. Partial exploration in 1910 yielded nothing

of any note, but the mound had been recorded as long ago as 1759 by the antiquary William Stukeley, who thought it was Cunobelinus' grave. Its Roman date, however, is suggested by the steep profile and conical shape. Most such mounds in Britain date to the second half of the first century or to the second century AD (cf. pp. 255–7).

Return now once more to the A1124, go straight over at the roundabout, and turn left at the traffic-lights along Straight Road (signposted Mersea). After 250 m (275 yds), on the left-hand side of the road, is the so-called Lexden Triple Dyke [AM; A], originally some 1,500 m (1,640 yds) long. Excavation in 1961 apparently showed this to be of Roman date, but if so its purpose is unclear; it has been suggested that it was intended to provide partial temporary cover for the invading army before it built its fortress. But since a triple bank is unheard of in a Roman military context, and it continues the line of a known pre-Roman defence, it seems more much likely that it was thrown up immediately before Roman armies reached Colchester, and that it forms part of the complicated defences of the British settlement.

Continue down Straight Road to the first of the two roundabouts at the end and turn right (signposted Maldon, B1022). Just beyond the next roundabout, where you should continue taking the Maldon road, leave your car in the small car-park on the left: this marks the entrance to Gosbecks Archaeological Park, opened in 1995. Where the path ahead of you forks, take the right-hand one heading for an upstanding sign-board which you can see 250 m (275 yds) ahead of you. This leads you to the site of a Romano-British temple precinct, known largely from aerial photography (supplemented by trial excavation), which has been marked out here on the grass by weed-killer (plans to introduce more permanent indicator lines are under discussion in 2000). You first come to three parallel walls belonging to the roofed portico bordering the precinct (notice its impressive overall width): the outer wall would have been solid, the middle one a base for a colonnade supporting the roof, and the innermost a colonnade open to the piazza beyond. The square precinct measures 1,000 Roman feet (305 m) per side. From the sign-board walk diagonally across the portico towards the centre of the precinct and you come across almost at once two single

parallel lines 7.5 m (24 ft) apart. This marks the most unusual
feature of a broad ditch (and a substantial 3.35 m [11 ft] deep)
inside the porticoes built in the classical architectural idiom,
and in the reconstruction-painting displayed on the sign-board
they are shown as co-existing. The evidence for this is that
pottery found in the ditch, believed to be of the later second
century, seemed to indicate that the ditch remained open even
after the building of the porticoes. That however would mean
that the centre of the piazza would have been readily
accessible only at the entrance to the whole precinct (where
there is a break in the ditch), and it is surely more logical to
think that the ditch marked the boundary of the original pre-
Roman sanctuary and that it was filled in when the 'Roman'
version of the sanctuary was constructed *c*. AD 100.

Now make for the solitary tree ahead of you, noting on
your left the precinct entrance and the causeway across the
inner ditch. The temple, of usual Romano-Celtic type (in
ground-plan, a square within a square), is marked out just
inside and to the left of the ditch; interestingly, for reasons
that we do not know, it is not placed centrally within the
sanctuary. Since Gosbecks was the focus of cult in the late
pre-Roman Iron Age, and continuity of worship into the
Roman period is therefore certain, it would be intriguing to
know if there was a timber forerunner of the Romano-Celtic
temple below the stone one of *c*. AD 100. A trench across it in
1995 did not locate one, but it did demonstrate that the *cella*
was surrounded by freestanding columns in the classical
manner, rather than by dwarf columns on low walls (or indeed
by solid walls) attested in such temples elsewhere. The trench
also showed that the temple was decorated with Purbeck
marble wall veneer and with black and white floor mosaics
(only loose tesserae however survived), The existence of a
pre-Roman timber prototype for the 'Romano-Celtic' temple
has been considered conjectural, but it best explains the
origins and layout of the stone versions of the type, which are
exclusively of Roman date. Indeed, with the possible
exception of an example below Heathrow Airport's first
runway, no other Iron Age timber forerunners of the square-
within-a-square ground-plan are known in Britain, although
timber examples recently excavated in France and Germany

are beginning at last to confirm the origin of this temple type in the later Iron Age.

Now from the temple-site make in the direction of the two trees to the left of the solitary one. Leaving them to your right and following the path, you come after 200 m (220 yds) to the site of the Roman theatre, the largest known example in Britain (its diameter is 82 m [270 ft]), the plan of which has also been marked out on the ground. The exterior wall had four curious funnel-shaped projections, apparently staircases providing access to the upper tiers of seats. Especially from the far side you can still make out the low semicircular mound, flattened by 1,500 years of ploughing, which constituted the turf bank for supporting the seating: but as recently as 1950 it was reported as surviving to a height of 1.80 m (6 ft). The theatre's estimated capacity is at least 4,000. Of classical semicircular shape (as at Canterbury [p. 61], but in contrast to that at St Albans, p. 235), the building was erected about the same time as the temple (*c.* AD 100). It was originally constructed entirely in wood, and was then rebuilt *c.* AD 150 with timber seating resting on banks of cut turves, which were contained by an outer revetment wall of stone. This building, too, had a comparatively short life: for reasons unknown it was demolished 50 years or so later.

Presumably the theatre was used to stage religious enactments at the time of the principal holy festivals, although these may have been quite simple in view of the absence of an elaborate stage building. Gosbecks is therefore an example of a rural sanctuary with both temple and theatre, of a type common in Gaul but otherwise unique in Britain (another at Frilford in Oxfordshire, however, not now visible, was furnished with an amphitheatre rather than a theatre). An alternative hypothesis for the Gosbecks theatre, that it served principally as a meeting place for tribal gatherings, is less convincing. It has also been suggested, on minimal evidence, that the great Catuvellaunian king, Cunobelinus, lived in a hut enclosure adjacent to the Gosbecks sanctuary, and that its site was revered long after his death. Indeed it has also been proposed that the Romano-Celtic temple marked the site of his burial, and was subsequently the focus of a hero-cult in his honour (as at Folly Lane, St Albans: p. 229).

However that may be, the 'draw' of the Gosbecks sanctuary is indicated by the location of a high-class burial-ground a little to the west (Stanway), which in the 1990s produced some remarkable grave goods dating to around the time of the Roman conquest. The graves were probably those of leading local British aristocrats who were being buried here up to about AD 60. The most extraordinary was the so-called 'doctor's grave', complete with a small set of surgical instruments, divining (?) rods, and even a game board with the pieces set out as if in play. Still under conservation at the time of writing, these fascinating finds will eventually be displayed in the Castle Museum in Colchester.

Another Roman town which, like Colchester, was both founded near a pre-Roman settlement and sacked by Boudica, is one of the outstanding sites of Roman Britain. It is VERVLAMIVM near the modern **St Albans**** (TL 136073), which is still largely free from later buildings. Of the 203 acres (82 ha) enclosed within the walls (making it the third largest town in Roman Britain, after London and Cirencester), about 10 per cent has been excavated, mainly in the campaigns of Sir Mortimer Wheeler between 1930 and 1934 and of Professor Sheppard Frere between 1955 and 1961. More recent excavation has concentrated on burials outside the walls. Thanks to all this activity a very great deal is known about the development, prosperity and decline of this great Roman town.

Roman Verulamium takes its name from the late Iron Age stronghold in Prae Wood, which lay to the west of the Roman town. Coins inscribed VERLAMIO, 'the settlement by the marsh', were issued under King Tasciovanus of the Catuvellauni tribe, the predecessor of the great Cunobelinus, and even when the latter shifted his capital to Colchester, the Prae Wood settlement continued to flourish and to mint coins. A sizeable fragment of coin-mould can be seen in the Verulamium Museum. However there is some evidence to suggest that while Cunobelinus was intent on expansionist policies centred on Colchester – policies which ultimately attracted the attention of Rome and were one of the pretexts for the Claudian invasion – the western Catuvellauni were more pro-Roman in their sympathies. It is, for example, surprising that no early Roman forts are known in the whole of the region occupied by modern Hertfordshire, such as we would expect if this part of the tribe was hostile to Rome. Although a military post has been postulated in the area occupied by the village of St Michaels, guarding the crossing of the river Ver (it is the obvious choice for a fort site, at the point also where Watling Street makes a major change in alignment), no certain trace of it, despite extensive searching, has ever been found. This might suggest that the Hertfordshire area was left to its own devices as a 'client kingdom' (the status certainly accorded to the territory of Togidubnus of the Atrebates and Prasutagus of the Iceni), in which the local pro-Roman king would encourage his people to adopt also pro-Roman attitudes and the trappings of a Roman life-style.

Dramatic evidence in support of this hypothesis was discovered to the north of Verulamium in 1992, when excavation at Folly Lane (A on Fig. 47, but off map) discovered a man's cremated remains in an underground wooden chamber, a method of burial in accordance with Iron Age princely custom. He was accompanied by an astonishing range of exotic grave goods which had largely perished in the cremation fires, including silver-ware reduced to no more than pellets of molten metal. The associated pottery is of the early Roman period, and the burial can be dated to around AD 55. What is more, the site of the tomb was subsequently marked by a Romano-Celtic temple, presumably dedicated to a hero-cult in honour of the dead man. It is not impossible that the Folly Lane site marks the burial of the last monarch of the western Catuvellauni, a pro-Roman client king who fostered precociously Roman-style buildings in both town and country in the years immediately after AD 43. Unfortunately, although the name of Adminius has been suggested as the occupant of the Folly Lane tomb, we have no direct evidence for the identity of the deceased.

The first Roman town seems to have been laid out by AD 49 or 50: St Albans can therefore claim, with Colchester and London, to be one of the oldest towns in Britain. Verulamium was a *municipium*, according to Tacitus, i.e. a self-governing community, the chief magistrates of which were given the privilege of Roman citizenship after their year of office. Some of the streets and a row of rectangular timber-framed shops belonging to this first town have been found by excavation, as

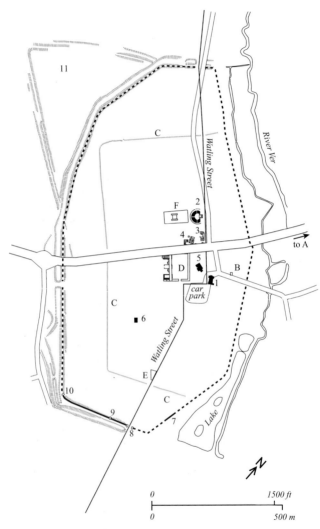

A-F *Roman structures no longer visible*
1-11 *Roman structures visible*

47 *St Albans (*Verulamium)*, location map*

well as part of the stone-built public baths, the earliest such example in Britain (B on Fig. 47); but Boudica and her followers saw to it in AD 60 or 61 that the entire settlement was razed to the ground.

In 1955 a first-century defence-circuit (a ditch, presumably accompanied by an earth bank: C) was located well inside the area later enclosed by the town walls, and it is likely that this delineated the *municipium* from immediately after the Boudican destruction. Recovery from this attack was, however, slow, and rebuilding on a large scale in the town was not in progress until the late 70s. The new forum and basilica (D) were dedicated in 79, during the governorship of Tacitus' father-in-law Agricola, whose name partly survives on a fragmentary inscription now in the Museum. By the beginning of the second century the town had overspilled the early defence-circuit, which had been filled in, and many of the public buildings had been erected in stone. New earth defences enclosing a vast area of nearly 500 acres (over 200 ha), the so-called 'Fosse' earthwork, may have been thrown up as early as the second quarter of the second century (11 on Fig. 47). This is earlier than elsewhere in Britain (except at the *coloniae*), and possibly a mark of the town's municipal status, just as the first-century rampart and ditch had been. It used to be considered an unfinished project, but the discovery of defensive ditches in the SE quarter of the town, predating the third-century defences there, suggests otherwise. The monumental and elaborate stone gateways at the SE and NW, one facing London and the other Chester, are probably contemporary with it.

The theatre (2 on Fig. 47) was also built in the first half of the second century, probably late in the reign of Hadrian (*c.* 135). Private dwellings remained in timber – although some were receiving elaborate wall-plaster and even, occasionally, figured mosaics – until another fire, probably accidental, destroyed the town in about AD 155. It does not seem to have greatly interrupted the prosperity of Verulamium, however, and town-houses were now built in stone for the first time, many of them floored with splendid mosaics: it is clear from finds here and at surrounding villa-sites that a school of mosaicists was operating in the town at this period. In the third century, monumental arches were erected on Watling Street to mark the limits of the Flavian town; then, probably *c.* AD 275 (although a date earlier in the third century has also been proposed), the visible stone defences with contemporary earth bank behind and internal turrets were erected to enclose a different area from that enclosed by the Fosse earthwork.

No mosaics and not many structural alterations can be attributed to the third century, but we need not assume from this that the town was in decline. A burst of renewed activity in both private and public building points to continued prosperity in many parts of the town in the fourth century, down at least to *c.* 380–90, although some houses and even public buildings (like the market) were already abandoned and disused. Private buildings continued to flourish even longer, and dramatic evidence for the continuation of organized life well after the legions had left Britain was found by Professor Frere. One house with mosaic and hypocaust cannot be earlier than *c.* AD 375, and it was in use long enough for a tessellated floor to be extensively patched and for its kitchen oven to be completely rebuilt. The house was then totally remodelled, presumably not before *c.* 400. Another house still occupied in the late fourth century was later demolished, and a substantial barn built on its site. Even when that was demolished, a wooden water-pipe with iron joints at 1.80 m (6 ft) intervals was laid, testifying to the remarkable survival of both constructional skills and civic discipline. In the absence of coinage, which ceased about 430, the date of this pipe-laying cannot be established, but it must have occurred well within the fifth century.

Roman Verulamium lies to the west of the modern town of St Albans, which grew up around the shrine of Alban. He was executed for his Christian beliefs, perhaps in AD 304 (although the precise date is unknown), and buried on the hill where the Abbey now stands. Excavations in 1982–4 and 1994–5 have confirmed the presence of a late Roman cemetery immediately south of the Abbey, but there was no sign of Alban's tomb when the area under the high altar was investigated in 1991. Unlike other deserted Roman town-sites in Britain, the reason at St Albans why the Roman town and its post-Roman successor occupy different sites is clear. The martyr's tomb was almost certainly marked by a shrine, later replaced by a succession of churches on or very near the site of the present Abbey; and naturally it was around this church that the Saxon and later town focused.

You should start your visit to the Roman town by seeing the Verulamium Museum (1 on Fig. 47), which is signposted from the A4147 (St Albans–Hemel Hempstead) (open daily throughout the year, Monday–Saturday, 1000–1730; Sunday, 1400–1730). This contains one of the finest Roman collections in the country, and the range and quality of the objects amply demonstrate the taste and elegance of the people of Verulamium. The Museum has, however, rather lost its way in recent years, with the sweeping aside of the old display and the presentation of a disappointing new one. Precise provenances for the objects are rarely given; dates (apart from in the first section) are few and far between; and the arrangement of having a central rotunda with galleries opening off it in various directions affords no clear 'path' through the Museum for the visitor. However, the unusual feature of having drawers below each showcase in which the reserve collection is kept and made available to all for inspection is a welcome feature retained from previous displays at this Museum.

In the first rotunda, note especially the case ('The last King of Verulamion') which presents some of the outstanding finds from the Folly Lane burial (see above), including fragments of Italian wine amphorae, chain-mail armour, the band from a wheel with silver and enamel inlay, and similarly decorated horse-harnesses. Another case has an iron chain probably for shackling slaves, and the clay mould for striking Iron Age coins, mentioned above. The presence of soldiers, perhaps to help in the building of the first town, is suggested by a helmet and some pieces of breastplate (*lorica segmentata*) in another case here. Pieces of burnt daub and burning on a samian bowl document the Boudican fire at Verulamium, but the evidence here is much less graphic than in the Colchester Museum (p. 215). In the last case in this section are iron collars from the water-pipe of *c.* 430 (p. 232) and part of a late mosaic (*c.* 380/400), which featured a bust of Bacchus at the centre.

The central rotunda of the Museum contains the fragmentary inscription from the forum-basilica complex, dated to AD 79, which was found in 1955. The suggested

restoration of the lost parts is not fanciful, as Roman
epigraphy follows strict conventions and the gaps can be
reconstructed from other texts with a reasonable degree of
confidence. One of the fragments contains part of the name of
Agricola, governor of Britain from 78 to 85 (or 77 to 84) and
immortalized in Tacitus' biography. Only three other
epigraphic records of his activity in Britain are known, all on
water-pipes at Chester. Also displayed here is a pair of
superb-quality bronze statuettes, probably both made in the
second century. The Mercury, complete with his usual
attributes (ram, tortoise and cockerel), comes from a cemetery
ditch on the SW side of the town; it was found in 1970. The
splendid Venus, with flowing drapery gathered round her hips,
was made perhaps in Gaul (there is an almost identical
example in Augst Museum, Switzerland), and was found in
1959 in a fourth-century cellar below one of the shops near
the theatre. For some reason, together with other bronze
vessels, it never reached the melting-pot for which it was
clearly destined.

From the central rotunda radiate other galleries, each with a
separate theme. In one to the right ('Rites and Recreation'),
note in particular the 'lamp-chimney' (of uncertain function)
from a temple excavated by Wheeler in a triangular precinct
on Watling Street (E on Fig. 47). The temple is claimed as
being dedicated to the eastern mother goddess Cybele, but that
identification rests solely on the burnt remains of pine cones
(*pinus pinea*) in the temple court. These have been taken to be
an Italian import and so somewhat exotic, but the discovery of
cones of *pinus pinea* still attached to their fragile branches in
a pit just outside the London amphitheatre (p. 613) has
demonstrated that the tree, introduced by the Romans from the
Mediterranean, must have been grown in Britain. In any case
pine cones need not have been burnt solely in honour of
Cybele, and a cult of this goddess in Roman Britain as early
as the Flavian period (when the temple was built) seems
precociously early. A further gallery, to the left of the central
rotunda ('Food and Farming'), contains another famous
Wheeler find, that of a tile with animal paw-print and, behind
it, a deeply embedded pebble – suggesting that the tile-maker
had aimed a stone at a dog wandering over his newly made
tiles, laid out to dry before firing.

At the far end of the Museum are three superb floor-mosaics against the wall, once well lit by natural daylight, but now rather dimly displayed; they are also (2000) completely unlabelled. The earliest and most unusual is the Scallop Shell mosaic, laid between AD 130 and 150, brilliantly designed and executed with subtle and pleasing use of colour. The two mosaics on either side belong to the later second century: one is entirely geometric, and the other depicts at the centre a bearded Oceanus with lobster claws sprouting from his head (an alternative view that these are horns, and the bust that of a woodland deity, does not convince). Earlier in date, but far less skilled, is the dolphin mosaic on the floor; it comes from a timber-framed house burnt down in the fire of *c.* 155.

Moving to the left into the adjacent gallery, you come to another extremely competent and pleasing mosaic laid in the late second century. The central panel depicts a powerfully drawn lion making off with the head and antlers of a stag; it may have been prefabricated in the master mosaicist's workshop, since otherwise it is hard to explain why the end of the lion's tail has been chopped off. Equally impressive are the reconstructed panels of painted wall-plaster and, in one instance, also ceiling-plaster. These finds, the best of which are in the British Museum (Fig. 142), have added enormously to our knowledge of Romano-British interior decor. A 'Daily Life' gallery follows, and finally 'Death and Burial'. In the latter, note especially the high-status third-century burial of a child, in a lead sarcophagus excavated outside the London Gate. The accompanying finds were extraordinary – not only a tunic embroidered in gold thread, but even a murex shell, unique in Britain, which was used to produce the purple dye so prized in the ancient world.

Turn right and then left on leaving the Museum, and a three-minute walk will bring you to the Roman theatre (2 on Fig. 47), the only completely visible example in Britain (daily, 1000–1700 [1000–1600 November–March]). Discovered in 1847 and excavated in 1934, it was built in the second quarter of the second century, before the fire of 155, on a site previously reserved for it, as no earlier structures were found beneath. The first building had only a tiny timber stage and the entertainment must have taken place mainly in the *orchestra*. This area was used as the dance floor in the ancient

Greek theatre (*orchester* means 'dancer' in Greek) and the
modern use of the term is therefore misleading. The nature of
the entertainment at this period is uncertain, but its close
association with a large temple to the south (F; buried)
suggests that the theatre was sometimes used in religious
ceremonies. At a later period in the second century the stage
area was rebuilt in stone. But the most important alteration
took place in the early fourth century when the theatre was
enlarged by the addition of a massive outer wall. The stage
building was repaired some time after AD 345, and the theatre
as a whole probably continued in use until the last quarter of
the century.

Passing the ticket-office and turning left in front of the
'dressing room', go up the steps to the mound which
surrounds the remains: this is the spoil-heap from the
excavations made into a convenient viewing platform, and
formed no part of the original design. You will see at once
that the theatre consisted of a stage and an *orchestra*; the latter
is encircled with earth banks, partially re-erected, which
carried timber seating. The stage displays three periods of
work: originally it was wooden, and the posts which
supported it have been replaced by modern timbers. At this
stage the seating-banks curved round even more than they do
now, making the building a hybrid 'theatre-amphitheatre'
type, of which many examples are known in Gaul: the ends of
the curving walls can be seen under the later stage area. Then,
before the end of the second century (Phase II), the stage was
rebuilt in stone on a more impressive scale and given a
back-drop of columns; one has been reconstructed in modern
materials, based on ancient fragments, to give some idea of
the height of the stage-building. Then, about AD 200, another
wall was added in front of the stage, forming a narrow slot
into which the curtain was lowered and raised (the reverse of
modern procedure). In Phase II, timber seats were built in part
of the *orchestra*; but in the early fourth-century rebuilding
they were removed, and the area of the *orchestra* was reduced
a little by the addition of a curved wall in front of the previous
one retaining the seating-banks. The banks would then have
been enlarged to take more seats, but the retaining-walls of
both periods are now visible. The *orchestra* was entered by
the three wide passageways which interrupt the seating-banks,

but these entrances would have originally been vaulted and the seats carried over them. Finally, there are the outer walls of the theatre, at the foot of the bank on which you are standing. The inner wall with buttresses was the outer wall when the theatre was first built in the second century. It is clearly visible in the reconstruction drawing (Fig. 48), which represents the building in its third-century state, after the addition of the curtain-slot c. 200, but before the major alterations of c. 300. In these latter, the buttresses of the original wall were demolished to floor-level and a massive new outer wall was built, forming a corridor round the whole of the back of the theatre, and increasing its capacity still further as more seats would have been built above it. A substantial pier in the middle of this corridor on the SW side clearly post-dates the demolition of the buttress here and may have been built to support a crack in the vault above. The path leads behind the stage and back to the ticket-office again,

48   St Albans (Verulamium), reconstruction-drawing of the theatre c. AD 200

passing the base of one pier of a triumphal arch, built over
Watling Street in the third century.

Between the theatre and the modern road some of the
buildings excavated in 1957–60 remain exposed. On the left,
marked out in kerb-stones, is the plan of some timber-framed
shops belonging to the original foundation of *c*. AD 50,
destroyed by Boudica ten years or so later (3 on Fig. 47). This
is the earliest ground-plan of a Roman building to be seen in
Britain. The stark regularity of the plan and the timber-framed
construction were far in advance of anything Britain had
previously known, and it is likely that military construction-
experts supervised the laying-out of the earliest town. The
shops were separated from Watling Street, now under
Gorhambury Drive, by a covered pavement-walk. This is not
visible, as it lies buried beneath the flint wall of *c*. 300 (visible
in the verge), which belongs to the last series of shops on the
site. The shops themselves consist of a working-area in front
and living-quarters (the part nearer you) behind. The labels
here give the various trades of the occupants as suggested by
finds from the excavations. After the destruction of AD 60, the
area lay idle until redevelopment *c*. 75, but constant use until
the fire of 155 entailed the rebuilding of the shops on four
occasions in that period, resulting in a build-up of layers. This
can be seen by comparing the left-hand part of this site, which
represents the timber shops erected after 155, with the level of
the pre-Boudican building, about 1.05 m (3 ft 6 in) below.

A little further on, to the right of the path, are the
foundations of part of a town-house built in stone after the fire
of 155 (4). An earlier timber house, which yielded the dolphin
mosaic and the imitation-marble wall-plaster (both in the
Museum), was found below. The only features of note in the
visible remains are the tubes in one room belonging to an
unusual form of hypocaust, and the apse of a shrine, the rest
of which lies under the road. The apse was presumably
intended for a statue and the side-niche for a lamp, but the
shrine does not appear to have been finished and it was used
as a cellar until the late fourth century.

Now retrace your steps to the Museum and go into the
car-park beyond. Laid out in the pavement in the front of
the Museum entrance are some of the offices belonging to the
basilica (5), most of which lies under St Michael's church; the

forum lay beyond, in the area of the vicarage (D). From the car-park follow the signs across the grass to the 'Hypocaust' (6; same hours as the museum). Here the *tepidarium* of the bath-suite of a Roman town-house of the late second century is preserved inside a 1930s structure, but this cover-building is due (2001) to be replaced by a new one in the next year or two. Part of the floor is missing, which conveniently reveals the hypocaust beneath; the brick stoke-hole arch is perfectly preserved. The geometric mosaic consists of four rows of four motifs arranged in pairs. Stand on the long side of the room and note the third (horizontal) row away from you. The first and third panels, although identical in design, look different because they have been set on a different orientation: this was clearly due to a fault in the laying, and probably suggests that the individual panels were manufactured elsewhere and merely assembled here by less competent craftsmen. The floor of the adjacent room with a tendril pattern was laid later (in the late third century). Excavation photographs on the wall show the winged corridor house to which this bath-suite belonged; the Oceanus mosaic in the Museum came from a room in this house.

Bear right on leaving the cover-building, making in the direction of the abbey. Soon you will come to the railed-in remains of a fragment of town wall (Fig. 49; 7 on Fig. 47). The square block with the rectangular cutting built into the north face of the wall is not Roman but belongs to a medieval repair, probably because this part of the wall served a secondary purpose at that time which has ensured its ultimate preservation. Turn right and follow the line of the defences under the grass as far as the massive London gate, the plan of which has been marked out (8). It consists of two passageways for vehicles and two for pedestrians, with flanking towers on either side. The date of this gateway and the defences as a whole has been discussed above (pp. 231–2). From here stretches a long section of the stone wall, with the bank behind it, and the formidable ditch, here 20 m wide (65 ft) and 6 m (20 ft) deep, on the left [AM; A]. The facing-stones of the wall have gone and the core is much battered, but it still stands 2.50–3 m (8–10 ft) high, about half its original height. Half-way along are the foundations of a projecting tower (9), and another stands to a good height at

*49   St Albans (*Verulamium*), Roman town wall on NE, and the abbey beyond*

the corner (10). The railings now prevent access for a closer
look, but the projecting tower is bonded in with the rest of the
stone wall of the late third century and so presumably is
contemporary; but behind it is a stone internal turret, which
would normally be thought of as an earlier feature, replaced
by a later projecting tower. Present orthodoxy, however,
regards both tower and turret as contemporary. Projecting
towers are in fact only found at Verulamium on this south
face of the walls adjacent to the London gate, and they may
therefore have been a feature designed to impress on this side
only rather than being a systematic part of the defences. The
line of the walls, now overgrown, continues in the wood
beyond. The Fosse earthwork (11) lies on private land beyond
the modern road: permission to visit must be obtained in
advance from the Gorhambury Estate Office. Much of the
western half of the Roman town lies within this estate, and it
is scandalous that ploughing continues here each year,

inflicting long-term damage on archaeological deposits and associated Roman buildings.

When Boudica's revolt had been crushed and her tribe, the Iceni, had been reconciled to the idea of Roman occupation, a small Roman town was founded for them as their tribal capital. It was VENTA ICENORVM, 'the market of the Iceni', near the village of **Caistor St Edmund*** (TG 230035), some 3 miles (4.8 km) south of Norwich. The interior of the Roman town is now entirely under grass, but until ploughing was stopped in the 1980s the street-grid could often be seen as parched lines in the ripening corn. The clarity with which these appeared on an air-photograph of 1928 caused much excitement, and funds were raised which enabled the excavation of some of the internal buildings in 1929–35. These have been filled in.

The street-plan of VENTA was laid out about AD 70, but buildings remained very modest until the second century. Then a forum and basilica were built, but nothing is known of its plan: the one recovered from the excavations belongs to the middle of the century, and the bath-house near the west gate is of a similar date. There were repairs to both after burning at the end of the second century, and the forum was totally rebuilt on a smaller and simpler scale *c.* 270/90, after a long period of neglect and decay. Two stone temples were also found, but private dwellings were very humble and even in the third century were still not constructed in stone. Air-photographs have revealed a defence-system of earlier date on the south side of the town, but when the town walls were finally built, *c.* 200, they enclosed a smaller area than that envisaged by the street-grid. All this points to only a moderately successful town, and the 34 acres (14 ha) enclosed within the final defences make it one of the smallest *civitas* capitals in Roman Britain, smaller even than distant Caerwent in south Wales (44 acres [18 ha]), and only slightly larger than Carmarthen (31 acres [13 ha]).

Although nothing is visible within the defences, the latter are still prominent in their entire circuit. They comprised an external ditch (up to 24.5 m [80 ft] wide and 17 m [5 ft] deep) and a stone wall, 4 m (14 ft) wide at the base, backed by an internal bank and strengthened by projecting towers. Presumably there were the usual three phases in the

development of these defences, but excavation has yet to
prove it.

The site is reached by taking the Ipswich road (A140) out
of Norwich and turning to the left (signposted Caistor St
Edmund) at a roundabout immediately after the A140 has
passed under the Norwich bypass (A47). Turn right at the next
crossroads, on entering the village, and park at the car-park on
the right 100 m beyond the church, $\frac{1}{2}$ mile (800 m) further on.
From here the broad mound of the south defences of VENTA
are visible: take the wooden steps to the top of the defences,
and then turn left to follow the path along the inside of the
walled circuit. Flints poke out of the grass along the entire
length of the south rampart, and a long stretch of the flint
rubble-core is exposed east of the south gate; there is also an
impressive drop to the faint hollow of the ditch below. A
depression half-way along marks the site of the south gate,
which consisted of a single portal and two guardrooms. It
soon became choked with rubbish and the guardrooms were
deliberately filled in before AD 300. Near the SW angle, away
to your left, is the site of the amphitheatre, of which nothing is
visible; first detected from the air, its arena was defined by
geophysical survey in 1995 as measuring 40 m by 33 m
(44 yds by 36 yds). Another stretch of rubble masonry, up to
1.80 m (6 ft) high, has been exposed just before you reach the
SW corner. You will soon pick up the line of the west
rampart; the ditch was omitted on this side as the river Tass
flows nearby. A depression opposite the field-gate marks the
site of the west gate. Just beyond this an isolated Roman
tower still stands to an impressive height of 3 m (10 ft),
displaying four courses of triple bonding-tiles. As can be seen
by looking at them in section, these are only superficial: they
do not extend throughout the thickness of the rubble-core. The
towers were presumably later additions to the wall and so are
not bonded with it; but it is still extraordinary that the stone
robbers who removed the wall behind left this tower relatively
unscathed. About 6 m (20 ft) north of this, a semicircular
mound projecting from the line of the wall marks the site of
another tower. If all four walls at Caistor St Edmund were
furnished with towers at such close intervals, there must have
been over 40 in all; but there is no sign of them on the north

or south sides, and the west defences may have received special treatment.

Another fragment of stone core (with a modern support) appears at the NW angle, and then again at the beginning of the north wall, after which rubble walling is visible all the way to the north gate (keep along the outside of the defences). If you move inside the rampart at the point where there is a tiny break, mid-way between the NW corner and the north gate, you come immediately to three 'scoops' inside the back of the wall, of uncertain function; but the first at least, 1.50 m (5 ft) long and 30 cm (1 ft) deep with rounded corners, cannot have been accidental.

Now descend the bank and go into the field with the farm. The site of the north gate is marked by a field-gate immediately on your right. Now follow the best preserved stretch of all the walled circuit at VENTA, with considerable stretches of impressive flint wall still standing in places 5 m (16 ft) high. Its original maximum height, excluding the parapet, was probably only 1 m (3 ft) taller; and in fact half-way between the north gate and the NE corner there is even a short stretch where a fragment of the parapet survives (as nowhere else on town defences in Roman Britain) – the masonry projecting above the top string course. In two places also small sections of the facing flints at the base of the wall are preserved, and part of the tile bonding-courses, again here only surface-deep.

Now climb the steps to the top of the wall and round the NE corner. No masonry is visible along the east side of the defences, but you can make your way to the church drive along the line of the well preserved ditch. The site of the east gate lay near the war memorial. The church has Roman tiles built into the porch and elsewhere. As you complete your circuit of the walls, just before you reach the car-park, note the breach at the SE corner, in front of which is a substantial piece of fallen defences; the core of the walls, again standing to a considerable height, is visible here in the adjacent stretch.

Each of the three towns so far described in this chapter had a different administrative status: *colonia*, *municipium*, and *civitas* capital. The fourth and last settlement, that of **Caister-on-Sea** (TG 517123) [AM; A], is of uncertain function. It lies 3 miles (4.8 km) north of Great Yarmouth,

400 m (440 yd) east of the bypass roundabout in the western outskirts of the village (turn left at the church if coming from Great Yarmouth). The coastline has changed a great deal since Roman times: Caister was then at the mouth of a large estuary stretching some way inland, and where Yarmouth now lies was sea. The site was originally interpreted as a small harbour town founded probably in the second half of the second century, but the presence of stone walls belonging to the early third century, unparalleled for a town (other than the *coloniae*) at such an early date, and its similarity with the earliest forts of the Saxon Shore system (such as Reculver [p. 45] and Brancaster [App. 1]), have prompted the re-interpretation of the site at Caister-on-Sea as a fort. Nevertheless, the principal excavated building does not appear to have a particularly military character, and military finds, while present, do not predominate. One possibility, if Caister did have a military function when the walls were built, is that this transferred to the fort at Burgh Castle on the other side of the estuary mouth (see below), when the latter was constructed in the later third century, and that Caister reverted to having a largely civilian character again from then on. The site is therefore something of an enigma. The settlement was still flourishing until *c.* 370/90; there is then a hiatus before a middle/late Saxon village (*c.* AD 650–1066), chiefly represented by over 150 burials to the south of the Roman walled enclosure. The Roman name of the site, which was excavated between 1951 and 1955, is not known.

Immediately inside the entrance gate to the remains are two concrete circles (often concealed in the grass) and a long wiggly concrete line. The circles mark the sites of post-holes for the timbers which carried a wooden bridge over the ditch outside the defences. The concrete line represents a timber palisade which surrounded the settlement before the walls (although this is hardly substantial enough ever to have served a defensive purpose, despite what the site information board states). This was replaced by the broad stone wall, originally backed by a clay rampart, which was erected to defend the settlement soon after AD 200. It enclosed a square area of 8.75 acres (3.5 ha), but only this portion of the south defences, and the western guardroom of the south gate, are visible now.

The purpose of the three circular flint bases just inside the wall (and clearly preceding it) is uncertain.

Inside the defensive wall are the remains of a long strip building, later included in a larger courtyard building. It was apparently not built before the mid/late third century, but was probably preceded by a timber structure; it went through several modifications, and was still in use in the fourth century. By this time the cobbled corridor on the south had been filled in. The small curved wall in one corner of the first room (the end nearest the Roman guard-chamber) is believed to have been a latrine; but the room was a high-status one, with floral designs on its painted wall-plaster. There is a brick-built hearth in the centre of the next room; two other, secondary hearths were also found in this room, together with evidence for iron-working, but none of this is now visible. Two rooms further on is an unusual hypocaust, of the channelled type in the centre but with *pilae* set round the edges. The hypocaust was filled with rammed clay mixed with quantities of wheat when it fell into disuse (giving rise to the idea that it served as a granary), but there seems no reason to doubt that the chamber in its visible form was intended to function as a normal heated room. There are recesses for wall-flues in the east and west walls near their junction with the north wall. A doorway is visible in the latter, later blocked by the brickwork still partially in place; the blocking is dated by a coin of Constantine found at its base to not before the early fourth century. The room's furnace was in the adjoining cubicle, in one corner of which was found a heap of tiles. Interpreted by the original excavator as the base for a water-tank (unlikely since the tiles were unmortared), its true purpose is uncertain. There was a second corridor and a courtyard to the north, and a further fragmentary structure adjacent, but these are now largely buried. The only other features to note on the site are two shallow depressions, one a late Roman pit, the other a Saxon metal-working hollow, and the pebbled main street, with central depression for drainage, leading down to the south gate and so out to the harbour.

The purpose of the long strip building is controversial. Originally identified by the excavator as a 'seamen's hostel' (polite terminology for what others called a brothel), both the use of painted wall-plaster in the first four rooms, and the presence of a hypocaust in another room, suggest a period of domestic occupation; the presence of small finds associated with women, such as hair pins and a necklace, also points to the same conclusion. If Caister really was a fort, then presumably this formed an officer's accommodation, which could explain the hypocaust, the painted plaster and the small finds appropriate to female use; a courtyard building might point to a CO's house (cf. Piercebridge for a similar late example: p. 398), although the plan of the building at Caister is not very coherent. The presence of a water-tank (not visible) and evidence of metal-working have also led to the suggestion that it was the fort's *fabrica* (workshop) at some stage, but this seems less plausible. If, however, the site was no longer a fort but a civilian town by the late third century, the structure is presumably the wing of what became a large and comfortable town-house.

In the second half of the third century the peace and security of SE England was threatened for the first time since the Roman invasion. At this time, a series of strong forts, known as the forts of the Saxon Shore, was built from the Wash to the Solent, and several have already been described in Chapter 1 (pp. 39–56), and another in Chapter 2 (p. 149). Three more of these forts existed on the East Anglian coast (not to mention that at Walton-on-the-Naze in Essex, which has slipped completely into the sea). Those at Brancaster, near Hunstanton in Norfolk, and at Bradwell-on-Sea in Essex, have left little trace above ground (see App. 1), but the site at **Burgh Castle**** (TG 475046) is very fine [AM; A]. The Roman name, GARIANNVM (or less likely GARIANNONVM), probably means 'babbling river', the river being the Yare on which Burgh Castle stands. The garrison was a detachment of Stablesian cavalry from what was formerly Yugoslavia. The fort lies only a short distance today from the remains of the Roman site at Caister-on-Sea, but in Roman times the two places lay on opposite sides of a large estuary. Take the Lowestoft road (A12) for about 2 miles (3 km) out of Great Yarmouth, until a roundabout is reached; Burgh Castle is signposted from there (turn right at the T-junction). The footpath leads in ten minutes to the fort, which you see on your right. Roman occupation must have spread some way beyond the walled enclosure, since many objects have been

retrieved by systematic field-walking in the fields around: a
geophysical survey might provide more details. Strike across
the field east of the fort towards the walls; ignore for the
moment the gap marking the east gate, but make first for the
SE corner tower away to your left.

Beyond the corner tower is the short but picturesque portion
of the south wall, part standing, part toppling, part fallen
(Fig. 50). The standing part retains all its facing-flints,
separated by rows of tile bonding-courses (at Burgh only
surface-deep), and forms a magnificent stretch of Roman
masonry, 3.20 m (10 ft 6 in) thick at base and 4.50 m (15 ft)
high – probably its original height except for a parapet. The
fallen tower here has a socket in the middle of its top, either to
support a superstructure of wood or, less probably, for
anchoring a *ballista*, which hurled stone balls and other
weapons on to the attacker. The base of this tower shows
traces of the timber framework used in the foundations of the
wall. The use of timber posts is also implied by a series of

50   Burgh Castle, late Roman fort, the south wall looking east

vertical square holes which can be seen on the inside of the stretch of south wall nearest the river. From here you can walk round the inside of the three remaining walls of the fort: that on the west has totally vanished, but what was presumably a timber wharf was found in the nineteenth century at the foot of the low cliff facing the river. The thickness of the wall was reduced on the inside face by a series of offsets, which can be seen (partially restored) in the eastern portion of the south wall.

Now walk round the walls on the inside. The main gate of the fort was in the long east wall, but only a simple gap remains today. Eventually you reach the centre of the north wall and its leaning tower. This originally protected a narrow postern gate, but hardly anything remains of it now. The particular interest of this tower lies in the curving profile of its back, and in the matching mortar curve of the main body of the wall from which it has fallen. The reason for this is as follows. When the decision to build Burgh Castle was taken, the plan was to have the conventional internal turrets and no projecting towers: one such turret has been found in excavations but is not now visible. After about 2.15 m (7 ft) of the curtain wall had been built, the order went out that towers were to be added. For this reason, only the top half of each tower is bonded into the wall; the lower half merely stands up against it. The curving portion marks the joint between the bonded and unbonded parts of each tower, and, having observed it with ease in this example on the north, you can examine the rest of the standing towers (Fig. 51) for this feature as you make your way round the outside of the walls, back to the SE corner. Throughout, the defences stand to a spectacular height, even though many of the facing-stones have been robbed.

The construction of the towers as an afterthought gives a clue as to the dating of GARIANNVM. It is later than the early examples of the series, such as Reculver, or Dover as originally built, which had no towers, but is earlier than Saxon Shore forts such as Richborough, Portchester and Pevensey, where towers were an integral part of the scheme. A date around AD 275 is the most likely for the building of Burgh Castle. It does not seem to have been occupied much beyond the middle of the fourth century.

51   Burgh Castle, late Roman fort, a tower on the east wall

The comparative lack of prosperity in the Icenian tribal capital is reflected by a similar situation in the surrounding countryside, where villas never reached the size or degree of Romanized luxury displayed by those of SW England. It is not surprising, therefore, to find no villa-site visible today in the territory of the Iceni. Further west, the Fens were drained for the first time by the Romans and the area was extensively cultivated, but villa-estates are non-existent here and it has with good reason been suggested that the area may have been an imperial estate, the property of the emperor. The artificial drainage system, however, designed to link natural watercourses, remains to bear witness to Roman engineering skills in this region.

The main channel is the Car Dyke, which excavation has shown on average to have been 2.50 m (8 ft) deep, 9 m (30 ft) wide at the bottom and 15 m (50 ft) at the top. It was probably cut at the beginning of the second century (some think a little earlier), and it used to be interpreted as a canal for transporting grain to the north, for the network extended at least as far as Lincoln. More recent work, however, has shown that in parts the Lincolnshire Car Dyke was not continuous but was interrupted by gravel causeways making navigation impossible. A survey of the Dyke further south has demonstrated that the central sector here is higher than at its confluence with the rivers Welland to the north and the Nene to the south, suggesting that it was intended exclusively as a catchwater drain. A navigable channel would have needed a level course throughout to maintain water at a constant depth. Long stretches of the Car Dyke can be traced both in Cambridgeshire and Lincolnshire with the help of OS maps, but it is rarely more than a wet ditch and hardly likely to generate much excitement.

One convenient place to view the Cambridgeshire Car Dyke is near **Waterbeach** (TL 485664), a few miles north of Cambridge. From the latter follow the Ely road (A10) for 6 miles (9.7 km), until you reach a turning to the left (Waterbeach Road) opposite a pub, signposted Landbeach and Cottenham. Park as soon as it is safe, and then walk back to the A10, cross the dual carriageway, and look out for some railings just north of the pub. The Roman drain shows as a wet ditch below and beyond the railings. Excavation nearby in 1997, at its junction with the Cam, showed the Car Dyke here to be 24 m (79 ft) wide and 7 m (23 ft) deep; a timber building and two pottery kilns (second–fourth centuries) were found on the bank.

Further west, one Roman villa of which an unusual feature has been preserved is that at **Bancroft** (SP 827403), Bradwell, on the NW edge of Milton Keynes. Turn off the A422 ('H3') at the second roundabout east of the A5 along V6 (northwards), then left along Millers Way ('H2'). Next take the sign for Bancroft Park (Constantine Way). The second turning on the left leads you into the car-park just after the Roman Park Residents' Club. There are no signposts to the site. The villa, partly excavated in the 1970s and then more comprehensively in 1983–7, is a good example of a medium-sized 'winged corridor' villa. First built in stone in the second century to replace an earlier timber structure or structures, it underwent various modifications and enlargements, most notably at two separate periods in the fourth century, when

geometric mosaics were added in many rooms and the main
bath-suite was rebuilt and enlarged. In front of the villa a
formal garden was laid out in the fourth century with an
ornamental fishpond on the main axis. Bancroft is one of the
most extensively excavated Roman villas in Britain: six
outlying farm buildings have been located to the north, three
rectangular (one at least probably a barn), and three circular in
the pre-Roman tradition; all except one belonged to the
second century. A fourth-century mausoleum, 300 m (330
yds) NW of the villa, is also known.

At one stage it was hoped that the whole site would be
consolidated and left exposed, but this has not proved
possible. The only visible Roman structure is the fourth-
century stone-lined fishpond which stood in the centre of the
walled garden, but the walls of the main villa itself have been
rebuilt at a higher level in modern materials (their 'ruined'
appearance is potentially misleading), as has an octagonal
structure (a shrine?) in the garden. The main bath-suite of the
villa is easily recognizable from the tiny size of its rooms and
its double-apsed *caldarium.* The way the structures on the
west (uphill) side have been presented is most misleading.
The square store-room at the back, built *c.* AD 300, was a
freestanding building, later demolished when an even tinier,
secondary set of baths was added on this west side of the
house: as presented, however, the walls show both features as
though they were contemporary and interconnecting, which
they were not.

The mosaics from the Bancroft villa were lifted in 1983 and
are in store, except for one geometric floor now in the centre
of Milton Keynes. Enter the shopping complex called The
Centre at the corner framed by the church in one direction and
the council offices in the other (Silbury Arcade). Keeping
Marks and Spencer on your right, carry on walking for five
minutes until you come to a large open-air fountain court on
the right; the mosaic is displayed in a corridor looking into
this court. It dates to the early fourth century and comes from
a vestibule in the villa's main bath-suite. Stylistic affinities
strongly suggest that this Bancroft floor was the work of
itinerant mosaicists from Cirencester, 58 miles (93 km) away
as the crow flies; but still later mosaics at Bancroft (*c.* 350/75)

were probably laid by Durnovarian craftsmen from
Dorchester, even further away (120 miles [194 km]).

Villas become more plentiful and more imposing in the
territory of the Catuvellauni, especially around Verulamium,
but only one site, Dicket Mead near **Welwyn*** (TL 2315), has
been permanently preserved. A pair of buildings with front
and rear corridors, together with part of a third building, was
excavated here in 1970, 1,235 m (1,350 yds) south of a
Roman villa discovered in 1930 on the other side of the river
Mimram (this was the key site of Lockleys, in its earliest
phase one of the first stone-built villas known in Britain). The
Dicket Mead villa, by contrast, was built in the early third
century and occupied for about 150 years. None of these
structures is now visible, except for the small bath-house at
the end of one of the long buildings at Dicket Mead, which
has been preserved *in situ* in a concrete vault beneath the
A1(M) motorway. Discovered in 1960 and opened in 1975, it
can be visited on Saturdays and Sundays (as well as Bank
Holidays) from January to November between 1400 and 1700.
It is also open daily (also 1400–1700) during the Easter and
summer school holidays and at half-terms (for the precise
days, telephone 01707–271362). Access is from the west side
of the A1(M), just north of Welwyn. If northbound, come off
the A1(M) at junction 6, and then take the second exit at the
first roundabout, and the last exit ('London: A1(M)') at the
second roundabout. If alternatively you are travelling
southwards on the A1, take the last exit at the first roundabout
on leaving the motorway, and then go right at the fork,
following the road round; then take the third exit at the second
roundabout. In both cases the bath-house car-park lies
immediately on your left after this second roundabout.

The first feature you encounter on entering the site is the
superbly preserved stoking-area for the baths; the main flue
opening (and the relieving arch above), together with a
receptacle for hot water situated over the flue, still stands
some 1.50 m (5 ft) high. The wall to the left of the stoke-hole
is clearly secondary. Now move to your left round the
building. The hot room (*caldarium*) comes next, with a
fragment of floor *in situ*. Its supporting *pilae* look to be of
more than one period (one very burnt *pila* has been
strengthened by an additional pier alongside it). A hot-water

pool lies opposite, with cement floor, pink mortar rendering on the wall, and flue-tiles embedded in the thickness of the wall; its drain outlet is also visible. The *pilae* of the warm room (*tepidarium*) have been entirely removed (the impressions of one base remain), and the wall separating this room from the hot room was neatly robbed out after the baths ceased to function, but enough remains to show that it was pierced by two flue openings (to allow hot air to pass from one room to the other). Note in particular the scar in the wall close to the hot bath, where the stonework has been robbed, but where the mortar which lined it can be seen on either side. The tiled floor of the cold room has been relaid. The intact cold immersion-bath, with steps down into it and a terracotta drain, was clearly added later to the original baths (the straight joints between the two are obvious); so too was the hot-water pool on this same side of the baths, mentioned above. The tile closest to the entrance into the hot-water bath has the impression of a shoe in it, a feature best seen from the panel entitled 'Constructing the vault' on the far side. The bath-house was built, along with the rest of the villa, early in the third century and was demolished at some stage in the fourth century; it had an active life, therefore, of a little over 100 years. There are plans afoot (2001) to construct a life-size simulation of the whole building, on the greensward at the entrance to the tunnel under the motorway.

If the East Anglian countryside is not exactly overflowing with the remains of villas, the area is at least rich in Roman funerary monuments. Most of these are in the form of earth burial-mounds, or *tumuli*, but an exception is the stone mausoleum at **Harpenden** (TL 119136). It lies in the private grounds of the Rothamsted Experimental Station, which is signposted to the right (west) of the St Albans road (A1081) just south of the town. Casual visitors are usually not unwelcome, but permission should be requested at the entrance lodge. From there keep straight as far as possible, and then turn right at the T-junction. Follow the road round to the right, keeping the manor on your left. Proceed on, following directions for the farm. Go past it, keeping it on your left, and then turn left immediately beyond it. The mausoleum is on the left of the road just beyond the farm.

Here you will see the immaculately kept foundations of a

52   Harpenden, Roman mausoleum

square building with an apse on one side (Fig. 52). The
interior, however, is circular, 3.35 m (11 ft) in diameter, and
has a square plinth in the centre: this must have been the base
of the tomb monument itself and no doubt carried an
inscription. Fragments of a statue, presumably of the
deceased, were found during excavations in 1937, and this
probably stood in the alcove. The function of the cross-wall
between the square base and the apse is puzzling: perhaps this
belongs to an earlier structure demolished when the
mausoleum was built, in which case the cross-wall would
have been invisible below the later floor. The thickness of the
external walls suggests that the superstructure of the
mausoleum was quite substantial, perhaps 6 m (20 ft) high. It
stood in the middle of an enclosure, about 30 m (100 ft)
square, in which two cremation-burials dating to the first half
of the second century were found. Nearly half of this
enclosure-wall also remains exposed; there was originally a
ditch beyond it.

Of the many sites in East Anglia where Romano-British *tumuli* are visible, I include only four here; one near Colchester has already been mentioned (p. 224), and the rest are listed in Appendix 1. The most interesting is perhaps that on **Mersea Island** (TM 023143), the sole British example where it is possible to go underneath the earth mound to inspect the site of the burial-chamber (for which an appointment to collect the key must be made in advance with the Colchester and Essex Museum on 01206–282928). Immediately after the B1025 crosses the causeway on to the island, turn left along the East Mersea road. The barrow lies behind railings on the left, just beyond a road to the right (Dawes Lane). A concrete tunnel made by the excavators of 1912 leads to the middle of the barrow; the site of the burial is marked by some tiles in the floor of the last chamber. These Roman tiles formed a cavity 46 cm (18 inches) high, and inside was a lead casket containing a glass bowl with ashes of human bones. These finds, probably belonging to the second half of the first century AD, are now in Colchester Museum (p. 217). The earth mound raised over the burial is 33.50 m (110 ft) in diameter and over 6 m (20 ft) high, and since 1966 has been cleared of undergrowth and carefully maintained. Mersea Museum, next to the church in West Mersea, is open 1400–1700 daily between May and September.

The Mersea example is an isolated barrow, but *tumuli* also occur in groups. At **Thornborough** (SP 732333) in Buckinghamshire two are found side by side. They are quite well preserved, one 4.90 m (16 ft) high and 36.50 m (120 ft) in diameter, the other a little smaller. When opened in 1859, the larger barrow yielded second-century samian pottery, bronze jugs, a glass vessel with cremated remains, and other finds; these are now in the Museum of Archaeology and Ethnology at Cambridge. From Buckingham follow the Bletchley road (A421) for just under 2 miles (3 km) until you cross the river Twin with the medieval bridge of *c.* 1400 on your left. The two *tumuli* lie in the field on the left beyond the bridge (reached by a stile from the car-park and picnic area; information boards). Excavations in 1972–3 before the building of the new bridge found seven first-century cremations with grave goods (pottery and glass vessels), and

evidence of at least two parallel roads leading to a ford across
the river. A third-century Romano-Celtic temple is known
100 m south of the bridge.

A larger group, this time of six barrows arranged in a single
row, can be seen at **Stevenage** (TL 237237) in Hertfordshire.
Each is 18 m (60 ft) in diameter and now about 3 m (10 ft)
high. Only two maintain what is probably their original profile
at the top; shallow scoops and other irregularities indicate that
treasure-seekers have interfered with the other four in the past.
One, for example, is known to have been dug into in 1741
when 'wood and iron' were found. The *tumuli* are situated on
the south side of Stevenage, and you should first follow signs
for Stevenage railway station. From its forecourt turn left and
go right the way round the first roundabout and back along the
dual carriageway (if travelling by car; if on foot, turn right!).
At the next roundabout take the third exit ('College') and you
will see the Six Hills, as the barrows are known locally, on
your right.

The largest and most impressive group of Romano-British
tumuli is at **Bartlow*** (TL 586448), on the Essex/
Cambridgeshire border. Here there were originally two rows
of three and four barrows respectively, but the former was
destroyed in the nineteenth century. The surviving four are
excellently preserved. They were explored in 1832–40, when
many fine grave goods were found. These indicated that the
barrows were erected between the end of the first and the
middle of the second century AD. Most of the objects
unfortunately perished in a fire in 1847, but some remaining
finds are in Saffron Walden Museum (April–October,
Monday–Saturday, 1000–1700: Sunday and Bank Holidays,
1430–1700; November to March, Tuesday–Saturday,
1100–1600; Sunday and Bank Holidays, 1430–1630). A relief
from Chester showing gladiatorial combat is among other
Roman material displayed here.

Bartlow is signposted from the A604 (Colchester road)
$\frac{1}{2}$ mile (800 m) east of the village of Linton, 10 miles (16 km)
SE of Cambridge. In Bartlow itself take the turning to
Ashdon. The footpath to the Bartlow Hills, the name by which
the barrows are known, is signposted on the left shortly after
passing the abutments of the disused railway-bridge (slight
lay-by). The footpath leads almost at once to a clearing with

three barrows. On your left is Barrow VII, some 7.5 m (25 ft) high. In it were found a lamp and mid-second-century pottery, and a wooden chest which contained a pot and cremated bones in a glass jug. Barrow IV, straight ahead, is the largest extant *tumulus* in Roman Britain, a massive heap 44 m (144 ft) in diameter and 13.75 m (45 ft) high. Very steep, it is easily accessible by a wooden staircase on the far side. Its grave goods were elaborate – a wooden chest containing glass vessels (for holding perfumes, food and the cremated bones), an enamelled bowl, and a folding stool with bronze fittings and a leather seat. The adjacent Barrow V beyond, which is 10 m (35 ft) high, produced finds similar to those of Barrow VII. Finally there is Barrow VI, the northernmost of the row, which lies in private ground on the other side of the former railway. One side of it, rising steeply and a little overgrown, can be seen from the railway footbridge, reached round the back of Barrow VII. A bronze bowl, an iron lamp and a toilet-instrument were found inside. Of the now-destroyed mounds, which a nineteenth-century engraving shows as already then much lower than IV–VII, part of I is just discernible as a very slight rise bisected by the fence, to your left as you return to the footpath; II is adjacent to it further to your left, mostly under nettles on the far side of the fence; and III, which lay to the right of the path, is invisible.

Chapter 5

Central England

Cambridgeshire (part of), Derbyshire, Leicestershire,
Lincolnshire, Rutland, Shropshire, Staffordshire and
Warwickshire

(Appendix 1 only – Northamptonshire and Nottinghamshire)

With the capture of Colchester in AD 43 and the establishment
of a base there for the Twentieth Legion, the invading army
split up. The Second Legion made for the West Country (see
Chapter 2), the Ninth advanced northwards towards Lincoln,
and the Fourteenth aimed for the Shropshire area. The precise
movements of these legions in the period AD 44–60 are still
far from certain, but a vast addition to our knowledge has
been made by aerial discoveries and excavation during the last
30 years. It is now known that the Ninth Legion was not

established in its fortress on the hill at Lincoln until about AD 60, although the possibility of an earlier fortress in the 50s on flat ground south of the river cannot be ruled out. Before that it was divided between a 28-acre (12-ha) vexillation fortress at Longthorpe near Peterborough (p. 290) and others which cluster to the NW and SW of Lincoln: no fewer than four vexillation fortresses are known here, and clearly not all were exactly contemporary, since we now have more vexillation fortresses than there are legions to put in them (although the proportion of auxiliaries which might be stationed in each is unknown). Smaller forts are known to have existed at several other places in the same area, but no trace of any of these early forts and vexillation fortresses is visible as an earthwork on the ground today.

Less is known about the progress of the Fourteenth Legion. One part may have advanced through Cambridge and Godmanchester (near Huntingdon) to Leicester, where the size of the early military establishment is still undetermined. Another part of the Fourteenth followed the line later taken by Watling Street (the modern A5), and here too there is a plethora of vexillation fortresses known (four along Watling Street, including Wall, and a fifth to the south at Metchley in the outskirts of Birmingham). None of these vexillation fortresses, however (with the exception of Metchley: App. 1), have left traces visible on the ground. Eventually, about AD 58, the scattered detachments were brought together and a fortress for the full Fourteenth Legion was established at Wroxeter near Shrewsbury.

The only one of these first-century forts worth visiting is that at the Lunt, **Baginton*** (SP 344752). Here an ambitious reconstruction scheme, between 1966 and 1977, turned a flat field into one of the most instructive military sites of Roman Britain. The village of Baginton lies 2 miles (3 km) south of Coventry and is best reached by the minor road to Coventry airport. This leaves the roundabout joining the Coventry bypass (A45) with the A46 and A423, SE of the city (Baginton is signed from the roundabout). At present (2001) the fort is open at rather irregular hours: between the beginning of April and the end of October, it is open Saturdays and Sundays (and Bank Holiday Mondays) only, 1000–1700. It is also open daily for a week during the school half-term holiday (approximately the first week of June), and also daily except Wednesday during the school summer holidays (the last week of July to the middle of September), in all cases between 1000 and 1700.

The site of Baginton was occupied only between AD 60 and 79/80, but within that period its history is extremely complex. It was apparently constructed in the aftermath of the Boudican rebellion, for no finds at present point to the existence of a fort here in the earliest invasion period. The first fort was much larger than the visible enclosure, although its exact size has not yet been established. In the second phase the internal buildings were rebuilt on a different alignment. Then a curious circular structure was erected (Phase IIb), covering in part two barrack buildings of the second stage of the fort. The original fort was then reduced in size (Phase IIc), and the new eastern defences made a highly unusual detour to avoid the circular structure; the western defences, too, were also far from regular. Finally, in Period III, the size of the fort was reduced once again, with a pair of ditches cutting through the *via principalis* of the Period II fort, and a new south gate built on the site of the demolished *principia* of the preceding fort. In AD 77/8, when the coin-series from the site ends, the fort was abandoned, the defences dismantled, and the timber carried away for use elsewhere. There is also surprising evidence for a short-lived re-occupation in the late third century, together with fresh defences. A fort at that date in inland lowland Britain is quite exceptional and is presumably a reflection of local insecurity.

The most impressive feature at the Lunt is the fine east gateway to the Period II fort and the section of earth and timber defences rebuilt on either side of it (Figs. 53–4). The plan of the gateway was learnt from excavation in 1966–7; its elevation is based on evidence of similar structures represented on Trajan's Column in Rome, but to what extent the latter reflects precise military knowledge or was subject to a degree of artistic licence and creative imagination, is a moot point. The gate was prefabricated in modern army-workshops and erected by the Royal Engineers during three days in September 1970, without the aid of modern equipment. The defences were refurbished, and a further long section built, in 1984–7, but these too at the time of writing (2001) are

53   Baginton, Roman fort,
on the rampart-walk

54   Baginton, Roman fort, reconstructed east gateway
(from outside)

showing signs of their age: in particular the defences have
slumped, leaving the timber breastwork standing proud, with
daylight visible between the two (cf. Vindolanda, p. 502).
Nevertheless the rate of decay is in itself a useful piece of
experimental archaeology – a reminder that Roman turf and
timber forts need extensive refurbishment and rebuilding
every 30 years or so, in turn explaining the complicated
sequence of successive timber forts detected on many sites
before the stone-built phase (which at Baginton never came).

From the gateway the *via principalis* leads you to the centre
of the fort where on the right the plan of the Period II HQ
building (*principia*) has been marked out. It lacks a cross-hall
but has the usual central courtyard and five administrative
rooms along the back. The room in the middle was the shrine
for the standards, and sunk into its floor is a strong-room, a
common feature of later stone forts. But the headquarters was
dismantled before the further reduction of the fort took place
in period III, for the latter's new south gateway, twin-portalled
like the reconstructed one, was built over part of the HQ
courtyard. The post-holes of this later gate have also been
marked out in concrete.

Next to the *principia* a timber granary, reconstructed in
1973, serves as the site Museum (Fig. 55): it contains a model
of the fort, information panels and a few finds, of which a

55   Baginton, Roman fort, the reconstructed timber granary

curious bowl with a central finial (of unknown purpose) is the
most unusual find (in the case to the left of the exit). The
archaeological evidence for the granary was provided by 105
post-holes at 1.50-m (5-ft) intervals, which represented the
timber uprights for supporting the floor above ground-level, as
customary in such buildings. Archaeology, however, provides
a ground-plan but rarely any evidence for the third dimension.
The simulation at the Lunt, therefore, is an outstanding
attempt at providing an illustration of the suggested
superstructure of a Roman building in Britain, one of the first
to have been attempted in this country – even if the evidence
is scanty for such details as the pitch of the roof, the position
and number of louvers, and the precise nature and appearance
of the wall-finish. The Roman granary which stood here
c. AD 67–77 is, however, unlikely to have looked substantially
different from the one before you now.

The granary and the HQ are two structures which follow
more or less predictable patterns known from other excavated
forts in Britain and elsewhere. Few other features at the Lunt
do, but none is more peculiar than the unique circular
stockade which the eastern defences bulge out to avoid. This,
also reconstructed (in 1977), encloses a circular arena 33 m
(107 ft) in diameter, dug out to a depth of 60 cm (2 ft) below
the rest of the interior of the fort. In the absence of parallels
for this feature, in any fort the length and breadth of the

Roman Empire, its purpose remains enigmatic; but the hypothesis that it is a *gyrus* or training-ground for horses and cavalry recruits seems convincing. Beyond it, the plan of some further barracks and granaries have been marked out in concrete and appropriately labelled.

The Lunt is therefore an impressive and fascinating site (although now after 25 years looking a little run-down), but it is important to stress that it is not a typical Roman fort. It has even been suggested that, at least for part of its existence, it was more of an army training-centre than a regular fort, but such a description may be a false and anachronistic borrowing from modern terminology, inappropriate to a Roman military post. Having puzzled over the function of the circular structure, do not go away thinking that every Roman fort had one. And having admired the reconstructions of the gateway and portions of the earth and timber defences, remember that the sinuous course taken by the eastern rampart is a feature unique in Britain and extremely rare on the Continent. Roman forts, from the mid-first century onwards, are almost always built to a regular playing-card shape with rounded corners and straight sides: it is ironical that of all the many Roman forts in Britain where such reconstruction could have taken place, it has been done at the most untypical example of all!

At four other fort sites in central England can something be seen of the surrounding rampart-mounds, but at three of them the remains are not impressive and they have therefore been relegated to Appendix 1: Greensforge and Wall Town were part of the garrison of Wales, while Brough-on-Noe in Derbyshire belonged to the southern edge of the Pennine chain of forts. So too did the fort of **Melandra Castle** (SK 009951), probably the Roman ARDOTALIA (which means 'the high brow', an apt description for its setting). It lies just west of Glossop and is signposted from the A626 $\frac{1}{2}$ mile (800 m) west of its junction with the A57, at the top of the hill; the fort lies on the left of the road 1 mile (1.6 km) from the A626. The fort, which can be visited at any time, is situated on a magnificent spur with a steep escarpment on the west, down to the river, and an extensive command of ground to the north; erosion is, however, endangering the SW corner, and the site is also marred by rubbish tips and signs of vandalism. The banks covering the stone walls of the fort stand to a prominent height throughout their circuit, often over 1.80 m (6 ft) high. Stonework is visible at the SE corner, opposite the car-park, where the fort wall and corner tower are exposed, and a small fragment of the NW corner tower is also upstanding. The gaps at all four gates are clear, but apart from a few blocks at the north gate no stonework is visible. In the centre of the fort the foundations of the headquarters building, first exposed in 1899, have been re-excavated and consolidated. It is not a particularly instructive example of its type, as the footings were poorly preserved, but the entrance (to the north) and three rooms at the rear can be made out, including a central shrine (*sacellum*) which had an *opus signinum* floor. The small garrison bath-house was discovered in 1973 7.5 m (50 ft) outside the fort between the north gate and the NW corner. Part of it had fallen down the slope, and the rest was excavated in annual campaigns up until 1998, but has now been backfilled. Excavations have shown that the fort was an Agricolan foundation *c.* 78, its clay and timber defences being refurbished in stone *c.* 110/20. The *principia* foundations also date from then, but the bath-house was (not surprisingly) of stone from the beginning, although twice altered and enlarged in the second century. The fort was given up and systematically dismantled about AD 140, clearly because of the renewed advance into Scotland under Antoninus Pius and the need to redeploy garrisons further north. A civilian settlement with timber buildings and its own defensive ditch, partly examined in 1966–9 before the housing-estate was built, also showed activity limited to the period AD 80–140. Thereafter this part of Britain was reckoned peaceful enough not to warrant the presence of a permanent military garrison.

Most of central England became civilian in character after the military had moved northwards and westwards in the last quarter of the first century AD, and many of the places which started life as forts were rebuilt as towns. The two legionary fortresses, Lincoln and Wroxeter, were no exception. The fortress on the hill at **Lincoln** ** (SK 976715) was founded, as we saw above, in about AD 60 or 61 for the Ninth Legion as part of the military reorganization that followed the revolt of Boudica, although there are hints of military occupation even before this, possibly on a quite separate site south of the river;

whether this was an auxiliary fort or an early abortive legionary fortress in unknown. In AD 71 the Ninth was moved forward to Yorkshire, and its place at Lincoln was taken by a legion newly brought to Britain, the Second Adiutrix. The earth and timber defences of the legionary fortress have been found in excavations, as well as part of the headquarters building (*principia*). In about AD 78 *Legio* II *Adiutrix* moved to Chester, and the military phase at Lincoln was over.

The site was then gradually resettled during the 80s and early 90s as a *colonia*, a town for retired legionaries and their families. Its Roman name, LINDVM, means 'the place by the pool', an allusion to what is now called Brayford Pool on the river Witham, immediately to the south. The first town clung to the hill-top, and when stone defences were erected early in the second century, they followed the same line as the legionary ramparts, and in fact used the latter to form the core of the bank behind the wall. *Lindum colonia* was a flourishing town, and occupation also increased on the slope facing the river: by the mid-second century elements of a street-grid were in place there too. Before very long, probably in the last quarter of the second century, this lower town too was walled, and the overall area enclosed by the defences was thus increased from 41 to 97 acres (17 to 40 ha). The defences of the upper town were made higher in the late second or early third century, but a more major rebuilding took place at the end of the third or the beginning of the fourth century, when the stone wall was made much wider, either by tacking on extra masonry on the inner face of the old, or by a complete rebuilding. The strengthening of the lower town was carried out where necessary at some later stage in the third century, with further major building work in the mid-fourth century. Much less is known about the interior of Roman Lincoln, but an impressive sewer-system and mosaic pavements point to a comfortable standard of living. In the fourth century it seems likely that Lincoln was the capital of one of the newly divided four provinces of Roman Britain, probably that of Britannia Secunda.

Many fine stretches of the defences of LINDVM still exist, but its chief pride are the three magnificent Roman gateways. A convenient place to start your visit is at the Eastgate Hotel, opposite the cathedral (1 on Fig. 56). Here, in the forecourt of

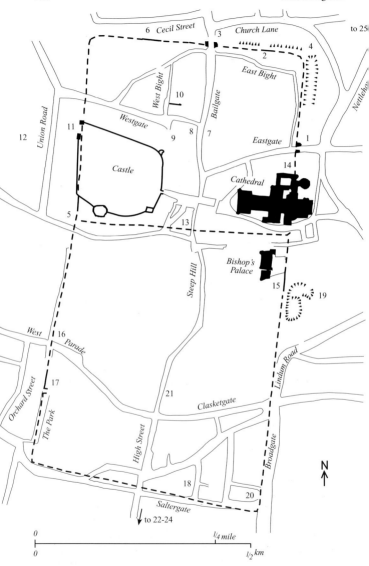

56   Lincoln, location map

the hotel, the north tower of the Roman east gate stands to a spectacular height. The entrance-door into the tower, the gate jamb from which the arch sprang, and the interior staircase giving access to an upper level, are all impressively preserved. This semicircular tower was matched by another (buried beneath the pavement and part of the cathedral green) which flanked the double carriageway of the gate proper, now under the road. These massive remains, however, only belong to the last phase of the gateway, in the early third century. Excavation within the tower in 1959–66 revealed the post-holes of the gateway of the timber legionary fortress of AD 61–78 and also the narrow stone wall, 1.20 m (4 ft) wide, which was built to front the timber gateway soon after the founding of the *colonia*, together with the fragment of an internal tower (a gate-tower?). The fortress post-holes are marked by modern timbers, and a fragment of the narrow wall and tower are also visible; they are labelled respectively 1 and 2 on the plan displayed on the retaining-wall.

In the grounds of the hotel, on the other side from the east gate, is a picturesque stretch of the Roman wall: walk round the back of the hotel and go under the bridge of the hotel extension ahead of you. Some brickwork is visible in its core at the far end, where the bottom three upright courses constitute, of course, modern repair. Now retrace your steps and walk down the narrow lane (East Bight) adjoining the remains of the east gate. After turning the corner, in private grounds behind railings on the right of the road (but visible from East Bight), you will see a massive piece of wall-core, 3 m (10 ft) thick (2 on Fig. 56). Although inaccessible, a facing-stone one course up from foundations here, on the north side of the wall, bears a sculptured phallus for good luck. This stretch of wall was backed by a large platform, marked out in the grass in modern materials (although it is often virtually invisible), which formed the foundation for a water storage tank. The Roman public baths, which were partially excavated in 1956–8 but are no longer visible, lay conveniently opposite, immediately behind the high boundary wall of East Bight in this corner of the city. The water was brought through a pipe-line from a uncertain source located NE of the city (see p. 275), but how it reached the top of the hill is still problematical. The old idea, that it was pumped uphill in a sealed pipe-line, is mechanically impossible, but a series of bucket-and-chain lifting devices, similar to that discovered in London (p. 633), might conceivably have been used. In the next property, beyond the hedge, are the foundations of an internal tower, attached to a piece of the original, second-century (narrow) gauge of stone wall. The contrast in width between this and the massive core of *c*. AD 300 immediately to the east is striking.

The lane soon leads to the famous Newport Arch (3), the north gate of the town and the only Roman archway still standing in Britain (Fig. 57). Built in its present form early in the third century, it was restored at various times in the eighteenth and nineteenth centuries and again in 1964, when a lorry partly demolished it. It is a fine relic, looking a little squat because of a build-up in road-levels, and consists of a main arch and a smaller one for pedestrians on one side, originally matched by a similar small arch on the other. Only the inner part of the gate is Roman; the rest of the masonry,

57 Lincoln, the Roman north gate (Newport Arch) from the south

including the pedestrian tunnel, belongs to the medieval structure. Like the east gate, it was flanked by projecting towers, and the lowest course of one of these, together with its projecting base-plinth, overlain by medieval work, can be seen in the small garden on the left (west) of the road. If the garden is open, turn left at the bottom of the steps: underneath the modern street you can see the massive block masonry of the Roman gate-piers for the pedestrian walkway, and the lower courses of the sub-Roman or post-Roman blocking (it may be of Norman date) in between. On the other side of the tower the lowest courses of the Roman city wall can be seen continuing westwards, depending on ivy growth.

Immediately east of the Newport Arch, a fragment of wall in the garden of Newport Cottage (52, Bailgate) can be viewed to the right from the property's front gate, and if you want to be even more thorough, there is a large but overgrown section of the ditch accompanying the wall on very private property in the back garden of The Fosse House, 21, Northgate, on the corner of Church Lane (4); go outside the Arch and turn right. Another preserved fragment of the upper defences, largely covered with ivy, is in the grounds of Hilton House at the south end of the west defences, immediately south of the castle walls (5), but this is also on private property and is not accessible except by prior arrangement.

From outside the Newport Arch, walk northwards for 20 m and turn left along Cecil Street. An arch on the left in Mary Sookias House opposite no. 24 leads to another fine stretch of city wall, 3 m (10 ft) high, uncovered in 1975–7 (6), but by 2001 somewhat dilapidated and in need of restoration. There are serious conservation problems with this stretch, and it may have to be reburied for its own protection. Here all but the lowest two or three courses of facing-stones above the projecting base-plinth have been robbed (and the base-plinth itself is currently invisible, choked by rubble). A row of putlog holes which held the scaffolding timbers during construction used to be clear, 2.50 m (8 ft) above the ground, but weathering has progressively reduced their visibility: only one, at the far right-hand (west) end, is now conspicuous.

Now return to the Newport Arch and go down Bailgate. A sign over the door at 29, on the right, draws attention to the existence of a Roman colonnade: it was 84 m (275 ft) long

and partly runs under the street further on (7), where some of
its 19 columns are marked out in the tarmac (a few remains of
the columns themselves are preserved *in situ* in cellars,
including three at 29, Bailgate, but these are on private
property and are not accessible except by special
arrangement). Some were double columns, marking important
entrances: this too is reflected in the overlapping stone-sett
circles in the street. The whole formed a magnificent and
grandiose façade to the forum on its east side.

Now turn right along Westgate and go down the few steps
on your left to reach part of the walling and an adjacent well-
shaft (with tile-built arches at the top) which lay on the east
side of the Roman forum (8). First found in 1979, the well
was fully excavated in 1984, when it was found to have a
capacity of about 3,000 gallons (*c.* 13,500 litres), but it had
been emptied of its contents and recut in the fifteenth century.
It belongs along with the other walling here to the late second
or early third century, when the original forum of *c.* 100/25
was refurbished. The Bailgate colonnade was almost certainly
added at the same time.

In the pedestrian area immediately adjacent to the Roman
well-shaft, the plan of a simple but sizeable apsed building of
timber has been marked out in modern materials (9).
Discovered when the Victorian church of St Paul-in-the-Bail
was demolished here in 1971, it stood in the middle of the
open space of the Roman forum. There can be no doubt that it
is a church, and below it was a simpler, smaller, rectangular
wooden building, which may conceivably also have been a
church (this is not indicated on the ground today). The earliest
burials post-dating the larger building have radio-carbon dates
of the fifth and sixth centuries, and a single coin of 388/92 on
its floor is also consistent with a date not before *c.* 400; it
might well be later. Graves cut into the wall of this later
church indicate that it had certainly been demolished by the
later eighth century. The church itself might, therefore, belong
to any time between *c.* 400 and *c.* 700. As for the earlier
timber structure, some prefer to push its dating back into the
later fourth century, and to see it as a tiny Roman church:
there is, however, no direct corroboration of this, and its
location in the middle of the forum is somewhat irregular if
the latter was still operating normally. It may be safer to

assume that both structures are sub-Roman, built in the decaying forum after the latter had ceased to function as such.

Now turn right from Westgate into West Bight, and then first right behind the Castle Hotel. Here stands the so-called Mint Wall (10), 21 m (70 ft) long and 7 m (23 ft) high and, for Britain, an impressive enough piece of upstanding Roman masonry; a further 2.50 m (8 ft) lies buried, the difference in height between the modern ground-line and Roman floor-levels. The Mint Wall is part of the rear wall of the city's civic basilica, in the form it took after a reconstruction in the late second or early third century. Three rows of triple brick bonding-courses can be seen, as well as some putlog holes (blocked with modern cement); the extra bonding-courses at one end may denote the beginning of a separate feature, such as a central apse. The other side of the Mint Wall can be seen from the yard behind the Castle Hotel, opening directly off Westgate. The adjacent forum to the south was partly revealed in excavations of 1978–9, together with the cross-hall and part of the courtyard of the timber *principia* of the legionary fortress below it.

Continue walking westwards along Westgate and turn left at the end along Union Road. On your left near the NW corner of the medieval wall, the site of the Roman west gate lies buried in the castle embankment. Its single arch was still intact when it was uncovered in 1836, as shown by a painting in the Usher Gallery (p. 274), but it collapsed soon afterwards (11). Opposite, in The Lawn, the Archaeology Centre (12) has displays about how archaeological evidence is studied (open daily throughout the year, Monday–Thursday, 1000–1630, Friday–Sunday, 1000–1600).

Now retrace your steps to Bailgate, turn right, and walk down Steep Hill. On the right, where a lantern has been affixed to the wall, is a piece of mellowed stone (13). The lower part of this fragment formed part of the Roman south gate of the upper town (the upper, larger blocks are medieval); when the walls were extended in the mid-second century, there was of course another south gate, at the foot of High Street, facing the river. A recent excavation on the other side of the street (at 44, Steep Hill) has found the wall of the east carriageway, and a fragment of the pier separating the two gates, so that we now know that the south gate was of double-

carriageway type. Excavation in 1984 south of here
demonstrated, in fact, that part of the approach to the upper
city was by means of a monumental stepped street, in the
manner of some Mediterranean cities where similarly steep
terrain demanded it.

Now retrace your steps a little and turn right into the
cathedral precinct. Under a stairway leading off the NE corner
of the cloisters is a portion of Roman mosaic, found nearby in
1793 (14). On the south side of the cathedral are the remains
of the Bishop's Palace [AM; April–September, daily
1000–1800; October, daily 1000–1700; November–March,
Saturday and Sunday only, 1000–1600]. At the extreme south
end of the Bishop's Palace, a stretch of defences 4.25 m
(14 ft) high, bordering the former palace garden, which has
long been taken to be Roman work, has now been shown to
be medieval (15). The only Roman feature visible here are the
foundations and two or three courses of walling, running
down the slope (rather than laid horizontally, as is the
medieval work above it) for nearly 6 m (19 ft). This formed
part of the defences of the lower town some 50 m (55 yd)
south of its junction with the upper city.

Until the important excavations of the 1970s very little was
known of the walls of the lower Roman town, and none of its
gates had been found. One stretch of defences was located in
1971 north of West Parade, while building a new police
headquarters, but these have been destroyed. A plan of what
was found there is, however, displayed on the façade of the
building in West Parade, opposite The Park (16), and a tiny
fragment of walling belonging to a fourth-century platform
added at the back of the wall is visible immediately below the
display board.

At the same time that this was being excavated, an
impressive stretch of the lower defences, including the west
gate, was being uncovered in 1970–2 a few metres further
south, and this has been consolidated in the forecourt of the
Municipal Offices in Orchard Street (17). We now know that
the first wall surrounding the lower *colonia* was built towards
the end of the second century and was only 1.50 m (5 ft)
thick. It was, however, well constructed and seems to have
stood here unrepaired until the fourth century, although in
selected places elsewhere on the lower circuit the rampart was

widened to 11 m (36 ft) at some time during the third century, presumably in those sections where the original wall had collapsed. An interval tower was added on the inside of the wall in the mid- or late third century, but it was demolished towards the mid-fourth century when the wall was pierced to make a gateway here. This was originally planned as a single passageway 4.90 m (16 ft) wide and 9 m (30 ft) long, together with a central stone block serving as a gate stop; but it was modified during construction by shortening the passageway and adding massive projecting rectangular towers. The backs of these flanking towers still stand to a considerable height, and here can be seen the rear portion of the two guard-chambers which each contained. The fronts of the towers are less well preserved, but it can be seen that their foundations incorporate material which has been pirated from other buildings in the town. One piece built into the south side of the north tower is a fine second-century cornice, from a temple or some other public building. It has been replaced on site by a cast, but the original, viewable on request, is in the Municipal Offices. Some large blocks at the front of the towers here have lewis holes in them to assist in lifting.

At the same time that this gate was constructed about the middle of the fourth century, the defences were strengthened still further. North of the gate the old late second-century wall was completely replaced at this time, but to the south new masonry was tacked on to the back of the early wall, and to save material the width was reduced by a series of offsets, thus creating the present step-like effect. The wall here stands to a height of 3 m (10 ft); the stonework was not robbed in medieval times, because it was protected by the clay mound which backed the wall and which was increased to a width of 24 m (80 ft) in these late fourth-century changes. It has now been removed to display the splendid masonry of the rear face of the wall. Coins on the road surface indicate that the gate remained in use into the fifth century.

Another stretch of *colonia* wall, showing a similar sequence to that in Orchard Street, was excavated in 1973–4 on the south side of the circuit, under the Stonebow Centre in Saltergate (18): here again the original narrow wall (dated here however to the late third century, at variance with the evidence elsewhere – possibly an indication that the original

lower walls took decades to complete) was thickened by
additional masonry in the mid-fourth century. These Roman
defences, which also plundered material from other buildings
(including part of a monumental inscription), stood over
2.25 m (7 ft 6 in) high, and were crowned by a further 1.50 m
(5 ft) of medieval wall. A narrow postern gate for pedestrians,
2 m (6 ft 6 in) wide, was also found (whether contemporary
with the original wall or the fourth-century thickening is
unclear), but the main south gate must lie further west, on the
line of High Street. The postern has been preserved in the
basement of the modern building, but at the time of writing
(2001) access to it is restricted to occasional Saturdays each
year: advance arrangements to view have to be made with the
Lincoln Museums Service. Currently (and shamefully)
Lincoln lacks an archaeological museum, but plans to build
one behind the Usher Art Gallery in Lindum Road are well
advanced (19). A shapeless fragment of wall-ditch, on the line
of the eastern defences here, is visible in its grounds.

Very little else is visible in the lower *colonia*. The church
of St Swithin's adjacent to Saltergate contains a Roman altar
(20), and the flue arch of a hypocaust found in 1925 and
perhaps belonging to a bath building can be found in the
basement of the premises next door to the Job Centre, in High
Street near to its junction with Clasketgate (21). At the time
of writing (2001), the site is occupied by a night club called
Po Na Na: the Roman arch can be inspected on request (at the
discretion of the management) between the hours of 2100 and
0200 only. On the other side of Clasketgate, a few paces
further down High Street and also on the left (east), the
finding in 1845 of a monumental inscription dedicated to
Mercury, together with several column bases, indicates the
probable site of an imposing temple under no. 287, now
occupied by Ruddock's shop; the site of the Roman building
is marked by a plaque on the wall.

Outside the Roman walled city, four other Roman items
may be briefly mentioned, three of them reached by
proceeding south along High Street. About 300 m (330 yds)
south of Saltergate, on the left next to the railway station, a
Roman gabled tombstone can be seen to the right of the door
into the tower of the church of St Mary-le-Wigford (22). It
commemorates a Gaul called Sacer son of Bruscus, his wife

Carssouna, and son Quintus, and was presumably robbed as building stone from the nearby Roman cemetery; the gable inscription was added in the eleventh century. As with similar examples elsewhere in Britain, the very fact that the pagan inscription was left visible instead of the stone being reversed suggests that there was a certain prestige value in medieval times attached to recycling the relics of the mighty Roman Empire, as though the tenacity of a former regime might rub off on the new rulers. A quarter of a mile (400 m) further on, also on the left, at 385, High Street, is the twelfth-century structure of St Mary's Guildhall (23), now the offices of Lincoln Civic Trust (open Mondays, Tuesdays and Thursdays only, 0900–1300). Inside is a shorn-down stone believed to represent the base of the first Roman milestone south of the Roman town walls, and also a preserved section of the Roman surface of the Fosse Way, with the rut-marks of Roman carts still visible in it. Adjacent to St Mary's Guildhall is the church of St Peter-at-Gowts (24). High up in its tower, facing High Street, above the second window down, is a very weathered Roman relief, re-used in the medieval church fabric just like the Sacer tombstone mentioned above. Its details are barely visible without binoculars, but a recent suggestion is that the winged figure represents the shadowy figure of Arimanius (Ahriman), a figure in the complex Mithraic religion who represented darkness but who was also linked with the god of infinite time; the sculptured figure is, however, too worn for absolute certainty.

Finally, on the other side of Lincoln, a section of the Roman aqueduct pipe, encased in pink *opus signinum* mortar, can be seen inside the entrance to Safeways supermarket (25), on the left of Nettleham Road (the road heading NE out of the city from the Eastgate Hotel, branching off almost immediately from Northgate; follow it for 1 mile [1.6 km]). Found during construction of the supermarket, this is the only surviving fragment of a substantial aqueduct, mentioned above (p. 267), which supplied water to the Roman city. One untested hypothesis is that the aqueduct brought water from possibly as far away as 20 miles (32 km); more likely it conveyed water from a source somewhere on the Jurassic Ridge north of Lincoln, and crossed a valley 50 m north of the supermarket under pressure in an inverted siphon (which

would account for the encasement of the pipe in mortar) to a
collection point north of the city. It would then have needed to
be raised up to the level of the collection reservoir in East
Bight, possibly by a bucket-and-chain lifting mechanism of
the type recently found in London (p. 633). Part of the
aqueduct NE of Safeways was carried on stone arches, the
piers of which have been discovered in excavation but sadly
not preserved. One of the many puzzling features about this
aqueduct is the absence of lime deposits in the pipe, to be
expected in this limestone-rich area if the pipe was in use for
any length of time. It is not impossible that the system
malfunctioned soon after completion, and that this Romano-
British attempt at sophisticated water engineering was a costly
white elephant. Only further research will show.

Whereas the legionary fortress at Lincoln became a *colonia*,
that at **Wroxeter**** (SJ 568088) [AM; April–September,
daily, 1000–1800; October, daily, 1000–1700; November–
March, Wednesday–Sunday, 1000–1300 and 1400–1600] was
turned into the tribal capital of the Cornovii, VIROCONIVM
CORNOVIORVM. The ditches of the 40-acre (16-ha) legionary
fortress have been identified from the air (and subsequently
tested by excavation), and timber barracks belonging to it
have been excavated beneath the baths in the heart of the later
town. Finds indicate that the military base, at first garrisoned
by the Fourteenth Gemina legion and then (after its
withdrawal from Britain in AD 66/7) by the Twentieth, lasted
from about AD 55/60 to 87, by which time the legion had
returned from its base at Inchtuthil in Scotland and was then
posted forward to Chester. The civilian settlement which must
have grown up during this military phase then developed into
a fully fledged *civitas* capital, which subsequently expanded
and flourished: when the earth defences were thrown up in the
later second century, they enclosed an area of 170 acres
(71 ha), making Wroxeter the fourth largest Romano-British
town. Quite apart from the excavations in the central sector,
much has been learnt of the plan of the town from aerial
photography (the site lies in open fields), and more recently
from geophysical prospection, part of an ambitious
programme of fieldwork carried out in the 1990s which also
involved study of tracts of the surrounding territory. This has
indicated the density of urban settlement in much of the town

(a population of 5,000 is suggested for Wroxeter at its zenith), and a number of buildings have been identified, including a possible church 100 m SE of the baths.

The site is reached, if you are coming from the west, by turning off the A5 ring road at a roundabout on the SE side of Shrewsbury, following the B45061 for Wellington, and turning right $\frac{1}{2}$ mile (800 m) after Attingham. If you are coming from the east, turn southwards off M54 at junction 7, and then first right for Uppington, after which you turn left on to the B45061. Before entering the main site on the left, continue walking along the road a little further and look over the fence on the right (1 on Fig. 58). The long line of column-stumps which you see here formed part of a portico on the east side of the forum. The whole of the latter was excavated in the 1920s but only this part has been left exposed. The excavations produced one of the largest and finest inscriptions from Roman Britain, recording the erection of the building by the *civitas Cornoviorum* under the Emperor Hadrian in AD 129/30. The original is in Rowley's House Museum, Shrewsbury (weekdays, 1000–1700; Sunday, Easter–mid September 1200–1700), but there is a cast in the site Museum. The excavations also showed that a bath building had been started in the late first century in what later was to become the central piazza of the forum. This was probably an extramural military bath-house belonging to the legionary fortress, built by the Twentieth on returning from Scotland *c.* AD 86, but demolished before completion a year or so later because of the decision to move the legion on to Chester; it was probably intended to replace an earlier, smaller bath building within the fortress. The alternative view, that it is a civilian bath-house built in the first flush of civic pride, but left unfinished because of technical or financial problems, seems much less likely. Visitors with time to spare may like to continue walking southwards to the church of St Andrew, which re-uses Roman stone in its north wall (the massive blocks), in its font (a re-used Roman column base) and at the entrance gate (a pair of Roman columns). If you continue on past the church, the road passes through a section of the Roman town defences, visible here as a broad bank.

Now return to the car-park and enter the main site to visit the excellent site Museum (2 on Fig. 58), furnished with some

unusual exhibits and very full information panels. Apart from
the cast of the forum stone, another inscription of great
interest is displayed here. It reads: 'Cunorix, son of Maqqos-
Colini' ('Son of the Holly'), and is dated on linguistic grounds
to AD 460–75. Macus and Maqqos mean 'son' in ancient Irish,
and Cunorix is probably an Irishman settled by the Romans in
Britain to help stave off other invaders; such men were known
as *foederati*, 'allied'. Other important exhibits in the museum
include the painted plaster from the vault of the baths'
caldarium (note the scored guidelines to help the painter); the
stack of samian bowls from the forum gutter, for long a key
deposit in our understanding of the chronology of second-
century samian pottery; part of a bronze discharge certificate
for an auxiliary soldier, dated to AD 135; some lead-weighted
javelin heads, a novelty introduced to fourth-century warfare;
and an apotropaic relief in stone of a winged phallus on legs
pulling a chariot.

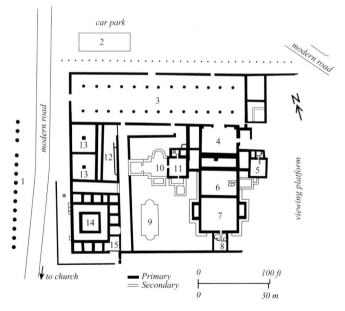

58   Wroxeter, Roman baths and adjacent buildings, site plan

When you have finished visiting the Museum, go out on to the veranda and look over the rest of the site. The most conspicuous feature is the fine upstanding piece of masonry known as the Old Work, which has miraculously survived medieval stone-robbing and the vagaries of over 1,800 years of British weather. It is part of the south wall of a large aisled building, 74.50 m (245 ft or 250 Roman feet) long and 20 m (66 ft) wide, which occupied all the area between the Museum and the rest of the site, and which formed a covered exercise-hall (*palaestra*) for the baths (3). Along with the rest of the baths, construction started in the 120s and was then suspended for reasons unknown; it was only 30 or so years later that construction began again in earnest and was brought to completion. The floor of the covered hall was of pink *opus signinum* mortar, and the aisles had simple geometric mosaic pavements, although that in the south aisle was repaved *c.* AD 300 with a herringbone brick floor (*opus spicatum*); this survived in an excellent state of preservation, but it has not been left exposed. There was then a long sequence of floor-levels within the hall as it gradually decayed, until finally, probably some time in the fifth century, it had to be dismantled. In the building-rubble several timber structures have been traced, suggesting that at the time the area was used as a market. Then in the sixth century, after total demolition of the remaining shell of the great stone hall, more timber buildings, some of considerable pretensions, were erected on its site. Precise dating evidence is lacking, but life must have continued here into the seventh century before Wroxeter was finally abandoned. None of these sub-Roman structures can be seen today, nor have their plans been marked out; instead it is the great covered excercise-hall with its two rows of columns, together with some remnants of its original outer walls, which can be traced on the ground today.

Walk down to the far end and enter the bath-house through the site of the double doors which partially filled the present gap in the Old Work. In the north (*palaestra*) side, which is especially well preserved, putlog holes of two sizes are clearly visible, with a specially placed, larger flat stone slab over each opening. On the underside of the gap in the Old Work can be seen the two rounded impressions left by the relieving-arches (now vanished) which lay above the lintels of the two doors;

59   Wroxeter, Roman baths, the Old Work reconstructed

the doors were not, therefore, as high as the present gap in the
structure. Higher up are three great tile arches which form
deep recesses and which were originally supported by
columns or pilasters. All these features can be better
understood by a glance at the drawing of the suggested
reconstruction (Fig. 59).

Now turn your back on the Old Work and examine the rest
of the baths complex. You are now standing in the *frigidarium*
(4). On the left and right were cold-water pools (grey gravel)
and in front of you are the thresholds, one very worn, which
led into the *tepidarium*, which is divided into two parts by a
cross-wall. From here onwards you are walking below the
original floor-level, for none of the baths' floors has survived
(note the brick drain under the *frigidarium* behind you). On
your left are two smaller rooms, one with two *pilae*-bases and
an adjoining stoke-hole (5), with firing chamber and the steps
down to it. Later the door to the firing chamber was blocked
and a still-extant window (a rare *in situ* survival for Roman
Britain: cf. Chesters, p. 481, for another) was inserted. Note
on the high platform above the stoke-room there is a
herringbone brick floor, one of very few visible examples of
this widespread technique (*opus spicatum*) in Britain. The
rooms which this chamber heated formed a subsidiary set of

intense dry-heat rooms and were matched by a similar set on the other side, less well preserved.

Ignore the latter for the moment and move from the second (main) part of the *tepidarium* (6) into the *caldarium* (moist heat: 7), on either side of which are recesses for hot baths. All the *pilae* here are modern, as all the original tiles had been robbed and only their impressions remained; so too is the floor. The original walls of these rooms had also disappeared, and they are also marked out in modern materials. Soon after the baths were built, an outer wall of grey sandstone partly encased the *caldarium*. Probably cracks developed in the inner wall, and the new wall was then built to prevent heat-loss. At the end of the *caldarium* is the stoke-hole (8; Fig. 60); this was probably originally intended to heat both the warm rooms, but later the *tepidarium* was given a separate furnace, and part of the internal channel flue of this secondary addition is represented by the Roman masonry visible on the floor of that room. Watch out for a flat-lying tile in the oblique flue here – it has the oval finger-impression of the person who made it some 1,700 years ago.

On leaving the *caldarium* by its stoke-hole at the far end, note that the mortar rendering on the exterior of the bath-

60   Wroxeter, the baths and the Old Work, seen from the hot room's stoke-hole

house survives well here. At this point you may like to mount
the viewing platform to your left for an excellent overall view
of the site. Now retrace your steps across the grass, past the
caldarium, to the small open-air swimming-bath (*piscina*)
with an apse at each end (9). This was not a regular feature of
all Roman baths in Britain, and it is in fact the only visible
example in the country apart from that in the legionary baths
at Caerleon (p. 303). It did not have a very long life, perhaps
because the British climate never made it popular, and at the
beginning of the third century it was demolished; most of its
paving stones were ripped up for use elsewhere, and it became
a rubbish tip. At the same time an extension to the main
bath-suite prevented access to this corner of the establishment.

The *caldarium* of this extension (10 on Fig. 58) is clearly
recognizable by the semicircular wall north of the *piscina*. On
the outside of this apse, at eye-level, can be seen a stone with
pieces of iron crampon remarkably still *in situ*, together with
the lead bedding which holds it there; the metal tie was
designed to anchor the block to an adjacent one. The stoke-
hole of this *caldarium* is represented by the two large blocks
to the west, while the room on the east, with another furnace-
chamber approached by steps, was the *tepidarium* of the
extension (11). This room was originally intended, however,
to be one of a pair of dry-heat rooms flanking the *tepidarium*
of the main suite, matched by the similar pair of rooms on the
other side mentioned above. The reason for building the
extension is not known for certain, but the furnace of the main
caldarium of the baths appears to have gone out of use by
c. 300, and with it the main heated rooms (perhaps because of
the structural problems and possible heat-loss alluded to
above). The enlarged side-suite may therefore have been
designed to replace, on a smaller scale, the now abandoned
caldarium and one of the *tepidaria* of the grandiose original
baths. A nineteenth-century print of this side-suite, showing
many *pilae* in position and parts of the suspended floor, is
displayed in the site museum; it indicates how much the baths
have deteriorated since they were first exposed nearly 150
years ago.

Now leave the heated wing and move westwards towards
the area with pink gravel. The long room nearest to the baths
(and reachable directly from it, or from a side alley) was a

public latrine (12), recognizable by its long, tile-lined sewer along one wall; covered by seats, the sewer originally ran round all four walls. The adjacent chambers with square bases in the centre to support their roof were shops (13) facing on to a main street opposite the forum. Next to them, separated by an alleyway, is the *macellum* or market, consisting of a series of small rooms ranged about a courtyard (14). It was built, like the forum, in the Hadrianic period, over the levelled remains of the legionary defences and subsequent civilian timber structures. It was then remodelled *c*. AD 300 when the corridor was floored (like the south aisle in the baths exercise-hall) in herringbone brickwork, but this is not visible. Another latrine occupied the L-shaped room at its SE corner (15).

The other tribal capital in central England, **Leicester*** (SK 583044), was RATAE CORIELTAVVORVM, the *civitas* capital of the Corieltauvi. RATAE means 'fortification' in Celtic, a root still surviving in the Irish word 'rath'. There was pre-Roman occupation of the site and a military post of uncertain size in the early years of the Roman conquest, but as yet very little is known of either phase. The street-grid of the town belongs to the early second century, and the first earth defences probably to later in the same century. These enclosed about 100 acres (42 ha) and were later refurbished in stone, but no scrap of the Roman walls remains visible. There is no evidence for the addition of projecting towers. Inside the town, the remains of just one Roman building has been left exposed; like Wroxeter, it preserves a magnificent stretch of Roman masonry 9 m (30 ft) high, the Jewry Wall.

The site, which lies in the western half of the modern town near the church of St Nicholas (on St Nicholas' Circle on the Central Ring ring road), was excavated in 1936–9. The intention had been to erect modern swimming-baths on the site, but as it was believed at the time that the Jewry Wall was part of the basilica and that the supposed adjacent forum was later covered by public baths, it was decided to preserve what was thought to have been the earliest administrative centre of Leicester. It is now known, however, that the forum and basilica lay on an adjacent site to the east partly under St Nicholas' Circle, and that the Jewry Wall, like the Old Work at Wroxeter, is part of the *palaestra*, or exercise-hall, of the public baths.

It is best to visit first the Jewry Wall Museum (daily,
April–October, Monday–Saturday, 1000–1700, Sunday,
1400–1700; November–March, 1000–1600, Sunday,
1300–1600), which overlooks the Roman remains. The most
spectacular exhibits are four examples of frescoed wall
decoration, and three mosaic floors recovered from various
town-houses. First to confront the visitor is the wall-plaster
from a villa in Norfolk Street, which lay outside the town in
Roman times. Painted *c*. AD 150/200, its scheme consists of
panels framed in red and yellow on a white ground
(white-ground painting first appeared in Rome in the late first
century BC, but became fashionable only in the second century
AD). To the right are some substantial columns and their
stylobate coming from the Roman forum; near them note
especially the case with a tile from Cave's Inn (Roman
TRIPONTIVM), found in 1965, which demonstrated for the first
time that the name of the local tribe was not the Coritani, as
had been erroneously handed down to us by the manuscript
tradition, but the Corieltauvi – a form of the name since in
part corroborated by another more recent find, an inscribed
lead sealing from Nottinghamshire.

In the next section is an outstanding geometric mosaic from
Blackfriars, first found in 1830 and relaid in the Museum in
1977. Dated to not earlier than *c*. 125/40 by pieces of samian
pottery used as red tesserae in the floor, the pavement has a
highly pleasing, intricate design and a restrained, tasteful use
of colour. Displayed behind it is another frescoed wall from
the Norfolk Street villa, with a modern attempt on the right to
show how it might have appeared when freshly painted; but
no classical artist, not even a Romano-British one, would have
painted the bizarre monster suggested for the central panel.
The frame of this, incidentally, with its overlapping yellow
border, probably reflects the form of wooden frames used in
portable panel paintings. The smaller fresco panel to the right
comes from the ceiling of another of RATAE's public buildings,
the market-hall. Also displayed here are two further mosaics,
one (in poor condition) depicting a peacock at the centre;
more striking are the wall frescoes of the mid-second century
which come from the corridor of a town-house found in 1958
immediately north of the forum (Blue Boar Lane). They
depict human figures, birds, garlands and candelabra, set in an

61   Leicester, Roman wall-plaster from a house in Blue Boar Lane

architectural framework on a red and black ground (Fig. 61),
and are among the most sophisticated examples of classically
inspired wall painting in Britain. The general scheme adopted
here, ultimately derived from first-century Italian models, was
widely imitated in provincial painting in the north-west
provinces during the second century.

In the final section note especially the weathered but good-
quality limestone portrait of a young man, from Hinkley; a
box flue-tile inscribed with a metal comb, 'Primus made 60
[of these]' (whether in a day or in a week is not recorded!);
and an instructive case with human bones showing ancient
medical problems, including evidence for arthritis and
tuberculosis. Also documented here is a surgical operation,
the drilling of a hole through the skull (a process known as
trephination), which was believed in antiquity to help relieve
excessive head pain, but which was only used (not
surprisingly) as a last resort. In this case, as the absence of

regenerative bone growth around the hole demonstrates, the patient died soon afterwards.

On leaving the Museum, take a look at the plan of the Roman baths which is displayed on the terrace. The visible remains belong to two periods, the first about AD 145–50, when the Jewry Wall itself and the rooms nearest to it were put up; for reasons unknown it seems never to have been finished. After a short hiatus, the building was completed with alterations and additions, perhaps *c.* 155–60, when the three large halls in front of you were built. These distinctions are not indicated on the plan, but the gravel marking the lines of the walls is coloured yellow for the phase 1 walls, and grey for the later additions. The apsed hot baths and furnaces marked on the plan were destroyed when the Museum was constructed. Keep to the right and make first for the superb Roman drain with a single capstone *in situ*; its walls constitute a good example of Roman construction consisting of coursed masonry with a triple bonding-course of bricks. The capstone marks Roman ground-level: all the remains here except for the Jewry Wall is reduced to foundations only. Beyond the drain, at a higher level, is part of a town-house.

Now walk over to the impressive Jewry Wall [AM; A], which may owe its preservation to incorporation into the Saxon predecessor of the present St Nicholas' Church. The origin of the name Jewry Wall is uncertain, but it is believed to be a corruption of 'jurat', a medieval term for an alderman or city councillor. It is an imposing stretch of masonry, with tile bonding-courses and one of the two arched doorways in a fine state of preservation. The course of large blocks of Derbyshire millstone grit to the right indicates approximate Roman floor-level. The square holes were designed to hold wooden scaffolding during construction, and would have been plugged with other material which has now fallen out. Below the Jewry Wall is another section of drain: this ran underneath the bath building's *frigidarium*. At the far end, close to the metal staircase, is an outfall-channel leading into another drain from a tiny room at a higher level, presumably a small immersion-bath (certainly not a latrine, as suggested in the current guide leaflet). Now turn and face the Museum. On the small mound in front of you are some bases of hypocaust *pilae*, another indication that most of what is visible at this site is at sub-basement level; it formed part of a small *tepidarium*, and the two adjacent rooms to its left were probably also *tepidaria*. Finally, at a lower level beyond, there are three more heated rooms (*caldaria*), with apses for plunge-baths on either side. The precise sequence of rooms which the bather would have followed is not fully understood (mainly because the remains are largely destroyed to sub-floor level), and the Leicester building is not, therefore, as good an example of a public bath-house as that at Wroxeter (p. 279).

After you have left the site, take a look at the other side of the Jewry Wall. In addition to the pair of arched doorways, two arched recesses are visible here, as well as a niche in the middle, presumably for a statue. The lower courses of the north wall of the *palaestra* hall can be seen from Welles Street (follow St Nicholas' Walk to the far end and turn left). In the churchyard are some further displaced columns coming from the adjacent Roman forum.

The only other remnant of Roman Leicester is a stretch of fairly impressive earthwork known as the Raw Dykes. Only 120 m (130 yds) of it survives now, but some 900 m (996 yds) of it was still visible in the early nineteenth century. Excavation has shown that it consists of a shallow channel 2.4 m (8 ft) deep with the upcast forming a bank on one side; there was a deeper cut, 1.5 m (5 ft) deep and 0.9 m (3 ft) wide, at the bottom. It seems to have been part of the aqueduct serving RATAE (the construction is not dissimilar to that serving Dorchester: p. 108), taking waters from a nearby stream, but differences in level show that on reaching the city it must have been raised by water-wheels or by a bucket-and-chain lifting device to a higher level, for efficient gravity distribution to sites in the Roman town like the baths. The Raw Dykes lie about 1 mile (1.6 km) south of the Jewry Wall. From St Nicholas' Circle follow directions for 'Rugby (A426)'. Just after turning left on to the A426 proper, stop just before the railway-bridge. The earthwork lies on the right-hand side of the road, facing a large Toyota car showroom.

The rest of the Roman towns in central England did not have colonial or *civitas*-capital status, and were generally much smaller in size. One settlement, however, at **Water Newton** (TL 122908), was quite extraordinarily large and complex, and it is possible that it was promoted to self-

governing status in the later Roman period. It began, as with
so many of the towns of Roman Britain, as a village outside a
military fort, established in the conquest period (perhaps
c. AD 45) to guard the crossing-point of the main trunk-road to
the north, Ermine Street, over the river Nene. When the army
moved on c. AD 70 it flourished and expanded in piecemeal
fashion, first as ribbon development along Ermine Street, but
then over a vast area both north and south of the Nene: at its
apogee in the fourth century, the town of DVROBRIVAE ('the
fort at the bridge', indicating its military origin) sprawled over
some 250 acres (60 ha), a size rivalled only by Cirencester
and London. But whereas the last two were carefully planned
administrative centres, Water Newton was the product of
spontaneous, unplanned growth, and aerial photographs show
that there was no neat grid-pattern of streets. Another
difference was that the defences, when they came, enclosed
only about 44 acres (18 ha) at the heart of the town. Limited
excavation suggested that its earth rampart was of the late
second century, as commonly in Romano-British towns, and
that the stone wall in front of it was contemporary; this,
however, seems unlikely (if both were really built at the same
time, they probably belong to the third century at the earliest).
Towers, visible on air photographs, were presumably added in
the fourth century. A cemetery of the third to the early fifth
century, with 160 inhumations and two stone sarcophagi, was
discovered on the SW side of the town in 1998 during
drainage works along the A1.

    The site is now accessible only to southbound traffic on the
east side of the A1, $2\frac{1}{2}$ miles (4 km) south of its junction with
the A47 (Leicester–Peterborough): park in the second (larger)
lay-by south of the more southerly of the two turnings to
Water Newton village (AA phone). You are now at the south
corner of the Roman town. Particularly striking is the
magnificent *agger* of Ermine Street striding up to the SE gate
and right through the middle of the town: it will be
appreciated that the modern road has swerved to the west and
south of the Roman line at this point. The SE defences can be
made out as a low mound to your left (as they are for most of
their circuit), but for a better view of these, it is best to walk
back along the verge northwards along the A1 to the field-gate
recessed from the road. The SW defences of the town,

together with thistles marking the line of the accompanying ditch, are clearly visible from here, and the line of Ermine Street as it crosses the town can be made out as a raised mound on the skyline. Very little controlled excavation has been carried out within the defences, but aerial photos taken when the site was under crop (it is now permanently in pasture to avoid further damage to the buried structures) revealed much – a large public building, possibly an official inn for travellers, or else a market-place, and at least one temple, as well as other structures, residential or commercial in character. But the shanty town, as mentioned above, spread far beyond the walls, and extensive excavation, especially over the past decade, has yielded detailed information about the buildings and activities there: this was one of the main industrial areas of Roman Britain, the centre of one of the most successful potteries in the island. From the mid-second century down into the late fourth century it produced a wide range of colour-coated vessels, both decorated and plain (known as Nene Valley or Castor ware), which were traded over much of the province. The mosaics of the surrounding countryside, the silver plate of a Christian church or house-chapel in the town, now in the British Museum (p. 651), the high-quality small finds from even the humblest buildings – all are indicators of the prosperity and high living standards of the Nene valley region in late Roman times.

Some of the rich establishments in the hinterland of Water Newton, such as that underlying Castor village (App. 1), may well have been connected in some way with the potteries, and perhaps owned by businessmen who had made their money in the industry; but others were traditional villas dependent on farming the fertile soils of the Nene valley. Few of these villas and farms have been excavated (many are known from the air), and of those that have, only one has something preserved *in situ*. That is the site, now largely marked out in modern materials, at Lynch Farm, **Orton Longueville** (TL 149977), which was excavated in 1972–4. It lies in the recreation area known as Nene Park Ferry Meadows, which is signposted from the A605 (Corby–Peterborough) 2 miles (3 km) east of its junction with the A1 (near Water Newton), and 3 miles (5 km) west of Peterborough (roundabout). Follow the road round to the left as far as the roundabout after the barrier at the entrance to the park: here take the last exit for the parking area, where you should park as close as possible to the Visitor Centre. About 150 m past the latter, bear right when the path forks, and you will see an information board ('Roman Point') at the top of the slope ahead of you, immediately to the right of the path.

The earliest feature here is the corner (which has been marked out) of a first-century military ditch, part of two multiple ditch-systems which may have belonged to marching-camps or perhaps camps built in training, although neither type usually has more than one ditch. The earlier system is contemporary with the 28-acre (12-ha) vexillation fortress which lies facing you, immediately across the river at Longthorpe; it is now buried below a golf-course. This was a key base in the subjugation of the eastern Midlands, where legionaries and auxiliaries were brigaded together between c. AD 45 and 62, the base from which Petillius Cerialis made a desperate and disastrous attempt to stem the Boudican advance in 60/1 before Suetonius Paullinus could return from Anglesey (p. 301). Later, probably in the third century, a large aisled barn was put up, built of timber on pitched-stone footings. Its roof was supported on two rows of posts, now marked out as concrete circles. The barn was used no doubt, like its modern counterpart, for storing crops and farm implements, but several furnaces were found (one is still visible at the far end of the barn), indicating as well small-scale production of ironwork. Such aisled buildings were extremely common in the countryside of Roman Britain, either as outbuildings in courtyard-type villas, or else as independent farm buildings, sometimes even with subdivisions for living accommodation; but apart from that at the Rockbourne villa (p. 131), this is the only permanently accessible example of its type in Britain. A well and a small square timber building on stone footings with a timber veranda or colonnade (possibly a temple) are the other visible associated features, but a corn-drier and a stone tank probably used as a fishpond had to give way to the waters of the artificial pleasure-lake. These were clearly the outbuildings of a farming estate, possibly the same as the one which included ditched stockyards 400 m (440 yds) further east, but the main villa buildings have not been excavated. In the fourth century decline set in here, probably because of flooding, and the stockyards were used as a cemetery for 51 burials (which are not now visible).

Towns such as Water Newton which were situated on trunk roads also served as 'posting stations', where the traveller could expect to find a hotel and a stable for his horses. Another example, this time on Watling Street, was LETOCETVM ('grey wood'), now the village of **Wall*** (SK 099067) [AM; April–September, daily, 1000–1700; closed October–March]. The village is signposted from the A5, which now bypasses it. The earliest occupation at Wall was military, but the full details of a complex series of fortifications in and around the village have yet to be unravelled. The earliest was a vexillation fortress, approximately 30 acres (12.6 ha) in size, which was presumably the base for part of the Fourteenth Legion from about AD 50–8, before it moved on to Wroxeter. Finds however indicate that the same site continued in use until about AD 70. In the second century there was a small fort on the crest of the hill by the church. The importance of Wall as a military site would have attracted civilians to settle along Watling Street. The resulting settlement was a sprawling one but was not enclosed by defences. Only in the late Empire, perhaps c. 300, was a small area enclosing 5 acres (2.1 ha), astride Watling Street on the highest point of ground, provided with a wall and earth rampart and surrounded by triple ditches. Its precise character is unclear as no buildings have been excavated within it, but it seems to have enclosed the remaining population of LETOCETVM in the fourth century, since the areas of settlement which lay outside, including the inn (*mansio*) and the baths, were abandoned. Only these last two buildings can be seen at Wall today.

The bath-house was excavated in 1912–14. It is extremely complicated in its present, final form, in which five separate phases have been recognized. The first building, revealed by excavation in 1956 but not now visible, belonged to the first century and was presumably military. The Phase II bath-house, perhaps early second-century, occupies about one-third of the area of the final building and is the part first reached from the custodian's hut. In Phase III (third-century) a new undressing room and cold immersion-bath were added. In Phase IV there were internal changes and a covered exercise-hall was built, and in Phase V (perhaps at the same time as IV) the main stoke-hole was rebuilt. Phases IV and V probably also belong to the third century, since no appreciable finds were attributable to the fourth century, and the baths seemed to have been abandoned by then. Visitors who want to work out all the various phases on the site should study the plan displayed in the adjacent Museum or in the site guide.

The visitor first reaches the *tepidarium* and *caldarium*, built in Phase II. The *pilae* here have now been backfilled for their own protection. At first a small rectangular alcove projected from the exterior wall in front of you, and the broken ends of it are visible roughly in the middle of the long wall (its right-hand end is marked by the brickwork pier); it was demolished in Phase IV and the wall made continuous. Turn right towards the hedge. The next room was the entrance-hall and cold room of the Phase II baths: the latter occupies the far right-hand end of the grass-covered area where the grass slopes down to the gravel. Then comes a tiny hot bath with brick seat and lead outflow-pipe (now backfilled); beyond it (where the display panel on the workings of a hypocaust is) was a small room for dry heat, its hypocaust also now filled in. Portions of *opus signinum* lining can still be seen adhering to the walls. The bath was inserted in Phase IV; in the Phase II building this had been a single room, and was in fact the southern limit of the bath-house at this stage. The date of the room next to the hedge is unknown. It has a stoke-hole to warm the adjacent hot room, but five *pilae*-bases discovered here indicate that it too was heated at some stage. A flue opening (now blocked with modern cement) is visible in the north wall to allow hot air to circulate in the adjacent room.

Now return to the other end of the bath-house and go round the projecting stoke-yard which supplied heat to the main heated rooms. You can now examine the far side of the wall running down the middle of the building, which was the outer wall of the Phase II bath-house. Traces of three of its external buttresses, designed to take the thrust of the vaulted roof, can be seen here. The one nearest you is the most conspicuous, and another will have been noted projecting into the grass on the other side. The wall here has been much altered in later phases, and a new stoke-hole was inserted in Phase V. Note the brickwork cheek here, later blocked up. Beyond, the four flues in the far room indicate that there were two adjacent heated rooms here, although no *pilae* are visible in either room. Now continue on round the outside of the building, noting three parallel walls on your right. Two belong to a veranda of the adjoining covered exercise-hall, added in Phase IV, while the third wall (the one nearest you) is part of an earlier building underlying the hall. Rounding the corner and moving on to the gravel path marking the line of a street, you come to the broad threshold blocks of the main entrance to the baths and so cross into the courtyard. On the far side are three rooms added in Phase III. The one on the right, with a slab in the centre, was a room of dry heat (*laconicum*): the hypocaust-flues beneath are visible (as noted above). The next room is the undressing room. In Phase IV a niche was inserted, presumably for a statue; until recently this was still covered with salmon-pink plaster (it has now been replaced by a modern copy), but parts of the original rendering are still in place in the opposite corner of the room. Lastly, between the undressing room and the hedge is a cold immersion-bath, now also backfilled for its own preservation.

The substantial stone courtyard building on the other side of the Roman street, still standing up to 1.80 m (6 ft) high, was first uncovered in 1910–12 and was re-excavated in 1974–7. Its small and generally squarish rooms are arranged around a corridor and a central court, where the semicircular apse probably once held a fountain (Fig. 62). The projecting walls on the south side facing the baths are usually interpreted as buttresses, but they look too substantial for that: perhaps they are the remains of shops, independent of the building behind. Now enter the latter by the corridor on its east side, nearest the hedge. The wall forming the far side of the corridor makes a straight joint with the outer wall of the building: its east wall and the SE corner look therefore earlier than the rest of the masonry, unless this was a construction quirk during building. The three square holes present in the walls in the NE part of the building are a curious and unexplained feature: they are unlikely to mark the position of Roman internal down-pipes (the present outflows may be modern, to prevent them filling up with water); but equally to interpret them as emplacements for a timber superstructure seems illogical – not only would we expect more of them but the thickness of the walls implies

62   *Wall, Roman 'small town', the* mansio *or inn*

a stone superstructure. The room at the far north corner
(nearest the church) has fragmentary remains of a channelled
hypocaust. The double walls on the north and south sides of
this room are clearly not of the same period: only the inner
ones are contemporary with the insertion of the hypocaust.

Excavation has shown that the building was constructed
about AD 120 and replaced two phases of similar timber
building on the same alignment. The formal arrangement of
the rooms, the high quality of the construction work, together
with the presence of painted wall-plaster and window glass,
the thickness of the walls suggesting that it was a two-storey
structure, and the comparatively early date for a building in
stone at a civilian settlement, all strongly suggest some public
function, probably as a small inn (*mansio*) for travellers; but it
had a short life and seems to have been destroyed before the
end of the second century.

The Museum, two doors along Watling Street, contains a small collection of mostly unremarkable finds, but the bronze head from a statuette of a black African wrestler, half melted down, and the stones deriving from a cult-centre, perhaps where horned gods of the indigenous 'Celtic' tradition were worshipped, are of particular interest.

Another posting-station on a great trunk-road is the village of **Great Casterton** (TF 002091) on Ermine Street. It lies in the county of Rutland, 3 miles (4.8 km) NW of Stamford. It is now bypassed by the A1; so if you are heading north, turn off along the Oakham road (A606), and if you are going southwards, take the B1081 for Stamford. In the village, follow a lane signposted to Ryhall and Essendine, and you will see on your right, just after the houses, the surprisingly impressive remains of the town's defences. No stonework is now exposed, but the mound of the rampart is here 1.50 m (5 ft) high, and the enormous shallow ditch in front of it is 18 m (60 ft) wide. Elsewhere the rampart has been largely ploughed away, but the great ditch can be followed all the way down the east side of the town. Beyond the field wall, where it swings away to the right, it is much fainter. Excavations in the 1950s revealed that the town wall was first built, with a bank behind it, at the close of the second century, and that there was a deep V-shaped ditch 2.15 m (7 ft) in front of it. These walls enclosed about 18 acres (7.5 ha) but nothing is known of the buildings within, apart from a late first-century bath-house. Soon after the middle of the fourth century the defences were drastically reorganized, and it was then that the wide ditch visible today was dug. The second-century ditch, which lay much closer to the wall, was then filled with the material excavated from the new ditch. The filling provided a foundation for rectangular projecting towers which were added to the wall at this time. Some of these may have carried the Roman catapult machines, *ballistae* and *onagri*, which hurled stone balls and iron-tipped bolts at the enemy. The purpose of the new broad ditch, cut out of solid rock, was probably to keep the enemy at a range suited to the Roman artillery machines.

Outside the town, but close to the corner where the defences are visible, a short-lived fort was discovered from the air in 1959. Excavation showed that it was built soon after

the conquest and occupied until about AD 80, after a slight
reduction in size *c*. 70. It is not visible on the ground. Further
away to the east a villa has been excavated, now also filled in.
It was built as late as *c*. AD 350–65, enlarged
c. 370–80 and burnt at the very end of the fourth century.
There is evidence that even then agricultural activity
continued at the site, and it is likely that life went on behind
the shelter of the town walls into the fifth century.

The next town of any size on Ermine Street north of Great
Casterton was situated at **Ancaster** (SK 983436), and the
course of the Roman road between the two is followed by
modern highways. For the first 12 miles (19 km) north of
Great Casterton, Ermine Street is represented by the dual
carriageway of the A1, but then you should turn off along the
B6403, and keep straight on for Ancaster. For the last 6 miles
(9.6 km) the road is very straight: it is a fine piece of highway,
with the B-road running on top of an *agger* about 1.20 m
(4 ft) high.

At Ancaster, Ermine Street is crossed by the A153
(Grantham–Sleaford). Beyond this crossroads, in the field on
the right of the B-road, is the SE corner of the defences of the
Roman town, here represented by a mound and a broad ditch,
less impressive than at Great Casterton. A stone wall 2.3 m
(7 ft 6 in) thick and backed by a contemporary earth rampart
was built to enclose an area of about 9 acres (3.6 ha) some
time between AD 200 and 225. It was defended by one or
more ditches, but the visible broad ditch (which was
accompanied by a slighter, outer one) is certainly of fourth-
century date. Two fan-shaped towers, paralleled on the Danube
but elsewhere only once in Britain (at Godmanchester), have
been discovered at Ancaster at the NW and NE corners.
Probably added in the fourth century, they are not now visible.
Little is known of buildings within the town; but what is clear
is that this defended enclosure embraced only a fraction of the
original civilian settlement along Ermine Street, which at its
apogee *c*. AD 200 covered some 60 acres (24 ha).

The Roman antiquities of Ancaster can be traced by means
of the Ancaster Trail, and some of the numbers on its route
(but not the entire route) will be mentioned below: the
defences mentioned in the last paragraph, for example, are
no. 8 on the Trail. The line of the western defences can be

gauged by going into the churchyard, no. 7 in the Trail, on the
other side of Ermine Street (note the replica of a Roman relief
depicting three mother goddesses which is built into the
churchyard wall; the original, found close by in 1831, is now
in Grantham Museum). Beyond the church tower there is a
drop in ground-level and the path cuts through the site of the
rampart. The change in level is also clear in the garden
adjoining the churchyard on the south (left).

Now turn right along the path beyond the church to reach
the modern cemetery (Trail no. 6). This was the site also of a
late Roman inhumation cemetery of *c*. AD 290/370 excavated
in the 1960s: the almost total absence of grave goods and the
consistency of the east-west alignment of the burials
suggested that it was the burial-ground of early Christians.
Two stone sarcophagi of Roman date have been left here, one
each in the mid-point of the modern cemetery's boundaries to
left and right. Underneath these burials were located two
V-shaped ditches, at right-angles to the path and in the area
closest to it: these belonged to a first-century military fort of
which very little else is known. The fort presumably occupied
the elevated knoll still clear in the SE corner of the graveyard,
and from which the ground drops away appreciably to the
north and east. Outside Ancaster, a 10-minute walk away, lies
the site of a Roman marching-camp of 28 acres (11.3 ha),
found from the air in 1974, but there is nothing visible on the
ground. If you want to visit it, take Water Lane opposite
Ancaster Post Office, turn right at the bottom, and so up to the
railway. The camp lies in the field on the right immediately
beyond (Trail no. 4). A badly weathered Roman relief,
possibly showing a Genius (presiding spirit), is housed in
Ancaster Primary School.

The last two towns to be mentioned in this chapter, Caistor
and Horncastle, lie in NE Lincolnshire. The status of both is
uncertain, but the presence of defensive stone walls, which
constitute the visible remains at both places, implies that the
places were of some importance in the late Empire. Earlier
they doubtless served as market-centres, but their late Roman
military character is suggested by their strong walls and their
proximity to an exposed coastline: geological survey, for
example, has shown that Horncastle stood on an estuary in
Roman times. Excavation here in 1984–5 confirmed a late

third- or early fourth-century date for the defences, and those of Caistor must be contemporary. The towers were probably part of the original scheme. At Horncastle the wall was backed as well by a contemporary earth rampart. Both are candidates for identification as the Roman BANNOVALIVM ('the strong rampart'), but there is no way of deciding between the two.

The remains of the walls at Caistor are insignificant (see App. 1 for the details), but those of **Horncastle** (TF 260695) have left more numerous and more interesting fragments. The walk round these only takes about 20 minutes, as the area enclosed by the defences is very small (5 acres or 2 ha, cf. about 8 acres [3.3 ha] at Caistor). There was, however, considerable Roman settlement outside the walled area to the south which was excluded by the late defences. A convenient starting point is Market Place, where a plan of the modern town marking the Roman remains can be studied. Walk down nearly to the end of Church Lane; on the left, at the back of a car-park opposite the churchyard steps, is a piece of wall-core forming the base of a modern brick wall, badly overgrown in 2000. Turn left along Wharf Road. A fine stretch, 6 m (20 ft) long and 1 m (4 ft) high, including part of the inner face, is displayed in the vestibule of the Branch Library on the left (viewable from a side window in Lindsay Court when the library is closed). Go up Bull Ring, turn left into High Street and so back to Market Place. Turn right down St Lawrence Street. On the right, immediately before a public toilet, is a bookshop called Jabberwock, in the inside of which a small section of wall can be viewed through a glass door. If the owner is not busy, he may be able to show you the low stretch of wall visible in his back garden, together with the fine north corner tower which is visible at the far end, still standing about 3 m (10 ft) high.

Now return to Market Square and walk over to Woolworths. Two properties further to the right, underneath the plaque announcing Bridge Street, is the Banovallum [*sic*] Suite (tel: 01507–527637); in the rear of these premises is a low stretch of wall-core. Now return to Woolworths, go down Manor House Street, and turn right along a private road adjacent to the Manor House. From the field on your left, behind a neat hedge to the left of the first tree, can be seen a

stretch of the inner face of the wall at the west angle, some
1.80 m (6 ft) high; it lies in private property. Continue on
down to the end of Manor House Street, where another stretch
of wall, also 1.80 m (6 ft) high, is visible at the entrance to the
health centre. About 7 m (21 ft) further on a cross-section of
the wall's core, squared off to form the back wall of a now
demolished lean-to, was also visible in 2000, but this area
may be subject to redevelopment.

You should now return along Manor House Street and go
into the churchyard, keeping straight along the path to the
other side. Immediately past the bollards a tiny fragment of
wall-core is visible at pavement-level facing 1 St Mary's
Square. Next to house no. 12 is a side-gate giving access to
the longest and highest stretch of wall at Horncastle, although
once again only core is visible; but normally this door is kept
firmly locked. With the permission of the respective owners, it
is possible to follow this piece of wall, past a short brick
interruption and through another gate into another back-yard,
and see the wall rounding the south corner. The lowest course
of the Roman wall is also visible on the left of the road,
before disappearing under the houses.

Chapter 6

Wales

including Cheshire

Wales posed something of a problem for the Roman administration: the area was too hostile to be left alone, as it provided a threat to the security of the towns and villas of the peaceful lowlands. It had therefore to be conquered and garrisoned, and the cost of this can hardly have been offset by the minerals, especially gold and copper, which the Romans exploited. Even after its final pacification, Wales remained a garrisoned zone, and although Romanization in the form of villas and a couple of towns reached the extreme south and SW, life for the indigenous population in most places must have been changed little by the Roman conquest.

We know a good deal about the military campaigns against the Welsh tribes from the pages of the historian Tacitus, but he gives no place-names and few geographical details, and it is therefore impossible to reconstruct each campaign with precision. The first attempts were made by Ostorius Scapula, governor between AD 47 and 52, with further advances under Veranius in 57 and Suetonius Paullinus in 58/9 until the latter was halted by the rebellion of Boudica in East Anglia. We do not hear of any further campaigns in Wales until AD 74, when Julius Frontinus finally subdued the Silures, the tribe occupying most of south Wales except the SW corner. The Ordovices of north Wales were not finally quelled until 78 by Frontinus' successor, Cnaeus Julius Agricola.

The archaeological record for these campaigns is sparse. Several temporary campaign camps (the so-called 'marching-camps') have been discovered by aerial photography and patient fieldwork, and most if not all of those mentioned later in this chapter, or listed in Appendix 1, belong to this early period. So too does the 48-acre (20-ha) campaign base dating to the 50s and 60s at Rhyn Park, Chirk (Shropshire), of which nothing is visible on the ground, and another base, a vexillation fortress of 26 acres (11 ha), at Clyro near Hay-on-Wye (see App. 1). The strategic importance of the latter site, and the finds of pottery, which indicate that occupation had ceased before c. 75, make it clear that this was a base, established c. 55/60, for large expeditionary forces in their attacks on the Silures.

After the final pacification of Wales in 77/8, literary sources for the situation in Wales are lacking, and the rest of its history under the Roman occupation has to be deduced from archaeological and epigraphical evidence alone. The whole area was controlled by a carefully designed network of forts, fortlets and roads, but much research remains to be done both on the identification of new sites and on the elucidation of the periods of occupation for those sites already known.

The two corner-stones for the garrison of Wales were the legionary fortresses at Caerleon and Chester, which, together with York, formed the three permanent bases of the legions in Roman Britain. **Caerleon**** (ST 340906) was the home of the Second Augustan Legion, situated 3 miles (4.8 km) NE of Newport, or $1\frac{1}{2}$ miles (2.4 km) from intersection 24, 25 or 26 on the M4, from which it is clearly signposted. This was the Roman ISCA, a Celtic word meaning 'water' or 'river', and still surviving in the modern river name, the Usk. The fortress was established by Frontinus in AD 74 or 75 with an earth rampart and timber buildings. Refurbishing of the defences in stone began in the late 80s and continued at least until 100. The barracks were gradually given stone footings from *c.* 100/20, but the superstructure of these and many other buildings probably remained half-timbered throughout the fortress's life. For much of the second century large parts of the legion were on duty elsewhere – helping to build first Hadrian's Wall and then Antoninus' frontier, and later fighting for Severus and his sons in Scotland: plans may even have been afoot to transfer the entire legion northwards, until Caracalla decided to abandon Scotland in 212 or 213 shortly after his father's death. There was some substantial rebuilding and other repair in the third century, but by about 290 the fortress was no longer garrisoned to full strength and some of the principal buildings, including a substantial portion of the *principia*, were demolished: part of the legion was transferred probably now to Richborough in Kent (p. 39), perhaps even taking with them building materials for recycling. Some buildings were, however, occupied up until the middle of the fourth century, indicating that a skeletal force was maintained in the former fortress up until *c.* 350. Regular excavations since 1926 have furnished many important details of the layout of the 50-acre (20-ha) fortress, but only two significant portions of the interior remain visible today.

The first, part of the legionary bath-house (1 on Fig. 63), can be reached from the car-park of the Bull Inn, which is on the right of the main road soon after entering the village [AM: 0930–1700 daily, but closed Sunday mornings until 1300 between November and March]. Although military bath-houses in Britain were normally situated outside fort defences to minimize fire-risk, in a stone-built legionary fortress this was not so; indeed in Caerleon as elsewhere the baths were of necessity stone-built from the time of the fortress's foundation, whereas the rest of the buildings were initially of timber. Only part of the baths has been conserved under the modern cover-building (which opened in 1985); and although it represents only a fragment of the original structure, what there is impresses by the sheer size and solidity of the masonry. Excavations between 1964 and 1981 revealed a detailed structural sequence between its original construction *c.* 75 and its final disuse *c.* 230, curiously some 60 or so years before the garrison left ISCA: by that time, especially if the legion was well below full strength, soldiers may have turned to the smaller extramural bath-house recorded in the nineteenth century near the castle mound.

Stand first on the catwalk with the ticket-desk behind you, and look down on the great swimming-bath (*natatio*), which formed part of the original construction of *c.* 75. The steps in front of you mark the end of the pool in this first phase. In a major renovation of the baths *c.* 150, however, the pool was shortened by the building of a new cross-wall, with bonding-courses using flat roofing-tiles (*tegulae*). The buttress in the centre was a later addition to strengthen the wall, as is clear both from the absence of bonding-courses and from the straight joints with the wall which it abuts. You can also see from here that the long walls of the swimming-pool were increased in width in the later rebuilding: this is especially clear in its south wall to your right, which presents the appearance of a double wall, of which the outer part is the later addition. Now walk down the catwalk on your right to the far end. An excellent model of the baths is displayed here, as well as an accompanying plan which shows how little of the baths are still visible – about one-sixth of the original complex. In particular, note that no part of the covered exercise-hall (*basilica*), so prominent in the model, is currently accessible.

Next pause half-way along the catwalk on the far side of the swimming-pool and watch out for the central lead drainpipe away to your left. The wall containing it is also part of the rebuilding of *c.* 150, when the original *natatio*, a massive 41 m (135 ft) long, was shortened at both ends to a pool only 26 m (85 ft) long. The contrast between the comparatively untidy mid-second-century masonry of this wall, and the original lining of the pool 75 years or so earlier,

will also be noticed. The two phases of the long wall in front
of you, already noted, are particularly clear from here. At the
far end of this catwalk you can also see the remains of the
semicircular fountain house which adorned the *natatio* in the
first phase, but was demolished when the pool was shortened
c. AD 150. The stone dolphin fountain-spout, displayed in the
case immediately above, formed part of this structure, and the
likely form of the niche (*aedicula*) containing it is suggested
by the miniature version of it displayed in the showcase with
the sculpture of the dolphin.

Now turn and face the rest of the baths, with the
swimming-pool behind you. Three elements can be seen here
in front of you: a pool with paving slabs under the catwalk to
your right, inserted into an earlier, larger pool of which the
stripped remains are also visible; the great drain, a most
impressive early document (*c.* AD 75) of Roman water

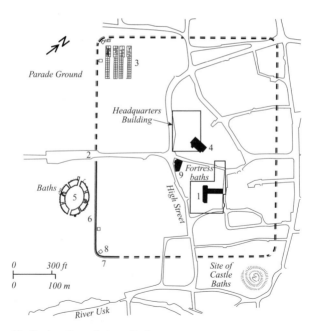

63   Caerleon, Roman fortress, site plan

technology in Britain, 2 m (6 ft 6 in) high and with vaulted
cover still largely intact, curving away in front of you; and, to
your left, a large heated changing-room added *c.* AD 150, most
of which lies buried outside the cover-building. Some of its
pilae and impressions of others in the mortar floor are visible
in this room. Fragments of painted plaster and wall veneers in
Purbeck and other stones are displayed on the catwalk to your
right, tantalizing hints of the scheme of interior decor now
largely lost to us.

Next go down the catwalk and pause in front of the central
arched 'opening', simulated in thin gauze to give an idea of
the dimensions of the superstructure of the building. You are
now standing above the cold room (*frigidarium*) of the baths,
of which less than half is preserved inside the cover-building.
A rectangular pool is visible straight ahead, with semicircular
alcoves to left and right; to your left, in the large pit beyond
the drain cover, earlier floors of this room are visible in
section, as they are also in similar pits further to your left and
to the right. All three holes were created by stone robbers
anxious to extract the massive stone piers which took the
weight of the vaulted roof of the *frigidarium* here. Note that
the final flooring has been cut away to reveal an earlier floor,
and the corner of a Phase 1 wall and associated floor can be
detected below that. There were major refloorings of the baths
(apparently to combat flooding problems caused by a high
water table) *c.* 100/10 and again *c.* 150. Part of the paving of
the room in its final phase is visible to your right, as is the
central opening to the drain (in the alcove behind you); but
both the circular drain cover and the large fragmentary
wash-basin decorated with a Medusa head come not from this
building but from the extramural Castle Baths, excavated in
the nineteenth century. By contrast the mosaic on the wall to
your right was found in the intramural legionary baths (in
1877), but in a room outside the preserved area. If belonging
to the first phase of the baths (as is thought), it ranks among
the earliest mosaics from Roman Britain (*c.* 75/80); but the
work, which depicts a clumsy representation of the tip of a
Bacchic wand (*thyrsus*), is heavy-handed (notice especially
the poorly drawn guilloche), presumably by an inexperienced
legionary craftsman, and not a specially imported Continental
mosaicist. The position of the entrance to the covered

exercise-hall (*basilica*), which also lies buried outside the
cover-building, is indicated in the far corner. Not now visible,
this hall, similar to later civilian examples at Wroxeter
(p. 279) and Leicester (p. 283), was an afterthought added to
the bath-house in the 80s.

The dimensions of the *tepidarium* and *caldarium* which lay
south of the cover building have been established by
trenching, and an outline plan of the baths can therefore be
ascertained. They are in the mainstream of legionary
bath-development at this period (the second half of the first
century), and would undoubtedly have been designed by a
military architect trained, if not in Rome, then perhaps in
Germany or Switzerland where the closest parallels occur.

The second visible portion of the fortress, its west corner,
can be reached by continuing along the main road and forking
left at the church. You are now following the line of the *via
principalis* and soon pass through the site of the SW gateway
(2 on Fig. 63). At the car-park you are outside the fortress,
with the amphitheatre on your left. Ignore that for the
moment, and take the path on your right which runs adjacent
to the fortress-ditch, its original V-profile now obscured by
silt. The path passes the site of the parade-ground and some
buildings of the civilian settlement (*vicus*) under the playing-
fields on your left, but a more extensive part of the *vicus* lay
on the north side of the fortress. After about 150 m, cross the
ditch by the path and you find yourself in the west corner of
ISCA [AM; A] (3 on Fig. 63).

What you first see as you walk down to the far end are four
circular oven-bases which back on to the rampart, and the
impressions of three more under the grass. These were once
domed structures, of tile, masonry and mortared rubble
(although the domes themselves may have been temporary, of
clay and straw, broken down and made up again with each
firing). They were probably covered by wooden sheds. They
belong to the original fortress of AD 75 but were superseded
about AD 150 by more substantial square stone structures, with
furnaces and built-in flues. Two of these cookhouses are
visible, constructed up against already existing stone internal
towers which are also visible. The first lies half-way along the
fortress-bank here: note how the masonry of the cookhouse
abuts the earlier tower (witness the straight joint), especially

clear on the right-hand side. Continue walking down to the far corner, noting the drain lining the *intervallum* road. The cookhouse adjacent to the corner tower is better preserved than its twin: the emplacements of two circular ovens can be seen at a higher level, and note also how the poorer-quality walling of the cookhouse contrasts with and abuts the finer masonry of the corner tower.

Adjoining the cookhouse and contemporary with it is a latrine. The most prominent feature is its stone-built sewer running below floor-level on three sides (it would have been surmounted by a row of seats), and the worn channel (clearest at one corner) which would have carried water for the necessary ablutions (p. 18).

The interior of the fortress at this corner was occupied by rows of barrack-blocks arranged in pairs facing each other (Fig. 64). Only one is visible now, the plans of three others being misleadingly laid out at a higher level in modern materials. This is only a fraction of the total: to get some idea

64   Caerleon, Roman fortress, reconstruction-drawing of the west corner

of the fortress's size, you have to imagine 24 of them
stretching in a row from here to the north corner; then there
were 24 more at the other end of the fortress, and a further 16
in the centre, flanking the headquarters building: Caerleon
church, the tower of which is visible from here, overlies part
of the *principia* and thus roughly marks the central point of
ISCA (4 on Fig. 63). As can be seen from the plan before you
(Fig. 65), a barrack-block consists of spacious quarters at one
end of the building (that nearer you) for the officer, a
centurion, and his junior staff, and 12 pairs of rooms for the
rest of his company, fronted by a veranda. The larger room of
each pair provided the living- and sleeping-quarters for about
six men, while the smaller was used for storing their arms and
equipment; each barrack was thus designed to hold a *centuria*
of 80 men. The barracks here were built around the middle of
the second century to replace earlier ones of timber, but
various modifications were made in the third century to the
centurion's quarters; not all the dividing walls visible today,
therefore, belong to one period. The reconstruction-drawing
(Fig. 64) shows the barracks built entirely of stone; more
probably, as noted above, the superstructure was only
half-timbered resting on stone dwarf-walls.

   Another outstanding Roman monument at Caerleon is the
amphitheatre [AM; A], dug by Sir Mortimer Wheeler in

65   Caerleon, a legionary barrack-block   *66   Caerleon, the amphitheat*

1926–7, and still the most instructive example of its type in Britain (5). It was constructed about AD 90 and so is almost contemporary with the most famous amphitheatre of all, the Colosseum. But whereas the latter was designed purely for the gratification and enjoyment of the Roman masses, its comparatively humble counterpart in distant Caerleon was primarily used for military exercises and displays, although no doubt blood-sports and gladiatorial combat were also staged here. There were various modifications in the middle of the second and at the beginning of the third centuries, until its final abandonment on the departure of the garrison.

You can see at once that the amphitheatre has been hollowed out to create the arena, the upcast earth being used to form banks on which timber seating was erected. These banks were encased in masonry both internally and externally, where buttresses gave added support. Move now anti-clockwise round the monument. The stoke-hole (with massive stone voussoirs) for heating a small bath building is visible close to the outer wall on this west side: these baths preceded the amphitheatre by a few years and were extensively rebuilt in the early third century, as we know from numerous stamped and datable tiles found in its roof collapse. From here descend the broad flight of steps in the adjoining entrance (Fig. 66) towards the arena. In front of the brick piers turn right through a perfectly preserved brick arch to see a staircase, also substantially complete, which led up to a 'box' for high-ranking officers. The latter was suspended over the small room where competitors waited their turn, through which you now pass as you enter the arena. The companies which built the amphitheatre inscribed their names on some stones set in the arena wall; presumably they were left visible when the rest of the arena wall was covered with mortar. The casts made to replace the original stones have now become largely illegible through weathering. That easiest to find is a short distance to the left of the entrance you have just passed through, a reddish block seven courses above ground-level; it originally read 'Xth cohort, century of Julinus [built this]', but only the letters IVL are decipherable now.

Continuing anti-clockwise, follow the arena wall round to the south entrance. This, and its better-preserved counterpart on the north, were the principal entrances to the arena, and were originally vaulted to carry an upper tier of seats. The outer half of the passage was originally roofed by a section of concrete vaulting, between two large stone arches: two piers supporting the latter are complete to impost height, and that on your left even has the springer and one voussoir of the arch itself preserved. Continue round the arena, past one of the four narrow stairways giving access to the seating, until you reach another of the competitors' 'waiting-rooms', this time complete with stone benches. The brick apse with the semi-dome, an alteration of the early third century, was perhaps designed for a statuette of Nemesis, the goddess of Fate; a lead curse-tablet invoking her, on display in the Museum, was found in the amphitheatre (a *nemeseum* is also known in the Chester amphitheatre: p. 319). From here you can complete your tour of the building with a visit to the north entrance, which displays massive external piers of masonry (one again standing to capstone height), with sockets for the bars barricading the arena. The arena wall to the right of the entrance still bears some traces of its mortar rendering.

On leaving the north entrance, follow the outside of the amphitheatre round towards the stile in the fence beyond. At the rear of the possible *nemeseum* already noted can be seen another pair of staircases which led up to a second officers' 'box' here; that on the right is particularly well preserved, but access to it had been denied at some stage by the insertion of a blocking wall.

Beyond the amphitheatre a fine stretch of the fortress's stone defences, still over 2 m (7 ft) high, has been consolidated (6). Mostly it is the core of the wall that is left, as only a few rows of facing-stones near the base have survived later stone-robbing. Keeping to the outside of the wall you soon come to the south corner of the fortress, where the wall still stands 3.60 m (12 ft) high, only a metre or so lower than the probable level of the sentry walk. An arched sewer-outlet (now blocked) can be seen at the foot of the wall after rounding the corner (7); it implies that a latrine awaits discovery inside the rampart here (comparable no doubt to the one excavated at the west corner). Now retrace your steps to the field-gate and mount the rampart; skirting an interval tower you come to the south angle tower, excavated in 1982 (8). Note how the whole of the south corner of the wall bows outward from the original line: this sector of defensive wall collapsed at some stage in the second century and was rebuilt on a slightly different orientation. A mint coin of AD 86 in the foundation trench of the corner tower showed that the rebuilding of the defences in stone started earlier than has been thought hitherto. The date of the finishing touches to this major refurbishment is indicated by the splendid dedication slab of AD 100, now in the Museum (Fig. 67).

Caerleon Legionary Museum (9 on Fig. 63), situated on the main road close to the church, houses an outstanding collection of military antiquities, superbly displayed (Monday–Saturday, 1000–1700 and Sunday, 1400–1700 throughout the year). The classical-style portico belongs to the original Museum established as long ago as 1850, but a new building behind this façade was opened in 1987. Space precludes more than a brief notice here of a few of the outstanding exhibits. After four cases of finds from Usk, a predecessor fortress built in the 50s a few miles upstream from Caerleon, you pass the first of many interesting tombstones in the museum, recording a mother and son. The latter, Tadius Exuper(a)tus, had 'died on the German expedition', a reminder that from time to time detachments of the legion were sent on duty overseas. The maze mosaic on your right, from the Caerleon *principia*, is one of very few mosaics from a military context in Britain (the fragment displayed in the baths is another: p. 305). The amphorae here are a cylindrical wine-carrier from Italy (form Dressel 2/4), a globular oil-carrier from southern Spain (Dressel 20), and a small 'carrot'-shaped amphora, believed to be a date-carrier imported from Palestine.

At the foot of the ramp are stones illustrating the cosmopolitan composition of the legion: they record soldiers who hailed from Lyon, Nice and Digne in France and from Xanten in Germany. In a showcase on the back wall towards the far corner is a bronze 'saucepan' (*trulleus*), stamped not only with the name of its Gaulish maker Maturus, but also with that of an auxiliary unit, the first *ala* of Thracians: whether a soldier from this unit was serving, however briefly, with the legion at Caerleon, or whether the *trulleus* had changed hands in the course of its life, we can only guess. The same case has a very rare silver tip from a legionary banner (*vexillum*); part of a first-century wine amphora imported all the way from Crete, with painted inscriptions (*dipinti*) on the neck naming the legion, and on the shoulder a slogan reading among other letters *perprimum*, 'absolutely tops' (referring to the wine); and a fragment of tablet with ink writing, similar to the famous series from Vindolanda (p. 510), recording guards being despatched to fetch pay, and others being sent to forage for building timber.

The fine inscription to Trajan on the wall above (TRAIANO in line 2) was dedicated in AD 100 (Fig. 67), as indicated by his holding a third consulship in that year (COS III in line 5): note how the third stroke was clearly added later (it is not quite vertical), indicating that the stone was prepared in 99, when Trajan was still COS II, but not erected until the following year. To the right are other inscriptions important for documenting third-century building activity in the fortress, especially the long text recording the restoration 'from the ground up' (*a solo*) of the barracks of the Seventh Cohort in AD 253/8. A

67   Caerleon, Roman fortress, building inscription of AD 100

slab near the floor here has been partially repainted in modern times to give an impression of its likely original appearance. Some of the centurial stones from the amphitheatre (p. 309) are also displayed on this wall and on the stand behind you. On the latter is also a splendid example of a stamped *tegula* – trodden on twice (accidentally?) while still damp, and so still bearing to this day the impressions of the hobnailed shoes of the culprit.

The wall to your right here has material illustrating religious cults at Caerleon (inscriptions to Mithras and Diana, and the lead curse-tablet to Nemesis: p. 310). A section on funerary customs comes next, with more tombstones, a striking head of the eastern deity Attis (common in funerary symbolism) from the top of a tomb, and a rare example of a cremation burial, from the Roman cemetery on the other side of the Usk. The burial was placed in a lead canister, still with a pipe protruding upwards from it; the latter was intended to receive libations from ground-level offered by periodic visitors to the grave. The cases in the centre of the room contain *inter alia* some interesting fragmentary glass, including one piece engraved with the figure of a gladiator, and another, mould-blown in the form of a negroid head, signed by its maker C. Caesius Bucaddus; it also features a figure of Helios, the sun god, on its base. Another example taken from the same mould is known from London; both were imported from a Continental glasshouse. The striking ivories of a tragic mask and of a maenad and cupid, displayed nearby, perhaps decorated a box or a piece of furniture.

Finally, there are some exceptional finds from the legionary baths: the great drain, for example (p. 304), yielded no fewer than 88 gemstones lost by bathers from their signet-rings, the largest collection from a single find-spot in Britain until 117 were found in a jeweller's haul at Snettisham, Norfolk, in 1985 (now on display in the British Museum). Also lost in the drain was a superb and very rare bronze strigil (the instrument for scraping dirt and dead skin from the body), inlaid with gold and silver with scenes from six of the 12 labours of Hercules. This outstanding find, inscribed in Greek 'it washed you nicely', must have been made in Italy or the Greek East, and was presumably the prized possession of some high-ranking officer.

Before leaving the Museum, ask a custodian to show you
(if there are staff to spare) the full-size replica of part of a
barrack room in the 'Capricorn Centre' at the rear. Modern
reproductions of armour and equipment are also available to
try out here – an imaginative piece of experimental
archaeology which adds an important extra dimension to our
understanding of the everyday concerns of the Roman soldier.

Caerleon's sister fortress at **Chester**** (SJ 404665), the
Roman DEVA (the name of the river, the Dee, on which it
stands), is even more built over. With the exception of the
amphitheatre, its surviving remains are isolated fragments
which require a good deal of patience to track down. This is
hardly surprising in a city like Chester, the strategic position
of which, first recognized by the Romans, has ensured its
continued importance to this day. Excavation since the 1970s
has added many fresh details of the fortress's development
and history, about which (considering the intensity of post-
Roman occupation) we are remarkably well informed.

It is now known that there was at least one military base of
unknown size at Chester in the 50s (possibly as early as the
first campaign against the Deceangli in 47), with an
orientation somewhat different from that of the later fortress.
It was replaced by a 60-acre (24-ha) earth and timber
legionary fortress *c.* AD 76–8, and three lead water-pipes
bearing the name of Agricola show that the finishing touches
had been put by 79. Excavations at Abbey Green in 1975–7
found the turf rampart still standing to wall-walk level, which
was, rather surprisingly, only about 2.15 m (7 ft) above the
foundations. If this was normal elsewhere, it is possible that
the reconstruction at Baginton (p. 260) gives a misleading
impression of height, but allowance has to be made for the
slumping and compression of the earth rampart at Chester
over time. The initial garrison, as we know from tombstones,
was the Second Adiutrix Legion, but this was replaced, in 87
or a little later, by the Twentieth Valeria Victrix, which then
remained at Chester throughout. Rebuilding in stone, first of
the defences and of the internal buildings immediately
afterwards, started before the beginning of the second century
and continued until *c.* 120. For the rest of the second century
large parts of the legion were seconded for duties elsewhere,
including the building of the two frontier barriers in northern

Britain, Hadrian's Wall and the Antonine Wall. Under
Septimius Severus and his successors the legion (when not
engaged on Severus' Scottish campaigns) seems to have been
in full strength again at Chester, and extensive rebuilding and
refurbishing of both the defences and the interior buildings
occurred in the first two decades of the third century. Many
barracks seem to have been in 'mothballs' from *c.* 250 to 300
(presumably because legionary detachments were again
widely redeployed elsewhere), but they were reoccupied in
altered form from *c.* 300, when further repairs to the defences
were made.

  Rescue excavation, especially between the mid 1960s and
the late 1980s, has recovered much of the plan of the
fortress's buildings, but little is now to be seen. Many of the
surviving fragments are on private property, and prior
permission is needed to visit them. Only the most easily
accessible have been included here; the rest are listed in
Appendix 1 (p. 658).

  The best place to start your tour is to ascend the walls at the
Eastgate (1 on Fig. 68), which lies on the site of a Roman
predecessor. Immediately north of this, a fine portion of what
is certainly the Roman fortress wall can be seen by
descending the staircase to the car-park in Mercia Square (2).
Returning to the wall-walk and continuing northwards, you
can see the lowest four courses of another stretch of Roman
wall just in front of the medieval alignment by leaning
forward from the wall-parapet. Descend once more from the
walls by another wooden staircase a little further on, and walk
back to the south end of the car-park to study another well
preserved stretch, incorporated in the bottom of the medieval
walls but once more on a slightly altered alignment.
Excavation here in 1983 showed that the standing wall was no
earlier than *c.* 150 (it probably belongs *c.* 200), but sandstone
fragments belonging to a different structure suggested that the
visible wall was a replacement for the first stone defences of
the early second century. After turning the NE corner (King
Charles' Tower, 3), you can follow the Roman walls, here in a
superb state of preservation, to Northgate. Shortly before the
latter, excavations in the late 1970s revealed a Roman internal
tower and a battery of six ovens inserted in the third century
into an earlier rampart building (4), but these have now been

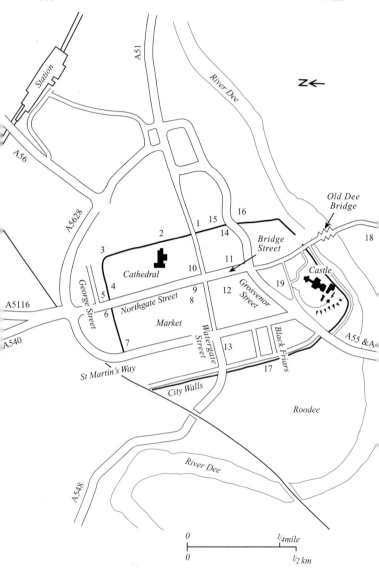

68   Chester, location map

backfilled. The tower still stood to rampart-walk height, preserved beneath the earth bank behind the defences. The bank was altered and widened in the early fourth century, rendering the tower and bread ovens obsolete.

Come off the walls at Northgate (5) to view this same stretch on the outside from the canal bridge. The wall here, 5 m (16 ft 6 in) high to the moulded cornice (the walkway at the top is modern), is one of the most impressive stretches of Roman defensive work in Britain. The slope inwards towards the cornice is due to partial post-Roman collapse and was not a feature of the Roman walls, which would have been vertical. The visible masonry here belongs to the original stone structure of the early second century, with an unusually elaborate cornice moulding marking the beginning of the wall-walk. Parts of the walled circuit were repaired in the early third century, and there were further alterations *c*. 300, when the bank behind was lowered and widened and part of the rear face of the wall made freestanding; but this affected other parts of the fortress circuit and not the stretch immediately east of Northgate. Tombstones robbed from the nearby cemeteries were used as building material in these alterations; many found elsewhere in the northern defences between 1883 and 1892 are now in the Museum.

Some 40 m (45 yds) west of Northgate, at Northgate House (6), a 7-m (23-ft) stretch of Roman wall, found to be in danger of collapse, was dismantled and rebuilt in 1989–90. At the NW corner (7), Roman and medieval walls part company, and the Roman NW tower was found in 1964–5 standing 4.50 m (15 ft) high. Unfortunately it had to give way to the inner ring road, but its plan is outlined on the pavement below St Martin's Gate. From here the Roman west wall followed the line of the inner ring road, while the medieval circuit embraced a wider area to the west and south.

Return to Northgate and enter the street of the same name, which was the Roman *via decumana*. Some Roman bases and a Tuscan capital (the column shaft is medieval), together with Roman gutter-stones, can be seen (not *in situ*) outside the Coach and Horses pub at the corner of Northgate Street with Princess Street, and there is a Roman grooved slab (for holding a balustrade?) behind the public library, off Princess Street. These are *disiecta membra* of fortress buildings recovered in this area prior to redevelopment, Northgate Street bisecting the site of what was probably the hospital, and a possible stores-depot lying between the library and the bus station. Some lines of these buildings are marked out in the modern pavement.

Between the Town Hall and the central cross of the Rows lies the site of the *principia*, the HQ of the fortress, of which two fragments are accessible. One, excavated in 1970 and visible from Hamilton Place (8: turn right beyond 'The Forum'), is part of the row of offices along the north range of the building, including the shrine where the legionary standards were kept (*sacellum*), and, below it, the impressive underground strong-room (*aerarium*), cut in the rock to a depth of 1.8 m (6 ft) below normal floor-level. This probably belongs to the Severan rebuilding of the fortress in the early third century. The other is a massive base for one of the columns of the third-century cross-hall, together with two ends of column shafts projecting out of the cellar walls, in the basement of Jigsaw, at 23 Northgate Row (9). An assistant may be able to let you into the basement to see the column base and the column shafts if the shop is not busy. At no. 14, Miss Selfridge (10), the uninspiring remains of an isolated hypocaust may be viewed (ask an assistant). The area around St Michael's Row was occupied by a large internal bath building, of which a well preserved hypocaust is on show in Spud-U-Like at 39, Bridge Street (ask the manager): part of the floor and its supporting *pilae* are visible (11). In Pierpoint Lane off Bridge Street (12) is the entrance to the 'Dewa Roman Experience' (daily, year-round, 0900–1700). This contains a selection of Roman material, mostly from Mediterranean contexts without relevance to Chester, but a number of test-pits, dug in 1991 as part of an archaeological evaluation before the Experience opened, can also be seen, with tantalizing fragments of Roman walls (as well as post-Roman structures), but the excavations are inevitably too small to reveal the nature of the Roman building or buildings which occupied this part of the fortress. Now return to the central cross of the Rows and turn right. A column at 35, Watergate Street, possibly from the residence of a tribune, one of the junior officers of senatorial rank, is readily accessible (provided the staff are not busy) at the back of a toy-shop called Toycraft (13).

Retrace your steps to Bridge Street, and turn left along Pepper Street in order to reach Newgate, from which the SE angle-tower of the fortress can be seen (14); opposite, a public garden contains some re-erected Roman columns and a re-assembled hypocaust from the bath building mentioned above. Just north of the angle-tower, in an inspection-chamber which is in the back yard of the Off the Wall pub, 12, St John Street, is another stretch of the fortress-wall (15). The Roman date of the wall here is not in doubt, as the medieval circuit takes a slightly different line.

The most interesting monument of Roman Chester is undoubtedly the amphitheatre, on display since 1972 (16) [AM; A]. Only the north half is visible, and a proposal in the 1980s and again in the late 1990s to excavate the remainder has been shelved (although there is talk of excavating the west entrance, unaffected by the eighteenth-century Dee House). Chester's amphitheatre cannot therefore rival the Caerleon example, even though Chester's is substantially larger: its estimated size is 102 m by 91 m (335 ft by 298 ft) – the largest amphitheatre, in fact, known in Roman Britain (cf. London's, p. 614). Its site, just outside Newgate, has been known since 1929 but proper excavation began only in 1960. This showed that a timber amphitheatre, with an arena the same size but with only half the seating capacity of its successor, was replaced in stone after a few years, perhaps c. AD 86. Its outer wall, supported by massive buttresses, has been mostly robbed, but the arena wall itself is well preserved; it would have been topped by semicircular coping stones, of which some lie on the grass near the Newgate entrance. One major and one minor entrance to the arena are visible, on the north and the east. That on the north was closed by large wooden doors hung on the stone gate-posts which are visible on either side, next to the arena wall; behind were flights of steps leading up to the seats, but only those on the right survive. The massive stone pier at the outer side of the north entrance is also striking. Adjoining this entrance at the arena end on the west is a small shrine of Nemesis, the goddess of Fate: an altar to her (originally replaced on the site by a replica, now stolen), and two column-bases, perhaps once supporting dedications, were placed here at the end of the first century.

The east entrance consists of a level passage and then a few steps down to a room at arena-level. Stairs on either side of it led to the seats and also to an officers' box raised above this room; the steps on one side, much worn, are still visible. The superbly preserved jambs flanking the door to the arena will also be noticed, as will the foundations of the amphitheatre's outer wall together with one of the external buttresses. Another coping stone from the arena wall also lies here. The position of the subsidiary staircases giving access to the seating (which was wooden, supported on banks of sand) has been marked out on the grass, together with the plan of the outer, buttressed wall. The arena floor showed traces of repair in about AD 300 after a long period of disuse (coinciding with what is known about reoccupation of the fortress barracks about this time). There was also a curious timber platform in the centre of the arena, carefully avoided by a drain which ran from the north entrance right through the centre of the arena, neither of which is now visible.

Two other extramural monuments complete this survey of Roman Chester. Part of a substantial Roman wall, up to 3.30 m (10 ft) high, is situated behind a public toilet on the Roodee racecourse (17). It can be seen from a distance at the foot of the steps which go down to the course a few metres south of Black Friars, but a closer look can only be obtained with the permission of the course manager. Excavation here in 1884 showed that at least a further 4.50 m (15 ft) lies buried below ground-level, but flooding prevented its true height from being established. The wall as a whole has been traced for some 250 m (275 yds) in a north-south direction. It was for long taken to be a quayside (the Roodee was the site of a Roman harbour), but that is now considered to be unlikely because of impossible differences in level between its top and the estimated high-water mark. Recently it has been re-interpreted as a Roman defensive wall, probably of third-century date, which surrounded the civilian settlement on the west side of the fortress. The only alternative is to see it as a simple revetment wall, defining a terrace for safe building only 9 m (30 ft) wide west of the fortress's ditch on this side. Whatever the correct interpretation, it seems a hugely ambitious and expensive project – the construction of a wall over 8 m (26 ft) high here, so much taller than the fortress-wall itself. The Roodee 'quay' remains, therefore, a complete enigma. The other monument is a small Roman quarry-face (18) with a much weathered figure of Minerva holding spear and shield, standing in an *aedicula* (a pair of columns surmounted by a pediment); the item between Minerva's head and the right-hand capital is an owl, Minerva's bird. This can be found in a public garden (Edgar's Field, but not labelled as such), on the south side of the river, on your right immediately after crossing the Old Dee Bridge.

Finally, no visit to Chester is complete without seeing the Grosvenor Museum in Grosvenor Street (19), which along with that at Caerleon (p. 311) contains one of the finest displays of Roman military and sculptural material in the country (Monday–Saturday, 1030–1700; Sunday, 1400–1700). The first Roman gallery illustrates the life of the Roman soldier. There are helpful models of the Chester *principia*, a gateway and a barrack-block, and a fine diorama of the whole fortress in its setting at the far end of the gallery (since this was made, however, the civilian settlement is known to have been much more extensive than is shown here). Among the finds displayed in this gallery, note especially the lead water-pipe bearing the name of Agricola, father-in-law of the historian Tacitus – a rare epigraphic witness of his activity in Britain (cf. also p. 234), one which also shows that the finishing touches were presumably being put to the fortress *c.* 78/9; lead pigs displayed in the same case, including one from Halkyn Mountain (20 miles [32 km] NW of Chester), recording it as lead produced by the Deceangl(i), the tribe occupying this area; and, on the other side of the room, a model of the legionary supply depot at Holt, 8 miles (12.8 km) south of Chester. This made bricks, tiles and pottery for the Chester garrison, and some of the artefacts shown in the next case, including fine examples of antefixes (made to cover the gap left by *imbrices* along the roof edge) – a lion head, a head of Jupiter Ammon (with the attribute of the horns), and the running boar, emblem of the Twentieth Legion – were made at Holt. A tile found casually at Holt in 1991 is scratched before firing in five or six different hands with an expense account for soldiers, among them Junius,

Maternus and Bellettus (the last an otherwise unattested name). Note also here the examples of hollow terracotta tubes, each provided with a nozzle for interlocking into its neighbour: they were used to provide the framework for pouring the concrete vaulting of the legionary baths, and are attested in Britain also in baths at the fortresses of Caerleon and York, and from Chesters on Hadrian's Wall. This method of vault construction (a temporary framework or 'centring' of timber was more normal) was invented in Sicily in the third century BC and was very common in north Africa from the later second century AD onwards. Why it should also turn up being used in Britain for legionary bath-houses is something of a mystery: the presence of African architects serving in the legions is one possibility.

The second gallery contains a wealth of sculptured and epigraphic material, much of it extracted in the nineteenth century from the fortress's north wall (p. 317). First to greet you is a gaudily painted cast of the tombstone of an *optio* (deputy centurion) in the Twentieth Legion, who came from Emerita (Merida) in Spain (a fellow Emeritan, G. Lovesius Caldarus, is recorded on a tombstone displayed nearby, on the left long wall). Such painted casts are a reminder of how garish (to our eyes) Roman inscriptions and sculptures would have seemed when newly finished. Other stones here reflect the cosmopolitan composition of legionary recruits – a man from Brescia in north Italy, for example, others from Italy and Croatia who served in the Second Adiutrix in the early days of the Chester fortress, others again from Thrace (Aprus, in European Turkey), from eastern Turkey (Osroene), and even from the upper Euphrates (Samosata).

Sculptural representations to the right in this room display a knowledge of classical mythology – the dying Adonis beside a tree, Actaeon being devoured by his own hounds (for seeing Diana at her bath), Hercules rescuing Hesione – but the standard of figural representation, probably in the hands of army craftsmen, leaves a very great deal to be desired. Stones such as these illustrate well an important aspect of the level of cultural assimilation in Roman Britain. Classical culture came to Britain during the Roman occupation, but the frequently abysmal artistic expression of it must have made visiting Romans from Italy, among them legionaries serving in the

Chester garrison, dismiss it as downright 'provincial'. Many of the stones, however, may date to the third century, when recruitment into the legions from the local British population became commonplace, and when knowledge of sculptural standards elsewhere in the Empire would have been limited.

The two fortresses of ISCA and DEVA were, as already noted, the corner-stones for the control of Wales, although the Chester command must have had responsibilities as well in northern England. Wales itself was studded with carefully sited forts, and to some of these I will now turn.

In the south is the fort at **Brecon Gaer*** (SO 002297) [AM; A], the Roman CICVCIVM or CICVTIVM: its name refers to the 'breast-shaped' spur on which the fort sits. The site is best reached by following the A40 west of Brecon for 4 miles (6.4 km) and taking the first road on the right, to Aberbran. Turn right at the T-junction in this village, and continue straight on for $1\frac{3}{4}$ miles (2.8 km). Shortly after the second turning to the left, after crossing a stream, you will come to an unsignposted crossroads. (This point can also be reached by taking a minor road from Brecon to Battle and turning left in Cradoc, signposted Aberbran and Aberyscir.) Here you must turn back hard on your right to Y Gaer farm (no signpost). Follow the road round to the farmyard, leaving the farmhouse to your left. Park here, walk through the gate between the first and second barns on your left in the farmyard, and turn right; you will then see a fine stretch of the stone defences of the fort away to your left. Passing through two further metal gates in quick succession, you soon reach the fort's interior.

The fort was built c. AD 75/80 with turf ramparts and timber buildings: its large size, covering $7\frac{3}{4}$ acres (just over 3 ha), underlines the importance of the post, set at the junction of several roads. Its garrison at the turn of the first century (and perhaps from the foundation) was a Spanish cavalry regiment of Vettones, 500 strong, recorded on two tombstones from the site. A stone wall was added to the defences at some time between 140 and 160, and the principal internal buildings (the headquarters building, the commandant's house and the granaries) were also reconstructed in stone at about the same time. The gates seem to have been rebuilt towards the end of the second century, perhaps (it is claimed) after destruction, but the fort was evacuated soon afterwards. There was a brief reoccupation at the end of the third century when the south gate was repaired. A trickle of finds goes on into the fourth century, and the fort was probably held by a caretaker garrison of just a few men during this period; a small internal bath-house may belong to this phase. Evidence for a widening and heightening of the rampart bank at some late period, probably sub- or post-Roman, obliterating corner towers and gates in the process, has also been noted. The fort was extensively excavated by Sir Mortimer Wheeler in 1924–5, but only three gateways, two angle turrets, and part of the fort wall remain visible today.

Turning left once you are inside the fort field, and following the walls clockwise, you first come to the NE angle tower. The lowest part of the tower's walls, considerably wider than the rest, has been interpreted as foundations for the tower walls above. More probably there are two phases here, the lowest courses representing the first stone rebuilding in the Antonine period, and the upper walls representing a subsequent phase when the tower was substantially rebuilt (c. AD 200?). Later still (perhaps the end of the third century?) the outer curtain wall at the corner needed a complete reconstruction: note the irregular masonry of the inner face here, and the straight joints it makes with the pre-existing masonry of the tower on either side.

You next arrive at the east gate. Just one guardroom with its entrance is now visible; the carriageway and the other guardroom lie buried. Move on now, past the dilapidated SE corner tower, to the fine south gate (Fig. 69). Both guard-chambers are excellently preserved, together with the two carriageways. The latter are as usual separated by a central pier, here pierced by a doorway. Two of the pivot-holes for hanging the gate at the front of the east (left) passageway can be seen with difficulty, as well as a drain under one of the carriageways. The stone sill across the front of the western (right-hand) carriageway was inserted in a secondary period when the road level was raised. Now walk through the gate inside its enclosure and turn to the left to examine the fort wall at this point. The two bottom-most courses here belong to the original stone fort of c. 140/60, but this had slumped outwards, perhaps through subsidence, and needed complete rebuilding in a secondary phase. Above it are the rough

69   Brecon Gaer, Roman fort, the south gate (from the east)

foundation courses and then two rows of the facing-stones of this rebuilt curtain wall. The ground-level at the time of the rebuilding would have been level with the lower of these two facing courses, since the foundations lower down would not have been exposed. This in turn implies a raising of the road-level in the carriageways (as noted above), a re-hanging of the gateways, and adjustments to the gate-tower entrances. At the same time as the rebuilding of the curtain wall here, the east guardroom was reduced in size by increasing the thickness of its south wall. Note how this later masonry abuts against part of the original guardroom's east wall, and that the stone curtain wall is double the width of its counterpart in the west guard-chamber, which by contrast needed no such drastic repairs or reconstruction.

Finally, you come to the west gate, which is less well preserved but unusual in having projecting rectangular guard-chambers. This feature is extremely rare in second-century forts in Britain (it is much more common in Germany), although three gates at Castell Collen (p. 329) and those in the exceptional *classis Britannica* fort at Dover (p. 51 and Fig. 6) had projecting rounded fronts to their gate-towers. The west gate at Brecon Gaer has the customary two carriageways, the central pier, and the pivot-holes for the gates. It should in theory have been the fort's main gate, since the *principia* faced it, but the steepness of the slope outside probably meant that it was used less often than the more accessible north gate. Certainly the considerable civilian settlement, including the original garrison bath-house, is known to lie on the north side of the fort.

At least five Roman roads met at the fort of Brecon Gaer: one followed the river Usk SE to Caerleon, with intermediate forts at Pen-y-Gaer (App. 1), Abergavenny, and Usk (App. 1); a second ran south to Cardiff via Pen-y-Darren (Merthyr Tydfil), Gelligaer (see below) and Caerphilly; a third ran SW to Neath (p. 328) through a fort at Coelbren (App. 1); a fourth road went north to Castell Collen (p. 328); and a fifth ran west to Llandovery (App. 1) and beyond. The forts in this network where there is still something substantial worth seeing will now be mentioned in turn, although the remains are hardly spectacular at any of them.

The fort at **Gelligaer** (ST 133973), on the second road listed above, lies immediately to the left of the first house west of the church in this village, on the north side of the B4254: park in a lay-by here next to a small public garden. The rear wall of this garden lies on the SE corner of the Roman fort, and the mound of the south rampart, together with a slight depression marking the ditch, is conspicuous to your left here. The east rampart by contrast is marked by the line of the field boundary straight ahead of you. The fort was built in stone during Trajan's reign early in the second century (as we know from gate inscriptions datable to AD 103/11), and the entire plan of its buildings was recovered by excavations in 1899–1901. Despite shortcomings in the excavation methodology of the day, the plan recovered remains a textbook example of a small stone auxiliary fort in Britain (it covers 3.7 acres or 1.4 ha). No stonework, however, is visible today. On the fort's east side (to the right when looking from the B4254) was an annexe, also defended, which contained the regimental bath-house. The annexe stretched as far as the churchyard, but hardly any trace of it is visible now. A tile kiln was excavated in 1913 in one corner of the graveyard. The Roman name of Gelligaer is unknown.

The Trajanic fort may not, however, have been the earliest on this site, because the excavator described how the stone wall was added to the front of an existing rampart, and also reports the existence of timber gates and other buildings which must have preceded the stone phase. It therefore seems likely that the earliest fort on this site was late Flavian (c. AD 90/5?), rebuilt in stone some 10 or 15 years later. There was a gap in occupation in the second century, probably during the Antonine occupation of Scotland (c. 139–65), and then renewed occupation at Gelligaer down to the end of the second century. A further short-lived phase of military activity around the late third and early fourth century was of uncertain scope and purpose.

Now walk along the B4254 away from the church and turn right into Rectory Road. A metal kissing-gate gives access to the north rampart of the fort; note the depression marking the site of the north gate, just beyond the point where an oblique cart track has eroded the rampart. To your left beyond here, outside the fort, lay the gravelled parade-ground, identified by excavation in 1913: it measured some 116 m by 49 m (380 ft by 160 ft).

The visible fort was not, however, the earliest at Gelligaer: a larger fort, covering 6 acres (2.4 ha), with earth ramparts and timber buildings, lay on a completely different, though adjacent, site to the west, on the other side of Rectory Road. Virtually nothing is traceable of this fort on the ground today, but if you walk westwards again along the B4254 and pause at the first field-gate on your right after Rectory Road (just beyond the speed de-restriction signs), you can see the SW defences of this early fort faintly visible in front of you. The rampart turns a corner west of here and runs away to the NE, just beyond the field boundary to your left. Excavation has shown that this fort belongs to the AD 70s, but quite why its site was spurned in favour of a completely fresh one later in the first century (the requirements of a smaller garrison?) is unknown. Further north, on Gelligaer Common, five practice camps are known; two of these can be traced quite easily with the help of a 1:50,000 OS map (sheet 171, ST 138993 and 131991; another is at ST 116986).

The fort at **Neath** (SS 748977), the terminal point of the third Roman road from Brecon listed above (p. 326), was not identified until 1949, although it had long been known that the Roman NIDVM must have been at or close to the present town. The strategic importance of its position, accessible by sea, guarding an important river-crossing on the east-west coastal road, and controlling a valley which penetrates far inland, was obvious. Yet the occupation seems to have been brief: from about AD 75 for a few years, then a second turf and timber fort *c.* 80/90 lasting until *c.* 110, and then a stone rebuilding *c.* 115–25 after a short gap. There was further military activity between *c.* 140 and 170, and evidence of a further, partial reoccupation *c.* 275 (until *c.* 320).

Two gates (the south and east) of the stone reconstruction, both with double carriageways and guardrooms, have been preserved in a housing-estate served by a road called Roman Way. To reach this from the centre of Neath, follow directions for Pontardawe (A474) and Swansea, taking the bridge straight ahead (not right) over the river, and then going left at the first roundabout (signposted M4, Swansea and Neath Abbey). Roman Way is a turning on the left after $\frac{1}{2}$ mile (800 m), opposite the school. First turn left for the east gate, with the defensive ditch dug out in front of it (the road from the gate must have crossed it on a timber bridge); then follow the modern road round to the south gate. Only the east guard-chamber and the central dividing wall of this double-passageway gate survive (the rest is under the main road), and its south wall, marked now by the pebbles, was found to have been completely robbed. Also worth noting are the two impressive courses of large rusticated blocks at the NW corner of the guard-chamber, and the drain running under the adjacent carriageway.

The road running due north from Brecon Gaer aimed for a fort at **Castell Collen** (SO 055628), which overlooks a large bend in the river Ithon just NW of Llandrindod Wells. The fort-platform is reached by a road which leaves the A4081 (Llandrindod–Rhayader) on the right at an unsignposted crossroads, immediately after crossing the river ('no through road' sign). Follow this road as far as the red-brick farmhouse, where you should ask for permission to visit. The Roman fort lies in the field immediately behind and to the left of the farmhouse (keep straight at the end of the track, leaving the gate to the farmhouse drive on your right, then through or over a metal gate, then through a second metal gate on your right, and then across the stile at the wire fence). The banks and ditches of a square fort are impressively visible in their entire circuit, with an apparently isolated bank and ditch lying to the west of it (on your right, nearest the farmhouse). The latter was part of the defences of an original large fort (5 acres [2 ha]), probably holding a part-mounted garrison 500 strong or an infantry unit 1,000 strong. It was built in turf and timber *c*. 75–8, and later faced in stone. This probably took place in the mid-second century, with the help of the Second Legion Augusta (on the basis of a fragmentary building-slab, found re-used in the bath-house). The guard-chambers of three of the gates had projecting semicircular façades, a touch of pretension unusual in Roman forts at this date. A recent alternative proposal is that stone rebuilding occurred early in the second century, as at Gelligaer, if the very speculative ascription of another fragmentary inscription to the Trajanic period, restoring also its garrison as the 4th Cohort of Delmatians, is correct; but elaborate semicircular gates are unheard of at this period, and the unit, of 500 infantry, is too small to occupy a 5-acre (2-ha) fort. At the end of the second century, however, the area of the fort was reduced to 3.6 acres (1.45 ha) by the building of a cross-wall, and the outer defences (the now isolated bank and ditch) were no longer used. There were apparently some further repairs to the defences in the late third century, implying short-lived re-occupation in the fourth century. Its Roman name is unknown.

Some traces of the stone buildings in the centre of the fort, excavated in 1911–13, still remain, albeit in a very dilapidated condition. The first is a rectangular building of unknown function, by the trees in the NW corner of the reduced fort. The HQ building (*principia*) in the centre comes next, and is the most intelligible, with its range of five rear rooms (in front of you as you stand on the rampart of the reduced fort): the strong-room in the centre is marked by a clump of dark green reeds. The long walls away to your left (north) near the solitary tree belong to a granary; least intelligible of all is the commandant's house, which lies to the right (south) of the *principia*. The excavations were never backfilled, so the site provides telling evidence of the archaeological methodology of the time. This is especially true of the commanding officer's house, where both diagonal trenches to locate the walls initially, and then wall-following trenches to recover the plan, are still clearly visible, with many unexcavated mounds in between. It is the partial, selective nature of such early archaeological work that makes the re-excavation of such sites, in accordance with more modern techniques (including the examination of deposits untouched within many of the rooms) still very rewarding.

The garrison bath-house was excavated outside the SE angle in 1955–7 (not visible), and metal detecting and geophysical work in 1995–7 has revealed some details of the attendant village (*vicus*) on the south and east sides of the fort, with evidence for a possible pottery kiln near the baths, and small-scale metal-working (bronze waste) close by. The heyday of both fort and *vicus* appears to have been in the second century.

Llandrindod Wells also claims the distinction of having the largest known group of military practice camps in the whole Roman Empire (its closest competitor is Chester, where 15 have been identified by aerial photography to the north and east of the fortress, but none of these is traceable on the ground). The troops stationed at Castell Collen were responsible for digging, presumably at various times, no fewer than 18 of these small camps, roughly 30 m (100 ft) square. Very little of them is left, but if you have the time or the enthusiasm, you can trace the eight examples of which visible traces remain on Llandrindod Common, south of the town to the west of the A483 (see Bibliography). The easiest to locate is reached by a lane leaving the A-road steeply up to the right, 600 m (650 yds) south of an Esso filling-station (signed Dolberthog Farm, bed and breakfast). Park immediately on the right (metal gate): now very faint, the camp is situated on the crest of the field here, opposite the entrance to Castalia (coarse reeds in parts of its ditch help to identify it).

The course of the Roman road running west from Brecon Gaer (the fifth road above, p. 326) is not clear until the village of Trecastle on the A40. Here in its western outskirts (opposite the bus shelter) you can take the unsignposted minor road to the left (south), and then after $\frac{1}{2}$ mile (800 m) turn right along a modern road which roughly follows the Roman alignment. After 2 miles (3 km) it becomes impassable (metal gate), and you need to walk a further 2 miles (3 km) along a track which more or less follows the Roman alignment before you pass the fine Roman marching-camps of **Y Pigwn*** (SN 827313), in a wild and desolate position over 400 m (1,350 ft) high. This approach is not, however, recommended unless you are interested in tracing the line of the Roman road. The camps are much more easily approached from the west. Continue along the A40 for 4 miles (6.4 km) beyond Trecastle and take the narrow unsignposted road on the left, immediately after the sign announcing the hamlet of Halfway. Keep along this road for 2 miles (3 km), through two metal gates, past a farmhouse on the left, and up a steep twisting hill, until you reach a T-junction. Turn left here (signposted 'No Through Road') and leave your car by the farm on your left after $\frac{1}{2}$ mile (800 m). It is then 20 minutes' walk along the track ahead of you to the camps.

The camps are temporary ones belonging to the early years of the Roman conquest, and were occupied at the most for a few campaigns. There are two camps here, one inside the other (Fig. 70). The outer one covers some 38 acres (15 ha), big enough to house the equivalent of an entire legion, and the

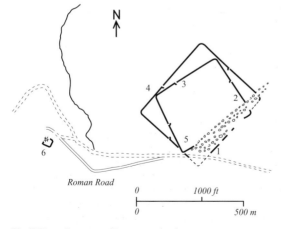

70   *Y Pigwn, Roman marching-camps, site plan*

inner one 25 acres (10 ha). The latter, as will be seen, is later in date, but probably only by a few years, as both are likely to fall within the period of hostilities against the Welsh tribes, between AD 47 and 78. Keep walking, bearing left wherever the track forks, until you see on the left the large series of lead-working mounds which have destroyed the south ramparts of both camps. Leave the track at this point (1 on Fig. 70) and follow the north edge of the workings for about 350 m (380 yds), looking out on the left for the rampart of the inner camp. This can be easily spotted by the coarser, browner grass which grows in its accompanying ditch (2). From here, with the help of the plan, you should be able to trace the ramparts of both camps. Their north sides are particularly fine (over the crest and down the slope beyond), with the north gate of the smaller camp (3) in an excellent state of preservation, its *clavicula* boldly visible (Fig. 71). Note also how the ramparts come very close to touching at the NW corner (4). By now your eye should be 'in', and you will be able to see that, at the SW corner (5), the inner rampart actually projects over the line of the outer as the former rounds the corner, showing that the smaller camp was constructed after the larger one. Furthermore, the ditch of the inner camp can be clearly seen cutting through the rampart of the outer. Another earthwork is known 500 m (550 yds) to the west on the other side of the track (6), with a superb view

71   Y Pigwn, the north entrance of the inner camp, with clavicula

down towards Llandovery, where there was a fort (App. 1).
The rampart is about 37 m (120 ft) square and its north corner
is obscured by a low medieval *motte*, but it is difficult to trace
on the ground today. It is either a signal tower or a very small
fortlet. Three small practice camps are also known $\frac{1}{2}$ mile
(800 m) to the NW, also beside the Roman road, but these are
not visible on the ground.

The Roman road running NW from Llandovery passes the
only known Roman gold-mine in Britain, that at **Dolaucothi***
(SN 664394). This site, set in lovely countryside owned by the
National Trust for Wales, is of great interest for the light
which it sheds on Roman extraction processes and investment
in mining technology, more clearly than at any comparable
site in Britain. It is well signposted from the Lampeter–
Llandovery road (A482), both from the north and the south: it
lies just south of the village of Pumsaint. The Visitor Centre
and exhibitions are open between March and November
(1000–1800), and in high summer (late May to late
September) guided tours of the underground workings of the
1930s are also available; but outside these hours and
throughout the winter the site is freely accessible (take a torch
with you if you want to examine the openings of some of the
mining adits more closely). The primary interest lies in the
complexity of the mining activity, but it is important to stress
that distinguishing Roman workings from nineteenth- and
twentieth-century operations is not always easy in an industry
where the technology has changed little until recent times.
Indeed the history of gold-working here has been extended
still further by a recent French survey of the site, which has
demonstrated that opencast extraction commenced at
Dolaucothi as early as the Bronze Age.

In the Roman period, gold-bearing pyrites were removed by
means of both opencast workings and underground galleries,
which have been traced to a depth of 45 m (145 ft) at one
point. Water was brought to the site by means of two main
aqueducts, the Cothi, 7 miles (11 km) long, and the Annell,
4 miles (6.4 km) long; both were simple channels built on a
shelf cut into the hillside (the platform for the Annell leat was
c. 1.70 m [5 ft 6 in] wide). Short stretches of two other leats
of uncertain length and destination have also been located.
The water was used partly for washing the ore after crushing,

and partly for the process known as 'hushing'; this involved releasing a great wave of water from a tank located immediately above an opencast working, either to remove natural overburden or to dispose of mining debris. 'Firesetting', in which the rock was first heated and then subjected suddenly to cold water, causing the surface to crack, was also employed.

Of the settlement associated with these mines little is at present known. A bath-house to the west of the main workings may have served the miners' village suspected in the same area. Military supervision, in the form of a turf and timber fort of 4.75 acres (2 ha) discovered under Pumsaint village in 1972/3, was established in the Flavian period (c. AD 75), presumably at the time when the gold-mines were first being worked by the Romans. It was rebuilt in stone c. AD 100/10 on a much reduced scale (covering only 2.2 acres [0.9 ha]), but it had already been abandoned by c. AD 130, when military control of the mines was clearly no longer deemed necessary, and the working was no doubt handed over to private lessees. A separate civilian settlement and possible bath-house serving the reduced fort was identified by geophysical prospection on its east side in 1999. How long Roman exploitation of the gold at Dolaucothi continued must await future work: a little third- and fourth-century pottery is known, but the bulk of the considerable Roman mining investment here seems on present evidence to have taken place in the last quarter of the first century and throughout the second century, rather than later. The Roman name of the site was probably LVENTINVM, a name that may mean 'the washeries', referring to the washing of the gold-bearing ores.

The car-park leads to an opencast area, where the (modern) mining buildings and a 1930s mining adit lie. Towards the back of this area, note the full-size reconstruction of a Roman water-wheel, based on a fragment found deep in the mines and now on display in the National Museum at Cardiff (p. 356). It was designed to prevent flooding making the mines unworkable below ground. Most known Roman water-wheels raise the water by having scoops attached to the outer rim; this one is unusual in having triangular openings in the side of the wheel to let the water in, and boxed compartments within to keep it contained. When each triangular opening was horizontal again, a half-revolution of the wheel later, the water was able to be discharged into a trough at a higher level, whereupon the process could be repeated by means of further water-wheels until the water was removed to the surface. The wheels were powered by hand, a thankless task especially in such brutal working conditions: no wonder that the human labour was largely provided by slaves and convicts, and that the sentence *damnatio ad metalla* in the Roman world ('condemnation to the mines') was so feared.

Now take the path which leads between the mine-shaft headgear and the metal sheds, to the right of ticket-office on entry. After an initial climb, follow the asphalt road to your left and the yellow arrows on green backgrounds (ignore for the moment directions to 'The Roman Mine'). You come very soon to an opencast trough christened 'Niagara' by the 1930s miners, presumably because water cascaded down it from the top of the slope in the rainy season (this is Station III on the marker post). It is impossible to tell whether this opencast was the work of Roman miners or rather was cut in the nineteenth century: as already noted, mining techniques changed little in the interim.

Now follow the steps up to your right and on to the broad grass track leading upwards. From here, especially in winter, you have a good view of the village of Pumsaint in the middle distance, where the fort lay. Immediately after this you come to the 'Lower Roman Adit' (IV), which was cut by hand (pick- and chisel-marks are visible in the walls), and so predates modern blasting. Adits of this shape are known from Roman workings at Rio Tinto in Spain, and so too this might be of Roman date; but certainty is impossible. At the next level comes the 'Upper Roman Adit' (V), with a neat opening 2 m high and the same wide, as well as smooth walls, impossible to make with explosives. Whenever it was made, whether in Roman times or later, it represents an enormous labour-intensive, back-breaking effort.

Next take the route climbing the hill to your right until the path divides, one set of steps descending to the right to another mining adit (accessible on the guided tour). You should keep straight here, following the yellow arrows, through a gate and into a field with remains of the short-lived mining operations of 1938 (VI). From here look across to the

hillside in front of you. To your left, in the trees, the mining
adits shown in Fig. 72 are visible, especially in winter; to the
right, in pasture, and on a level just above the top of the adit,
can be seen a slight shelf in the hillside which marks the line
of the Cothi aqueduct. The Annell aqueduct ran on a level
higher up on the same hillside, but its remains are hard to
detect on the ground from here.

Immediately after marker VI comes another asphalted road
which you should follow to your left (more remnants of
twentieth-century processing lie in the field to your right:
VII). At the T-junction turn right, and just as the road bends
up to the right, take the stile on your left. Follow the field
boundary on your left as far as stile IX. Turn your back on it
for the moment and look across the pasture field to the other
side. The slightly raised bump in the surface in front of you
here marks the embankment for the west side of the Cothi
aqueduct, which ran on an artificially prepared shelf across the
field here. To the right of it, at an oblique angle to the
aqueduct, is a series of shallow scoops down the hillside,
which almost certainly represent washing tables on which the
mined ore was placed to separate gold-bearing elements from
the rest of the debris. It has been suggested that to ease this
process gorse may have been placed on the washing tables to
trap the gold, which was later released by burning the gorse.
The presence of the washing tables implies that there was a
sluice gate in the side of the aqueduct at this point, so that
water could be diverted as required for the washing process.

You should now follow the line of the aqueduct to the far
side of the field, and look over the double fence which
unfortunately prevents your progressing any further. In the
field beyond, a large depression in the hillside marks the site
of the enormous tank which formed the principal collection
reservoir of the main Cothi aqueduct: of the dozen or so tanks
of Roman date identified by fieldwork at Dolaucothi, this is
the largest. Its west side is now a gorse-covered mound, but
excavation has shown this to have been a retaining wall some
16.75 m (55 ft) wide at base, consisting of a turf inner lining
and a series of stepped shale revetments on its outer edge to
provide stability on a steeply shelving site. The reservoir
measured some 43 m (140 ft) long and at least 11 m (35 ft)

wide, and is estimated to have had a capacity of a quarter of a million gallons (1.25 million litres).

Next retrace your steps to cross stile IX. Immediately afterwards (marker post X), you cross over a further series of three washing tables (before the rock-cut gully on your left, which is believed also to be a Roman feature). Walk a few paces up to your right here and you come at once to a gap in the large earth bank marking the west and south sides of another water-tank, smaller than the last but still impressive: it measured about 25 m by 9 m (80 ft by 30 ft) and could contain about 100,000 gallons (500,000 litres). Its rear (east) face is rock-cut, and the gap in the mound you have just walked through marks the site of a sluice-gate at the start of the washing tables. Excavation has shown that the mound marking the tank's west retaining wall was 8 m (26 ft) wide, made up of alternating layers of clay and shale lined on the inner face with waterproof clay. The Cothi aqueduct entered the tank on the north (short) side, now much eroded, and left it on the south (to your right). These and other earthwork features at Dolaucothi are most easily traced in winter or early spring, before bracken growth obscures some details.

Rejoining the path you come almost at once to marker post XI and two further impressive mining adits (Fig. 72), which are almost certainly Roman in date, following veins of quartz at an oblique angle into the hillside. After this the path passes the Mitchell Adit of the 1880s (XII), and after crossing another stile, descends once again to the opencast area and the present car-park.

One other remarkable piece of evidence remains to be noted. Opposite the car-park is a prominent mound, for long taken to be a medieval *motte*. Just to the east of it, 20 m (65 ft) from the asphalt road which bypasses the site, is an upright stone, known since time immemorial as Carreg Pumsaint ('Five Saints Stone'). A survey in 1982 of the area immediately adjacent interpreted the site as a water-driven mill complex for crushing and grinding the ore, seen as medieval or modern in date as the technology required (cam-operated and using trip hammers) was thought to be unknown to the Romans. A medieval date was also assumed for Carreg Pumsaint itself, which the shallow groove-like depressions on the side identify as a mortar stone used in this

72   Dolaucothi, Roman gold-mines, entrances to mining tunnels

process. Excavation in 1991 and 1993, however, has demonstrated not only that the '*motte*' is in fact a huge conical spoil tip of discarded mining waste, but also that the activity, including that of the mill complex, was datable by radio-carbon samples to the early Roman period rather than later. A water-powered grain-pounder was known to Pliny the Elder, writing before AD 79, and evidence from Spain and Portugal indicates that water-operated cam-driven mills were operating there before the end of the first century, with examples of granite blocks very similar in form to that of Carreg Pumsaint. They functioned as mortar stones or anvils in connection with ore crushing. Carreg Pumsaint is therefore now to be considered Roman rather than medieval, and the nearby mounds may conceal a precociously early example of a water-assisted ore-crushing plant, which places Dolaucothi at the cutting edge of ancient technological innovation.

Our knowledge of the road-system and its accompanying forts is less complete for north Wales than it is for the south; in particular there is a wide area to the west and south of Chester where the courses of roads are assumed, but have not been traced in detail on the ground. There was a road running west towards the coast along the Upper Severn from the town at Wroxeter, and fort-platforms are visible along this route at Forden Gaer and Caersws (both App. 1). There are also two fortlets in this part of Wales: one on a deserted hilltop at Pen-y-crogbren and another, 7 miles (11 km) due south, in an isolated position at Cae Gaer (both App. 1). The earth ramparts of the latter are impressively preserved, but as the site lies in Forestry Commission property prior permission to visit must be obtained.

Moving further into the NW corner of Wales, we come to an important fort at **Tomen-y-Mur*** (SH 705387), near Trawsfynydd in Gwynedd, the Roman name of which is unknown. Even if there was nothing to see here, the site would be worth visiting on account of the wild beauty of its natural setting, with superb command of the surrounding countryside in nearly every direction. The wind often blows here, so exposed is the position, and we can sympathize with the soldiers whose lot it was to serve in this remote spot. Yet its very remoteness has ensured the good state of preservation of the surviving earthworks, and there is much of interest.

Tomen-y-Mur is reached by an unsignposted minor road on the east side of the A470 immediately south of its junction with the Porthmadog road (A487), 3 miles (4.8 km) north of Trawsfynydd village. Follow this road for exactly 1 mile (1.6 km) and park in the car-park on the right, opposite the cattle-grid sign. Cross the cattle-grid and you will see immediately on your right (A on Fig. 73) an unusual monument: it is one of very few known amphitheatres attached to an auxiliary fort in Britain. Until recently unique, it has now been joined by others (probably) at Newstead [p. 557] and Inveresk in Scotland, and at Catterick, and possibly Binchester, in England; so providing entertainment as well as a place for weapons-training for auxiliary units may well have been more common than was once thought. The arena at Tomen-y-Mur is now marshy and the surrounding banks are much depleted, but its character is clear.

Now retrace your steps and take the stile provided (white direction arrow) into the field where the fort lies. Earlier editions of this book referred to problems of access here, but all this has now changed and visitors are welcome in this area

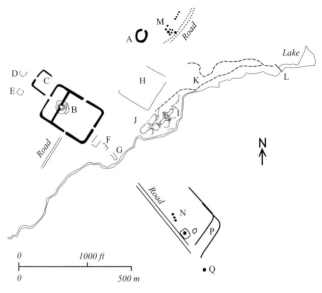

73   Tomen-y-Mur, Roman fort, plan of Roman earthworks

of Snowdonia National Park. A fragment of amphitheatre
bank excluded by the stone field-wall will be noted to your
left. Now make for the ruined farm buildings and the
conspicuous circular earthwork on the skyline: the latter is a
Norman *motte* which, as the plan shows (B), sits on the
middle of the Roman rampart belonging to the second phase
of the fort. For here, as at Castell Collen (p. 329), the original
earth and timber fort of 4.2 acres (1.7 ha), built by Agricola
c. 78, was reduced in size at a later date. In this instance the
reduction in garrison occurred early in Trajan's reign, *c.* 110,
when the new, reduced fort was given a stone wall. Its small
size (3.3 acres [1.35 ha]) indicates that its garrison can only
have been an infantry unit 500 strong. It is the defensive
circuit of this smaller fort which has still left prominent traces,
with some stonework emerging from the banks; these are
often crowned by later field-walls which are built of robbed
material from the fort wall. Occupation at Tomen-y-Mur was
short: the fort was abandoned *c.* AD 140, no doubt because

troops were needed for the Antonine advance into Scotland, and it was never reoccupied. All the Roman military activity at Tomen-y-Mur, therefore, belongs within a space of 60 years.

The track leads to the gap in the rampart marking the position of the NE gate, beside the ruined farm. Going inside the fort and turning right, keeping the *motte* on your left, you will soon see the rounded rampart-mound on the NW side of the original, full-size fort, free of field-walls. A small defended annexe (C) lay beyond the rampart on this side, but it has left scant traces on the ground. About 100 m (110 yds) beyond the NW gate, if you can surmount the fence in your way, can be found a small earthwork (D) with two entrances and a *titulus*: it is a practice camp built by the troops as part of their training. Another small earthwork to the south (E) is probably another example, especially as it was not provided with entrances.

Now follow the fort perimeter round to the middle of the SE side, and leave the fort by the SE gate, keeping the field-wall which runs at right-angles to the fort on your left. You are now walking along the line of the Roman road which headed SE towards Caer Gai (p. 343), lined on either side with the stone buildings of a small civilian settlement. Just after crossing the line of a broken field-wall, by the trees on your right, a tumble of Roman stones marks the position of the garrison bath-house (F), partly explored in the nineteenth century. A little beyond is an earth embankment some 2.40 m (8 ft) high, which formed the abutment for a wooden bridge (G) carrying the Roman road across the stream; the corresponding abutment on the other side of the stream has been completely eroded.

You should now strike back across the field in the direction of the amphitheatre. Nearing the latter, you will see a prominent stile over the field-wall to your right. This allows access to the field beyond and in particular to the site of the level parade-ground, artificially prepared out of the boggy terrain (H). A small bluff here gives you an excellent overall view of the parade-ground, the fort and the Trawsfynydd lake beyond. The parade-ground appears to have been unfinished. Banks were made round three sides, increasing in height down the slope to ensure that the top was level throughout. The intention was then to excavate earth just north of the area and cart it down the slope until the ground was level with the banks, but this was only half completed, and so both the delimiting banks and the excavation-pits are still visible. Hillock I, with flanking terraces, and Earthwork J are both of unknown purpose; it has been suggested that the former might have been a temple to the protecting goddesses of the parade-ground, the *Matres Campestres*, whereas J probably marks the site of a small medieval or post-medieval settlement. Recent fieldwork has demonstrated the presence of two short aqueducts (K) which brought water from a small artificial lake 700 m (765 yds) to the NE, formed by the building of an earth dam (L). The more southerly leat must have supplied the bath-house, and the other, probably on timber supports, may have headed for the fort. The evidence for these can just be traced on the ground with a discerning eye as slight terraces.

Finally, just before rejoining your car, walk along the asphalted road past the amphitheatre, and climb the knoll in front of you where the modern road swings left. Several mounds here, some more easily traceable than others, are small earthen *tumuli* marking the sites of burials, a few with surrounding ditches (M); a further group of four, barely detectable, lies in a row 50 m further north. They are similar to the *tumuli* in the better preserved military cemetery at High Rochester (p. 543) and, like those, presumably conceal cremation burials beneath. The tombs line the main Roman road, visible here as a broad terrace at the slighter lower level, which joined Tomen-y-Mur with the forts at Bryn-y-Gefailiau (App. 1) and Caerhun (p. 344) to the north.

This by no means exhausts the list of Roman earthworks in the vicinity of Tomen-y-Mur, and visitors with plenty of time to spare may like to explore further by crossing the stream and proceeding SE on the alignment of the Roman road (set by the line between the SE gate and the bridge abutment, G). Three more disfigured mounds, clearly further tombs (N), lie 500 m (550 yds) SE of the SE gate, just before a modern wall passes obliquely across the line of the Roman road. On the other side of the wall, on the left (east) of the Roman road, is a prominent burial mound on a square platform (O), perhaps the tomb of a commanding officer. After negotiating a medieval bank and ditch immediately beyond this tomb, you cross the line of the south ramparts of two successive and overlapping

marching-camps to your left (P), of which only the outer is
just visible; the rest of these camps have been ploughed out.
Immediately beyond this, the Roman road swerved to avoid
the low knoll ahead of you, which is crowned by another
Roman burial-mound (Q). Disturbance on the top of all these
tumuli makes it likely that they have been dug into in the past
by grave robbers. An OS map will be needed if you want to
find two practice camps further afield. Llwyn-Crwn (SH
712382) measures about 37 m by 34 m (122 ft by 112 ft) and
is 0.6 m (2 ft) high in parts; Braich-ddu (SH 717383), near a
disused slate-quarry, is about 23 m (75 ft) square with four
gates and internal *claviculae* almost touching one another.
Another group of five practice camps, with *tituli* rather than
claviculae, is known at Doldinnas (SH 735378), 2 miles
(3.2 km) south of Tomen-y-Mur. As usual with this class of
antiquity, their remains are slight although still clearly visible
on the ground: along with those on Llandrindod Common (p.
330), they are in fact the best preserved group of such practice
camps in Britain. A yet further group of four practice camps
were discovered from the air in 1996 $\frac{1}{2}$ mile (800 m) SE of
Doldinnas, on the west side of the lake called Llyn Hiraethlyn
(SH 741368), but these are scarcely visible on the ground. The
southernmost camp, however, 24.50 m (80 ft) square, can be
detected with a sharp eye, and a tiny camp immediately to its
NE, 12.80 m by 12.50 m (42 ft by 41 ft), with *tituli* outside its
west and east entrances, still stands 0.5 m (1 ft 7 in) high.

The Roman road which passes all these earthworks was
heading over the mountains for the fort at the SW corner of
Bala Lake, known as **Caer Gai** (SH 877314). The farm of that
name which obscures the fort's northern corner is reached by
an unsignposted turning on the north (left) side of the A494,
$\frac{3}{4}$ mile (1.2 km) north of Llanuwchllyn (it is the second turning
on the left after the minor road to Trawsfynedd). After the
track bends sharply to the right, you will see the field-wall,
which incorporates part of the Roman stone core, crowning
the full length of the SE defences of the fort. Continue on and
park to the right of the farmhouse itself (enquire here for
permission). Go through the metal gate beside the drive
leading to the farmhouse and keep straight. After passing
through the next field-gate you come out to the SW side of the
fort, its ditch and rampart very conspicuous (with a modern

wall on top). The post, which covered $4\frac{1}{2}$ acres (1.8 ha), was probably founded *c*. 78 by Agricola during his campaign against the Ordovices, and was then occupied until *c*. 125, the original turf rampart being revetted in stone presumably at the beginning of the second century. The garrison at this time was the First Cohort of Nervii (originally from Belgium) 500 strong, as we know from an inscription found in 1885 and now in Cardiff. Two practice camps are known nearby, one of them still visible (Pont Rhyd Sarn, App. 1). Another, larger, fort was discovered from the air in 1975 $5\frac{1}{2}$ miles (9 km) away, at the NE end of Bala Lake, together with a polygonal stores-base and two marching-camps of earlier date on the same site (at Llanfor, nothing visible); all these installations probably pre-date the Flavian fort at Caer Gai.

The road north from Tomen-y-Mur led to **Caerhun** (SH 775704) in the Conwy valley, after an intermediate station near Betws-y-Coed (Bryn-y-gefeiliau, App. 1). The fort at Caerhun, KANOVIVM as we can read on a Hadrianic milestone in the British Museum, is situated $4\frac{1}{2}$ miles (6 km) due south of Conwy on the river of the same name. 'Conwy' in fact derives from KANOVIVM, which probably means 'the reedy [river]'. It is reached by a lane on the left (east) of the B5106 to Trefriw, 50 m after its junction with the more southerly of the two turnings to Rowen on the south side of the village of Tyn-y-Groes (signposted Pontwgan and Rowen). The lane you need is signposted '13th century Caerhun church'. The history of the place holds some puzzles: the usual earth and timber fort of *c*. 78 is usually thought to have been replaced in stone *c*. 140, but the odd treatment of the gates, two of them with single guardrooms only, is more characteristic of the third century. Certainly coins and pottery indicate that occupation lasted into the fourth century, with evidence of increased activity in the 360s or 370s (probably in response to the mounting threat posed by Irish seaborne raiders). No fourth-century structures, however, were apparently detected by the excavators of 1926–9; they uncovered the entire plan of the fort except for the NE corner, underlying the church and churchyard. All the excavations have been filled in, and only the mound of the rampart, very well preserved on the south where the lane bisects it, can be seen at the site today, with the occasional piece of stonework peeping through the turf.

A road headed eastwards from Caerhun in the direction of
St Asaph in the vale of Clwyd, where Roman finds have been
made and a fort is suspected, probably the Roman VARIS. But
our knowledge of the Roman occupation of NE Wales has
been advanced in recent years by the discovery of a further
site near **Prestatyn** (SJ 062817), 5 miles (8 km) NNE of
St Asaph. Although two successive forts in adjacent positions
have been claimed to have existed here, both trial excavation
and geophysical research show that both are a myth. The
small Roman settlement excavated here is probably, therefore,
best interpreted as civilian and not military. There may have
been a harbour here on a now vanished inlet, and the site's
primary role was probably commercial, serving the lead-mines
at nearby Meliden. Of this settlement a small bath-house has
been excavated and consolidated for permanent view.

The site lies on the west side of the A547 mid-way between
the centre of Prestatyn and the village of Meliden, 2 miles
(3.2 km) to the south: take the turning called Melyd Avenue
(cul-de-sac), at the bottom of which, in an area intended to be
a housing-estate which was never completed, you will find the
tiny three-roomed bath-house (there is no signpost). The walls
of the cold room, nearest the road, and of its adjacent
semicircular immersion-bath with outflow pipe, were badly
robbed (its walls are now partly restored). An oblique stone-
built structure, floored with tiles, is part of a drain, probably
taking excess water away via a perforated cover-slab in the
centre of the floor above. The two heated rooms beyond the
frigidarium are better preserved, built of neatly coursed rows
of white limestone and red Cheshire sandstone (with a single
tile bonding-course on the south [left] wall, and on the inside
of the east wall). The *pilae* supporting the floors are of brick,
some stamped by the Twentieth Legion Valeria Victrix (LEG
XX VV), which were made at the legionary brickworks at Holt
near Chester; four stamped examples used to be visible, but
only one is now clearly legible. The *pilae* of the *tepidarium*
are all modern (they are stamped with the date of 1986 in
Roman numerals!). The stoke-hole of the *caldarium* at the far
end employed an inscribed slab re-used from elsewhere: three
letters (?COR, the last not certain) survived but are not now
legible. First located in 1936, the bath-house was re-excavated
in 1984–6, when it was found that the two heated rooms were

built earlier (*c.* AD 120) than the *frigidarium* and its cold
plunge. These were added later (*c.* 150/60), as can be clearly
seen from the straight joint between the two. But two heated
rooms alone do not make a bath-house; the earliest cold room
must have been of timber, as at Bearsden (p. 582). Water was
brought to the baths on a wooden leat supported on posts; also
found nearby were several timber buildings, including a
bronze workshop with remains of crucibles, slag, and,
unusually, clay moulds for brooch production. Both the baths
and the workshop were abandoned by *c.* 160.

A road running west from Caerhun, and another probably
striking NW from Tomen-y-Mur, met at **Caernarfon****
(SH 485625), a place of the utmost strategic importance not
only in Roman times but later too, as the famous Edwardian
castle at the river mouth demonstrates. The Roman name,
SEGONTIVM, means 'the forceful river'. The remains of the fort
lie in the outskirts of the town on the A4085 to Beddgelert:
follow first the A487 (Portmadoc), and then keep straight up
the hill (Bedgelert Road) when the A487 swings to the right.
The Museum and fort are open daily all the year round [AM;
April–October, Monday–Saturday, 1000–1700, Sunday,
1400–1700; November–March, Monday–Saturday,
1000–1600, Sunday, 1400–1600].

The main phases of SEGONTIVM's history were first revealed
in excavations of 1920–3 by Sir Mortimer Wheeler, but
important further excavations in the fort's SE sector in 1975–9
have amplified and modified Wheeler's work. Founded by
Agricola *c.* 77/8, the 5.5-acre (2.25-ha) fort started life, as
usual, in earth and timber form, probably designed for an
infantry cohort 1,000 strong. There were two refurbishings of
this timber fort, probably in the late Flavian and Trajanic
periods, before stone rebuilding, including the defences, took
place in stages during the second century, from *c.* 140
onwards. The Twentieth Legion from Chester helped in
reconstructing the internal buildings, bringing with it the red
Cheshire sandstone (used for the granaries, the commandant's
house and two barracks in the NW corner). There was a further
major refurbishment in the early third century. An inscription
of 198–209 refers to the rebuilding of an aqueduct 'collapsed
through age', and there is no reason to take this phrase other
than at face value; it also tells us that the garrison at the time

was the First Cohort of Sunici (from Germany), which was
only 500 strong. The fort walls, the south gate, and probably
the north and west gates visible today date from this period.
There was a gap in occupation in the late third century,
probably when the usurper Allectus withdrew troops to defend
his short-lived bid for power as Carausius' successor in the
separatist British 'Empire', and there was another gap in
occupation during the mid-fourth century. Final extensive
rebuilding took place after AD 364, but the coinage ends
abruptly under Magnus Maximus (383–8), when the garrison
was withdrawn. By then SEGONTIVM had enjoyed an almost
continuous occupation longer than any other known fort in the
whole of Wales.

The entrance to the site (1 on Fig. 74) is close to the east
gate (underneath the road) and an adjoining section of fort
wall. First the excellent site museum should be visited, where
some of the main finds from the fort are exhibited. Note
especially the inscription of AD 198–209 mentioning
restoration of the water supply (referred to above); the finds
from the Temple of Mithras (see below); and the facsimile of
a gold foil worn to protect the wearer against the evil eye,
inscribed in Greek with a series of magical words, which was
found outside the fort around 1828 (the original is in
Caernarfon Public Library).

Behind the Museum, you will see the foundations of several
barrack buildings (2) which fill up the whole of the rear
portion of the fort: these consist of quarters for officers at one
end and a long section, originally divided by partitions, for the
men. The first pair you come to, between the museum and the
modern reservoir (2 and 3 on Fig. 74), are part of the second-
century layout (the fourth-century additions in the more
southerly [2] were removed by Wheeler to display the earlier
plan). Then turn right towards the north gate. The three
barracks on your left (4–6) belong to the third-century
rebuilding in their visible form. Next on your right is the
surviving part of a granary (7), in an unusual position in a fort
of this date, and supernumerary to the customary two
granaries which lie buried under the Museum and adjacent
properties. It was dated by Wheeler to the second century, but
its unorthodox position (partially blocking, furthermore, the
intervallum roadway), and the fact that it is not laid out

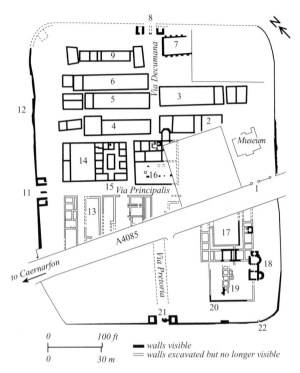

74   Caernarfon, Roman fort, site plan

parallel with the rampart (a surveying fault?), suggest that it is
not earlier than the third century. Next to this are the paltry
remains of the north gate (8) with twin roadways and guard-
chambers; the central pier dividing the carriageways is no
longer visible.

Now turn left and follow the defences. The barrack to your
left (9) is displayed in its fourth-century form, when the
original barrack-plan was breaking up into several smaller
units; but this is still a different type from the contemporary
'chalet'-type barracks known at Housesteads (p. 494) and
elsewhere on the northern frontier. Rounding the NW corner
(where the site of a corner tower [10] is marked by the
hollow), you pass on the left the barracks already noted. Next

you arrive at the west gate, which displays masonry of several
periods (11). It started with the normal twin passages and
guard-chambers, but in the fourth century the gate was
reduced to a single carriageway, and the other roadway (on
the left) was converted into a new guardroom. The original
guardroom here was then filled up, but it has been cleared out
again now. The contrast in masonry styles between the
gateway in its third-century form and the larger masonry of
the fourth-century addition will be noted. One pivot-hole from
the third-century gate can be seen.

Now go down the slope outside the fort and turn right, to
see a fine stretch of the stone curtain wall, 15 m (50 ft) long
and 2.5 m (8 ft) high, with some of its facing-stones still intact
(12). Return now to the gate and walk in a straight line from it
to the modern houses, along the line of the *via principalis*.
The area of barracks on your right between here and the road
has been excavated but is not now visible (13). On the left,
first of all, is a long shed with a large adjoining yard –
interpreted by Wheeler as the fort's *fabrica*, or workshop (14).
Beyond is the commandant's house (*praetorium*), as it
appeared in its original second-century form of four ranges of
rooms around a central courtyard (15); the fourth-century
changes have been removed. The building used a mixture of
stones: the far right-hand (NE) corner uses a few blocks of red
Cheshire sandstone, but the rest is of local stone. An isolated
masonry plinth in a room at the far end was perhaps the base
for a statue.

Finally, you come to part of the central building of the fort
and the most interesting of all, the *principia* or headquarters
building (16). The front part consists of a courtyard, of which
the well and some paving-flags are visible; the central part
was a roofed assembly-hall later subdivided for office use; and
the rear range consisted of five rooms (two are under the
modern house), of which the central one contained the chapel
where the military standard was kept. Under it, originally
vaulted, a strong-room was built in the early third century
with steps leading down to it. At the same time a heated room
was tacked on rather crudely at the rear; it overlay one end of
a second-century barrack which must have been re-shaped
to accommodate the *principia* extension. Wheeler claimed, on
the strength of an inscription (there is a cast in the museum),

that it was the record-office of the quartermaster (*actarius*)
who dedicated an altar to Minerva, but in fact the altar was
found among late third-century debris in the strong-room
rather than specifically in the heated room. In fact the date of
the extension might rather belong to the fourth century. The
channels for hot air to circulate below floor-level can be seen.

The rest of SEGONTIVM lies on the other side of the A4085
and part of it was re-excavated in 1975–9; this has been
consolidated and left exposed. It is reached via the metal gate
on the other side of the road opposite the *principia*. The
largest structure, badly robbed, was a spacious courtyard
building with three and presumably once four ranges round a
central court (17): only a few rooms and a couple of drains
could be consolidated and left exposed. Built *c*. AD 140, its
purpose is uncertain: it seems too large to have been the
hospital, yet it is clearly not the commandant's house, which
is in the central range (15) where it ought to be. One
suggestion is that it was the residence of the *procurator
metallorum*, the official responsible for the overall
administration of the rich copper-mines of Anglesey and the
north Wales coast; but this is no more than a guess. The
presence of this large building, however, out of the ordinary
for a 'normal' fort, suggests a reduction in the garrison at
Caernarfon during the second century.

In the late third or early fourth century, after the demolition
of the courtyard building, a small but substantially built bath-
house (18) was erected, still standing up to six courses high: it
comprised (from north to south) a furnace, a hot (apsed) room,
and then the tepid and cold rooms with an apsed immersion-
bath containing cold water. The bath-house was however
never finished, since hypocausts were never installed. In
Britain, bath-houses normally appear inside the walls of
Roman forts only in the late Roman period, and this is a good
example: the earlier pressures on space had been relaxed by
the presence of smaller garrisons. However, an even smaller
bath-house further west (19), of which only one corner
(including a blocked doorway) has survived later demolition,
was built as early as the mid-second century and is
contemporary with the large courtyard building. The presence
of a bath-house inside the defences, one moreover taking up
valuable space and not tucked up alongside the rampart (as at

Bar Hill: p. 580), is highly unusual in Britain at this early date; it reinforces the impression that SEGONTIVM was not a typical fort but had a special role to play in the Roman occupation of NW Wales. The structure served, however, not as a garrison bath-house but for the occupants of the courtyard building (17), and its exclusivity is emphasized by its enclosure at a subsequent period (at some stage in the third century) within a separate boundary wall, of which a long stretch is also visible (20).

The south gate (21) originally consisted of a double-carriageway flanked by a solid tower on one side and a guardroom and tower on the other, but one of the carriageways was later blocked by a rough wall still in position. At the same time, the inside of the guard-chamber was cut in two by a partition wall.

The outside of the fort wall, consisting of core only (except for three courses of facing high up at the SE corner) can be studied on the east and south sides by taking the path almost opposite the entrance to the Museum, and following the walls round into the children's playground. The Roman east wall is at first masked by modern refacing. An arched drainage culvert will be spotted at the base of the south wall, just after rounding the SE corner (22).

Building operations around the fort have revealed traces of a large civilian settlement, including a temple to Mithras; the position of the latter is marked by a plaque on a house at the far end (on the left) of Lon Arfon, 150 m east of the fort (turn first left off the A4085). Neither temple nor any building in the *vicus* is now visible. There is, however, an impressive enclosure-wall known as Hen Waliau ('Old Walls') situated 300 m west of the fort (SH 482625). To reach it from the Museum, walk westwards along the A4085, turn left (Segontium Road South) and then right down the hill (Hendre Street, avoiding Gelert Street). Turn right on reaching the main road at the bottom (Portmadoc Road) and you come soon to a fine stretch of walling, still standing 5.80 m (19 ft) above Roman ground-level, in the grounds of a private house, facing the pedestrian lights. A gateway, blocked up with modern material, is also visible here, and a longer stretch of its outer face, somewhat overgrown, is visible in the grounds of the Health Clinic next door. The wall, 1.8 m (6 ft) thick, belongs to an enclosure covering some 70 m by 50 m (230 ft by 165 ft). There is no sign of gate-towers or other projecting towers, and it is probably best to regard this defended enclosure as a stores-compound (it was probably built in the early third century).

The provision of such massive walls reflects an insecurity which grew even greater in the later Roman period, as emphasized by two important additions to the Welsh defences at Holyhead and Cardiff. The forts so far described all belong to the detailed Roman plan, worked out in the first century but modified in the second, for garrisoning Wales by means of regularly placed forts. The new forts, however, at Holyhead and Cardiff, belong to the late third or the fourth century and were clearly designed to combat an enemy expected from the sea, and not from the Welsh mountains.

The late Roman fort at Holyhead, **Caer Gybi*** (SH 247826) in Welsh, owes its preservation to the church of St Gybi which stands inside its walls. Follow directions for the town centre, forking left at the War Memorial up the hill (one-way system). Turn right into Williams Street and follow the road round to the left, turning right again at the National Westminster Bank. Then turn first right yet again at the telephone kiosks for the short-stay car-park beside the north wall of the Roman fort.

The small cliff on which the fort stands was originally much less steep (it was cut back in the nineteenth century) and the walls continued down to the beach, with the shore-side probably left open: it is, therefore, a defended beaching-point for the Roman fleet using Holyhead harbour, of a type also known on the Rhine and Neckar in Germany in the fourth century. The walls are 1.6 m (5 ft 6 in) thick, built of small stones partly laid in herringbone pattern, and still 4–5 m (13–16 ft) high where best preserved, on the north and west sides. Even details of the rampart-walk are clearly visible, especially on the north when viewed from the churchyard. Putlog holes for Roman scaffolding are also detectable, especially on the outer face of the north wall (seen from the car-park). Three round towers can be seen, but only that at the NW corner is substantially Roman: the others have suffered in various degrees from medieval and modern rebuilding. The original entrance, on the south, is now much obscured by later work; the gap in the north wall is not of Roman origin. The date of Caer Gybi is not precisely known, but it probably belongs to the second half of the fourth century. Why other similar structures are not known on the Welsh coasts is something of a mystery: perhaps the copper-mines of Anglesey were believed to merit special protection.

The defence of NW Anglesey centred on Caer Gybi must have been assisted by a series of watchtowers from which warning of impending attack could be signalled, and one of these, excavated on the summit of **Holyhead Mountain** (SH 218829) in 1980–1, has been consolidated and left exposed. To reach the site, turn right from the car-park at Holyhead fort, left at the bottom, and then third left at the Marine Hotel. Keep straight for $\frac{1}{4}$ mile (400 m), and then turn left at the first mini-roundabout, signposted South Stack (Walthew Avenue, which becomes New Park Road). Keep straight as far as the T-junction. Turn right here (still signed South Stack), and then after a further $\frac{1}{2}$ mile (800 m) watch out for Old School Road on your left. Ignore that, but continue on for another $\frac{1}{3}$ mile (500 m) until the other loop of Old School Road joins the main road. Turn right here (unsignposted) and keep climbing for $\frac{1}{4}$ mile (400 m) (fork left whenever you are in doubt); you should park near a post-box and a house called Bryn Heulog.

From here take not the track but the footpath near the post-box, and keep straight: an eventually well-defined path leads in approximately 15 minutes to the entrance of **Caer Y Twr** hill-fort (SH 218830) [AM; A]. The stone ramparts of this 17-acre (7-ha) enclosure, probably built in the early Roman period but in the tradition of the late Iron Age, are well preserved – up to 3 m (10 ft) high, with remains of the rampart-walk still extant in places. Aim now for the OS triangulation pillar clearly visible from here: a further 10-minute walk will bring you to the summit of **Holyhead Mountain** (SH 218829) and to the two surviving walls of a square Roman watchtower, which lies next to the OS pillar. Measuring some 5.45 m (18 ft) square, it has walls 1.50 m (5 ft) wide on wider footings. The scanty pottery, not well stratified, and a small coin hoard deposited c. AD 395, pointed to occupation in the second half of the fourth century, when the fort at Caer Gybi was presumably also garrisoned. Not surprisingly there are fine views of Holyhead harbour, but the view northwards is blocked by Carmel Head, on the summit of which another Roman watchtower (SH 293924), so far unexcavated, is suspected.

By leaving the tower behind you and continuing down to the bluff just below, where the mountain falls steeply to flattish moorland, you can make out the hut circles of an indigenous settlement on the SW slope of Holyhead Mountain (SH 212820) [AH; A]. Excavation has shown that there were 20 huts in all, occupied between the second and fourth centuries. They lie to the left of the track and to the right of the rectangular reservoir.

The 9-acre (3.50-ha) fort at **Cardiff Castle*** (ST 181766), in the heart of modern Cardiff, is a much more massive affair, closely similar to the Saxon Shore forts of SE England. It was built in the late third century, probably under Carausius in the 280s, and was provided with semi-octagonal towers and two single-arched gates, each protected by guard-towers. It was occupied until the time of Valentinian (364–78). The fort is particularly striking for the reconstruction – pioneering in Britain at the time and rarely imitated since – of the north, east and part of the south walls, which was carried out at the expense of the Marquess of Bute at the end of the nineteenth century. His statue stands in a public garden across the road from the fort's NE corner.

The original Roman facing is visible at the foot of the walls, especially on the south; sensibly, it is separated from the reconstructed walling above by a row of pink stones. On the north and east stretches, openings near ground-level give a glimpse of the Roman core which lies behind. The reconstruction gives a clear idea of what a Saxon Shore fort may have looked like in the late third century, the north gate being especially fine (Fig. 75). It must, however, be noted that although its gate-towers might have been reconstructed to approximately the correct height, the adjacent curtain wall is certainly too high. More likely its crenellations would have been level with the first-floor windows in the gate-towers. This late stronghold is the fourth in a succession of Roman forts on approximately the same site, starting with a very large one *c.* AD 55 (a vexillation fortress?), and followed by more conventional forts in the Flavian period and early in the

75   *Cardiff, late Roman fort, reconstructed north gate*

second century. This last partly extended north of the late Roman enclosure, but was levelled in the late third century to make room for the visible fort.

The National Museum of Wales, which has an archaeological section, is nearby: it is open all the year round (Tuesday–Sunday, 1000–1700). Of especial note here are the models of the fort and a gateway at Gelligaer (p. 326); finds from the Twentieth Legion's tile-works at Holt (p. 321); and the lead pig from the Flintshire lead-mines naming the private contractor C. Nipius Ascanius, probably *c.* AD 75. Interestingly, the same man is known to have worked earlier at Charterhouse, as we know from another pig of AD 60 in the British Museum. Note also the fragment of water-wheel, and a wooden panning cradle, both of which come from the gold-mines at Dolaucothi (p. 333).

Cardiff, like Holyhead, cannot have stood alone and must have been linked with a series of signal-posts to give warnings of imminent pirate raids; but much is likely to have been lost in the nineteenth-century expansion of Cardiff and its satellite towns. One enigmatic building, however, at Cold Knap, **Barry*** (ST 099664), might be relevant here. Excavated in 1980–1 and subsequently consolidated and left exposed, it lies in the western outskirts of modern Barry, from the centre of which you should follow signs for The Knap and Porthkerri Park. In Lakeside, turn left before the railway-bridge along Bron-y-Mor. The Roman site lies (unsignposted) facing the beach at the end of this road, behind (i.e. west of) Water's Edge Residential Home. Well constructed throughout of

76   Barry, Roman courtyard building from the east

coursed lias limestone, it consists of 21 rooms and corridors arranged on all four sides of a central rectangular court, with walkway around (Fig. 76). There is a cellar at the SE corner of the structure where the masonry still stands 1.75 m (5 ft 9 in) high; it has a pebbled floor with a rectangular cutaway in one corner, a tiled entrance threshold in the east wall, and five curious slits in its west wall. Excavation has shown that the south range was planned first and the rest then followed, but this detail is not clear now; the veranda on the beach side was apparently an afterthought. The building was enclosed by a U-shaped rock-cut ditch, partly found on the east side. The work was carried out at some time in the late third century, roughly contemporary with the visible fort at Cardiff. Curiously, however, the building seems never to have been put into commission. There was no sign of floor-levels, plaster rendering or occupation debris, and one wall had collapsed directly on to builders' levels. The structure's intended function is therefore a complete enigma. It is a substantial building, of Mediterranean courtyard type, constructed of stone to roof height, and with a tiled roof. All this suggests an official function (private buildings in Roman south Wales generally have slate roofs) – it is certainly not a private villa. Its position on the sea, and in particular on a small harbour (in Roman times the sea came in where the nearby boating lake now is), might indicate that it was a *mansio*, a lodging-house for government and other officials, of the type still visible at Wall (p. 293) and Vindolanda (p. 501); indeed the harbour might even have had a certain importance as a departure point for crossing the Severn estuary. An adjacent one-roomed square structure was discovered when the residential home was built, and a bath-house seems to have been destroyed without record nearby; but nothing else is known of Roman settlement at Barry (no late Roman military post is suspected, for example). Why the building project was aborted before completion we shall probably never know; but conditions must have taken a dramatic, unexpected and very sudden turn for the worse if they really were responsible for the '*mansio*' builders' change of heart.

The fort at Cardiff was designed especially to protect the civilian population of the Glamorgan plain and the Severn estuary. Only in this part of Wales was there the spread of

Romanization in the form of towns and villas so familiar in
the English lowlands. Or rather not quite. For long Caerwent
(between Newport and Chepstow) was the only known
Roman town in our area, but a totally new light was shed on
the penetration of Roman influence in SW Wales by the
discovery in 1968 that **Carmarthen** (SN 416214) was also a
walled town replacing an earlier fort, and not a fort
throughout the Roman period as had hitherto been believed.
Presumably the Demetae, the tribe which occupied this corner
of Wales, were rewarded for their comparative lack of
resistance to Roman arms by the creation of a *civitas* capital.
Excavations between 1968 and 1990 suggested that the town
was properly laid out with a street grid *c.* 120/50, developing
from civilian sprawl alongside an earlier fort to the west. This
early fort had been demolished *c.* 100 and replaced by a
smaller structure, implying a reduced garrison, which finally
left *c.* AD 120 (the site of the fort is crossed by King Street
and Spillman Street, between St Peter's Church and the
medieval castle). Its Roman name was MORIDVNVM, 'the fort
by the sea'. The town was given clay-bank defences at some
stage during the third century, revetted in stone at a later date
in the same century, and these enclosed an area of some 31
acres (13 ha). Inside have been found a Romano-Celtic temple
(but as yet no other public buildings) and fragmentary
domestic buildings of timber and stone (including tessellated
floors and hypocausts), which continued in use to the end of
the fourth century at least.

The only feature of Roman date visible today, however, is
part of the amphitheatre, situated on the east side of the town.
Two miles (3.2 km) east of the centre of Carmarthen, on the
outskirts of the town, the A40 from Llandeilo comes to a
roundabout. Take here the road signposted Abergwili. The
Carmarthen Museum, splendidly displayed in the former
Bishop's Palace, lies on the left immediately after this
roundabout (Monday–Saturday, 1000–1630). At the next
roundabout take the turning for 'Town centre'. The
amphitheatre is to be found on the right (north) of this road,
$1\frac{1}{2}$ miles (2.4 km) from the Carmarthen Museum: watch out
for a telephone kiosk and a sign ('Amphitheatre Moridunum')
set parallel to the road (and therefore easily missable),
adjacent to Priory Close. The north bank of the amphitheatre,

which was hollowed out of the hillside, still stands to its
original height, some 7 m (23 ft) above the arena floor, but
arrangements on the south side are less certain: either the
south bank has become very eroded, or else this was a hybrid
building of the 'theatre-amphitheatre' type known elsewhere
in the NW provinces (cf. Verulamium, p. 236), with a stage
on the south side rather than seating. Further excavation will
be necessary to resolve the point. The arena itself apparently
measured about 45 m by 27 m (150 ft by 90 ft). Excavations
in 1968 and 1971 found traces of the timber beams which
supported the seating, as well as a complex drainage-system,
but the arena wall had been totally robbed and the wall you
see today is modern. This amphitheatre, probably built around
the middle of the second century, is a remarkable witness to
the extent of the penetration of Roman influence in this far
corner of the province, itself so far from the heart of the
Roman Empire.

The other town at **Caerwent**** (ST 469905) [AM; A] is
one of the most impressive sites not only in this chapter but in
the whole of Roman Britain. It was VENTA SILVRVM, the
'market of the Silures' tribe which proved so hostile to
successive Roman armies in the first century. It was only a
small settlement of 44 acres (18 ha), hardly more than what
we would call a village, but it had all the usual amenities –
forum, basilica, temples and baths – that one expects of any
fully-fledged Roman town, whether *civitas* capital or not; only
a theatre and/or amphitheatre of the expected complement of
public buildings are yet to be found. Estimates of population
are not easy, here or anywhere else: a suggestion that it lay
between 2,500 and 3,500 may be on the high side if the
proposed figure of 5,000 for Wroxeter, a town four times the
size, has any validity (p. 277). The excavations which
uncovered much of the plan of the town took place between
1899 and 1913, contemporary with the large-scale work at
Silchester (p. 115). The two sites have yielded fuller
topographical plans of Roman towns in Britain than anywhere
else (Wroxeter, however, now rivals them: p. 276), although
at Caerwent six of the 20 *insulae* making up the town were
touched hardly or not at all by the Edwardian excavators.

VENTA SILVRVM was probably founded towards the close of
the first century, and may well have succeeded an earlier fort

on the site (there is a natural flat plateau at the centre of the
later town); no trace of it, however, has yet been found. Urban
development was initially slow. The first town defences,
comprising an earth rampart and ditch, came not earlier than
AD 130, and probably (in line with other Romano-British
towns) at the end of the second century. The visible stone wall
was no doubt built (as elsewhere) at some stage in the third
century, although current orthodoxy, reflected for example in
the explanatory panels on site, reckons that this did not
happen until *c*. AD 330. Caerwent would in that case be out of
step with every other major town in Roman Britain, all of
which seem to have received their stone defences before the
end of the third century. Polygonal towers, in theory to
provide extra defensive cover, were added some time not
much later than 350, curiously on the north and south walls
only. The basilica was turned over to metal-working at about
the same time, but coin finds at Caerwent are plentiful until
near the end of the fourth century, and only then do houses
such as that excavated west of Pound Lane show evidence of
abandonment and decay.

Your tour of the defences can conveniently begin at the
Coach and Horses pub close to the east gate (1 on Fig. 77).
The latter, like its counterpart on the west, probably had a
double-carriageway and flanking towers, a fragment of which
can be seen south of the main east-west road. It is not bonded
with the rest of the wall and so is earlier in date: in all
likelihood the gates and their guard-towers were built
freestanding of stone at the same time that the first earth
defences were erected. The wall that stretches southwards
from here is on average 3 m (10 ft) high, although only the
core is visible since most of the facing-stones have been
robbed. Now go through a wicket gate and round the SE
corner (the mound is a Norman *motte*: 2 on Fig. 77). After a
short while you cross a farm track: before that, watch out for
short stone projections on the inner face of the wall, believed
to mark the position of access stairs to the wall-walk, of
which a dozen examples have been identified around the walls
at Caerwent.

Some stone steps on the far side of the farm track give
access to the top of the defences again, and here, where the
earth bank makes a detour, are the remains of the south gate, a

single arched passageway in a fine state of preservation (3).
The piers on either side are still complete, together with the
springers and even some voussoirs of the arch. Note how the
gate-piers appear to be freestanding (clearer on the left than
on the right), with the curtain wall abutting on either side. At
some time in the fourth century – a reflection of the growing

77   Caerwent, Roman town, site plan

troubles which had caused the new fort at Cardiff to be built –
the gate was entirely blocked up (except for openings left for
drainage at the bottom), and this blocking-wall remains in
position. Now return to ground-level to view the gate from the
outside. Here you can see clearly the straight joints between
the earlier gate-piers and the later curtain wall (especially on
the right), and also a second drainage-channel through the
blocking-wall, which was not visible on the other side.

From here also you can admire the superb stretch of walling
and tower which are at their best preserved at this point, some
5 m (17 ft) high, and still largely with their facing-stones
intact (Fig. 78). Two rows of putlog holes which held
scaffolding during construction are clearly visible, and note
also how the tower sits up against the wall without being
bonded into it. Further on you pass other towers in varying
stages of completeness. Putlog holes are also visible in these,
in some cases penetrating the full thickness of the tower wall.
Hollow towers are unusual in a British context – they are a
feature shared by the Multangular Tower and its fellows on
the river frontage (only) of the fortress at York, for example,
where their purpose was undoubtedly to impress. Were the
towers at Caerwent, absent for no apparent reason on the west

78   *Caerwent, Roman town wall and projecting towers, south side*

and east sides of the defences (illogically, if serious military tactics determined their construction), also no more than hollow mockeries, designed for show alone? On the other hand, the last tower before the SW angle (4) once had, on its eastern side, a postern door, presumably for 'defenders' to slip out in emergency; it was later blocked, and this blocking can be easily spotted both by its narrower width and by the straight joints on either side.

Rounding the SW angle and following the west wall, you reach the modern road again and the footings of part of the west gate (5). This, like all the other known gates at Caerwent, projects forward from the line of the later stone curtain wall: each was probably flush with the outer edge of the earth rampart bank when the gates were first built, but was later left protruding when the rampart was cut back to receive a stone facing.

Next, walk to your right along the road to Pound Lane (on your left), where are the foundations of a couple of VENTA's houses (6). The patch of gravel nearest the wall marks the site of the Roman street, which was much wider than its modern counterpart. Its side gutter and part of the drain into which it discharged, improvements dating to the fourth century, are visible here. The house nearest the road started life in about AD 150 as two long buildings with shops facing the street and living-quarters behind (an earlier occupation phase lies invisible beneath). In the early third century both were joined together into one property, and then in the mid fourth century the east strip-house was demolished and the survivor given two more wings, on the north and later on the east, to enclose a courtyard (now largely buried under the adjacent garden): not all the visible walls are of the same period. One has a sub-floor opening made up of overlapping tiles: this looks like a hypocaust-flue, implying the intention to provide underfloor heating in one or more rooms here; but it was never finished. Part of the house was used for iron-working (a blacksmith's forge) in both the third and fourth centuries.

The visible masonry of the second house belongs entirely to the fourth century (apparently the plot was open before then), but only part of one wing, and the fragment of another emerging from the grass, are visible. A room at the far left as Pound Lane starts to bend to the right was heated, and furnished by a fine geometric mosaic featuring a *cantharus* at the centre and dolphins on each side; it is now reburied. At the end of the fourth century both houses were taken over by squatters, who built stone hearths over the ruined walls and dug pits into the floors.

Further north along Pound Lane, across the grass on the left, lies another Roman house, excavated in 1981–4 and consolidated in 1987 (7). It represents an important addition to the plan of the Roman town, since this *insula* was not touched by the Edwardian excavators. A spacious courtyard house was erected here in the early fourth century over the demolished remains of two third-century predecessors; the plot was vacant before then. The main court (the grassed area) has a veranda on three sides (that on the east is still buried), and rooms opening off it. A large room at the SW corner has three curious pitched-footing walls in close proximity to one another. Either this room had a raised dais at one end (a dining-room?), or it was used for storing foodstuffs which needed a raised floor for ventilation; but if the latter, it is odd that only half the room was so equipped. The adjacent room in the middle of the west side had a hypocaust, although little survived: both flue and brick *pilae* have, however, been further damaged by disgraceful vandalism. The hypocaust of a room opening off the north wing used to be better preserved, but now also has been vandalized. The brick-lined flue for heating it, in its south wall, was clearly a late insertion, since it sliced through at an oblique angle part of the partition wall between two rooms in the north wing. From here it is assumed that access was gained to the corridor round a second internal court (also grassed), and so northwards to another group of rooms; but no doorways survive, and it is not impossible that there were two houses back to back here ('semi-detached', to use modern terminology). The substantial room at the far end, probably a dining-room, had another hypocaust (with stone *pilae*); part of a second garden court lies to the right. Its portico had a geometric mosaic and Tuscan capitals on stone columns, traces of which were found in the excavations (as were fragmentary mosaics in some other rooms), but are not now visible.

Return now down Pound Lane to the main road and turn left. A little further on is the war-memorial which marks the centre of the Roman town. It stands virtually at the SW corner of the site of the forum and basilica, and on the other side of the street, adjacent to the church, the public baths lie buried. The church porch (8) contains two Roman inscribed stones (if locked, the key may be obtained from the vicarage, a modern house some way east of the east gate: ask locally for directions). The larger (Fig. 79) is a statue base in honour of a certain Paulinus, presumably a benefactor of VENTA; no doubt it originally stood in the forum. Having commanded the Second Augustan Legion at Caerleon, Paulinus went on to become the governor of two Roman provinces in what is now France, Narbonensis (with its capital at Narbonne) and Lugdunensis (governed from Lyon). The end of the inscription, which can be dated to shortly before AD 220, reads EX DECRETO ORDINIS RES PVBL(ica) CIVIT(atis) SILVRVM, 'by decree of the local senate (*ordo*), the State (literally 'Republic') of the Community (*civitas*) of the Silures (had this set up)'. It is an important illustration of the machinery of self-government accorded to the old tribal groupings in Britain, whereby Siluran aristocrats and other leading notables continued to have power and influence in the governance of

79   Caerwent, inscription in honour of Paulinus, in the church

their own community in its transformed, Romanized form.
The other stone is a dedication to Mars Ocelus, a British
war god assimilated with his classical counterpart. A plan of
the Edwardian excavations which revealed so many details of
Caerwent's Roman buildings is displayed just before the
entrance to the churchyard.

The next Roman building exposed within the walls is a
religious precinct (9 on Fig. 77). It lies on the left of the
modern road as you return towards the Coach and Horses, and
is reached through a large iron gate opposite a bus shelter.
Excavation has shown that the whole of the visible complex
was built *c*. AD 330; previously the site had been occupied by
mundane timber and later stone buildings, with a secular
rather than a religious function. You first come to a long
narthex with an apse at one end, entered across the broad
threshold to your left, its western end nearest the forum. The
internal projecting piers probably mark the position of
decorative pilasters adorning the walls at these points, adding
a touch of architectural pretension to the interior; there was a
mosaic panel in front of the apse (the rest of the floor
consisted of plain tessellation); and no doubt a statue was set
up in the apse itself.

Half-way along this narthex you turned left to enter the
sacred precinct proper (*temenos*): the small rooms attached to
the north side of the narthex facing the temple (priest's rooms,
or shops selling votive offerings?) were secondary additions.
The temple itself had a projecting porch at the entrance; these
walls are flanked by rectangular platforms and other
secondary foundations, the purpose of which is obscure
(statue bases, or shelves to place votives?). Beyond is an
excellent example of a Romano-Celtic temple, a type
ubiquitous in southern Britain in Roman times but of which
very few are now visible, consisting of the central shrine (the
cella, here with a rear apse) and surrounding ambulatory. The
interior of the latter has four pairs of small projecting pilaster-
like piers similar to those in the narthex; by contrast the outer
wall of the temple has projecting buttresses which look
structural rather than decorative. The religious precinct, in
honour of an unknown deity, was still maintained in the late
fourth century, its presumably pagan ritual continuing despite
the advancing strength of Christianity.

From the rear of the temple precinct, follow the grass round to your left, and you are presented immediately with a sight which is unique in Britain – the only substantial portion of a Romano-British forum and basilica complex exposed on permanent view (10). First excavated in 1907–9, the site was re-excavated in 1986–95, when coins in the construction levels showed it to have been begun very late in Trajan's reign or at the beginning of his successor Hadrian's (*c.* AD 115/25); there was no sign of any timber forerunner below. You first come to a rectangular structure of massive sandstone blocks projecting from the east side of the basilica's south aisle. It served as the foundation for a pretentious three-way arch, marking a monumental entrance to the basilica on this side. Crossing over a massive threshold block, still with the remains of huge pivot-holes for the door, you pass into the south aisle of the basilica. This was a great covered hall, the central part loftier than the aisles, and originally some 20 m (65 ft) high. On the small size by comparison with other Romano-British *basilicae* (but in keeping with Caerwent's scaled-down version of the classical 'Roman' city), it originally measured some 80 m (260 ft) long, of which about two-thirds are now visible. London's basilica (to give, by way of example, the opposite end of the Romano-British spectrum) was more than twice as long. No emplacements to mark the position of the sandstone columns separating nave from aisles remain *in situ*, but enough fragments were found during the excavations to be certain that the columns were in the Corinthian order and were over 9 m (30 ft) high. The excavators thought that the basilica was open on the forum side rather than fully enclosed, but this would make it out of line with what is known of Romano-British basilicas elsewhere, and more in keeping with counterparts in the Mediterranean world: was an Italian architect despatched to VENTA, unaware of the vagaries of the British climate, or at any rate was an Italian architectural blueprint being slavishly followed? The basilica seems to have served its original function as a civic hall down to the middle of the fourth century, when blacksmiths' hearths were inserted into the nave. Around AD 390 it was systematically demolished, at a time when evidence elsewhere at Caerwent points to abandonment and decay, and normal civic life was finally breaking down.

Immediately on your right when entering the south aisle of the basilica is a narrow stoke-hole, with two massive blocks used as cheeks to enhance the through draught; the flue served to fire a hypocaust inserted in the room beyond in a late period (probably the fourth century). No *pilae* are visible there now, but you will appreciate that at the time of this conversion the floor-level would have been considerably higher than the second-century one, which is marked by the huge threshold blocks at the main entrance from the nave of the basilica. This threshold contains a broad groove to receive a sliding screen, enabling the room to be partitioned off: it probably served as the *tribunal* where law suits could be heard, but was no doubt used as well for other meetings. The square sockets also visible in this threshold indicate that in a secondary period the sliding screen was replaced by massive wooden doors, requiring bolt holes (the sockets) to fasten. Another substantial threshold leads from the *tribunal* to an office on its north side.

Now return to the basilica's south aisle, and cross another large threshold block into the NE corner of the forum. To your right is the remaining portion of the double step which originally ran the full length of the basilica's south side. In front of them are impressive remains of the eaves-drip gutter hewn out of enormous blocks of sandstone, seen here running along both the north and east sides of the forum. A drain running under the basilica discharged into this gutter at the corner. Beyond it are occasional large blocks which formed part of the forum paving at some stage, but most of the surviving paving, on its east side, is made up of smaller and thinner slabs. To the left, a single shop of the east range of the forum has been preserved; there were probably eight in all on this side. Judging from the square base in one corner (an oven for cooking or heating food), and the personal items like gaming counters and tweezers found in this room, it may have been a fast-food restaurant or snack bar.

Now retrace your steps across the basilica and pass finally into the six rooms, mostly offices, which made up the rear range of the basilica-forum complex: these are preserved for their entire width, from which the original extent of the

basilica and forum can be readily appreciated. The central
room of such ranges at *fora* elsewhere normally served as a
shrine for the protecting deities of the town and as a focus for
the cult of the emperor, but no specific evidence for such a use
was found at Caerwent. Yet another superbly preserved
threshold will be noticed giving access from the basilica to the
second room from the east; but the principal focus of interest
here is the largest chamber in the rear range, the second from
the west (11 on Fig. 77), its south wall still standing 2 m (6 ft
6 in) high (with four putlog holes in it). Excavation has shown
that this room was the *curia*, the meeting place where the
local senate (*ordo*) met: the decision to erect the statue to
Paulinus, recorded on the inscription in the church (p. 365),
will have been taken here. The four stone bases against the
east wall formed the foundation for a dais where the presiding
magistrates (*duoviri*) would have sat. Cuttings in the floor for
the timber supports of the tiered wooden seating on either side
for the rest of the senate were found in the excavations, as
well as some remnants of a T-shaped mosaic floor (not now
visible) in the centre and west end, areas not covered by
seating. The last room, at the NW corner, later subdivided into
two, has a second foundation on its inner edge, interpreted as
a bench: it may therefore have been a waiting-room for those
due to appear before the *ordo*.

Next retrace your steps back to the main road and turn left
in the direction of the Coach and Horses. The right-hand
(west) wall bordering the latter's car-park (12) was found in
1997 to be built on Roman foundations: a stretch 11 m (36 ft)
long and up to four courses high has been left visible beneath
a modern dry-stone capping. Note that three distinct phases of
walling are visible here: the left-hand 2-m portion came first,
distinguished from the rest by a clear break in the masonry; to
the right you will see that the lowest two courses project
wider than the upper courses, indicating that an earlier wall
had been partly demolished and a new wall built on the
remains of its predecessor. The nature of the building to
which this wall belonged is not known. Associated finds dated
from the early second to the mid-fourth century.

Now take the lane which leads from the east gate
northwards towards the bypass. The core of the east wall is
visible for a long stretch north of the gate. Follow the path

round to the left and make towards the Northgate Inn. The foundations of the wall in the second property from the corner are currently (2001) almost entirely obscured by rubbish, but further on, just beyond the next fence, comes a field in which the mound covering the rampart is striking, and the stone foundations of two further towers emerging from it are visible (13). A short piece of stonework of the defences themselves can also be seen here shortly before the inn.

The north gate is visible, with difficulty, by looking over the wooden fence adjacent to the inn on its far (west) side (14). It is very similar to the better preserved south gate, with late blocking-wall and some voussoirs of the right-hand arch still in position. Other parts of the north wall can be seen running along the back gardens of private houses. Apart, however, from a well preserved tower near the NW corner, excavated in 1972 (15), which can be seen from a private drive off the A48 just west of the road coming from the centre of the village, the rest of the walls from here, round the NW corner and down the west side as far as the west gate, are of difficult access. The ditch which formed part of the defences throughout the entire circuit is at its best preserved state here (16). Finds from Caerwent are mostly in the Newport Museum, which has a small but attractively presented Roman section; this is centred around a mosaic depicting rather crudely drawn Seasons and animals in panels, found in a house near the west gate (Monday–Thursday, 0930–1700, Friday, 0930–1630, Saturday, 0930–1600).

Apart from a few farms around Caerwent and a scattering of villas on the Glamorgan plain, civilian life continued in Wales in much the same way as it had before the Roman conquest. There is, therefore, a whole host of native sites built or adapted in the Roman period which could be mentioned. In contrast to southern Britain, many pre-Roman hill-forts continued to be occupied and even re-fortified. The most famous and impressive is **Tre'r Ceiri** (SH 373446) in the Lleyn peninsula. It is approached from the south by a public footpath signposted on the right of the B4417, 1 mile (1.6 km) SW of Llanaelhaearn (on the A499), or from the west, at the end of the minor road from Llithfaen. It is an exhausting climb, 275 m (900 ft) or so above the road. The path enters the enclosure by its SW entrance, which has traces of external towers on each side. The whole girdle of its dry-stone walls is still in an astonishing state of preservation, 4 m (13 ft) high on its outer face. The wall-walk is still visible in the best preserved stretches on the north and west. There are traces, too, of an additional wall built further down the slope on the north and west sides, where the approach is the least difficult. During consolidation work in 1993 at the NW entrance, pottery datable to *c.* 150/290 was found in the core of the defences; it shows that whatever the date of the original perimeter, the defensive wall was substantially rebuilt during the Roman period. Inside are about 150 huts of various shapes and sizes, some circular, some D-shaped, some rectangular, many with subdivisions. Undivided circular huts are probably the earliest and some may be pre-Roman. The few objects found indicate that the main occupation was from about AD 150 to AD 400. The walls clearly owe something to the Roman model of defences, but they were not as strong: they could have kept brigands out, but not the Roman army, should they have been turned to such a use. Two Anglesey hill-forts also have stone ramparts erected during the Roman period: Caer Y Twr on Holyhead Mountain (SH 218830) [AM; A], which has been mentioned above (p. 353), and Din Sylwy in the NE corner of the island (SH 5881). You will need an OS map if you wish to find the latter.

Not all the indigenous population, however, lived on hill-tops during the Roman period: open villages of circular or rectangular huts also occur, often in large groups. Twenty huts still visible of a settlement occupied from the second to fourth century on the SW slope of Holyhead Mountain (SH 212820) have been mentioned above (p. 354), but there are many other examples of these, of which two further Anglesey examples [both AM; A] will have to suffice here. A rectangular and a circular hut, inhabited in the third century, were found at **Caer Leb** (SH 473674) in 1866. The double banks which surrounded them are still very prominent. Follow the A4080 westwards from Menai Bridge, and then take the first road on the right (unsignposted) immediately on leaving Bryn-Siencyn on the west. Caer Leb is on the left-hand side of this road after $\frac{1}{2}$ mile (800 m) (AM sign). The second site is **Din Lligwy** (SH 496862), which is signposted from the Llanallgo roundabout (junction of the A5025 with the A5108 to

Moelfre), 7 miles (11 km) SE of Amlwych; it lies on the left of the minor road after 700 m (750 yds) (park-place). This charming site is the fortified residence of (probably) a native chieftain, and consists of two circular and four rectangular huts (probably not all directly contemporary), enclosed by stone walls in the shape of a pentagon. The circular hut at the far end and the rectangular one next to it preserve their entrance thresholds. The buildings still stand to a maximum height of 1.80 m (6 ft), and appear to have been built in the second half of the fourth century. It is a far cry from the civilized luxury of the villas of southern Britain.

Chapter 7

The Pennines and the Lakes

Cumbria, Durham, Greater Manchester, Lancashire,
Northumberland (south of Hadrian's Wall), and North and
West Yorkshire

(Appendix 1 only – South Yorkshire)

1 Brough
2 Maiden Castle
3 Rey Cross
4 Bowes Moor
5 Bowes

Nearly the whole of the large area covered by this chapter was
inhabited by the Brigantes before the Roman conquest. Their
queen, Cartimandua, was friendly towards the new invaders,
but she ruled uneasily and civil war broke out on a number of
occasions. This resulted in the first official Roman contact
with the north of England, for in AD 48, *c*. 57 and 69, Roman
arms came to the queen's aid. The last of these interventions
was only moderately successful, and Tacitus pithily comments
that 'the throne was left to Venutius, the war to us', Venutius
being the divorced husband of Cartimandua. In AD 71,
therefore, the new governor of Britain, Petillius Cerialis, took
the Ninth Legion from Lincoln and advanced northwards, bent

on final conquest. The remarkable Iron Age fortress at
Stanwick near Scotch Corner, which in its final phase
enclosed an astonishing area of 741 acres (300 ha), was
interpreted by Sir Mortimer Wheeler, who excavated it, as the
place where Venutius made his last stand against a Roman
army in AD 71 or 72. A small section of stone wall and ditch
lies close to the hamlet of Forcett, 2 miles (3 km) SW of
Piercebridge, and about 5 miles (8 km) NW of Scotch Corner
(NZ 178124). The tumbled rampart, now reconstructed
[AM; A], was thought by Wheeler to have been 'slighted' by
a Roman attacking army, rather than falling down naturally
through decay; but more recent excavation near the heart of
the Stanwick enclosures has demonstrated the high level of
Roman imports in the final phase of occupation, making it
perhaps more likely that Stanwick was the pro-Roman
Cartimandua's stronghold rather than Venutius'.

The building of the legionary fortress for the Ninth at
York** (SE 603521) can be attributed to Petillius Cerialis in
or about AD 71 and, by the end of the first century, York had
established itself as the military capital of Britain and the hub
of the northern fort system. The early fortress had a rampart
of clay and turf with timber breastwork and towers and timber
internal buildings, but these began to be replaced in stone
towards the end of the first century, and one of the gateways
was rebuilt in stone in AD 107–8. We know this from an
inscription (in the Yorkshire Museum) which also documents
the last recorded appearance in Britain of *legio IX Hispana*.
Soon afterwards it was probably transferred out of Britain,
first to Germany and then to the East where it was disbanded
after an unknown disaster some time before AD 165. Its place
at York was taken by the Sixth Legion Victrix, which came to
Britain in 122.

The next rebuilding of the defences occurred towards the
end of the second or the beginning of the third century. The
weak foundations of the wall of 107–8 had caused partial
collapse, and total rebuilding on a more imposing scale was
necessary. This work is likely to have been carried out either
by the emperor Severus, who died in York in 211, or by his
son Caracalla (emperor 211–17). Further reconstruction was
done by Constantius I in the early years of the fourth century,
when the whole of the river front was given a grandiose series

of polygonal towers. These were clearly designed to impress, and the elaboration may be connected with the creation about now of a new post as commander-in-chief of land forces in Britain, the *Dux Britanniarum*, whose headquarters York was. Constantius died in York in 306, and his son, the famous Constantine the Great, was proclaimed emperor here. The Constantian rebuilding remained the basis of York's defences until the Danes built an earth bank and stockade in the late ninth century. The Roman name EBVRACVM (whence Anglo-Saxon 'Eoforwic' and modern 'York') means either 'the place of Eburos' or 'the place of the yews'.

Of the buildings inside this great legionary fortress, little is known except for parts of an internal bath-house and the headquarters building (both visible) and fragments of barracks. York, however, was more than a military centre in Roman times. The civilian settlement, which flourished and grew into a fully-fledged town on the south bank of the Ouse, was given walls of its own, and acquired the honorary status of *colonia* in the third century. From 208 to 211 it was the seat of the Imperial Court while Severus and his sons were engaged on their Scottish campaigns, and in 213, when Britain was divided into two provinces, it became the capital of *Britannia Inferior*. Little is known about the town's buildings, but some outstanding objects which have been found there are displayed in the Yorkshire Museum.

This Museum, and the most spectacular portion of the fortress's defences, are to be found in the public gardens on the north side of the river. To the right of the main entrance to the gardens (1 on Fig. 80), under a stone archway, are several Roman coffins; the slabs to the right piled up on one another are the constituent parts of a public fountain in the *colonia*, found in 1906 and then dismantled, but sadly never since re-assembled. Nearby, the foundations of a polygonal tower emerge from the grass: it was one of the series added to the fortress on this side *c*. AD 300. From here onwards runs a superb stretch of the fourth-century fortress-wall, standing virtually to wall-walk height with all its facing-stones and a row of bonding-bricks intact. The stretch ends at the west corner of the 50-acre (21-ha) fortress, known as the Multangular Tower and one of the best preserved Roman structures in Britain. Parts of the exterior have been patched with later material, but the join between the Roman work and the top 3.35 m (11 ft) of medieval masonry is obvious.

Before going inside the walls, it is convenient now to visit the archaeological Museum (1000–1700 daily, all year), which lies in the gardens nearby (2); the well-arranged Roman section is not huge but contains some remarkable finds. In the entrance-hall are two reconstructed panels of second-century wall-plaster from Catterick, the one on the right having been found superimposed on the earlier fresco on the left. The back

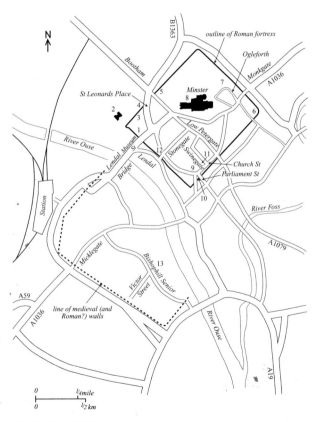

80   York, location plan

stairs to your left has a pair of well preserved fourth-century mosaics, one of them from York with Medusa at the centre and the four Seasons at the corners, and the other, also with a Medusa head, coming from an apsed room of a villa at Dalton Parlours, near Collingham, NE of Leeds.

In the first Roman room, the initial section (to the left) illustrates York's military origins. Note especially the tombstone of L. Duccius Rufinus, a standard-bearer in the Ninth Legion who came from Vienne in France (line 3); a tile stamp of the same legion; and some unusually elaborate silvered horse-pendants (from Fremington Hagg). Next, displayed high up, is the fine marble head of Constantine the Great, twice life-size, wearing an oak wreath; such impressive imperial statuary, a commonplace in many parts of the Roman Empire, constitutes a rare survival from Roman Britain. Also above your head here is the King's Square inscription, which dates the first stone fortress defences to AD 107–8 (p. 374). The fine quality of the lettering is typical of official inscriptions of Trajanic date (cf. Fig. 67). A case nearby illustrating finds from the pre-Roman stronghold of Stanwick includes Italian glassware and red samian ware from France as examples of the luxury imports attested there (p. 374).

The next section has a case in the centre with a good-quality marble statuette of an athlete, probably imported ready-made from the Continent, as was the fragment of mould-blown glass with a chariot scene in the same case. Even more unusual (for Britain) is the fine scrap of engraved glass with a painted inscription, in the case to your left, displayed alongside two inscribed bronze tags with punched letters in Greek. Both the latter were dedicated by Demetrios, one of them to the 'deities of the governor's headquarters', the other to 'Ocean and Tethys' (a goddess of the sea). The nature of these dedications and the fact that they are in Greek suggest very strongly that the Demetrios in question is a *grammaticus* (schoolmaster), known to have taken part in a visit to the western isles of Scotland on an official fact-finding mission *c.* 82 or 83, and clearly therefore a member of Cnaeus Julius Agricola's staff.

Among fascinating finds in the next two cases is the unique survival of a young girl's hair, found in a lead coffin under the railway station in 1875, together with two jet pins; there are also portrait roundels in the same material here, and in the

jewellery case further on, the star item is a beautiful jet bracelet of
graduated beads. The industry making jewellery out of black
Whitby jet flourished between the second and fourth centuries.
Another astonishing survival displayed here is the stocking from
Micklegate in 'sprang' technique (by which woollen threads are
stretched on a frame and interlaced). Above, on the wall, is the
most interesting of York's surviving tombstones (Fig. 81): it
portrays the entire family of Augustinus (mother, father and two
children), all wearing cloaks. The inscription records that both
children died before the age of two, but the carving clearly
represents them a little too old; perhaps this was a ready-prepared
gravestone bought 'off the peg', with only the faces left blank,
waiting to be carved. Of the rest of the material in this room, note
especially the stone from Malton (the suburb of Norton), with the
only epigraphic reference to a goldsmith's shop or workshop
(*aureficina*) in Britain.

*81   York, tombstone of
Augustinus and his family
(Yorkshire Museum)*

The second room ('death' and then 'religion') starts on the left with the inscribed sarcophagus (itself not a common item in the archaeology of Roman Britain) of Julia Fortunata, who came from Sardinia. It was commissioned by her husband, Verecundius Diogenes, who by chance is also known from his own sarcophagus (now lost) to have been a Gaul from Bourges, and to have been a priest in the imperial cult (*sevir Augustalis*) at York. The six cases along the left wall present spectacular grave groups from York: one has a chicken's egg; another is Christian, with a blue glass jug made in Cologne and a bone plaque inscribed 'Hail, sister, may you live in God'. The last case here contains five necklaces from a single grave, one of blue glass beads, one of coral and three of jet (of which one has unusual barrel-shaped beads), as well as a jet pendant featuring a Medusa head. A gypsum burial further on to the right, a practice sometimes adopted by Christians in their burials (the plaster 'preserving' the body for the resurrection; but not all gypsum burials are Christian), is one of very few such examples of a widespread practice in late Roman Britain to receive museum display. Of the religious dedications, the finest is that recording a temple of the Egyptian god Serapis (the temple itself has not been found), and beyond is a facsimile of the Ravenscar signal station stone (p. 437; the original is in Whitby), one of the last official dedications carved in the dying days of Roman authority in northern Britain.

Now you should return to the Multangular Tower, pass through the narrow gate beside and beyond it, and so enter the Roman legionary fortress. The interior of the tower can be seen on your right to be in a fine state of preservation, 6 m (19 ft) high. Scaffolding holes, an internal partition wall, Roman coffins and the medieval apertures above are all very clear. On the far side of the tower is an oven-base, excavated in 1925 under the Public Library and reset here. Its floor contained one tile stamped LEG(io) IX HISP(ana), and so the oven predates the withdrawal of this legion from York *c.* 120. To your left (3) is another fine stretch of fourth-century curtain wall, excavated in 1969–70. First, walk along by the rough inside face which would have been covered by an earth bank (the wall on the right is of thirteenth-century date). Half-way along are the fragmentary remains of an interval tower,

which is believed from the different quality of the masonry to
belong to an earlier phase of the defences, of either the second
or the third century. Then comes the peculiar 'Anglian' tower,
a barrel-vaulted structure built of roughly dressed stones to fill
a breach in the Roman wall. It is unique in Britain and
probably in Europe, and it cannot be dated more closely than
AD 400–870. Some believe that it is late Roman, others that it
was part of the reorganization of the defences in the seventh
century. Beyond, the fine sequence of rampart-banks behind
the wall has been carefully displayed – four successive levels
from Roman to medieval. Finally, you can go through the
Anglian Tower to examine the outer face of the fourth-century
wall. Not all of it has been exposed: much more of it lies
buried beneath the path.

Leave the gardens at the main entrance, turn left, and left
again at the traffic-lights. Another fragment of fourth-century
wall lies on the left by St Leonard's car-park (4). Once again
only the top portion is visible, but excavation in 1835 and
1928 showed that more than 3 m (11 ft) lies buried below
ground-level. It is worth climbing the mound beyond the
car-park for a splendid view of the long stretch of Roman wall
already noted, from the Anglian to the Multangular Towers.

Now cross the road and climb the steps to the top of
Bootham Bar, which occupies the site of the Roman NW gate
(5: a fragment of it, preserved in a room below the public
lavatory, is visible on application to the Museum). Turn left
and walk along the walls as far as Monk Bar, following the
line of the Roman defences all the way, and passing over the
site of the NE gate. Descend to street-level at Monk Bar and
ascend the walls again to see a long stretch of Roman
defences, including an interval tower and the east angle tower
(6), below you and just inside the line of the medieval city
walls. This Roman work is a century earlier than the remains
so far described, as they belong to the early third-century
rebuilding which was untouched in the Constantian
reorganization. This corner tower is on a much smaller scale
and does not project from the wall. The slightly raised mound
in the bottom is part of the bank of the first-century legionary
fortress and is thus the oldest portion of EBVRACVM still
visible, but it is usually obscured by luxuriant grass growth.
The foundations of the first stone tower, on a slightly different

alignment, were also found during excavations in 1926. In front, the Roman curtain wall still stands to a spectacular height of 4.90 m (16 ft), and even the moulded slab on which the parapet rested survives. The masonry is similar to the fourth-century work, but there are no brick bonding-courses, and the inner side is properly faced even where it would have been covered by rampart-mound. One of the stones on the outer face of the wall at the corner tower still bears an inscription, COH X, recording that the tenth cohort (of the Sixth Legion) built this section of wall; but this cannot be seen from the medieval walls. If you are lucky enough to gain access to the greensward containing these Roman defences (e.g. during grass cutting), the inscription is at approximately head-height.

Now retrace your steps to Monk Bar. Turn left and then right down Ogleforth. Past a corner the Treasurer's House will be seen on the right (April–October, daily except Friday, 1100–1700). Here an isolated Roman column-base is preserved, together with part of a Roman street surface (7). You have now arrived at the Minster and the site of the *Principia*, the Headquarters Building (8). Until 1966, when it was announced that the Minster was in serious danger of collapse, virtually nothing was known about the Roman building, but excavations carried out during the strengthening of the Minster's fabric have revealed a great deal. Most of the excavated remains are of fourth-century date, including several column-bases belonging to the great cross-hall. One of these, 6.75 m (22 ft) long and 1 m (3 ft) in diameter, was found virtually complete, and it has been re-erected opposite the south door of the Minster. What is particularly interesting is the date at which it fell: pottery sealed beneath the destruction rubble of the Roman cross-hall indicates that these columns were still standing in the ninth century, 400 years after the Sixth Legion had left York.

Enter the Minster by the south door; just inside is the access to the 'Foundations' Museum in the Undercroft and Crypt, opened in 1972, where many of the discoveries of the late 1960s have been imaginatively preserved (1000–1730 daily, but 0930–1830 July–August). After the first section with a display of Saxon stones, and the foundation of the Norman cathedral of 1086 on the right, you come to some fragmentary columns of the *principia*'s cross-hall. Only the west end of this great basilican hall is under the Minster: originally there would have been two rows of 16 columns, all of the same height as the example re-erected outside, which was found near here (see above). A corridor leads you to the neat Roman walling of a room which formed part of the single row of administrative offices at the rear of any *principia*. From the Treasury to your right, you look down on the *principia*'s back wall: glancing back to the front walling of the office just noted, you can appreciate the considerable depth back-to-front of these rear rooms (about 12 m [39 ft]).

Descend the steps from the Treasury and turn right through another tunnel to a section with a model of the *principia* and a case with finds. Then after passing a thirteenth-century well, you come down to Roman level again – the rough concrete floor here indicates the position of a Roman street running alongside the HQ. The original Roman culvert still draining it is visible here, together with the Roman wall of a structure (added to one side of the *principia*) still eight courses high. But your eye will have been caught by the wall behind, on which one of the finest and largest examples of Roman painted plaster from Britain is displayed: it came from an administrative room added at the back of the *principia* in the fourth century. High up on the left is a fine theatrical mask; in centre-left birds are depicted; at top right even a window-light survives, and further to the right is a male human figure. The rest is filled up with architectural details and abstract panels in brilliant colour. To its left, in the showcase, note the tile with a chi-rho scratched in it – tantalizing evidence, it seems, for Christianity in Roman York. Immediately after this section comes a further piece of the foundation of the cross-hall, together with what is believed to be part of the *tribunal* at one end. Maybe it was here that Constantine was proclaimed emperor by his troops after the death of his father in York on 25 July, 306.

The only other Roman structure visible within the fortress is the bath-house in St Sampson's Square (9). Leave the Minster by the south door and go down Minster Gates opposite (this and Stonegate follow the line of a Roman street). Turn left at Low Petergate and right at the traffic-lights along Church Street. The remains are preserved beneath the pub called Roman Bath. Here, after payment of a small fee to the bartender, you will be admitted to an underground display area: a vestibule with Roman tiles (two stamped) leads to a portion of the *tepidarium* (on your right) and the impressively preserved large apse forming part of the *caldarium* beyond. Part of the tiled cold immersion-bath belonging to the *frigidarium* has also been preserved (behind the *caldarium* apse, far corner, to the right of the catwalk). It is regrettable that the current display (2001) strews individual Roman tiles around in an 'artistic' display without regard for their original positions (confusing to the uninitiated); ghastly, too, is the modern mock-up of a hypocaust behind the apse, using tesserae cut from glazed ceramic tiles (and in part of a lurid turquoise colour) which no Roman would ever have seen. Excavations in 1930–1 established a fourth-century date for the bath-house, but whether this site was occupied by the main legionary baths from the late first century is unknown.

An impressive section of the east side of the Roman legionary fortress-wall near the SE angle (10) was found to be still standing more than 2.5 m (8 ft 2 in) high in 1987 during repairs to a shop in 16, Parliament Street (this is the fourth shop from the corner with Feasegate on the south side of Parliament Street). At the time of writing (2001), the basement containing this fine stretch of the defences is not accessible for Health and Safety reasons.

Also normally inaccessible is part of the sewer-system which served the fortress, discovered in 1972 on a building-site at the corner of Swinegate and Church Street (11). This structure, some 1.20–1.50 m (4–5 ft) high and excellently preserved, was traced for over 45 m (150 ft), together with six side channels. The sewer was in use from early in the second century to late in the fourth and produced various finds, including a rare piece of silk, woven in the west from imported Chinese raw material, as well as fascinating environmental evidence for latrine sediments, grain pests (indicating a granary nearby), and insects tolerant of the foul sewer conditions. Access to this impressive monument of Roman hygiene is through a manhole in the street, but visits will only be permitted if prior arrangements have been made, in writing, with the Museum.

Apart from an uninspiring fragment of wall-core visible in the (private) cellar of 17, Lendal (12), no other remains of the

fortress are now visible. Of the town across the river, nothing
has been preserved *in situ*, except for an uninteresting stone
wall of which the lowest three courses are probably Roman,
incorporated in a modern wall in Carrs Lane (13: off
Bishophill Senior opposite Victor Street). The line of the
Roman town walls probably coincided with the medieval
defences on this side of the river. Of scraps not *in situ*, a
column-base kept at the back of Holy Trinity Church,
Micklegate, a tombstone in St Martin's Church (also
Micklegate), and the tombstone of Baebius Crescens, a soldier
of the Sixth, in the Mount School (off The Mount), may be
mentioned. A unique burial-vault with coffin and skeleton still
in position exists under 104, The Mount, but it can only be
visited by prior written appointment with the accountants who
own the building.

The legionary soldiers based at York may have been
responsible for building at least some of the remarkable but
enigmatic earthworks at **Cawthorn*** (SE 785901), the
significance of which is still disputed. They were investigated
in the 1920s by Sir Ian Richmond, but later they became
heavily congested with bracken and forest cover, which made
the camps difficult to see, before this was cleared away in the
late 1980s. A programme of fresh small-scale excavations
which took place in 1999 and 2000 is leading to a partial
re-assessment of Richmond's work. Turn off the A170 for the
village of Wrelton, 2 miles (3 km) west of Pickering, and then
turn left, signposted Cropton, and then right at the end of the
village (signposted 'Cawthorne [*sic*] 2'). Three miles (4.8 km)
later, turn right at an unsignposted T-junction. Cawthorn
camps (car-park) is signposted on the left, $\frac{1}{4}$ mile (400 m) after
the turning to Keldy. Follow the first Roman helmet sign out
of the car-park, but when the path forks take the left one
(ignoring the helmet sign which sends you to the right). After
five minutes you reach the fine causeway striding up to the
south gate of D, the best preserved of the four earthworks at
Cawthorn (1 on Fig. 82). The south rampart and double
ditches separated by a flat mound are especially fine, and just
inside the south gate, to the right (east), a mound projecting
from the back of the rampart may incorporate a staircase to
the patrol-walk (see the discussion on Hod Hill, p. 99). This is
clearly not a temporary camp but a fully-fledged earth and

timber fort. Excavation in 2000 showed that plough damage
had largely removed interior buildings in the two areas
investigated, and that the defences were of two phases, the
outer ditch being a later addition.

Now return across the causeway and turn left, following the
outer lip of the ditches to the SE corner. Here you see the west
rampart of camp C, of unusual polygonal shape. The rampart
is slighter than that of the fort but still well preserved; note
how it is cut by the outer ditch of D, demonstrating that the
latter is later than camp C (2 on Fig. 82). Now follow the path
across the centre of C to the middle of the three openings on
its east side, protected by external *claviculae*. It is worth
turning right here for a short distance along the rampart to see
the superbly preserved *clavicula* at the southern-most of the
three entrances (3). Now retrace your steps and walk up to the
NE corner of Camp C, past a more damaged *clavicula*, before
following the path through the wood away from the camp.
This soon brings you out to a clearing where the superb
command of ground to the north which the camps enjoyed
over the North York Moors can be appreciated (4).

Very soon afterwards, you come to the NW corner of the
impressive rampart of earthwork A, here still some 3 m (10 ft)
above the bottom of the ditch outside. The whole of the north,
west and south ramparts of A are equally massive, but the east
rampart is only half the scale of the rest. The defences of B

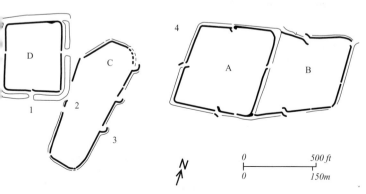

82   Cawthorn, plan of the Roman earthworks

are also on this lesser scale. The three visible entrances of A appear now to consist of internal *claviculae* only; by contrast B has double *claviculae*, external and internal together. Richmond believed that both were camps (*claviculae* at both suggest as much), and that camp C was erected to protect tents and baggage while its troops were engaged on constructing A. At least two of the entrances of A (the west and south), however, originally possessed double *claviculae*. Camp B was later tacked on as an annexe to A. Later still the ramparts of A were substantially modified and enlarged, as excavation demonstrated in 1999–2000. Was A in this secondary phase intended, therefore, to be a camp or a fort? The defences are now of fort-like dimensions on three sides, yet the entrances still have *claviculae* – unusual but not quite unparalleled in a Roman fort. One possible explanation is that these may have been in the process of adaptation (the external *claviculae* were cut by new ditches, leaving their outer parts isolated), but were never quite finished.

Two phases of interior buildings have been identified within A by the recent archaeological work: the earlier were composed of turf walls lined with wattle-and-daub (and four ovens just inside the rampart), the later with shallow stone footings and a stone floor at one point. Neither are appropriate inside a temporary camp, which normally shows, at best, evidence of pits and gullies and little else, as one would expect from a short-lived bivouac. So earthwork A at Cawthorn does look more like a fort than a camp, although whether it ever developed a full complement of buildings inside is unknown, and seems unlikely. Was the rebuilding of A at the more formidable level of defence aborted before completion (as the feebler east rampart suggests), and a new site chosen for the fort, that of D? Archaeomagnetic dating from the remains of the Phase-1 ovens in A confirm that they belonged to the first century AD, and overall the finds from all four enclosures, A–D, do not fall outside *c*. AD 80–120, as Richmond had already concluded long ago. Impressive though these short-lived Roman earthworks are, Cawthorn is a site which still defies neat classification and explanation.

The earthworks at Cawthorn lie on a Roman road known as Wade's Causeway, which ran from Malton to Whitby. Wade is a giant in local legends and he is alleged to have built the

causeway for his wife who kept cattle on the moor. A $1\frac{1}{4}$ mile
(2 km) stretch of this road has been excavated and preserved
on **Wheeldale Moor** (SE 805975) [AM; A]. From Goathland,
a village west of the A169 (Pickering–Whitby), take the road
leading southwards and then follow the AM signs: you have
the choice of walking to one end of the exposed sector (by
taking the turning left to Hunt House), or continuing on by a
roundabout route to the other end (turn left just before
reaching Egton Bridge: after 4 miles (6.4 km), before the
modern road descends into the first valley after the ford,
watch out for a wooden sign and display board on your left).
This used to be the most impressive piece of original Roman
highway in Britain (Fig. 83), but it is now sadly overgrown
and neglected: English Heritage and the North York Moors
National Park who jointly maintain it ought to be able to do
better. The large slabs which form the most impressive part of
the remains were only intended to act as the foundation layer
for a final surface of gravel or small stones, long since washed
away. In places kerb-stones still remain, and there are several
drainage culverts with large cover-stones: the first can be seen
running obliquely across the Roman road about 100 m from
the beginning of the preserved stretch.

The road on Wheeldale Moor headed southwards for the
fort at **Malton** (SE 791717): this was the Roman DERVENTIO,

83   Wheeldale Moor, Roman road

'the river in the oakwood', from the Derwent river on which it stands. This was a very large fort (8.5 acres [3.5 ha]), but little of it remains. From the centre of Malton take the Pickering road ('Old Maltongate'); turn right at the top of the hill for Orchard Fields where the fort lies. The NE rampart-mound is well preserved, the SE one less so. The fort was occupied from *c*. AD 78/9 (Agricolan) to the end of the fourth century, with rebuilding in stone *c*. 108 and *c*. 280. Excavation has also revealed a very large semi-permanent fortress of at least 22 acres (9 ha) beneath and beyond the fort, and this was probably the base for half the Ninth Legion in the campaigns of Petillius Cerialis *c*. 71–2 or of his predecessor Vettius Bolanus *c*. 69. Outside the fort was a substantial civilian settlement (*vicus*), with stone buildings, partly excavated in 1949–52 and 1968–70. One had a mosaic pavement and figured wall paintings, and the possibility of re-excavating this and exposing it to public view has been aired from time to time. The *vicus* was defended by a rampart from the late second century, visible as a low swelling to the right of the path at the east corner of the fort. Finds from Malton and the surrounding area are displayed in the Roman Malton Museum (Monday–Saturday, 1300–1600, from Easter to the end of October), which lies in the town-centre opposite the church, to the left of the Milton Rooms.

Several Roman roads radiated from York. The east-coast road via Malton and Wheeldale Moor has already been mentioned. South-westwards a road ran across the Pennines to Manchester (p. 389); en route the earthworks of a fort at **Castleshaw** (SD 999097) are still visible. This is probably to be identified with the Roman RIGODVNVM, 'royal fort', presumably a reference to an Iron Age settlement nearby, the seat of a Brigantian princeling at the time of Roman conquest. Turn off the A62 (Oldham–Huddersfield road), $2\frac{1}{2}$ miles (4 km) NE of Delph in Greater Manchester, along the road marked 'Castleshaw Centre' (Waterworks Road; gate-pier inscribed OCWW). Follow this road, leaving the first reservoir to your left, and then take the right fork (leaving the second reservoir also to your left) up the hill for 200 m; then park in the verge on your left just before the first house. The fort site (there is no signpost, only a low-level AM notice by

the field-gate) lies at the top of the hill in the field which lies
to the right of the road.

   The first fort, of which the earth defences are still partly
visible (its east gate is the first you reach), was probably an
Agricolan foundation, built *c*. 78/9 and abandoned about
15 years later. Trial trenching in 1957–64 revealed traces of
Agricolan timber buildings within (and there was a hint of
pre-Agricolan structures as well). The fort was a small one
(about 3 acres [1.3 ha]), and was presumably designed for
500 infantry if a full unit was posted here.

   About AD 105, a fortlet of 0.8 acres (0.35 ha), measuring
45 m by 50 m (147 ft by 180 ft), was built inside the fort. It
had a turf rampart on a stone base and two timber gateways;
the line of its southern defences coincided with that of the
fort. Thoroughly explored in 1907–8, after which untidy
spoilheaps were left all over the place, this fortlet was the
focus of extensive re-investigation in the 1980s. The
spoilheaps have now been removed, and the defensive circuit
recreated as a low bank, a quarter of its estimated original
height: the original ramparts were slighted on withdrawal
c. 120. The purpose of the fortlet, which like its predecessor
had a life of barely 15 years, remains enigmatic. Roof-tiles
from the Grimescar (Huddersfield) tilery of the 4th cohort of
Breuci have prompted the suggestion that part of this unit
manned the fortlet. That is certainly possible, but the products
of this tilery enjoyed a fairly widespread distribution in west
Yorkshire. A stone-built room with a hypocaust may have
been part of the commandant's house. The other known
internal buildings are a single barrack, a workshop (with
smithy), a courtyard building for administration (or for
accommodating visiting officials?), and a large granary
(discovered in the earlier excavations). The size of the granary
might indicate, perhaps, that the fortlet served as a collection-
point for the corn-tax levied from local farmers. None of these
buildings is now visible, but the lines of their walls have been
seeded with coarse grass to make their outline ground-plans
intelligible to the visitor.

   About 13 miles (21 km) SW of Castleshaw lay another fort,
Manchester (SJ 833976). This was the Roman MAMVCIVM, a
name possibly referring to the 'breast-like hill' on which the
fort was situated. Extensively excavated a century ago, and at

various times in the twentieth century, the site was further
explored in the 1970s and early 1980s, followed (in 1984–6)
by an enlightened programme of reconstruction. Heading
south from Deansgate in the centre of Manchester, turn right
along Liverpool Road just before the railway bridge
(signposted A57, Warrington). Directions for Castlefield
(brown signs) and Deansgate are widely signposted from the
outskirts of Manchester.

The fort's north gate lies in gardens opposite the
Manchester Museum of Space and Industry. Three simple
buildings in the civilian settlement (*vicus*) north of the fort are
marked out in modern materials. Early makeshift shacks with
signs of iron-working around them were demolished *c.* 120;
buildings on stone footings took their place *c.* 200 and were
occupied until *c.* 350. Pottery, bone, bronze and iron objects
were all made here. Beyond rises part of the north defences of
the fort together with the reconstructed gateway. The first fort
on the site (4.8 acres [1.9 ha]) was a turf and timber one built
under Agricola *c.* 79 and renovated *c.* 90; it was demolished
in the first quarter of the second century, probably *c.* 124
when troop movements, consequent on the decision to place
forts on Hadrian's Wall, involved the abandonment of many
garrison-posts further south. A slightly larger fort covering
5 acres (2 ha) took its place *c.* 160 as part of the consolidation
necessary after the Brigantian uprising of *c.* 155. This was
apparently also of turf and timber and was not refurbished in
stone until the early third century, later than usual in this part
of the province (although Ilkley among visible forts shares a
similar construction history: p. 391). What you see today,
therefore, is the twin-portalled gateway as it may have
appeared in the third century, with flat platform above but no
flanking guardrooms. The simulated gateway is noticeably
squatter than its reconstructed counterpart at South Shields
(p. 451), and may be nearer the original height, although such
conjectures are always problematical in view of the lack of
evidence. The inscriptions on each façade are bogus but
plausible. Only the robbed-out foundations of both gate and
wall survived. The only Roman masonry visible *in situ* are
three slabs of the base-plinth on the outer face to the left of
the gateway as you approach it (clearly distinguishable from

the modern blocks either side). A few facing-stones are ancient but the vast majority are modern.

Close by, off Duke Place, a section of the west defences just north of the site of the west gate has also been reconstructed, and a granary, based on the structure excavated here (which was not well preserved), has been marked out in modern materials inside. A statigraphic section across the site illustrating the chronology of the excavated deposits is displayed just inside the fort wall. Another fragment, of the east defences of MAMVCIVM, used once to be visible by retracing your steps past the north gate, and then turning first right: it lay at the end of this street (Collier Street) under a blocked railway arch. At the time of writing (2001), however, the whole area is derelict and inaccessible, pending future urban redevelopment.

From Tadcaster, 10 miles (16 km) SW of York, another road headed towards Ribchester on the western trunk-road, passing through forts at Ilkley and Elslack (App. 1). **Ilkley** (SE 116478), probably the Roman VERBEIA (the goddess of the river Wharfe on which Ilkley stands), has a small Museum, and a section of stone fort wall is also visible. The Manor House Museum (Tuesday 1300–1700; Wednesday–Saturday 1100–1700; Sunday 1300–1600; closed Monday), is situated on the north side of the A65 (Skipton Road), next to the church by the traffic-lights in the centre of the town. Among the exhibits are two interesting tombstones, one showing a seated woman with long tresses who came from the Shropshire area (she calls herself a Cornovian), the other (uninscribed) portraying a man, his wife and their little boy. A fragmentary Roman inscription, probably Severan, found in 1982 re-used in the foundations of the west wall of the church, is now displayed in the tower with Saxon stones from the churchyard.

Behind the Museum, and always accessible, is part of the fort's west wall, 1.25 m (4 ft) high, including the NW corner. Excavation in 1998 showed that it was defended by two ditches on this side. A modern plaque marks the site of the north gate. The prominence of the fort platform and its command of ground to the north will be noted, but the outlook to the south is somewhat blocked by Ilkley Moor. The fort was founded by Agricola *c*. 80, evacuated peacefully *c*. 120, reoccupied *c.* 165, and destroyed at the end of the second century. The first stone wall and stone internal buildings were then erected in the early third century. At first the stone wall had a clay bank behind it, but in alterations *c.* 290/300 it was made freestanding, as it is today. The garrison in the later second century was part-mounted, probably the Second Cohort of Lingones, originally recruited from eastern France.

A branch-road joined Ilkley with Manchester, and part of what has been assumed to be it, on Blackstone Edge near Rochdale (SD 9616), is remarkable for being paved with large stone setts. One mile (1.6 km) east of Littleborough the A58 makes a large U-bend. At the bottom of the U, as the road swings due north, a public footpath is signposted to the right (east) of the road, and a lighter strip of grass can be seen going straight up the moorland to the top of the hill. This is $\frac{1}{4}$ mile (400 m) beyond a house marked 'Blackstone Edge Old Road'. It is near the top of the hill that the stone paving becomes visible, 4.90 m (16 ft) wide, with a central groove. This is much worn, presumably by the brake-pole of carts as they tried to descend the hill without going out of control. At the top, where the road becomes level, the central slab flattens out. Earlier editions of this book treated this road without question as of Roman date, but the uniqueness of the monument in a Romano-British context, and the difficulty of finding Roman parallels anywhere for the central grooved channel, emphasize the need to question its long-accepted Roman date; it may well rather be part of an eighteenth-century coach road.

As mentioned above, the east-west road on which Ilkley stood was heading for **Ribchester*** (SD 649349), the BREMETENNACVM ('roaring river') of the Romans, and now a village on the B6245 6 miles (9.7 km) north of Blackburn. The main item of interest here is the little museum near the church, enlarged and refurbished in 2001 (Monday–Friday, all year round, 0900–1700; Saturday and Sunday, 1100–1700 all year round). This has a small collection of inscriptions, reliefs and other material. Watch out particularly for the pedestal in the far left corner of the first Roman room, which bears reliefs of Apollo and two female figures (of uncertain identification, but claimed by one scholar, Sir Ian Richmond, to be personifications of the area and the province); one face bears an inscription to the god, recording both the name of the fort (BREMETENN) and its garrison, a regiment of Sarmatian horsemen from the Danube. The inscription also mentions the emperor Gordian, thus dating the stone to AD 238–44. On the wall above the former entrance is a fine dedicatory slab datable to AD 222/35 in honour of an unknown god (the beginning is lost); a *templum* (temple) is mentioned in the penultimate line.

On the right-hand wall is a replica of the famous Ribchester helmet (the original is in the British Museum), one of the most elaborate and best preserved of all the 130-odd such helmets which have been found in the Roman Empire. They were worn not in battle but in special displays of horsemanship and cavalry manoeuvres, a sort of Roman gymkhana. It was found in 1796 close to the river, together with a bronze skillet (a kind of saucepan) and a collection of military horse-harnesses and other items – clearly a hoard, buried in uncertain times before the end of the first century and never recovered. Also on the right-hand wall is a late first- or second-century tombstone depicting a cavalryman riding down his barbarian foe – a common enough subject, here rather crudely rendered by an inexperienced sculptor, with ill-proportioned horse and perfunctory detail. Among the small finds, the most unusual is the rectangular stone slab with eight receptacles in it, possibly to take wax for lighting. At the back of the museum are some more inscriptions, including one with fine lettering in honour of Caracalla and his mother Julia Domna; note how the name of his brother Geta, murdered in 212 at Caracalla's behest, has been erased at the bottom of the stone, as it was throughout the Empire in a process known as *damnatio memoriae* ('damning of the memory').

On leaving the Museum, turn right, and right again before entering the churchyard. Go through the side gate into the churchyard and then turn immediately right. A short path here leads to the front ends of the fort's granaries, excavated in 1908; further work was carried out in 2000 during building of the new path alongside them. The granaries are buttressed, as usual, and one has a loading-platform outside, but it is clear from their unequal size and differences in construction that the buildings were not erected at the same time. That on the left has a ledge round the inside as well as central stone piers, clearly re-used, to support the floor, whereas the larger granary on the right has a central dividing wall, one row of piers in each half, and buttresses which do not line up with those of the other granary. The gutter stones are out of place here and many come from the *principia*. The granaries probably belong to different periods in the third century; hints of both timber and stone predecessors were noted in 1908. The site of the NW gate lies immediately beyond. The north corner tower of the fort has been exposed in the honorary custodian's garden; it may be possible to view this (weekends only) on application to the custodian (enquire at the Museum). The rest of the fort still lies buried, or rather the part spared by the river Ribble, which has removed the whole of the east corner and the NE and SE gates.

Now enter the churchyard by the main gate (the column under the sundial on the left is Roman), and walk over to the far side and through the gate beyond. Here the mound covering the SW defences of the second-century fort and its accompanying ditch are clearly visible, and the rampart can be seen rounding the west corner and running through the churchyard. The earliest fort of turf and timber was founded by Petillius Cerialis *c*. AD 72, and occupied with two subsequent refurbishments in timber into the early second century. This Flavian fort extended further north and was differently orientated from its second-century successor. Among the finds in the ditch-fill when its defences were demolished were two boxwood combs: their soil residues contained human head lice, astonishingly still preserved by the waterlogged conditions. The new fort erected *c*. AD 117/25, replacing these timber forerunners, had defences and a central range of stone (either from the start, or at least from *c*. 165), which was at least twice repaired. Occupation continued to the end of the fourth century, but at least part of the interior was empty of buildings then, and the northern *vicus* had been abandoned as early as *c*. 200. The first garrison, recorded on an altar in the Museum, was a cavalry regiment of Asturians from Spain, demonstrated also by the significant amount of horse-tack found in excavations. The third-century garrison of Sarmatians has already been mentioned. An extensive civilian settlement, largely of timber buildings, lies under the modern village and also NW of the fort. Here the presence of large timber-framed workshops on a regular layout with strip-houses beyond, all enclosed within an annexe, suggests a degree of military control during the second century over the planning, construction, growth and perhaps even the tenancy of the civilian *vicus*.

Retrace your steps past the museum and turn right along the river bank. On the right is a holly bush, and adjoining it at the far end is a Roman well *in situ*; it lay in the courtyard of the CO's house. Sometimes obscured by the density of the holly bush, it was clearly visible in late 2001. More substantial are the remains of the bath-house identified in 1837, first dug in 1927, and re-excavated between 1978 and 1980. Closed between November and Easter, it is accessible at any time during the rest of the year, either from the main road in the village (turn down Greenside and then take the first turning on the right), or from the path along the river, leaving the main road near the Museum (signpost).

The architectural development and function of the various rooms of this bath building are by no means clear, and it is not therefore a particularly instructive example of its type. Make first for the square room with scanty remains of hypocaust *pilae* of two different periods, some round, some square. This and the adjacent square room with the flagged floor at a higher level were both part of the earliest bath-house apparently erected *c.* 100, the rest of which now lies buried. Both rooms were heated in this first phase, as flues to enable the underfloor circulation of warm air are visible in the party wall between the two. Later (*c.* 160?) these openings were blocked with brickwork, when the room nearer the river became either a *frigidarium* or the *apodyterium* and received the flagged floor still partly visible. On the other side of the remaining heated room (which probably now served as a *tepidarium*), a fresh heated chamber (*caldarium*) was added. The well outside it is medieval. New flue arches were opened in the party wall between *tepidarium* and *caldarium*, and new stoke-holes were added to the north wall; that serving the *caldarium* shows signs of particularly heavy use. The detached circular sweating-room (*sudatorium*) is thought to have been added *c.* 120. The purpose of the cobbled area is uncertain (a base for a water-tank?). The baths were demolished *c.* 200/25, although the furnace area seems to have remained in use later as a smithy.

The Roman trunk-road to the north from York is still largely followed by the A1, which passes by or through the Roman towns at Aldborough (see below) and Catterick (App. 1). At Scotch Corner, then as now, the road splits. The left fork heads over the Stainmore Pass and is described below, while the right-hand fork (Dere Street) made for Corbridge and Hadrian's Wall via forts at Piercebridge, Binchester, Lanchester and Ebchester, all in County Durham. At each of these forts stone remains are visible today.

Piercebridge** (NZ 211157) lies 7 miles (11 km) north of Scotch Corner on the B6275. The modern road follows the alignment of its Roman predecessor, straight as a die, for the entire distance between the two (and again for some 5 miles [8 km] north of Piercebridge), until it swings to the left just before crossing the bridge into the village. Park on the right after the bend (by courtesy of the George Hotel), and walk back to the EH notice and the path leading to a Roman bridge over the Tees, discovered and excavated in 1972 [AM; A]. You first reach the tumbled remains of large stone blocks comprising both the bridge-piers and the flagstones on the river bottom, which have been left as found. The remains become more intelligible at the far end, where the paving, designed to prevent river-scouring, is excellently preserved. The stones were not held together by clamps, the interlocking of the stones themselves being enough to keep them in position on the river bed. Then the sturdy bridge abutment itself is reached: still intact, it consists of two courses of huge, close-fitting blocks (no mortar was used), complete with iron tie-bars and lead fixings *in situ* on the upper surface, and the cuttings to take part of the timber superstructure: for this was not an arched bridge entirely of stone but a wooden one resting on a stone base.

The position of the first bridge-pier (with cutwater to the west) is clearly detectable where the river-bed paving is missing, and the start of the second is marked by the straight edge at the point where the coherent stretch of paving stops; but in both cases the stonework of the piers themselves has vanished. There were two more piers in the preserved part of the bridge: the third is not detectable on the ground, but part of the stonework of the fourth can be made out *in situ* about 2.50 m (8 ft) from the entrance to the English Heritage enclosure. Most of the rear (straight), downstream face of the pier survives, consisting of nine blocks set together, marked with tie-bar slots and lewis holes.

Although the position of the abutment, which stood on the south bank, shows how far the river has shifted since Roman times, the precise position of the Roman north abutment is unknown. Either it is lost to the river, or it lies deeply buried in river gravel somewhere on the north bank – if the latter, the bridge may have had as many as 12 piers and to have been some 200 m (220 yds) long. The bridge was built probably towards the end of the second century, or early in the third, but already before the end of the Roman period the problem of the changing river course had become acute. It was found necessary to carry the road on a causeway, its sides revetted in limestone, which covered the abutment and the first two piers. Part of this causeway has been reconstituted in the form of a grass mound on the site today. Pottery from this causeway indicates that it was built not earlier than the first half of the fourth century.

These remains at Piercebridge, however, are not those of the first Roman bridge across the Tees: Dere Street originally kept straight and crossed the river mid-way between the visible Roman bridge and the post-medieval one. Presumably erosion and flood damage were responsible for the abandonment of this earlier Roman bridge, which appears to have been of timber: oak piles belonging to it were identified in the river bed in the 1930s and 1980s. Why that bridge was apparently not replaced by another of stone on the same spot we do not know; instead, a stretch of Dere Street was rebuilt with a dog-leg deviation 180 m (200 yd) to the east, in order to cross the river by the new (visible) stone bridge of *c.* 200.

Now follow on foot the road into the village (it is best to leave your car in the George Hotel car-park), and take the lane between the cottages nearest the south side of the church. Here an extensive area, excavated between 1975 and 1981, is laid out on permanent display. It is part of an exceptionally large fort of nearly 11 acres (4.50 ha) which was a totally new foundation *c.* AD 265/70, fully garrisoned until *c.* 320, and then reoccupied with a reduced force *c.* 350 until the end of the fourth century.

You first reach the heavily robbed remains of the east gate, with two solid gate-towers which projected behind the line of the wall, and a double-carriageway. On either side is a long stretch of the fort wall, also poorly preserved, but an impressive 2 m (10 ft) wide. On the berm separating it from the ditches were cut two rows of neat rectangular pits, indicated today by concrete markers. The pits are clearly deliberate and must be interpreted as *lilia*: they would have been filled with pointed stakes and covered with bracken to deceive an attacker into thinking he was on solid ground. The device, described by Julius Caesar, has also been detected in Scotland (pp. 572 and 574), and along the berm of Hadrian's Wall (pp. 464 and 465): the Piercebridge example shows that it was still in vogue over 300 years after Caesar was writing.

Backing the massive stone wall was a road (but no earth rampart), below which ran a well preserved drain or sewer. It curves across the line of the *via principalis* at the east gate, where it was joined by another. One large cover-slab here is clearly a re-used stone from an earlier building. Parallel with the drain for most of its course is part of a large, substantial stone structure, built on footings of river pebbles. Interpreted by the excavator as a luxury barracks (the rooms had painted wall-plaster, and two adjacent rooms at the far end have channelled hypocausts), it seems more likely to have been one wing of the commandant's house (*praetorium*). Part of its bath-suite has been excavated in the yard of an adjacent house and can be seen from afar by looking (obliquely, to the right of the lean-to) over the wall at the far end. The Roman walling is incorporated into the modern house here to a height of some 3.50 m (11 ft 6 in).

Now retrace your steps to the east gate and turn right, past the remains of an eleventh-century lime kiln. Ends of *vicus* buildings project from the grass beyond: that on the far right ended in a cellar (now under the grass) with niches in its walls, tentatively interpreted as the temple of an eastern version of the Jupiter cult, that of Jupiter Dolichenus. Pass into the footpath beyond, and turn left. A display board here explains about the *vicus* in the field in front of you, the plan of which, consisting of strip buildings lining both Dere Street and the road leading up to it from the fort behind you, has been largely established by aerial photography. It seems likely that an early fort, presumably a Flavian foundation, lies buried here astride Dere Street, but it had been superseded by the *vicus* already in the Hadrianic period. Yet there surely was a fort at Piercebridge for the rest of the second and the first half of the third century, although its precise whereabouts are unknown; most probably it lies buried below the visible, late third-century fort.

Next go through the gate before the barn into the farmyard on your left (asking permission to enter from the farmer), and turn right between the barns. In the field beyond, and just visible from the farmyard itself, is another portion of the fort, which has been left exposed since 1934; it was, sadly, very overgrown in 2001. Here the NE corner of the fort wall can be seen turning the corner, its superbly cut plinth and facing-blocks better preserved than in the stretch near the east gate. The sewer is also in a fine state here, one side of it over 2.15 m (7 ft) high; note the well preserved vault over the sewer where it enters and leaves the semicircular building erected over it. This structure, of which foundations and a doorway are visible, was the fort's latrine, with an estimated maximum capacity of perhaps 30. The holes in its rear wall 1.50 m (5 ft) apart, above the sewer, were designed to take timbers for the seating structure.

Now return to the footpath, turn left (past a display board about the latrine) and walk to the far end. Turn left past the Carlbury Arms for a fine view (opposite the bus-shelter) of the NW corner of the Roman fort, visible here as a boldly upstanding earthwork. The Roman name of Piercebridge is unknown, but one candidate (if it is not to be identified with the fort at Greta Bridge) is MORBIVM, which the late fourth-century document called the *Notitia Dignitatum* places between Doncaster and South Shields.

The next fort to the north is **Binchester*** (NZ 210313), the Roman VINOVIA or VINOVIVM, a name of uncertain meaning. From the old centre of Bishop Auckland (Market Place), turn left by The Sportsman Inn, signposted 'Binchester Roman fort' and 'Newfield'. Follow this for about 1 mile (1.6 km), and then take the access road to the Binchester Hall Nursing

Home. If coming from the north, the fort is signposted on the
A690 between Crook and Willington. The site (open
April–September only, Saturday–Wednesday 1030–1800) lies
beyond the nursing home car-park. Binchester was a large
cavalry fort covering nearly 9 acres (3.57 ha), founded by
Agricola, evacuated early in the second century, and
apparently re-occupied *c.* 160. Its north and east ramparts are
very prominent as earth mounds in the field beyond the farm,
while to the south lay an extensive civilian settlement. The
only building visible is a complex structure believed to have
been built in the mid-fourth century as the commandant's
house (*praetorium*), and subsequently much altered.

Opposite the ticket-office, take the steps down to examine
the main furnace and stoke-hole area (*praefurnium*) for the
heated rooms you will see presently: note the putlog holes and
details of the hypocaust beyond (through the grille). A
dedication to Jupiter Best and Greatest was found re-used in
this furnace in 1990; it is now in the Bowes Museum at
Barnard Castle. Return to the path, and after passing a
massive, uninscribed altar lying on the ground, you turn right
across an impressive flagged 'courtyard' and pretentious
triple-arched entrance (represented by the moulded blocks). It
is structurally later than the heated part of a bath-suite (under
the shed), but probably not by much. The excavators assume
that this courtyard was roofed over to provide a *frigidarium*
which the baths otherwise appear to lack; however, its
supporting walls look rather insubstantial for such a wide
span. Two rooms under cover here are interpreted, somewhat
uncertainly, as cold-water immersion-baths.

The shed covers one of the best preserved and most
instructive examples of a hypocaust in Britain. It belonged to
the baths of the *praetorium* in their final form in the second
half of the fourth century (*c.* 360?). The concrete floor of one
room is still in position, and the wall-flues for the rising heat
can be seen round the edges (Fig. 84). Underneath this floor,
in perfect condition, are 88 *pilae* of Roman tiles partially
blackened by the heat. Some of the larger tiles supporting the
floor are stamped N CON, for *N(umerus) Con(cangiensium)*,
the name of the unit which made them. Three fine arches, two
perfectly preserved, allowed the heat to circulate in the
adjoining room. The central arch and the floor of this adjoining

84   Binchester, hypocaust flue-tiles in the baths of the praetorium

room appear still intact in a drawing made when the building was first found in the early nineteenth century. The destruction was reputedly caused by later explorers who expected to find buried treasure underneath and ripped down the centre arch in their desire for quicker access. Further digging was done in 1878–80 and 1964, and the hut was put up in 1969; fresh excavation took place between 1976 and 1981 and again between 1986 and 1991.

The third heated room (*caldarium*) in its final phase had two immersion-baths. That straight ahead of you stands over the flue arch to the main furnace beyond, but remains of an earlier flue channel, as well as the straight joints of the recess with the masonry on either side, indicate that the immersion-bath here was a later addition to the main heated block.

On leaving the shed by the far door, the path passes an impressive stoke-hole with a double row of brick voussoirs. In the wall to the right, putlog holes are visible. On rounding the corner, one course up from ground-level, you will find a quoin sculpted with a now-headless dog (or fox). Now re-cross the paved court, turn right, and walk down to the fence at the far end. First you pass a fine stretch of Roman street (the course

of Dere Street passing through the fort) with guttering on the
far side. Then turn right along the blue-gravelled corridor, at
the far end of which (and in the room beyond) are some
demolished foundations of third-century structures. The
function and layout of the rest of the rooms here, which are of
fourth-century date and appear to have also formed part of the
praetorium, are not easy to interpret. The original arrangement
has been obscured by the radical changes of the late fourth
century, when this part of the building was turned into self-
contained flatlets of two or three rooms. Others were used for
iron-working and other processes, but this apparently occurred
when the *praetorium* was falling into disuse, probably in the
years after 400: the room with the single square slab adjacent
to the blue-gravelled corridor, for example, is interpreted on
the basis of bone finds as a cattle-slaughterhouse.

The next fort to the north, **Lanchester** (NZ 159468), the
Roman LONGOVICIVM, was built under Lollius Urbicus
c. AD 140 at a period when both Ebchester to the north and
Binchester to the south were empty; it does not seem to have
had a Flavian or early second-century predecessor. A large
fort (6.25 acres [2.50 ha]), it was designed to hold a nominal
garrison of 1,000 men. In the 170s this was a Spanish cohort
of Vardulli, part-mounted, who had the exceptional honour of
being Roman citizens. By *c*. 220 this had been replaced by the
First Cohort of Lingones, also part-mounted, a unit which
earlier had been stationed at High Rochester. Under Gordian
(emperor 238–44), building activity at Lanchester is attested
by two fine inscriptions now in the Fulling Mill Museum
of Archaeology at Durham (April–September, daily
1000–1600; October–March, Friday–Monday 1130–1530.
Its garrison at this time was still the Cohort of Lingones, now
reinforced by a unit of Suebians. The latter dedicated an altar
to their Germanic goddess Garmangabis which now stands in
the south porch of Lanchester church.

To reach the site of the fort, which lies 8 miles (12.8 km)
NW of Durham, turn off the A691 opposite Lanchester
church, taking the B6296 for Wolsingham. At the top of the
hill, bordering the left-hand side of the road, you will see a
long stretch of stone core belonging to the north wall of
LONGOVICIVM; just beyond it is a lay-by with a display board.
No facing-stones survive, but the stone core of the walls is

visible round nearly the entire circuit. In places it still stands 2 m (6 ft 6 in) high, but as recently as the late eighteenth century it was still standing to its full height, including a paved wall-walk. Little excavation has been conducted in the interior (the only visible feature is a hollow showing some pieces of stonework), but a geophysical survey in 1990–2 has revealed details of its layout and that of the attendant *vicus* with exceptional clarity. From south to north, the buildings in the central range comprised a commanding officer's house (with a possible granary and other structures built on top of it in the late Empire), a standard *principia* and two granaries beyond; the plans of eight barracks were also clear in the front part (*praetentura*) to the east. A cemetery for the *vicus* is known 350 m (380 yds) SW of the fort, in use between the mid-second and the late third century. Virtually no trace remains of the three aqueduct-channels which brought water up to 4 miles (6.4 km) from the NW (for the details, see the article cited in the Bibliography on p. 707). As so often with Roman forts, the superb position, commanding land in all directions, cannot fail to be noticed.

Between here and Corbridge there was a small fort on the Derwent at **Ebchester** (NZ 103554), the Roman VINDOMORA (possibly meaning 'the bright waters'), now a village on the A694 12 miles (19 km) SW of Newcastle. A clay and timber fort covering 4 acres (1.65 ha), of Agricolan date (*c.* AD 80), was in occupation until *c.* 140, when it was abandoned on the Antonine advance into Scotland. Reoccupied from about 163 after Scotland was given up, Ebchester's defences were probably rebuilt in stone now (rather than earlier). The fort remained in use until the middle of the fourth century, with at least two major rebuildings, probably at the beginning and the end of the third century. The third-century garrison was the Fourth Cohort of Breuci, as we know from an inscription now in the Fulling Mill Museum at Durham (p. 402) and from stamped tiles found at the site.

Very little excavation has taken place here, and not much is known of the fort's interior layout. The main visible relic at the site is a hypocaust in an apse-shaped room, not earlier than the late third century. Its position points to its being part of a bath-suite in the commandant's house; but the orientation of the structure, at variance with the rest of the fort layout,

suggests that it is a late insertion, possibly when the garrison
was much reduced and traditional fort layouts were breaking
down. The stone *pilae* and walls of the heated room are still
1 m (3 ft) high, and there is a stoke-hole to one side. Two of
the *pilae* clearly sit on an earlier wall, itself part of a heated
room: the brick foundations here represent a demolished
stoke-hole for an earlier heated chamber on the site. This
monument, however, lies on private property, and is not
therefore accessible to the public without prior written
permission. If you are interested in seeing it, write in advance
to Noel and Brenda Beveridge, Mains Farm, Ebchester,
enclosing a stamped addressed envelope. I stress that casual
visitors without an appointment are understandably *not*
welcome. We owe the preservation of the Roman structure to
the generous action of a former owner of Mains Farm,
Mr W Dodds, who found the remains in 1962 when digging
near his barn. A fragmentary tombstone found during
demolition work in 1985 is displayed with other finds in a
small private museum established by Mr Dodds and
maintained by the Beveridges. To reach the spot, turn off the
main road by the bus-shelter near the church. Mains Farm is
the first house on the left after the corner bungalow.

Opposite Mains Farm, a Roman altar and several other
Roman stones are displayed in the church, and in the
graveyard behind, the mound of the south rampart of the
defences can be made out; the school beyond sits on the site
of an annexe. More striking is the rampart-bank at the
NE corner of the fort, reached by turning left out of the
churchyard, crossing the main street (Vindomora Road), and
going into the public garden to the right of the Post Office.
A display board here helps you place the outlines of the fort in
the context of the modern village.

The Roman road which swung west at Scotch Corner
headed over the Stainmore Pass for the Eden valley. Closely
followed by the A66, it still forms one of the major east-west
highways in northern Britain. The route is littered with Roman
earthworks, and I will note them in the order in which they
occur when approached from the east. For the first 11 miles
(17.7 km) the A66 is dead straight and follows the Roman
alignment. The first change in direction occurs at **Greta
Bridge** (NZ 085132), where a fort was situated. Avoid the

bypass of the A66 and enter the village of Greta Bridge itself; after crossing the river you will see on your left the prominent mound marking the eastern defences. Then turn left along the road to Brignall just past the Morritt Arms Hotel, which sits on the north wall of the fort. The conspicuous remains of the earth rampart-mound and ditches of the southern defences are visible in the first field on the left, with the causeway across the ditch running up to the south gate. Its Roman name is uncertain (p. 399).

Little excavation has been done at Greta Bridge, and the length of occupation inside the fort is unknown: it may have been a new foundation only in the Antonine period of the mid-second century, while an inscription, now in the Bowes Museum at Barnard Castle, attests to building work under the energetic governor L. Alfenus Senecio in 205/8. Rescue work conducted in the civilian settlement in 1972–4, in advance of the building of a new route for the A66, found that the *vicus* lined, on both sides of the river, the main Roman road bypassing the fort to the north. That to the east of the river consisted of a timber building of *c*. AD 180–275, with industrial activity below not earlier than *c*. 150; after a fire came strip buildings with stone foundations in the last quarter of the third century (11 were excavated in all), with occupation not lasting far into the fourth century. How far this reflects the occupation history of the fort itself is a question only future excavation can resolve.

Only $5\frac{1}{2}$ miles (9 km) further west is the fort at **Bowes** (NY 993135), the Roman LAVATRIS, a name of uncertain derivation. This guarded the eastern end of the Stainmore Pass, as did the Norman castle which later obliterated the NW corner of the fort. Follow signs for Bowes village (now bypassed by the A66) and then for Bowes Castle. The churchyard occupies the NE corner (its east wall is on the line of the east rampart of the fort), and a cemetery the SE quadrant, but the rampart-mound of its south and west sides (in the field south of the castle) are still well preserved. Excavations in 1966–7 revealed that the original rampart raised by Agricola *c*. AD 78 consisted of huge river-boulders set in clay, with a rear revetment of turf and a front revetment of timber. In the second century a subsequent clay rampart was cut back to receive a stone wall; this was later replaced by a second wall, nearly 2.45 m (8 ft) thick, which was crudely repaired in the fourth century.

The path through the cemetery leads to a stone stairway where it crosses the line of the south rampart: the change in level to the ground outside is considerable. Descend the stairs and look over the cemetery wall: a large hollow with some pieces of stonework showing through marks the site of the extramural bath-house, plundered in the nineteenth century. An inscription now in Cambridge records that this building, *vi ignis exustum*, 'burnt by the violence of fire', was restored in the governorship of Virius Lupus (AD 197–202), when a cavalry regiment of Spanish Vettones was the garrison at Bowes. By 208 this had been replaced by the First Cohort of Thracians (originally from Bulgaria), who erected a dedication-slab to the emperor Severus and his sons Caracalla and Geta. This can be seen, poorly lit and nearly illegible, in the north transept of Bowes church (enter from north door – if, that is, the church is not locked, as sadly churches increasingly are in the present age). The name of Geta, as usual, was erased after his murder. Three other Roman stones are also displayed in the church, one of them inscribed (it was later re-used as a millstone). Some traces of the aqueduct-channel which brought water to the fort from the NW can be located with the help of a detailed map (see article cited in the Bibliography, p. 707).

One of the few spare-time pursuits open to an officer serving in such a distant outpost must have been hunting, and it was no doubt to appease the local moorland god that two rustic shrines were built in a wild and desolate spot, 2 miles (3 km) south of the fort, on the west bank of the East Black Sike near its confluence with the Eller Beck (NY 999105). One was rectangular and the other, 23 m (25 yds) to the south, was circular. In them were found, mostly in 1946–7, three altars (and fragments of others) dedicated to the god Vinotonus, equated with the Roman god of hunting and woodland, Silvanus. The best preserved, erected by the commander of the First Thracian Cohort, Caesius Frontinus, who came from Parma in north Italy, is now part of the collection housed in the Bowes Museum at Barnard Castle (1100–1700 daily throughout the year). Another altar, dedicated by a separate commander of the same unit, was found casually in 1986 mid-

way between the two shrines; it too is now in the Bowes
Museum. Very little can be seen at the site today, and it is
therefore listed in Appendix 1; but the walk across Scargill
Moor to find it is a splendid one, and a feeling of the past will
not be difficult to capture on this high and windy moor where
little has changed since Roman times.

The next fort west of Bowes was at Brough, 13 miles
(21 km) away on the other side of the Stainmore Pass. In
between was a series of signal towers designed to transmit
messages over rugged and inhospitable terrain. Six have so far
been identified with certainty (some are in App. 1), and there
are several other likely ones, but details of their typology and
chronology remain largely obscure. The idea, advanced 35
years ago, that they formed part of a much longer system has
not been substantiated by more recent discoveries.

The most accessible of these signal-posts is that on **Bowes
Moor** (NY 929125), 4 miles (6.4 km) west of Bowes.
Whether you are travelling east or west, pull off at the Bowes
Moor Hotel on the south side of A66, park there, and then
pass through the metal gate on the north side of the road,
opposite the hotel. Walk eastwards from here for five minutes,
and soon after drawing level with the P-sign on the north
carriageway, at the top of the slope ahead of you, you will see
the prominent remains of the signal station on the bluff next to
the road. This is larger than most signal stations, measuring
some 13 m (43 ft) east-west by 10 m (33 ft). The remains
consist of a rampart (made up of sandy soil revetted in
turves), 3 m (10 ft) thick, and a V-shaped ditch outside it. The
upcast from the latter formed a lesser mound on the outer lip
of the ditch, and this is clearly visible on the north, the best
preserved side of the signal station. There is an entrance on
the side facing the road, but the ditch here has been destroyed
by the modern road-widening, when excavation established
(somewhat surprisingly) a date for the station in the late third
or early fourth century. Inside the enclosure excavation in
1990 showed that the four timber uprights of the stout timber
tower rested on pad stones; a stone platform in the NW corner
may have been the base of a staircase.

To the west the outlook is very fine, and you may be able to
spot a slight 'pimple' on the skyline. This is the signal station
of Roper Castle, very similar to that on Bowes Moor. It can be

found with the help of a 1:50,000 OS map, after a long climb over boggy ground (App. 1). Eastwards from the Bowes Moor post, the view to LAVATRIS is blocked by a low spur, from which another signal station, not now visible on the ground, relayed messages to the fort. An experiment in 1977 showed that it took less than three minutes to relay a simple message by flags between the fort at Bowes and the fortlet at Maiden Castle (p. 410), 10 miles (16 km) apart, using the known intermediate signal stations en route.

Immediately north of Bowes Moor signal station, there is another, very slight Roman earthwork, the existence of which was only first detected (and from the air) in 1979. Barely 10 m from the upcast of the north ditch of the signal station, you will detect a short stretch of mound about 0.30 m (1 ft) high: a weathered modern concrete conical base stands on its line, and at the time of writing (2001) a 1990s excavation trench sectioning it has been left un-backfilled. This is part of a tiny camp 50 m (165 ft) square, of which the rest of the circuit is hardly now traceable on the ground: but if you walk parallel to the road westwards from this identifiable piece of its south rampart, you may just be able to detect the slightly lighter colour of the grass marking its course, and, towards its SW corner, a thin line of brown reeds marking the position of its ditch. Perhaps the camp was built by the building gang responsible for constructing the signal-tower, and was occupied therefore for only a very brief time.

One and a half miles (2.4 km) further west is the summit of the Stainmore Pass at 447 m (1,468 ft), and the remains of the best-preserved marching-camp in Britain, at **Rey Cross*** (NY 901124). The widening of the A66 into a dual carriageway in 1990–2 has made access to this camp much more difficult than previously. If travelling westwards, stop in the lay-by just before the summit, and walk on westwards for 200 m to a metal field-gate on the left, set back from the road (1 on Fig. 85). This brings you at once to the SE corner of the camp. If you miss this lay-by, there is another one $\frac{1}{2}$ mile (800 m) further on, at the Cumbrian border. For those travelling eastwards, park in the lay-by just past the summit: this is the new home of the Rey Cross, the base of a monument of *c*. AD 950, which was moved here from its original position within the Roman camp in 1992 (information

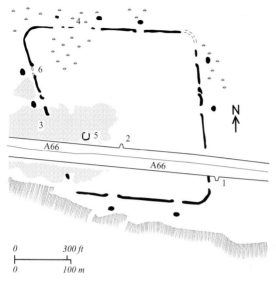

85   Rey Cross, marching-camp, site plan

board). From this lay-by walk back 350 m (385 yds) to
another metal field-gate set back from the road which gives
you access to the major part of the Roman ramparts (2 on Fig.
85). Obviously to see all of the Roman camp you will need to
exercise extreme caution in crossing the dangerous A66, but
with the help of the plan (Fig. 85) you should be able to trace
the outline of this magnificent earthwork.

   Limestone quarrying (3) has removed the southern half of
the western defences and the SW corner, and this accounts for
the confusing unevenness of the terrain here. Part of the
northern rampart has also disappeared (4), having slipped into
the bog. Elsewhere it is traceable by the lighter colour of the
grass but above all by the boldness of the rampart, 6 m (20 ft)
wide and often over 1.80 m (6 ft) high. No fewer than nine
tituli survive, each defending an entrance; two more must
have been destroyed by the road. Rather surprisingly, there is
virtually no surface evidence of a ditch, which only appears
near the NE angle. Excavation in advance of road-widening in
1991, however, showed that a ditch did exist but had been

completely obliterated by the peat; it also demonstrated that
the ramparts had been revetted by turves on the outer face and
by large stones on the inner.

Rey Cross is probably big enough (at 20 acres or 8.15 ha)
to have held the best part of a legion, and since the course of
the road, which itself must have been built in the first century,
bends slightly in order to pass through two entrances into the
camp, the earthwork belongs to the earliest Roman campaigns
in the area. It probably held the tents of the majority of the
Ninth Legion under Petillius Cerialis during his campaigns
against the Brigantes in AD 72 and 73. A small earthwork now
difficult to spot (5), curiously respected by the nineteenth-
century quarrying, may conceivably have been another signal
station like that at Bowes Moor – a hypothesis that needs
testing by excavation. Certainly there is evidence for third-
and fourth-century activity at the summit, as the 1991–2
excavations showed, when some of the camp's entrances were
apparently blocked with boulders: one of those on the west (6)
still has them in position. Clearly the strategic position of this
earthwork, controlling this key east-west communication link,
was not lost on Roman commanders later than the time of
Petillius Cerialis.

One mile (1.6 km) west of Rey Cross the A66 leaves the
Roman alignment, and soon afterwards a minor road goes off
to the left, signposted South Stainmore, Barras and Kaber (if
coming from the west, turn off the A66 at this point). Park
where convenient here and cross over to the north side of the
A66, which is dual-carriageway at this point. Opposite the
turning to South Stainmore is a sign reading 'Public
Bridleway, Maiden Way' (take the right-hand of the two
metal gates). Ten minutes' walk away, and clearly visible on
the bluff to your right overlooking the road, is the Roman
fortlet of **Maiden Castle** (NY 872132). This small post,
enclosing less than $\frac{1}{2}$ acre (0.17 ha), and perhaps therefore
only holding about 50 men, was a link in the signalling
system between Brough and Bowes and also a convenient
stopping-place for convoys after the long haul up from
Brough. It commands a magnificent view over the Eden
valley, with Brough Castle visible in the middle distance.
Eastwards its view is blocked by the Stainmore Pass, but it is
in sight of the Roper Castle signal station (see above) and

thence messages could be relayed to Bowes; more straightforwardly, there may have been a signal station also at Rey Cross (see above). Limited excavations in the 1930s pointed to a foundation date in the middle of the second century, and it was occupied into the late fourth century. The remains now consist of four stony banks about 1.80 m (6 ft) high, representing the original stone defences. There are two gates. A single ditch appears on the north, marked by the inner set of reeds. The outer row of reeds indicates the line of a cart-track which probably follows a Roman branch road bypassing the fortlet.

The fort at **Brough** (NY 791141) lies $\frac{1}{2}$ mile (800 m) south of the A66, under the castle. Avoid Brough village but follow directions for Kirkby Stephen, turning left on leaving the A66, then immediately right for Church Brough, then left at the T-junction and first right. The castle [AM; A] has obliterated the fort's northern half; how much of the impressive rampart and ditch of its southern half is the work of Roman soldiers or Norman castle-builders is unclear. A dedication-slab of AD 197, now virtually illegible, is visible inside the south porch of the church, and casts of a tombstone in Greek of a 16-year-old from Commagene (Turkey) are displayed inside the tower. The fort was occupied from c. 79 to c. 120, and from c. 160 onwards. A cremation cemetery was found in 1971 under what is now the A66, approximately 500 m (550 yds) east of the fort, and a civilian settlement has been identified between the two. The Roman name was VERTERIS, meaning perhaps 'at the summits'.

Westwards from Brough the land becomes cultivable again and the Roman earthworks are consequently more damaged. Of the next fort, at Kirkby Thore, for example, nothing is visible on the ground, and little remains now of the marching-camp at Crackenthorpe, the earthworks of which were reported in the eighteenth century as being well preserved (App. 1). One unusual Roman relic does, however, exist nearby, $\frac{1}{2}$ mile (800 m) SE of **Temple Sowerby** (NY 619264). Apart from the better example at Chesterholm, this is the only undoubted Roman milestone in Britain which occupies its original position. It stands about 1.40 m (4 ft 6 in) high, looking a little sorry for itself in its iron cage; it lacks any

explanatory sign. It is situated on the verge of a lay-by on the
north side of the A66.

The next fort to the west is **Brougham** (NY 538289), and
once again, significantly of course, Romans and Normans
agreed in their choice of a strategic position. Brougham Castle
[AM; April–September, daily 1000–1800; October, daily
1000–1700] lies 2 miles (3 km) SE of Penrith, just off the
A66. It has removed the northern quarter of the Roman fort,
but the rest can be traced as a slight bank and ditch in the field
south of the castle, especially near the crossroads with the
B6262. A first-century date is unproven, as all the finds date
from between the second century and the close of the fourth.
Its Roman name was BROCAVVM, perhaps meaning 'the fort at
the pointed rock'. More interesting than the remains of the
fort itself, however, are the ten inscriptions preserved at the
castle, formerly displayed in the Inner and Outer Gatehouses
but now housed in a site Museum next to the ticket-office.
One is a well-carved tombstone of Crescentinus, who died
aged 18 (Fig. 88), set up by his father Vidaris, possibly a
Germanic name. Note the pine cone in the pediment, a
common funerary symbol. Next to it is the relief of a boy in a
cloak with the inscription: 'Annamoris, his father, and
Ressona, his mother, had this put up'. Also displayed here are
three stones found during excavation in the fort's cemetery in
1966–7, when over 200 burials, mostly cremations, were
uncovered (now under the A66). A fragment of another
tombstone is built into the ceiling of a short passage in the
second floor of the keep. The deceased in this case is a certain
Tittus . . . who lived 32 years 'more or less' ([*plu*]*s minus* in
the penultimate line). This form of words is sometimes used
on Christian tombstones.

From Kirkby Thore a Roman road, known as the Maiden
Way, ran straight to Hadrian's Wall near Greenhead, and
en route is the fort of **Whitley Castle*** (NY 695487). There
is practically no stonework visible here today, but the
remarkable system of ditches protecting the fort on the SW
makes it an outstanding site comparable only with Ardoch in
Scotland (p. 587). From Alston take the Brampton road
(A689) for $1\frac{1}{2}$ miles (2.4 km) until it descends to cross a
narrow bridge over a stream. A quarter of a mile (400 m)
later, immediately after a farm on the left, park at the lay-by

on the right (telephone box). Take the path through the wood opposite ('Pennine Way' signpost), and cross the stream by the bridge. You will then see the fort on the skyline to your left, five minutes' walk away. You first reach the NW defences with its gate, passing the site of the external bath-house (excavated in 1810) to your left: the fort ditches here appear to respect it, suggesting that the outer ones were added (here and no doubt elsewhere) in a secondary phase.

Turn right inside the fort, and cross the stone field-wall in front of you. The site of the fort's *principia* is marked by uneven ground on the other side of this field-wall in the centre of the fort. Beyond lies the conspicuous rampart-mound of the magnificent SW defences, furnished with as many as seven ditches (Fig. 86). Presumably such excessive defence was thought necessary because of the relatively close proximity of a range of hills on this flank; the absence of a gate on this side betrays the same defensive thinking. Part of the SE side of the fort is also very impressive. One of the highest forts in Britain

86   Whitley Castle, Roman fort, aerial view from the SW

(320 m or 1,050 ft), it departs from the normal playing-card shape, forming a rhomboid to take full advantage of the hillock on which it lies.

Of Whitley Castle's history little is known, as virtually no excavation has been conducted here. It was originally built in the middle of the second century, and a couple of dedication-slabs indicate building activity in the period AD 213–19, either because the fort had been destroyed or after a period of neglect. The spectacular ditches reached their greatest extent now, and it is possible that the fort was enlarged on the NW at this time, to reach its present size of 3 acres (1.2 ha). The stone walls, of which occasional fragments are exposed in the turf banks, must have been rebuilt in this third-century phase; whether the original second-century fort was given stone defences from the start (as seems likely) has not been established with certainty. One of the inscriptions tells us that its garrison was the Second Cohort of Nervii, originally recruited from the lower Rhine. The Roman name of Whitley Castle is uncertain, but it may be EPIACVM (which should mean, intriguingly, 'the property of Epios'). One of its functions was probably to control the nearby lead-mines.

Brougham lay on the major western artery to Carlisle and Scotland. The platform of the next fort to the north, VOREDA, is clearly visible beside the A6 (Old Penrith, App. 1). From here a road ran south-westwards through the northern part of the Lake District, and although its full course is unknown, it probably headed for the upper waters of the Derwent and linked up with the fort at Papcastle (App. 1) and ultimately with Maryport (p. 418) on the coast. On the way it passed an intermediate fort at **Troutbeck** (NY 383273), and although there is little to see of the fort itself there, the site is worth visiting for other Roman military earthworks in its immediate vicinity. Immediately opposite the junction of the A5091 (for Dockray and Ullswater) with the A66, turn off the latter northwards at Hill Crest (bed and breakfast). Proceed along this road (it is the old course of the A66) to a metal field-gate 100 m beyond the turning to Far Howe. Walk 25 paces north of this gate and you come to the south entrance of a marching-camp (3 on Fig. 87), which enclosed about 1.6 acres (0.3 ha) and is the smallest of the three temporary camps at Troutbeck. The entrance was defended by double *claviculae*, with

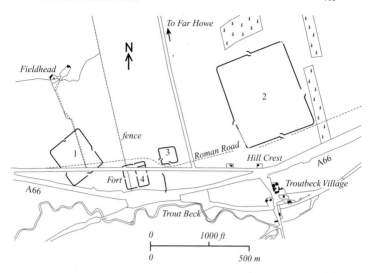

87   Troutbeck, Roman fort and marching-camps, site plan

extensions of the rampart curving both inwards and outwards
to protect the entrance, and in theory to enforce oblique entry
for an attacker. The external *clavicula* alone is clear at the
south entrance, but both can be seen at the west entrance. This
is the only other break in the rampart of this camp, which can
be traced with ease for its entire circuit (only the SW angle
has largely disappeared). Notice also, when looking east from
its east rampart, how the boundary wall lining the drive to Far
Howe rises and falls as it approaches the former A66: this
marks the line of the embankment (*agger*) of the Roman road
which can be seen approaching the SE corner of the camp.
Another much larger camp (2 on Fig. 87), covering some
24 acres (9.7 ha), lies in the distance 250 m (275 yds) away,
on higher ground behind Hill Crest; only its north side, with
the entrance again defended by external and internal
claviculae, is well preserved.

  Now continue westwards from the field-gate to the brow of
the hill 125 m (135 yds) further on: here lies the fort of
Troutbeck (4), of which the east rampart in particular is
visible as a broad mound to the left of the road. It has never

been excavated, but it is clear from the surviving earthworks that it was reduced in size in a secondary period. The fort's west rampart is just visible to the left of the road beyond the brow, opposite the lay-by with the stile and footpath sign. A further 200 m brings you to the drive to 'Fieldhead' on your right; park here and walk back 60 paces. At this point the line of the east corner of Camp 1 crosses your path, clearly visible as a lighter strip in the surrounding brown moorland. The entire ramparts of this 10-acre (4 ha) camp are remarkably well preserved, with four entrances protected by internal *claviculae*: its SE entrance is visible immediately south of the road at this point. The date of all these earthworks is uncertain, but the exclusive use of *claviculae* suggests a date in the Flavian period or early in the second century.

From Carlisle another road ran more directly to the Cumberland coast at Moresby near Whitehaven (App. 1), and both the forts which line this route, and a third slightly off it, have left traces on the ground. Of these by far the most prominent is that at **Old Carlisle** (NY 260464) (for Papcastle and Caermote, see App. 1). Take the A595 for 10 miles (16 km) out of Carlisle and watch out for the B5305 to Wigton. Do not take that, but turn first right after it (minor road signposted 'Wigton 1.5'), stopping at the farm on the left (bed and breakfast). The fort lies two fields behind the farm; alternatively, it can be viewed from afar from the main road a short distance west of the junction. No stonework is visible, but the fort ditches and the mound covering the stone walls and earth rampart are superbly preserved on the west and the west part of the south sides, and the causeways leading to the east and south gates are also very bold, but there has been much disturbance on the north. An extensive area of ridges and mounds in the pasture between the fort and the A595 belong to the civilian settlement, and these showed up with sufficient clarity in the parched conditions of 1974–5 for them to be planned with reasonable accuracy. But no excavation has taken place in either fort or settlement, and the length of occupation is unknown. Most of our information is derived from the 26 inscriptions ploughed up in the fort or its vicinity: from these we learn, for example, that the garrison of MAGLONA ('High Place') in the late second and early third century was the Ala Augusta, a cavalry regiment 500 strong, and that the inhabitants of the civilian settlement (*vikani*) set up an altar to Jupiter and Vulcan in the mid-third century.

Other coastal forts apart from Moresby were at Burrow Walls near Workington, Maryport and Beckfoot. These were designed to protect the Solway coast and the western approaches to Hadrian's Wall, and the system of milefortlets and towers continued along the coast from Bowness, where the Wall ends, to beyond Maryport, and possibly as far as St Bees Head. Of this entire system nothing is visible on the ground today except for the milefortlet at **Swarthy Hill** (NY 067400), 4 miles (6.4 km) north of Maryport. Take the B5300 off the Carlisle road $\frac{3}{4}$ mile (1 km) north of Maryport (Silloth and Allonby), and park in the first car-park on the right, just after the turning to Crosscanonby. A stairway up the bluff here leads to the partly reconstructed remains of Milefortlet 21 (counting from Bowness). The site was discovered from the air in 1968 about 70 m north of where it had been predicted on measurement to be, and was totally excavated in 1990–1. The milefortlet consisted of a rampart of sand revetted with turves (mostly ploughed out; the visible mounds are modern), and a surrounding ditch, omitted on the cliff side. The milefortlet had two gates, and the four post-holes found at the west have been marked by modern timbers; these would have supported a tower above. The east gate was differently constructed, with sill beams resting on the earth into which timber uprights were inserted; the difference probably implies that there was no tower above this gate. The central roadway between the two gates was flanked on the south by three earth-walled buildings, now reconstituted in modern materials (one has an oven), and a long building on the north with five post-holes supporting the roof; all backed on to the rampart. The front wall of the north building left no traces (it may have been of sill-beam construction), and internal partitions into four cubicles can be postulated by the presence of a hearth or oven in each. Evidence here and elsewhere on the Solway frontier suggests that the milefortlets and towers had largely outlived their usefulness by the end of the second century: that at Swarthy Hill seems to have been occupied for less than two decades. A small piece of reconstructed milefortlet rampart nearby provides a suitable viewing platform over the site.

Of the forts along the Solway only that at **Maryport***
(NY 038373), has left any visible surface trace. Turn right off
the A596 in the town (signposted Maryport town centre), and
then take the first turning on the right. Keep going straight as
far as possible, and follow the road round where it bends to
the left. Keep straight again as far as the T-junction at the cliff
edge. Turn right here: the road leads up to the car-park of the
Senhouse Roman Museum, which occupies a nineteenth-
century coastal battery alongside the Roman fort. Here a
modern viewing-point (opened in 2001), loosely based on the
type of watchtower depicted on Trajan's Column in Rome,
but not intended as a simulation of a Cumbrian one, provides
an excellent vista over the fort and its attendant *vicus.*

A Flavian fort at Maryport in the 70s, Agricolan, if not
indeed Cerialan, is highly probable, but it was almost certainly
on a different site, perhaps closer to the river-mouth. The fort
before you, at $6\frac{1}{2}$ acres (2.58 ha) one of the largest on the
Hadrianic frontier, was built under Hadrian, probably *c.* 124
and occupied, no doubt with periodic interruptions, until the
close of the fourth century. The Hadrianic garrison was the
First Spanish Cohort, part-mounted. The Antonine garrison in
139 was the First Cohort of Delmatae, and later in the second
century the First Cohort of Baetasians was at Maryport, soon
to be transferred to Reculver (p. 46). Both of these units were
500-strong, as may also have been the Spanish cohort, and
certainly Maryport does not show any sign of having been
reduced in size, as might be expected if the garrison size was
halved. Yet Maryport's size suggests something more than a
500-strong garrison: it is not impossible that the fort had some
additional role as a supply-base for the western part of the
Hadrianic frontier, if the size of the strong-room in its
principia, excavated in the seventeenth and eighteenth
centuries, is anything to go by: it is the second largest
example in Roman Britain, after that at South Shields. The
Roman name of Maryport was most probably ALAVNA, from
the river at whose mouth it stands (still surviving in its
modern name, the Ellen).

From the observation-post, you see the fort spread out
clearly below you, with its unusual square (rather than
playing-card) shape, and breaks in the prominent rampart-
mound for its four gates. Apart from antiquarian exploration,

the only archaeological work conducted inside the fort took place in the east corner in 1966. Outside, to the north (to your left), lay the civilian settlement, known partly from nineteenth-century excavations, partly from aerial photography, and partly from geophysical survey conducted in 2000. The last revealed the plan of the *vicus* in extraordinary detail, with intensive ribbon development of strip-buildings for 300 m (325 yds) alongside the Roman road leading NE of the fort, and other buildings, including temples, inserted behind those on the street frontage. A large prominent building outside the north angle of the fort might have been the *mansio*. The area of the cemetery has been identified to the north (away to your left), west of the Roman road. The village appears even without excavation to be one of the most complete and well preserved on the northern frontier, with an estimated population of perhaps 500 people.

In 1870, a remarkable find was made on the edge of this *vicus*, 320 m (350 yds) NE of the fort. Deliberately buried in pits, a haul of no fewer than 17 inscribed altars was found, probably taken from a nearby sanctuary of Jupiter when the latter became too over-crowded with dedications. The one

88   Brougham, tombstone   *89   Maryport, altar*

illustrated (Fig. 89) is dedicated to the personification of the Emperor's Victory by Titus Attius Tutor, commander of the first Cohort of Baetasians (originally from the lower Rhine) who had the honour of being Roman citizens (as indicated by the letters C R in the inscription: serving auxiliary soldiers were normally not).

This and many other fine inscriptions, lovingly collected since the sixteenth century by successive generations of the Senhouse family, are displayed in the adjacent Senhouse Roman Museum, the largest private collection of Roman inscriptions in Britain. Opened in 1991, the Museum is open daily, July to October 1000–1700; Tuesdays and Thursday–Sunday, April to June 1000–1700; Friday–Sunday, November–March 1030–1600. The altars from the pits naturally get pride of place: uniquely, we have here virtually the complete record of the successive commanders (six of them) of the First Cohort of Spaniards in Hadrian's reign – three probably from Italy, one from France, one from Austria and one from Tunisia. There are some unusual sculptured stones, including a relief of the horse goddess Epona riding side-saddle, an engaging piece showing a naked, horned warrior god, and the striking serpent stone, a phallic grave marker from Maryport's cemetery.

Further south, in the Lake District, is the fort of **Ravenglass*** (SD 088958). Turn off the A595 17 miles (27 km) south of Whitehaven for the village of Ravenglass. Park when the road bends sharply to the right and take the lane signposted 'Public Footpath, Walls Castle'. After $\frac{1}{4}$ mile (400 m) you will come to 'Walls Castle', the Roman bath-house still standing to an astonishing height of 3.80 m (12 ft 6 in), making it the best preserved Roman structure in the north of England [AM; A]. The first room, possibly for undressing, has a niche in one wall and three doorways. These have shallow relieving arches, but the lintels beneath have disappeared; they may have been of wood but are more likely to have been large slabs of stone, now robbed out. Large putlog holes are visible here, especially in the wall on the left. Go through the doorway on your left into another room, where the lower part of a splayed window and a stretch of pink mortar rendering are well preserved. Now return to the changing-room and go through the door on your left. Its relieving arch is especially clear on the far side because it is not there covered by mortar rendering. Part of a splayed window survives in the far wall, and a large putlog hole in the wall to your right. Now go through the door into the final room, where more putlog holes and the remains of another splayed window (in the left-hand wall) will be noted, as well as the worn threshold between it and the changing-room. Excavation in 1881 revealed more of the building extending under the field to the east, including hypocausts, but the bathing arrangements and the identity of the various rooms are still in doubt.

The baths stand at the NE corner of a 3.5 acre (1.5 ha) fort, the platform of which is clear in the field beyond, to the right of the track. Much of the north rampart and ditch, and the whole of its east side can be clearly made out; the south side is crowned by a line of trees. The western part of the fort is bisected by the railway. Excavation in 1976–8 beyond the railway-line, on the cliff edge where marine erosion is taking place, indicated that the fort was built *c.* 130 to replace an earlier fortlet, and was occupied until *c.* 400 with periods in the mid-second and in the third century when it lay idle. The barracks remained of timber throughout, and the turf rampart of the defences was provided with a stone wall only in the third century. A fragmentary bronze discharge diploma, given to a veteran of *Cohors I Aelia Classica* in AD 158, was found on the foreshore in 1995: it confirms a lead sealing found 20 years earlier that this was the second-century garrison of Ravenglass, the *Classica* denoting the unit's special naval capability (*classis* means 'fleet') as befits its coastal location. The diploma also reveals that Ravenglass's Roman name was not GLANNOVENTA ('the field by the shore'), as hitherto assumed, but ITVNOCELVM ('the promontory at the water').

Nine miles (14.5 km) NE of Ravenglass, and half-way down the west side of the notoriously steep Hardknott Pass, is the Roman fort of **Hardknott Castle**** (NY 219015) [AM; A], one of the outstanding sites of Roman Britain. The fact that this is the best preserved Roman fort in Britain outside Hadrian's Wall matters less than its spectacular position: it is a veritable British Mycenae, with magnificent views of Eskdale to the west, the pass to the east, and the Scafell range to the north. The visitor approaching from the east cannot miss the fort, so commanding is its situation, but from the west it can be more easily missed as there is no signpost: it lies a short distance left (north) of the road, mid-way between the valley and the summit of Hardknott Pass (there is a small car-park to the left of the road just past the bath-house).

From the time of Camden, who wrote about it in 1607, Hardknott Castle has made a strong impression on its many visitors. One visitor in 1892 (R S Ferguson) called it 'an enchanted fortress in the air', and it needs little imagination to visualize the fort in its heyday. Excavations were carried out between 1890 and 1894, and again during consolidation work between 1958 and 1969. A fragmentary inscription, found in 1964 at the SE gate and now displayed in Tullie House Museum, Carlisle, revealed that the fort was built in the reign of Hadrian and was garrisoned by a Cohort of Dalmatians (from Croatia), probably the Fourth. Pottery finds show that the fort, which covers an area of just over 3 acres (1.3 ha), was given up *c.* 140 on the Antonine advance into Scotland and was never re-occupied. It therefore had an active service life of barely 20 years. There is no evidence for an attendant civilian settlement (*vicus*), not surprising in view of the brevity of the occupation and the inhospitable location. The Roman name of Hardknott is unknown: attempts to identify it as MEDIOBOGDVM, 'the fort in the middle of the bend' (of a river) – not in any case a particularly appropriate description of its location – now seem less likely since the discovery in 1995 that Ravenglass is not GLANNAVENTA, the adjacent fort to MEDIOBOGDVM in our lists (p. 421).

The track up to the fort passes the shell of the external bath-house, with cold, warm and hot rooms in a simple row. Hypocausts found here in the nineteenth century have now disappeared, and only the lowest courses of the brick-built stoke-hole survive. A circular room for intense dry heat (*laconicum*), with its own stoke-hole, is detached from the main building. You then arrive at the SE gate, which has twin passageways (a fragment of the central pier remains), but no guardrooms; indeed none of the gates at Hardknott has guardrooms. Of the other gates, two also have double-carriageways, but that on the NW has only a single portal; one pivot-hole for hanging one of the doors survives at the SW

gate. The entire circuit of the fort wall and all four corner
turrets stand to a superb height of up to 2.20 m (6 ft 7 in)
(Fig. 90), and the earth rampart behind also survives in part.
The corner turrets lack doorways, and the ground-level inside
must therefore have been reached by means of ladders from
the wall-walk above. A single ditch is identifiable for a short
stretch at the north corner, and it may have continued along
the NE side where it is lost to the bog; elsewhere the hardness

90   (top) *Hardknott, the fort wall*   *91*   (above) *Hardknott, the HQ building*

of the outcropping rock precluded ditch-digging. Note how
the curtain wall has been partly rebuilt with fallen stones: a
slate course commendably separates original masonry from
rebuilt work. Such practice is widespread in the restoration of
ancient monuments in Europe, but has been rarely tried in
more conservative Britain.

In the centre of the fort is the *principia* or headquarters
building (Fig. 91). It contains L-shaped store-rooms flanking
the courtyard, the cross-hall with a *tribunal* at one end, and
three administrative rooms at the back. The middle one would
have been the chapel of the standards. To the west (left) of the
HQ is the commandant's house, but only the north wing and
one wall of the east wing are visible now, and it appears
therefore never to have been finished; there are however traces
of further walls on the nineteenth-century excavators' plans,
and it is possible that more of the building survived then. To
the east is a pair of buttressed granaries, originally a single
building with a single partition-wall, but later re-roofed as two
when an extra dividing wall was built (that to the east). The
internal floor-supports and remains of loading-platforms will
also be noticed. The rest of the fort would have been filled up
largely with wooden barrack blocks, fragments of which were
located in the 1960s excavations. It is very likely that the
superstructure of the *principia* and *praetorium* was also of
timber, rather than of stone to roof height.

Finally, you should round off your visit to Hardknott by
walking up to the parade-ground, an artificially levelled area
completely free of stones, 190 m (200 yds) east of the NE
gate. Measuring some 140 m by 80 m (460 ft by 260 ft), it is
with that at Tomen-y-Mur in Wales (p. 341) the finest
example in Britain, indeed in the whole of the NW provinces
of the Roman Empire. Note in particular the careful
embanking on the SE side (nearest the road), and the sloping
mound on its NW side; the latter is up to 9 m (30 ft) high.
This is usually interpreted as the *tribunal*, the mound for the
commanding officer, but it seems unnecessarily massive, and
its sloping form is ill-suited to that purpose; an alternative
suggestion is to see it as a temple to the protecting goddesses
of the parade-ground, the *Matres Campestres*, and to identify
the *tribunal* with the much lesser mound in the middle of the
SE side. The engineering effort required to create such a level

platform for the parade-ground in this difficult terrain was enormous, and it has been estimated that at least 5,000 cubic metres (6,500 cubic yds) of soil and rock would have been needed to be removed in order to effect it.

After Hardknott, the fort at **Ambleside** (NY 373034) [AM; A] is a grave disappointment. It was excavated in 1913–15 and 1920, after which two gates and the central range of buildings of the stone fort were fenced off and kept open. The stonework was rarely well preserved, and as the tops of the walls have been turfed and not consolidated (with the exception of one building, the granary), one gets the impression that the site is very overgrown. The National Trust, who manage it, ought to be able to do better. The remains lie in Borrans Field, situated on the south side of the short A-road which links the A593 at Rothay Manor with the A591 at Waterhead Hotel, bypassing Ambleside. Borrans Field is easily missed as the signpost announcing it is low-level, designed for pedestrians. Be very careful about parking, impossible on this busy road: if coming from the south, turn first right past Borrans Field into a residential street, and if coming from the north, take the first turning on the left after Galava Gate Self Catering. The Roman name for the fort is generally reckoned to be GALAVA ('powerful stream').

You first come to the scanty remains of the double-passageway east gate. Then turn left past the site of the SE angle tower to the single-carriageway south gate, facing the lake: a pivot-hole in its threshold and a short length of fort wall to the west can be seen here. In the central range of buildings (stile), that on the left is the commandant's house. The *principia* in the centre is similar in plan to Hardknott's, with L-shaped rooms, *tribunal* in the cross-hall and three rear rooms. Here, however (unlike at Hardknott), the central room was later given an underground strong-room, approached by steps. On your right are the buttressed granaries with long internal sleeper walls to support the floors; some of the buttresses on the far granary have chamfered plinths. Ventilation holes are also visible in the two outermost long walls. A charred deposit of grain found during excavation in 1989 revealed that the granary contained good-quality spelt wheat, but that half the sample had been damaged by weevils.

Hints of an earlier granary were noted below. The visible stone fort was built in the second century, probably *c.* AD 120/30, and continued in use well into the fourth. Preceding it, on a slightly different site, was a clay and timber fort, now invisible. Its excavator claimed an Agricolan date for it, but no pottery is earlier than *c.* AD 90. Little is known of the *vicus* lying north and east of the fort; its main period of use seems to have been the second century.

The next fort to the east of Ambleside, Low Borrowbridge near Tebay (App. 1), lay on the main western trunk-road from Carlisle to Manchester. On this road is a Roman milestone at **Middleton** (SD 624859). It now stands near the top of a slope in the second field south of Middleton church, which is situated mid-way between Sedbergh and Kirkby Lonsdale on the west side of the A683. The Roman inscription on it reads simply MP LIII, 53 miles (from Carlisle), but its discoverer re-erected it 180 m (200 yds) from its find-spot and carved another inscription lower down on the stone. This records that the milestone was dug out of the ground and set up again by William Moore in the year 1836.

Nine miles (14.5 km) south of Middleton a road branched off the Carlisle to Manchester trunk-route along the valley of the Lune to **Lancaster** (SD 474619), the Roman name of which is unknown. The history of the succession of Roman forts which crowned the hill overlooking the river at the highest point of the modern town is very complex, and excavation has not been made easy by the presence of the castle and St Mary's church on top of the Roman site. A late first-century fort with turf rampart and timber buildings saw stone rebuilding, possibly of the defences, in the early second century (the evidence is a Trajanic inscription). This was then levelled and the site cleared for a new enlarged fort, not later than AD 160, with some stone and some timber buildings. It was outside the defences of this fort that a bath building was excavated in 1973–7, and subsequently consolidated and left exposed. The main feature here is a well preserved hypocausted room with solid stone *pilae*, some preserved to their full height, and the recesses in the walls through which the hot air was drawn upwards (Fig. 92). The furnace-flue which heated this room shows clear signs of rebuilding; it also heated the other room with a hypocaust here. A drain can also

92   Lancaster, Roman fort, bath building cut by later fort ditch

be seen to the left of the heated room. The bath structure dates
from *c.* 120/30 but was disused by *c.* 160; later it formed part
of an adjacent courtyard building (not visible), occupied *c.*
250–300.

The bath building was totally demolished in the fourth
century when the last of the forts on the site was built. This
had massive stone walls (and at least one tower) like some of
the Saxon Shore forts of southern England, and was clearly
designed, like the fort at Cardiff, to strengthen the late Roman
coastal defences. It does, however, belong to a rather later
period than both Cardiff and the Saxon Shore forts, as a
slightly worn coin of *c.* AD 326 in the construction layer
suggests a date of *c.* 330/50 for it. It is to this fort that the
large and rather shapeless chunk of masonry core known as
the Wery Wall belongs, standing about 2.50 m (8 ft) high
(under the trees, incorporated into the railings), which formed
part of a projecting semicircular tower on the NW side of this
late defensive enclosure. It was accompanied by a ditch which

slices through the earlier bath building, as the V-profile cut in the side walls of the main heated room vividly demonstrates (Fig. 92). To reach the site, park in front of the castle and go up the steps between it and Priory Church, and then turn right behind the church. As the path descends, a gap in the hedge leads you into the field on the right, at the far end of which is a railed-in enclosure with the remains. The footpath is also signposted from St George's Quay, off Bridge Lane. Finds are housed in the City Museum in Market Square (Monday–Saturday, 1000–1700).

The long catalogue of forts in the Pennines and the Lakes has now come to an end, and we can turn aside from the military to consider the civilian aspects of life in northern Britain under Roman rule. Nearly all the forts had villages (*vici*) clustered around them, but no stonework is visible at any of them today. On the larger scale, the *colonia* at York has been mentioned, and there were three other towns in Yorkshire, at Aldborough, Catterick (App. 1) and Brough-on-Humber (nothing visible). **Aldborough*** (SE 405661) [AM; April–September, daily, 1000–1300 and 1400–1800; October, daily, 1000–1300 and 1400–1700], a village near Boroughbridge off the B6265, was ISVRIVM, the tribal capital of the Brigantes. A small town grew up here at the end of the first century, probably on the site of a fort. An area of 55 acres (23 ha) was enclosed by an earth bank and ditch in the second half (and probably the last quarter) of the second century, and this defence was given a stone wall in the middle of the third century. A hundred years later towers were added but none is now visible.

Very little remains of the town wall in the section kept by English Heritage, which was excavated in the early nineteenth century. First a portion of the back of the wall is visible, originally obscured by an earth rampart-bank. Then comes an internal tower. Further on is a second stretch of wall, and part of another tower, which have been largely rebuilt. The position of the wall elsewhere is marked by a pair of concrete strips, and at the end of the path fragments of an angle tower are visible. To the left, under the trees and down the slope, is a quarry worked by the Romans.

Of the interior of ISVRIVM (named after the river Isura, now the Ure), little is known in detail, but the large number of polychrome mosaics recorded from the eighteenth century onwards reveal its wealth, especially during the fourth century. The two mosaics still visible, however, are datable to the second century; they are reached by a footpath from the town wall. One, found in 1848, is in perfect condition. It is an entirely geometric composition, featuring an eight-pointed star in the centre. The swastika and meander pattern in the surround is a rarity in Britain, otherwise paralleled only on a Lincolnshire mosaic (Winterton), datable on archaeological grounds to *c*. AD 180. The second mosaic, which is badly damaged, was discovered in 1832. Its main panel depicted a lion under a tree, but only the tree, a paw and part of the mane survive. A third mosaic, first uncovered in 1846 and consolidated in 1979, is known from a dining-room in either the same or an adjacent house; this floor, however, dates to *c*. AD 300. It was too fragmentary to leave on display, but part of the figured panel in the apse was clearly intended to represent the Muses, as the scene is labelled 'Helikon', their mountain home – unusually (for Britain) in Greek. This fragment is on display in the site Museum. Another illustration of classical learning at Aldborough is another, cruder pavement illustrating the myth of Romulus and Remus being suckled by the she-wolf (although the creature looks resolutely male), now in Leeds City Museum (Tuesday–Friday, 0930–1730; Saturday, 1000–1600).

Some of the smaller finds from Aldborough are displayed in the site Museum. Otherwise, a figure of Mercury in the church, and an earthwork which in all likelihood is the amphitheatre, a short distance outside the south angle of the defences (Studforth Hill), are all that can be seen of ISVRIVM outside the English Heritage enclosure. The latter can be reached by returning to the crossroads with the B6265 and turning left: the elliptical banks with central circular depression are clearly visible from the second field-gate on the left of the road.

The mosaics at Aldborough suggest a considerable degree of Romanization, and this is apparent also in the large number of villa-sites known in the East Riding of Yorkshire. At the height of their prosperity, in the fourth century, many seem to have been fitted with mosaic pavements, painted plaster and hypocausts. The most remarkable mosaics of all, uncovered in

1933, come from a villa at Rudston near Bridlington, and are
now displayed at the rear of the East Riding and Hull Museum
at **Hull*** (weekdays, 1000–1700; Sunday, 1330–1630). The
most famous is the fourth-century pavement with a central
roundel depicting Venus, the goddess of love and beauty, but
there is nothing beautiful about this wild creature (Fig. 93).
Her face is hard, her body lacks any sense of proportion, her
stance is ungainly. Wearing nothing but armlets, her hair
streaming behind her, she has dropped a mirror while a triton
holds up what is meant to represent a torch (although it looks
more like a primitive back-scratcher). Surrounding the central
roundel are the equally naive depictions of three (originally
four) shaggy huntsmen (probably meant to represent
venatores, the professional animal fighters in the
amphitheatre), and four crude animals, two of them labelled
with Latin names ('the lion [called] Fiery' ['Spear-bearer' is
less likely] and 'the bull [named] Homicide'). The level of
draughtsmanship suggests that the mosaicist had never seen a
leopard (the spotted animal) or a lion. Interestingly, the motif
above the bull, a crescent on a stick, is a symbol of one of the

93   Rudston, Roman villa, Venus mosaic (Hull and East Riding Museum)

professional amphitheatre troupes in what is now Tunisia, and suggests that these figures were taken from a copybook, ultimately derived (probably at several removes) from one circulating in north Africa. It is doubtful whether either mosaicist or patron realized its true significance. The border at the top of the mosaic features a bust of Mercury in the centre, identifiable from his distinctive wand (*caduceus*), but the mosaicist has clearly not understood what are meant to be wings emerging from his cap. The whole floor is a fascinating illustration of the artistic level to which a local craftsman (doubtless more at home with non-figural pavements) could sink in his attempt to copy ambitious classical subjects beyond his technical ability. It also says something about the taste of the villa owner who commissioned it, happy to show off his classical learning however ineptly depicted.

Another Rudston mosaic, a fragmentary but lively aquatic scene, is displayed on the wall facing the Venus pavement, while on the floor to the right is a geometric mosaic from Brantingham near Brough-on-Humber, set on a reconstructed hypocaust (note also the Spanish oil amphora in the niche at the back). Passing now to the right into the next room, you come to part of another Brantingham mosaic of *c*. AD 350, discovered in 1962. The central circle contains the bust of a personification wearing a mural crown (seen upside-down in this display), while water-nymphs recline in the surrounding lunettes. Note also the four amphorae depicted around the central panel (as water-carriers, they were appropriate attributes for nymphs): the first and third (counting from the left) are more competent than the other two, which were clearly the work of a less accomplished craftsman. At either end of the pavement were depicted four female busts with top-knots, of which one panel is displayed on the wall. The subject matter of this mosaic has been much debated. A recent attempt to see the Nine Muses here does not convince, because the headgear of the central figure and that of the other eight is clearly different, and the top-knot does not look like a misunderstood feather (the usual attribute of Muses). The mural crown of the central figure ultimately goes back to the personification of the Tyche ('Good Fortune') of the city of Antioch, a type created *c*. 300 BC, and the bust here must stand either for a city (Brough-on-Humber? Aldborough?), or for a region (Brigantia?), or (less likely) for a province (Britannia), or even for the entire inhabited world (Oikoumene). Identification of the other eight busts remains enigmatic. The interpretation of another female bust, also with a *nimbus* ('halo'), reconstructed from plaster fragments and also displayed here, is equally problematic; it came from the wall or ceiling decoration of the same room in the Brantingham villa.

The next room in the Museum houses a mosaic depicting a charioteer, with the four Seasons in the corners and birds in the oblong panels. It also comes from the Rudston villa, but this was found only in 1971. The chronology of both this and the Venus floor is controversial. The much more competent level of workmanship of the charioteer and Seasons indicates undoubtedly that they were laid at a different time in the fourth century from the Venus mosaic, but there was no archaeological evidence for its date. Stylistic considerations, often misleading when taken on their own, might suggest that the charioteer floor dates to *c.* 325/50, and the Venus mosaic to perhaps 350/75, as proposed by Dr David Smith their publisher; but archaeological evidence suggests that the bath building which yielded the Venus and aquatic mosaics went out of use *c.* 330. If so, there is a real possibility that the Venus floor (*c.* 300/25?) is in fact earlier than the charioteer mosaic (*c.* 325/50?), a demonstration of the dangers of basing chronological conclusions on grounds of style alone.

The bust of Spring (top right) is an especially delicate rendering which compares favourably even with examples from the more Romanized parts of Britain (e.g. Lullingstone, p. 88). Note too how the bottom left-hand corner has been repaired in antiquity, not exquisitely, but not disastrously either. Evident traces of burning, especially above the charioteer, suggest that the villa perished in a fire. Note also the threshold panel on the floor showing a pair of leaping leopards (with blue spots!), and the striking fresco decoration from the same villa on the walls.

Moving left past the Venus mosaic again, you enter another gallery, where parts of an astonishing, vast mosaic originally measuring 15 m by 6 m (50 ft by 20 ft) are displayed, found in a Roman villa at Horkstow in Lincolnshire in 1797. The panel in the centre on the floor is a much less skilled representation of a theme – Orpheus charming the beasts – which Cirencester mosaicists attempted with greater success (cf. pp. 180 and 197). Around the (lost) central Orpheus, the animals were here placed in framed segments, of which a bear and an elephant (the latter clearly not drawn from life – the mosaicist had never set eyes on one!) can be seen in the displayed portion. On the wall at the far end, originally part of the same floor, is a chariot race simplified to its bare essentials: even the turning posts (*metae*), customarily three in number, have been reduced to two. It would be wrong to think from this that the circus was a familiar part of the Romano-British scene, since this panel, unique in the province, is more likely to have been drawn from a copybook of stock themes than provide an accurate reflection of a regular pastime of the villa-owner. Similarly, it would be wrong to assume from the Rudston Venus mosaic that exotic animals such as leopards and lions were ever displayed and despatched in the local Romano-British amphitheatres.

Among other finds displayed in this gallery, note especially the theatre inscription from Brough-on-Humber, referring to the gift of a *proscaen*[*ium*] from M. Ulpius Ianuarius. It is assumed therefore that this tiny walled area on the banks of the Humber (enclosing only 13 acres [5.25 ha]) was the *civitas* capital of the Parisi, PETVARIA by name, and that it included among its civic amenities a theatre, however small. Judging from the inscription, which is on stone, the building itself must have at least partly been constructed of stone. Some, however, believe that the known walled enclosure at Brough is military (the theatre inscription was found re-used in a later building), and that a separate civilian town awaits discovery nearby.

Finally, on the first floor en route back to the entrance, note a geometric mosaic from Rudston contemporary with the Venus and aquatic floors. This one has only a geometric pattern, and at first sight it looks much more competent; but pause especially to note the rows of black stepped triangles which frame the central tableau. Those at the top and right-hand side are neat and regular, but those of the other two sides are larger and irregular, presumably the work of an apprentice. The whole of this remarkable ensemble of fourth-century mosaics from Humberside forms a striking testimony not only

of the popularity of this medium on the northern fringes of the
Roman world, but also of the classical tastes of the prosperous
villa-owners who commissioned them, and of the varying
levels of competence of the local Romano-British mosaic
craftsmen at their disposal.

A number of other villas are known in this area of NE
England, but none has left any substantial visible traces on the
ground, with the exception of that at **Beadlam*** (SE 634842),
where part of one building has been consolidated [AM; A].
The villa lies on the A170 1 mile (1.6 km) east of Helmsley
and 200 m west of the turning to Pockley, and is reached via
the first field-gate on the south side of the road west of this
turning (past the bridge, at the bottom of the slope); there is
no signpost. The field here had long been known to contain
'old buildings', but only excavations in 1966 revealed their
Roman date. In 1969 two wings of the villa were excavated
down to the latest levels, and further excavations took place
between 1972 and 1978.

The visible north building is in fine condition, 37 m (40
yds) long with walls standing several courses high. In its final,
visible form it is a simple example of the winged corridor
villa, of the type we have met with so frequently in the villas
of southern Britain; this developed from a rectangular
barn-like building at its core, to which other rooms around
were added in a secondary phase. The coins found are
predominantly fourth-century, and it seems certain that the
first stone building here dates to the first half of the fourth
century, with later modifications continuing until the late
fourth century. The first room you come to has recesses for
flue-tiles in the walls and a channelled hypocaust below the
floor, its cover-slabs still intact. The position of its stoke-hole
is indicated by the arch in the east wall, more clearly seen
from the adjacent room. Another channelled hypocaust, with
one box flue-tile still *in situ*, can be seen further east in the
wing; it was floored by a geometric mosaic (now in store) of
c. AD 350, which had partially collapsed into the hypocaust.
Its stoke-hole was in the west wall (traces of brick) but is now
completely destroyed. In the room beyond, a small built
fireplace, marked now by the slight recess, was inserted in the
middle of the west wall in a secondary period.

A badly robbed west block, which also had projecting rooms and a corridor along the front, as well as a small bath-suite at one end, and the east range, where the original rectangular building was later replaced by a single, shorter room with an apse, have both been backfilled. Geophysical work in 1992 found a further small square building to the south as well as an enclosure ditch round the villa. Plans to return the mosaic to the site and to erect a cover-building over the north range have been indefinitely postponed.

Most of the Yorkshire villas are concentrated in the East Riding around the Vale of York, but isolated examples have been found away to the north, near Piercebridge and Durham, and also to the west at Gargrave near Skipton. Elsewhere, agricultural communities continued to live in native farmsteads and villages, and numerous examples of these can be seen. Just two will be included here. They are quite well preserved, but consist of nothing more than a series of grass ridges, and so they are unlikely to prove of any great interest except to the specialist. At the pretty village of **Grassington** (SE 004651), there is a large area of ancient fields, covering more than 240 acres (100 ha), to be seen. Each cultivation-strip measures about 115 m by 22 m (375 ft by 75 ft), and is defined by well preserved banks. Both the size of the system and second- to fourth-century pottery make it certain that the fields were laid out and farmed in the Roman period. Some small scattered circular houses have been noted among the fields, but unlike Ewe Close (see below) no sign of nucleated settlement. Grassington lies about 7 miles (11 km) north of Skipton on the B6265. Turn off this road along Main Street and fork left along Chapel Street. Park immediately in the lay-by on the left. After 200 m a track goes off to the right near a telegraph-pole and two houses called Oak Bank and Wood View. Follow this as far as a wooden gate and stile, immediately after the track has made a sharp bend to their right. The first gate in the wall on the right of the track beyond this point leads into the field where the ancient banks lie.

The other native site is at **Ewe Close** (NY 610135) in Cumbria. It is near the village of Crosby Ravensworth, which is signposted from the B6260 (Appleby–Tebay). Turn right by the telephone booth in Crosby (signposted 'Shap $3\frac{1}{2}$') and immediately left by the end house. Take the left-hand track of

the three at the fork (metal gate, to the left of that marked
'Dale Banks'), and then follow this for 1½ miles (2.4 km),
keeping straight wherever possible, through another metal
gate, until the track peters out in a field. At this point you will
notice a broad grass terrace running away from you slightly to
the left, up to the skyline. This is the main west-coast Roman
trunk-road, ancient forerunner of the M6, in its stretch
between the forts at Low Borrowbridge (App. 1) near Tebay
to the south, and Brougham near Penrith (p. 412) to the north.
As a point of orientation, make for the three large boulders set
close together which you will see ahead of you, just to the left
of the line of the Roman road. At the brow of the hill you pass
(D on Fig. 94) the native settlement of Ewe Close. A lot of
ridges and banks marking farmyard enclosures and
stockyards, and a few hut-circles (A) indicating dwellings, are
all that can be made out of these confusing and complicated
earthworks. The banks conceal stone walls, and some
stonework is visible in places emerging from the grass. The
well (B) is marked by a thick patch of thistles. If all the
structures are contemporary, there were clearly several
farmsteads grouped together here in a small agricultural
village of a type which was commonplace in the Romano-
British countryside.

In the closing years of the Roman occupation, when the

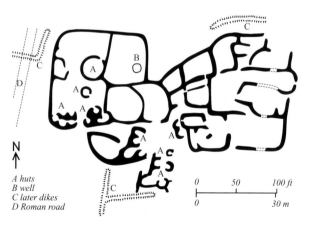

94   Ewe Close, native settlement, plan of earthworks

province of Britain was being threatened both by barbarian incursions from the north and by Saxon pirates from across the North Sea, a series of signal towers was built along the Yorkshire coast. Five of them have been found, from Huntcliff in the north to Filey in the south, and more must undoubtedly have existed (perhaps as far north as Hawthorn and Hartlepool, and extending southwards to Beacon Hill on Flamborough Head). All were built to a highly standardized pattern – a central tower 15 m (50 ft) square with foundations generally 2.5 m (8 ft) wide, implying a multi-storey structure perhaps some 20 m (65 ft) high; a surrounding wall with projecting corner towers; and an outer ditch where necessary. They were designed to give early warning of impending naval raids, and the news was then transferred by beacon-fire and messenger to military units stationed at Malton and beyond, which then tried to co-ordinate resistance to the attack. Excavation has shown that they had a short life, of only 20 years or so. Once thought to be the work of Count Theodosius *c.* AD 370, after the 'great barbarian conspiracy' of 367, it now seems more likely on coin evidence that they were built by the usurper Magnus Maximus: he defeated the Picts in AD 382, and the next year made a bid for the imperial purple, stripping troops from Britain when he invaded Italy in 387.

There is very little to see at any of these sites today. At Huntcliff (NZ 687219), a plaque marking the location of the site and a probable fragment of its defensive ditch can be seen on the cliff path, the Cleveland Way, 2 miles (3 km) east of Saltburn. The one at Ravenscar (NZ 981018) underlies the Raven Hall Hotel, the building of which in 1774 yielded one of the latest official inscriptions from Roman Britain, its letters very untidily carved. Now in Whitby Museum, it records that 'Justinianus, commander, and Vindicianus, controller, built this tower and fort from the ground up'. The signal station at Filey (TA 125817), dramatically located on the highest part of the Carr Naze, was excavated in 1857 when five stone bases in the central tower, to hold stout timbers supporting the upper floors, were removed to Crescent Gardens in the town where they can still be seen; the central block bears a relief sculpture of two animals. An accurate plan of the signal station was recovered in 1923. Re-excavation in 1993–4 (now backfilled) revealed that in the intervening

70 years virtually all the Roman structure had sadly been lost to erosion.

Today, only at the **Scarborough** example (TA 052892) [AM; April–September, daily, 1000–1800 (August 0930–1900); October, daily, 1000–1700; November–March, Wednesday–Sunday, 1000–1600] can the plan of one of these signal-towers be made out. It lies on the edge of the cliff east of the castle, but the site was later occupied by a series of medieval chapels and no Roman masonry is now exposed. The outline of the signal station has, however, been marked out in concrete, and the surrounding ditch has been dug out on the south and partly on the west. The east side of the remains has slipped into the sea.

This chain of signal stations represents the last desperate attempt in the late fourth century to maintain peace and security in Roman Britain. Then came the end, at some of them dramatically. At Goldsborough (App. 1), the skeleton of a short man lay face down across a hearth fire. His hand was twisted behind him, perhaps because he had been stabbed in the back. Another man lay at his feet, sprawled on top of the skeleton of a powerful dog. The days of Roman rule in Britain were numbered.

Chapter 8

Hadrian's Wall

Hadrian's Wall cannot fail to stir the imagination. It has fascinated countless people, scholars and ordinary visitors alike, from the time of Gildas (who died in AD 570) and Bede (in AD 735) to the present day. The remains are, in parts, strikingly well preserved, and they are situated amid some of the most spectacular scenery in the British Isles. The deepest impression on a visitor to the Wall, however, is made by the sheer magnitude of the undertaking, which expresses so well an essential aspect of Roman civilization: here was a regime that not only had the confidence to make the bold decision of building a wall from sea to sea, but also had the vast resources of manpower and money, as well as the tremendous organizational ability, that were required to build it and manage it for close on 300 years. From the engineering point of view especially, the achievement is staggering: over 770,000 cubic metres of stone needed to be quarried, carried to the spot and set in place, and it has been estimated that transport alone would have involved for each of the approximately seven years of its construction an average of 900 carts and their drivers, in addition to 1,800 oxen and more than twice that number of horses and mules. The great Wall of Hadrian is not just the most exciting relic of the Roman occupation of Britain; it is perhaps the largest and most remarkable single building programme ever undertaken in these islands at any time.

Hadrian's barrier, however, is much more than a single wall running across the Tyne-Solway isthmus: it is an immensely complicated group of works, and the problem of their precise relation, function and date has only become reasonably clear, through careful excavation, over the past 75 years. Some background information is therefore essential to a proper understanding and enjoyment of its remains.

About AD 105, the last group of forts held in southern Scotland was finally given up and the frontier was fixed along the 'Stanegate', the name by which the Roman road from Carlisle to Corbridge was later known. Once considered the work of Agricola, it now looks much more likely that it should be dated to c. 90/105, either late in Domitian's reign

or early in Trajan's. Forts were built along it in the period
c. 90–115, and the road was probably in time extended
westwards and eastwards, although less is known about these
parts than about its central sector. In 118, soon after Hadrian
became emperor on the death of Trajan, there was a rebellion
in Britain and the 'Britons could no longer be held under
control'. We have no details beyond these words of Hadrian's
biographer, but there was apparently a frank reference to the

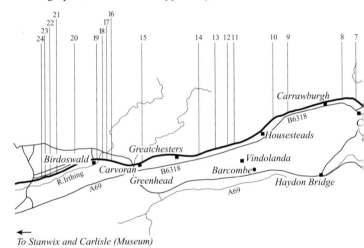

To Stanwix and Carlisle (Museum)

trouble on a victory monument near the mouth of the Tyne (its
precise position and appearance are unknown), celebrating the
construction of Hadrian's Wall: its inscription admitted that
'the barbarians had been dispersed and the province
recovered'. The tribes involved were surely the Brigantes of
northern England and probably also the Selgovae and
Novantae of southern Scotland. In 122, with order restored,
the emperor came to Britain to assess the situation for himself.
As a consequence of this famous visit, Hadrian's Wall was
constructed: in the absence of any suitable natural frontier
(once the decision had been taken not to overrun the whole
island), an artificial one had to be created.

The original plan was relatively uncomplicated. The
existing Stanegate forts were to hold the main fighting

sible *forts* only are marked
the map with a square.

1 Byker
2 Denton Hall
3 Heddon-on-the-Wall
4 Planetrees
5 Brunton
6 Chesters Bridge Abutment
7 Black Carts
8 Limestone Corner
9 Coesike
10 Sewingshields Crags
11 Highshield Crags
12 Peel Crag

13 Winshields
14 Cawfields
15 Walltown
16 Poltross Burn
17 Gilsland
18 Willowford
19 Harrow's Scar
20 High House
21 Piper Sike
22 Leahill
23 Banks East
24 Hare Hill

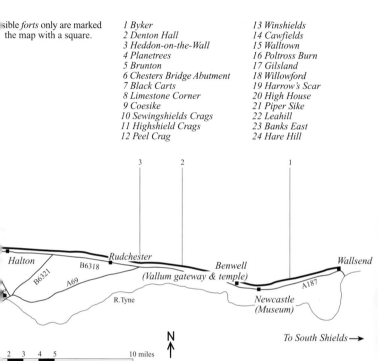

garrison, but the actual frontier was to be marked by a ditch
and a wall on the commanding ground a few miles to the
north. The **Ditch**, on average about 8.25 m (27 ft) wide and
2.75 m (9 ft) deep, accompanies the Wall on its north side,
except where cliffs make it unnecessary. The **Wall** was to run
from Newcastle upon Tyne to Bowness on the Solway. From
Newcastle to the river Irthing, over half its length, it was to be
built of stone, 3 m (10 ft) thick and perhaps 6.50 m (21 ft)
high, including the parapet. Evidence is mounting to suggest
that the wall on both sides was rendered in smooth white
mortar, scored with lines (probably painted red) to give the
impression that the Wall was made of 'large-block' masonry;

if so, the neat coursed blocks so familiar today would have been invisible when the Wall was first completed. West of the river Irthing, where limestone was difficult to obtain, the Wall was to be of turf, 6 m (20 ft) wide at base and probably about 5 m (17 ft) high, including a timber breastwork.

At intervals of one Roman mile (1,482 m or 1,620 yds) fortlets, known as **milecastles**, were constructed, each having two gateways (one through the Wall) and some barrack accommodation: milecastle 48 (Poltross Burn) is unusual in having a full complement of two stone barracks, perhaps for 32 men, but many of the others which have been excavated had accommodation, it seems, for half that number or less. These milecastles were built of timber west of the Irthing, of stone elsewhere. Between each were two **turrets**, everywhere built of stone and about 4.25 m (14 ft) square internally. The ground floor often contains hearths and was no doubt used as a mess-room and resting place for soldiers off-duty. Some have a low stone foundation, probably best interpreted as a base for a wooden staircase (rather than ladders). The top of the turret is often thought of as flat with a crenellated parapet, as in the Vindolanda reconstruction (p. 502), but there is evidence that some turrets at least had tiled roofs, in which case there was presumably a wooden observation platform erected around the top below roof-level, of the type indicated on Trajan's Column in Rome and as rebuilt in several places on the German frontier. Each turret, estimated at about 12.20 m (40 ft) high, was used primarily for watching enemy movements north of the Wall, and signalling back to the Stanegate if the trouble was more than the local milecastles could cope with. *Ballista* bolts and catapult-balls are known from two or three turrets, raising the possibility that artillery was mounted in at least some of them. Milecastles, which also had a tower the same height as the turrets over their north gate (but probably not their south gates), are numbered from the east, and the same number, followed by *a* or *b*, is given successively to the two turrets to the west of each milecastle.

Inscriptions make clear that the Wall and its associated turrets and milecastles were built by detachments from all three of the British legions. Differing construction styles, especially in the gateways of milecastles, have been claimed as the work of identifiably separate legions, but fresh evidence has questioned such attributions. The construction parties were divided up into various groups, some working on the foundation of the Wall, some on the turrets and milecastles, others on the Wall superstructure, and others, perhaps not legionaries, on digging the Ditch.

Some time after work had started, probably in AD 124, an important alteration was made to the original scheme. This was the decision to move the main fighting force forward from the Stanegate on to the Wall itself, where it was housed in a number of **forts**, originally 12 in number (including an already existing fort at Newcastle), but eventually 16. At the same time, or shortly afterwards, other decisions were taken: to narrow the Wall from 3 m (10 ft) to 2.45 m (8 ft), to extend the Wall from Newcastle eastwards to Wallsend, and to replace the Turf Wall in stone for a stretch of 5 miles (8 km) west of the Irthing (as far as the natural geological fault, after which limestone is absent). Up to this time, many of the turrets and a few of the milecastles had been built to the broad gauge, in the expectation that the forthcoming curtain wall would be of the same width. But the building of the actual curtain wall was lagging far behind: parts of it had been built west of Newcastle (such as the Denton Hall and Heddon-on-the-Wall stretches: pp. 470 and 471 below), and work was also in hand in the sector east of the river Irthing in Cumbria and in a number of other places. All this results in a very complicated sequence, which, grossly over-simplified, might be summarized as: (i) from Wallsend to Newcastle, the Wall is narrow (8 ft [2.4 m]) on a narrow foundation; (ii) from Newcastle to a point approaching the North Tyne, the Wall is broad (10 ft [3 m]) on a broad foundation, although there are exceptions, probably the result of later rebuilding; (iii) from the North Tyne to the Irthing the Wall is narrow on a foundation sometimes narrow, sometimes broad; (iv) for 5 miles (8 km) west of the Irthing the Wall is narrow on a narrow foundation; (v) for the rest of its course the Turf Wall was not rebuilt in stone until later, certainly not before 160 and possibly not until c. 200; it had an 'intermediate' width of 2.75 m (9 ft).

Very soon after the forts had been built, or as soon as they had been planned, an earthwork known as the **Vallum** was constructed a short distance south of the Wall. It consisted of a flat-bottomed ditch, about 6 m (20 ft) wide at the top and 2.45 m (8 ft) wide at the bottom, and some 3 m (10 ft) deep; on either side was a berm of 9 m (30 ft) flanked by two turf mounds 6 m (20 ft) wide and originally 1.80 m (6 ft) high. The whole Vallum was thus about 37 m (120 ft) across. This earthwork in some ways is the most remarkable of all the components of Hadrian's frontier. It is a formidable obstacle, evidently designed not to be crossed, but its form, and in particular its flat-bottomed ditch, shows that it is not a proper military defence. Its purpose was probably to delineate the area under strict military control, above all to prevent civilians or other unauthorized persons from wandering too close to the military zone: this they were allowed to enter only through the large Vallum gateways opposite every fort. Nevertheless the earthwork, quite without parallel on other Roman frontiers, seems to be excessively elaborate for such a purpose, and it bears all the eccentric hallmarks of being an original creation of none other than that erratic genius, Hadrian himself. And when the emperor ordered, nobody dared disobey.

These two additions of forts and Vallum to the original scheme give us some indication of the hostility with which the whole idea of a frontier-wall was received by the local peoples. Hadrian's biographer says that the Wall divided the Romans from the barbarians, but it is more exact to say that its purpose was to separate the Brigantes of northern England from the tribes of southern Scotland, to prevent collusion between them, and so, it was hoped, to lessen the scale of any future uprising. The placing of the striking force on the Wall-line shows that pressure from the north needed to be dealt with more speedily and effectively than was possible when the main body of troops was on the Stanegate; and the building of the Vallum shows that the tribesmen behind the Wall were sufficiently restless to warrant an additional deterrent to their contacting friends in the north.

The main purpose of the Wall, then, was to provide a fixed frontier to the Roman province of Britain, and to separate two sets of potential trouble-makers. It also served as a potent propaganda symbol of imperial power, its newly white-washed rendering making a striking gash across the landscape. No doubt it was this frontier that the second-century writer, Aelius Aristides, was thinking of when he wrote that it 'gleamed with more brilliance than bronze'. These were its political roles. In military terms, it acted as a superb cover for movements against an enemy unable to predict from which point troops might emerge. The Wall itself was never meant to be used as a fighting-platform; indeed some even think there was no patrol-walk along the top (no other frontier has one), but the Wall's width would in that case have been unjustifiable (the Raetian wall in Germany, for example, is a mere 1.25 m [4 ft] wide). Not only have coping stones been found occasionally on stretches of Wall not directly associated with turrets or milecastles, but Roman bronze 'souvenirs' of the Wall, such as the Rudge cup and the Amiens skillet, which name some of the forts along it, also show the Wall with crenellations (to argue that only the forts had crenellations and that the wall-walk did not seems unduly perverse). The garrison, probably some 11,000 when all posts were fully manned, was provided by auxiliary units of the Roman army; legionaries built the Wall but never patrolled it, except as a temporary measure.

A few words must also be said about the history of Hadrian's Wall. It was begun in 122 (120 according to an alternative suggestion) under the supervision of the governor Aulus Platorius Nepos, then a close friend of Hadrian. Most of it was finished by about 128. In 139–40, when the Antonine Wall was built, Hadrian's Wall was evacuated. The mounds of the Vallum were breached in places and its ditch filled in. Milecastle gates were removed. The forts were given caretaker garrisons, possibly skeleton detachments of legionaries. Twenty years later, however, probably in 161/2, the Antonine Wall was abandoned and Hadrian's Wall was fully recommissioned: the milecastle gates were re-hung and the Vallum was restored in most places to its former state. It was now that a continuous road running behind the frontier, the Military Way, was built, and, as noted above, it was either at this time, or else about 200, that the rest of the Turf Wall was rebuilt in stone. At least that is the current orthodoxy, but it is curious, indeed inexplicable, that the Military Way did not form part of the original Hadrianic frontier, in view of its obvious practical convenience.

More controversial is the date of the first destruction of Hadrian's frontier. The historian Dio records that in 180 the

British tribes crossed 'the Wall' and inflicted much damage. This must refer to Hadrian's Wall rather than a barrier out of commission, and archaeological evidence points to destruction at this date at Corbridge and at two of its neighbours on the Wall, Rudchester and Halton: if so, it looks as though the tribes burst through the centre and left the rest of the Wall unharmed. The great destruction, however, has often been taken to be one of 196–7, when Clodius Albinus stripped Britain of its troops in a bid to become emperor, which failed near Lyon in 197. Virius Lupus, sent by Severus to recover the province, had to buy off the Maeatae of southern Scotland, and this has been taken to mean that they had already destroyed the Wall and its works. If so, it is very odd that the Wall lay in ruins for ten years or more, for it was not until the governorship of Alfenus Senecio (205–8) that restoration was begun. It is, however, much more likely that the Wall was not destroyed in the troubles of 196–7, and that the work of c. 205–8 was merely a massive refurbishment of the ageing frontier. In this Severan reconstruction, some of the turrets were demolished, and others not reoccupied (only a quarter of the 45 turrets so far examined show evidence for later use, and some had been disused from about the 170s or 180s); the gateways of the milecastles were narrowed, and the Vallum was not restored, for some of the forts' civilian suburbs were allowed to grow over its filled-in course.

The expeditions of Severus to Scotland in 209–11 gave peace to the Hadrianic frontier for a long time. Apathy set in and some of the forts were certainly in a state of neglect and disrepair by the end of the third century. A thorough rebuilding and reorganization was set in motion by Constantius, who came to Britain in 296 to regain the province from the usurper Allectus. While units were no doubt withdrawn from the Wall to serve in Allectus' army, it is far from certain that the Wall was destroyed at this time: signs of burning may be due to demolition-work by army construction-gangs rather than to enemy action. Similarly, the extensive repairs carried out by Theodosius in 369–70 may have been necessitated by frontier neglect and decay rather than enemy destruction in the so-called 'barbarian conspiracy' of 367–8. Obviously the amount of reconstruction necessary on each occasion (Severan, Constantian, Theodosian) must

have varied, but the Wall of Hadrian was certainly rebuilt in
places from its foundations, as will be seen. Destruction in
383, when another pretender, Magnus Maximus, tried for the
throne, is equally uncertain. Some forts were certainly
occupied after this date, and by now soldiers had their
families with them inside the protection of the walls: the
mostly undefended *vici* outside were abandoned. By 400 the
final garrison had gone, and the work of the Wall was
finished. The slow process of decay and destruction began,
only to be halted in the twentieth century.

Very substantial remains of Hadrian's great frontier still
survive, and I can hope to do no more than indicate here
which are the best preserved or most instructive portions. For
those who wish for more, the first two works listed in the
Bibliography for this chapter are indispensable; in particular,
the OS *Map of Hadrian's Wall* will be found most useful even
for the briefest of visits. A taste of the Wall can be had in a
day (Chesters, Vindolanda and Housesteads should be seen),
and a fair sample can be taken in three days (visit all sites
with a double asterisk). All the places mentioned below can
be visited, with the aid of a car, in six to seven days.

Hadrian's Wall itself ran from Wallsend to Bowness, a
distance of $73\frac{1}{2}$ miles (80 Roman miles [117 km]), but its
flanks also needed protection. On the west, the system of
milefortlets and towers continued for another 40 miles
(64 km) down the Cumbrian coast, the sea here probably
providing a sufficient barrier, although a continuous palisade
as on the Hadrianic German frontier is not impossible (see
p. 417 for the only visible milefortlet). On the east, the
extension of the Wall to Wallsend was made to prevent an
enemy slipping across the river, and there may have been one
or more posts on the south bank between Wallsend and the
Tyne mouth. The latter was guarded by a fort at South
Shields, and this remarkable site provides an essential starting
point for a visit to Hadrian's Wall.

Part of the fort at **South Shields**** (NZ 365679), found in
the late nineteenth century, has long been visible, but recent
work, first in the late 1960s and then continuously since 1978,
has added enormously to our knowledge of the site. Thanks to
the enlightened attitude of Tyne and Wear County Council,

much of the fort is now consolidated and exposed, and parts of it reconstructed (Easter–September, Monday–Saturday, 1000–1730, Sunday, 1300–1700; October–Easter, Monday–Saturday, 1000–1600). It is important to remember, however, that a good deal of what is visible at South Shields is not typical of a Roman fort. The stone second-century fort covering 3.9 acres (1.5 ha) was indeed regular, but in the early third century it was enlarged to enclose 5 acres (2.03 ha), and much of the area inside its walls was converted into a store-base for Severus' campaigns in Scotland: initially, probably *c.* 205/8, the northern half of the fort, separated from the rest by an internal stone partition-wall, was almost entirely taken up with 14 granaries, and there were at least two more in the southern part. A year or two later, *c.* 210, the number of granaries was increased still further; with an additional one converted *c.* 220/25, the final tally was a remarkable 24 (a phenomenon unique in the Roman Empire), of which parts of 11 are currently visible. Only *c.* 290/300 did some semblance of normality return, when the *principia* was restored to the central range and many of the granaries were given up or converted into barracks.

The Roman name of South Shields was ARBEIA, possibly deriving from the Aramaic word for 'Arabs' (Arbaya) used in Mesopotamia: if so, it is possible that there was a specialist unit stationed here at the start in the second century, accustomed to dealing with the dangerous shoals of the river Tyne, and not only in the fourth century, when a *numerus barcariorum Tigrisiensium*, a detachment of 'Tigris boatmen', is specifically documented as its garrison. Otherwise one has to assume, if this etymology is correct, that the name Arbeia was only used in the late Roman period, replacing some earlier appellation which fell into disuse; and since the third-century garrison was not a specialist eastern unit but a cohort of Gauls, this latter alternative is perhaps preferable.

The fort, on a prominent plateau overlooking the Tyne, is well signposted from the southern approaches to South Shields with 'Roman helmet' indicators, until the very last moment when you enter the main shopping street after turning right at a roundabout (Asda store). Here you should take the first turning on the left straight up to the top of the hill: the entrance to the site lies on your right.

The site Museum should be visited first (1 on Fig. 95). The room on the right has some splendidly displayed small finds: note especially, on the left, two replicas, one of a helmet cheek-guard decorated with the figure of one of the Dioscuri (Castor or Pollux), and the other of an elaborate shield-boss belonging to a soldier of the 8th Legion Augusta, a detachment of which seems to have been sent to Britain in response to a military emergency in the late second century. Both pieces, the originals of which are in the Newcastle Museum of Antiquities and the British Museum respectively, come from the river Tyne just north of the fort, probably from a shipwreck of that date. In the centre of this room, apart from the model of the third-century *principia*, is displayed the very rare find of a ring-mail shirt, found in a barrack in the SE corner of the fort in 1997, where it had been burnt in a fire *c.* AD 300. Apart from the less well preserved example at Wallsend (p. 458), and a now lost find from Housesteads, these are the only mail shirts to have survived from Roman Britain. While extremely durable when finished, they were time-consuming to make: it has been estimated that a shirt of 54,000 rings would take 215 man-days to manufacture.

The room on the left contains the principal inscriptions and other stones from the site, three of which are especially important. That near the entrance gives the name of the fort's third-century garrison, the Fifth Cohort of Gauls, who dedicated an aqueduct in AD 222; while the pair of fine tombstones at the far end belongs to the later second century. That on the right commemorates Regina, an ex-slave who gives her origin as CATVALLAVNA, that is, a member of the Catuvellauni tribe whose capital was at Verulamium (St Albans). She became the wife of her former master Barates, who hailed from Palmyra in Syria, and by chance part of his tombstone has also survived (it is on display in the Corbridge Museum). The wicker chair in which Regina sits and the wool-basket on her left give us a rare glimpse of the kind of furniture in use in Roman Britain. Even better preserved is the tombstone of Victor, who came from Mauretania (in what is now Morocco). He is shown reclining on a couch at his dinner, while a tiny slave holds up a wine jar filled from the bowl on the floor. A stylized tree is engraved behind Victor. Both tombstones, recording an African and the wife of a

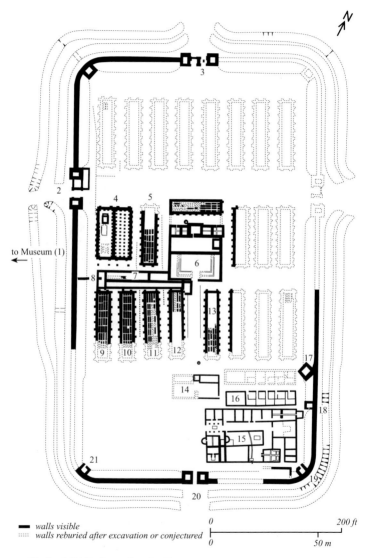

—— walls visible
∷∷∷ walls reburied after excavation or conjectured

95   South Shields, Roman fort, site plan

Syrian, reflect the cosmopolitanism of life on the northern frontier (as indeed in many other parts of Britain). Furthermore, stylistic comparisons suggest not only that both tombstones were carved by the same man but that he himself also came from Palmyra, a suggestion further reinforced by the assured use of Aramaic at the foot of Regina's tombstone.

On leaving the Museum cross the scanty remains of the fort wall and turn left to the splendid west gate, reconstructed in 1986 (2). This and the one at Manchester (p. 390), built in 1984, are the only examples so far in Britain of reconstructed fort-gateways in stone, an exercise first tried in Germany over a century ago. The decision to reconstruct on the same site as the original gateway rather than elsewhere was controversial, but the loss was minimal (only footings survived, and they of course were comprehensively recorded before destruction), by comparison with the very considerable gain of being able to visualize the approximate original appearance of such structures. Many details of the superstructure, as well as its exact height (in my view it has been rebuilt higher than the original would have been), are of course guesswork. In particular it is by no means certain that gate-towers (or interval towers for that matter) were roofed rather than provided with open flat tops and crenellation (cf. Fig. 75, p. 355). The Romans probably used both types of construction, perhaps in different regions and at different times, but the archaeological evidence for superstructure is generally too exiguous for clear conclusions to emerge. The gate contains supplementary Museum displays, including a model of the fort at the moment of its enlargement to form a stores-base (the original south wall is shown in the process of demolition), and there is an imaginative simulation of a quartermaster's stores on the second floor of the north tower. There is a fine view of the fort from here. An unusual item on the floor below is an arch headstone painted in white lime to show imaginary voussoirs: it is a reminder that some of the stonework which we see today bare and unadorned would have been decorated, however simply, in antiquity.

From the west gate you can follow what remains of the stone rampart round past the NW angle-tower to the north gate (3), the fort's principal gate until the radical transformations of the third century. It too had twin portals and guard-chambers, but the west passageway was subsequently blocked with a wall still partly in position, and the other arch, apparently in danger of collapse, had to be propped up with the massive pier of blocks visible in the middle of the eastern portal. The squared masonry of the gate-towers and the central pier is very fine, and part of the iron collar for hanging one of the gates even survives in the west portal. The drains below both carriageways will also be noted: note how the vertical stone with the hole in it in the eastern passageway (for a drain) would have been below the late Roman road surface at a higher level, which has been removed during excavation.

Until recently the first stone fort at South Shields was reckoned to be of Hadrianic date, but it is now known that the visible stone defences and gates, and the first stone headquarters building, are no earlier than the Antonine period in the middle of the second century. Fragmentary traces of a turf and timber fort of two periods have been detected below, dating to c. 120/60. A Hadrianic fort at South Shields was a vital prerequisite for securing the eastern flank of Hadrian's Wall; the fact that it was built in turf and timber when the forts on the Wall-line c. 124 were in stone probably indicates that its building pre-dates this decision, perhaps c. 120 rather than later.

Some of the structures in the northern third of the fort were uncovered in 1966–7 (it was occupied entirely by granaries for much of the third century), but they now lie under the grass. Retrace your steps past the reconstructed gate and turn left on to the street which is level with the Museum exit. The first building on your left is a double granary which belongs to the original stone fort of the mid-second century (4). In the fourth century the floor of one of the granaries was removed and two tile-kilns were inserted. One, in excellent condition, was re-excavated in 1980 in the hope that it could be consolidated, but it was found to be too fragile to withstand winter frosts and has been reburied under a protective earth mound (a photograph displayed on site shows its excavated state). The plan of the other has been marked out in modern materials. The bases of the portico designed to give shelter during delivery of supplies are visible in front of the granary. The next building is also a granary (5), one of many provided

when the fort became a supply-base for the emperor Severus'
northern campaigns: this one was added in the second of the
two stages of this conversion, *c.* 210. In contrast to the
Antonine granary, which had its floors supported on piers, the
third-century ones, here and elsewhere at South Shields, use
low longitudinal 'sleeper' walls to support the floors.

After it comes the headquarters building (*principia*), a
structure with a long and complicated history elucidated
during re-excavation in 1984–5 (6). You first enter the
courtyard of the fourth-century headquarters building of
c. AD 290/300: the two columns belong to the colonnade
which once flanked it, and part of its gutter can also be seen
(Fig. 96). This building replaced a partly demolished second-
century *principia* which faced in the opposite direction: its
rear range of five rooms, with buttresses along the back wall,
are marked out in pebbles in front of you. Beyond this lies the
cross-hall, which remained in the same position throughout
the life of the building. The *tribunal* of such halls, however,

96   *South Shields, Roman fort,* principia *and reconstructed west gate*

always lies on the right of anyone entering from the courtyard, and so when the HQ was turned round a new *tribunal* had to be built. That on your right (confusingly indicated in identical-type pebbles to those used for the second-century rear range) belongs to the *principia* of *c.* 300, while that on your left is the masonry of the second-century *tribunal*. Beyond lies the massive strong-room, added *c.* 205/8 when the *principia* was first turned round to face in the opposite direction, and retained in the further alterations of *c.* 290/300. It has double-thickness walls of cramponed blocks (some re-used from the second-century fort), and a sump in the bottom to keep it dry. Its size, much bigger than in a normal auxiliary fort, emphasizes the continued importance of South Shields even after the conclusion of Severus' campaigns: pay-chests for the garrison of more than one fort were surely stored here, if only on a short-term basis before distribution to their respective HQs. The administrative rooms on either side were given hypocausts (of the channelled variety) in the fourth century; traces are visible. Beyond the back wall of the third/fourth-century *principia* lies a well. This was in the courtyard of the second-century HQ but remained in use even after the building switched direction. Some of the square bases which supported the colonnade flanking this early courtyard can be detected beyond, on the north and east sides, as well as the gutters which flanked the entrance to the second-century *principia*. When it was replaced *c.* 205/8 by a fresh HQ facing in the opposite direction, a new granary was built in the area of the courtyard of the second-century *principia*, using the latter's walls on three sides and having a new (buttressed) wall only on the fourth. Its plan has been marked out in pebbles, and part of the sleeper walls and a reconstituted fragment of floor (which originally, of course, extended the full length of the granary) are also visible. Later still, *c.* 220/5, yet another granary was inserted into the shell of the cross-hall (which was left standing), although no walls belonging to the granary phase are indicated on the ground there now. The total requisition of the *principia* at this date by granaries raises the question of where the nerve-centre of the mid- and late third-century fort was, to which an answer will be provided presently.

Now retrace your steps to the double granary, and look at

the buildings on the other side of the street you have been following. Marked out here in pebbles is the plan of a building of uncertain function (7), as it is unique in a military setting anywhere in the Roman Empire. In a civilian context it would be taken as a version of a 'winged corridor' villa – a series of rooms divided by timber partitions, with a corridor along the front, and projecting wings at either end to the south (partly obscured under the later granaries). First investigated in 1949 and completely excavated in 1998, it predates the Antonine stone fort, and was therefore apparently a lone stone building inside the otherwise turf and timber forts of *c*. 120/60, an anomaly which future work may be able to elucidate; current thinking sees it as sole survivor of an abortive Hadrianic stone fort. There was a hearth in each of the rooms (six have been marked out). The stone wall partly visible over its west end, and continuing up to the fort wall (8), is part of the short-lived dividing wall of *c*. 205/8, when the newly-built granaries in the back half of the fort to the north were partitioned off from the rest of the fort's buildings.

As you walk again along the *via principalis*, five further granaries (and part of a sixth under what is currently [2001] the spoilheap) are visible to your right. The first two (9 and 10) belong to Severus' stores-base of 205/8, and the others (11–13) were added in the additional major alterations of *c*. 210, when (as noted above), the number of granaries in the fort was increased still further from 18 to 23. The date of these additional changes, following so soon after the first, was suggested by the find of six lead sealings with busts of the emperors Severus, Caracalla and Geta, datable to 198/210, which were found in 2000 in construction levels between the third and fourth granaries here. Fragments of the Antonine barracks which preceded the granaries (and which were laid out east-west) have also been consolidated and can be seen below, especially under the second and third granaries (10 and 11). Part of the flagged floor of the fourth granary (12) survives *in situ*. When the fort returned to something approaching normality *c*. AD 300, these granaries were divided up by internal partition walls to provide barrack accommodation, but this phase has now been entirely removed (its walls were very fragmentary) to expose the third-century granaries.

Now turn right after the fourth granary (12) to the southern part of the fort. The total conversion of the Severan *principia* to granary use *c.* 220/5, mentioned above, entailed the building of a totally new *principia* in the southern part of the fort (14). The new *principia* also has an underground strong-room approached by steps, and two administrative rooms next to it; two more must lie on the other side of the strong-room under the grass. A shallow cross-hall lies in front of the rear rooms across the width of the building, but the customary courtyard in front of that was omitted.

The history of the development of the fort in the SE quarter has been elucidated by excavations in the 1990s. An Iron Age round house of before 100 BC was overlain two centuries later by an area of rammed gravel, assumed to be part of the parade-ground outside the Hadrianic fort (neither are now visible). After the enlargement of the fort, two phases of barrack buildings here, of 205/8 and 222/35, were succeeded *c.* AD 300 by an imposing courtyard residence, which was clearly the commanding officer's house (15). It had a grandiose aisled entrance hall on the west with columns and a pool, and a spacious dining-room at the east end of the courtyard, with a built Π-shaped bench (unique in Britain) to receive three mattresses, in the traditional arrangement of a *triclinium*. Such fittings can be seen in Mediterranean towns such as Pompeii, but this is a unique survival from Roman Britain, and suggests an officer of considerable social standing and probable Mediterranean origin, who translated the amenities of his native land to his temporary home on the distant northern frontier. Figured wall paintings adorned one of the courtyard verandas. The building, which also contained a small bath-suite in the SW corner, and a stable and another dining-room (heated) in the south wing, continued to be occupied into the third quarter of the fourth century at least. It is this elegant house which has been partly and imaginatively reconstructed in recent years, together with a barrack block alongside (16) belonging to a slightly earlier phase in the fort's history (*c.* 220/5), when the garrison was the Fourth Cohort of Gauls. Access to these reconstructions is at present (2001) restricted to guided tours of six or more people, but this may well change when the current programme of work in the SE sector is completed.

Now retrace your steps to the columns of the headquarters building and walk round the back of the spoilheap to your right, to examine the eastern defences. First come the bases of two ovens, and then you will see a fragment of curving wall inside the line of the main defences (17). This, discovered in 1978, represents the SE corner (and part of an angle-tower) of the second-century fort, and demonstrated conclusively that the fort was enlarged when it was converted into the Severan store-base *c*. 205/8. The whole of the stone defences south of this point, therefore, including the south gate (20, of single-passageway type with flanking guardrooms which do not project forward from the line of the wall), belongs to the early third century. Next comes the fort latrine (18), with central flagged floor and stone seat-supports. The drains which flushed it, their cover-slabs partly *in situ*, can be seen beyond heading for it. The fort wall is mostly reduced to foundations, and is severely robbed on the south side, but the base-plinth at the SE corner (19) survives, and the back wall of the SW angle-tower stands a few courses high (21). The earth rampart backing the wall has been entirely levelled. Much of the defences here was first uncovered in the nineteenth century in advance of housing development and then re-exposed in 1977–9. Here ends your visit to this remarkable site: only at Wallsend, Housesteads and Caernarfon in Britain is a comparable proportion of a Roman fort's interior layout available for permanent inspection.

The fort at **Wallsend**** (SZ 300660), the Roman SEGEDVNVM ('strong fort' or 'victory fort'), was covered by housing in the nineteenth century, and its outline was discovered by careful trenching only in 1929. Nothing, however, was known of the fort's interior until excavations commenced in 1975 in advance of proposed redevelopment, and the consequent archaeological work until 1984 resulted in the important recovery of the first almost complete fort-plan from Hadrian's Wall in its various phases, excavated under modern conditions. The proposal to cover the site with fresh housing was shelved; the site was grassed over and the fort perimeter was marked out, but only the *principia* was consolidated and left accessible.

There matters rested until 1997, when an ambitious and imaginative scheme to present the whole of the fort in more

vivid fashion, to reconstruct the fort bath-house, and to create
a museum and a look-out tower alongside, was started. The
project, now triumphantly crowned with success, cost
£9 million, funded mainly by National Lottery and European
and Regional Development monies; it opened in June 2000.
The site is open daily throughout the year, April–August
1000–1700; September–March 1000–1530. If coming from
South Shields it is easy to find: follow signs for Tyne Tunnel
and then 'Segedunum'; from Newcastle take the A187 for
Wallsend, and again follow the 'Segedunum' signs.

First visit the attractive Museum, built around a simulated
courtyard of a fort's headquarters building. The fort model in
the centre opts for open flat tops for the gate- and interval
towers, in contrast to the sloping tiled roofs chosen for the
South Shields gate (p. 451): either is possible. The shrine
(*aedes*) is re-created beyond, with a facsimile of the
Hildesheim silver treasure from Germany (not strictly
relevant) and life-size replicas of standards (that with the
dragon is a copy of one found at Niederbieber in Germany).
In the left-hand gallery note especially the tantalizing
fragment of an inscription referring to Wallsend's bath-house
(*bali*[*neum*]), and, at the far end, the impressive life-size
reconstruction of part of a cavalry barrack (see below). A rare
fragment of ring-mail shirt (cf. also one at South Shields:
p. 449) is displayed here, together with a modern mail shirt
(try it for weight).

In the gallery to the right of the '*principia* courtyard' are
some poor copies of frescoes found in the *praetorium* of
Echzell fort near Frankfurt; the dice tower is a replica of one
discovered in the 1980s near Düren in NW Germany. Of
especial note here, found in the hospital's latrine, are the
upright seat-support and a seat, both of stone: surviving
lavatory seats from Roman Britain are extremely rare
(probably because they make good paving slabs when
robbed). Also displayed here is a uniquely complete miniature
lead shrine with folding doors, decorated with a figure of
Mercury inside, and intended to hold a talisman or a favourite
divinity as a portable good-luck charm.

Next take the lift to the Tower Panorama for a unique
bird's-eye view over a Roman site in Britain: the fort of
SEGEDVNVM is spread out before you, with the vista of the

Tyne beyond, providing at a glance a superb idea of the layout of a Roman fort such as one can get nowhere else in the Roman Empire. The outline of the entire fort is marked out, including the part to the right of the road outside the archaeological park; at the far left (SW) corner is the reconstructed bath-house; while beyond in the middle distance is the life-size simulation of a stretch of Hadrian's Wall.

On your way to the bath-house, you pass a fragment of the Wall on your left (1 on Fig. 97), outside the fence, heading for Swan Hunter's yard. During the construction of the yard in 1903 a stretch of Wall was excavated but could not be preserved: it was dismantled and re-assembled in Wallsend Park, where it remained until 1991. Then the stones were

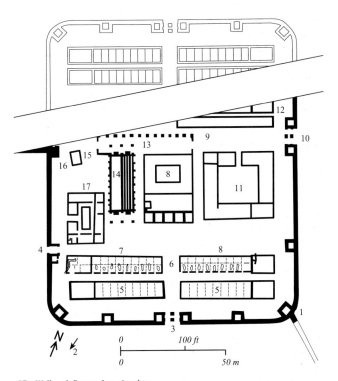

97   Wallsend, Roman fort, site plan

brought back to the fort site and rebuilt here, about 60 m
(65 yds) from where they were found a century ago, to give
visitors an idea of the direction which the final stretch of
Hadrian's Narrow Wall took as it headed for the Tyne at its
eastern terminus.

The rebuilt bath-house (2) in front of you is not on the site
of SEGEDVNVM's bath-house, which was located in 1814 and
destroyed, virtually without record, 125 m south of the fort. In
the absence of details from Wallsend, what you see here is
based on the surviving remains of the Chesters bath-house
(p. 480) reproduced in mirror image. It is only open for 20
minutes every hour on the hour, in order to conserve heat: for
this is a full working bath-house, not just a 'cold' shell. Of
course many of the details of this simulation are controversial,
not least its height: my own instinct is that the building as
reconstructed is too high. The changing-room with its bench
and niches is modelled on the Chesters' *apodyterium*; turn
right for the (modern and) ancient latrines. Straight ahead
leads you to a vestibule, with two rooms to the left for dry
heat, and the vaulted *frigidarium* with a cold immersion-bath
off to your right. The statue of Fortuna in the niche here is a
cast of one found in Birdoswald (now in Carlisle); such
statues were often found in bath-houses where the naked body
was thought to be in especial need of protection. The interior
decoration is fanciful but plausible: paintings of fish are
common in bath-houses on the Continent. The cupid with
mirror riding on a dolphin here is in fact a copy of an image
on a mosaic pavement in a house at Bulla Regia in Tunisia.
The warm and hot rooms (*tepidarium* and *caldarium*) follow,
the latter with a hot-water immersion-bath; also here is a stone
wash-basin (*labrum*) with a Medusa head at the centre,
modelled on one from the Castle Baths at Caerleon in south
Wales (p. 305). The painting of this room was in progress in
2001. Floors are in simulated *opus signinum* throughout.

Now walk up to the south gate (3) and begin your visit to
the fort itself, shown in its layout of *c.* AD 200. During the
third and fourth centuries its garrison was the Fourth Cohort
of Lingones, nominally 500 strong, a part-mounted unit
(*equitata*). The fort wall, the south and SW gates (4) and the
interval towers have been marked out in pebbles, as have also
the first two cavalry barracks inside (5). The next pair either

side of the central roadway (*via quintana*: 6) are the most instructive cavalry barracks visible anywhere in the Roman Empire (7–8). The outer walls are of stone (they were of timber in the Hadrianic fort), but the internal partitions were wood-framed. The more southerly of each pair of rooms has an oval urine pit (and sometimes stone flagging); the more northerly generally has a hearth. Both the pits and the hearths have been marked out on the ground. Note also the L-shaped latrine pit in the officers' block at the west end of 7. The complete excavation of these cavalry barracks in 1997–8 demonstrated for the first time in Britain what had earlier been surmised from evidence on the German frontier – that men in cavalry or part-mounted units lived with their horses alongside in a specially adapted barrack-block, and the elusive 'stable blocks' sought and tentatively identified by earlier excavators of forts all over the Empire are a myth. Three men lived in each of the nine cubicles, and their three horses in each neighbouring room: each barrack therefore housed a squadron of about 30 (including officers). The original Roman walls visible in part interrupting this arrangement belong to the fragmentary remains of the later third- or fourth-century infantry barracks (of the 'chalet' type best seen at Housesteads: p. 494), built only after the third-century cavalry barracks had been demolished.

Next continue along the *via quintana* to the headquarters building (*principia*: 8), walk straight through it to the *via principalis* (9), and then turn and face it. It is of the usual plan consisting of forecourt, cross-hall (entered also from the east, across a worn threshold block), and five rear rooms. The *principia* by the third century had had its original (Hadrianic) colonnade walled off to form two L-shaped rooms, perhaps stores (with moulded base-piers for the roof supports), and the customary *tribunal* in the cross-hall had been removed. A water-tank had also been placed in the courtyard, and a strong-room had been inserted under the central regimental shrine in the rear range. A freestanding, second water-tank behind the *principia* is also visible.

Now turn left and walk along the *via principalis* to the east gate (10). The few masonry blocks visible here are not precisely *in situ*: the gate was recorded before destruction in

1912 during the erection of a hotel, and the surviving pieces were transferred to Wallsend Park, whence they have now returned. The commanding officer's house (11) is only marked in outline; it had badly suffered from the early twentieth-century hotel built above it. Facing it are parts of two infantry barracks (12). Now retrace your steps to the centre of the fort and note the buttressed wall to your right, which was part of a covered cross-hall (13): it straddled the *via principalis* and was built up against the *principia* (8) and granaries (14). The hall, which was not part of the Hadrianic fort but was added some time during the later second century, is probably of the type described as a *basilica equestris exercitatoria* on an inscription from Netherby in Scotland, and is therefore usually thought to have been used for drill and other training manoeuvres, especially (in a fort with some cavalry) involving horses (*equestris*). The on-site information board, however, says that it was for 'ceremonial and religious gatherings', for which there is scant evidence. Common on the German frontier, this is one of only seven examples attested in Britain, and the only visible one apart from a fragment at Birdoswald (p. 525).

A little further west is a large stone tank (15), originally with four freestanding piers supporting its roof, two of them later incorporated in a cross-wall, when the tank seems to have been made smaller. Beyond, the south guard-chamber of the west gate has been marked out (16), but not unfortunately the point of junction with Hadrian's Wall (Wallsend was a fort, like Chesters, which lay astride the Wall). It was here in 1929 that a brilliant excavation by F G Simpson, by tunnelling under the street, showed that this was Narrow Wall and of one build with the fort; he thus demonstrated for the first time that the extension of the Wall from Newcastle to Wallsend, and the fort of SEGEDVNVM itself, were afterthoughts which belong to the second-phase planning of Hadrian's Wall, *c.* 124.

Now walk back towards the granaries (14), as usual buttressed buildings, and with a pair of loading platforms and a portico (represented by the three bases) at either end. This arrangement dates back to the original Hadrianic granary, but the northern portico and loading platforms must have been demolished and disused from the time that the 'drill-hall' was built *c.* 180/200. Unusually, only one part of this double granary has longitudinal sleeper walls for under-floor ventilation: a possible explanation is that the western half was a storehouse for less perishable foodstuffs (e.g. wine and oil), which unlike grain did not require the customary raised and ventilated floor.

The final building (17) is the hospital, one of the better preserved structures with a good deal of Roman masonry visible (Fig. 98). It was added to the fort *c.* AD 180/200, there being a smaller timber building of Hadrianic date below, of unknown purpose. The hospital consists of four ranges of rooms around a central courtyard: the circular stone slab in one corner of the latter, and the modern facsimile in another, were designed to take rain-water from the eaves, and to direct it into the adjacent channel, which brought water from the tank already noted (15). It and two other water channels converged on the room at the SW corner of the hospital, the

98   Wallsend, Roman fort, hospital with latrine in foreground

latrine. The stone toilet seat which you saw in the Museum came from this room.

Turn left out of the Segedunum car-park, right at the first roundabout after 200 m, and then first right into Plantation Street. Here a 35-m (115-ft) stretch of Hadrian's Wall was rebuilt in 1991–2, complete with the narrow string courses at intervals typical of Hadrianic work (cf. pp. 497 and 522), and a parapet above (cf. p. 445) (Fig. 99). Excavation here revealed not only the foundations of the Narrow Wall, conserved *in situ* alongside the reconstruction, but also some close-set pits on the berm in front of the Wall. These were smaller than the rectangular pits called *lilia* ('lilies') of the type described by Julius Caesar, found at Byker (p. 465), but were presumably also designed to provide an extra line of defence in front of the Wall. The positions of these pits have now been indicated by wooden posts, sawn off for safety; presumably they were sharpened to a point in antiquity, as

99 Wallsend, Hadrian's Wall (foreground) with modern simulation

Caesar described. Two rows of less formidable holes immediately adjacent to the west have not been marked out on the ground.

In 1999, a further 50-m (165-ft) stretch of Hadrian's Wall was uncovered further west, and was still under excavation in 2002. This was found to be still up to eight courses high, with core and facing-stones bonded with clay. The south face had collapsed at one point at least twice, and been rebuilt from the foundations: similar evidence elsewhere on the Wall line points to the same conclusion, that long stretches (probably a large majority) of what we see today are not, strictly speaking, *Hadrian's* Wall. The second of these rebuildings in the Wallsend stretch occurred some time in the later third century, when the Wall had been rebuilt with large, re-used blocks with lewis holes and tie-beam (crampon) sockets. Part of a window head and a piece of architectural decoration are among the recycled pieces used at this period. A culvert flowed through the base of the Wall here, and may have contributed to the frequent subsidence. The south face eventually collapsed again, and six courses of facing were found where they had fallen; further collapse has also been found on the north of the Wall. Meticulous examination of a stretch of Hadrian's Wall like this, and the considerable results which it is yielding, are all the more important because most of the Wall as we see it today was consolidated by masons from the then Ministry of Works during the 1960s and 1970s without proper archaeological supervision and record, and much vital information was undoubtedly lost.

After Wallsend the next visible fragment of Hadrian's Wall is in the eastern Newcastle suburb of **Byker** (NZ 271648), where a short stretch of the Narrow Wall was uncovered during building work in 2000; it hardly however merits a visit. One of our earliest antiquaries, William Stukeley, was so impressed with what was then still remaining of the Wall on Byker Hill that he sketched it on a visit in 1725, but only the foundations and a single course were found to have survived 275 years later. Also found, most interestingly, were multiple *lilia* (oblong defensive pits) on the berm north of the Wall, systematically arranged in three rows. Together with the appearance of smaller pits at Wallsend (see above: p. 464), the discovery raises the important question as to whether such

lilia are to be found along the entire length of Hadrian's Wall
– or at least in those parts where the outlook to the north was
not precipitous. A miserable 9-m (30-ft) stretch of Hadrian's
Wall here, half of the length excavated, has been
unsympathetically preserved in a pedestrianized area (with no
sign, and no marking out of the berm or the *lilia*); this is on
the south side of the main street of Byker (Shields Road),
almost opposite Lloyds TSB (Warworth Street). When coming
from Wallsend, go westwards along the A187 until you reach
a large roundabout with B & Q on your left. Take the third
exit here (ignoring the turning for Byker village), signposted
'Shields Road Shopping Centre'. The fragment of Hadrian's
Wall lies 200 m on the left. The same roundabout can be
reached 2 miles (3 km) from the centre of Newcastle along the
A193 (then take the first exit).

Nothing is visible of the key fort of Pons Aelii, 'Aelius'
[i.e. Hadrian's] Bridge', in the heart of **Newcastle upon
Tyne*** (NZ 250639), although a few Roman buildings in the
vicinity of the castle have been marked out in modern
materials. The Museum of Antiquities in the University of
Newcastle, however, is one of the outstanding Roman
collections in the country, especially important for the many
inscriptions displayed here which form the basis for our
knowledge of the Wall's constructional history (Monday–
Saturday, 1000–1700; take King's Walk from Haymarket and
turn left at the top after going through the arches). Space
precludes a detailed description of all the exhibits, but
attention is drawn here to a few items of especial interest; in
addition, some of the stones from forts north of the Wall are
mentioned in Chapter 9 (Figs. 123–4), and various other
exhibits are noted in passing later in this chapter. Especially
important are the scale-models of the Wall and its structures
as they may once have appeared (Fig. 2). Although details of
the superstructure are inevitably conjectural, the visitor to the
Wall with these in mind can better appreciate the original
appearance of the ruined buildings.

The case on the left after entering has a rare example from
Britain of a long wooden stake (the so-called '*pilum murale*'),
found at Greatchesters, which was used to protect the
ramparts of temporary camps whenever an army unit, away
from its base fort, stopped for the night (see p. 9). The

interlocking hollow tubular pipes from Chesters in the same
case must be vaulting tubes of the type already noted in
Chester (p. 322). The technique, common in Africa, was
presumably introduced to the Wall by legionary craftsmen,
because elsewhere in Britain such tubes are only attested in
legionary fortresses. Note also here the pair of bronze harness-
ornaments from South Shields, with attractive curvilinear
patterns documenting the survival of the Celtic love of
ornamental design well into the Roman period, as does even
more clearly the Aesica brooch (see below).

The second bay on the left has a famous inscription (it is
one of a pair) from milecastle 38 (Fig. 100), which simply
records the full name of the emperor (Hadrian, lines 1–2), that
of the governor (A. Platorius Nepos, line 4), and who the
builders were (men from the Second Augustan Legion, line 3).
It was this inscription, found in the 1750s, which finally
proved that Hadrian built the Wall, although the implications
were not fully realized until nearly a century later: for until
John Hodgson published his considered views in 1840,
antiquarians had believed that only the Vallum was Hadrian's,
and that the Wall was built for the first time by Septimius
Severus. Also here is an inscription from the granaries at
Benwell fort, which shows that detachments of the British

100   Milecastle 38, inscription (Newcastle upon Tyne, Museum of Antiquities)

fleet (*classis Britannica*), based in Dover, also helped, along with the three legions, in the building of Hadrian's Wall. The head of Antenociticus, also from Benwell, is displayed alongside (see p. 469). The wall-case here has a striking face-pot, and a fine handled bowl (*patera*), from the possible shipwreck site (p. 469) in the Tyne at South Shields; it is dedicated to Apollo Anextiomarus, a Celtic deity (with his Roman equivalent) otherwise known only from the Continent.

The next bay has a case with replicas of the jewellery from Greatchesters (Aesica), of which the gilded bronze brooch, Roman in form yet with swirling curvilinear decoration wholly in the Iron Age La Tène tradition, is a justly renowned masterpiece; but the accompanying trumpet brooch of silver made *c.* AD 150, massive and vulgar, steals the show for sheer ostentation. The building slab from High Rochester on the wall to your left here mentions Q. Lollius Urbicus as governor, the man who supervised the building of the Antonine Wall in Scotland. He was an African from a tiny town in Algeria (Tiddis) who rose eventually to be Urban Prefect at Rome – a good example of spectacular social and political advancement for a provincial from the backwoods, which the Roman administrative system made possible.

Two impressively grandiloquent inscriptions of the early third century from Risingham (see further p. 537) are at the back of the Museum; passing between them you reach the important series of altars and other reliefs from the three shrines to the enigmatic god Mithras found on the Wall. One from Housesteads shows Mithras being born from an egg, a variant not commonly depicted in mithraic iconography Empire-wide (the standard version shows him emerging at birth from a rock). The originals of the altars and statues displayed as casts in the Carrawburgh *mithraeum* (p. 485) are also here, together with an impressive full-scale reconstruction of the temple.

In the case by the entrance to the post-Roman room is a replica of an elaborate shield-boss and a fine decorated helmet cheek-piece: both come from the Tyne at South Shields (see further p. 449). Of the Roman stones on display in the rest of the Museum, there are several outstanding inscriptions from High Rochester, mentioned in more detail in the next chapter (pp. 542–6): the dedication slab of AD 216 (Fig. 123), the building slab of the Twentieth Legion flanked by a macho Mars and Hercules, the inscription of 225/35 mentioning an artillery store or emplacement (*ballistarium*); and finally the charming relief of Venus and nymphs near the exit door (Fig. 124).

The next Roman structures visible along the line of Hadrian's Wall are in **Benwell** (NZ 216647), on the A186 2 miles (3 km) west of the centre of Newcastle (follow signs for 'City (West)'). Nothing can be seen of the fort of CONDERCVM (which means 'fine view'), but two structures which lay outside its walls have been preserved; neither are signposted from the A186. One is the tiny temple of a native god, Antenociticus [AM; A], for which you need to turn south off the main road near the summit of the hill in Benwell, opposite Westgate Community College – not at the traffic lights but further west past the petrol station, just before reaching the brow of the hill (Weidner Road). You should then go first right and immediately left into Broomridge Avenue (ignore EH signs hereabouts if there are any, because they are frequently re-orientated by local residents to confuse visitors!). The temple is then on your left. Excavated in 1862, and re-excavated in 1937, it has an apse to the south where the cult statue stood (what may be its base has been replaced here), and there is a doorway in the east wall; traces of another door were found in the nineteenth century in the north wall, but are no longer visible. The column set upside-down in the corner has an inscription reading SEV[erus?] still on it; they are clearly Roman letters, but the inscription is meaningless as it stands. Perhaps this was a trial piece from a stone-cutter's workshop nearby; it was not actually found in the temple. Alongside the inscription on the column is what may possibly be a crude carving of a horned god, but this is not certain.

Of three altars known from the temple, two call the god Antenociticus and one Anociticus, the latter presumably a stonemason's error. All are now in the Museum at Newcastle, but two have been replaced by casts (now illegible) at the site: that on the right has a clearly defined *focus* (the saucer-shaped depression on the top) to receive offerings, and reliefs of a sacrificial chopper and a libation jug on the sides. Also in Newcastle is the head of the god himself, which survived from the cult statue (along with fragments of limbs). It is a powerful rendering, and well displays, like other pieces of Romano-British sculpture (such as the Bath pediment: p. 161), the strong influence of Celtic traditions, here represented by the large baggy eyes and especially the deeply grooved, snake-like hair, arranged in a neat symmetrical pattern.

Returning from the temple to the A186, you should turn left, rising to the top of the hill where the fort lay: one-third of it is under the reservoir to the right of the road. Take the first turning on the left (Denhill Park, but currently [2001] not signposted). At the bottom of this looped road is the sole visible example of one of the Vallum gateways which existed opposite every Wall fort [AM; A, but if you need a closer inspection the key is available from 31, Denhill Park]. The ditch of the Vallum was not dug in the centre, and the sides of the resulting causeway have been revetted in stone with an opening left for drainage. Excavation here in 1934 showed that the Vallum ditch was about 3 m (10 ft) deep; it is only half that today. The roadway over it (note several periods of metalling, displayed in step-fashion) was closed by a large doorway, of which one pier and a pivot-hole survive. These gateways ensured a strict control over movements into and out of the military zone.

One mile (1.6 km) further west along the A186, immediately after the second roundabout (keep straight over at both), a fragment of Hadrian's Wall may be seen on the left-hand side of the road. About 300 m further on, also on the left, is the much longer stretch at **Denton Hall** (NZ 195656) [AM; A]. This is a good example of the Broad Wall, and bonded into it is turret 7b. The pivot-hole for hanging the door and the bolt hole for fastening it are visible in the doorway. Inside the assumed base for the stairway will be noted: flat-lying stones make it clear that this was no higher (although it is not clear why it needed to be so high if such platforms truly served as staircase bases). There are slight remains of a hearth in the angle between base and the turret's west wall. Excavation in 1929 revealed that the turret was still in use in the fourth century. Immediately after here comes a roundabout on the A186 where the A1(M) goes off to the south; keep straight on, following the A69 which now replaces the A186. A portion of Wall excavated here in advance of destruction by the roadworks in 1988 found a section of plaster rendering fallen from it: cream-coloured, it was marked with grooves to give the impression of seven courses of false ashlar blocks (p. 441). Other paltry fragments of Broad Wall foundation can be seen on the left of the road at West Denton [AM; A], just after the roundabout.

You are now on the Hexham road (A69). Very little is visible of the Wall or its attendant works for nearly 2 miles (3 km), but turn off the A69 for Heddon, turn left, left again at the entrance to Heddon village, and finally first right. Behind the hedge on your left, reached by a stile at the far end, about 100 m of Broad Wall have been consolidated at **Heddon-on-the-Wall** (NZ 136669) [AM; A]. Note how the bank on your right at the entrance to the EH enclosure is full of stones clearly derived from the Wall. The lip and part of the profile of the Ditch can also be made out before reaching the consolidated stretch, as well as a post-Roman lime kiln on the Wall-line itself. It has been claimed that some of the white mortar visible on certain stones on the south face of the Wall here are remains of 'white-washing' (see above, p. 441), but where this has been discovered in more recent excavations it has generally been removed by the elements after a few years.

From here proceed into the centre of Heddon, turn right at the T-junction, and then right and left at The Three Tuns along the B6318. This is the Military Way, built in 1751. For many miles the Wall is invisible, as it was dismantled at that date to provide a foundation for the road. One and a half miles (2.4 km) beyond Heddon is a crossroads ('Wylam', left; 'Stamfordham and Ponteland', right), and immediately west of it the fort of **Rudchester** (NZ 113676), straddles the B-road. This was the Roman VINDOBALA, meaning 'white peak' or 'bright peak'. The earth mound which covers its stone defences is not impressive; it is best viewed at the SE corner (turn left at the crossroads and look over the first field-gate on your right). Four and a half miles (7 km) west of Rudchester, and $1\frac{1}{2}$ miles (2.4 km) past the reservoirs, both Vallum on the left and Wall Ditch on the right become conspicuous. Take the road signposted 'Stocksfield' and 'Stelling Hall' on the left, and stop at the gap in the hedge on the left by the telegraph pole. The Vallum is not very impressive here, but the gaps in the flanking mounds and the

causeways across its ditch are clearly visible. This is one of
the few places along the course of the Vallum where the
breaches made about AD 140 were not later repaired. It is
worth walking back to the B-road to look at the picturesque,
tree-grown stretch of Wall Ditch, which is in good condition
at this point.

Two and three quarter miles (4 km) further west is the fort
of ONNVM, **Halton** (NY 998684): turn left (imposing gate-
piers) over the cattle-grid before a bend-sign, $\frac{1}{4}$ mile (400 m)
after Halton Red House on the right. The road passes through
the southern part of the fort, but only the mounds of its
ramparts and uneven ground marking the sites of interior
buildings can be seen today. Although barracks, a granary and
an internal bath-house were uncovered (and backfilled) in
1827 and 1936, the layout of the interior buildings of this fort
is now much better understood as a result of a geophysical
survey undertaken in 1995–2000. This also located another
bath-house south of the fort and *vicus* buildings lining a
north-south road for 250 m. Exceptionally for Hadrian's Wall,
this fort had an annexe attached to its SW corner.

After another $\frac{1}{2}$ mile (800 m) comes a roundabout where the
A68 crosses the B6318. There was a gateway through the
Wall at this point (Portgate), taking Dere Street into Scotland:
its route is described on pp. 534–52. Here it is convenient to
make the 2-mile (3-km) detour southwards to **Corbridge****
(NY 982648), and visit the remains of the Roman town $\frac{1}{2}$ mile
(800 m) west of the modern one [AM; April–September,
daily, 1000–1800; October, daily, 1000–1700; November–
March, Wednesday–Sunday, 1000–1300 and 1400–1600]. Its
Roman name was not Coriosopitum or Corstopitum, as used
to be thought on the basis of corrupt readings in manuscript
sources; the Vindolanda tablets (p. 510) now reveal its true
name as CORIA, a Celtic word meaning simply 'army'. Most of
the structures in the exposed portion belong to the third and
fourth centuries, when Corbridge was a flourishing town and a
military supply-depot for the Wall. Below them lies a
succession of earlier forts. The earliest was for long thought to
have been an Agricolan foundation of *c*. AD 79, but the
Agricolan site is now known to lie $\frac{3}{4}$ mile (1 km) to the west,
where part of a large stores-base was excavated in 1974 on the
line of the A69. The contemporary structure uncovered nearby

in 1955–7 now falls into place as the bath building of this early fort. The Agricolan base was, however, demolished on the withdrawal from Scotland *c.* 87, and the first turf and timber fort on the main Corbridge site was erected.

The garrison of the first Corbridge fort was probably a cavalry regiment, the *Ala Petriana*, then 500 strong but later doubled in size. To it belonged a certain Flavinus, whose tombstone, depicting him riding down his barbarian foe, is now in the south transept of Hexham Abbey church (other stones are displayed at the north end). The fort was burnt and rebuilt *c.* 105, kept in use during the building of the Hadrianic frontier, but given up *c.* 130. It was then rebuilt in stone *c.* 139 with the Antonine advance into Scotland, and probably remained in use for about 25 years.

The present site, which represents only a small part of the final settlement, is bisected by the Stanegate (1 on Fig. 101). The first portion of this road, still lined by its side gutters, represents the final fourth-century level, which is a couple of metres higher than the original first-century surface. On the left, immediately below the road and half-buried by it, are the lower parts of some columns. These supported a porch in front of the two large third-century granaries beyond (2), the best preserved examples of their type in Roman Britain. Substantial portions of the floor remain in position. The ventilation-openings between the buttresses are also clear, and one in the right-hand wall of the second granary, still with its vertical stone support *in situ*, is still in perfect condition.

Immediately next to the granaries is an elaborate fountain (3) consisting of three elements: an aqueduct-channel, originally covered with stone slabs; a hexagonal fountain house, of which only a few blocks remain; and a basin into which water discharged. Its sides became so worn down by the washing of clothes and the sharpening of knives that the fountain can hardly have worked properly in its final years. The crampon holes, originally filled with lead, for fastening the blocks together, will be noted. The fountain house was furnished with an inscribed pediment (on display in the Museum) which indicates that it was built by men from the Twentieth Legion, on detachment from Chester probably in the third century. Note the statue bases on either side of the fountain, and also, partly destroyed by the criss-crossing drains, a small fragmentary square room at the lower level in front of the fountain. This and a portion of corridor adjacent to the right (a drain crosses the latter obliquely) belong to a building, possibly the hospital, of the stone fort of *c.* 140 which underlies the site (4).

The third structure on this side of the Stanegate is a vast, unfinished building, perhaps a storehouse, consisting of four wings enclosing a courtyard (5). The fine quality of the massive masonry blocks, which would have been dressed off flush when completed, will be noted. The archaeological evidence for dating this building has been scanty. It now seems possible that construction was under way in the late 160s or during the 170s, but it was only ever completed on the side facing the Stanegate. Possibly it was a casualty of the

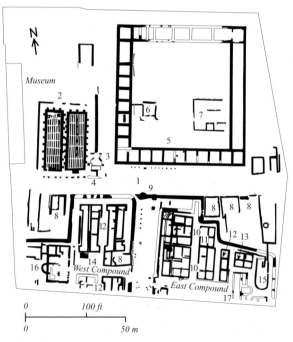

101   Corbridge, site plan

upheavals which followed the enemy destruction of Corbridge
in 180. Fragments of two other buildings are visible within the
courtyard. The rooms nearer the granaries formed part of the
rear range of the HQ building of the second-century stone
fort, including the central shrine (*sacellum*); this alone had not
been demolished during the erection of the grand storehouse,
and it was then converted to other uses, probably domestic
(6). The other building exposed within the courtyard is part of
the commandant's house (*praetorium*) of the fort (7).

At the far end, you should mount the steps and survey the
jumble of fragmentary remains on the south side of the
Stanegate. Serious subsidence into the early fort ditches below
has contributed to the crazy effect. It is well to have a good
look at the helpful reconstruction-drawing which is displayed
here. From this you will see that the area consisted of two
military compounds, surrounded by enclosure-walls. These
take an irregular course to avoid temples (8) and other
buildings fronting the Stanegate. The compound-walls can be
recognized by their more massive construction (1.50 m or 5 ft
wide), and the projecting plinth at their bottom. At the
beginning of the fourth century the compounds were united by
building a wall, broken by an entrance (9), along the
Stanegate. The buildings inside these compounds – officers'
houses (10), barracks (11), workshops (12), a latrine (13), a
water-tank (14), a possible club-house (15) – can be
understood with the help of the excellent information panels.
A small administrative building in the west compound,
adjoining the path near the Museum, has an underground
strong-room approached by steps (16); a badly preserved
building, also with an apse, may be its counterpart in the east
compound (17).

The superb Museum, opened in 1983, contains a replica of
the Flavinus tombstone (p. 473), an important hoard from an
armourer's workshop of *c.* AD 105, excellent models of the
granaries and the fountain building, some informative
inscriptions (two partly recoloured to give an idea of their
original polychrome effect), and many fascinating sculptures.
One is a rugged, unrealistic portrayal of a lion devouring a
stag (a tomb monument), another is part of a frieze
representing the crowned sun god riding on a winged horse
towards a pedimented building, in which stands Castor or

Pollux. Along with other sculptures it came from a temple dedicated to Dolichenus, an eastern deity equated with Jupiter, and he is named on an altar also in the Museum. A poorly preserved pedimental relief depicts Romulus and Remus being suckled by the she-wolf – a potent symbol of *Romanitas*, and it is striking to find it expressed in this distant outpost on the northern fringes of the Empire. At the far end are two large tombstones of children, striking for the perfunctory nature of their reliefs (one is illustrated on the spine of this book). Other fragmentary sculptures testify to the remarkable diversity and elaboration of the buildings that must once have graced this distant settlement of the Roman Empire.

Return now to the B6318. For 3 miles (5 km) west of Portgate the Ditch on the north of the road, and the Vallum on the south, are in an outstanding state of preservation. The Wall itself is buried beneath the road, but the two then part company: after descending the first part of a 1:8 hill 1 mile (1.6 km) before Chollerford, watch out for the broad entrance to Black Pasture quarry on the right. Park here and take the wooden stile over the wall on the opposite side of the road, marked 'Public Footpath Fallowfield'. In the field here, to your right, is the interesting stretch of Hadrian's Wall at **Planetrees** (NY 928696) [AM; A]. It preserves the junction between a stretch of the Broad Wall and a portion only 1.80 m (6 ft) wide, standing on broad foundation. The reason for this is uncertain, but it is probably an example of a stretch totally rebuilt at a later date, perhaps *c*. 205, when evidence elsewhere on the Wall (pp. 484 and 512) suggests that substantial rebuilding, sometimes to foundations, had become necessary. A drainage culvert is also visible here.

You are now approaching the North Tyne and the central sector of Hadrian's Wall, where the scenery becomes more beautiful and the Roman remains better preserved. A long stretch of the Wall, over 2 m (7 ft) high and incorporating a well preserved turret (26b), is only a short distance from Planetrees. Turn left along the A6079 at the bottom of the hill and you will see **Brunton** turret (NY 922698) [AM; A] signposted on the left (parking place). It is the most westerly section of Broad Wall on a broad foundation, for it was when the curtain-builders had got this far that the order came to change the width from 3 m to 2.45 m (10 ft to 8 ft). This

Broad Wall can be seen on the west side of the turret; to the east of it, however, the Wall is only 2 m (6 ft) wide, and this may represent a re-building of Severan date, as suggested at Planetrees. The turret preserves its door-sill and pivot-hole, and an uninscribed altar and the lower part of a corn-mill can be seen inside.

Return to the crossroads and turn left for Chollerford. Most visitors now go on to Chesters, but if you have half an hour to spare park immediately before the river-bridge and take the path on the left which leads to **Chesters bridge abutment***(NY 922698) [AM; A]. The Wall, here on its broad foundation, ends in a tower adjacent to the massive masonry apron forming the abutment. Consolidation work in 1982–3, which included removal of the stones formerly on the abutment to a display area under the trees, has demonstrated that the visible work belongs to a major rebuilding, and that the Hadrianic bridge abutment lay further east. Once thought to have occurred *c.* 220, this rebuilding has now been redated (on evidence from the west bank excavations of 1990/1) to the mid Antonine period. It can now therefore be seen, very logically, as part of the programme of works carried out when the Military Way was added *c.* 162/5, when the Hadrianic pedestrians-only bridge had to be replaced by a road bridge.

Part of the river-bed paving of Hadrianic date is visible in the base of the Phase 2 tower, and the outline of a diamond-shaped pier of the Hadrianic bridge, with cutwaters in both directions, can be made out in the apron immediately west of the tower, where it was incorporated in the later masonry. The Hadrianic bridge may have had stone arches; the later one by contrast certainly had a timber superstructure on stone piers. One pier is buried in the river bank, and two other piers and the west abutment have been detected in the river itself, which has shifted some metres to the west since antiquity; by contrast the Hadrianic stone bridge had probably eight (smaller) piers. A water channel (a later addition) can be seen running through the tower, once covered by the huge slabs which lie shattered on its south side. A barrel-shaped stone in Chesters Museum with eight radial sockets was once interpreted as evidence for a water-mill at this point, but it is probabaly nothing of the sort; a counterweight for a crane, or a pile-driver, are alternative interpretations of it. Other

features to note at the Chesters bridge abutment are a phallus
carved for good luck on the northward outer face of the
abutment; the massive projecting foundation stones of the
south abutment, set obliquely to the edge of the masonry
apron above; and a cylindrical tapering stone with square base
and rounded raised knob on the top, lying on the apron, one of
a pair of bollards (a more fragmentary one is under the trees)
which are believed to have originally flanked the approach to
the bridge ramp.

Turning left at the Chollerford roundabout, you will soon
see the entrance to the Roman fort of **Chesters****
(NY 912702) [AM; S except that it is open from 0930 daily,
April–September], a charming spot, set in a lush estate beside
the North Tyne. The remains of the fort were mainly
excavated by the remarkable John Clayton (1792–1890),
owner of the Chesters estate in the nineteenth century, who
was responsible for buying up, and thereby saving from
destruction, much of the central sector of Hadrian's Wall. The
buildings at Chesters are on the whole well preserved, even if
detailed evidence for their chronology was largely removed
without record, according to the normal standards of the day.
Chesters was a cavalry fort, and both the *Ala Augusta* (in the
Hadrianic period) and the Second *Ala* of Asturians are
recorded as its garrisons. Its Roman name was CILVRNVM,
thought to mean the fort of 'the deep pool'; but 'Cilurnigi' are
now attested on an inscription found in Spain in the 1990s as
a branch of the Asturians, and it is possible that CILVRNVM is
connected with them. If so, the name may not be the original
Hadrianic one of the fort, unless the *Ala Augusta* was also
composed of Asturians.

The path first leads to the north gate (1 on Fig. 102): of its
two portals, the west has been cleared down to the original
Hadrianic level, the other preserves a sill of later date. Pivot-
holes for hanging the gates and a water channel under the east
carriageway (possibly an aqueduct inlet rather than an outfall
drain) are also visible. In the next enclosure is part of a double
barrack building, the rooms of which would have been
originally divided into two by a timber partition (2). As usual
there are more spacious quarters for officers, at the far end.
The pieces of column lying around supported the veranda

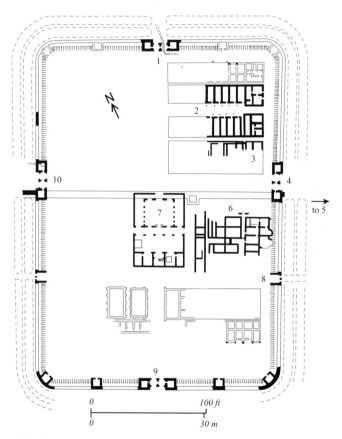

102   Chesters, Roman fort, site plan

along each side of the street, which has a gutter to collect water from the eaves.

Beyond, in the same enclosure, is a building of uncertain purpose with a stone-flagged floor, traditionally interpreted as a stable (3). The recent realization that horses in cavalry forts shared accommodation with their riders (see p. 461) has

thrown this interpretation wide open; too little of the building
here has been excavated for it to be confidently interpreted as
a cavalry barrack. The east gate, entirely Hadrianic in form as
all later masonry was removed in 1867, is very well preserved
(4): the cap from which the rear arch sprang is still in position
on the south side.

Now leave the fort and walk down to the river, passing a
fragment of the Wall on your way. You will soon reach the
bath-house (5), one side of which still stands to a height of
3 m (10 ft). Recent survey has demonstrated that it was laid
out in units of 10 or 20 Roman feet (a Roman foot measures
296 mm rather than the 305 mm of the imperial foot), and that
its walls are three Roman feet thick. A porch, added in a
secondary period, gives access to the large changing-room
(Fig. 103). The seven niches probably held wooden lockers
for clothes, and no doubt there was once a second row above.
Exposed in a small trench is one of the bench supports for a
row of seats along this wall in its primary phase: you will

103   Chesters, Roman fort, changing-room in the bath-house

appreciate that both the present level (grass) and the final
Roman pavement-level, represented by the stone flags, are
considerably higher than the primary Roman floor. An
information panel explains the unusual tile and tufa barrel
vault which roofed this room. On the river side is a heavily
buttressed latrine. All that remains of it are the foundations
and the lower part of the sewer: the floor-level and the
supports for the seats have gone. From the changing-room the
bather would cross the worn threshold, and turn left into the
cold room with its cold immersion-bath. Then he had a choice
of hot rooms, although not all belong to the original building.
Returning to the lobby he could either keep straight ahead and
then turn right for the hot-dry room, or turn left for the long
room of moist heat, which was originally divided into two
parts, the *tepidarium* and the *caldarium*. Its floor and
hypocaust have completely disappeared, but the stoke-hole
survives at the far end, together with part of the supports on
either side for hot-water boilers. On the right, the imposing
wall of the hot-water immersion-bath still has the lower part
of its window. Another set of warm rooms runs parallel on the
river side.

From the bath-house you may like to wander down to the
river. The outfall drains of the baths' latrine are clearly visible
from here, as well as the large buttress at the SE corner and a
further V-shaped drain beyond. If the water is low a bridge
abutment and two piers may be visible; the eastern abutment
can be seen on the far side (see above). Excavation here in
1990–1 demonstrated the presence of a tower west of the
abutment itself (as on the other bank), flanked on its south
side by a huge ramp built at an oblique angle to take the road
(the Military Way) up to the level of the bridge: part of its
stone revetment wall is visible (but not the tower). This
belongs to a secondary phase, after the bridge had been
converted to vehicular use in the middle of the second century
(see above). Late fourth-century coins found above the final
metalling of the road on the ramp indicate that it was still used
down to the very end of the Roman period.

Returning to the fort, you first reach the hypocaust of the
commandant's private bath-suite (6). Its floor is supported by
a mixture of brick and stone pillars: the irregularity is due to
partial reconstruction, probably in the fourth century. The

104   Chesters, Roman fort, inside the HQ (drawing by Alan Sorrell)

hypocausts in the living-rooms are also additions to the visible
building, the original plan of which is not clear: some
fragments of wall-foundation detectable here and there at a
lower level presumably belong to an earlier commandant's
house. Beyond the *praetorium* comes a long narrow structure
of unknown purpose.

   In the centre of the fort is the headquarters building (7), the
most instructive example visible in Britain. The entrance led
to a courtyard surrounded by a covered colonnade on three
sides. The gutters and part of the courtyard paving are visible,
and on one of the flags near the well a phallus has been carved
for good luck. The courtyard led to the covered cross-hall,
with a *tribunal* on the right from which the officer could
address his assembled troops. Beyond are five administrative
rooms, the central one of which contained the statue of the
emperor and the regimental standards (Fig. 104). In the third
century, a strong-room, still covered by its vaulted roof, was
inserted below the floor (Fig. 105). It now projects

considerably above ground, but the effect is exaggerated: although the floor of the third-century chapel of the standards above the strong-room was probably slightly raised, third-century floor-levels elsewhere were much higher than now, as the excavators removed the later floors and doors to expose the Hadrianic masonry.

Finally, you should visit the rest of the defences: a single-portalled gate on the east side (8, near the commandant's house), an angle-tower, two interval towers, and the south and west gates all remain exposed. Of the south gate (9), one portal was blocked up soon after being built, but its blocking-wall has been removed to reveal the Hadrianic masonry; the other remained in use, resulting in a build-up of road-levels and the raising of the east portal. Its rear threshold, much worn, is built of re-used gutter-stones. The west gate (10) was found entirely blocked up, but once again the blocking-walls were removed by the nineteenth-century excavators. A tank fed by a leat bringing water from the west can be seen in one guardroom, and beyond it an oven. A portion of Hadrian's Wall is also visible, adjoining the south guardroom: Chesters fort lay astride the Wall, and three of its gateways, therefore, opened into enemy territory.

A tour of the Chesters Museum, crammed full of important sculptured and inscribed stones, completes your visit to this site. Most of what it contains was found during John Clayton's excavations at the five Wall forts which he bought and explored, from Chesters to Carvoran. The arrangement has been deliberately left as an example of early twentieth-century museum display (it opened in 1903), in itself an interesting educational experience. Of many outstanding pieces, note especially, in the room to the left, two inscribed terracotta incense-burners from Coventina's well at Carrawburgh (p. 485); the corn-measure from Carvoran (p. 519); an arm-purse from Barcombe quarry (p. 498) with three gold and 60 silver coins, lost there in the Hadrianic period; a fragmentary altar found in 1978 which demonstrated that the Hadrianic garrison at Chesters was a cavalry unit, the *Ala Augusta* (line 3); and the fragmentary tombstone of a man wearing a toga, found in 1990. In the main hall, your eye will especially notice the arched entrance to the sanctuary at Housesteads of the Germanic god Mars Thincsus; the relief of cross-legged Cautes, torchbearer of Mithras, from the *mithraeum* at Housesteads; the relief from Carrawburgh inscribed to Coventina, and another showing the nymph in triplicate (triplism being much favoured by indigenous Celtic religions: cf. pp. 182 and 490); and the remarkable if headless statue from Chesters of Juno Regina standing on a bull, witness of a Syrian cult (she was the consort of Jupiter Dolichenus), and possibly also of an eastern sculptor.

Now continue westwards along the B6318. At the top of the hill, after the turning to Wark, you will see a fine piece of Wall and turret 29a at **Black Carts** (NY 884712) [AM; A]; they deserve closer inspection. Turn off, therefore, along the next lane on the right. The back wall of the turret is still 3.35 m (11 ft) high, but the front has been reduced to ground-level. The adjacent Wall is built to the narrow width, and so this is the first visible turret with wing-walls of the broad gauge on both sides (p. 443). Two 'centurial stones', recording the erection of stretches of Wall by working-parties of legionary *centuriae*, used to be legible here, but they can only be traced now in very favourable conditions (raking evening sunlight). One, on the bottom course of the south face, 12 blocks west of the end of the turret's wing-wall, read 'from the sixth cohort, the century of Gellius P(h)ilippus (built this)'. The other, on the bottom course of the north face 88 block east of the start of this stretch, read COH I NAS |BA ('from the First Cohort, the century of Nas. . . Ba[ssus] [built this]'. The fact that both were on the bottom course of the wall (and one on the north face), whereas they were originally set on the south face at a height convenient enough to be clearly visible, suggests that at least part of the Black Carts stretch of Wall is not Hadrianic but the work of a later reconstruction, when the centurial stones were incorporated into the fabric as though they were normal building-stones. The Ditch is conspicuous here, but is even more striking on the other side of the lane, where another long stretch of the Wall has been consolidated.

After Black Carts, the road climbs again. After the bend, on the downward slope, there is a lay-by on the right near an iron gate. This leads at once to the stretch of Ditch on **Limestone Corner** (NY 875716), here unfinished because of the hardness of the rock. It is an imposing sight, and a sobering reminder of what Roman engineers were capable of achieving without the

use of explosives. A substantial block in the middle of the
Ditch here has dowel holes in it preparatory to splitting it by
metal wedges into smaller pieces and so to its subsequent
removal – a rare visible document of Romano-British
quarrying technology. Returning to the B6318, walk back
eastwards for 200 m to a field-gate on the south side of the
road, for access to a fine length of the Vallum here.

A mile (1.6 km) further on, after passing another superb
stretch of the Vallum (Fig. 106), you will come to the car-park
adjoining the fort of **Carrawburgh*** (NY 859712), of which
only the lofty earth rampart-mounds are visible. Its Roman
name, BROCOLITIA, may mean 'covered with heather',
although this is not certain. It was added later than the main
series of forts, about AD 130–3, covering the Vallum in the
process. Outside the fort is the fine little Temple of Mithras,
excavated in 1950 [AM; A]. First built soon after AD 205, it
was extended a decade or so later, and underwent three further
major repairs or rebuildings before its final desecration in the
early fourth century, possibly by Christians. The visible
remains represent the building in its final form (Fig. 107). An
ante-chapel containing the statuette of a mother goddess is
separated from the nave by a screen (some concrete posts,
representing wooden uprights, remain). Low benches, revetted
with a wooden interlace, flank the nave, where stand smashed
representations of the torchbearers and four tiny altars. The
originals of the sculptures and the inscriptions are now in the
Newcastle Museum (together with a full-scale reconstruction
of the building), but casts have been sensibly placed on site –
a practice, widespread in Germany, which has been little tried
in Britain, perhaps for fear of vandalism (cf. p. 319). The
stone walls visible half-way along the benches mark the limits
of the first *mithraeum*, which was only half the size of the
present building. At the end are the three impressive altars,
and in the shelf behind them would have stood the bull-
slaying relief. A few words about Mithraism and a
reconstruction-drawing of a ceremony in progress will be
found on p. 619.

The shrine of the local water nymph, Coventina, is
represented by a square stone basin 150 m to the north
enclosing the source of her spring: its site adjoins the field-
wall and is surrounded by wooden rails. Contrary to what is

105 (top) *Chesters, Roman fort, the headquarters building*   *106* (above) *Carrawburgh, the Vallu*

sometimes stated, it is not a Romano-Celtic temple, as an
outer wall only defined the precinct and was not structurally
part of a building: the central well was almost certainly open
to the sky. An enormous array of votive offerings, including
stone altars, gold and silver rings, brooches and other bronze
objects, two terracotta incense-burners, and over 13,000 coins,

was found during its excavation in 1876. To reach it, return to the car-park and enter the fort by the stile, cross to the far side, and out again by the site of the west gate. The shrine lies beyond the field-wall which crosses your path, but there is little to see, and the ground surrounding Coventina's well tends to be extremely boggy except in the driest of summers.

Two and a half miles (4 km) after Carrawburgh, the road swings to the left and crosses the Vallum at the start of a wood. Go on up the slope as far as the first field-gate on the left set back from the road, and park here (take care not to obstruct farm vehicles). Now walk back $\frac{1}{4}$ mile (400 m) to the dip, take the field-gate on your left signposted 'Sewingshields, Public Footpath', and strike across the field until you reach the Wall Ditch. Walking westwards you soon come to turret 33b, **Coesike** (NY 821705), which furnishes an excellent illustration of the fate which befell many of the turrets in the later second century and at the beginning of the third century. The original structure has wing-walls of the broad gauge as well as the usual 'staircase-platform' and doorway. Excavation in 1968 and 1970 found very little pottery of the second half of the second century, suggesting that the turret went out of use soon after the recommissioning of the Wall in the 160s, and its doorway was blocked up. Then in the Severan reorganization it was decided that this turret was no longer required and it was demolished. Hadrian's Wall was then partly reconstructed over the wing-walls and in the recess on the north, where it has bulged and sagged (to the right of the pole in Fig. 108). A centurial stone reading > GRAN[niani], 'the century of Gran[nianus] [built this]', can be seen on the north face: it is the first surviving block from the east in the third course here. The implications of this have been discussed above (p. 484).

Those with time to spare may like to continue walking westwards. No Wall is exposed in this sector, but the Ditch is very striking, especially where it stops abruptly opposite the site of milecastle 34 (clump of trees). From here onwards as far as Greenhead, the cliffs rendered it unnecessary except for a few stretches. Turret 34a, demolished to foundations, has been consolidated immediately beyond the next field-wall. If you continue walking westwards from here for another 15 minutes, skirting round the north side of the farm in the

107 (top) *Carrawburgh, Temple of Mithras*   108 (above) *Coesike, turret 33*

coppice, you reach another length of consolidated Wall on
Sewingshields Crags (NY 805702), together with what is left
of milecastle 35 [AM; A]. The Crags are spectacular here, 325
m (1,068 ft) above sea-level, and there are fine views in all
directions, but the Wall, excavated in 1978–80, is not
preserved to any great height. Reduced in width by one or two
offsets above its narrow Wall foundation (in turn resting on
Broad Wall footings), the superstructure here is only some
2 m (6 ft 6 in) wide, considerably less than the norm for the
Hadrianic narrow gauge. The whole stretch seems to have
been rebuilt more or less from foundations, probably early in
the third century (as at Peel Gap and elsewhere: see below,
p. 512) – the 'offset' courses below representing the original
Hadrianic Narrow Wall.

Milecastle 35 is much robbed and the jumble of structures
inside it is at first sight confusing. The earliest is the small
rectangular structure (Hadrianic) at the SE corner, later
overlain by another, also visible (?Severan). The west
building, presumably a barrack, is not before the early third
century; note its small square hearth near the centre with
traces of burning. In the fourth century this was demolished
and other structures, given over entirely to metal-working,
were erected on top. The milecastle had evidently ceased to
have any military function by then; indeed the metalworkers'
principal access was over the demolished remains of the
milecastle's east wall. The oven in the NW corner also
belongs to this fourth-century phase. Note that there is
(uniquely) no north gate, at least in the third century, when
total rebuilding of the Wall removed all traces of the
Hadrianic arrangement; but although at times Hadrianic
builders did indeed rigidly stick to their blueprints, and were
blind to the demands of local topography, no building gang at
any period would surely have been idiotic enough to build a
gate here, leading nowhere except to a precipice.

Visitors with time to spare may like to walk on for a further
$\frac{1}{3}$ mile (500 m) as far as the consolidated remains of turret 35a,
another example, like 33b and 34a, of a turret demolished at
the end of the second century when the Wall was built across
its recess. Thereafter the Wall has not been consolidated until
the Knag Burn gateway (p. 494) over 1 mile (1.6 km) further
on. Visitors with cars, however, will want to retrace their

steps to Coesike, and drive westwards for $1\frac{1}{2}$ miles (2.4 km) to visit the most famous and popular of all the Wall forts, **Housesteads**** (NY 790688) [AM; S]: if it is high summer and you want to visit the site in comparative peace, be sure to arrive early. Its Roman name was VERCOVICIVM (the meaning is uncertain). The third-century garrison was an infantry cohort of Tungrians (originally recruited from Belgium), 1,000 strong. The fame of Housesteads is mainly due to its dramatic setting, on the edge of a craggy precipice in a lonely part of Northumberland, and also because it is one of the most intelligible and most extensively explored of all Wall forts. The defences were uncovered by John Clayton in the mid nineteenth century, and the interior was extensively stripped by R C Bosanquet in 1898–1901, when a complete fort plan was revealed for the first time – not only for Roman Britain but in the entire Roman Empire. Subsequently, individual buildings were excavated again at various times in the twentieth century, especially between 1967 and 1981, prior to consolidation and display.

The little Museum has a few items, notably a model of the fort, a statue of three now-headless mother goddesses, and a famous relief of three anonymous godlings (the triplism, once again, typically Celtic). Presumed to be *genii cucullati* ('hooded spirits'), they wear the hooded cloak (the *birrus Britannicus*) – one of Britain's few exported goods which was much prized elsewhere in the Empire.

On leaving the Museum, first make for the few buildings of the large civilian settlement exposed beyond the south gate. You then retrace your steps and enter the fort through a modern breach in the southern defences. The first building on the left is the commandant's house (2), but walk past that for the moment to visit the double-portalled south gate (1 on Fig. 109). The gate-stop in the eastern passageway survives, but the flagging here is modern, to resist the tramp of visitors' feet before the south gate was closed as the principal entry point to the fort. The blocking in the original doorway to the eastern guard-chamber (including a Roman column) is late medieval (sixteenth- or seventeenth-century), when a bastle house (built of course with stones from the Roman fort) was tacked on to the front of the fort defences and the guard-chamber was taken over by a corn-drier.

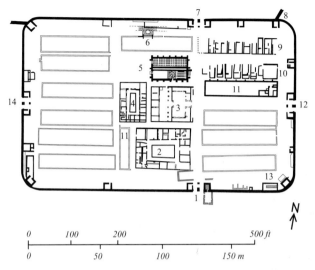

109   Housesteads, Roman fort, site plan

Next return to the commandant's house (*praetorium*: 2),
best approached now via the prominent wooden staircase, but
originally entered through a room in the middle of the east
wing. In its visible, third-century form it consists of four
wings around a courtyard, but only the north and west wings
are of Hadrianic origin. The lower part of the modern wooden
stairway at the SE corner of the building covers a large
flagged area interpreted as stables, with drainage channels (to
ease mucking-out), and with a water-tank in one corner. There
was separate access from the street. The stone flagging in the
courtyard, partly made up of re-used material brought from
other buildings, belongs to the final period of the house, when
the comfortable life-style of the commandant was no longer
relevant to the changing military situation, and the building
was split into at least two separate flatlets.

At the top of the stairs, in the NE corner of the house, is the
kitchen with an oven: this served a dining-room further along
the corridor. The next room along from the latter, originally
part of a small bath-suite, was provided with a hypocaust in the
fourth century: its stone *pilae*, some of them broken

110 Housesteads, Roman fort, the commandant's house from the NE

columns probably robbed from demolished verandas (one
with a capital can be seen in the far left corner), are well
preserved, and part of the floor is in position (Fig. 110). A
paved passage at the west end of the courtyard-corridor has
two phases of floor, including the post-hole of the door at the
lower level. It leads to a small toilet, made in the third century
when the larger latrine immediately adjacent (on the south
side) was filled in, and its doorway blocked up: cross over to
the grass and lean over the west wall of the larger latrine to
observe the blocking set on top of the original threshold. The
sewer in this latrine is very fine; note especially the massive
re-used slab covering it where it leaves the west side of the
building, two rooms away down the slope. At the SW corner
of the *praetorium* are two further rooms, heated from the
beginning, with fragmentary remains of hypocausts. It is
worth looking at the outside wall of the house here, where the
junction between the original Hadrianic masonry and the later
addition of the south wing is very clear.

Now return to the south gate and turn left up the *via principalis* to visit the headquarters building (*principia*), which also dates mainly from the third century (3). It contains the usual courtyard, cross-hall (with *tribunal* to the right and statue-base to the left) and five administrative rooms, but it is not well preserved. Behind it is the hospital, apart from that at Wallsend the only visible example of its kind in Britain (4). This too was a courtyard building, originally with a veranda which was later demolished when the flagging was laid in the whole central area. The hospital was entered on the west side with the operating theatre occupying the north end. The east wing contains small wards alternating with corridors, but the building is poorly preserved here and the doorway arrangements are uncertain. The room at the SW corner with a deep stone-lined pit and accompanying drains was apparently for ablutions, and that next to it was a small latrine.

Next to the headquarters is a pair of granaries (5), probably third-century in their visible form. One has been marred by the insertion of an eighteenth-century corn-drying kiln, but elsewhere the pillars that supported the now-vanished floor may be seen. Note that the building as originally constructed (the Hadrianic arrangement) was a double granary without dividing walls but with a central row of seven piers to support the roof. When the building was divided into two (no doubt to lessen the strain on the roof), and re-roofed as two separate granaries, the Hadrianic piers supporting the floor were isolated and rendered useless: they can be seen in the narrow eaves-drip between the two granaries. You will also note here how the central buttress on the east side is original, but that both the lesser buttresses and the new longitudinal walls dividing the granary into two have straight joints with the original outer walls. The granaries were entered from the west, where there are wide thresholds and loading bays.

After the granaries you reach the north wall of the fort. Built up against the back of this is a long base for a staircase up to the rampart-walk and, immediately in front of it, and partly buried under it, are the footings of a small square structure (6) with a hearth-base. This is turret 36b, demolished *c*. AD 124 when the order came to place forts on the Wall itself. It will be seen from the position of this turret that Hadrian's Wall was originally designed to run a little behind

its present course, back from the precipice. Now turn right to
the north gate (7). Originally a roadway sloped up to it from
outside, but this was removed in 1853 to expose the massive
foundations. A water-tank rests against one of the well
preserved guardrooms. From the NE corner (8), the Wall can
be seen running down to the Knag Burn, where a customs
gateway, flanked by a pair of guardrooms, was inserted in the
fourth century.

In the NE portion of the fort three buildings are visible, all
of them in their final, fourth-century, state. Nos. 9 and 10 are
barrack-blocks, excavated in 1974–7 and 1959–60
respectively. Both were conventional barracks during the
second and third centuries, with the more spacious officers'
blocks at the east end, but no masonry of these periods is now
exposed. The structures which replaced them in the final
phase were very different, consisting of individual one- or
two-roomed chalets, most built as freestanding units, although
the more westerly group in no. 9 have party walls. All are
north-facing, but their lengths vary considerably. Most appear
to be open to the north, but were closed off there by timber
shutters rather than a stone wall. Many have flagged floors
and benches, and the most easterly compartment of 10 has an
oven, of 9 a hearth. Some were rebuilt and modified in the
second half of the fourth century. The structure to the south
(11) is a long store-building with a bath-suite inserted at one
end. Enter it by the stoke-hole on its north side: on the top
block of the corner pier facing you to the left, a phallus has
been carved for good luck.

At the east gate (12), note the deeply rutted threshold of the
north portal; that on the south was blocked up in the third
century and became a guard-chamber, while the original
guardroom became a coal-store. At the SE corner is one of the
most fascinating buildings at Housesteads, the best preserved
latrine in Roman Britain (13: Fig. 111). The soldiers would
have sat on seats erected over the deep sewers on either side,
and used the water running along the channel in front of them
for their ablutions (see p. 18). Two basins were provided for
rinsing their hands. It is a remarkable monument to Roman
hygiene, the level of which was not matched and surpassed
until the late nineteenth century. In a secondary period, to
improve water supply to the latrine, the door into the corner

111   Housesteads, Roman fort, the latrine at the SE corner

tower was blocked up (access was henceforth from the wall-walk alone), and a reservoir was built in front of it to gather rain-water from its roof. Its sides are worn down, apparently caused most likely by the washing of clothes. Water overflowing from this tank was then channelled into another channel which entered the latrine from its east end (originally the latrine had been entered from that end, but the original door was now blocked up because of the new arrangements). Note how the water channel in front of the seats is on a gentle incline, so that its point of discharge is lower than the point of entry. The sewer can be seen curving away to dispose of its contents outside the fort's SE corner. The four isolated steps to the west of the latrine are the bottom treads of a staircase to the rampart-walk; an estimated projection of the steps on paper gives a wall-walk height of 4.20 m (14 ft).

Continue following the fort wall clockwise. The earth rampart originally backing this was partly removed in the third century to make room for new buildings; at the same time the wall was widened and faced with stone on the inside too. After passing the south gate again and rounding the SW angle (one oven and part of a second are visible in a building here), you reach the west gate, still standing to a spectacular height (14), with massive masonry piers, socket holes for the doors, and an L-shaped slot in the central pier for securing a beam fast behind the door.

The walk along Hadrian's Wall westwards from here is always a popular one, although other stretches equally fine but less well known exist elsewhere (especially on Highshield Crags and at Walltown). This stretch is owned by the National Trust, whose policy is to leave a turf capping on the Wall for the convenience of visitors. The tremendous views over a vast tract of the Northumbrian fells make the walk particularly memorable, but structurally there is not a great deal to note. After emerging from a picturesque coppice, you will notice a few offsets on the inside face of the Wall, marking the junction between different portions of slightly differing widths. These probably represent sections of Wall rebuilt or repaired by different groups of workmen in the nineteenth century, and are not an ancient feature at all.

Milecastle 37 is soon reached. The visible stone barrack, for a maximum of perhaps 16 men, was matched by timber buildings and hearths in the western half. The north gateway is very fine. The massive masonry of the gate-piers, together with the two springers *in situ* and some voussoirs (found fallen, and now re-set), are all of Hadrianic date. Before recent excavation and consolidation, these gate jambs were clearly out of the perpendicular, and this used to be interpreted as the work of barbarian destruction *c*. 197 – however hard it was to believe that a crowbar-wielding attacker would have paused to be so thorough on his way through to supposed pillage and plunder. Re-excavation has shown, however, that the gate-piers slumped out of position soon after their erection because too inadequate a foundation had been prepared for them. The opening as a result had to be entirely blocked soon after it was built to prevent the arch collapsing, although later, in the early third century, a new blocking-wall (what you see now) was erected, pierced by a narrow postern gate. The north wall of the milecastle on either side of the gate is a good example of the original Hadrianic

work, without later repairs or rebuildings. Note how two thin
levelling courses, characteristic of Hadrianic work, can be
seen to the left (and one to the right) of the gate. It has been
estimated from the projected height of the arch that the Wall
to wall-walk height would have been 4.5 m here
(14 ft 9 in), but that assumes that there were no further
courses of walling above the top of the archway (cf. the
estimate of 5 m [16 ft 4 in] at Poltross Burn, p. 520).

Thereafter, the Wall can be followed over Cuddy's Crag
with its famous view to the east, and on over Hotbank Crags
(327 m or 1,074 ft), where Crag Lough comes into view,
before it drops down to Milking Gap and the site of milecastle
38 (whence the stone in Fig. 100 came). No turrets are visible
on this stretch. Visitors with cars, of course, will have to
retrace their steps to Housesteads.

A mile (1.6 km) west of Housesteads car-park (where the
National Trust information centre displays a few finds from
the 1980s excavation of the Wall at Castle Nick, Sycamore
Gap and Highshield Crags), take a turning to the left
signposted Bardon Mill. Turn right at the T-junction and you
will soon come to a road to the right signposted Vindolanda
Museum. The site of Vindolanda can be reached from this
direction, but it is better to approach it from the west (see
below). Ignore therefore this turn, and continue on for $\frac{1}{3}$ mile
(500 m), before stopping in the second lay-by on the right.
Walk on for 200 m, and take the drive on your left at the
entrance to the third house (yellow way-markers). Turn sharp
left, through the gate, and make across the field to the metal
gate straight ahead of you. When in the next field, strike
obliquely to your left, cross the broken-down field-wall, and
join the grass path moving upwards to your right, parallel with
the road. Five minutes later, on a track not for the faint-
hearted, you pass a first quarry and then two minor outcrops,
before reaching the Roman quarry of **Barcombe** (NY
776662). This is one of very few quarries in Britain where we
can be certain that the workings are Roman rather than later.
In the main face here note a vertical fault line to the left of
centre: to the left of it are three vertical Roman wedge marks
and traces of a fourth, made by hammering metal wedges into
the rock to split it. About 1.50 m (5 ft) to the right of the fault,
at eye-level, you can still see the numeral XIII inscribed in the

rock by a Roman quarry worker; to its left are the letters JV, added in the nineteenth or twentieth century. A running boar, now weathered to oblivion, has been recorded further to the right: the emblem of the Twentieth Legion, it indicates the likely source of the men who worked the quarry. At the left-hand edge of this quarry face, 4 m (13 ft) from the fault line, a rather crudely drawn phallus, a symbol of good luck, has been cut in the rock by the quarrymen. The view of Vindolanda from here is breathtaking. This is not the only Roman quarry on the hill (the arm purse with coin hoard, now in Chesters Museum [p. 483], was found nearby in the nineteenth century), and further on the earthworks of a Roman signal station can be seen (NY 783668), but to locate it you will need a 1:50,000 OS map.

Return now to the B6318 and follow it westwards for another $1\frac{1}{2}$ miles (2.4 km) to the Steel Rigg crossroads, where you should turn left. As the road descends, the outlines of two temporary camps can be made out in the field facing you, on the other side of the stream. About 30 examples are known in the Wall region. Some were used in training, but these two probably sheltered troops engaged in building or possibly reconstructing the Wall. Readers interested in this class of antiquity can trace them in detail with the help of the catalogue and plans in *Roman Camps in England* (see Bibliography, p. 712).

Next turn left along the Stanegate Roman road. Note the stump of the Roman milestone of **Smith's Field** (NY 756662), mid-way between the first and second passing-places on the left: its upper parts were re-used in gate-posts, and its fragmentary inscription was recorded in the eighteenth century but is now lost. Soon after you come to the fort at Chesterholm, now usually known by its Roman name of **Vindolanda**** (NY 771664); it probably means 'bright moor'. The site is open daily from 1000, closing at 1600 (February and November), 1700 (March and October), 1730 (April and September), 1800 (May and June), or 1830 (July and August). Here an ambitious programme of excavation over the last 30 years, the work almost entirely of private initiative dependent on private funding, has uncovered a substantial part of the fort and its attendant settlement (*vicus*), and much else besides, which has turned Vindolanda into one

of the outstanding sites of Roman Britain. For since 1968
Vindolanda has produced a constant stream of remarkable
discoveries: it has the only visible example in Britain (apart
from a few buildings at Housesteads) of the sort of village
which sprang up round nearly every fort soon after its
foundation; it is the only site in Britain with two substantial
military bath-houses preserved; it has by far the largest
number of visible Roman lavatories (seven) at any Roman site
in the country; it boasts a curious series of circular stone
'huts', unique in the Roman Empire in a military context; and
it has produced from the pre-Hadrianic forts, now buried, an
astonishing archive of written material of exceptional
significance and of international importance.

A presumed early fort of Agricolan date beside the
Stanegate so far eludes discovery; it may have lain on a
completely different site, as at Corbridge (p. 472), or simply
not have existed. The earliest known occupation at
Vindolanda comes from a sequence of at least four successive
turf and timber forts of *c.* AD 90/125 which partly underlay the
later, visible civilian settlement. The first stone fort was
erected *c.* AD 124/5 with its axis on a different orientation and
a little further east; and this was replaced by a new fort of
AD 223/5 on substantially the same site. Shortly before that
happened, however, part of the interior of stone fort 1 was
remodelled with a series of circular huts, and the excavators at
Vindolanda currently think that the more 'conventional'
buildings of the fort at this stage, including visible buildings
interpreted as 'barracks' and the 'commanding officer's
house', lay in a defended annexe to the west of the fort
proper; in other words, according to this interpretation, some
of the '*vicus*' buildings at this period were not in fact civilian
but military. This cannot be right. No third-century fort
anywhere in the Empire is known with such an irregularly
laid-out series of military buildings as that currently proposed
for this 'annexe' in the first quarter of the third century at
Vindolanda, and in any case the circular 'huts' need not have
filled the whole of the fort interior in this phase (it has been
calculated that if they did there would have been 220 of
them!). The rebuilt fort of AD 223/5, more or less conventional
once more, remained in use into the late fourth century and
beyond, even though the *vicus* outside seems largely to have

been abandoned after *c.* 270. Nevertheless unbroken
occupation at Vindolanda is attested for more than 300 years.

The part of the site you come to first is the *vicus*, the
civilian settlement which grew up outside the Hadrianic/
Antonine fort and its third-century successor. Much of the
visible masonry belongs to the major reconstruction in the
third century (*c.* 225), but some elements of the second-
century *vicus* are also visible. First on the left is an excellent
example of a Romano-Celtic temple (1 on Fig. 112),
consisting of a central square shrine (with benches on three
sides) and an outer ambulatory. It was excavated in 2001,
when a fragmentary altar was also found; unfortunately the
name of the god venerated did not survive. Built *c.* AD 100, it
seems to have been demolished before the end of the second

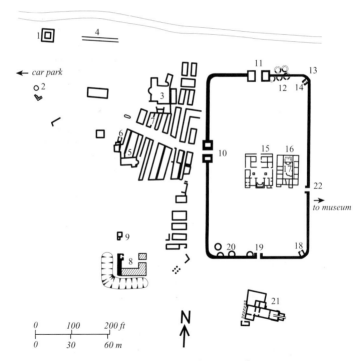

112   Vindolanda, Roman fort and civilian settlement, site plan

century. The discovery is of exceptional interest because
temples of Romano-Celtic type have not hitherto been found
further north than the Midlands: one wonders whether the man
responsible for commissioning the Vindolanda shrine was an
officer from further south in Britain, or from France or
Germany where the type is also common.

  After passing a well and a water-tank (2 on Fig. 112),
where the fine upright slabs are deeply worn, aim to the left
towards a military bath-house (3), passing a substantial
building with a flagged floor on your left, and a water conduit
(4) further uphill towards the fence: the latter seems to have
been part of the main aqueduct leat serving Vindolanda, at
least from the west. The bath-house, built *c.* 225 and so
contemporary with the visible stone fort, stands within a
fenced enclosure and is not therefore accessible: it is best to
observe it from the north side, near the steps. Its walls are in
part extraordinarily well preserved, standing up to 2.50 m
(8 ft) high; indeed antiquarian reports make it clear that part
of the vault was still standing in the late seventeenth century
before it fell prey to stone robbers. In front of you is the main
furnace-chamber with steps leading up to a boiler tank
mounted over the stoke-hole, which heated the adjacent hot
moist room (*caldarium*). The *tepidarium* lies beyond, with
most of its *pilae* intact, and you can also see the top of the
hot-water bath in the apse. A covered drain runs through the
hot room, under the flue, and then curves away. To the left of
the hot room is another heated room, with a separate stoke-
hole and part of its floor *in situ*; it was probably a hot dry
room (*laconicum*). Beyond it is the cold room (*frigidarium*)
and a cold immersion-bath. Moving now to your left down the
slope you come to a latrine, flushed by the drain already
mentioned; it is joined here by another that brought waste
water from the cold bath and passed under a long rectangular
room. The latter is interpreted as a changing-room, and, like
the latrine, is secondary to the main block; in the original
baths the *frigidarium* no doubt doubled as the changing-room.

  Now make towards the paved street which divides the *vicus*
into two halves. The first building to the right of the road is
probably a *mansio*, a hotel for travelling officials and anyone
else who could afford it (5). The label currently describes it,
however, as the commanding officer's house of the early

third-century fort, but for the reason given above I think this most unlikely. Before you enter it, note on the right what may have been a small brewery (6), with two semicircular vats and interconnecting flue, heated by a pair of stoke-holes in front. The *mansio* has a paved room in the right-hand wing, interpreted as the principal dining-room because of the adjacent kitchen (with oven in one corner), but it is surely too small for that purpose. A bath-suite at the far end has flue arches and stone-flagged floors partly *in situ*, as well as stone *pilae* and recesses in the walls to take hollow box flue-tiles *(tubuli)*. Straight joints make it clear that the bath-suite was originally freestanding and that the rest of the *mansio* was tacked on to it later. At the same time an extra room (a new *caldarium*) was added to the baths, with a new furnace (the original stoke-hole was probably removed when the additional heated room was built). The apsed pool in the original *caldarium* is also secondary. The latrine in the middle of the east wing had seats over the sewer surrounding the central block (the floor), but this one was apparently not flushed with running water.

Now cross the road to the house with a central corridor (7), originally one large dwelling, split into two in the late third-century alterations. The triple drains in one room have been interpreted as serving a butcher's shop or similar, but this is far from certain. Crossing the road once again you come to the remains of two long strip-buildings, but their current interpretation as barrack blocks serving an early third-century fort is doubtful (see above). A substantial oven at the far end of one of them at a higher level belongs to later houses and workshops now removed.

The rest of the structures between here and the west gate contain nothing of particular interest, so it is best to turn southwards now to the stone turret, stretch of turf wall, and timber milecastle gateway which were built here in 1972–4 to give visitors a three-dimensional idea of what the Wall and its works may once have looked like (8). As noted above (p. 442), it is far from certain that stone turrets had a flat platform at the top; note also how the turf wall and timber breastwork have parted company despite constant monitoring and repair – a salutary reminder that earth and timber forts in general in Britain needed substantial refurbishment (if not total rebuilding) at least every 30 years. Just before reaching the replicas are two stone-built tombs, one with a cist grave at its centre, contained within walled enclosures (9), while the stout modern posts behind the reconstructed turf wall mark the site of the south gate of the pre-Hadrianic fort, on a different alignment to the stone fort beyond.

The visible fort at Vindolanda, occupying 3.6 acres (1.5 ha), is the product of a complete rebuilding *c*. AD 223/5 (we know the precise date from an inscription), when its garrison was the Fourth Cohort of Gauls. Of the earlier stone fort below ('stone fort 1'), of Hadrianic and later date, parts of the *principia* and of the west and east defences have been identified. Also belonging to stone fort 1, but in a later phase, are the extraordinary circular stone huts (see below), which replaced conventional barracks at the north and south ends of the fort for a short time *c*. AD 200.

Of the third-century fort of *c*. 225 ('stone fort 2'), the west and north single-passageway gates, with towers containing guard-chambers unusually projecting beyond the line of the fort wall, were excavated and conserved in the 1930s. In the west gate (10), the recesses in the passage near the outer end were for the big stone piers of the gate structure, now robbed. The guard-chambers were both entered from inside the fort rather than from the passageway; one of these doors was later blocked. Now walk across the grass to the north gate (11), where the base of one of the gate-piers with a pivot-hole for hanging the door is still *in situ*. To the right are parts of three circular stone huts of *c*. AD 200 (12). They clearly predate the fort wall of 223/5, which has sliced through them: more of them can be seen outside the north wall. Excavation has shown that they were arranged in three neat rows of five in this NE sector; one has been found further west (not visible), and four more can be seen inside the south defences. It is therefore possible that a considerable part of the fort was occupied by these huts for a brief period in the early third century. Although no defences on either the north or the south sides have so far been located with certainty beyond the visible defences of AD 223/5 (finding them is an urgent research *desideratum*), they must surely have existed.

The function of the huts is baffling, since they are without parallel in a military context in the entire Roman world. They

recall similar structures which appear as outbuildings at some
Roman villas, reflecting Iron Age traditions (the circularity)
but built in stone. It has been suggested that the Vindolanda
huts were for British 'prisoners of war' captured by Severus'
army in Scotland, but no army at any period in history builds
purpose-made structures for prisoners, of a type to make them
feel at home. More likely these were intended as temporary
accommodation for pro-Roman local Britons (civilians) who
for some reason needed the protection of the military in an
emergency; but in the absence of parallels the true context for
their construction eludes us.

Now go out through the north gate and turn right, past the
remains of more circular huts, to examine the NE corner (13).
Here the wall stands over 2 m (7 ft) high, and two outlets are
visible at the base, where sewage and waste water discharged
from one of the fort's latrines. Retrace your steps through the
north gate and round to the NE corner, where this latrine, first
located in 1972, has been excavated and consolidated (14). In
an excellent state of preservation, it has a central flagged floor
and a Π-shaped sewer surrounding it. Built later than the fort
wall, which it abuts, it occupies (as does the latrine in the SE
corner) the position where one would expect a corner tower in
a second-century fort; but by the third century, here as
elsewhere, some of the features regarded as standard to fort-
design 100 years earlier were being modified.

Now walk to the centre of the fort, where the headquarters
building (15), excavated in the 1930s, is excellently preserved,
containing many interesting features not visible in that at
Chesters. A few foundations of the second-century *principia*
of stone fort 1, which faced in the opposite direction, can be
seen in places, but the visible layout belongs entirely to the
third century: this is the *principia* of the fort built in AD 223/5.
In the front half of the building, several rooms round a small
courtyard containing a well were turned into store-rooms
during a major reorganization in the fourth century: parts of
their ventilated floors remain, built of stone flags resting on
sleeper walls. Beyond is the usual cross-hall with its *tribunal*
on the right; the latter remarkably still preserves its moulded
edge, and the steps leading up to it. Look out for a phallus
carved for good luck on an ashlar block, re-used in the drain

close to the *tribunal*. Of the administrative rooms in the *principia*'s rear range, two features are unusual: the Π-shaped pit for storing pay-chests and other valuables; and the ornamental stone screens providing fronts to service counters in the flanking rooms on either side. A heated room was added to the rear range in a secondary period, projecting from the rear of the building as at Caernarfon (p. 349).

Now walk along the *via principalis* towards the east gate to visit the commandant's house (*praetorium*), partially explored in 1831 and totally excavated in 1997–8 (16). Three splendid altars to the presiding spirit of the house (*genius praetorii*) were found here in 1831 and are now in Chesters Museum; a fourth, with more weathered text, was found in 1997 and is in the site Museum (interestingly it was dedicated by a tribune of Legio I Minerva, which was stationed not in Britain but at Bonn in Germany). As consolidated, the commandant's house is in its early fourth-century state, with some later alterations *c.* AD 370.

At the SW corner of the *praetorium* is a structure with a drain (a water-tank?) and a little further on is a latrine, with the drain passing through to flush it: both were later additions to the main building as straight joints make clear. Now enter the building at the SE corner into a room with a flagged floor on low sleeper walls, similar to rooms in the *principia* and probably, like those, used as a store-building, the raised floor providing ventilation. There is a similar small square room adjacent, its entrance threshold still *in situ*. The three massive buttresses against the east wall of the building, clearly secondary, imply problems of subsidence at some stage in the *praetorium*'s life. Now pass into the heart of the building, an open courtyard indicated by the grassed area. Much of the southern half of this was occupied in its final phase by a building with an apse to the west (17: Fig. 113). The date is late, after AD 370 and probably *c.* AD 400, but that it is Roman rather than sub-Roman is suggested above all by its careful stone construction. Its plan at this date suggests that it must have been a church (western apses being not uncommon before the sixth century); so this little building can claim, together with the probable church at Colchester (p. 222) and the baptismal font at Richborough (p. 44), to be one of the earliest visible Christian structures in Britain.

A room in the south range of the *praetorium* has a
hypocaust (stone *pilae*), and the room at the NW corner
contains walling and a threshold which belong to an earlier
structure, which continues into the grass to the north. Between
praetorium and visible *principia* is another early wall, at a
still lower level and on a slightly different alignment
(probably the result of a surveying error). This is part of the
outer east wall of the Hadrianic *principia* of stone fort 1. The
wall is made up (highly unusually) of squared stones at
intervals and adobe (mud and straw) construction on a stone
foundation between, reminiscent of a style of masonry more
associated with Roman north Africa than with anything
elsewhere on the northern British frontier.

At the centre of the *praetorium*'s north wing is a heated
room fired from the west, marked by a long flue with
platforms on either side (the base for a hot-water pool?). The
floor supports inside are a miscellaneous jumble of re-used

113   Vindolanda, Roman fort, the praetorium *from the east, with church in
courtyard*

blocks, a column drum etc., in keeping with a late date
(*c.* 370?) for this insertion. The four buttresses along the
room's north wall are an afterthought (straight joints), as is
another hot bath on the south side of the room. This was at
first rectangular and then made semicircular, but later still the
bath substructure was filled in, and half of this blocking
remains *in situ*. The larger room into which this late bath was
inserted was itself originally heated: you can see the blocked-
up brick flue-arch (its original stoke-hole) in the room with
the flagged floor at the NE corner of the *praetorium*. Outside
the latter is a rectangular structure with a drain running
through it, a latrine block replaced in a final phase by a
smaller successor immediately adjacent (served by a second
drain at a higher level). Finally, a room in the east wing
adjacent to that with the flagged floor has a hypocaust fired
from its south side (there are signs of burning on the flue).
The floor supports are, unusually, roughly-hewn stone slabs
piled in irregular fashion, and there are gaps in the floor-
support ledge closest to the walls for the hot air to escape
upwards (clearest at the NW corner); that in the NE corner,
however, was blocked up by the time of the latest floor-laying.
The threshold block in the corridor here is obviously not in its
original position.

Now follow the fort wall to the SE corner, where there is
another latrine (18), with stone flags on either side resting on
low walls (indicating that one stepped up from the floor-well
to reach the seats over the sewers on each side); the arch of
the outflow sewer is also visible in the fort wall behind. From
here you soon reach the south gate, a simple opening without
flanking guard-chambers (19). Excellently preserved on its
east cheek are the tooling marks made by Roman masons
when dressing the stones; a rusticated block at the base of the
inner pier is also impressive. Part of the threshold block for
the gate also survives, flush with the outer face of the fort
wall. On the right of the gate, inside the fort wall, is half of
one of the circular stone huts already noted, sliced by the
construction of the south defences here *c.* AD 223/5: a
complete hut and parts of two more are visible inside the
fort's SW angle (20).

Outside the south gate on the right are foundations
(probably carrying a timber or an adobe [mud] superstructure)

of yet more *vicus* buildings, and the fort wall stands to an impressive height of nearly 2 m (7 ft) near the SW angle. But the real surprise in this quarter was the discovery in 2000 of a second military bath-house, erected *c.* AD 95/100 to serve the now-buried pre-Hadrianic turf-and-timber forts outside which it lay (21). These baths had a life of barely 50 years, being finally demolished and stripped *c.* AD 145. They belong to the so-called *Reihentyp* or 'row type' of military bath-house common in Europe (other visible examples include those at Hardknott in the Lake District and Bar Hill in Scotland: pp. 422 and 580), as opposed to the 'block' type of which Vindolanda's third-century bath-house is a good representative example. The *apodyterium* is now reburied; to its left are fragmentary remains of a small *laconicum* with two stone *pilae* and adjacent stoke-hole. The walkway passes over the central part of the bath-house: the cold room (*frigidarium*) lies to the right, with a red mortar (*opus signinum*) floor and a drain in the centre. Beyond it, below the end of the walkway, is a cold-water immersion-bath; curiously, there is no step down into it as customary (perhaps originally it was of timber), and the two blocks on the floor, not in alignment with one another and clearly placed there in a secondary period, appear to have served as a makeshift step. The floor of the pool itself, again unusually, has stone flags in the centre and *opus signinum* at the sides; was a smaller pool enlarged at some stage? Beyond it, down the slope in a detached block, was the latrine, with three steps leading down into it. It was flushed by a drain running from the centre of the *frigidarium*, which passed under the cold pool: the massive cover-slab of this drain can be seen in the narrow gap between the two buildings. Another drain descending the hill away to your right (west), its cover-flags still in position, does not seem to have connected with the latrine sewer.

To the left (east) of the *frigidarium* a narrow lobby also floored with *opus signinum* led the bather into the heated rooms, visible on the left of the walkway. The floors have gone but the *pilae* of both *tepidarium* and *caldarium* are very well preserved; most are of brick (many have circular control marks made with the finger on one side), but the *pilae* nearest the outer walls are of stone (Fig. 114). Frost damage will in time necessitate the substitution of the brick *pilae* with

modern replacements; many were shattered in the winter of
2000/1. Four substantial stone piers separate *tepidarium* from
caldarium, one still with mortar rendering on it. Beyond, a
long straight flue runs into the heart of the *caldarium* from the
furnace area on the east, but the latter, now very close to the
edge of the slope, is not well preserved.

From here retrace your steps through the fort's south gate to
the east gate, a simple opening like the south gate without
guard-chambers (22). To the right note the foundations of the
demolished period 1 (Hadrianic) fort wall, projecting up to a
metre (3 ft) in front of its successor. From here you descend to
the stream and the charming house which now contains the
Vindolanda Museum. Outside it, beside the stream, are
attempts to simulate what a shop, a house and a shrine in the
vicus would have looked like, as well as replicas of the altars
now at Chesters (and one in the Fulling Mill Museum at
Durham: p. 402) which were found at Vindolanda in the past.

114   Vindolanda, bath-house of the pre-Hadrianic fort, from the west

The first gallery in the Museum contains jewellery and glass, including a rare painted fragment (imported from the Cologne glassworks?) depicting a gladiatorial combat. The next room concentrates on the astonishing writing tablets (the objects themselves are in the British Museum) which have been the single most sensational discovery of the excavations. They come from the waterlogged levels of the pre-Hadrianic forts and can be closely dated between *c.* AD 90 and 120. Nearly 400 bear legible texts, the majority of them written in ink on thin leaves of wood, and still the discoveries go on (60 more were found in 2001). Some are letters of recommendation; some are private letters, one mentioning the despatch of sandals, woollen socks and two pairs of underpants; several are copies of letters sent by Flavius Cerialis, prefect of the Ninth Cohort of Batavians, who was stationed at Vindolanda *c.* AD 100, or are letters received by him; the most famous of all the documents is the invitation to Sulpicia Lepidina, Cerialis' wife, to come to the birthday-party of Severa, probably the wife of the commandant at another fort. Other tablets are official accounts, including financial records, reports on the strength of the garrison (documenting how many are seconded for duties elsewhere, or listed sick), and lists of foodstuffs such as barley, goats' meat, young pig, ham and venison, as well as wine and beer; one is even an official memorandum on the fighting capability of *Brittunculi* ('little Brits'), a disparaging diminutive. It is hard to overestimate the importance of the information which this unique military archive has yielded – about Roman army organization, about clothing and diet, about the private, everyday concerns of the ordinary soldier – quite apart from the light that they shed on the correct form of place-names, on styles of handwriting, and on the nuances of grammar, spelling and syntax.

Moving to your left and keeping straight, you come to a room with a staggering collection of wood and leather finds which have survived exceptionally well in the waterlogged pre-Hadrianic levels. The leatherware includes a perfect apron-pouch for tools, large fragments of clothing, and part of a tent-piece. Note also the rare survival of woven textiles, and an ox-head skull punctured by holes in target-practice. The woodwork includes pieces of doors, furniture such as a stool, and utensils such as a perfectly preserved wooden bowl, of a type which must have been ubiquitous in the ancient world but which rarely survives. The room opening off this gallery continues the same theme – more than a dozen wooden combs, one still in its leather pocket, a wooden spade, a now bristleless scrubbing brush. Also here are a charming bronze two-nozzled lamp on a stand, and a prancing horse on an attachment, probably used to decorate a wagon, but also interpreted (erroneously) as part of a military standard. The next gallery contains further remarkable wooden and leather objects, including a huge collection of Roman shoes; one is a superb lady's slipper, complete with a stamp in triplicate of the maker's name, L Aeb(utius) Thales. Some miniature altars and an array of tiles from the pre-Hadrianic bath-house excavated in 2000 are also displayed here. Two decorated balustrade slabs from the fourth-century *principia* give entrance to the final room, which concentrates on the theme of foodstuffs and cooking.

Before retracing your steps to the main entrance to Vindolanda, walk up to the farm road from the Museum and turn left: just beyond the stream on the right is a Roman milestone, standing complete but uninscribed (the original text may have been painted). It is one of very few Roman milestones in Britain still in its original position.

Now return to the B-road and go straight across it and up to Steel Rigg Roman Wall car-park. You now have the choice of going west or east. Westwards, a 15-minute walk takes you up to **Winshields** (NY 744676), the highest point on the Wall (trig-point, 1,230 ft or 375 m), with spectacular views as far as the Solway on a clear day. At the start the Ditch is rarely better preserved, and the overgrown remains of milecastle 40 are detectable just after the field-gate, but no Wall is visible until a long stretch just before the summit [AM; A].

Eastwards from the Steel Rigg car-park, on **Peel Crag*** and **Highshield Crags**** (NY 755676), there is much more of the Wall to see. Excavation and consolidation work from 1982 to 1990 has rendered this sector one of the most dramatic and rewarding on the whole Wall line. The level stretch on Peel Crag is partly dry-stone nineteenth-century work, as restored by John Clayton's workmen (in places it is only 1 m [3 ft] wide!). East of here, the Wall drops into Peel Gap, where excavation in 1986 discovered an unexpected supernumerary turret, and where you should cross over to the south side of the Wall (Fig. 115). The distance between milecastles 39 and 40 is one of the longest on the Wall, and the planners evidently decided to add a third turret in the stretch between the two, as an afterthought, after the Wall was built. Unlike all other turrets on the stone Wall, therefore, it is not recessed into the Wall but abuts it, as the straight joints make very clear. The turret is, however, unusually situated in a blind gap, with poor visibility except back to the Stanegate, so it was probably intended specifically to prevent people slipping over the Wall here unobserved, out of sight from adjacent turrets. The problem which prompted its building was, however, a short-term local difficulty which soon passed, and it is hardly surprising that the turret's door was soon blocked and that it was later demolished and ignored in the third-century reconstruction of the Wall in Peel Gap.

Evidence for the various phases of Hadrian's Wall is especially clear here: the Broad Wall foundation, the Narrow Wall base course, projecting slightly below the three or so courses of regular Narrow Wall standing on it, and then the Severan Wall of the early third century above that (Fig. 115). The distinction here between the hard white mortar of the Severan work and the second-century pinkish mortar was strikingly clear prior to consolidation work in 1987, but has now been replaced by modern mortar throughout. The excavation here and elsewhere on this stretch has in fact dramatically confirmed just how extensive the early third-century rebuilding of the Wall was, at least in this central sector – something suspected from evidence elsewhere (e.g. p. 484), but only fully confirmed by the excavations of the last two decades (cf. also Sewingshields, p. 489).

After climbing the hill on the far side, there is another stretch of largely rebuilt Wall, and the four 'offsets' visible here are probably breaks in the work of nineteenth- and early twentieth-century repair gangs. The second offset you come to does, however, serve to mark the site of the west wall of turret 39a, excavated by the distinguished Wall scholar, F G Simpson, in 1911. Its demolished walls are just below the turf here and are sometimes partly visible; so too are two courses of long slabs at the base of the Wall, which represent third-

century masonry built across the recess when the turret was
demolished (cf. Coesike, p. 487). It is clear from excavation
photographs of the time that the 'Hadrian's Wall' which you
see above these long slabs was in fact built by Simpson's
workmen in or after 1911.

A third of a mile (500 m) later you dip down again into
Castle Nick, milecastle 39 (front cover photograph). As at
Sewingshields the buildings within are all fragmentary, and
belong to at least three periods. At first the buildings within
were of timber, but these were soon replaced on the west by a
conventional long barrack in stone, of which one corner is
visible near the milecastle's north wall. In the third century,
this barrack was replaced by smaller rooms set at right-angles
to the milecastle walls; later additions impinge on the central
roadway. There were similar small stone structures occupying
the east side of the milecastle as well. Occupation continued

115   Peel Gap, turret   *116   Sycamore Gap, Hadrian's Wall*

into the late fourth century. Broad Wall foundations are visible on the inside on the milecastle's north wall. Its gateways are made of small stones, as the usual massive blocks were probably too awkward to transport to this remote spot. In the Severan period the gateways were reduced in width, and this later stonework remains in position at the south gate. The insubstantial footings suggest that gate did not bear the weight of a tower above, and it was probably the norm along the Wall that only the north gate had a two- or three-storey tower.

On the crag east of the milecastle are three small irregular stone buildings ('shielings' or shepherds' huts) erected in the shelter of the Wall in the medieval period: pottery from them dates from the fourteenth to the sixteenth centuries. Beyond them, just before the prominent knoll named Mons Fabricius (after a noted German scholar in Roman frontier studies), a short stretch of Wall foundations (in the broad gauge) can just be made out immediately south of the line which the Wall eventually took. It is now somewhat overgrown, but if you climb the knoll and look obliquely back towards the Wall, the foundation can be made out below you. Clearly the original plan was to swing the Wall eastwards down into Sycamore Gap on a more gentle curve, but, as built, the Wall turns abruptly 90° to descend the steep slope.

The Wall descending into Sycamore Gap is a splendid sight (Fig. 116). Erected on carefully stepped foundations, keeping its horizontal coursing as it takes a dramatic dive down into the gap, this stretch is steeper and even more impressive than similar examples elsewhere in the consolidated sector (e.g. Thorny Doors, p. 515; Walltown, p. 517). It is worth walking through the modern breach at the foot of the gap to examine the drainage culvert at the lowest point; note also how the very hard basalt whinstone blocks, distinct in colour from the limestone courses above (and much more difficult to quarry), are employed at the base of the Wall for extra stability. When first exposed in 1987 some traces of hard white mortar on the outer face of the Wall as it climbed eastwards out of the gap were still visible (immediately on the right of the path where it starts from the breach). The mortar was clearly not just in the joins but also covering the facing-stones. The feature was also detectable in parts on the inner face, and has given rise to the suggestion, since confirmed by work elsewhere on the Wall, that by the time of the Severan reconstruction (and probably also from the start), Hadrian's Wall was 'white-washed' throughout its entire length, to make it an even more forbidding sight. More than a decade of rain and frost, however, has now removed virtually all traces of this rendering. Return now to the inner face and climb up on to Highshield Crags where the newly consolidated sector ends. The broad foundation, in places with a single building course present, is clearly visible here as the Wall climbs up to the crags again, with the Narrow Wall foundation cutting into it. The original white, very hard Severan mortar is still visible in places here, still resistant to frost damage (a great tribute to its quality), and can be easily distinguished from the modern grouting in grey and pink mortar; but it will need gradual replacement over the coming years. Some traces of the superficial 'white-washing' are visible here on the inner face, especially on the bottom course, at the end of the first of the two stretches of broad foundation.

From Steel Rigg, turn right on to the B-road and then second right (signposted Cawfields). On the left, between road and stream, the rampart-mounds of the fortlet of Haltwhistle Burn are visible, built under Hadrian but only briefly occupied. On its north side, at the point where the road swings to the left, is a small practice camp, right by the road. Park here, and walk along the track leading straight on. Immediately on the right, the low defences of another tiny camp can be made out. Both are too small to have served other than as training exercises in camp-building. Next you cross the Vallum, which is most striking as it stretches away to the right in a fine state of preservation. Then the Military Way is clearly visible, laid in the 160s to link forts and milecastles. Finally you reach the Wall at **Cawfields** (NY 716667) [AM; A]. (If you prefer not to walk the whole way, follow the asphalt road round to Cawfields car-park and then take the path to the Wall.) Here is milecastle 42 (Fig. 117), especially impressive for the massive masonry of its south gate, which stands 1.80 m (6 ft) high, thus preserving the bolt-hole. It is worth walking eastwards from here at least as far as the gap at Thorny Doors, where you should go through the iron gate to admire a magnificent piece nearly 3 m (10 ft)

high, and nowhere else higher on the whole Wall (since the
Hare Hill fragment in Cumbria was largely rebuilt in the
nineteenth century: p. 529). So steep is the slope here that the
foundation of the Wall must be stepped, for the courses are
laid nearly at right-angles to the lie of the ground. In places
such as this, you can fully appreciate just how tremendous an
engineering achievement Hadrian's Wall is.

There is much of interest, too, in the stretch from Thorny
Doors all the way to the minor road $\frac{1}{2}$ mile (800 m) away. First
follow the inside of the Wall, noting the offsets which mark
the varying thicknesses of the Wall in different stretches.
Then cross to the north side at the second stile after Thorny
Doors, and you soon come to a remarkable stretch where the
wall is stepped to ensure great stability (cf. p. 518). Just
before the minor road the foundations of turret 41a will be
reached. This was demolished and the Wall rebuilt over it in
the third century: the line of both the inside face of the
original north wall of the turret and the third-century masonry
filling can be seen, as elsewhere on the Wall (e.g. Coesike,

117 Cawfields milecastle

p. 487). This point can also be reached by taking the turning to Cawburn off the B6318.

Return from Cawfields once more to the B-road, turn right and first right (unsignposted). Bear right at the fork, and after the third gate across the road you come at once to the south gate of the fort of **Greatchesters** (NY 704668), with an altar (a libation jug in relief on one side) still standing in the east guard-chamber. This was the Roman AESICA, a name echoing the Celtic god Esus, perhaps worshipped hereabouts. A good deal is visible here – most of the south and west ramparts and their gates, the NW and SW corner towers, and one of the arches of the underground strong-room in the *principia* – but the ruins are in a sorry state, overgrown and neglected. The place is perhaps worth a visit to show how exposed masonry deteriorates when it is not treated, and to enable us to appreciate precisely what the consolidation of the Wall by the National Trust and by what is now English Heritage has achieved. Greatchesters would look very different with intervention from them. The fort was a later addition to the Wall than most, as it was not built before AD 128. The main item of interest is its west gate, which still has a blocking-wall in position across one portal: note how this sits on a threshold with pivot-hole, probably marking the third-century level; by contrast the Hadrianic threshold in the other portal is nearly 0.90 m (3 ft) lower. Nineteenth-century excavators at other forts often removed such masonry to expose the thresholds beneath; only at Birdoswald elsewhere on the Wall is such blocking of a fort gateway still visible *in situ*. A 6-mile (9.7-km) leat brought water to the fort from the north: parts of it can be traced with the help of the OS map of Hadrian's Wall (see also Bibliography, p. 715).

Follow the B6318 for another 3 miles (5 km) until a signpost to **Walltown**** (NY 673664) [AM; A] appears on the right, $\frac{1}{2}$ mile (800 m) east of Greenhead. Follow the English Heritage signs. The path from the car-park leads to a hollow between the trees, but it is better to climb up the slope on your right, until you reach turret 45a. This was built as an independent signalling-tower, probably early in Hadrian's reign when the Stanegate was still the frontier, and was later incorporated into the Wall. From here westwards for some 400 m the Wall is at its very best. First comes a magnificent

dive into one of the Nine Nicks of Thirlwall, and the effortless
climb up the far side (Fig. 118). A 'centurial stone' reading
COH III was built upside-down into the outer face of the
Wall, although it is now (2001) virtually illegible: it lies west
of the great dip, on the bottom course above the foundation
offset, 46 blocks west of the point of ground where the Wall,
having reached the summit and stayed level for 3 m, begins to
slope down again westwards (for the implication, see p. 484).
Then, still standing to a stately height of 2.10–2.40 m (7–8 ft),
the Wall weaves a sinuous course round whinstone outcrops.
At one point where it has to change direction suddenly on a
steep slope, the inner face is stepped slightly to ensure stability.
Finally, this exciting sector is abruptly ended on the edge of a
quarry, which has disgracefully removed the Wall for $\frac{1}{4}$ mile
(400 m). If you have time you may like to follow the Wall
eastwards from turret 45a. Most of it is visible, unconsolidated,
all the way to Greatchesters, but it lacks the grandeur of the
Walltown stretch. Turret 44b, above Walltown Farm, still nine

118   Walltown Crags, Hadrian's Wall as it may have appeared, looking east

courses high, stands unusually in a 90° angle, as the Wall
changes direction here.

After Walltown, before rejoining the B6318 near
Greenhead, the Roman Army Museum is worth a short visit.
The Museum is open daily from 1000, closing at 1600
(February and November), 1700 (March and October), 1730
(April and September), 1800 (May and June), or 1830 (July
and August). There are a few original finds on display here
(mostly 'overflow' material from Vindolanda, a site under the
same management), but several models, life-size mock-ups
and reproductions of Roman armour, as well as a Hadrian's
Wall video, are informative and entertaining.

On leaving the Museum, it is worth walking down the path
along its north side, as far as the metal gate, for an excellent
view of the north rampart of the fort of **Carvoran**
(NY 665657), standing high and bold under its turf capping.
The stonework of the NW angle-tower, first uncovered in 1886
and re-excavated and consolidated in 1997, is also visible.
Virtually no excavation has ever been carried out at this fort,
although some is scheduled for 2002/3; regrettably, a request
for permission to reconstruct a section of the fort wall (a
practice common in Germany at the forts of its Roman frontier)
has so far been turned down by English Heritage. Aerial
photography suggests that there was a pre-Hadrianic fort
(*c.* 90?) below the visible one, but on a slightly different site.
Geophysical work in the 1990s has revealed an extensive
civilian settlement at Carvoran, especially to the east and south,
where buildings lined the Stanegate for over 180 m (200 yds).

Carvoran, the Roman MAGNIS (meaning 'stones' or 'rocks'
in Celtic), has also produced a rich haul of inscribed stones
and other chance finds over many years, now mainly divided
between the museums at Chesters and Newcastle. The
garrison attested here in 136/8 and 163/6 is the First Cohort of
Hamian archers, a specialist unit from Syria; not surprisingly
dedications to Syrian deities such as the 'Syrian goddess'
(*dea Syria*) and Jupiter of Baalbeck are also known. Also
from Carvoran and now in Chesters Museum is the very rare
find of a bronze dry-measure (*modius*), designed to hold,
according to its elegant inscription, the equivalent of $17\frac{1}{2}$
sextarii (9.5 litres). It was inscribed in AD 90/1, as the
consular date given in the reign of Domitian makes clear; but

the name of Domitian himself has been erased, an excellent
example of the process of *damnatio memoriae*, whereby all
records naming a 'bad' emperor were systematically
eradicated. The reason for the rather curious amount of the
contents (a little more than a *modius*, which was made up of
16 *sextarii*) is that it was probably the amount of a soldier's
weekly ration of corn, which another source indicates
amounted to just under $2\frac{1}{2}$ *sextarii* per day. If this is right, it
demonstrates (along with other evidence) that the seven-day
week was already in operation in the first century AD.

After Carvoran, the dramatic parts of Hadrian's Wall are
behind you, and you leave the crags for the gentler slopes of
Cumbria. Go right in Greenhead, and follow the signs for
Gilsland, turning right along the B6318. After $\frac{1}{2}$ mile (800 m),
just before the first turning to Longbyre, a fragment of
Hadrian's Wall (here cut by the modern road) is visible high
up in the embankment on your left. Just before the railway-
bridge at the beginning of Gilsland, turn left to the hotel car-
park and visit milecastle 48 at **Poltross Burn*** (NY 635662)
[AM; A], the most instructive on the Wall. Both gates were
narrowed in the Severan reconstruction, and the blocking-wall
and pivot-hole are clearly visible at the north gate. There is an
oven at the NW corner and, in the NE, a staircase to the
rampart-walk: a projected calculation of its treads upwards
has suggested that the wall-walk here was 15 Roman feet high
(16 ft 4 in or 5 m). The outlines of the two stone barracks
survive. The milecastle was built with broad-gauge wing-
walls on either side; one of these can be seen, together with a
fragment of Narrow Wall on broad foundation. The latter
feature continues as far as the Irthing.

Go under the railway-bridge, turn left at the junction in
Gilsland, and stop on the brow of the hill. On your left an old
'Ministry of Works' board (wicket-gate) advertises the sector
of Wall in the former vicarage garden of **Gilsland** (NY
630662) [AM; A]. Here it only stands 1–1.20 m (3–4 ft) high,
but there is no better place to study the Narrow Wall on a
broad foundation. The first stretch in the grounds of a
neglected house is rather overgrown with moss and nettles,
but beyond the fence the Wall is well conserved. This stretch
has some superb drainage culverts, because of the proximity
of a stream, and the first of these (the most westerly) is the

culvert through which the stream itself originally passed. Here too it can be seen most clearly that the Narrow Wall does not merely rest on broad foundation, but on three courses of Broad Wall. It seems that construction of the curtain wall was actually in progress here when the order came, in 124 or 125, to reduce the width of the wall, and rather than demolish what was already constructed, the builders merely carried the Wall on upwards at its new width.

On the other side of the road, the Wall is impressively visible on its broad foundation all the way to **Willowford*** (NY 622664) [AM; A] and the bridge over the Irthing. First comes an excellent example of a turret (48a) with wing-walls built to the broad gauge. Nearer the farm a cart-track runs in the Ditch, and turret 48b is visible. By contrast this has a wing-wall only on the east side, whereas on the west there is a tapering width to accommodate the Narrow Wall beyond. This detail suggests that turret 48b was actually in the process of construction when the order came to narrow the Wall: the east wing-wall had been built expecting Broad Wall to meet it, but the west side was modified to accommodate a new, narrower specification for the curtain wall.

Then comes the final slope down to the Irthing. The bridge abutment here, less impressive than the example at Chesters, is a complicated structure displaying work of three periods. Starting from the wicket-gate on the north side of the Wall, you will first see a large masonry embankment which protected the ground here from erosion by the river. The latter has now shifted far away. Then come two culverts which were probably flood channels for a river in spate. The recesses for the timbers of the bridge superstructure, as well as the cramp-holes to bind the stones together, can be seen in the pier here: all this masonry, as well as the culverts and the projecting embankment, belong to the Phase II (Antonine) bridge, after the stone arches of the Phase I (Hadrianic) bridge had been removed. Now round the bridge pier and a paved section of the river bed. Parallel to it is a bridge abutment; on its south end note the block with a fragmentary phallus on it, re-used from the curtain wall, and there is a re-used moulded block in the fill of this abutment too. The pier and the abutment, which blocks one of the culverts, belong to the Phase III bridge, which carried the Military Way: it approached the bridge on a

sloping ramp, which extended east of (and buried) the square
tower with a central internal floor support. The tower (built of
re-used blocks, with massive foundation stones) belongs to the
Phase II bridge of *c*. 140, and the edge of its abutment is
represented by the diagonal line of stones which was
incorporated in and buried by the later ramp. The masonry
between the two abutments must be a later addition (straight
joint) to the Phase III abutment. The south face of the Wall
here shows considerable signs of the frequent rebuildings it
underwent. The date of the Phase III bridge is currently
assigned to the late second or early third century on the basis
of pottery; but it makes sense to ascribe it to *c*. 165, in line
with the chronology now established at the Chesters bridge,
and see it as part of the works associated with the building of
the Military Way, and the consequent need to convert what
had been only a pedestrian bridge into one for vehicular
traffic. If this work was really not carried out at Willowford
until *c*. 200, carts and wagons must have crossed the Irthing
somewhere else, on a temporary timber bridge.

Walkers can now cross the Irthing via a newly built
footbridge, and climb up the bank opposite, now much steeper
than in Roman times. Motorists must return to Gilsland, turn
left and left again after the bridge; then follow the B6318 for
about $1\frac{1}{4}$ miles (2 km) until Birdoswald is signposted on the
left. From the car-park $\frac{1}{2}$ mile (800 m) later, you walk up
towards the Birdoswald fort. Before visiting that, take the gate
into the field on your left opposite the start of the path to the
Visitor Centre. You can then walk along a fine stretch of the
Wall eastwards to the Irthing.

The Wall here is Narrow on a narrow foundation, for it was
not built in stone until late in Hadrian's reign. Where it
survives high enough, the thin string course typical of
Hadrianic work after 124 will be spotted. The earlier Turf
Wall, which this stretch replaced and which for 2 miles
(3.2 km) west of the Irthing takes a slightly different course
to that of the Stone Wall, is not now visible except for a short
sector west of Birdoswald mentioned below. This sector of
stone Wall has an above-average frequency of drainage
culverts: at the start of this stretch, look out for a diagonal
cross (probably the numeral X) scratched on a block two
courses up from the bottom, just before the first drainage

culvert. This is one of half a dozen such stones to have been found in the area of Birdoswald, and it and other numerals have been recorded from elsewhere on the Wall: they presumably represent tally-marks, either made in the quarry, or else (more likely) by stonemasons building the Wall. Five blocks above it, note that a phallus has been carved in relief for good luck, one of two in this stretch (the other, mid-way between here and the milecastle, or 52 m [57 yds] beyond the centurial stone mentioned below, is now very difficult to spot). At the time of the consolidation of this stretch of wall, in the 1960s, six examples of centurial stones were found, still in their original positions on the inside face of the Wall. Only one of these is still readily identifiable, and its position, on the top surviving course, is indicated by a small metal strip projecting near the base of the Wall. It can be found one-third of the way along this stretch, 152 m (167 yds) from the start of it, or 245 m (268 yds) before the milecastle. It reads COH VIII | >IVL PRIMI, 'Eighth Cohort, *centuria* [the V-sign on its side] of Julius Primus'. Other inscriptions from this stretch of Hadrian's Wall, between milecastles 49 and 54, consistently refer to the Sixth Legion, so we can be fairly certain that Primus belonged to this legion, which carried out this late Hadrianic change of plan (see above).

Your walk ends at the poorly preserved milecastle 49, **Harrow's Scar** (NY 620663) [AM; A]. Parts of its walls and one gate are visible, but most of the stonework inside belongs to a post-Roman farmstead. Not surprisingly the south gate was later narrowed by a blocking-wall still partly *in situ*: the steepness of the slope outside suggests that this gate would only ever have been suitable for pedestrians. It will be noted that there are no wing-walls at this milecastle; in fact its side walls abut Hadrian's Wall here. This is because, as noted above, the original Turf Wall and the turf and timber milecastle here were replaced in stone *c.* 135, after the main construction programme of the original Wall (120–30) had been completed. This change initially affected only the first 5 miles (8 km) west of the Irthing.

Now retrace your steps and visit the fort of **Birdoswald**** (NY 616663) [AM; March–October, daily, 1000–1730; November, 1000–1600; the fort is also accessible outside these hours]. Its defences are arguably more interesting and better preserved than those of any other Wall fort. To the right of the path leading to the exhibition area, an interval tower on the fort's northern defences is marked out, demolished in the third century when it was replaced by a larger cookhouse with ovens. Beyond is the NW corner, still standing 1.80 m (6 ft) high. Climb up the bank to have a look at the angle-tower; there are two second-century ovens, often rebuilt, within. Its doorway has been blocked, probably in the fourth century. After a short break comes an interval tower with a flagged floor of Severan date and another blocked doorway.

Now retrace your steps to the Visitor Centre, where the history of the fort together with some of the finds are displayed in a clear and imaginative way. Much of the defences as we see them today were uncovered in the mid nineteenth century; there were other excavations in the 1920s and 1930s, and then a major series of campaigns between 1987 and 1992 which exposed the interior buildings now visible and the west gate. Little is known of the Hadrianic short-lived turf-and-timber fort which lay astride the Turf Wall; it was quickly replaced by a stone Hadrianic fort, and a new alignment was taken for Hadrian's Wall, meeting up with the fort's northern defences. Birdoswald was an infantry fort for a unit nominally 1,000 strong: a milliary cohort of Dacians (originally from Romania) was the garrison here in the third and fourth centuries.

Now go round to the back of the former farm buildings to visit the interior structures excavated in 1987–91. On your left are two excellently preserved granaries (Fig. 119), built in 205–8 (as we know from an inscription). The customary buttresses are here only on the south side of each granary, and the sleeper walls supporting the floors can be seen – only partially in the south granary, where the flagged floor has been replaced on completion of the excavation. Note that the fourth stone up on the east side of the fourth buttress of the north granary (counting from the east) is inscribed IVLIVS. The ventilation slots in the south wall of the north granary and the north wall of the south granary will also be noted. At the very end of the fourth century, the latter had been used by squatters for domestic occupation (hearth); later, after its collapse, the long-ruined north granary (which had collapsed c. 350), became the site of two successive timber buildings, the later

119   Birdoswald, Roman fort, granaries from the east

(perhaps fifth/sixth century) a substantial sub-Roman hall. The
massive posts for this, in their original post-holes, mark out its
plan and size.

On the other side of the *via principalis*, in front of the
former farmhouse, are a number of structures of varying dates.
On the east was a third-century workshop (*fabrica*), with a
workbench, a drain, an area of hardstanding and a rudimentary
kiln (at the west end); but all this was overlain by a sixteenth-
century house (distinguishable from the Roman masonry by
the pitched footings). Next to it, to the west, was another
workshop which during excavation produced plentiful
evidence for iron-smithing. This was again a third-century
structure; it replaced a Hadrianic store-building. Its slight
subsidence, still visible, is due to slippage into the Ditch of the
original Hadrianic Turf Wall which lay below at this point.

Beyond it, in the grass verge right next to the farmhouse,
the single long wall marks the southern extremity of a large
hall (*basilica*), divided by two rows of piers into a 'nave' and

side 'aisles'; other parts of its plan, and its overall dimensions
(16 m by 43 m [52 ft by 140 ft]), have been established by
judicious trenching in the yard beyond. Belonging to the
original Hadrianic fort, and used throughout the military
occupation down into the fourth century, it is assumed to have
been a covered drill-hall. It is clearly of the same type as that
already noted at Wallsend (p. 462), but it and the other British
examples are all found astride the *via principalis*, not
occupying a separate building unit within the fort interior.
Indeed in this one respect, the Birdoswald *basilica* is unique
in the military archaeology of the Roman Empire.

You now come to the west gate, one of the most instructive
on the Wall. From the inside, you can see that this was a
single-portal gate in its final phase, with pivot-holes for
hanging the doors, door-stop, and a paved road leading up to
it. To your left (south) is the original south portal at the lower
level, with a late blocking-wall in position over the original
threshold of this carriageway below: the blocking-wall was
dismantled during excavation to study the threshold, but has
been carefully reconstructed. The iron socket for holding the
gate is still *in situ* at this lower level. Note the original large-
block inner and outer gate-piers at the south end. The original
guard-chamber can be seen beyond. To your right is the north
guardroom of the west gate, used as a smithy from the third
century; beyond, in the rampart backing further north, are
three second-century ovens.

Now go through the west gate and across the causeway
outside the fort, and then turn left on to the grass. The culvert
draining the late causeway across the ditch can be seen, but the
most remarkable feature is the superb cut masonry with
projecting base-plinth, all laid without mortar, which comprises
the outer wall of the original south guardroom of the third-
century gate-tower. Masonry of this quality is an extreme rarity
in Roman Britain, and its appearance here is something of a
surprise: it was not specially cut for the gate here, and was
certainly dismantled from another monument elsewhere (a fine
grave monument? or a Victory monument?) and re-assembled
here. Despite its impressive appearance it may not have been
intended to be seen, if the whole of the fort's exterior was
covered in white plaster, as seems most likely.

Passing through the gate into the field beyond, and

continuing along the west rampart, you come first to the lesser
(single-portal) west gate and then reach the SW angle. Here the
bottom two courses are probably Hadrianic, the next three (set
back a little, giving a step-like appearance) are Severan, and
the top two are the work of a fourth-century repair. Long
interpreted as graphic evidence for alleged destructions of the
Wall and its works in 197 and 296, this more likely indicates
the extent of the rebuilding sometimes necessary when
refurbishment of the defences was carried out after long
periods of neglect.

Next comes the south gate. Both thresholds of the Hadrianic
gate, together with pivot-holes, are visible; the later blocking-
walls have been removed. The irregular masonry of the wall on
the left belongs to a fourth-century rebuilding. Both the
flanking guardrooms have kilns and ovens. Next, it is worth
walking to the edge of the promontory for the view over the
Irthing. The name of the fort, BANNA, which means the 'horn'
or 'spur', must refer to its dominant position overlooking the
river. Evidence of the ditches of the labour camp built when
the Hadrianic turf fort was first being constructed, was found
here in 1932 and 1996, and produced important remains of
leather tents in their waterlogged deposits.

Now follow the fort wall round the SE angle (the corner
tower is visible, excavated in 1992). A stretch of partially
tilting wall either side of the lesser east gate, excavated in
1992, can be seen here. The large blocks on the top with lewis
holes for lifting them are part of a third-century repair: blocks
coming from the Willowford Bridge have been re-used here.
The east gate is excellently preserved. In both portals remains
of two successive pivot-holes can be seen, probably Hadrianic
and (above) Severan. The massive jamb of the right-hand
(north) portal still stands to its full height and the springer of
the arch is in position. In the fourth century, this portal became
a guardroom, and part of its back wall is still visible. The door
of the original, adjacent guard-chamber was then blocked up
and a new door opened in its south wall, giving access to the
portal now used as a guardroom. At the same time fresh
masonry was inserted between the back and front central piers.
Finally, at the north end of the east rampart, near a post-Roman
kiln, comes an interval tower.

Extensive geophysical work in 1997–8 has not only

provided a reasonably detailed plan of buildings in the rest of
the fort interior not excavated; it has also yielded a vivid
picture of a densely packed area of some 30 buildings in a
civilian settlement (*vicus*) east of the fort, as well as ribbon
development along a road leading west, where the cemetery
also lay. More remarkably, the geophysics also demonstrated
that buildings lined, for at least 100 m, a Roman road heading
northwards for the fort at Bewcastle (App. 1), on the
'barbarian' side of the Wall Ditch. Such settlement is a telling
witness to what must have been the many years of unbroken
peace on the northern frontier, especially in the third and early
fourth centuries: these structures otherwise would simply
never have been built.

Westwards from Birdoswald you will get your last view of a
substantial length of Hadrian's Wall. Turret 49b is also
exposed here. Then, $\frac{1}{2}$ mile (800 m) later, look out for the first
track on the left (metal gate), with the sign **High House**
(NY 603657). Just after passing through a fence on this track
you will see a low broad mound and accompanying Ditch
stretching for a short distance on the left. This is the only
visible fragment of the Turf Wall: be careful not to confuse it
with the high mounds and ditch of the Vallum which lie
immediately beyond and which are a striking sight here in both
directions. Return to the minor road and stop after the slight
bend $\frac{3}{4}$ mile (1.2 km) further on, at the gate on the right at the
top of a slope. The Wall Ditch is boldly preserved here on your
right, but so also is the Turf Wall Ditch which can be seen over
the stone field-wall on the left of the road at the same point.
The lines of the Turf and Stone Walls converged a few metres
further on and remained identical, with one short exception, all
the way to Bowness.

Soon afterwards, three Turf Wall turrets are passed. These
were built of stone from the beginning and the Turf Wall came
right up to either side: when the latter was replaced in stone, it
too stood up against the existing turrets, and its masonry is
never bonded with that of the turrets. First comes turret 51a,
Piper Sike (NY 589653) [AM; A], excavated in 1970 and the
least well preserved. A flagged platform can be seen inside,
usually thought to have been a base for a staircase to the upper
storeys. The straight joint between the turret and the later stone
Wall can be seen on the west side. Turret 51b, **Leahill** (NY

583650) [AM; A], like Piper Sike, seems not to have been used
after the second century; it too has a stone base within and a
fragment of the Wall abutting it on the west side. Finally,
$\frac{2}{3}$ mile (1 km) further west, comes the imposing turret of **Banks
East** (NY 575646) [AM; A], turret 52a. Unlike the other two
this was occupied into the third century. Here the plinth that
was a characteristic of Turf Wall turrets is perfectly preserved
on the north, and the Stone Wall of Hadrian abuts on each side:
this is part of the 5-mile (8-km) stretch west of Birdoswald
which was rebuilt in stone as an afterthought already in
Hadrian's reign (p. 522). Two hearths and a 'staircase
platform' can be seen within the turret, and a fallen piece of
superstructure lies nearby. The view to the south is very fine.
Four drainage culverts are visible in the adjacent stretch of the
Wall, three west of the turret, one to the east. A path leads
eastwards for 100 m to the single surviving corner of the tower
on Pike Hill which, like the one at Walltown (p. 517), seems to
have been built early in Hadrian's reign before the Wall was
conceived. Despite being so close to turret 52a, it appears to
have continued in use right into the fourth century. Curiously,
it was this fragmentary tower that was the first ever piece of
the Wall to come into state guardianship, under what was then
the Office of Works, in 1933.

After Banks East, turn right at the T-junction $\frac{3}{4}$ mile (1 km)
later. About 320 m (350 yds) further on, on the left, the first
track on the left leads very soon to the fragment of Wall on
Hare Hill (NY 564646) [AM; A]. At 3 m (9 ft 10 in) high, it
happens to be the highest surviving fragment anywhere along
the Wall line, but the facing-stones on the north side, including
a centurial stone, are Roman but not original, having been
collected elsewhere and set here only in the nineteenth century.

This is the last visible piece of the Stone Wall before its
terminus on the Solway. Further west, although short stretches
of Ditch or Vallum can be traced in places, Hadrian's Wall
has little of interest for the visitor. Westwards from milecastle
54 ($1\frac{1}{2}$ miles [2.4 km] west of Banks East), the Wall remained
in turf until reconstructed in stone either $c.$ 165 or $c.$ 200,
when the gauge was neither 3 m (10 ft) i.e. broad, nor 2.45 m
(8 ft) (narrow), but 2.75 m (9 ft). One stretch of this
Intermediate Wall, in red sandstone, used to be exposed
during the summer months at Walton, but it has now been

reburied for its own protection because of the friable nature of the sandstone.

The five remaining forts have left little visible trace. That at **Stanwix** (NY 401571), now a suburb of Carlisle, was the largest fort on the Wall. It was the Roman VXELLODVNVM, 'high fort'. Here was stationed the commander-in-chief of the Wall garrison and a cavalry regiment 1,000 strong, the *Ala Petriana*. Only one cavalry unit of this size was allowed per province, and in Britain's case the prestigious unit was stationed here – a sign of the significance of Stanwix in the whole Wall command structure. The position of this headquarters so near the western end may seem surprising, but when the 40 miles (64 km) of Solway posts, which were an integral part of the Hadrianic frontier, are included, Stanwix is near the centre of the system. It is also in this part that the Wall's command of ground to the north is weakest. In 1984 the footings of the north wall of the fort were found further north than expected, making the fort over 9.75 acres (4 ha) in size. A length of 24 m (80 ft) was uncovered, including an interval tower; the date was apparently Antonine, when the fort must have been expanded in size. A tiny fragment of this curtain wall has been consolidated and left on display, in the car-park at the rear of the Cumbria Park Hotel on Scotland Road (turn off the A7 eastwards along Milecastle Crescent); this lies a little to the north of St Michael's Church. Part of the mound of the fort's south rampart is faintly discernible near the southern boundary of St Michael's churchyard.

Across the river, at **Carlisle*** (NY 396561), lay the flourishing town of LVGVVALIVM, preceded by and incorporating a series of military structures of which much has been learnt through excavation prior to redevelopment over the last 30 years. Particularly striking were the timber remains, excellently preserved in waterlogged conditions, of the south gate of the early fort (which lay under and to the south of the castle). Dendrochronology has established that this fort was founded by Petillius Cerialis in AD 72/3. A defended annexe lay to the south: part of its ditch was excavated in 1989 before building an extension to the Tullie House Museum. The Flavian fort was demolished *c.* 103/5, but the finds from a succession of second-century timber buildings with industrial workings, and from the stone

barrack-type structures put up in their place in the third
century, suggest a continued military presence. It is uncertain,
however, if this was still a conventional fort in the third and
fourth centuries. To the SE lay a surprisingly large town
covering some 80 acres (33 ha), but little is known about it.
All that can be seen of Roman Carlisle today is an enigmatic
stone-lined pit, probably a water-tank, exposed in the garden
of the Tullie House Museum. It may be part of a public
building (substantial foundations are known in nearby Abbey
Street), but whether *mansio* (inn), forum or market building is
uncertain. The grass here is laid out to show the position of a
Roman street.

The Tullie House Museum (open daily, Monday–Saturday
1000–1600; Sunday 1200–1600) contains another impressive
display of sculptured and inscribed stones and of small
objects, superbly displayed after refurbishment in 1991, and
too rich and numerous to describe in detail here. A full-scale
mock-up of Hadrian's Turf Wall confronts you on entry to the
Roman section; be sure not to miss, on the pier facing it, the
fragment of wooden inscription, unique of its kind, from
milecastle 50 on the Turf Wall. It contains part of the name of
Hadrian and of his governor A. Platorius Nepos, and is the
timber counterpart of the stone inscription from milecastle 38,
in Newcastle (p. 467). Among other exceptional items
displayed in this collection, there are some important finds
from waterlogged levels, mostly from Carlisle, such as
wooden tent pegs, wooden barrel staves, a well preserved
basket, and a rare first-century wooden training sword. There
is a fine model of the south gateway of the Cerialan fort, and
half of the actual door-sill (with a post-socket to the left).
Another exceptional discovery, made in 2001 and not yet on
display, is a hoard of second-century Roman armour,
including a scale shoulder guard, its iron scales held together
by bronze wire, which appears to be a unique survival from
anywhere in the Roman world.

Tullie House contains rich collections as well relating to
civilian and religious life on the northern frontier. There is a
particularly impressive range of dedications and statues to
deities, which illustrate with exceptional clarity the process of
assimilation between Roman and native religions (a process
referred to by Tacitus as *interpretatio Romana*), with

dedications to Mars Ocelus, Mars Belatucadrus, Mars
Cocidius, etc. Be sure not to miss, at the end of the corridor
by the steps down from the Turf Wall simulation, the case
displaying the little silver plaques of the native warrior god
Cocidius, from Bewcastle north of Hadrian's Wall (his
principal shrine). One depicts the god with stick-like legs,
spear, and largely featureless face – yet he is standing beneath
an arch with columns and a capital, vestigial elements of the
language of Roman architecture, even if the native
silversmith's depiction of them is perfunctory. In the 'Roman
life' section, finally, note the poem inscribed on stone (from
Bowness), vowed to the mother goddesses by Antonianus, in
which he promises to gild his inscription, letter by letter, if his
prayer is answered; and some of the wooden ink writing
tablets from Carlisle, from contexts of AD 72/3 to AD 125, of
which more than 50 have yielded fragmentary texts
(Vindolanda does not quite have a monopoly on these). In one
of those on display the name of the province is mis-spelled
('Britania', with a single n), and another is addressed to M.
Julius Martialis, 'either at Trimontium [Newstead] or at
Lug(u)valium [Carlisle]'. Despite the vagueness of the postal
address, its find-spot suggests that the tablet successfully
reached its addressee.

Note: this map does *not* mark all the
sites between Swine Hall and Chew
Green (described on pp. 534–52), or
those on the Antonine Wall (see Fig.
128), or the individual sites along the
Gask Ridge (pp. 592–5).

Chapter 9

Scotland

and England beyond Hadrian's Wall

§1: Between the Walls

Driving north into Scotland along Dere Street (A68) is an
exhilarating experience. For a great distance the modern road
sticks very closely to the Roman alignment, rising and falling
dramatically over the hilly terrain. Agricola came this way on
his first campaign into Scotland, in AD 80, and Dere Street
was constructed in the wake of his advance, probably in 81.
Thereafter the route was used by many Roman armies
marching into Scotland, and numerous earthworks which they
constructed can still be traced along its route today. Apart
from the permanent posts, the remains of some 15 Roman
marching-camps are visible on an 18-mile (29-km) stretch
south of the Scottish border: there is no more instructive area
anywhere in the Roman Empire to study this particular class
of military antiquity. Inevitably, however, with such short-
lived encampments, their chronology is often difficult to
establish: the camps further north in Scotland, because there
are fewer available candidates there who might have been
responsible for building them, are on the whole better dated.
Some of the Northumberland camps are no doubt Agricolan
(although only two are demonstrably so), but the area north of
Hadrian's Wall saw intensive military activity both before and
after the construction of that barrier, and many of the camps
were probably constructed at various times in the course of
the second century.

For the first 7 miles (11 km) from Corbridge, the A68 does
not swerve from the Roman alignment. Then they part
company for 1 mile (1.6 km), taking different routes to cross a
stream, before joining forces again for another 4-mile (6.5-km)
stretch. At about 14 miles (2.5 km) from Corbridge, watch out
for a crossroads signposted Bellingham (left) and Knowesgate
and Kirkwhelpington (right). Turn right here and after
300 m look out for the Roman milestone of **Waterfalls**
(NY 913815), standing as a lonely sentinel on the skyline to
the south (right) of the road, to the right of a small coppice.
The milestone, uninscribed, is not *in situ*, having been moved
from its original find-spot on Dere Street in 1760 to
commemorate the raising here in 1715 of the Jacobite
standard by the Earl of Derwentwater (in support of James II's

son as monarch, in preference to William of Orange).
Derwentwater was later executed for treason. Having fallen
over again, the Roman milestone (the 'Derwentwater stone')
was re-erected by the Redesdale Society in 1980.

Half a mile (800 m) later, where the A68 bends sharply to
the right, take the slip road on the left signposted 'The Steel',
as far as the metal gate with the tall gate-piers. A gate in the
field-wall on your left here (signposted 'Public bridleway')
gives you access to the temporary camp of **Swine Hill**
(NY 904826), which lies immediately in front of you on the
other side of a rivulet. Its prominent NE corner is marked by a
concrete post, as are all the other corners and the three
entrances (in the middle of the north, east and south sides)
with their internal *claviculae*: it is therefore easy to trace the
outline of this small and well preserved camp. The west
rampart is confused by modern ridges and the south side is
rather low, but the north gate is in excellent condition.
Enclosing some 6 acres (2.4 ha), the camp would have been
large enough for about 1,000 men. At a later date a much
smaller square camp occupying less than an acre was inserted
in the NW angle, its north and west sides utilizing the
ramparts of the earlier camp, but with new defences
constructed on the south and east. These, though surviving to
a lesser height, are also just traceable on the ground, together
with two entrances (both with *tituli* rather than *claviculae*) in
its east side.

The next village on the A68 is Ridsdale, $\frac{3}{4}$ mile (1 km) after
which you should park in the first lay-by on your left, soon
after the turning to East Woodburn and Monkridge. Walk
northwards on the A68 for another 200 m until you reach the
'11% gradient' sign. Cross the field-wall at this point and
follow the ridge round the left edge of the small quarry of
Parkhead (NY 902856). At the second solitary tree on your
left, descend the steep slope until you see a revetted enclosure
and a sign erected by the Redesdale Society in 1983.
Immediately behind the sign (sometimes partly concealed by
bracken in high summer) is what remains of the enigmatic
rock-cut figure known to antiquarians as 'Rob of Risingham'.
It survived intact until the eighteenth century when the
landowner, fed up with visitors intruding on his land, hacked
it down; sadly all that is therefore left is the lower part of the

120   Parkhead, 'Rob of Risingham'   *121   Yardhope, rock-cut warrior god*

figure's legs and a small animal's head in the left hand
(Fig. 120). Luckily an engraving was made before destruction,
and this has been reproduced in miniature in the modern stone
relief erected here. The figure must be a deity and is usually
thought of as male (but the sex of figures is not always made
explicit in the hands of incompetent sculptors), and it clearly
carried a bow as well as the animal head. The figure is often
identified as Cocidius, a local war god whose cult was popular
in the northern frontier region (cf. p. 532), but that
interpretation is almost certainly wrong (his usual attributes
are spear and shield). More probably he should be seen as
Silvanus, a deity of the woodlands; indeed on a battered
dedication from Risingham itself (now in private ownership at
East Woodburn), erected to Silvanus and Cocidius together, a
deity who is clearly meant to represent the former is shown in
relief carrying a bow. Alternatively, 'Rob of Risingham'
might possibly be a crude representation of the classical
goddess of the hunt, Diana: she is often shown carrying a bow
and dressed in a short tunic, leaving the legs exposed (and
holding an animal head in her left hand). We do not know if
the figure was accompanied by a rustic open air-shrine, as at
South Yardhope (p. 552), but that is a strong possibility.

   Continue along the A68 for another mile (1.6 km) as far as
West Woodburn. Within the village, as you descend the hill,
you will see a lane on the right signposted 'East Woodburn 1,
Monkridge 4.5'. Take the farm-track opposite it, on the left of

the A68, and after $\frac{1}{2}$ mile (800 m) the prominent grass mounds which cover the stone ramparts of the Roman fort of **Risingham** (NY 890862) are unmistakable on your right, opposite the farm. This was the Roman HABITANCVM, 'the property of Habitus', although who precisely Habitus was (a local British warlord?) is a matter for speculation. Occasional pieces of stonework are still visible, mostly at the west gate and the NE angle, and there are faint traces of multiple ditches on the south and west. If you wish to inspect the site more closely, ask for permission at the farm.

Risingham was a permanent fort, founded not by Agricola but by Lollius Urbicus in the mid-second century. Little is known of this earliest structure, when a part-mounted cohort of Gauls was its garrison. The visible fort, which served as an outpost for Hadrian's Wall, dates from the early third century. At this time the original fort was entirely rebuilt with massive defences, including polygonal projecting towers flanking the south gate. Two fine building-inscriptions, now in the Museum of Antiquities in Newcastle, record this work. One, within a circular wreath, records the restoration of the south gate; the other, from the headquarters building, is extraordinarily long (nearly 5.75 m [19 ft]) and fills the whole of the back wall of the Museum. It is dated to AD 213 and records the new garrison as the First Cohort of Vangiones, brigaded with 'Raetian Spearmen and the Scouts of Habitancum'. Further alterations and repairs at Risingham occurred in the fourth century. Dere Street passed immediately to the west of the fort (the A68 in West Woodburn is not on the Roman alignment), and crossed the Rede on a stone bridge. Substantial remains of its south abutment were recorded in the early nineteenth century but are no longer visible. A column which once stood flanking the carriageway at the start of this bridge (cf. Chesters, p. 478) can, however, still be seen, in the front garden of the Grey Horse Inn in West Woodburn.

Now return to the A68, and continue northwards along it. After crossing the Rede, and climbing the hill out of West Woodburn, the road swings to the right and then left to rejoin the line of Dere Street. At the brow of the hill here is an unsignposted crossroads. Turn left (National Park marker) and go through the metal gate. Immediately on your left is another

uninscribed Roman milestone, again not in its original
position. It was found propping up the roof of a nearby farm
building and was re-erected here by the Redesdale Society in
1971. Its original position, as recorded in 1702, was 1 mile
(1.6 km) south of Risingham (at NY 896847, High House),
which is exactly 2 Roman miles north of the place where the
Waterfalls milestone (p. 534) was found.

Returning to the crossroads with the A68, go straight across
it, along a minor road. After $\frac{1}{4}$ mile (400 m), it bends sharply
to the right, and a grass track goes straight on (metal gate).
Park here, and walk along the grass track. After 50 m, just
inside the field on your right, you can see the NW corner and
a well preserved section of the north defences of the
temporary camp of **West Woodburn** (NY 895874), here about
70 cm (2 ft 3 in) above the ditch bottom. The prominent
cluster of dark reeds marks the ditch at the NW corner. A
short stretch of west rampart can be seen as far as the stone
field-wall to your right bordering the asphalted road. Keep
walking along the track. Just before the next field-wall on
your right 150 m (165 yds) further on is the slight depression
marking the site of the north entrance, defended by a *titulus*
now virtually invisible. Thereafter, in the field beyond, the
rest of the north defences and the east side of the camp have
been severely damaged by ploughing. The camp as a whole
probably enclosed 27 acres (11 ha), a little less than full
legionary size; it might have held the tents of some 4,500 men.

The next Roman earthwork northwards on Dere Street is a
temporary camp called **The Dargues** (NY 860937). One mile
(1.6 km) after the A68 is crossed by the B6320, a minor road
is signposted 'Highgreen 4'. Carry on down the slope and
over the burn, and you will see two houses facing each other
across the road. Stop here and walk northwards along the A68
to the next field-gate on the left, and from it you will see the
east rampart of the Roman camp clearly visible 20 m away.
Half the size of West Woodburn, this camp enclosing 14.5
acres (6 ha) is in somewhat better condition. The east rampart
survives only in a series of short stretches. That on the north
is clear but much eroded, immediately beyond the line of the
wire fence, although its ditch, once very clear, was
disgracefully ploughed out by the landowner, the Ministry of
Agriculture, a few years ago. The west rampart is low, but the

line of its ditch, marked by dark rushes, is very obvious. The
clavicula of a gate can just be seen near the stone wall
dividing this field from the next. The rest of the west rampart
is visible from here, but the whole of the south rampart is
virtually invisible, although the line of the ditch (marked by
dark rushes) is clear. The farm has obliterated the whole of
the SE corner. If you cross the modern road here and look into
the field on the other side, the low *agger* of Dere Street is
clearly visible, as far as the house to your right, and as far as
the line of the wooden fence and gate away to your left: note
how the latter rises and falls over the embankment of the
Roman road.

Half a mile (800 m) after The Dargues, the A68 again
leaves Dere Street, swinging away sharply to the right. There
is a parking-place on the left of the road at the bend. Cross the
road and look over the stone wall. You are now at the NW
corner of the Roman fort of **Blakehope** (NY 859945), but
very little of it is visible. Excavation in 1955 showed that its
turf rampart had been burnt down before the Hadrianic period
and was never rebuilt. It may therefore be an Agricolan fort,
one of the *praesidia* (fortifications) that Tacitus says were
built in AD 81 as part of the consolidation of southern
Scotland. The dark reeds clearly mark the position of its
single ditch for the whole of the west and north ramparts, and
the causeway leading to the north gate is marked by a break in
the line of reeds. The turf rampart accompanying this ditch
now only survives as a low broad mound. Do not,
incidentally, be confused by the higher 'ramparts' visible to
the left near the power-line poles; these are modern banks
connected with drainage ditches.

Half a mile (800 m) later the Newcastle road (A696) joins
the A68. Turn left and go on for another mile (1.6 km).
Shortly after the road passes through a wooded area, a
driveway on the left with cattle-grid is labelled 'Bagraw'.
Park here and walk northwards for 75 paces. On your right (it
is less clear to the left of the road) you will see the south
rampart of the double camp of **Bagraw** (NY 848967), rather
broken but still up to 1 m (3 ft 3 in) high. Now walk on a
further 250 m, as far as the point were the road bends and dips
slightly to the left. At the point where the second 'keep in'
white arrow is painted on the road for north-bound motorists,

you can see clearly on your right the well preserved south
rampart of the inner of the two camps. Now cross the road to
the metal gate on your right a little further on, and look over
the wall obliquely across the field beyond. This field, now
pasture, has been ploughed in the past, but the west rampart of
Bagraw camp is still clear, stretching away into the distance.
Passing through the gate and walking along the track ahead of
you, look out on your left for the faint remains of the *agger* of
a Roman road bisecting the camp north-south in the pasture
field to your left. The very existence of such a prominent road
in the centre of the camp probably indicates more than casual,
short-term use: Bagraw may have been used by armies on
campaign over quite a long period of time. Beyond, where the
track dips and bends to the left, the east side of the camp is
visible with difficulty in rough grass on the left, inside a
former plantation. Now retrace your steps to the gate, cross
the A68 to its west side again, and look towards the gate in
the stone wall away to your left on the far side of the field.
You are now looking along the west rampart of the camp,
here visible as a prominent ridge, with Dere Street bordering
its west side. Bagraw camp in its final form was rectangular
and elongated, to make it fit on to a narrow shelf of ground.
Originally a square camp (the northern half) enclosing 9 acres
(3.6 ha), it was later doubled in size by the addition of a
second set of ramparts tacked on to the original south side.

A mile (1.6 km) further on, soon after the Redesdale Arms,
a turning on the right between gate-posts ('Horsley House')
leads to Horsley-on-Rede church, in the porch of which is a
rather weathered altar erected to 'Victory and Peace', found at
Featherwood (p. 550). After a further $\frac{1}{3}$ mile (500 m), just after
you have passed the sign announcing the village of Rochester,
turn off the A68 to the right by the war memorial. The house
opposite it has two stone catapult-balls and several Roman
gutter-stones built into its porch; one of the stones has a
groove suggesting that it took a vertical screen, of the type
known from the headquarters building at Vindolanda (p. 505).
It has been claimed that the catapult-balls are too heavy, at
around 50 kg (110 lb), to be hurled from Roman artillery
machines, but it is hard to see what else they can have been.
All of these items came from the nearby fort of **High
Rochester**** (NY 833986), the Roman BREMENIVM ('the place

of the roaring stream'). There are stone remains visible here, more substantial than at any other site in Britain north of Hadrian's Wall; and after the final withdrawal from Scotland, this little post bore the distinction, if such it was, of being the most northerly occupied fort of the Roman Empire. It was founded as a turf and timber fort in the Flavian period by Agricola, and at least once refurbished; it was then rebuilt in stone by Lollius Urbicus *c*. 139, and rebuilt again at the beginning of the third and in the fourth century. Recently found pottery evidence suggests that it was not finally abandoned until the later fourth century. Two-thirds of the fort's interior was uncovered (and backfilled) in 1852–5, the first large-scale excavation of a Roman fort in Britain, but the plan made then is far from intelligible in all its details. Small-scale work was carried out in the 1930s, but major advances in our knowledge have been made by a five-year research programme, based on geophysical survey and selective small-scale excavation, in the 1990s.

From the war memorial the road leads up to the tranquil hamlet of High Rochester and the site of the fort, which encloses 5 acres (2 ha). This is entered by the south gate, of which a displaced block is visible in the right-hand verge. Park inside the fort and walk back through the south gate, taking the stile on your right. The rampart-mound is prominent along the whole of this southern side of the fort, but the stone wall crowning it is modern. Just west of the road, however, the huge stone blocks of an interval tower, still nearly 2 m (6 ft) high, are clearly visible. The front side, where the fort wall originally stood, has been robbed, and the rear door is blocked. The tower dates from the last, fourth-century, rebuilding. The defensive ditches are also at their most impressive here: note how the upcast from them is piled up on the berm between the ditches to make crossing them an even more forbidding task.

Now mount a second stile at the SW corner, and you come to two stretches of stone defences with facing-stones still partly intact, as well as another short piece of wall apparently on a separate alignment: this represents ancient collapse and subsidence. The use of large irregular slabs here suggests that this stretch is largely also the work of a fourth-century rebuilding of the defences. Immediately after a modern track

cuts through the Roman rampart, you come to the west gate.
The flanking towers of massive masonry, flush with the fort
wall, make an impressive sight, and the moulded cap of one of
the gate jambs as well as a springer of the arch survive. The
visible masonry probably belongs to the third century, either
c. 205/8 or *c.* 216 when inscriptions attest building activity at
the fort. The gate consists of a single passageway: no doubt a
double-portal gate of standard second-century type lies buried
below. *Ballistaria* mentioned on two third-century inscriptions
may refer to shelters or emplacements behind the ramparts on
which the catapults and stone-slinging machines were kept;
these will have hurled the stone balls built into the porch by
the main road. They appear to show that already by the early
third century (if not before), auxiliary units included powerful
artillery among their weaponry, thought to be largely the
preserve of the legions in earlier centuries.

Now continue walking to the NW angle of the fort, where
more Roman work, up to 1.80 m (6 ft) high, is visible. Work
here in 1935 and 1992 revealed evidence for at least three and
probably four phases of fort wall, and three different sizes of
stonework are still distinguishable. At first the coursed walling
(third-century) rests on three lower courses which project at
the base and are earlier (second-century); but the large-block
walling to the left (north) is clearly different again and
belongs to the latest (fourth-century) phase. An annexe,
probably late Flavian, has been identified by geophysical
survey attached to this NW side of the fort: its single ditch
encloses an area of *c.* 80 m by 60 m (260 ft by 200 ft).

Now cross over the stile, and follow the defences round to
the north gate; some blocks of its east jamb are visible. You
can admire the command of terrain from here, and you should
also be able to pick out the entire outline of the Roman
temporary camp of Birdhope (see below). It lies on rough
ground to your left, on the other side of the stream but before
the modern army huts. In front of you traces of the multiple
ditch-system (four ditches in the final phase) are still visible.
Geophysical work in 1994 found considerable traces of a
civilian settlement with associated roads, outside the eastern
part of the north defences. From here you can follow the
defences round the NE corner and pass through the metal gate
(the site of the east gate) back on to the hamlet green.

Dere Street, the Roman road you have been following from Corbridge, skirted BREMENIVM to the east, and close to it, some 500 m south of the fort, is the rare sight of an extensive Roman cemetery still clearly visible on the ground. To find it, go down the road from the hamlet of High Rochester, and stop opposite the last house on your right, facing a metal gate. Go through this and follow the metalled path, making first for the house on the skyline (Petty Knowes). Shortly before reaching it, take the grass path which forks off to the right. After 200 m you will come to a small rubbish pit on your left. Leave the path here and climb up to the ridge behind, where you look down on the site of a Roman quarry, its floor occupied by a (later) low Roman burial-mound (*tumulus*). Now follow the ridge round to your left, at the end of which, between here and the field-wall beyond, can be seen a remarkable group of some 75 low circular earth mounds, best seen when the sun is low in the sky. Each is surrounded by a circular ditch (often marked by coarser grass, moss and reeds), and some are provided with a further low upcast mound encircling the ditch on the outside. Excavation of 17 of these tombs in 1978–9 confirmed that they were indeed Roman, dating from the early second to the late third century, and that each marked the site of a single cremation burial. Grave goods were few. In some cases there was evidence that the body had been cremated on the spot, the ashes being then raked into a burial pit, and the small *tumulus* erected over it. Burials of similar type have been noted at a number of military sites, including Halton and Greatchesters on Hadrian's Wall, and Tomen-y-Mur in Wales, but nowhere else in Britain does such a complete Roman cemetery survive as a visible field monument on the ground.

Now return to the track and continue along it until you reach the metal gate across your path. Immediately beyond it you will see Dere Street, visible as a low, broad *agger*, crossing your path. Turn right here and follow it for a few metres: when you are level with the end of the rocky outcrop to your left (Lamb Crag), you will see a Roman stone tomb on the right (west) side of Dere Street. Known locally as the Roman Well, it is circular and consists of two courses of large blocks on a projecting foundation course (the latter visible only on its east side) (Fig. 122). The fact that both courses of

walling survive to exactly the same level throughout suggests
that the tomb has not been robbed (stone-robbing is never so
systematic), and so the upper part of the tomb was probably a
tumulus of earth. A coin of Alexander Severus from the
central fill, reported together with burnt material when the
tomb was first exposed in 1850, suggests another *in situ*
cremation burial and a likely third-century date. One of the
stones of the lower course on the west side is decorated with
the head of an animal. It has often been claimed that this is a
fox and so a reminder of the hunting pastimes of the deceased,
but it is in fact a *bucranium* or ox-skull, common in Roman
funerary symbolism, as the animal's long horn on the left
makes clear (its other horn is damaged). Much less well
known is the existence of a corresponding relief, a pine cone
(also ubiquitous in Roman funerary art), which can be seen at
the cardinal point opposite the *bucranium*, on the side facing
Dere Street. Three square tombs, also of stone, which lay
immediately adjacent to the south, were entirely robbed out in

122   High Rochester, Roman tomb on Dere Street, looking north

the nineteenth century, but with a keen eye you can make out three more tombs, all of them low earth *tumuli*, immediately north of the stone tomb. The first is about 8 m in diameter, and beyond it, in the direction of the fence and the rivulet, are two smaller ones about 3 m in diameter. The site of High Rochester fort is visible in the distance.

High Rochester, like Risingham, has produced a wealth of Roman inscriptions. Most of them are in Newcastle, but some are in the Fulling Mill Museum of Archaeology at Durham (p. 402), and another is in Cambridge. One of them in Newcastle, found about 1744, is a well preserved and well executed example of a dedication-stone (Fig. 123). Similar inscriptions would have appeared on every major building, civilian and military, in Roman Britain. The full translation of this one reads: 'For the Emperor Caesar Marcus Aurelius Severus Antoninus Pius Felix Augustus, Most Great Conqueror of Parthia, Most Great Conqueror of Britain, Most Great Conqueror of Germany, high priest, in the nineteenth

123   High Rochester, inscription of AD 216 (Newcastle upon Tyne, Museum of Antiquities)

year of his tribunician power, twice acclaimed Imperator, four times consul, proconsul, father of his country, the loyal first cohort of Vardulli, Roman citizens (CR), part-mounted (EQ), one thousand strong (∞), styled Antoniniana, built this under the charge of . . . the emperor's propraetorian legate'. The building it adorned is unknown. The date of the stone is AD 216, as we know the year of the magistracies held by the emperor, who is here given his full official titles. He is better known as Caracalla. The inscription also gives the name of the garrison, and another stone from the site, also in Newcastle, tells us that they were brigaded with a unit of scouts (*exploratores*): the Spanish Vardulli cannot have been at anything near their full strength, for 1,000+ is far too many men to fit into such a small fort.

Yet another inscription, also in Newcastle, came from the east gate and declares that a *vexillatio* of the Twentieth Legion (from Chester) built it. Crude figures of Mars and Hercules flank the inscribed panel. Particularly fascinating is a poorly executed but ambitiously conceived slab with a lively scene representing Venus and two water-nymphs disporting themselves in their bath; they seem a little offended by our presence (Fig. 124). The central figure, with her somewhat pear-shaped figure, tiny bosom, and streaming hair, recalls another Romano-British depiction of the same goddess in a different medium, the Venus on the Rudston mosaic in Hull (Fig. 93); yet for all their poor execution, the iconography of both figures is firmly rooted in the classical tradition.

On regaining the A68 from BREMENIVM, turn right. If you want to see a Roman altar (itself well preserved but the inscription is illegible), take the first track on the right: the altar is built into the wall near the front door of the last house on the left of this track. Return once more to the main road and continue further into the village. Here on the right an enterprising project has turned an empty field into an experimental archaeology centre called 'Brigantium' (daily, 0900–1700), where a number of ancient structures of different periods have been intelligently and imaginatively reconstructed. The most impressive is a circular hut with stone walls and thatched roof, modelled on one excavated at nearby Woolaw, which lies a little over a mile (1.6 km) to the NW (NY 813987). It is of a type which was a commonplace in the

124   High Rochester, Venus and nymphs (Newcastle upon Tyne, Museum of Antiquities)

landscape hereabouts in Roman times, the homesteads of the indigenous population. Also here is a section of original stone foundation slabs of Roman Dere Street, relaid from its find-spot at Featherwood (although *contra* the information panel, its final surface would not have been grassed over but would have consisted of rammed gravel, resting on the stone-slab substructure which would have been largely invisible). Nearby are a couple of simulated Roman tombs of the *tumulus* type visible at High Rochester (but disregard the Latin of the inscriptions). Other 'attractions', including the reconstruction of a Roman timber bridge and a simulation of the Yardhope shrine, are planned for the near future.

At the west end of the village of Rochester, take another road, involving a sharp right turn off the A68 (signposted 'No Through Road'). Continue straight along this, avoiding the modern camp, go through the metal gate, and park immediately after, at the point where the tarmac road swings to the right. Keep walking straight until you see a white-star marker-post on the grass track on your left, and then walk on a dozen paces beyond it. Looking to your left here towards the modern army camp, you may be able to make out an indistinct slight 'bump' in the terrain, with occasional tufts of coarse grass to its left, marking the line of a ditch. This is the southern rampart of one of three temporary camps that have been identified at **Birdhope** (NY 826988), known as camp 1 and the largest of the three (30 acres or 12 ha); its eastern side runs along the track you are on from this point onwards, but is obscured below a modern bank, and little of its north and west sides remain. To your right is the hamlet and Roman fort of High Rochester. You should leave the grass track here and strike now obliquely to your left, heading for the star-marker on the horizon. This stands close to the SE corner of Birdhope 2 temporary camp, which covers 7.7 acres (3 ha) and is in a fine state of preservation. Its entire circuit is easily traceable by the lighter colour of the grass growing on the ramparts and the coarser grass growing in the ditch. There were entrances in the middle of each side defended by *tituli*, but the latter have virtually all disappeared into the bog. The substantial rampart suggests that the troops encamped here were staying for some time. If you turn left on reaching the SE corner and follow the rampart along its south side, you come to the depression marking the south entrance. Just beyond here, inside the rampart on your right, the extremely sharp eye may be able to detect the faint south rampart and SW corner of Birdhope camp 3 (of which little else is known), at best no more than 30 cm (1 ft) high; the line of its ditch is marked by a mere dark stain on the surface (its SW corner is some 25 m before the SW corner of Birdhope 2). This camp must have been levelled by the builders of camp 2.

The rest of the Roman earthworks along the Northumberland sector of Dere Street lie within the Redesdale army camp, and as the area is used as a firing-range, access is only possible on days when firing is not taking place (no red flags; incidentally, do not touch, let alone pick up, anything you find within the ranges). The possibility of access can be checked one day in advance by telephoning the Range Control Officer on 01830–520569. The entrance lies $\frac{3}{4}$ mile (1 km) beyond (west of) the turning to Birdhope. Two roads lead north from the centre of the camp. The more westerly passes through the Roman marching-camp of Bellshiel (App. 1); but it is better to take the eastern road, which is the second exit on

the roundabout at the entrance to the modern camp
(signposted 'Otterburn Camp R4 and Ranges'). The road
winds a little on leaving Redesdale Camp and then swings left
to join Dere Street (ignore now the turning to 'Otterburn
Camp R4'). It now follows Dere Street, dead straight, for
nearly three miles (5 km).

Immediately after joining the alignment, look out for a
star-marker near a fence, a little to the east of the road; the
post stands outside the SW corner of **Sills Burn South** camp
(NY 826996), and a further marker can be seen in the distance
indicating the position of the camp's SE corner. A further
star-marker, roughly in line with the point where the wood on
the hill beyond ends, marks the location of the camp's NW
corner. The camp is small, rectangular and unusually narrow,
to fit on the narrow shelf between Dere Street and the burn to
the east. There are *claviculae* at the north and south gates.
Excavation in the 1930s and in 1993 showed that whereas the
east rampart was built of earth compacted with stones, the
north defences were composed of an earth-fill faced with
cheeks of cut turves – suggesting a relaxed view of camp-
building rather than any rigid blueprint. In view of its
position, without good visibility, it is not impossible that this
was a practice camp for troops on exercises from High
Rochester, although it is rather large for such an earthwork. It
encloses an area of 4.5 acres (1.8 ha), in theory enough for
800 men under canvas. Also on Dere Street, 150 m further on,
pull into the lay-by on the right of the road. Just beyond it a
white star-marker lies just outside the west rampart of **Sills
Burn North** camp (NY 826999) on your right, and another
just visible beyond marks its NW corner. Like its neighbour
the camp is in good condition, although ploughing has
removed the east rampart. It encloses 4.6 acres (2 ha).

Shortly after this a road goes off to the right to Silloans
farmhouse: there are two star-markers either side of the road,
and just beyond them the western half of the south rampart of
Silloans camp (NT 823005) is clearly visible to your left (a
concrete post and a trig-like marker are on its line). Do not,
incidentally, confuse this with a slighter 'rampart' on a
somewhat different alignment beyond: this is an eighteenth-
century enclosure bank. Since Dere Street passes straight
through both the north and south gates of the camp and

destroys the *tituli* which once defended them, and as Dere Street was constructed *c*. AD 81, Silloans is almost certainly one of Agricola's marching-camps in his Scottish campaign of AD 80. The ramparts here enclose 45 acres (18.5 ha), enough for a legion and several auxiliary units. The north rampart of the camp is virtually untraceable, but its west part can just be made out to the left of the road, at a point level with the loop-shaped banked road (a gun emplacement) on your right.

Two miles (3 km) further on, the road bends to the right near Featherwood farmhouse. Turn left at the fork just after this. At the next junction, $\frac{3}{4}$ mile (1 km) later, a road goes off on the right signposted 'Ridleeshope CQB'. A few yards along this is the west rampart of **Featherwood East** camp (NT 820056), the SW corner of which is marked by a star-post to the right of the road; another marker close by stands just outside the west rampart. Keep straight on along this road and down the slope beyond, where the road becomes untarred, and you will see two further star-marker posts marking the east rampart and the NE corner of the camp. The earthwork encloses about 40 acres (16 ha), and has a gate and *titulus* in each side.

Return now to Dere Street. After a further $\frac{1}{2}$ mile (800 km) is **Featherwood West** camp (NT 813057), of the same size but less regular than its neighbour; it had five entrances. As the road climbs, watch out for the sign indicating to the right 'Ridleeshope BSA/BSR'; 25 m before this, on the left of the road, is a wooden gate in the barbed-wire fence. Just beyond it lies the prominent east rampart of Featherwood West camp, with a star-marker lying just in front of it. It was on the line of Dere Street near here that the altar now in Horsley Church (p. 540) was discovered in 1914, just three years after the British army purchased this vast tract of land to serve as a major military training ground.

Soon after the road turns sharply to the left, there is another junction. Turn right here and keep climbing for about $1\frac{1}{4}$ miles (2 km). When you come over the pass (at 510 m [1,674 ft]), you will have a dramatic view of the **Chew Green*** (NT 788084) earthworks on the other side of the valley. They are perhaps more impressive from afar than from closer quarters, for they are extremely complex (see plan, Fig. 125). As their excavator Sir Ian Richmond wrote, the group 'rewards the

connoisseur in such sites rather than someone visiting Roman
earthworks for the first time, striking though the first
impression can hardly fail to be'. Further complications are
added by the much slighter enclosure-banks of post-Roman
date: they have also been indicated on Fig. 125, as have the
position of star-marker-posts (the small crosses), which may
help you get your bearings on the ground. There is a car-park
near the burn at the foot of the valley, and an information
board on the track leading up to the site.

The sequence of earthworks, established by Richmond in
1936, is as follows. Camp I occupies the best ground and is
the earliest construction here. It is probably an Agricolan
marching-camp of *c*. AD 80, at 19 acres (7.7 ha) big enough
for about 3,000 men. Some years later a small permanent
convoy-post (II) was built on the site occupied by the later
fortlet (V), but it is known only from excavation and is not
now visible. Later still a temporary camp (III) was built to the
north of the main earthworks, levelling the north rampart of I
where it fell within the new encampment. The ramparts of III
are not, however, particularly well preserved. Richmond
thought that the troops in III then constructed IV, a strong
semi-permanent camp, with four gates all with internal
claviculae, but the chronological connection between the two

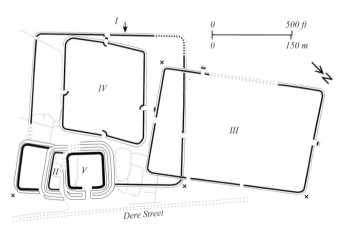

125   Chew Green, plan of the Roman earthworks

is not demonstrable, and at 14 acres (5.5 ha) Camp III seems
unnecessarily large for such a purpose. The longer-term nature
of Camp IV's occupation is suggested by the more substantial
size of its ramparts, still generally over 1 m (3 ft) high (and at
the SE corner some 3 m [10 ft] high above the ditch bottom),
as well as by the pits and metalled streets which were found
inside. Some have interpreted it as a fort (there are some
similarities with Cawthorn A: p. 385), but it seems to have
housed tents, not timber buildings, and should therefore be
considered a camp. Later still came V, a small permanent
fortlet surrounded by triple ditches except on the south. These
form the most conspicuous remains at Chew Green. The
building in the middle at an oblique angle is medieval,
probably a Norman chapel (not only Roman travellers have
needed sustenance on this journey over a bleak stretch of the
Cheviots). On the fortlet's south side are what Richmond
interpreted as two annexes used as waggon-parks, with
entrances on Dere Street, but the steepness of the terrain
makes them unsuitable for this purpose, and they may in fact
be remains of earlier fortlets, each successfully cut by the
ramparts of its replacement. This route must have seen heavy
traffic during the occupation of Scotland, and fortlet V was
probably designed to house a small force assisting and
protecting convoys over the remote moorland. The chronology
is quite uncertain. The closest parallels for the fortlet seem to
be Antonine rather than earlier, and if the similarity of IV to
Cawthorn A is real, it might belong to the late first century or
early in the second.

From Chew Green walkers will be able to follow Dere
Street into Scotland to the next site, Pennymuir, 3 miles
(5 km) to the north. On the way they will pass a Roman signal
station on the summit of Brownhart Law (App. 1). The
motorist, however, has to make nearly a complete circle to
reach Pennymuir. Return the way you have come as far as the
junction, turn right, and you will eventually reach the A68.

One more Roman site is, however, worth seeing within the
Redesdale army ranges, that at **South Yardhope** (grid
reference withheld by request of the Ministry of Defence). It
lies about 12 miles (19 km) as the crow flies SE of Chew
Green, but it is more conveniently approached from the east,
outside the ranges. From the village of Holystone (reached

from the B6341 Elsdon to Rothbury road), take the turning
signposted Holystone and Campville, and then immediately
left, marked 'Ranges'. Two and a half miles (4 km) further
on, after passing through forestry and then open moorland,
turn left at the junction signposted Otterburn Camp, just
before the gate across the road indicates the start of the firing-
ranges. After crossing the Long Tae Burn at a hairpin bend,
the road straightens and starts to climb. Park in the first of the
two lay-bys on the left of the road, opposite a small burn.
From here strike across the heather and bracken to the right of
the road, following the east (left) side of the burn, up towards
a long horizontal outcrop of rock which lies before you. Make
for the solitary tree beside the burn just below the crest of the
ridge, and then climb a little further, beyond and to the left of
the tree, to a spot where a number of large boulders outcrop.

On your right here you will see a relief depicting a warrior
god brandishing a spear and a circular shield, carved out of
the living rock at chest height (and facing east) (Fig. 121 on
p. 536). He stands to the right of the entrance to his shrine,
which is partially blocked by a large displaced stone; the
chamber is square and partly rock-cut, but the wall to the left
of the entrance is built of placed blocks. Note that the left-
hand wall has been partially cut into to receive a block, and
that in the rear wall the stones at the bottom right-hand corner
were also cut and placed, to square up the chamber at this
point. The purpose of the two ledges in the right-hand wall is
uncertain, but the upper may have served to prevent the ends
of timber planks slipping; the timbers may have been placed
across the shrine to form a makeshift roof (no doubt covered
with heather and bracken). The rock-cut god is clearly a Celtic
version of Mars: perhaps he is Cocidius, whose cult, centred
on the outpost fort at Bewcastle (App. 1), the FANVM COCIDII
of the Romans, was popular in the Hadrian's Wall area; but in
the absence of an inscription this must remain guesswork.
The god is placed in a 'keyhole' field, perhaps intended to
indicate the plan of his shrine; Roman pick-marks are clearly
visible in the rock to the left of and below the figure. Perhaps
it was carved here by troops operating out of the Roman
marching-camp at North Yardhope, which lies a mile (1.6 km)
to the west (App. 1).

Return now to the A68 and follow this over the Scottish
border. Watch out for the A6088 on the left: you need the first
turning on the right 3 miles (5 km) further on, signposted
Edgerston Tofts and Hownam. At the crossroads 4 miles
(6.4 km) later, take the road labelled Hownam and Hindhope.
After another mile (1.6 km) comes the junction (cattle grid
and wooden building) at the bottom-left corner of the sketch-
map (Fig. 126). Dere Street can be seen striding off to your
left, alongside the wooden shed. To your right is another
group of Roman temporary camps, the best preserved in
Scotland: **Pennymuir*** (NT 755139). The largest, Camp A,
encloses 42 acres (17.5 ha) and could have accommodated
rather more than a single legion. Its rampart is in excellent
condition, 4.50 m (15 ft) wide and up to 1.25 m (4 ft) high.
The east half of the north side, near the road, is outstanding,
and the whole of the west side, with two *tituli*, is also
impressively visible. Most of the south and east sides have
been destroyed. Camp B is smaller and later than A. Its west
rampart is also well preserved. The defences of C were on a

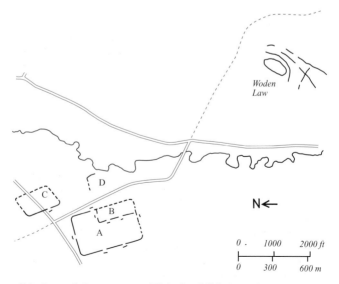

126   *Pennymuir, Roman camps, and Woden Law (hill-fort), site plan*

less massive scale and the surviving portion is no more than 30 cm (1 ft) high. Its west side is now only detectable from the *titulus* at the entrance to its SW corner. Camp D has been almost obliterated. Dating camps is notoriously difficult, but this group, from their size and form, is believed to represent military activity at the time of the Antonine occupation of southern Scotland.

At Pennymuir you can rejoin Dere Street and motor along it, through the ford of the Kale Water, to the road junction on the other side. From here a 20-minute walk takes you to the native pre-Roman fort of Woden Law (NT 768125). A series of earthworks on the NE side of the hill-fort were interpreted by Richmond as Roman 'siege-lines': he thought that their unfinished nature, the insignificance of the hill-fort and the tactical uselessness of some of the lines suggested that Roman troops, bivouacked at Pennymuir, erected these earthworks at various periods as part of their peacetime training. No Roman pottery has been found at Woden Law, however, and the 'Roman' ditches lack the usual crisp V-shaped military profile; so it is best to interpret these earthworks as part of the outworks strengthening the Iron Age defences of the hill-top, and nothing to do with Roman armies.

We have followed Dere Street into Scotland and seen the many forts and camps that line its route. Its destination was Inveresk on the Forth (App. 1), but apart from another marching-camp (Channelkirk, App. 1) no further visible remains lie beside it north of Pennymuir. The reason, quite simply, is that Scotland becomes more cultivable, and Roman earthworks have suffered as a result. Brief mention must be made, however, of the site at **Newstead** (NT 570344) on the Tweed. The succession of large and very strongly defended forts discovered here make it clear that TRIMONTIVM was a major stronghold, the king-pin of the occupation network of southern Scotland. Founded by Agricola *c.* AD 81, and at intervals deserted and then rebuilt, it was finally abandoned about 100 years later. Excavations in the early years of the twentieth century yielded a remarkable haul of metal tools, military equipment and weapons (Fig. 127), now in Edinburgh, and more limited work during the late 1980s and the early 1990s revealed extra details of the military activity outside the fort itself. There is very little to see at Newstead

127   Newstead, Roman fort, parade-helmet (Edinburgh, Museum of Scotland)

today, but a 'visitor trail' has been enterprisingly installed
which makes interpretation of key elements of the Roman
topography intelligible, and in any case the beautiful back-
drop of the triple Eildon Hills which gave the fort its Roman
name makes a visit to the site worth while. The most northerly
of these hills (405 m = 1,327 ft) is, incidentally, crowned by a
native hill-fort, in the centre of which is a Roman signal
station (App. 1).

    To visit the Roman fort at Newstead, turn off at the
roundabout on the A68 9 miles (14.4 km) north of Jedburgh,
at first eastwards along the A6091 for Melrose, and then turn
immediately right for Newstead. At the entrance to the village,
there is a first information board at the 'millennium stone', a

pink granite shaft commemorating the year 2000. Now turn right at the health centre, park in front of the gate barring access across the former B6361, and then keep walking straight along this road. An information board on the viewing platform here points out the sites, to the right of the road, of the extramural bath-house and an inn-like building assumed to have accommodated travellers on official business (a *mansio*). These lay in a defended enclosure tacked on to the fort itself, the so-called 'West Annexe'. The line of trees on the right of the road lies just inside (and at an oblique angle to) the west defences of the Roman fort proper. The actual line of these defences is marked by a change in contour, where the flat ground gives way to a gentle slope; but neither defensive earthwork nor ditches are visible.

A little further on, lying just inside the fort's NW corner, is an imposing commemorative stone erected in 1928. The former B-road changes direction slightly here to run on top of the former north defences of the fort, and a second information board reports on the fort itself and the extramural buildings arranged on terraces on your left, apparently themselves within a fortified enclosure (the 'North Annexe'). Another information board with viewing platform further on draws your attention to the alleged position of a very small amphitheatre, opposite the lay-by as the road descends towards the railway viaduct. The amphitheatre is suspected from the bowl-like shape of the hill-slope here, and was apparently confirmed by trenching in 1993 and 1996: these found an enclosing bank of earth and cobbles, presumably revetted in timber (although no post-holes were found), and an 'arena' measuring about 37 m by 23 m (40 yds by 25 yds). If correctly identified, it is not (despite the display panel) the only amphitheatre in Scotland, as what is almost certainly a timber one has been found by excavation at Inveresk near Edinburgh. Beyond this point, on the right at the former lay-by, another information board indicates the location of the East Annexe, where a parade-ground is suspected.

Finally, for the assiduous, some Roman stone finds displaced from the fort at Newstead have ended up being built into a summerhouse just east of Newstead. Return to the roundabout on the A68, head north, and then take the first turning on your right after crossing the river, following the

approach road (immediately on your left) for Drygrange
House, now a nursing home. Park at the house (where you
should ask permission) and take the steps leading down to the
right, outside the building. Do not follow the grass path to
your left but go beyond the trees before turning left: pass
through the metal gate into the field beyond. Strike obliquely
across it and you will find the summerhouse behind a large
tree. A stone gutter and two basins from the Roman fort at
Newstead are built into the front façade, and a trough in the
right wall; but they are hardly worth the effort of tracking
them down.

In the centre of Melrose, the Ormiston Institute (open
Easter–October, Monday–Saturday 1030–1230 and
1400–1630; Sunday, 1400–1630) has a routine collection of
finds, but selection of material from the locally gathered
Cruickshank Collection (now the property of the Museum of
Scotland) and a superb gemstone with an alleged portrait of a
beardless Caracalla (the identity is far from certain),
found just inside the fort's north gate during fieldwalking in
1998, was on display here in 2001. In Melrose Abbey
Museum (in the care of Historic Scotland) are some further
finds from Newstead.

Two other sites in the eastern half of southern Scotland are
worth a brief mention, Lyne and Castle Greg. The fort at **Lyne**
(NT 188405), near the upper reaches of the Tweed, lay on an
east-west road linking Newstead with the western trunk route.
Four miles (6.4 km) west of Peebles on the Glasgow road
(A72) is the junction with the B712 to Broughton. Half a mile
(800 m) beyond this, watch out for Lyne church in the fields
to your right, and a house on the road, also on your right; you
want the track immediately before this cottage, to Lyne
church. Park where the track ends, with the church to your
right, cross the stile, and turn left: the fort, which covers
$5\frac{1}{2}$ acres (2.3 ha), lies 200 m beyond (west of) the trees. There
is not a great deal to see here. The rampart has been nearly
levelled by agriculture, but survives as a bold mound at the
NE, NW and SW corners and as a ridge along the west side.
Of the ditch-system only the outer ditch on the east and south
sides is visible today. This was originally V-shaped but is now
flat-bottomed. Its edges are lined by two surprisingly well

preserved mounds, formed by piling up the earth excavated
from the ditch. The causeway leading to the site of the east
gate is also notable. The central buildings of this fort were of
stone, but the rampart was of turf only. Excavations in 1901
and 1959–63 revealed that it was built in the 150s and
occupied for only a few years. It is, however, only one of a
series of Roman works in the vicinity. There was a tiny fortlet
150 m to the north, two temporary camps to the east, and an
Agricolan fort of *c*. AD 81 on a bold eminence at Easter
Happrew, $\frac{1}{3}$ mile (500 m) ESE on the other side of Lyne
Water. All these are normally invisible from the ground, but a
crop-mark of the north rampart of the Agricolan fort can
sometimes be seen from the second-century site in especially
dry summers.

   Castle Greg (NT 050592) in Midlothian is among the best
preserved examples of a Roman fortlet in Britain. It almost
certainly dates from the later first century. Measuring just
45 m by 55 m (150 ft by 180 ft), the single earth rampart and
double ditches of this convoy-post are in perfect condition.
The only entrance is on the east side, where the curving in of
the outer ditch to meet the causeway is typical of Flavian
earthworks. It lies 4 miles (6.4 km) SE of West Calder, on the
east side of the B7008, exactly $\frac{1}{2}$ mile (800 m) north of its
junction with the A70. You draw level with it on this B-road
150 m SE of the 'Camilty Forest' sign near the reservoir sub-
station enclosure. The Roman earthworks lie in open
moorland on the skyline to the east, about five minutes' trek
away through long grass and bog.

   Roman earthworks in the western part of southern Scotland
fall into two distinct categories. The most accessible sites,
such as the camps at Cleghorn and Little Clyde and the fort at
Castledykes, are so poorly preserved that they do not warrant
detailed description, and are therefore listed in Appendix 1.
On the other hand, three earthworks in superb condition lie in
very remote areas, and 1:50,000 OS maps and a good deal of
patience are needed to track them down. These are Redshaw
Burn in Strathclyde, and Durisdeer and Raeburnfoot in
Dumfries and Galloway (all in App. 1). The first two are
Antonine fortlets, similar to but later than Castle Greg, their
single gates defended by *tituli*. Raeburnfoot consists of a

fortlet inside a larger enclosure, both apparently Antonine. NE of here, on high moor between Eskdale and Borthwick Water, a remarkable stretch of Roman road can be followed for about $6\frac{1}{2}$ miles (10 km). In places the Roman engineers cut through the peat to the natural rock and used that as the road-surface. On Craik Cross Hill it passes the site of a possible signal station (App. 1).

One site in SW Scotland that is worth a visit is the 4-acre (1.6-ha) fort at **Bothwellhaugh** (NS 731577), reached from the M74 by taking either the Motherwell (A723) or the Bothwell (A725) exits and following signs to Strathclyde Country Park. Once inside the park, follow the lake-hugging road and head for the bridge over a stream towards the south end of the park, immediately beyond the only roundabout on this road. Follow the road round from here to the car-park on the right. The car-park sits on the east angle of the Roman fort, which has been known since the 1790s and was partly dug in 1938–9 and 1967–8. It is not, however, the fort itself which merits a detour (only the SE rampart is easily distinguishable now), but the remains of the garrison bath-house down by the river (the path from the car-park follows the line of the NE rampart, represented by the very slight bank on your right). Bothwellhaugh is an Antonine fort, perhaps (on the slender basis of size) for a part-mounted unit 500 strong. Limited excavation of the defences revealed more than one phase, as did also the baths, but the site as a whole had a short life of not more than 25 years.

The baths were discovered in 1973, excavated in 1975–6 in advance of the artificial flooding of the valley bottom, and then dismantled and rebuilt on a higher level here in 1979–81. You first come to the furnace area, rebuilt in a secondary phase: there are brick cheeks to the flue, and stands for a hot-water-tank on either side. Beyond is the *caldarium*, where the brick piers are also secondary; its *pilae* were originally of stone. The hot-water bath lies to the right, also with a hypocaust. A cobbled foundation showed here that a bigger pool had been planned but was never finished, but this detail has not been included in the reconstruction. Beyond the *caldarium* are two *tepidaria*, originally with stone *pilae*. The brick *pilae* were added later, and one of the stone floor-supports ended up horizontally in the flue passage of a new stoke-hole here, itself a secondary addition (note the straight joint between the existing cheek walls with the baths). The buttresses on both long sides of the bath building also appear to be secondary, although some of these structural abutments may reflect the habits of the 1979 builders, and not reflect faithfully those of the original Roman building. Two stone voussoirs lying in one of the *tepidaria* may indicate that the rooms had stone vaults. The cold room beyond has replacement stone flags in its floor; an elegant drain cover from here is in the Hunterian Museum in Glasgow. A drain below this *frigidarium* passes through to the far end of the building, where cobbled foundations indicate that the room was intended to be built on a bigger scale. The cold-water bath, its floor still original, opens off this *frigidarium* at an oblique angle. The straight joint it makes with the adjacent *tepidarium* may indicate that this too is a secondary addition. It is well built, with largish masonry blocks, and still stands up to four courses high.

Two sites near Hadrian's Wall can conveniently close this section on southern Scotland. Just as the eastern half of the Wall had outlying forts at Risingham and High Rochester (though a later addition to the original Hadrianic scheme), the western end was also protected by a series of advance posts of which Bewcastle in Cumbria (App. 1) was one and **Birrens** (NY 218753) in Dumfries and Galloway another. The latter, BLATOBVLGIVM (which probably means 'flowering hillock'), was founded in the Flavian period and also occupied under Hadrian. The visible fort was first constructed about 142, when the garrison was the First Cohort of Nervii from the Rhine, but it was burnt down and rebuilt in *c.* 157/8. This we know from an inscription, now in Edinburgh's Museum of Scotland, which also records a different Rhineland regiment, the Second Cohort of Tungrians, as its garrison. It was finally given up in the 180s. There is not much to see at Birrens today, but the rampart survives as a bold mound on all sides except the south, where the stream has eroded it, and there are faint traces of a system of ditches on the north. Aerial photography shows further buildings and roads to the west, but it is not clear if this is a defended annexe or a civilian village (*vicus*). Leave at junction 20 of the A74(M), and follow signs for Eaglesfield and Middlebie (B722). Ignore the turning for Ecclefechan but take the next left for Middlebie immediately afterwards. After just over $\frac{1}{2}$ mile (800 m) the minor road crosses a stream on a stone bridge. The fort lies in the first field on the left after the stream: go up the slope to the field-gate and stile (small lay-by), opposite Birrens Cottage. From here you come at once to the north defences of the fort of BLATOBVLGIVM.

Much more interesting than Birrens are the nearby practice siege-camps of **Burnswark*** (NY 185787). Turn left in Middlebie, signposted Ecclefechan, and keep going for $1\frac{1}{4}$ miles (2 km), over the stream, until the road makes a 90° turn to the left, $\frac{1}{2}$ mile (800 m) before Ecclefechan. Turn right here (not signposted) and keep straight on for 2 miles (3 km). When the metalling ceases, take the right fork and park when the wood on your left ends. A field-gate here leads immediately to the SW corner of the first (south) Roman camp. This is in an excellent state of preservation. The entire, roughly rectangular, circuit can be traced with ease. The gates in the middle of the south, east and west sides are protected by normal-sized *tituli*, but the three entrances on the north are shielded by enormous mounds, known locally as The Three Brethren. They were built to support the Roman catapult machines which were used in assaulting the native hill-fort on the prominent summit ahead. Excavations here in 1898 found 67 Roman lead sling-bolts, and it was then believed that a real attack did indeed take place. More recent work, however, in 1967–70, has shown that the native ramparts (now largely invisible) were not standing when the bullets were fired, and it is clear that the 'attack' was only a training-exercise. In the NE corner of the Roman camp is a small fortlet, of mid second-century date, and excavation has shown that the camp was built after it. From the native fort at the top you can see the outline of another Roman camp on the north side of the hill. This is unfinished and it too must have been built for practice, as it is too far below the native fort to have served any useful purpose in its bombardment. From the top, too, you can admire the spectacular views in all directions, and on a clear day Hadrian's Wall is visible.

§2: The Antonine Wall

While the great Wall of Hadrian is a familiar monument, especially to the many thousands who trek its course each year, the other Roman frontier-barrier in these islands is not so well known, even though substantial stretches of it still survive. Almost immediately after the death of Hadrian in 138, the new emperor Antoninus Pius ordered a fresh advance in Britain and the building of another wall, this time entirely of turf. The literary evidence is confined to a single sentence: 'he [the emperor] conquered the Britons through Lollius Urbicus the governor and after driving back the barbarians built another wall, of turf [*muro caespiticio*].' Archaeological evidence shows that the campaign was already planned in 139 and was completed by 142/3, when a coin depicting Britannia, much as she appears on our own coinage, was minted. The reason for building another wall, apart from the emperor's desire to win military prestige, was apparently trouble in southern Scotland, but of the details we know nothing. At any rate Hadrian's Wall was evacuated, and the whole of southern Scotland was refortified and regarrisoned.

The Antonine Wall is a much simpler structure than the Hadrianic frontier. It ran for 37 miles (60 km) from Bridgeness on the Forth to Old Kilpatrick on the Clyde (Fig. 128). The Wall had a stone foundation 4.25 m (14 ft) wide, on which rows of cut turves were laid to a height of about 2.75 m (9 ft). The sides of the turf Wall sloped inwards, so that it was only about 1.85 m (6 ft) wide at the top, on which was probably built a timber patrol-walk about 1.50 m (5 ft) high. On the north the Wall was accompanied by a massive ditch 12 m (40 ft) wide and at least 3.70 m (12 ft) deep. On the south ran a military service-road, the 'Military Way'.

One might have thought that the planners of the Antonine frontier would have learnt from the mistakes of Hadrian's Wall, and that the new frontier would show none of the hesitancy and changes of plan that the Hadrianic frontier betrays. That is not the case. The original scheme, as John Gillam brilliantly realized in 1975, was to have only half a dozen forts about 8 miles (13 km) apart, similar to the distances adopted on Hadrian's Wall. A system of fortlets

between each was also intended, and nine milecastle-type
structures, five of them found only in 1977–81, are known. No
fresh fortlets have come to light in the last 20 years, however,
and it is possible that a full complement was planned but
never completed. Instead a decision was taken to increase the
number of forts, and at least two of the fortlets were directly
replaced by forts in this secondary phase. As finally built, the
Antonine Wall probably had 19 forts (of which 17 have been
identified) attached to the south side of the Wall at roughly
2-mile (3.2-km) intervals – closer than on any other frontier in
the Roman Empire, and presumably a measure of the hostility
with which the Wall was greeted by local tribes. These forts
were defended by turf ramparts, except for two examples
(Balmuildy and Castlecary) which had stone walls: indeed
Balmuildy even had stone 'wing-walls' on either side, as
though talk of a stone barrier was in the air at the start of the
project, and the fort-builders there believed that a stone Wall

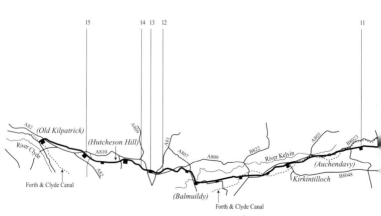

128   Antonine Wall, location map

was in prospect. Once again, therefore, as on Hadrian's Wall, there is evidence for muddled thinking in the planning of the Antonine frontier. Barracks inside the forts were of timber, but the central range of buildings usually had stone foundations. Some had defended annexes attached to one side of the fort defences, sometimes added as an afterthought. Two lessons from Hadrian's Wall were, however, grasped: a stone base was provided throughout for the Wall of turf, for greater stability, unlike on Hadrian's Turf Wall; and not surprisingly there was no Vallum.

One particular puzzle with the Antonine Wall is the apparent absence of signalling installations. Watchtowers, whether freestanding or incorporated into a continuous barrier (as with the turrets on Hadrian's Wall), formed an integral part of Roman frontier-systems everywhere else in Europe, and it seems inconceivable that none existed on the Antonine frontier. They were clearly not of stone as on Hadrian's Turf

1 Kinneil
2 Callendar Park
3 Watling Lodge
4 Tentfield Plantation
5 Rough Castle
6 Seabegs Wood
7 Castlecary
8 Garnhall

9 Tollpark
10 Croy Hill
11 Bar Hill
12 New Kilpatrick
13 Bearsden
14 West Bearsden
15 Duntocher

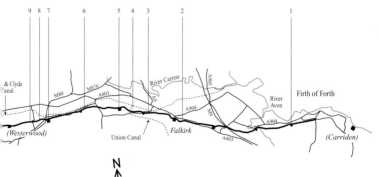

Wall, but if they had been of timber on the Antonine Wall, it is not impossible that no post-holes denoting the presence of a timber tower above have ever been found in the various sections which have been dug across the Wall's stone base. An alternative possibility is that the timber uprights of such hypothetical towers rested directly on post-pads on the stone Wall base without the need for post-holes. Timber towers for signalling surely did exist on the Antonine frontier; they have simply so far eluded discovery, although one was suspected during an excavation in 1989 at Callendar Park. Another curiosity is a further installation on the Antonine frontier which consists of a platform attached to the rear of the Wall, about 5.50 m (18 ft) square, of which six certain examples have been recognized on the ground. Because evidence of fire was found outside one of them, they have been misleadingly called 'beacon-stances', but their use in signalling is questionable, and at present it is best to admit that the precise nature and function of these 'expansions', as they are also called, is obscure.

The Wall itself, and some at least of the forts, were built by detachments from all three of the British legions. Their work is attested by 18 stone tablets or 'distance-slabs'. Each construction party would have set up one of these at the beginning and the end of its allotted stretch. A particularly fine example was ploughed up in 1969 (Fig. 129). The inscription, spread out over different portions of the stone, reads: 'For the Emperor Caesar Titus Aelius Hadrianus Antoninus Augustus Pius, father of his country, a detachment of the Twentieth Legion Valeria Victrix built 3,000 feet'. In the centre is a Roman standard-bearer bowing in respect to the personification of the province of Britain, who is putting what may be a victory wreath into the beak of the eagle on the standard. On either side is a grotesque portrayal of an ancient Briton, as seen through Roman eyes. Each kneels in captivity, his hands tied behind his back. Below is the running boar, the symbol of the legion. This splendid stone is now in the Hunterian Museum of the University of Glasgow, along with many other finds from the Wall (see below, p. 584).

A few words must be said about the fortunes of the new frontier. It has long been thought that there were two separate occupations of the Antonine Wall, which were punctuated by

129   Antonine Wall, distance-slab from Hutcheson Hill (Glasgow, Hunterian Museum)

a few years *c.* 155 when a revolt among the Brigantes further south called for emergency measures, including the temporary abandonment of the Antonine Wall. Recent research by Nicholas Hodgson has demonstrated that the idea of two occupation phases on the Antonine frontier is largely a myth. He has also suggested that the beginning of the decommissioning of the Antonine frontier might have begun as early as 158, when a single inscription on Hadrian's Wall indicates new building activity. There was indeed serious trouble among the Brigantes *c.* 155–8, and troop reinforcements arrived from Germany to help deal with it; but any rebuilding at this time in the Pennines could have been carried out without the need for actually giving up the Antonine Wall as early as 158. Such an act would surely have entailed too great a loss of face for the emperor Antoninus Pius, who had taken the decision to invade Scotland and to build the new Wall. The Emperor died, however, only three years later (161), and it seems more likely, therefore, that the decision to abandon the Antonine Wall, in response to mounting pressure on the frontiers in Germany and elsewhere, was taken by Antoninus' successors (the joint Emperors Marcus Aurelius and Lucius Verus) in 161 or later, and that Hadrian's Wall did not become fully recommissioned before *c.* 163/4. Whatever the precise chronology, Antoninus' massive engineering work had an active life of less than 20 years, and the Antonine Wall and the attendant reoccupation of Scotland must be regarded as a failure. There are traces at a few of the Wall forts of a mysterious later occupation, and it may have been the intention of the Emperor Severus, who campaigned in north Scotland in 208/9, to reoccupy the Antonine Wall; if so, the plan came to nothing.

A suitable base for exploring the remains of the eastern half of the Antonine Wall is, of course, **Edinburgh***, where archaeological finds from all over Scotland are housed in the Museum of Scotland, Chambers Street (Monday–Saturday, 1000–1700; Tuesday, 1000–2000; Sunday, 1200–1700). The archaeology galleries, for all their stylish presentation, have opted for a controversial thematic approach, and searching out the Roman artefacts in showcases which have objects from widely different periods presented all together is no easy task. The collection of finds from James Curle's Newstead excavations, for example, which were once displayed as a unit, are now widely scattered throughout the archaeology galleries. Specific chronology is rarely stated: visitors have to work hard with the 'time-line' chart provided in each case.

The entrance hall to the archaeology galleries contains the rare find (not just for Scotland but for the whole of Roman Britain) of a marble head, from Hawkshaw, perhaps of a governor or general (it does not look like an emperor). In different cases of the first section ('A Generous Land') are exceptional individual finds from Newstead, including a superb bronze jug imported from the Mediterranean, a stave-built wooden bucket, a wooden cart-wheel, and the astonishing survival of a 'hair-moss' hat, made by the same technique as basketry (an identical example has come from Vindolanda). Chronological uncertainties disappear in the next section, 'Roman Invaders', where the impressive Bridgeness distance-slab, from the eastern terminal point of the Antonine Wall, takes pride of place. The scene on the left of the inscription, showing the Roman cavalryman riding down his barbarian foes, is a commonplace on Romano-British military gravestones, but that on the right, depicting the official Roman state sacrifice of bull, pig and ram (*suovetaurilia*), is iconographically unique in Roman Britain. Out of a whole host of significant finds presented in the next section, space precludes mention of all but a few star items, but watch out especially for three famous parade-helmets from Newstead (for their use, cf. p. 393), and for the astonishing array of late Roman silver from the native hill-fort of Traprain Law, which dates to long after Roman withdrawal from Scotland, towards the end of the fourth century. Whether the hoard represents loot from plundering the heartlands of the province further south, or official 'gift exchange' from some desperate army commander anxious to buy off an invasion, we shall probably never know. In the final section, on Roman death and religion, the stunning masterpiece is the rugged sculpture found by chance in the river bed at Cramond in 1996. A massive 1.5 m (5 ft) long, it shows a recumbent lioness with prominent, jagged teeth devouring a stylized, bearded head of a man with an understandably glum expression. This dramatic and powerful sculpture, symbolizing the destructive power of death, and presumably the work of an army sculptor, must once have graced a military tomb at this distant outpost on the northern fringes of the Roman Empire.

Cramond (NT 190767), now a delightful village about 6 miles (9.6 km) west of the centre of Edinburgh and $1\frac{1}{2}$ miles (2.4 km) north of the A90, is not on the Antonine frontier itself, but since the latter was flanked by deep estuaries which had to be guarded, the forts to the east of the Wall at Carriden (very close to Bridgeness), Cramond and Inveresk (App. 1), were an integral part of the defensive system. The fort built at Cramond about 142 shares the same history as the Antonine Wall: its harbour must have provided a good anchorage for transport ships, and Cramond may have served as a key supply-depot for the Wall. Unlike forts on the barrier, it was thoroughly repaired and reorganized at the beginning of the third century, when it was used as a base for Severus' Scottish campaigns. Even after his withdrawal, the fort and civilian settlement were still inhabited.

One stretch of wall, which belongs to a workshop built under Severus, is still visible, and the outlines of other buildings within the fort have been marked out and labelled, including barracks, a latrine block, a granary and the headquarters building; the site was excavated in 1956–61. Part of the headquarters building was converted into a granary in a secondary period, as the buttressed wall makes clear – reminiscent of the conversion of the *principia* at another supply-base for another Wall, South Shields (p. 448). The NE corner of the defences can also be made out, but there were no ditches on the north side, and the excavators suggested that an annexe may have been located there. In Cramond take the road signed 'Cramond village and Kirk' (No Through Road), and park opposite the driveway immediately north of the church, before the road descends steeply to the harbour (signed 'Roman fort'). Beside the car-park near the Cramond Inn at the foot of the hill was the fort's bath-house, part of it standing over 1.80 m (6 ft) high; it was excavated in 1975–6, but has been backfilled through lack of funds for its consolidation and display. A civilian settlement east of the fort has also recently been located.

At the harbour a pedestrian ferry (daily except Friday, April–September 0900–1900; October–March 1000–1600) takes you across the river: it was here that the Cramond lioness (p. 569) was found. A ten-minute walk along the seashore on the other side will bring you to Eagle Rock [AM; A], which juts out on to the beach. On its east face, now protected by a grille, a figure standing in a niche has been cut out of the natural rock. It is now very worn, and all details have been obliterated. When first discovered the carving was thought to represent an eagle, and it has also been interpreted as Mercury, protector of travellers; but it is more likely to be a figure of a Genius (protecting spirit), wearing a mural crown (with schematic representation of town walls) on his head and holding a cornucopia in his left hand and a sacrificial dish (*patera*) outstretched over the altar in his right. It was probably cut by Roman soldiers to bring good luck to ships entering and leaving Cramond harbour.

The eastern end of the Antonine Wall has been largely

obliterated by the modern development of Bo'ness. About
$2\frac{1}{2}$ miles (4 km) west of the Wall's terminus, on the A993 west
of Bo'ness, lies the sixteenth-century Kinneil House and, to its
right, Kinneil House Museum. The house is clearly signposted
in the western outskirts of Bo'ness. Follow the road round to
the left of the house, and bear right at the fork. Park in front
of the Museum and follow the Antonine Wall path, clearly
signed to the right of the Museum, which leads you behind the
house and out in to the greensward beyond. Strike diagonally
across this to the left and take the path into the field beyond.
A signboard to your right on a gentle knoll points to the
remains of the milefortlet of **Kinneil** (NS 977803), the only
exposed example of the nine such fortlets so far identified on
the Wall (the 'one every mile' claimed on the signboard may,
as noted above, not turn out to be an accurate prediction).
Located in 1978 and completely excavated in 1981, the fortlet
was found to measure some 18.5 m by 21.5 m (61 ft by 71 ft)
internally, with timber gates set in the north and south
ramparts. The road through the former, of rammed pebbles, is
flanked by two drains, one capstone being still in place.
Strangely, post-holes were located on only one side of the
gate, but they must have been matched by a corresponding set
on the other side for the gate to have functioned. Two small
wooden buildings were traced within the fortlet, in addition to
a well in the NW corner which yielded some well preserved
shoes. Ploughing was found to have dealt unkindly with the
fortlet defences except at the NE corner, where the stone base
on which the rampart turves were erected still survived, as it
does along much of the north defences and a short stretch of
the Antonine Wall proper to the east. The kerb-stones visible
here are all original. Elsewhere the line of the ramparts and of
the Antonine Wall has been marked out with modern paving
slabs, and the timber gateways and buildings are represented
by wooden posts set in the original post-holes. The Antonine
Wall Ditch to the north is here only a gentle hollow.

The finds in Kinneil House Museum (Monday–Saturday
1230–1600, all year) include a model of the fortlet (although
its internal buildings do not correspond with what was
excavated on the ground), some shoes from the well (see
above), and a poorly lit altar from Westerwood. At the rear is
at present displayed (2001) an excellent model of a section of

the Antonine Wall and two working miniature replicas of Roman catapult machines; this display may not, however, become permanent.

Whereas the Antonine Wall itself has suffered badly over the centuries from cultivation and now only remains in a very few places, the great Ditch is a more formidable obstacle to the plough, and often survives impressively in places where the Wall has completely disappeared. One example of this is the substantial portion of Ditch visible in **Callendar Park** (NS 896796), beyond the greensward on the south side of the A803, $\frac{1}{2}$ mile (800 m) east of the centre of Falkirk. It can be reached by turning off the A803 into Callendar Park, and then left (Seaton Place); go down to the far end, and then walk northwards. The rampart is not detectable here, but the Ditch is impressive: it is about 1.80 m (6 ft) deep and can be traced here for $\frac{1}{3}$ mile (500 m). Excavation in 1989–90 discovered for the first time on the berm between Ditch and Wall the presence of *lilia*, defensive pits which would have been fitted with sharpened stakes and then covered with heather and bracken, which have since also been discovered on the berm of Hadrian's Wall (pp. 464 and 465). Since the Antonine Wall berm has rarely been the subject of detailed archaeological investigation, we do not know if this was a feature along the full length of the Wall, but it may well have been.

Further west, where the line of the Wall descends to Kemper Burn, a Roman heated structure, which must have been part of a bath-house, was partly revealed in 1980 but then backfilled; some kerb-stones of the Antonine Wall base discovered nearby are, however, still visible. Return to the A803 and turn left, turn left again at the roundabout immediately west of Callendar Park, and then take the third turning on the left (Kemper Avenue); the Wall lies at the far right-hand end of the car-park on your left. The Ditch lies buried under the car-park, and the baths are under the grass between the line of the Wall and the modern estate wall which lies beyond.

Far more impressive is the stretch at **Watling Lodge**** (NS 863798) [AM; A], one of the outstanding remains of the Antonine frontier. Here the Ditch survives in something like its original dimensions, some 12 m (40 ft) wide and 4.50 m (15 ft) deep, and gives a magnificent impression of the formidable nature of this man-made obstacle. To reach it, turn off the A803 $\frac{3}{4}$ mile (1.2 km) west of Falkirk (and immediately east of the Rosemount roundabout) along the canal (Glenfuir Road); it is signed 'Infirmary'. Then take the second turning on the right (Tamfourhill Road, the B816). The Ditch lies behind trees immediately on the left of this road.

After Watling Lodge the Ditch is again impressively visible in a newly cleared stretch immediately to the left of the road and visible from it; the Wall itself also becomes visible here. Then the road turns slightly to the left, so crossing the line of the Wall: there is an information panel here on the north lip of the Ditch (Tamfourhill). A little further on, beyond the next crossroads (Maryfield Place), you enter the stretch called **Tentfield Plantation** (NS 856797). Here both Wall and Ditch survive in fine condition and they can easily be followed, though much overgrown with bracken and trees, as far as the former railway-line 1 mile (1.6 km) away. Half a mile (800 m) after entering this stretch, watch out on the left for the turning to Rowan Crescent. Opposite the more easterly of the pair of signs labelling this road is one of the two 'beacon-stances' or 'expansions' which survive in this portion. It consists of a raised mound projecting from the back of the Wall, and can be clearly made out even in summer when it is covered with bracken. A narrow path leading from the main road to the Wall Ditch runs along its east side. The other 'beacon stance' in this stretch is rather more difficult to find: it lies 50 m east of the former railway (now a disused access road to nearby quarries).

Beyond, the Roman frontier can be traced all the way to Rough Castle, but it is more convenient to approach this from the west. Continue, therefore, along the B816 to the T-junction at the end and turn right. After 1 mile (1.6 km), after passing under two railway-bridges, watch out for the Antonine Primary School on your left. You need the next turning on the right, Foundry Road (it is signposted 'Rough Castle' but only from the opposite direction). If you are coming from the north, having left the A803 in Bonnybridge, this is the first turning on the left after crossing the Forth–Clyde canal. After crossing the railway, the road bends to the left and then becomes untarred. After it bends to the left again, stop at the metal pedestrian gate on the left and walk back 18 paces. The large mound which you will see projecting from the back of the Antonine Wall almost as far as the stone wall is a 'beacon-stance' or 'expansion', much overgrown with bracken in summer. There is another on the left, less well preserved, immediately before the access track to Rough Castle keeps straight on, and the main track swings 90° to the right. Excavation revealed its stone foundation, 5.50 m (18 ft) square, and heavy burning alongside it suggested its use as a beacon-fire for long-distance signalling. All four of these 'expansions' near Rough Castle have good command of the only known Roman road running beyond the Wall to outpost forts in the far north, and if they were really used in signalling (which is far from clear), it has been suggested that they may have received and transmitted messages from and to this road.

From here onwards both Wall and Ditch survive in superb condition all the way to Rough Castle. From the NE corner of the car-park follow the path across the partially filled Ditch to the metal gate: from here turn back to enjoy the spectacular view of the Ditch striding away westwards and of the Wall itself, which is here 1.50 m (5 ft) high and nowhere in a better state of preservation (Fig. 130). Retrace your steps to the south side of the Ditch and follow it eastwards, taking the path down to the stream and crossing the latter on the wooden bridge. Now follow the bottom of the Ditch to your left (the ground can be boggy in wet weather) until you reach the substantial causeway interrupting its line. This marks the roadway leading to the north gate of the fort at **Rough Castle**** (NS 844798) [AM; A], which lies to your right. First, however, turn your back on the fort, and walk north-westwards for about 30 m: here you will find some rows of small defensive pits. These pits, described as *lilia*, or 'lilies' by Roman military writers, were given pointed stakes and were then covered with brushwood and leaves, in order to deceive an approaching enemy into thinking that the ground was solid, and so to capitalize on the resulting confusion. At the time of their discovery in 1903, the find (of ten rows of pits, with over 20 in each – not all are now visible) was unique in Britain, but since then other *lilia* have been located elsewhere, notably at Piercebridge (p. 398), and more recently at Wallsend and at Byker at the eastern end of Hadrian's Wall

130   Antonine Wall and Ditch near Rough Castle

(pp. 464 and 465), as well as at Callendar Park on the
Antonine Wall (p. 572).

Rough Castle was a very tiny fort, occupying only about 1
acre (0.4 ha), the second smallest on the Wall, but the earth
rampart and ditches are very well preserved on all three sides,
and so are the Antonine Wall and Ditch which form its north
side. The post was garrisoned by men from the Sixth Cohort
of Nervii (originally raised in the Lower Rhine area) under the
command, unusually, of a centurion from the Twentieth
Legion, Flavius Betto. Crossing through the site of the north
gate into the interior, you can make out the position of the
small square headquarters building in front of you at the
centre of the fort, with occasional pieces of stonework
peeping through the turf. This, together with a stone granary
and part of an officer's house to the west, was excavated in
1902–3 but has been backfilled. The gaps in the ramparts for
the west gate to your right and the south gate straight ahead

are clear. Now walk to your left through the site of the east
gate (the double ditches defending the fort on this side are
clearly visible on your right), and keep straight on. You are
now in the east annexe. The site of the garrison bath-house
lies to your right here just beyond the fort ditches, but the
defences of the annexe itself are not now very conspicuous. A
little further on, however, the low mound of its east defences,
and the single ditch beyond, can be made out to the left of the
path. At this point, follow the line of these annexe defences to
the right of the path, as far as the prominent mound straight
ahead, which belonged to the annexe's south rampart. From
here you can see the well preserved defences of the south side
of the fort curving round at its SE corner.

Now make your way diagonally over to the west gate of the
fort, where the rampart and two ditches are again very well
preserved, and so down to the stream, which you cross on a
second bridge. Follow the path to your right and head back
towards the car-park. On your right, mid-way between the
path and the electricity pylon, you can make out the low broad
mound of the Military Way, the Roman road running behind
the Wall, and this can be followed, clearly visible, all the way
back to the car-park.

Return now to the B816, turn right, and then first left along
the south side of the Forth–Clyde canal. After $\frac{1}{3}$ mile (0.5 km),
soon after the houses stop, an information panel on your left
announces the **Seabegs Wood*** stretch (NS 814793) [AM; A].
Both Wall and Ditch are very well preserved here, having
now been cleared of the undergrowth which once obscured
them (Fig. 131), and also clearly visible 50 m (55 yd) behind
the Wall, forming an avenue between the trees, is the low
broad mound (*agger*) of the Military Way, the best preserved
stretch of it on the Antonine frontier. Immediately beyond the
preserved stretch of Wall and Ditch here, on a raised knoll
now in pasture, is the site of one of the nine known fortlets on
the Antonine Wall (nothing visible).

Another $1\frac{1}{2}$ miles (2.4 km) will bring you to the complicated
road-junction at Castlecary. Where the B816 crosses the A80,
turn left along the road signposted Walton, and then
immediately left. Park by the former school (now a private
house) where a Historic Scotland notice and plan help you to
locate what little remains of **Castlecary** fort (NS 799783)

131   Antonine Wall and Ditch, Seabegs Wood

[AM; A]; the board lies just outside its NE corner. Part of the
west and east ramparts survive as low ridges, and a hollow
near the fence with a few stone blocks represents the site of
the north gate (just inside the modern wall at the T-junction
where you turned left, but not visible from the road). The fort
had double ditches and an annexe on the east side, and was one
of only two forts on the Wall equipped with stone defences.

Avoid the dual-carriageway of the A80 and take the road
into Castlecary village. Turn right (north) off it at Castlecary
House Hotel: there is a Historic Scotland signpost, but it is
visible only for those coming from the west. Ignore the coach
park on your left and keep straight into a works compound.
A metal gate into the field on your left here leads to the
beginning of the long stretch of Ditch at **Garnhall**
(NS 784782) [AM; A].

Now return to the B816, turn right, and continue along it
for another $\frac{1}{2}$ mile (800 m). Turn right again (signposted

Wardpark North) and stop when the road bends to the right
(there is a gate on the left at this point). Park here, and go
through the gate into the field here, which preserves a fine
stretch of the Antonine Ditch at **Tollpark** (NS 778779) [AM;
A]. The Wall is not visible here, but the Ditch survives on
both sides of the road. Westwards it is in very good condition
and can be followed for 2 miles (3.2 km) to Westerwood fort
(App. 1) and beyond, until it is interrupted by the railway-line.
Further west, on both sides of Croy Hill, the Ditch again
becomes visible, but this portion is best approached from the
west.

From Tollpark continue northwards, cross the canal and
turn left along the A803. In Kilsyth take the B802 for Airdrie.
After crossing the canal again and climbing the hill, turn left
for Croy village and then first left at the very beginning of the
village (Nethercroy Road). Follow the track round to the
metal bar. Park here and walk straight ahead, past a disused
quarry, and immediately after passing through a metal gate
you come at once to the beginning of the Ditch on **Croy Hill**
(NS 734765) [AM; A], which continues to remain
impressively visible for nearly $1\frac{1}{2}$ miles (2.5 km). Here too is a
particularly good position from which to appreciate the fine
command of the Wall over ground to the north, since the
view, for once, is not obstructed by trees, electricity pylons or
factory chimneys. The line chosen was on the northern slope
of an almost continuous range of hills. This enabled the Wall
to dominate completely the broad depression now drained by
the Forth–Clyde canal, and still to be at a safe distance from
the loftier hills on the horizon. The path follows the line of the
Wall, here almost entirely denuded, but two closely spaced
'beacon-stances' are visible 150 m from the start of this
stretch. The first is crossed by the path half-way up the first
ascent: you reach it when you are level with the third power-
line pole on the south side (your right) of the Wall Ditch. The
second 'expansion' lies on the flat ground where the path
levels off before climbing again. This one in particular is a
substantial earthwork, but as elsewhere on the Antonine
frontier these mounds tend to be obscured by bracken in
summer and it is best to visit them in winter for maximum
visibility. Then the Ditch, here hewn resolutely from the solid
rock, swings down and away to the left (don't be misled by

the natural, wider crevice which goes straight on), and it can be followed, round the projecting crags, as far as the point where tumbled remains of rock interrupt its course. Then comes a 25-m (80-ft) stretch where the Ditch-diggers gave up in despair at the hardness of the rock. On the summit of Croy Hill, 143 m (470 ft) above sea-level, and one of the highest points of its course (cf. Winshields on Hadrian's Wall, 375 m or 1,230 ft), a fortlet was located in 1977, and 50 m to the east the site of a fort has long been known, but nothing can be seen of either on the ground. Thereafter the Ditch is excellently preserved, 12 m (40 ft) wide and 2.50 m (8 ft) deep, as far as Dullatur station.

Now return to the B802 and turn right. The next stretch, on Bar Hill, is signposted at the first lane on the left, but for motorists a western approach is more convenient. Cross the canal again and turn left for Twechar. At the beginning of the village turn left again over the canal; immediately after crossing it you will note the Antonine Wall Ditch clearly visible to the left of the road. Bar Hill is signposted 200 m further on, on the left. Park here and walk up the rough road which in 20 minutes leads you to the 3-acre (1.2-ha) fort at **Bar Hill**** (NS 708759) [AM; A] (keep straight at the first fork, and then left at the direction-arrow). First excavated in 1902–5, the fort was further examined in 1978–82, after which the bath-house and the headquarters building were consolidated and made permanently accessible. As a result, the interior of the fort at Bar Hill is now the most instructive on the Antonine Wall, although the defences are nothing like as well preserved as those at Rough Castle.

An information board here gives salient details of the fort's history and layout. The headquarters building (*principia*) follows the usual tripartite division of courtyard, cross-hall with *tribunal* (marked out to the right), and rear rooms (here three in number), of which the central one as usual was the regimental chapel; there was a stone-lined strong-box below. The well in the courtyard caused much excitement when excavated in 1902: it contained coins, arrowheads, a wooden bucket and pulley-wheel, two inscriptions and column-shafts, together with their capitals and bases – vivid evidence of the systematic demolition of the fort, presumably on the final withdrawal of the garrison in the 160s. The stone granaries and workshop (?) in the central range, and the timber barracks elsewhere, have not been re-excavated.

From the front of the *principia* walk due east to the site of the east gate: the causeway leading out from it across the faint hollow of the ditches is clear. This causeway, like that at the west gate, was protected by a *titulus*, not usually found in permanent structures such as forts (cf. p. 9), but these are not now visible. Now follow the low mound of the defences round the NE corner over the slope, to reach the fragmentary remains of an elongated, rectangular bath-house which lay in the NW corner of the fort. The Antonine Wall is exceptional in having several examples of bath-houses built within the fort defences, a feature normally found in Britain only in the fourth century. The stoke-hole at the east end for the heated rooms is partly preserved; the surviving hypocaust, however, with stone *pilae* and slab floor, belonged to a hot dry room with its own stoke-hole to the west. The changing-room and a latrine lay beyond. There were apparently no immersion-baths in this modest bath-house.

Unlike the other known forts on this frontier, Bar Hill is detached from the Antonine Wall, whose Ditch is clearly visible 50 m to the north. From the bath-house follow the fort rampart round the NW corner and down the west side. Two faint ditches are visible just beyond the causeway marking the site of the west gate. Two garrisons are known at Bar Hill, the First Cohort of Baetasians and the First Cohort of Hamii from Syria, indicating that a change of garrison occurred during its brief occupation. Both these cohorts were infantry units nominally 500 strong.

Further west Wall and Ditch have left no substantial remains for the rest of their course, except for four short sections of the stone base of the Wall which have been preserved near its western end. The two longest can be seen in **New Kilpatrick Cemetery** (NS 557724), which lies on the north side of the B8049 (Boclair Road), $\frac{1}{2}$ mile (800 m) east of its junction with the A81 in Bearsden. Keep straight ahead at the entrance gate and you will soon see the first stretch ahead of you; the second is reached by turning right at the T-junction, and then first left. Each stretch has a drainage culvert running across it, and the first also has a 'step' in it to ensure stability for the turf superstructure. On the B8049 2 miles (3.2

km) east of New Kilpatrick cemetery, the garden centre called
Dobbies behind The Tickled Trout pub has built a short
stretch of 'Antonine' Wall and Ditch as a visitor attraction,
but both the use of vertical turf facing for the earthwork and
the absence of timber breastwork are historically inaccurate,
and mar the attempted simulation.

From New Kilpatrick cemetery, go straight across the A81
at the traffic-lights, then turn left at the T-junction and go on
up the slope. Almost at the top, on the right just after Grange
Road, is a Roman bath-house excavated in 1973–5, which has
been on permanent display since 1982. You should park either
in Grange Road or in the car-park which lies about 300 m
further on, on the right.

The bath-house [AM; A] lay in a separately defended
annexe immediately east of the small fort at **Bearsden****
(NS 545721), now under a housing-estate (Fig. 132). The bath
building is much more intelligible and a better preserved
structure than the one inside the fort at Bar Hill; in places it
stands seven courses high. Very unusually for Britain (it is a
feature paralleled on the German frontier), both the central
cold room (*frigidarium*) and the undressing room were built of

132   Bearsden, Roman fort, bath-house from the NW

timber (presumably to economize), but the heated rooms were
stone-built as the steam would soon have warped wood. The
timber posts marking the outline of both *frigidarium* and
apodyterium stand in the original socket holes for the uprights
of the timber-framed structure. The *frigidarium* had a stone-
flagged floor, now mostly replaced by modern slabs (the frost-
damaged Roman ones are clearly distinguishable). A
star-shaped hole in a modern slab at the bottom of a slight
incline in this floor represents a drain cover. Opening off the
frigidarium is an apsidal immersion-bath for cold water (the
red cement lining here and elsewhere is modern), while on the
other side is a heated room, probably for dry heat (*laconicum*),
with its own stoke-hole. This is clearly a secondary addition,
since it is built around the timber posts of the original
frigidarium wall, as recesses in its south wall show, and it also
abuts the north wall of the first, tiny *tepidarium* adjacent
(straight joint). Note how 'header' stones project from the
wall in the *laconicum* to provide support for the wall cladding
in front, to allow hot air to rise between the two – a system
better seen in the *caldarium*. There is an irregular hypocaust
within, with some support walls thicker than others.

In the first *tepidarium* is a tiny semicircular hip bath,
probably an afterthought. Later the bath was eradicated and
the hypocaust filled in; the flagged stone floor (with another
five-'petalled' drain cover) belongs to this phase, when the
room probably served as a vestibule. Beyond are two further
heated rooms (second *tepidarium* and *caldarium*), their
hypocausts now filled in for protection. The wall-cladding
slabs resting against 'header' stones in the wall are well
preserved here, an interesting alternative method of creating a
wall-void for the hot air to rise rather than the more
conventional box flue-tiles. The stoke-hole projects into the
room for greater heating efficiency and is set at an oblique
angle: this was not the primary flue, however, which was set
centrally in the wall (its blocking-wall is partly *in situ*). There
is a hot-water bath to one side, and next to it a rectangular
base, perhaps a stand for a water-tank, surrounded by a
cobbled area. It was probably a secondary feature as it is not
bonded with the bath-house wall.

Also visible here, to the north, is the outline of a buttressed
room. This was planned to be another heated room (it had

provision for a stoke-hole, with a substantial springer stone for its arch still in place), but the hypocaust was never installed. It was demolished during construction when a change of plan occurred: indeed its size, position and proportions fit so ill with the rest of the visible building that one wonders whether it was intended to form part of an aborted bath-house conceived on a slightly grander scale. The masons' feather-tooling marks, especially a criss-cross pattern, are clearly visible on the outside of this room and on the *laconicum* to the west. A small latrine, with its door threshold somewhat worn, has also been preserved (except for its south wall, destroyed by a modern sewer); it was built up against the east rampart of the annexe, and flushed by two overflow drains which can be seen leading away from the baths. Its sewer has now been filled with gravel (for safety), but the customary water-channel is visible, running in front of the sewer and the (timber?) seats raised above it. Wheat, barley, coriander and opium poppy (the last two used for seasoning) were identified in sewer deposits from here. The stone base for the earth rampart of the annexe defences is partly preserved beyond. The $2\frac{1}{2}$-acre (0.9-ha) fort to the west had buildings entirely of timber except for two buttressed granaries in stone, but it appears not to have had a central *principia* or quarters for a full garrison.

Now continue westwards and turn right at the traffic-lights. Just after the A809 branches off to the right (Drymen), go first left (Whitehurst), then second left (Iain Drive) and first right (Iain Road). Take the steps near the end of this road on the left, which lead up to a small park. The Wall Ditch is visible in the trees to the left of the path as you enter, and 100 m further on, an iron cage to your right protects a piece of the stone base for the Wall at **West Bearsden** (NS 534725), exposed in 1964 with an accompanying section of Ditch (now backfilled). The stone base was totally overgrown in 2001. Finally, the tiny fragment exposed on the western slope of Golden Hill, **Duntocher** (NS 494727), may be mentioned, as it is the most westerly piece of the Antonine frontier still visible. Turn left (south) off the A810 at the roundabout in the eastern outskirts of Duntocher, along the A8014. After the right-hand bend, as the road twists to the left, turn right at the undertakers (Milton Douglas Road) and follow this (it

becomes Roman Road) until just after a church on the right. A
gate here leads to Golden Hill and a railed-off portion of Wall
base, including a culvert. Excavations in 1948–51 on top of
the hill (from which there is a superb panorama) revealed that
an Antonine fortlet preceded a very small fort here, the
smallest on the entire frontier: it covered only $\frac{1}{2}$ acre (0.2 ha).
In view of speculation about the planning of the Antonine
frontier (p. 563), the fortlet's stone foundations, which served
to stabilize the turf rampart above, were re-exposed in 1978
with a view to their permanent display; they have, however,
been backfilled, and no trace of fort or fortlet is now visible.
The fortlet had been demolished and replaced by the fort even
before the actual Wall was built in this sector, and it is likely
that the latter was for the most part built from east to west.
The same conclusion was reached when the terminal fort at
Old Kilpatrick, now built over, was excavated in 1923–4 and
again in 1931.

No visit to the Antonine Wall is complete, however,
without including the Hunterian Museum in the University of
Glasgow* (Monday–Friday, 0930–1700; Saturday,
0930–1300), where the Roman collection is small but richly
rewarding. The most important items here are the distance-
slabs from the Wall, of which the Museum possesses all but
two. One of them has been described and illustrated above
(p. 566), as has that housed in the Museum of Scotland in
Edinburgh (p. 569); the remaining one is in the Glasgow Art
Gallery. What impresses about these often highly decorative
stones is the variety and vitality of the army sculptors who
fashioned them, clearly given a free rein with regard to the
size and degree of elaboration that each produced. The
'centurial stones' recording building work on Hadrian's Wall
were tame by comparison; indeed no other frontier in the
Roman world has produced such a varied assortment of
ambitious commemorative stones, the sole purpose of which
was to record, after construction, a specific length of Wall
completed by the unit in question. It is also curious, to say the
least, that these elaborate stones were devised for a Wall built
of turf, which would not of course have been able to sustain
their weight. How they were presented is still unknown (none
has been found *in situ*): one assumes that low stone pedestals
were built immediately behind the Wall, or even recessed into

the back of the Wall, on which they were displayed. Among other inscriptions, make sure you do not miss the building-slab on which the name of the man who supervised the building of the Antonine Wall, Q. Lollius Urbicus (governor of Britain at the time), can still be partially read. As noted in the previous chapter (p. 468), he hailed from Tiddis in Algeria, where the forum still contains statue-bases erected by members of his family, and where the imposing family tomb built by Lollius himself can still be seen. He went on to become one of the most powerful men in the Empire, as Prefect of the City of Rome (*praefectus Urbis*).

Also in the Hunterian are finds from many of the other sites mentioned in this chapter: a model of the fort at Bearsden, the drain cover from the Bothwellhaugh bath-house, a fountain-head and a sculptured head of Fortuna from the Bearsden bath-house, and altars naming the First Cohort of Baetasians as the garrison at both Bar Hill and Old Kilpatrick (a unit we have met also at Reculver and Maryport). There are also, from Bar Hill, the remarkable haul of objects from the well in the *principia* (p. 579), and a striking pair of roughly hewn heads, most implausibly claimed to represent Silenus (the invariably bald-headed, wine-loving companion of Bacchus); more likely they depict otherwise unknown rustic divinities. Also here are four iron nails from the Inchtuthil hoard, discussed in the next section (below). Note also, to the left as you enter, the group of five altars (from Auchendavy fort) erected by a single centurion of the Second Augusta Legion, M. Cocceius Firmus, and, at the far end, altars to Fortuna from the bath-houses at Balmuildy and Castlecary. Throughout the frontier regions of the Roman world, as noted above (p. 460), this goddess was constantly remembered in fort bath-houses, not just because 'Lady Luck' was a popular talisman for every fighting soldier, but because the naked body in the bath was considered especially in need of protection from the malignant influence of the Evil Eye.

§3: Romans in the far north

Although Scotland north of the Antonine Wall never strictly became part of the Roman Empire, military campaigns were

carried out there on a number of occasions, and these have left
their traces in the form of marching-camps, forts, fortlets and
watchtowers. Our knowledge of Roman operations in the area
has been vastly increased over the past 50 years by the aerial
discoveries of the late Professor Kenneth St Joseph of
Cambridge University, supplemented by more recent work by
G S Maxwell and others. The majority of the earthworks seem
to be the work of either Agricola (AD 83–5) or the Emperor
Severus (AD 208–11). Other generals campaigned north of the
Forth–Clyde isthmus, however, including Lollius Urbicus in
142/3 and Constantius Chlorus in 306 (and possibly Ulpius
Marcellus c. 186), but their camps have not been securely
located. It is not, however, the shadowy records of these
invasions, or even Severus' punitive expeditions, which
capture the imagination, but the great campaigns of Cnaeus
Julius Agricola in AD 83 and 84. Here is a man who still lives
for us in the pages of Tacitus, and archaeology is able to
clothe with specific forts and camps the bare narrative handed
down to us. As a result we can begin to understand Agricolan
strategy a little better. He had no intention of entering the
Highland mass; the valleys leading from this were carefully
blocked by forts at Drumquhassle (Loch Lomond), Malling
(Lake of Menteith), Bochastle (pass of Leny), Dealgin Ross
(Strathearn), Fendoch (Sma' Glen) and Inchtuthil (Dunkeld
Gorge). The idea was to prevent the Highland tribes from
breaking into Strathmore and using that as the base for
inevitable attacks further south. Strathmore and Strathearn
were themselves carefully protected by a line of forts, no
doubt linked with harbour installations on the east coast which
still await discovery. But this grand plan was never allowed to
be brought to fruition. Agricola was recalled in the winter of
AD 84/5 (or 83/4 according to an alternative chronology), and
the emperor Domitian soon ordered withdrawal, which was
complete by 86/7. Tacitus bitterly comments that 'Britain was
thoroughly subdued and then immediately let slip' (*perdomita
Britannia et statim omissa*).

Not a great deal survives on the ground of the Agricolan
and later earthworks, as they lie in a fertile part of Scotland
which has been intensively cultivated, and most of our
knowledge is derived from aerial reconnaissance and
excavation. The outstanding visible site is the fort at

Ardoch** (NN 839099), which was founded by Agricola, but the visible remains date from AD 142/3 and later when it became an outpost fort for the Antonine Wall. And what remains there are! Ardoch is one of the most spectacular sights of Roman Britain, but not in the way that Chedworth or Pevensey are. There is not a scrap of stonework to be seen at Ardoch today: instead it is the system of multiple ditches, surviving especially on the north and east sides of the fort, which bears vivid witness to the presence of Romans in the far north, and shows above all the steps they were prepared to take in order to provide a defensible position in an area known to be hostile.

To reach Ardoch, turn off the A9 11 miles (17.5 km) north of Stirling, along the A822 for Crieff. After 1½ miles (2.4 km) you reach the village of Braco, where the road bends to cross the river Knaik. After the road swings first to the right and then to the left on crossing the river, there is a lay-by on the left. Park here and walk back to the bridge, where a wicket-gate to the left of the entry road to the Ardoch estate (1 on Fig. 133) leads you immediately to the site of the Roman fort (the building outline visible in the grass at its centre is medieval). Walk northwards and you will soon come to the NW corner of the fort (2). From here you can see the whole of the north rampart of the fort and the five ditches defending it. Not all of these are of the same date, as the fort was originally slightly longer on this north side and its rampart was protected by just three ditches, now the outermost. In fact the whole of the north rampart of this earlier fort, and especially its NW and NE corners, is still prominently visible between the second and third ditches (counting outwards). When the fort was reduced in size, two further ditches were dug in the deserted end of the larger enclosure and the former north rampart was left isolated; note how the approach to the new north gate was not straight as normal but at an oblique angle, and that the gap for the original north gate, again very unusually, is off-centre (3). The date of this alteration is not certain, but all the ditches probably belong to the Antonine period. Professor David Breeze, however, in a bold attempt to explain the somewhat odd final arrangement of the ditch-system, has suggested that the two outermost ditches on the north and east belong to the Agricolan fort; that, however,

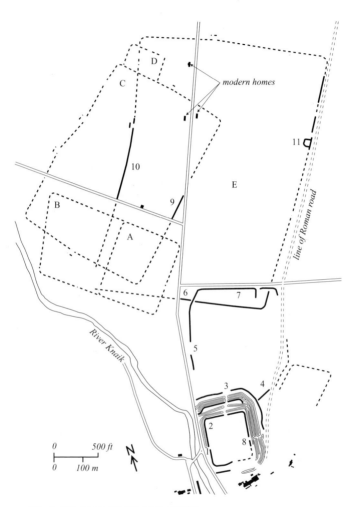

133 Ardoch, Roman fort and camps, site plan

would give the first-century defences a most peculiar outline
not readily paralleled elsewhere. The irregular ground-plan of
the ditches at the NE corner is probably to be explained by the

addition of further ditches during the Antonine occupation; in any case all five on the east must have been thought necessary in the final phase, as obsolete ditches from an earlier fort or forts would certainly have been filled in. Nothing can be seen of the Agricolan fort which lies below, but pottery belonging to it was found in the excavations of 1896–7. A tombstone now in the Hunterian Museum in Glasgow informs us that at some stage the First Cohort of Spaniards was the garrison here.

On the north side of the Antonine fort an additional enclosure existed, and its defences can also be traced on the ground (4). Long considered as an annexe contemporary with the Antonine fort, it may rather have been a separate enclosure, the south side of which was destroyed when the additional fort ditches were added on the north side. From the fort's north gate head towards the field-gate near the A822, where the ditch (dark reeds) on the west side of this enclosure is visible (5), and follow the latter northwards. The accompanying rampart is at first low, then rather bolder, before both are lost for a stretch near the two large oak trees. Its line can soon be picked up again further north, its rampart now bold and clear, but don't be misled by the lower mound running up obliquely from the right to join the 'annexe' defences (its irregular course betrays its post-Roman origin). If the bracken cover is low you may be able to detect on your left, just before the 'annexe' earthwork turns a corner at its NW angle, the south rampart of a 130-acre (53-ha) temporary camp (probably of Severan date) cutting through it (6). The continuation of the north rampart of the enclosure can be clearly traced adjacent to, and south of, the minor road to Auchterarder. Its function is uncertain, and it has an odd layout: in particular no gates are preserved to enable the earthwork to be more easily classified. The enclosure may have been a construction camp used during the building of the Antonine fort at Ardoch, or else perhaps a marching-camp of that date associated with the Antonine military control of this area.

Return now to the fort's north gate (3), from which you can either follow the ditches round to the east side or else cut across the interior to the break in the east rampart (8). Here the defences are even more staggeringly well preserved than

134   Ardoch, fort ditches on the east side, looking north

those on the north (Fig. 134). The fort rampart is high and
bold, and the causeway striding magnificently up to the east
gate is the only break in the superb quintuple ditches. Note
how the causeway is not dead straight but has a dog-leg in it
at the outer end, in theory to break the charge of a potential
attacker. Here it is the outermost two ditches which have been
added later.

Ardoch provided an admirable camping-ground, and it is
not surprising that a series of further temporary camps are
known immediately north of the fort (Fig. 133). A 13-acre
(5.4-ha) camp and a subsequent enlargement to one of 30
acres (12.5 ha) were probably the work of Agricola (A–B on
Fig. 133). Both were overlapped by a 63-acre (26-ha) camp
(C), to which a small annexe was added (D). Then a camp of
130 acres (54 ha) was constructed, overlapping all the other
works on the site; this is the one mentioned above (E). The
130-acre (54-ha) earthwork is probably Severan (AD 208/9),
and probably also the 63-acre (26-ha) one, although it would
be surprising if there was no Antonine activity here while the
adjacent fort was being built and occupied.

Two further fragments of these camps are visible NW of
here, but the rest of the camps are either no longer visible or
are difficult to trace on the ground. Continue northwards along

the A822 for $\frac{1}{2}$ mile (800 m) and take the B827 on your left to
Comrie. About 30 m from the road junction, on your right, is
a short section (9) of the east rampart of the 63-acre (26-ha)
camp; a gap in the fence allows access (AM; A). Continue on
along the Comrie road for a further 200 m exactly. Just before
the electricity sub-station, the road cuts through the west
rampart of the 130-acre (54-ha) camp (10); a fragment of its
south defences has been already noted in the field north of the
fort (6). Some 275 m of its overgrown rampart, with a gate
and *titulus* at the far end, can be seen here running away to
your right. The few other surviving parts of the 63-acre
(26-ha) and 130-acre (54-ha) camps are more difficult to trace,
as is the Flavian signal station of Blackhill Wood (11; see
Appendix 1).

Six miles (9.6 km) NE of Ardoch lay another fort,
Strageath, which was also an Agricolan foundation re-used as
an outpost fort of the Antonine Wall (nothing visible).
Between the two lies a smaller post, the fortlet known as
Kaims Castle (NN 861129). The A822 is straight for 1 mile
(1.6 km) north of Ardoch. One and a quarter miles (2 km)
after it swings to the right, you will see two houses facing
each other across the road; that on the right is named Kaimes
Lodge (if you are approaching from the north, this is $\frac{1}{4}$ mile
[400 m] after the turning to Aldonie). The impressively
preserved earthworks of the Roman fortlet lie behind the
house on the left and are reached through an adjacent field-
gate to its left. The rampart is about 25 m (80 ft) square and is
surrounded by a circular ditch. A single entrance faces the
road. Excavation in 1900 produced no secure evidence of
date, but the fortlet is now known to be part of a system of
forts, fortlets and towers which formed a genuine but short-
lived frontier system (*limes*) under Agricola in the 80s. The
visible earthworks may therefore belong to this period, but
what is not known is whether the fortlet was re-occupied and
rebuilt during the Antonine period, when the nearby forts of
Ardoch and Strageath were recommissioned, to serve as
outpost forts for the Antonine Wall. Certainly in the first
century, Kaims Castle was linked to the fort at Ardoch by
means of three signal stations; another north of Kaims
suggests a link also with the fort at Strageath, and that in turn

guarded the western end of another remarkable group of Roman watchtowers, to which we must now turn.

No fewer than 11 watchtowers are known on an 8-mile (13-km) stretch of Roman road on the **Gask Ridge** (NN 916148 to NO 028207). Most of them are now ploughed-out or obscured by undergrowth, but five are relatively easy to locate. The Roman road is partly followed by a modern minor road which leaves the A9 five miles (8 km) west of Perth (signposted Kinkell Bridge). Continue westwards for $1\frac{3}{4}$ miles (2.8 km) until, after a bend to the left and then one to the right, a track goes off on the left at the top of the hill. The first watchtower, **Midgate** (no. 1 in the series: NO 021205), lies on the right of the road opposite this: it was situated on the more westerly of the two knolls here, and although not much survives of its earthworks the fine view will be appreciated. The other knoll was crowned by a small fortlet, but of this too little remains on the surface. Access from the road via the grass track between the two knolls is at present (2001) hindered by a barbed-wire fence.

Each watchtower on the Gask Ridge consisted of a circular platform between 10.50 m and 15.25 m (35 ft and 50 ft) across, surrounded by a circular ditch and an outer bank of upcast material. There was a single entrance on the side facing the road. In the centre of the platform was a timber tower about 3 m (10 ft) square and presumably two storeys high. In three examples, the tower was surrounded by a rampart as well as the usual ditch and upcast mound (Fig. 135). The close spacing of these watchtowers, very similar to those on the German frontier, makes it very likely that they formed part of a Roman frontier, probably under Agricola and his successor c. 83–6. Although only a few scraps of pottery have come from excavations of the watchtowers (a couple of sherds appear to be Flavian), numismatic evidence from the forts of northern Scotland indicate that there were no first-century coins later than AD 86, and it seems likely that the Gask frontier was given up at the time of the Domitianic withdrawal from northern and central Scotland in 86/7. The creation of the frontier was presumably due to Agricola and his generals in 82 or 83 (an earlier date is impossible): as a result the earthworks of the Gask Ridge represent military installations which had an active service life of five years or less.

135   Gask Ridge, reconstruction sketch of a watchtower

Now continue on from Midgate for $1\frac{1}{2}$ miles (2.4 km), over the crossroads, and stop at the gate-piers with finials on the left. Go down the track opposite for 100 m, watching out for the point at which the wire fence in the edge of the wood to your right ends. Here you should strike into the wood at right-angles to the track. After 75 m you cross a slight north-south earthwork, a post-Roman boundary marker, and 20 m further on you come to the impressive earthworks of watchtower no. 3, **Witch Knowe** (NN 997195), largely free of trees. Waist-high wooden posts mark the outer edge of its substantial ditch.

Next continue westwards along the tarred minor road until it swings away southwards and leaves the Roman line. Park at the metal gate, and after a ten-minute walk along the Roman road, watch out for a clearing on the left of the road and a small metal direction arrow. Here, maintained by Historic Scotland, is watchtower no. 5, **Muir o'Fauld*** (NN 981189) [AM; A], the most rewarding of all the Gask Ridge towers to

visit. The rampart, the outer ditch, even the mound of spoil
deposited on the outer lip of the ditch, as well as the causeway
across the ditch on the north, linking the tower to the Roman
road, are all very clear. Also detectable are the post-pits of the
four substantial timber uprights at the centre which mark the
position of the tower itself.

Walkers and cyclists will want to continue along the Roman
road to the next watchtower just over a mile (1.6 km) further
on, but motorists should return to their cars and follow the
minor road westwards to the next junction, where you should
turn right ('Trinity Gask $\frac{1}{2}$'). At the top of the ridge you rejoin
the line of the Roman road again: at this point an Historic
Scotland sign alerts you to 'Ardunie watchtower 1 mile'
(along the Roman road to the west), but this is not worth a
visit if you have seen the others on the Gask Ridge mentioned
here (part of its ditch is faintly visible). Instead follow the
minor road for 200 m until it swings away to the left. Park
here and walk for 10 minutes along the Roman road to find
the watchtower of **Kirkhill** (NN 967188) to the right of the
road: a metal direction arrow and a wooden bridge over a wet
ditch lead you into a plantation, on the far side of which is an
area of cleared pasture in which the watchtower lies [AM; A].
The ditch (partially filled with dark green reeds on the NW
side), the outer mound, and the gap in the latter on the north
to allow access to the adjacent Roman road are all very
conspicuous. The stunning command of ground to the south
from here will be noted.

Continue now along the minor road to Kinkell Bridge,
where you should turn right along the B8062. After nearly 2
miles (3 km) the B-road bends sharply up to the left near a
group of cottages, and a wood begins on your right. At the top
a track goes off to your right. If you can negotiate the gate
here, follow the track for 50 m and you will see the prominent
earthworks of the watchtower of **Parkneuk** (NN 916184) in a
clearing on the right, much obscured by tall bracken growth in
summer. This makes some of the details difficult to detect, but
the ditch is especially well preserved on the south, nearest the
road. On returning to the wooden gate, strike left into the
wood and you come immediately across the prominent but
somewhat overgrown bank of a Roman temporary camp: this
formed part of its north side, with the ditch accompanying it

(on the forest side). The rampart is also clearly visible on the other side of the track. Its line lies mid-way between the wooden gate and the modern road, but you need to be inside the gate if you wish to examine it at close quarters.

Another temporary camp lies a short distance to the south of the Gask Ridge, at **Dunning** (NO 025148), a village which can be reached directly from the A9 via the B9141. Half a mile (800 m) from the village on the Perth road (B934), the road is bordered by Kincladie Wood on the left-hand side. After a slight rise the road descends into a dip. As it rises again, stop at a small clearing in the wood; the fence is currently (2001) negotiable at this point. This leads immediately to a well preserved stretch of rampart, 1–1.20 m (3–4 ft) high, with ditch to the right; it tends to be overgrown with brambles and nettles in the summer, which makes the going difficult. There is an entrance next to the road, defended by a traverse (*titulus*) which is surmounted by a substantial tree; but this is not as readily distinguishable as the *tituli* at Kirkbuddo (p. 601). If you are coming from Perth and have taken the first turning to Dunning, you will approach this spot from the opposite direction: the wood is on your right, and the clearing is about $\frac{1}{4}$ mile (400 m) after the start of the trees, just as the road dips downwards.

Dunning was a large camp of 117 acres (47.3 ha), but outside the wood (where it survives for a length of 130 m [430 ft]), it has been completely ploughed away. An attempt has been made to link the site, which lies close to Duncrub Hill (known in earlier times as Dorsum Crup), with the battle of Mons Graupius, Crup being claimed as a corruption of Craupius or Graupius; but this theory fails to convince, not least because the true battlefield is likely to have been much further north. The camp type and size are usually reckoned to be Flavian, but pottery found in 1992 near the top of the ditch at the now destroyed west entrance indicates that the camp was visited and presumably used in the Antonine period, *c.* AD 140. Another excavation, however, in 1988, immediately across the road from the clearing, appeared to show that the ditch had been recut, implying secondary re-use. On present evidence, therefore, the most likely hypothesis is that Dunning was a Flavian camp briefly recommissioned in the Antonine period, *c.* 139–63.

Both the chief Roman operators in northern Scotland needed bases. Severus built a 24-acre (10-ha) fort on the south bank of the Tay at Carpow, a few miles east of Perth (nothing visible), and Agricola's legionary fortress lay on the same river much further upstream, at **Inchtuthil**** (NO 125396). From Perth follow the Blairgowrie road (A93) for 12 miles (20 km) until the A984 crosses it near Meikleour. Turn left here and continue for 3 miles (4.8 km) until the B947 to Blairgowrie goes off to the right. At this point, take the track leaving the left-hand side of the A984 and keep straight along it wherever possible. One mile (1.6 km) later, after bending to the right at the edge of the Tay, you should fork right at the cottages, past the (normally open) metal gate, and then park before the grass track swings round to the right.

On your right here you can see the rampart and ditch defending the so-called Redoubt (5 on Fig. 136), probably a stores-compound; at present (2001) it is rather overgrown. When the track turns the corner to the right, keep straight on: provided you can negotiate successfully the electrified fence (2001) across your path, you will soon come to the site of the east gate and the conspicuous hollow marking the ditch on

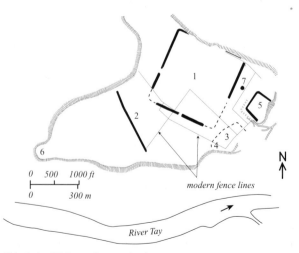

136   Inchtuthil, Roman fortress, site plan

this side of the legionary fortress (7 is a burial-mound, possibly of Bronze Age date). Rather more impressive is the massive rampart of the south defences, reached by going over to the far side of the pasture and through the field-gate at its SW corner, and then turning left to another gate near the trees. The southern defences are crossed immediately after the second gate. Of other earthworks, the north end of the 'Western Vallum' (2) is still prominent (this was built to enclose the tents of soldiers building the fortress), but nothing is now visible of the compound on the SE (3) which contained offices, stores, a barrack-block and a spacious residential building for the officers supervising construction work. The temporary bath-house was also here (4); a permanent one was due for construction within the fortress. The native fort (6) is of post-Roman date.

The surviving earthworks at Inchtuthil are not striking, but along with the towers of the Gask Ridge this is one of the few places in Britain where one can look at remains and associate them with the great governor of Britain made famous by the biography of Tacitus – Cnaeus Julius Agricola. This was the spot he chose to be the hub of his proposed operations to secure a stranglehold on the Scottish tribes, and the base fortress of the legion he had commanded earlier in his career, the Twentieth Valeria Victrix. In the 53 acres (22 ha) enclosed by the defences of the fortress (1 on Fig. 136) nothing is now visible, but excavation between 1952 and 1965 by the late Sir Ian Richmond and the late Professor J K St Joseph has revealed the complete if partially reconstructed plan of the timber buildings erected there. Construction was started in AD 82 or 83 and was almost complete when the order came to abandon and strip the site a handful of years later – probably in 86 or the beginning of 87. Agricola was not there to oversee the change in policy: he had left Britain in 83 or 84 to an embittered retirement in Rome. Some 64 barracks, four houses for junior officers, six granaries, a large hospital, a drill-hall, a workshop and a headquarters building had all been finished. The last is so small that it must have been regarded as a temporary structure from the start, with a larger *principia* planned to be built around it. Apart from this, no legionary bath-house or commandant's house had been erected, but in other respects the fortress was complete. There were four timber gateways and a single ditch, and the original turf rampart had already been modified by the addition of a stone facing-wall – one of the first forts or fortresses in Britain to be so defended.

No other legionary fortress, of timber or stone, has produced such a complete and intelligible plan as Inchtuthil's; and now a quantity surveyor's eye (Elizabeth Shirley's) has underlined the magnitude of the logistical operation involved in its construction. Although such calculations without the surviving bill of quantities are inevitably open to a margin of error, her conclusion is that the construction of the Inchtuthil fortress would have taken 2.7 million man-hours, the equivalent of 5,000 men working for two and a quarter months, or 1,000 men for nearly a year – to say nothing of the problems of supplying the raw materials. The Inchtuthil fortress is eloquent testimony to the sheer organizational capability of the Roman army.

Then, after all the effort, came withdrawal, barely five years after the fortress was started: not a mere abandonment, but a thorough destruction in order to let nothing of value fall into enemy hands. Foundation trenches were filled with nails bent by extraction from timber posts. The hospital drain was jammed with gravel. Unused pottery and glassware were deliberately pounded into tiny fragments in a gutter of the main street. The stone from the circuit wall was systematically dismantled. The unfired stone bath-house for officers outside the walls was stripped and demolished. Most dramatic of all was the discovery of a hoard of one million, mostly unused, nails of all sizes (together with nine cart 'tyres' of iron), which had been buried in a pit in the workshop. The nails have now been distributed round the world: examples are on display in the Hunterian Museum in Glasgow (p. 585) and in the Museum of Scotland in Edinburgh. Some were even bizarrely offered for re-sale on a Canadian web-site in 2000, 'available for benefit to your church or religious organization' as authentic Roman nails of (not long after) the time of Christ's crucifixion.

Another fort which belongs to the chain of Agricolan posts in Scotland of which Inchtuthil was intended to serve as the command base was that at Fendoch, close to the mouth of the Sma' Glen. The site was trenched by the late Sir Ian

Richmond in 1936–8, whose reconstructed plan served as the
model of turf and timber fort plans in Britain until superseded
by more recent open-area excavations, such as that at
Elginhaugh near Edinburgh, where an entire Agricolan fort
was laid bare in advance of destruction. Fendoch like
Inchtuthil was occupied only for a brief period, from
c. 82/3–86/7.

There is virtually nothing to see on the ground today at
Fendoch, but one of its dependencies, a watchtower designed
to give early warning of an impending raid by signalling back
to the fort, is visible as an earthwork at the very entrance to
the **Sma' Glen** itself (NN 908285). It is easily reachable after
a 15-minute climb from the road. Park at the lay-by situated at
the junction of the A822 with the B8063, 17 miles (27 km)
west of Perth, and go through the wooden gates on the west
side of the road. Of the three hillocks facing you here on the
other side of the stream, you need that furthest to your left.
Cross to the other side of the stream (negotiable with extreme
care along the strip closest to the road), and then find a narrow
sheep path which takes you along the south side of the first
two hillocks and then up to the third hill, which comes into
view ahead of you. The very well preserved earthworks of the
watchtower crown this third hillock, and are clearly visible
even when the heather is at its most prolific. Although never
excavated, it clearly consisted of a central wooden tower and
a surrounding bank and ditch, much like the contemporary
signal towers of the Gask Ridge (p. 592). There is a superb
view northwards up the Sma' Glen (the position has been
described as a 'cork in the mouth of the bottle' of the glen),
and the site of the fort itself is also clearly visible from here: it
is the level grass platform behind the middle of the three
electricity pylons, unusually set at the foot of a considerable
mountain. No doubt the hindrance to visibility from the fort in
this direction was overcome by the presence of another
watchtower on the top of this hill, although it has not been
archaeologically detected. The fort platform itself (NN
919283) can be reached by taking the first track to the right
along the B8063, $\frac{1}{4}$ mile (400 m) from the junction with the
A822. As it lies on private land, you should ask permission to
visit from Fendoch Farm. Only the very faint ridge of its

ramparts and the ditch hollow at the SW angle can be made out on the ground today.

North of Inchtuthil over 20 marching-camps have been identified from the air, but at only three of them are there substantial traces still visible on the ground. The camps are distinguishable, mainly on grounds of size, as belonging to five main classes varying from 30 to 130 acres (12.5 to 54 ha). Each group presumably represents a different campaign, and all have been associated with one or other of the two great generals who are known for certain to have pushed Roman arms this far north into Scotland. One was Agricola, the other the emperor Septimius Severus, who campaigned in these parts in AD 208–9. Unfortunately our literary evidence is too scanty to tell us if Lollius Urbicus (142/3), Ulpius Marcellus (186) or Constantius Chlorus (306) ever ventured into these parts, and on archaeological grounds marching-camps are notoriously difficult to date. The largest camps, of 130 acres (54 ha), represent the movements of a vast army, fitting for an imperial show of force, and they are plausibly linked with the campaigns of Severus. The one at Ardoch, the only visible example (p. 591), overlies as we have seen a camp belonging to the 63-acre (26-ha) series, and was apparently constructed before silt had collected in the latter's ditch: if so, the 63-acre (26-ha) camps may also be Severan, perhaps marking the line of the first expedition, in 208. A computer-generated model has suggested that a 63-acre (26-ha) camp was capable of holding as much as two legions, about 10,000 men; if that is right, the 130-acre (54-ha) camps would have sheltered a vast army approximately double that size.

The only 63-acre (26-ha) camp still partly visible, apart from the fragment of one at Ardoch already noted, is at **Kirkbuddo*** (NO 491442). Take the B961 from Dundee for 3 miles (5 km), then go along the B978 (Kellas) for 7 miles (11 km) and left again for 1 mile (1.6 km) along B9127 (Inverarity). A quarter of a mile (400 m) after the road has entered a wood, park at the slight lay-by on the left of the road, where the road swings slightly to the right. The SW rampart of the camp is clearly visible in the forest to the north of the road at this point. It is in a superb state of preservation (the top of the surviving bank is a full 1.80 m [6 ft] above the ditch bottom), and it is worth walking along its entire surviving length. There are two entrances in the rampart here, protected by prominent traverses (*tituli*) a short distance to the west (your left): the second entrance is marked by a heather-covered gap, and for the mound of the traverse you have to strike through the conifers to your left. There is no trace of the rampart in the pasture beyond, a striking reminder of the destruction wreaked by agriculture over the past two centuries on once-prominent earthworks: Kirkbuddo camp was in perfect condition when first recorded in the eighteenth century. The continuation of the SW rampart, and part of the SE rampart with a *titulus*, are preserved in the wood on the other side of the B-road; but both the denseness of the trees and the substantial nature of the fence along the road currently (2001) prevent access.

The other two camps of which substantial remnants survive, Normandykes and Raedykes, have been assigned to the 110-acre (45-ha) series, although the size of Raedykes (93 acres = 39 ha) is considerably less than the others and is not closely matched elsewhere. Of **Normandykes** (NO 831995), only the east part of the north rampart survives impressively; the remainder has been ploughed away. In the western outskirts of Peterculter (8 miles [13 km] SW of Aberdeen), take the minor road on the left (south) side of the A93, signposted 'Kinnerty and Peterculter Golf Club', immediately before the B979 to Westhill goes off to the right. Turn left at the bottom of the slope, and then keep straight, ignoring turns to left and right, for exactly $\frac{1}{2}$ mile (800 m). Turn left along the track at this point (just after the 'end of 5-ton lorry restriction' signs), and park at the disused railway-line. Keep walking straight to the end of the grass track, and then make across the field facing you up to the left-hand corner of the wood and the radio mast (obviously go round the edge of the field if it is in crop). The earthwork lies just inside the edge of the wood, and is unmistakable: the rampart-mound is still in a superb condition, and the ditch too lacks the silt which so often obscures its true profile elsewhere. A formidable obstacle, this is one of the best preserved fragments of a temporary camp anywhere in Britain.

Much more of the camp at **Raedykes*** (NO 841903) is visible, and this impressive site is an outstanding witness to the energies and determination of a Roman army campaigning

on the fringes of the then known world. The camp has an
irregular plan to suit the terrain, but it is basically rectangular
with a change of direction in the middle of the north rampart.
There were six entrances with *tituli*, two in each of the long
sides and one in each short side. It lies $3\frac{1}{2}$ miles (5.6 km) NW
of Stonehaven and is reached by taking an unsignposted minor
road to the right (north) off the A957, opposite the red pillar-
box in a wall. Fork right immediately and keep going until the
road swings sharply to the right. Keep straight on here, along
a track leading to Broomhill cottage. Park at the corner where
the track turns into the farmyard and keep walking straight,
passing through the metal gate. The camp's rampart, in part
denuded, and its accompanying ditch, are very clear in front
of you, although here and elsewhere at Raedykes rabbits are
wreaking havoc with the Roman earthworks. After crossing
the wire fence across your path the rampart becomes better
preserved, although this stretch is heavily covered with
bracken in summer. Some 25 m (80 ft) after crossing the
fence, a dip in the rampart and the causeway across the ditch
mark the site of one of the camp entrances, but the *titulus* in
the field beyond is much obscured by more recent activity.
Although ploughing has removed part of it, the camp rampart
can then be followed all the way up to the NE corner. Here
you will be rewarded with the fine sight of the rampart and
ditch curving to the left at the NE corner of the camp, the
rampart-top 3 m or so (10 ft) above ditch-bottom. The north
rampart can then be followed for its entire length, part of it
crowned by a wire fence from the point where the line
changes direction and swings to the right. No ditch however
survives along this north side, as ploughing has come right up
to the rampart line; it has also removed the *titulus* which once
defended the north entrance (at the point where the rampart
changes direction). Excavation in 1914 demonstrated that the
east rampart and part of the north had been deliberately made
more massive than elsewhere because the ground was less
steep and the camp more prone to attack on those sides. The
slighter west rampart is now largely covered with gorse.

The 110-acre (45-ha) camps continue northwards almost as
far as the mouth of the Spey, but apart from Glenmailen near
Ythan Wells, where part of the south rampart survives along a
field boundary (App. 1), no trace of any is visible on the

ground. This is not the only camp-size found in this part of
Scotland: that at Glenmailen overlies a 35-acre (14-ha) camp
with distinctive gateways, which is certainly Agricolan;
another similar example lies 15 miles (24 km) further NW
(Auchinhove); and what may be another Roman camp of
Agricolan date has been detected at the mouth of the Spey (at
Bellie). But the most intriguing find of the past 30 years was
the discovery in 1975 of a camp at Durno, 20 miles (32 km)
NW of Aberdeen, which covers about 144 acres (60 ha), the
largest yet located north of the Antonine Wall. Is it just
mathematical chance that its size represents the sum total of
the two known camp-series in the area, one of 110 (45 ha)
acres, the other, certainly Agricolan, of about 35 acres
(15 ha)? Could Durno, therefore, be the camp where Agricola
assembled his forces before the final battle of his long Scottish
campaigns? This intriguing possibility was suggested by the
late Professor St Joseph; the camp's size, if calculations
allocating about 30 acres (12 ha) for a legion of 5,000+ men
are accurate, represents an army of some 24,000 men, perhaps
two legions and 14,000 auxiliaries – on the large size, but a
not impossible figure for an Agricolan army. If true, then
Normandykes and Raedykes may well be of Agricolan date
rather than later. More 110-acre (44-ha) camps need to be
found further south before we can be absolutely certain, but at
present it is thought that the campaigns of Severus and his
sons did not reach this far north. Certainly Mount Bennachie
near Durno is a worthy candidate for the location of Mons
Graupius, and it was probably somewhere in this region that
the historic confrontation of AD 83 or 84 took place, when
Agricola defeated the Caledonian tribes under the leadership
of Calgacus. Ten thousand barbarians were killed, with only
360 losses on the Roman side. Then indeed, as Tacitus made
Calgacus say in his speech before the battle, 'the end of
Britain lay revealed' (*nunc terminus Britanniae patet*).

Chapter 10

London

The vast urban conglomeration known today as London owes its origin to the Romans. There is no evidence to suggest that in pre-Roman times there was any coherent nucleated settlement in the area now occupied by the City of London. But from soon after AD 43, when the first buildings were planted here, the city has expanded and flourished, and the almost continuous succession of occupation layers from that

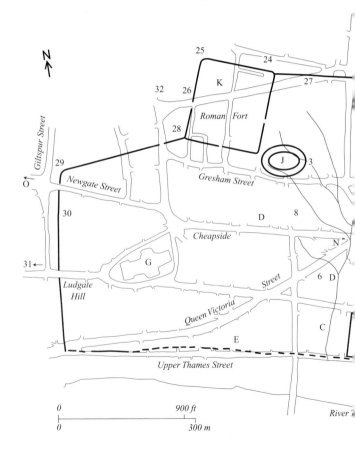

day to this has resulted in a steady rise in the level of the ground: Roman London lies buried between 3 m and 6 m (10–20 ft) below the modern pavement level. A notable early student of the City's Roman antiquities was Sir Christopher Wren, who recorded Roman buildings during the rebuilding of London after the Great Fire of 1666; there was notable fresh impetus in the nineteenth century, when finds were systematically collected for the first time by men such as Charles Roach Smith (whose objects were passed to the British Museum). The challenge of war-damaged London

Both letters (indicating 'site of') and numbers (meaning 'remains', i.e. something visible) are referred to in text. The outlines of the Walbrook stream and of the fort and Roman city wall are also shown.

after the blitz was heroically met by W F Grimes, who achieved much with limited resources in the late 1940s and 1950s, but the crying need for a proper archaeological team to investigate London's archaeology was not met until the establishment of Department of Urban Archaeology in 1973, now the Museum of London Archaeology Service. Between them they have been responsible for dramatic advances in our knowledge of London's past over the past 30 years, and an astonishing stream of stimulating fresh discoveries, some of them mentioned below, emerges yearly from their work. Roman London is a fast-changing scene.

A bridge across the Thames was essential to the Romans from the earliest stages of their occupation. The exact position of the Roman bridge, 60 m (200 ft) downstream from the present London Bridge, has now been established by the discovery of two Roman roads on the south bank converging on the same point, and of a box-structure on the north bank interpreted as a bridge-pier support (F on the map on p. 604–5). Somewhat surprisingly, however, the dating evidence from dendrochronology points to construction around AD 50 rather than earlier. Most therefore think on present evidence that Roman London was not founded on its present site before *c.* AD 49/50, but this may well change with new evidence, especially as revetment activity along the Thames can be dated as early as AD 47/8.

Yet the absence of a bridge over the Thames for seven years from AD 43 is inconceivable: either evidence for the first structure has been obliterated, or else the first bridge was a temporary affair, perhaps a pontoon. Neither seems entirely likely, however, and an alternative solution, based on the pattern of known early Roman roads in the London area, is that the earliest Roman activity was not focused in the City of London at all but at Westminster, where the Thames was shallower and narrower. An early bridge there would surely also have been accompanied by an early fort (probably under the Houses of Parliament, although other sites have been suggested). If so, the need for a military base may have passed by the time the shift of site had occurred. A V-shaped ditch and pre-Boudican timber buildings, possibly military, discovered at Aldgate in 1972, might conceivably belong to an early fort in the City of London, but this has not been confirmed by further discoveries in more recent years, and at best remains hypothetical.

About AD 50, therefore, on current evidence, the site of a new bridging point was chosen across the river, dictated by what was then the tidal limit of the Thames, and also by the solid gravel banks on either side of the river at this point. On the north bank were two low rounded hills, Ludgate Hill to the west (crowned today by St Paul's: G) and Cornhill to the east, later to become the site of the city's great forum (A). In between was the Walbrook stream (C), now canalized and invisible. Very quickly the economic potential of the site was fully realized. Streets were laid out, and substantial timber buildings were constructed, some with wall-plaster and roofing-tiles. Nor were all new buildings necessarily built in new-fangled fashion with rectangular ground-plans: several examples in four different parts of the city are known where the pre-Boudican houses are wattle-and-daub circular huts in the purely Iron Age tradition, including, remarkably, no fewer than 11 examples, each c. 5 m (16 ft) in diameter, which were uncovered in 2001 on one site in Gresham Street. Docks were built, and the large amount of Claudian material found in the City suggests London's immediate importance, no doubt as the principal supply-base for the armies campaigning further north. Rapid communication with these was ensured by the great trunk-roads, which fanned out from London from the early years of the occupation.

In AD 60 or 61, the first city came to a sudden and dramatic end: it went up in flames at the hands of Boudica and her followers. The historian Tacitus, who gives us the first literary reference to LONDINIVM (the precise meaning of which is uncertain), says that it was already packed with traders and a hive of commerce, although not yet graced with the title of *colonia*. London soon rose from the ashes. At Cheapside reconstruction had already started by AD 62, while at Regis House a massive quayside with vast oak beams, almost certainly built with the help of army expertise, was laid out in AD 63 on the Thames, with accompanying warehouses – part of a 30-year development programme which turned London into a major river port. At Plantation Place south of Fenchurch Street (H), excavation in 2000 found an earth-bank defence, erected over the demolished remains of the pre-Boudican city, and double ditches, which were traced for 70 m (230 ft) running in a north-south direction before turning west. They are currently interpreted as part of an emergency, short-lived fort placed here in the aftermath of the Boudican revolt, but to place a fort actually over part of the town (rather than near it) might seem a little drastic, and an alternative possibility is that these are the first urban defences of London. If so, their precociously early date, like those of Verulamium, might suggest that London received the status of *municipium* soon after AD 61.

It is also likely that London became the capital of the province at the same time. Certainly the chief financial official in the provincial administration, the *procurator*, was based here in the early 60s, since its holder Classicianus, who probably died in office, is known to have been buried in London (p. 625). Although Claudius had intended Colchester to be the capital of the new province, close to the site of the most important pre-Roman settlement, it seems probable that London with its more favoured geographical position usurped that role under Nero.

The Flavian period (AD 69–96) saw an outburst of building activity, and the first public buildings in stone. The amphitheatre (J) was built in timber *c.* 70, and refurbished in stone 40 or so years later. The first forum and basilica were built *c.* 75/85 and replaced by a much larger complex *c.* 100/120 (A). A huge bath building on Huggin Hill (E) was started *c.* 75/80, and the smaller baths in Cheapside are also Flavian (D); and by about AD 85, a large building formerly identified as the Governor's Palace (B) had already been erected. Some ordinary houses started to get rebuilt in stone from *c.* AD 100. Finally, at the beginning of the second century (*c.* 120), a stone fort was established on the NW side of the city (K), smaller than a legionary fortress but, at 11 acres (4.5 ha), over twice the size of most normal forts. Its garrison, which included men from all three of the regular British legions, would have fulfilled a variety of functions, supervising the transference of military supplies and acting as the governor's bodyguard. That London had a fort at all is remarkable, since there are few parallels for one in a civic context, one notable exception being Carthage in north Africa. London had by Hadrian's day become the political, financial and commercial capital of Britain, and the Roman genius in selecting its site is attested by its continuing role today.

Another fire swept London *c.* 125–30, this time accidental. About the middle of the century serious flooding, caused by subsidence, troubled some low-lying parts of the city. But expansion was not greatly interrupted, and when walls were built at the end of the second century they enclosed an area of 330 acres (138 ha), by far the largest city in Britain and the fourth largest north of the Alps. At a time when most other towns in Britain were receiving only earth-bank defences (with the exception of the prestigious *coloniae* who already had stone walls), London was equipped with a great girdle of stone defences around all sides except the river front, and these were backed by a (contemporary) rampart of earth. This exceptional state of affairs suggests that LONDINIVM received a promotion to the rank of *colonia* at this time (even though documentary evidence is lacking), and that the stone walls were erected as a gesture of civic pride. This may have occurred under Commodus (emperor 180–96), or at the beginning of Septimius Severus' reign: the year 197, when Britain was probably divided into two provinces, and LONDINIVM became the capital of *Britannia Superior* (Upper Britain), might have been a suitable moment for such a promotion – perhaps at the same time as York, capital of *Britannia Inferior*, and also a *colonia* by 237 at the latest. It is inconceivable that York could have been promoted to colonial status before London.

The other dates known in the history of Roman London may be briefly noted. After 268 the city walls were completed when additional stone defences were built along the Thames. About 286, the rebel emperor Carausius established the first mint in London, and in 294 (again dendrochronology allows for precision) a large and impressive building, probably a river-front palace, was begun by Allectus but never finished. In 296 the city was looted by Allectus' troops after he had been defeated by Constantius. The mint closed down *c.* AD 326 (although it was briefly revived in the 380s), and about the middle of the fourth century London was given the honorary name of AVGVSTA. By then, however, there is plentiful evidence for decline. The forum had been demolished *c.* AD 300 and left as an open space. The amphitheatre was disused and was gathering rubbish in the course of the fourth century. Some quaysides were abandoned and partly dismantled around the middle of the third century and were not rebuilt; in any case the late third-century riverside wall would have smashed through the heart of docklands. 'Dark earth' has been encountered on several domestic sites, indicating abandonment and decay. On the other hand investment in the city defences continued with the erection of projecting towers after 350; a large aisled building of *c.* AD 360, possibly a Christian cathedral-church, has been partly uncovered near the eastern city walls (Colchester Place: M); and evidence from the Lower Thames Street house (10) suggests that life continued there well into the fifth century. Then came the Dark Ages and the ensuing Saxon period, when the centre of London shifted briefly westwards to the Covent Garden area, where Lundenwic was founded – the only hiatus in the importance that the City has enjoyed from Roman times to the present day.

The nature of modern development inevitably means that opportunity for large-scale excavation of Roman levels in London is rare, and even when areas of a reasonable size are available, Roman levels have often been partially or completely removed by later activity. A notable exception to this was the excavation in 1994–6 at 1, Poultry, in the heart of the City (N). Here a remarkably complete picture of the successive development of a small part of Roman London over four centuries was obtained. The site, which lay on the west bank of the Walbrook, 100 m north of the Temple of Mithras (D; p. 617), was bisected by a major east-west Roman road, 7.5 m (24 ft 6 in) wide later widened to 9 m (29 ft 6 in); there were neat timber box-drains lining it. Another street went off at an oblique angle. The earliest structures lining these roads were destroyed in the Boudican fire, and these were soon replaced with a series of four wooden strip-buildings on the north side of the main road, and timber water-tanks behind for industrial processing; two more roads were added at right-angles. One was a baker's premises with oven, another a metal-smith's workshop. All were destroyed in the Hadrianic Great Fire of London *c.* 125/30. They were once more rebuilt, still in timber, and continued to prosper throughout the second and third centuries, when the parts behind the timber street frontages (presumably the shopkeepers' houses) were finally rebuilt in stone. One was provided with its own miniature bath-suite in the early fourth century; an adjacent house received geometric mosaics before *c.* 350. So even when public buildings like the forum and amphitheatre were no longer functioning, private individuals, the small traders and shopkeepers, were continuing to thrive. The area, however, fell into decay by the late fourth century, and became covered with 'dark earth'. This important excavation was the subject of a special exhibition at the Museum of London in 2000–1, and a selection of the small finds will eventually be displayed after further study in the Museum of London.

Another focus of archaeological attention in the 1990s and at the turn of the millennium has been the extensive cemeteries of London which ring the city beyond the defences on all sides except the north (which seems to have been marshy). One remarkable discovery in 1999 in the Spitalfields cemetery on the NE side of the city will be noted below (p. 640). Another excavation in 1999 in the west cemetery on the road leading up to Newgate (O) found 29 cremations and 18 inhumations, including two in intact oak coffins, one of re-used timbers. They had survived because of waterlogging: this part of the cemetery lay on the banks of the Fleet river. One was datable to *c.* 50–100, the other belonged to the third century. One of the coffins is being prepared for display in the Museum of London, and there is talk of having a selection of finds on show in the new building which will cover the site. This is Atlantic House, on an island bounded by Faringdon Street, Charterhouse Street and Shoe Lane.

Another burial to hit the headlines was a cremation excavated in 1996–7 in a cemetery lining Watling Street in Southwark, on the south bank of the Thames. Here remains of pine cones, dates, figs, almonds and chickens were offered to the deceased, an adult female, on her funeral pyre. Eight lamps, of which one features a gladiator and three the Egyptian dog-headed god Anubis, were buried with the human ashes, along with eight unusual high-footed bowls with wavy ('pie-crust') rims. The cremation probably occurred a few years after AD 100. The press leapt on the tentative suggestion that this might be the burial of a female gladiator, who are attested at Rome and in Turkey but not in Britain; but this is probably reading too much into the subject matter of a single lamp (in any case bearing a commonplace decoration). The Anubis lamps were chosen presumably because that god controlled entry to the (Egyptian) underworld: a further speculation that the lady was priestess in an Egyptian cult is also unnecessary. This exceptional grave-group is destined for future display in the Museum of London.

The settlement to which this Southwark cemetery belonged has also been the focus of intensive recent research. An excavation in Borough High Street in 1995–6 in advance of the building of the new Jubilee Line station at **London Bridge** (1, off the map on pp. 604–5) revealed a story very similar to that uncovered at 1, Poultry. The Roman settlement at Southwark developed quickly, *c.* 50–5, at the same time as London, and an early fire shows that Boudica probably struck here too. Strip-buildings along the Roman road heading for the bridge were rebuilt after the fire, with premises among others for a baker and a butcher. These timber buildings were replaced in the second century by masonry shops, including a smithy. A selection of finds from this excavation is now on permanent display at the top of the escalators in the Jubilee Line station of London Bridge.

The natural topography of the Roman city, briefly mentioned above as consisting of Ludgate Hill and Cornhill separated by the Walbrook, has been largely obliterated by post-medieval and modern development. On the top of the eastern plateau stood the most important public building of Roman London, the **forum** and **basilica** (A on map, pp. 604–5). This vast structure lay in the area which is now bounded on the north by Cornhill and Leadenhall, on the south by Lombard Street and Fenchurch Street, and is roughly bisected by Gracechurch Street. Some parts of it had been observed in 1880–2 during the construction of Leadenhall Market, and then at various stages during the twentieth century, especially in 1977 and again in 1984–8. The first stone forum-basilica, measuring 104 m by 53 m (340 ft by 174 ft), was constructed *c.* AD 75/85, and may have been deliberately intended as a stop-gap, since it was almost wholly contained within the courtyard of the

later forum. It would not be surprising if it had in turn
replaced a timber predecessor of *c.* 62/5, but no trace of one
has been recorded. Less than 20 years after the first stone
forum-basilica had been completed, work began on a
magnificent complex five times the size which was gradually
built all around it from *c.* AD 100 to *c.* 120/30. The whole
complex measured 167 m (545 ft) square, and the basilica
alone was 167 m (547 ft) long, 52.5 m (172 ft) wide and
probably 25 m (82 ft) high – not only bigger than any other
example in Britain, but probably at the time the largest Roman
building north of the Alps. Building work did not go
smoothly, and there is evidence for foundation trenches being
dug and allowed to collect rubbish before foundations were
laid, leading in turn to cracks and subsidence, with repairs and
patches needed shortly after construction; pellet excreta
indicate that tawny owls roosted in its rafters while the
building work was in progress. Nevertheless, with periodic
repairs, the basilica remained in use until *c.* 270/300, when silt
collected on some floors. About AD 300, the forum and
basilica were razed to the ground and the rubble levelled to
form an open space: by then London was no longer the
magnificent city of its heyday in the first half of the second
century. Of this great complex, only a single fragment of the
basilica has been preserved: a substantial brickwork pier on a
stone plinth, one of 15 which separated the south aisle of the
basilica from its central nave, is preserved in the basement of
90, Gracechurch Street (2 on the map on pp. 604–5),
currently (2001) a hairdresser's salon. A commemorative
plaque recording the forum and basilica can be seen in the
foyer of Marks & Spencer's store in Leadenhall Court.

A second public building is the **amphitheatre**** (J; 3), the
most exciting of all the discoveries within the walls during the
past 25 years, found in 1988 right next to the Guildhall. It is
now partly incorporated under the Guildhall Art Gallery in a
specially designed basement which is due to open in May
2002 (opening hours not available at the time of writing).
Guildhall Yard lies wholly within the Roman amphitheatre's
arena, which shaped the early medieval structures on the site
(much as at Lucca in Italy, as can still be seen today),
including the first Guildhall and the church of St Lawrence
Jewry. The outline of the arena wall, both known and as

projected, has been marked out in the paving which has been laid in Guildhall Yard.

The visible remains in the inspection chamber consist of part of the curving stone walls of the arena and one of the two entrances, the eastern one, on the major axis of the amphitheatre. This entrance, which would have been vaulted, is flanked on either side by a square chamber, each 4 m by 3 m (13 ft by 10 ft). The southern one has a stone threshold with two parallel slots in it for a sliding door and is interpreted as a wild-beast den (animal bones from the arena include bull and bear); the other may be a shrine, on the analogy of that in the same position at Chester in honour of Nemesis (p. 319); but there is no direct evidence in the London amphitheatre for such a use. Remarkably well preserved are the timber drains running through the entrance and round and across the arena. The seats were of timber on earth banks; there was no outer stone revetment wall, as is also the case at Silchester (p. 121). Overall, this amphitheatre is estimated to have measured 100 m (330 ft) long and to have had an arena 70 m (230 ft) long and 50 m (165 ft) wide: as such it is among the largest amphitheatres known in Roman Britain, with a capacity of perhaps 8,000. This stone amphitheatre was built c. AD 120 to replace an earlier timber one of the same size, erected c. AD 70. It was certainly still in use in the third century (AD 243 is the latest dendrochronogical date for a replacement timber drain, and there are late third-century coins); but by the 350s the amphitheatre was no longer functioning as such, and was already in use as a rubbish tip. Robbing of the arena walls for their stone started happening after AD 367, as coins in the robber trenches indicate.

The discovery of the amphitheatre in 1988 caused surprise because of its position: it lay inside the line later taken by the city walls, in contrast to every other known Romano-British amphitheatre, which is extramural. It lies in fact just outside the SE corner of the fort, also reckoned to have been built c. 120. If the fort had an earth and timber predecessor, which is not at present certain (although the fort site was certainly occupied in the Flavian era), then the link between amphitheatre and fort becomes even closer. It is possible, of course, that this was a building which was shared between the needs of the military and the civilian population; but it is not a truly monumental building, entirely of stone like many of the amphitheatres of the leading cities of Gaul, for example, and there remains therefore a possibility that this was only the military amphitheatre of LONDINIVM, attached to the fort, and that a monumental stone amphitheatre exclusively for civilian use, perhaps extramural, still awaits discovery.

A third public building is the so-called '**Governor's Palace**' (B), situated between Cannon Street and Upper Thames Street. Various massive foundations had been reported in this area, partly after the Great Fire of 1666, partly during sewer construction in Bush Lane in 1840–1, and partly during the building of Cannon Street station in 1868, which overlies the western portion of the palace. Further excavation took place in 1964–5 and again in 1998–9, in advance of office development. A large reception-hall, 25 m by 13 m (82 ft by 42 ft) internally, lay in the centre of the complex, and on its south side was a garden with an ornamental pool over 30 m (100 ft) long. The floor of the pool lay on a massive concrete raft 1.80 m (6 ft) thick. Rooms round two sides of this courtyard have been excavated; those on the east were probably offices, and what were taken to be the residential quarters faced the river. The ornamental pool alone points to its being a rather special building, and it was suggested in 1975 that it might be the provincial governor's official residence, constructed on the Thames much as its counterpart in Cologne was built overlooking the Rhine. The 1998–9 excavation has shown that the projected symmetry of the two wings round the court with the pool is erroneous, and has suggested that not all the walls recorded at various times belong to the same building complex. Nevertheless the structures here undoubtedly have an 'official', public character to them, and if not residential then they must have formed part of an administrative complex of some kind.

No remains of these buildings can now be seen, although one relic nearby ought to be mentioned. This is the **London Stone** (4), a shapeless lump of Clipsham limestone now built into the wall of the Overseas Chinese Banking Corporation, on the north side of Cannon Street next to St Swithin's Lane. It was first recorded in 1189 and is of either Roman or Saxon date. Sir Christopher Wren saw its foundation and believed that it was part of an elaborate monument connected with a

large complex further south. That complex is the so-called
'Governor's Palace', and the original position of the stone, in
the middle of Cannon Street a few metres from its present
site, seems to have been exactly on the north-south axis of the
large building. If so, its Roman origin seems very likely. One
suggestion, that it is part of a milestone from which distances
in Roman Britain were measured (*caput viarum*), was no
doubt inspired by the fact that Charing Cross station is used
today as the point of measurement for distances to and from
London. Although there was a 'golden milestone' (*milliarium
aureum*) in the Forum at Rome, we know of no equivalent in
the provinces, although such a milestone is not theoretically
impossible. It is unlikely that we shall ever know for certain.

Parts of several Roman bath-houses have come to light in
the city, but it is not always clear whether they were for public
or private use: an example is the small building found but not
preserved in **Cheapside** in 1956 (D). A much larger complex,
on **Huggin Hill**, Upper Thames Street, however, is certainly a
public bath-house (E). Excavation in 1964 and 1969 revealed
that in the original late first-century (Flavian) building there
were three unheated rooms, before two were given hypocausts
and a large apsed heated hall was added.

More extensive excavation subsequently took place in
1988–9 prior to further redevelopment; this greatly expanded
our knowledge of the bath building, in particular at its west
end. One wall still stood 2.50 m (8 ft) high, and a massive
caldarium was uncovered together with its furnace area and
two heated apses for hot-water pools; over 100 tile *pilae* for
supporting the floor of the *caldarium* still survived. The whole
building was disused and partly demolished as early as *c.* 140
(another public bath-house in London may have superseded
it), and some poorly constructed private dwellings were
erected within the shell of the building. Once again the
discovery caused controversy, with some calling for the
preservation of the baths as an ancient monument, others
believing that to do so would have wrecked the developers'
long-term intentions for the site at enormous cost, and would
also have ruined the good working relationships built up
between archaeologists and developers in the City of London
over many years – the lessons of the Mithras controversy of
1954 having been well and truly learnt. In the end a

compromise was reached, and the remains have for the most part not been destroyed but are preserved for posterity (but not for current viewing) beneath 3 m (10 ft) of sand. A similar fate befell another splendid monument of Roman water engineering in 1998, a stretch over 20 m (65 ft) long, and 3.30 m (11 ft) high of perfectly preserved Roman vaulted drain, which was saved intact but inaccessible below Monument House in Botolph Lane. It is sad that the prohibitive costs of land and its development in London's 'square mile' today very rarely allow such monuments to be permanently preserved as part of the nation's cultural heritage; yet as mentioned in my Preface (p. xviii) our European partners, most notably Germany, have often taken a different view of the correct order of priorities.

Excavations just north of Lower Thames Street and elsewhere along the Roman waterfront have provided graphic evidence of the commercial life of the city, in the form of massive timber quaysides and accompanying warehouses. In the mid-first century the Thames water-line here was 100 m or so (110 yds) north of its present line, but successive rebuilding and land reclamation advanced the line of the quays southwards by up to some 60 m (200 ft) before the end of the third century. Nothing is preserved of these wharves beyond a solitary timber post from a Roman quayside of *c.* AD 75, which is displayed in the forecourt of the **Church of St Magnus the Martyr** (5), on Upper Thames Street opposite its junction with Fish Street Hill (just south of the Monument). The substantial post was found near here in 1931.

Another important category of public buildings was temples. One early one is known beside the Flavian forum, demolished when the larger forum was built; and another, reconstructed as a full-fledged classical temple, has been partly excavated near the waterfront south of Queen Victoria Street. Only a single example has been completely excavated in London. That is the famous **Temple of Mithras*** (D; 6), the discovery of which in 1954 caused a sensation. Intense public interest demanded a temporary suspension of work on the modern building (Bucklersbury House) while 80,000 people flocked to see the remains. Questions were asked in the House of Commons about the possibility of preserving it, but in the end it was decided that the costs of keeping it *in situ* were too high. A compromise was reached, and the building was dismantled stone by stone and eventually reassembled in its present position in Temple Court, 11, Queen Victoria Street. This is 70 m (230 ft) NW of its original site on the west bank of the Walbrook stream (D).

The reconstruction visible today does give an idea of the outline of the temple, with its nave, two aisles and an apse for the main statue-group (and three external buttresses); the entrance threshold, much worn by the tread of Roman devotees, and the bases of the two rows of seven pillars that supported the roof, can also be seen. This is essentially the form of the temple as first built c. AD 240/50; the later phases, when the floor was successively raised and the columns were dismantled (entailing a re-roofing of the whole building), are not represented here. This was a substantial structure, nearly 18 m (59 ft) long and 8 m (26 ft) wide, larger than most *mithraea* in the western provinces. The semicircular apse is extremely rare in such temples, and one can understand why the building was provisionally interpreted as a church until the head of Mithras came to light.

There are, however, many misleading features about the 'new' Temple of Mithras as we see it today: the nave was originally much lower in relation to the side-aisles, and was reached from the doorway by two wooden steps; the earth floor of the nave and the wooden floor of the aisles have both been re-created in insensitive and inappropriate 'crazy paving' (to ensure zero maintenance costs); and a wooden water-tank in one corner has been rebuilt in stone. In addition, the present position of the temple on a lofty platform is quite the opposite of its original low-lying site: such locations (*mithraea* were built underground or in hollows where possible) were important to the whole myth-recreation central to Mithraic worship and ritual, since the killing of the bull by Mithras, ritually remembered in every act of Mithraic worship, had taken place in a cave.

The temple was graced with a beautiful set of imported sculptures, now in the Museum of London (p. 637) together with a Mithraic relief found here in the nineteenth century. Casts of the sculptures found in 1954 are enterprisingly displayed at the north, south and central entrances to Bucklersbury House (which is situated immediately east of

the temple), and can be seen on application to the security
staff at those entrances.

The reconstruction-drawing (Fig. 137) shows a suggested
view of what a Mithraic ceremony in progress in the temple
might have looked like. Mithraism was a secret 'mystery'
religion, open only to men and popular with soldiers,
merchants and officials. While borrowing some exotic
elements from the East (names, costumes and ritual words),
mithraism as we know it was largely created in Rome towards
the end of the first century AD. Thereafter it spread unevenly
throughout the Roman Empire, but was more popular in the
northern and western Empire than it ever was in the East.
There were various grades of initiation (the 'raven' and the
'lion' are shown in the nave in Fig. 137), seven in all: the
number of columns separating the nave from the aisles may
not be accidental. The aisles were normally furnished with
mattresses on which worshippers reclined: the standing
figures shown there in Fig. 137 may therefore be misleading.

137   Walbrook Temple of Mithras, a ceremony in progress

There was a ritual meal which celebrated Mithras' killing of
the bull, at which the bull's flesh and blood were often
substituted by other meats and wine: chicken bones were
plentiful in the London *mithraeum*. Antagonistic early
Christian writers not surprisingly saw this meal as a parody of
the Christian Eucharist. Like Christianity adherents were
promised eternal life: one painted inscription in a *mithraeum*
in Rome, addressed by a devotee to Mithras, reads: 'And you
have saved us by the shedding of the eternal blood' (referring
to the killing of the bull) – no wonder, then, that Christians
and Mithraists came into conflict. The only other temple of
Mithras visible in Britain is at Carrawburgh on Hadrian's
Wall (p. 485).

Mithraic worship continued in the temple into the early
fourth century, because an inscription in honour of the god
can be dated to AD 307/8, but soon afterwards the head of
Mithras and most of the other sculptures were buried in a pit,
and sealed by a succession of later floors. The latter implies
that the building continued in use, but presumably with a
different function. The fact that a sculptural group depicting
Bacchus and his companions (not a god usually found in
association with the otherwise eclectic mithraism) was found
not in the pit but on top of the latest floor in the temple has
given rise to the plausible suggestion that the building was
converted to Bacchic worship at some stage in the fourth
century. This was another 'mystery' cult by the time of the
late Empire, also promising eternal life to its adherents: the
inscription on this Bacchic group from the London temple,
'life to wandering men', perhaps hints as much. An
alternative, much less likely, view is to see this sculpture as an
'escapee' from the others associated with the Mithraic phase
of the temple (perhaps moved out of place by post-Roman
activity), and to see the building in its secondary use as a
Christian church; but there is not a scrap of material evidence
which supports such a hypothesis, and the physical take-over
of a *mithraeum* is not in line with what we know of Christian
practice elsewhere, which was normally to obliterate the
physical remains of its hated rival and to build a church as a
totally new building above.

About the middle of the second century the Walbrook
stream silted up, its revetted banks collapsed, and the area was

redeveloped to become one of the high-class residential
districts of the city. One well preserved geometric mosaic,
found in Bucklersbury (now Queen Victoria Street) in 1869,
aroused as much public interest as the Temple of Mithras did
nearly a century later: 33,000 people visited it in three days.
Measuring over 5 m (17 ft) long and of early fourth-century
date, it is now displayed in the Museum of London (p. 636).
Two much smaller geometric mosaics were found in 1933–4
during building work at the **Bank of England** (7). Both have
been lifted from their original positions: one has been reset in
the Bank's private museum, which contains other Roman
material (Monday–Friday 1000–1700 only); the other, much
restored, lies at the foot of the main staircase inside the Bank
but can only be viewed (for security reasons) by prior written
appointment through the Museum's curator. An earlier mosaic
discovery from the Bank of England site, in 1805, an
attractive square geometric panel with an unusual stylized
plant motif at its centre, is now displayed in the British
Museum next to the Classicianus tomb (p. 642). This belongs
to the early fourth century and was laid by the same workshop
responsible for the Bucklersbury mosaic. A disappointing
portion of third-century mosaic, which does remain *in situ*,
exists on the premises of 11, **Ironmonger Lane** (8). This is
currently (2001) occupied by Helaba Ltd, from whom written
permission to view it must be obtained in advance. The
mosaic was found in 1949 and restored in 1983. Finally, a red
tessellated floor, originally bisected by a wooden partition,
can be seen *in situ* in the crypt of **All Hallows Church** (9),
near the Tower of London. Another patch of red *tesserae* can
be seen nearby, but this has been relaid. Excavation in 2000 in
advance of a new visitor centre found further traces of walls
and floors of the building to which the red tessellated
pavement belongs. Several Roman finds from this and earlier
excavations are displayed in the crypt Museum (open daily,
1000–1600). The tombstone with a Greek inscription here was
brought to this country in recent times and is not a genuine
relic of the city's past.

Much more coherent and rewarding than these isolated
mosaics are the remains of a Roman house and attached bath-
suite in an inspection-chamber below 100, **Lower Thames
Street**** (10). In order to visit this outstanding site, enquiries

should be made well in advance by telephone with the
Museum of London (020–7600–3699). At present guided
tours are arranged to the site approximately once a month
(twice in summer), so you need to find out the day(s) and
time(s) these are taking place. With the exception of the
amphitheatre and some stretches of city wall, the surviving
fragments of Roman London are isolated relics, looking often
rather pathetic in their modern surroundings. Here, however,
is a more substantial building, and its appeal and intrinsic
interest are therefore the greater. It is also, of course, the
earliest dwelling-place of a Londoner that can be seen today,
and was indeed the only Roman house in London that had
been extensively explored until the explosion of
archaeological activity in the city over the past 30 years. Parts
of it had been discovered in 1848 and 1859, and even a small
portion preserved then beneath the Coal Exchange.
Excavation in 1969–70, and again in 1975–6, has revealed
that these earlier discoveries belonged to the bath-house of an
L-shaped private residence. Pottery suggests that the whole
building was constructed about AD 200, and it remained in use
for over two centuries: a group of 246 bronze coins points to
occupation after AD 395, possibly as late as the mid-fifth
century, and an early Anglo-Saxon brooch found in the rubble
of the collapsed roof implies that the house did not become
ruined until *c*. AD 500. Of the house itself parts of two
corridors serving the north and east wings, and some of the
rooms of these wings, have been explored, but the main
feature of the preserved remains is the fine bath-suite, situated
in the angle between the two wings. A worn door-sill leads
from a corridor of the house to a small undressing room with
a red tessellated floor. On either side are two heated rooms
with apses. On the bather's right (west side) was the
tepidarium, with a brick seat still visible in one of its walls;
this is the part that was preserved beneath the old Coal
Exchange. On the bather's left was the *caldarium*, which is in
excellent shape: 29 *pilae* bases for supporting the floor can be
seen, as well as the stoke-hole and flue-tiles in the walls for
the hot air to escape. The walls of the room are still about 1 m
(3 ft) high. On the south side of these heated chambers was a
large *frigidarium*, probably vaulted. Its original floor of red
tesserae was later covered after heavy wear with a layer of

pink cement, probably in the fourth century. At one end is a small cold-water immersion-bath.

The great defences of Roman London, which have left more numerous and more substantial fragments than the buildings they eventually enclosed, fall into three separate phases. Early in the second century, before the construction of the city wall, a large fort was erected NW of the built-up area (p. 608). This fort was one of the most important Roman discoveries made in the excavations of bomb-damaged sites after 1945: although the peculiar course taken by the city wall in the Cripplegate area had of course been noted, the reason for it was only revealed in 1949.

When the city wall was constructed, at the end of the second century, the existing north and west walls of the fort were incorporated into its circuit. The wall, some 2.45 m (8 ft) thick at base and 4.50 m to 6 m (15–20 ft) high, was made of courses of Kentish ragstone separated at intervals by tile bonding-courses. The rear face of the wall, despite the fact that it was to be covered immediately by an accompanying earth bank, was finished with the same neat precision as the outer face, but the thickness was reduced here by a series of offsets. The fort wall was only 1.20 m (4 ft) thick, and in those places where the line of the city wall coincided with the existing fort wall, additional masonry was tacked on to the latter's inside face (on the north and west sides of the fort) to make the defences overall the same width there as elsewhere.

The third phase in the city's defences happened in the late third century when the wall was completed along the Thames. Long suspected, the riverside wall was only finally located in 1975, when a stretch of 38 m (125 ft) was excavated in advance of destruction at the western end, near the Mermaid Theatre. The wall, erected on oak-pile foundations, was about 2.45 m (8 ft) wide and had a clay bank piled behind it. A great deal of re-used material was built into the wall here, most notably the astonishing haul of 52 sculptured blocks and inscriptions now in the Museum of London (p. 636). Many of these derived from a monumental arch decorated with relief sculpture, a commonplace in many provinces of the Roman world, but unique in Britain. Such wholesale recycling of earlier building stone was commonplace at the period, and no doubt reflected a practical way of disposing of monuments

demolished for the construction of the new wall: it need not
by itself indicate that Roman London as a whole was by now
in decay. The date of this wall has been established as after
AD 268 by the dendrochronology of the oak piles
underpinning the wall. This was a time when other places in
SE England were receiving fortifications for the first time
(town walls at Canterbury, and the Saxon Shore fort at Burgh
Castle, for example), and its construction may just precede the
period of Carausius' secessionist 'British Empire' from 286,
which could have provided a logical political context for such
a strengthening of London's defences. It certainly predates the
new palace complex close to St Peter's Hill off Upper Thames
Street started by Carausius' successor, Allectus, in 294 (in this
case precisely dated by dendrochronology), since dumps of
construction material from the palace were found to have
sealed the riverside defences at that point. But precisely when
between 268 and 294 the riverside wall was actually built is
still uncertain.

The fourth phase in the fortification of Roman London
came around the middle of the fourth century, when
projecting towers of solid masonry were added to the existing
landward wall, but in the eastern sector only. Many of them
used building stone pirated from elsewhere, including grave
monuments from nearby cemeteries. There are also towers in
the western sector, as we shall see at Cripplegate and
Newgate, but these are all hollow and belong to the medieval
period, *c.* AD 1250/1350. Curiously, they do not appear to
have had Roman predecessors, and one can only assume that
the programme for providing Roman London with projecting
towers round the whole of its landward walled circuit was
never finished, because there is no strategic or topographical
reason why the eastern side of the walls should have received
special treatment.

One final phase in LONDINIVM's defences is also known. In
1976–7 another stretch of riverside Roman wall was
uncovered and left on permanent display in the grounds of
the **Tower of London** (11 on map) (March–October,
Monday–Saturday, 0900–1700, Sunday, 1000–1700;
November–February, Tuesday–Saturday, 0900–1600,
Sunday–Monday, 1000–1600). Situated near the History
Gallery (turn left at the Water Gate), it is 20 m (70 ft) long

and over 2 m (7 ft) high. This, however, turned out to be of a different construction from the riverside wall located in excavations elsewhere: although partly constructed of re-used stones there were no timber foundation piles, and the wall had internal timber lacing, still detectable as cavities in the masonry which at one point have been filled by modern beams. A date for its construction in the 390s was clearly indicated by coins found in the bank of material dumped behind it, which had been piled up against the fresh and unweathered mortar of the newly completed wall. This work does not represent a wholesale refurbishment of the riverside defences at this late date, but the rebuilding of a short portion of them only; traces of their late third-century predecessor were also found.

Now go up the steps at the far (east) end and turn left up the slope. The ruins of the Wardrobe Tower sit on the site of a Roman tower, and behind it a low portion of Roman wall, 3 m (10 ft) long, survives (12). This of course belongs to the landward defences and is therefore about 200 years older than the masonry of the riverside wall. The rest of its line in this area, and the site of an internal interval tower (one of four discovered so far on the circuit), have been marked out on the ground in concrete.

The Tower of London forms a convenient starting-point for a tour of the remaining visible portions of London's Roman defences. Outside the Tower, on the north side of **Tower Hill*** (13) [AM; A], is a fine stretch of the Roman city wall, best viewed from the terrace near Tower Hill Underground station. Nearer the road only the base of the wall is visible, but to the north the Roman work survives in excellent condition – 15 courses of squared ragstone blocks, separated at intervals by four sets of bonding-bricks (the bottom two in triple rows, the upper two double). Higher up the wall is medieval. Set in the modern wall at the rear here is the cast of a Roman inscription; the original is now in the British Museum. Julius Alpinus Classicianus was the chief financial administrator (*procurator*) of Britain immediately after the Boudican revolt in AD 60/1, when he successfully urged on Rome restraint in dealing with the British people, bravely making a stand against the policy of harsh repression favoured by the provincial governor; his names indicate that he was a Gaul.

Classicianus died in London, presumably still in office, and his tomb was set up in one of the cemeteries outside the city walls. In the middle of the fourth century, it was broken up and incorporated into a projecting tower on the city wall not far from where the cast now stands. The upper portion, including part of his name, was found in 1852, and it was immediately claimed that the Classicianus named must be the same as the *procurator* mentioned by Tacitus. Scepticism later set in, as the coincidence was regarded as too great to be true, but in 1935 the lower part of what was clearly the same inscription was discovered in another part of the same tower. This reads PROC(*urator*) PROVINC(*iae*) BRIT(*anniae*), '*procurator* of the province of Britain', and all doubts about the man's identification were dispelled. It was set up by his wife Julia Pacata I(ndiana): she was the daughter of Julius Indus, a pro-Roman aristocrat of the Treveri tribe centred on Trier in what is now Germany (he helped raised an auxiliary unit for the Roman army which bore his name, the *ala Indiana*, which we have seen stationed at Cirencester in the early years of the conquest: p. 178). Julia Pacata and her husband Julius Alpinus Classicianus were, therefore, Romanized Gauls, capable of viewing the events of AD 61 in a different perspective from that of Rome. His career is also an example of the prominent role which trusted provincials from the north-western provinces were already playing in the governance of the Empire by the middle of the first century AD.

Immediately north of here is **Tower Hill Underground station** (14), where a fragment of wall found in 1967 is preserved high up in the tiled facing opposite platform 1 (westbound). A few yards further north, at 40–1 Trinity Square, is the Mercer building in **Wakefield House** (15), where a stretch of the outer face of the Roman wall is preserved in a basement. The plinth is visible here, and a triple row of bonding-tiles. This can, however, only be visited provided written permission has been sought in advance. Much more impressive is a fine stretch a little further north, in the courtyard behind 8–10, **Cooper's Row**** (16). This was first found in 1864 when it was incorporated in a warehouse. The latter was knocked down in 1961, since when the wall has been exposed and accessible. At the time of writing (2001), the site is once more being redeveloped, by Grange

Hotels, and the intention is that the wall will again be freely accessible at the centre of the new complex. It stands 10 m (35 ft) above ground-level here, but the upper part is medieval. The Roman portion, with considerable parts of the inner face and rows of tile bonding-courses still preserved, stands about 4 m (13 ft) high (Fig. 138). A display board will indicate clearly what is Roman and what is medieval. The outer face of the wall, more repaired but still showing the Roman sandstone plinth at its foot, can be seen on the other side. The southward continuation of the Cooper's Row stretch, at 6–7, The Crescent, 19.5 m long (64 ft) and 2.45 m (8 ft) high, is also preserved and can be seen through a glass window at the south end of the Cooper's Row wall.

Return now to Cooper's Row and go northwards, pass under the railway, and then turn immediately right into Crosswall. On the corner here, in Emperor House, **Crosswall** (17), is another stretch of Roman city wall, first exposed in 1980, 10 m (33 ft) long and 3 m (10 ft) high. Again, this is in

138   Cooper's Row, inner face of the Roman city wall

a private office building, and it is best to write to the occupier
in advance if you are keen to see it. Continue along Crosswall
and turn right into America Square. At 12, **America Square**
(18), another stretch of Roman city wall can be seen, 32 m
(105 ft) long and 2 m (6 ft 6 in) high; it is exposed in the
foyer of the office building, and is visible from the street.

Now retrace your steps to the western end of Crosswall,
and now turn right into **Crutched Friars** (19). At the end of
this street, on the right, just before Roman Wall House, in the
basement of the Market Bar and Restaurant (2, Crutched
Friars), a substantial piece of the wall survives, 6 m (20 ft)
long and 2.50–2.75 m (8–9 ft) high; it is freely accessible
whenever the bar is open. This is the wall's inner face, and
there is therefore an offset at eye-level and another at the very
top; there was also a further offset at the base of this stretch
(as the jagged edge of the bottom surviving course of the
brick bonding-courses shows), but the base of the wall has
here been destroyed by the modern construction work.

A miserable fragment of Roman city wall is preserved in
the London Guildhall University's **Sir John Cass'
Foundation** (20), 31, Jewry Street (the porter may be able to
arrange for a colleague to escort you, but it is better to arrange
viewing in advance by arrangement with the Provost's
secretary [tel: 0207–3201311]). A larger piece of wall exists
under **The Three Tuns** public house (21), 36, Jewry Street,
but the landlord will show it to you only if business is very
slack. Now retrace your steps towards Crutched Friars and
turn left down India Street, and right again into Vine Street. In
the basement of 35, Vine Street, **Emperor House** (22), is a
stretch of the external face of the Roman city wall, some 10 m
(30 ft) long and 3 m (10 ft) high, excavated in 1979–80. Also
visible here is the projecting rectangular foundation for one of
the D-shaped external towers added *c*. 350 (the tower itself
was demolished in medieval times), the only such example of
Roman date from the London defences permanently
accessible. The wall with its base-plinth and a portion of the
tower's footings is visible with difficulty through an
inspection-window in the yard to the right of the main
entrance to Emperor House; this is accessible at any time.
Closer inspection (from the staff canteen) is only possible by

prior written arrangement with The Secretary, Lloyd's Register of Shipping, 71, Fenchurch Street, London EC3M 4BS.

In the subway under **Houndsditch** (23, Aldgate end), a cross-section of the Roman wall with its accompanying earth bank, recorded here before destruction during the construction of the subway, is represented in modern tiling near exit 1. The Roman level here was found to be 4.2 m (14 ft) below the present-day one. This is item 6 on the 'London Wall Walk' itinerary, created in 1983 with information panels at the various points of interest: Emperor House (see above), for example, is the subject of panel 4, Cooper's Row panel 3, and so on. Thereafter, no remains of the city wall are visible until you reach the Cripplegate area. For those who wish to walk, the line of the wall is followed by Bevis Marks, Camomile Street, Wormwood Street and the road called London Wall. There were Roman gates at Aldgate and Bishopsgate.

The next surviving portion of city wall above ground is that in **St Alphage Churchyard** (24), reached from Wood Street: turn northwards off London Wall (and then first right). The brickwork battlements are Tudor and most of the rest of the facing is medieval, but one interesting Roman feature is visible here. Go up the stairway on the east side of the garden and look down at the outer face of the wall. At the bottom, on the left, there appears to be a vertical crack in the masonry, but in fact there are two walls of different periods side by side here. That on the right (outer) belongs to the Cripplegate Roman fort, and dates to the early second century; that on the left is the masonry added when the city wall was built in the late second century (as explained above, p. 623).

West of Wood Street, which passes through the site of Cripplegate, the north gate of the Roman fort, is the Barbican development. In the middle of this, starkly contrasting with the impressive modern architecture of steel, concrete and glass all around, is the church of St Giles, on the south side of which is a long stretch of city wall. This stands on Roman footings and incorporates Roman core, but most of the masonry visible here is medieval, including the lower part of a tower. Excavation in 1966 dated the latter to the mid- or late thirteenth century. You can observe this from a distance from the terrace on the south side of the church, but to view it at close quarters, return to Wood Street and take the gap in the otherwise continuous frontage of properties on your right (opposite 'Roman House'), signed 'Upstairs to Barbican Highwalk'. Go down two flights of steps, through the gate, and so up to the outer face of the city wall. The only Roman work visible is behind the tower, where neatly built squared stones and slight traces of a tile bonding-course (not, of course, the extensive brickwork above) can be seen in the lower part of the wall. The later tower protected the wall here, so making unnecessary the repair which has removed the Roman facing elsewhere. Also approximately of thirteenth-century date (*c.* 1250/1350 according to current thinking) is the spectacular **Cripplegate Bastion** (25) a few metres further west, which marks the position of the NW corner of the Roman fort and city wall.

Return now to Wood Street and so back to London Wall, then turn right (westwards) along its north side until you reach the ramp next to Bastion House descending to an underground car-park. To the right of the car-park entrance, behind the medieval bastion, is an insignificant fragment of Roman wall recognizable from the red tile bonding-course. Adjacent to this, the **West Gate*** (26) of the Roman fort is preserved in an inspection-chamber to the right of the car-park entrance, but it is now only opened at set times (normally once a month) on a guided tour starting from the nearby Museum of London. You are advised, therefore, to telephone the Museum well in advance (020–7600–3699) to find out the dates and times that it will be open. A portion is visible here of the original fort wall standing on its base-plinth, and behind, jutting up against it, is the masonry added when the city wall was built. Then comes a well preserved guardroom, originally matched by another which has not been preserved. In between were two carriageways spanned by arches. Some traces of the central dividing wall remain, and one of the carriageways is still blocked with a late Roman or post-Roman wall of crudely built material.

Adjacent to the remains of the west gate is the large underground car-park under **London Wall*** (27). At its east end is a well preserved fragment of the Roman wall, found in 1957 during clearance for the new road. It can also be more easily reached via a pedestrian staircase 150 m further east, on the south side of London Wall near its junction with Coleman

Street. Because the car-park is open 24 hours a day, this piece
of London's Roman heritage is accessible at any time. This
stretch of Roman wall lies east of the Cripplegate fort and so
is of a single thickness and build. Two offsets for reducing the
thickness are visible on the inside face; the outer is more
robbed, but the base-plinth is preserved. Like many such
surviving stretches of the Roman city wall, its underground
location is a salutary reminder of the relentless rise in ground-
level over the centuries.

At the west end of London Wall, on the corner with
Aldersgate Street, is the Museum of London, which should be
visited before proceeding further south (below, p. 632).
Almost opposite on the other side of London Wall, next to a
staircase up to Barbican Highwalk, is the pedestrian access to
Noble Street (28). Parts of the outer (fort) wall and the inner
(thickening) wall are exposed here for a considerable length,
including part of the foundations of an internal turret to the
left of the steps leading down to the Plaisterers' Hall, although
this portion is often overgrown. At the end of this stretch
comes the crucial junction between the fort and the city walls,
and it was here in 1949 that the existence of the fort was first
confirmed. The fort wall can be seen curving round, with the
conspicuous foundations of an internal tower of *c.* AD 120,
marking the SW corner of the fort. Projecting out from it and
disappearing under the modern brickwork is a short portion of
the Roman city wall added nearly a century later, *c.* AD 200.
The difference in thickness between the two will be noted, as
will a brick-lined culvert running through the thickness of the
city wall at this point.

Further west, incorporated in the new Merrill Lynch
European Headquarters, **Newgate Street** (29; still under
construction in early 2002), is an imposing fragment of
Roman wall, standing to perhaps half its original height. Next
to it is a substantial part of one of the hollow medieval
projecting towers of *c.* 1250/1350. First uncovered in 1909,
this and the Roman wall were preserved for nearly a century
in an inspection-chamber below the yard of the former
General Post Office. Excavations in 1999 examined the late
medieval city ditch here, which was backfilled and built over
in the mid-sixteenth century; among the discoveries was a
Roman barrel-lined well which produced a Gaulish pipeclay

figurine of Minerva. A permanent display of the history and
archaeology of the site is due to be presented in Merrill
Lynch's new building. Access to the remains of the Roman
wall and medieval tower is uncertain at the time of writing;
but access should be possible during office hours via the
Giltspur Street entrance. The wall turns southwards at this
point, and at Newgate there was a Roman gate. It had two
carriageways and large square flanking towers, and the whole
structure was about 30 m (100 ft) wide. Finally, a short
section of the base of the Roman wall has been preserved
under an extension to the **Central Criminal Court** (30), north
of Warwick Square. For obvious security reasons, this can
only be seen by prior arrangement, and you should write to
the Keeper of the Court at the Old Bailey if you wish to
inspect the relic.

Outside the immediate city limits, there is very little of
Roman interest. A red tessellated pavement *in situ* is reflected
in a mirror in the crypt of **St Bride's Church**, Fleet Street
(31, off map), and the position of a Roman ditch has been
marked out on the linoleum floor nearby. Further west there
was a Roman building under Westminster Abbey, and a
sarcophagus found there is now in the entrance to the Chapter
House. The so-called 'Roman Bath' in the Strand is of
sixteenth- or seventeenth-century date. Some of the finds from
the Roman suburb in Southwark are in the Cuming Museum,
155–7, Walworth Road (Tuesday–Saturday 1000–1700).
A tiny fragment of red mosaic has been relaid in the south
chancel-aisle of Southwark Cathedral. Slight traces of a
Roman building in Greenwich Park, part of a temple complex,
may also be mentioned (App. 1).

Roman London has yielded an astonishing haul of
fascinating finds, more than any other single site in Britain.
Some are in the British Museum, but the main collections are
housed in the **Museum of London**** (32), Aldersgate Street,
which is open daily from 1000 to 1750 (Sunday 1200–1750).
The superb Roman galleries here were totally refurbished and
re-designed in 1996, and now constitute what is
unquestionably one of the most stimulating, informative and
colourful displays of Roman material in the country: the
quality of the finds, as might be expected from one of the
western Roman world's leading cities, is exceptional. Space

prevents more than a list of some of the outstanding exhibits displayed in this Museum, and in any case such is the pace of discovery of extraordinary new finds that any account of the current Museum display is likely to be soon out of date. To take just one example: a particularly exciting find of 2001 (not yet incorporated in the permanent gallery) is that of a bucket and chain water-lifting device from Gresham Street, dated to the early second century AD (the well from which it came was built in AD 108/9, and it perished soon after in a fire, probably the Hadrianic one of *c.* 125). The chain to which wooden buckets were fastened would have been linked to a treadmill which provided motive power; each bucket scooped water from a lower level as it was dragged through the water, and discharged its load at the top of the loop as it was turned horizontally by the action of the moving chain. The ironwork of the chain remained in near-perfect condition, having been waterlogged for 1,800 years. Its weight without water is estimated at 120 kg (260 lb), and there were probably 20 buckets capable of containing 5 litres (1 gallon) of water each. This type of water-lifting device is described by Vitruvius, the first-century-BC architectural writer, but only fragments of such chains have been found elsewhere in the Roman Empire, and the new London find is therefore of international importance. An adjacent, even earlier well built in AD 63, dated like the later one by dendrochronology, also contained a bucket and loop mechanism, more fragmentary and constructed entirely of wood.

First in the Museum of London's Roman galleries comes a section on the army, with the Camomile Street tombstone of a legionary soldier (like Classicianus', found re-used in a fourth-century tower) greeting you on the right, and that of Vivius Marcianus of the Second Augustan legion (found on Ludgate Hill in 1669) on the left; a case with military equipment follows. Quite apart from the presence of a garrison in the Cripplegate fort, London was likely to have been a place where soldiers on official business of various sorts would frequently have been seen (as two of the Vindolanda tablets make clear). In the corner beyond, don't miss the case with graphic evidence of the first of London's great fires – that caused by Boudica and her followers in AD 60 or 61, with burnt daub, samian pottery, glass and grain as well as a decapitated head from the Walbrook, the last possibly but not certainly a victim of the uprising.

Now turn round to examine the display on writing behind you, with another cast of the Classicianus tombstone (p. 625) forming the backdrop. In the centre is a famous tile scratched with a verse graffito reading 'Au[gu]stalis has been wandering on his own every day for thirteen days' – usually claimed as the first recorded example of absenteeism by a British workman. Flanking it are two tombstones in white marble, one for M. Aurelius Eucarpus, perhaps a Greek (with unusually evident guidelines for the mason), and the other for L. Pompeius Licetus from Arezzo in Italy. Marble is an unusual material for tombstones (as for sculpture) in Roman Britain, and both inscriptions indicate both the wealth and the cosmopolitan mix of at least some of London's Roman inhabitants. Also here is the fascinating wooden writing tablet found in 1986, written with a *stilus*, a sharp metal instrument for writing in the wax – but here done so enthusiastically that the back of the wood behind the wax has been incised with the entire text. This is in fact the longest such text to have survived on a *stilus* tablet from Roman Britain. Precisely dated to 14 March AD 118, within months of Hadrian's accession, it is a rare legal document recording the sale of a piece of woodland called Verlucionium, somewhere in Kent (as the *civitas* of the Cantiaci is mentioned). It cost only 40 *denarii* for the equivalent of 4.6 acres (1.85 ha), which sounds like quite a bargain.

The next part of the gallery to your left illustrates the trading contacts between London and the Roman world, such as the amphora from Southwark still bearing its *dipinto* announcing the contents as 'L. Tettius Africanus' finest fish sauce from Antibes' in the south of France. Particularly rarely found in Britain are some of the items in the next case, such as the fragment of cameo glass (probably made in Rome), or the Mediterranean marble fragments imported from Paros and Euboea (*cippolino*) in Greece, and Dokimeion (Synnada) in western Turkey (*pavonazzetto*). More local trade is represented by the mast-step of the Blackfriars boat in the next case, excavated in 1962 (more of this boat was raised than there is space to display): this was carrying Kentish ragstone when it foundered within sight of London's Roman waterfront. The placing of a coin under the mast with a figure of Fortuna is a nice superstitious touch; but the luck of this particular vessel ran out some time around AD 150.

High up on the wall next on your left is the stunning fresco decoration of *c*. AD 150 from the Southwark 'palace', an administrative block of uncertain function on the south bank of the Thames. This elegant and delicately executed painting, with a cupid and no doubt other figures set against an architectural background with receding perspective, is ultimately a descendant of the so-called Fourth Style of Pompeian painting: indeed, in the absence of anything comparable in Britain, the closest parallels for this wall painting are in contemporary Italy. The alternate use of bright red and yellow is most striking, and the use of expensive cinnabar for a more lustrous red, at nine times the expense of ordinary red ochre according to Pliny, underlines the public character of the building it adorned.

The next case contains another famous exhibit, the so-called leather 'bikini' trunks ('monokini' is a more accurate description), but whether its wearer was an 'acrobat' (as the Museum label suggests), or was a performer in the low-brow theatrical variety shows which we know to have been popular elsewhere in the Roman Empire, or more mundanely was employed in some muddy job near the Walbrook (where the find was made), is left open to your imagination. Two more fragmentary examples of leather trunks, also displayed here, came from Queen Street within the City and from a third-century military site at Shadwell, a mile east of the Tower. Superb models of three of the structures discussed above – the forum, the first London bridge, and the Huggin Hill baths – follow; from the last, note the example of 'fried egg' pattern plasterwork, an imitation of the attractive *giallo antico* marble (from Chemtou, Tunisia) for those who could not afford the real thing. Near here a case displays a spectacular hoard of 43 gold coins in near-mint condition, buried *c*. 175/80 in a deposit safe at Plantation Place but never recovered. Why not we shall never know.

After moving up the ramp, and passing a case illustrating the second of the great Roman fires of London (*c*. AD 125), there follow sections illustrating crafts and then housing. The latter was still largely of timber until the end of the first

century, but increasingly in stone from then onwards. On the
left from Watling Court comes a floor of *c*. AD 100 in *opus
signinum* technique, with what for Britain is the unusual
feature of small black and white mosaic designs at intervals.
The general idea, although not this exact pattern, is closely
matched in countless examples around the central
Mediterranean, where this style had largely gone out of
fashion nearly a century before. Behind you is the spectacular
Bucklersbury mosaic, the largest and best preserved of
London's many mosaic pavements; it was laid early in the
fourth century (the Constantinian period) when a mosaic
workshop also responsible for the Bank of England mosaic in
the British Museum (p. 642) was active in London. The
treatment of the plant motifs in the four corners and in the
acanthus scroll on the threshold of the apse are highly
distinctive, unparalleled elsewhere in Britain. Interestingly,
this workshop seems to have gone out of business soon
afterwards, and by the mid-fourth century there may have
been none operating in the city: at any rate floors known to be
later in date, from Old Broad Street (showing Bacchus on a
leopard, in the British Museum but not currently on display),
from Southwark (Jubilee Line extension) and from 1 Poultry,
were laid by mosaicists based in Cirencester (the first two)
and the east Midlands respectively. Earlier in date (*c*. 150)
than the Bucklersbury floor but more fragmentary is the
mosaic from Milk Street displayed on the wall nearby, found
in 1976, with an elegant *cantharus* at its centre. Whether there
will also be space to house another polychrome geometric
pavement, found in Gresham Street in January 2001, remains
to be seen. The latter is of importance because it is one of the
earliest closely datable mosaics yet found in London: it comes
from the living-room of a timber-framed house destroyed by
the Hadrianic fire of *c*. 125.

   In the next section a fine sculptured panel shows four seated
female deities, one of the stones recovered from the late third-
century riverside wall in 1975. The deities are mother
goddesses, normally shown as a threesome, but here
accompanied by a unique and so far unexplained interloper.
Note also here the model of the monumental arch,
reconstructed from more blocks found in the riverside wall
(above p. 623 and below, p. 640). But your eye will have been

caught by the superlative sculptures found in the Temple of Mithras on the Walbrook which rightly enjoy pride of place in these galleries: it is the richest single haul of marble sculpture from anywhere in Britain.

Some pieces were found in the nineteenth century, and almost certainly come from the *mithraeum*, although the find-spots are vague and the building itself was not found then. The most interesting of these earlier finds is a small but complete slab depicting Mithras slaying the bull, accompanied by the torchbearers Cautes and Cautopates who represent light and darkness; signs of the zodiac appear in the surrounding circle. The remarkable sculptures found in 1954 deserve even closer attention. They had deliberately been buried in the floor of the sanctuary early in the fourth century, but the building as we have seen (p. 620) continued in use for some years after this. One of the sculptures is a marble head of Mithras in his Phrygian cap, and it was the discovery of this that conclusively proved the identity of the temple. It presumably formed part of the main bull-slaying relief in the apse. An enormous hand clasping the hilt of a dagger (in the rather dark case to the left) was also found, and this may have belonged to a similar group, but the scale of the completed work would have been too big for the Walbrook temple. It may indicate that an even bigger *mithraeum* existed somewhere else in London (third-century Ostia near Rome had 16 of them!). Other sculptures found in 1954, all of marble, include a figure of Mercury, a head of Minerva and a small damaged group of Bacchus and his companions (the last implying perhaps, as we have seen [p. 620], a re-use of the temple for Bacchic worship in the fourth century). But the most beautiful discovery of all is the head of Serapis, Graeco-Egyptian god of the underworld (Fig. 139). Like the head of Mithras it is an imported piece, probably Italian work around the end of the second century AD. On his head is a corn-measure, symbolic of the prosperity which the god can bestow both in this life and the next. The sensitive modelling of the face, the skill in the design and execution of the hair, and the splendour of the burnished finish make it a wholly exceptional piece in the context of Roman Britain. The presence of so many other deities within the temple may seem surprising, but all of them are in some way connected with the after-life and the promise of salvation,

139   Temple of Mithras, head of Serapis (Museum of London)

and such theological pluralism, paralleled in some Continental *mithraea*, is not out of place in the London Mithraic sanctuary. Finally, an enigmatic silver box and 'strainer' should not be missed (also in the case to the left). Scenes of combat between men and animals, including griffins, and between animals and other animals are represented; animals are also being lured into cages. This is fairly standard iconography for the capture and rounding-up of beasts for the amphitheatre; whether it has a deeper religious significance in this context has been much debated, but without agreement, and it is possible that the frieze on the box should be seen as purely decorative.

The case with the silver box also contains another famous exhibit, a jug on which can be clearly read the graffito LONDINI AD FANVM ISIDIS, 'in London next door to the temple of Isis'. Quite apart from documenting the existence of a temple of the Egyptian goddess Isis in Roman London (since confirmed by another inscription, found in 1975), the jug is one of the few written records of the city's Roman name (the earliest occurs on one of the Vindolanda tablets). What prompted the graffito to be written we shall never know. Was it the property of an inn, its 'address label' an attempted deterrent to thieves? The vessel was found in Southwark; either there was another temple of Isis there, or the jug did indeed go missing. One can endlessly speculate, but the true significance of the graffito it is impossible to establish with certainty.

The next case on the left has a facsimile of a famous gold medallion (worth 10 *aurei*) from Arras in France; the original is in Arras Museum. It was struck in 297 to celebrate the recovery the previous year of the British provinces, symbolized here by their most important city, London, after the ten-year separatist rule of Carausius and Allectus. It shows a personification of the grateful city kneeling before the emperor Constantius, who is described as the 'restorer of eternal light'. Behind the kneeling figure is the earliest portrayal of LONDINIVM, a schematic representation of one of the city gates. The medallion was minted in Trier (Germany), so it is unlikely that the die-designer had ever seen London, but it does show us that by that time the city wall of Trier, at any rate, had sloping tiled roofs to crown their gate-towers, rather than flat crenellated roofs.

The last section illustrates some of the plentiful evidence
forthcoming from numerous excavations in the cemeteries of
Roman London. The outstanding exhibit here, found in 1999,
is the lady buried in the Spitalfields cemetery on the NE side
of London in a lead coffin inside a limestone sarcophagus –
which for Roman Britain is in itself a mark of high status, and
only the third such burial in London. The lead sarcophagus
has a decoration of cable pattern and scallop-shell clusters. Its
occupant was female, in her early to mid-twenties, and was
1.64 m tall (5 ft $4\frac{1}{2}$ in, about 6 cm or $2\frac{1}{2}$ inches above average
for women in Roman London). Her wealth is further
suggested by the accompanying finds, including an
extraordinary glass phial and a pipette, perhaps made in the
Rhineland, several items of jet, and fragments of textile with
gold thread and silk embroidery, possibly from a cushion
placed under her head. Not surprisingly, her teeth show that
she had enjoyed a healthy diet, although cavities suggest that
she had a partiality for sweet things. Her cause of death is
unknown; her hip bones suggest that she had not borne
children. We probably know more about this anonymous
fourth-century Londoner than any other Roman inhabitant of
the city – even the likelihood, based on analysis of her tooth
enamel, that she had grown up in the western Mediterranean
area (Spain?) and was not therefore an indigenous Londoner
at all. The striking reconstruction of her face, based on the
bone structure of her skull, is not fanciful (only such details as
the colour of her eyes and hair are unknowable), and where
actual appearance is checkable such simulations have proved
to be extremely life-like.

At the very end of the Roman Gallery, almost as an
apologetic afterthought, are a couple of sculptured stones; one
shows part of the goddess Minerva with her spear and her
owl. They are a token representative of the many carved
blocks from the riverside wall, pillaged, as careful study has
shown, from just two major buildings. One was a decorated
monumental arch (a model of which was noted above), the
other an ornamental screen featuring at least five deities. The
carving is provincial, but in the best classical tradition: it is
vigorous, highly competent work, of a quality matched in
Britain only by some of the sculpture at Bath, and its subject
matter and decorative motifs were directly inspired by the

mainstream art of Italy. That such imposing monuments once graced the capital comes as no surprise; but so much has been destroyed in the post-Roman history of the city that finds such as this are rare. These sculptures represent a major addition to our knowledge of Romano-British art and architecture, and it is disappointing that space at the Museum of London is simply too limited to give them the museum presentation that they undoubtedly deserve.

The most important collection of Romano-British antiquities, including some finds from London, is the property of the **British Museum**** in Great Russell Street (Sunday–Wednesday, 1000–1730; Thursday–Friday, 1000–2030). After its rehousing in the splendid new Weston gallery in 1997, this superlative collection of Roman antiquities found in Britain at last has a spacious and airy home which can do justice to both the quality and the quantity of the exhibits it contains. Once again only a brief selection of the more outstanding items can be mentioned here.

The place to start is with the last showcases in the adjacent Iron Age room, which demonstrate the increasing links that Iron Age chieftains enjoyed with Rome in the century which separates Caesar's incursions from the invasion of AD 43: note, for example, the impressive Welwyn burial, found in 1967, with five Dressel 1 wine amphorae from Italy and an elegant silver cup from the same source. In the passage linking the two galleries are displayed two more Roman silver cups from Welwyn as well as a red gloss *terra sigillata* plate made at Arezzo in Italy, of *c.* 15 BC/AD 15. The latter comes from the Iron Age settlement at Skeleton Green, Hertfordshire, one of very few in Britain to have eschewed the traditional round house and opted instead for rectangular buildings in Continental fashion: for the use of the rectangular building-plan in Britain is essentially one of the legacies of the Roman conquest. The spectacular coin hoard from Alton of *c.* AD 25 in the same case is important for demonstrating that the full name of an Atrebatic king TINC, previously thought to be Tincommmius, is in fact Tincomarus ('big fish').

In front of you at the start of the Romano-British gallery is the massive altar (Fig. 140), 1.52 m (5 ft) high, dedicated to the 'Spirit of the Place, Fortune the Home-Bringer, Eternal Rome and Good Fate' – a good all-in spiritual insurance policy on the part of its dedicator, C. Cornelius Peregrinus. He was a third-century commander of the garrison at Maryport in Cumbria, and the stone is the first of the long line of inscriptions collected there by the Senhouse family (it was seen by Camden in 1599). Most are still there (p. 420), but this one got away, having been given by John Senhouse in 1683 as a present to Sir John Lowther at nearby Lowther Castle; the latter collection subsequently passed to the British Museum, in 1969.

To its left is the imposing reconstituted tomb of Classicianus, with the inscribed slabs discussed above (p. 625), and the Bank of England mosaic panel also mentioned above (p. 621); facing them are two tombstones from Lincoln in its early days as a legionary fortress, in memory of C. Saufeius, of the Ninth Legion, and T. Valerius Pudens, of the Second Adiutrix. Pudens came from Savaria in Hungary, Saufeius from Her(aclea), but which one, whether in Italy, Greece or Turkey, is uncertain. They can be precisely dated, because we know about troop distributions in these years: the first belongs to the decade *c.* 61–71, the second between 71 and 78, when the Second Adiutrix moved to Chester. It is interesting to find C. Saufeius lacking the third name (*cognomen*) of the typical three (*tria nomina*) which a Roman citizen normally possessed during the Empire: the phenomenon of the absent *cognomen* is rare after the mid-first century AD. The cast of an inscription from Bordeaux is next on the left, of AD 237, documenting M. Aurelius Lunaris from York, who gave thanks to his local guardian goddess Boudiga (essentially the same as the name of the rebel queen) for safe passage when he arrived in SW France. We do not know what business took him there: the idea that he was a trader in wine is inference, not fact. The inscription also provides secure evidence that York had received colonial status by this date (COL(*onia*) EBOR(*acum*) in line 3). A cast of the South Shields tombstone of Regina, wife of Barates, discussed above (p. 449), is also displayed here.

In the case facing these inscriptions are the finds from a remarkable British Museum excavation at Stonea in the Fens, where a substantial stone building of unique form (it was certainly not a villa) was investigated in a region where rural settlement is generally of native farmstead type. The square structure may have been the administrative centre of an imperial estate, which would explain why the sort of investment in stone-built villas which we would expect in this fertile tract of the Romano-British countryside was effectively stifled. The state of preservation of wooden finds from here is exceptional: note the wooden spade, similar to one at Canterbury (p. 62), a hay-rake, a willow handle and a (plain) ash writing tablet. Three adjacent cases illustrate life in the Roman army, with familiar objects already noted elsewhere in this book – the shield boss from the Tyne at South Shields, poorly illuminated, in one (p. 449); the handsome Ribchester helmet (p. 393) in another; and the Richborough bronze goose-head, possibly from a boat (p. 45), in a third case, along with a good example of a bronze discharge certificate (diploma) of AD 103, of the type which every auxiliary soldier received on retirement. A square tile with a graffito showing

140 Maryport, altar (British Museum)   *141 Uley, head of Mercury (British Museum)*

the shape of a lighthouse, helpful in understanding the original appearance of the one at Dover (p. 52), is also displayed here. A model of Housesteads fort (p. 490) is nearby, and beyond it, in the direction of the Iron Age room, is a handful of the hundreds of remarkable wooden tablets bearing ink handwriting, miraculously preserved in waterlogged deposits at Vindolanda, which have been discussed above (p. 510). The famous letter from Claudia Severa inviting her friend Sulpicia Lepidina to a birthday party is no. 11, in the centre here.

Near a pier in the middle of the Weston gallery is a case with emperor portraits: a bronze head of the Emperor Claudius from the river Alde in Suffolk, possibly deposited there by jubilant supporters of Boudica during the uprising of 61; a famous bronze head of the emperor Hadrian, found in the Thames in London; and a well preserved statuette of Nero from Holkham Hall, a rare survival since the majority of bronze representations Empire-wide of this manic matricide must have been melted down when a sentence of *damnatio memoriae* ('damning of the memory') was pronounced by the senate on his death. The wall-case nearby has an imposing bronze Hercules allegedly from Birdoswald in the centre, still with much of its gilt surviving; but serious doubts, which I share, have been raised about its authenticity. The marble statuette of Luna to the far left comes from the opulent Woodchester villa in Gloucestershire (p. 197). Marble statuary is not common in Roman Britain, and it is wholly in keeping with the luxury of this astonishing fourth-century villa that marble artefacts should have been found there.

Moving now into the second half of the gallery, diagonally across into its far right-hand quarter, watch out first for two cases illustrating a heady mixture of evidence for Romano-British pagan cults. Pride of place in one case goes to the finds from Uley (excavated in 1977–9), an important Gloucestershire rural shrine with a Romano-Celtic temple and surrounding buildings. Small votive bronzes of the god with his characteristic wand (*caduceus*) and winged hat made it clear that the divine honorand was Mercury, but the outstanding discovery is what was clearly the head of the cult statue of the god (Fig. 141), crisply carved in local limestone (probably *c*. 150), with somewhat stylized hair, but a vigorous, competent work, wholly in the classical tradition, and a cut above the average product of most Romano-British sculptural workshops. The other case here has items from the striking Barkway hoard, found in 1743, of silver 'leaf' votive plaques dedicated to Mars (and Vulcan); what is believed to be a strip from a sceptre-binding from the Farley Heath temple (p. 654), embossed with the naivest animal and human figures and magical (?) signs; and an extraordinary bronze 'nut-cracker' instrument, with a serrated inner edge and an outer one decorated with multiple busts of divinities – identified, perhaps over-dramatically, as a castration implement for the self-mutilation of priests serving the mystery cult of Cybele and Attis.

Beyond this are exceptional finds from other places discussed earlier in this book: the marble portrait busts from the Lullingstone villa (p. 84), for example, and the Christian wall-plaster from the unique house-chapel in the same villa, with a chi-rho on one panel (Fig. 143), and another wall painted with a row of six worshippers. The latter presumably contain portraits of the late fourth-century villa-owner and his fellow Christians, in the *orans* pose of hands outstretched in prayer. Above the chi-rho is part of a painted wall-frieze from Verulamium, an ambitious floral scroll on a pleasing yellow background, with two handsome peacocks and panther heads in attendance (detail, Fig. 142). This was the finest of the plentiful Roman wall-plaster from the 1950s excavations there, the finding of which revolutionized our knowledge of Romano-British interior decor. Also in this corner is a fragment of the beautiful circular acanthus scroll from the great mosaic at the Woodchester villa, closely similar in style to the one still visible in the dining-room of the west wing at Chedworth (p. 194), and like that one laid by Cirencester mosaicists in the fourth century. This fragment was presented to the British Museum by the great eighteenth- and early nineteenth-century antiquary Samuel Lysons, who was responsible for first uncovering the magnificent villa (p. 197).

One other mosaic too important to pass over in silence is not currently on display in the British Museum, although in 2000, to celebrate the millennium, the central roundel was displayed, out of logical sequence, at the opposite end of the Weston gallery next to the Iron Age room. This is the fourth-century mosaic from Hinton St Mary, Dorset, found in 1963,

142   St Albans (Verulamium), *wall-plaster (British Museum)*

which contains the earliest portrayal of Christ known in Britain: a chi-rho monogram appears behind his head, and pomegranates, symbols of immortality, are represented on either side. A recent persuasive suggestion is that the mosaicist's model for this head was a coin of Magnentius of AD 353, showing a bare-headed, clean-shaven man (pretender for the imperial throne, 350–3) with very similar treatment of the hair; the reverse depicts a chi-rho. If that is right, the mosaic presumably dates from some time after the striking of the coin, perhaps *c.* AD 353/55. It is a matter of the greatest regret that this crucially significant document of Romano-British Christianity is not currently (2001) on display, since the mosaic does not deserve to be consigned to the Museum's store-rooms. Plans to lay it in the Great Court, which some think is a sensible solution to the display problems that the mosaic undoubtedly poses, are currently (as this book goes to press) on hold. The central roundel in the other half of the floor depicts Bellerophon slaying the Chimaera, an allegory of the triumph over death and evil, which appears also on the mosaic at Lullingstone (p. 88) – significantly close to the Christian rooms there.

143   Lullingstone, chi-rho Christian wall-plaster (British Museum)

On the other side of the exit doorway to the gallery be sure not to miss the remarkable portion of superstructure from a mid-third-century aisled barn at Meonstoke, Hampshire, crated and lifted *in situ* and then transferred here. What you see is part of the blind arcade of false arched windows 1 m high, with pilasters between them bearing miniature Ionic capitals. It came from the upper storey of a building which had collapsed in the second half of the fourth century and lain undisturbed where it fell; enough even survived in the collapse of the roof edge to show that the angle of its pitch was a steep $47\frac{1}{2}°$. The evidence of clerestory windows in the level below, the use of decorative architectural detail in the preserved fragment on display, indeed the very use of stone to roof height in what was presumably a subsidiary structure on a villa-estate – all help to provide a necessary redress to the notion that every Romano-British rural outbuilding need have been (when not of timber) an unpretentious, half-timbered structure on stone footings. Subsequent discoveries of collapsed stone superstructures elsewhere, at Carsington

(Derbyshire) and Redlands Farm, Stanwick (Northants), have shown that the Meonstoke building was not unique.

Finally, in the four freestanding showcases in this last part of the gallery, are the superlative hoards of late Roman gold and silver from Thetford, Hoxne and Mildenhall, which eloquently demonstrate the wealth of some members of the Romano-British aristocracy in the fourth century, and their ability to afford silver tableware imported from overseas (none of it is likely to be British-made): for this is material of the highest quality, some of it (as in the case of the Mildenhall treasure) a match for the very best that the Roman Empire could provide. The fact that all three treasures have come from a comparatively narrow geographical range (in East Anglia), a region where not a single opulent late Roman villa is so far known, is nothing short of extraordinary.

The late fourth-century Thetford treasure, discovered in 1979, is the subject of the first showcase facing the Meonstoke façade, comprising a hoard of gold jewellery, a set of 33 silver spoons and strainers, and a shale jewellery box. All but two of the spoons are inscribed, a dozen of them in honour of Faunus, an Italian god of the countryside otherwise unattested in Roman Britain. Two of the spoons have gilt inlay, the larger decorated with a spirited rendering of a triton blowing a conch. A gold belt-buckle has a superb rendering of a dancing satyr. The jewellery is unworn and, in part, unfinished; it appears to have been the collection of a single jeweller, but its connection with the Faunus spoons, and the reason for the deposition (was it votive?; was there fear of pagan persecution in the 380s or 390s?; or fear of pirate plundering?), are enigmatic.

The Hoxne treasure, found in 1992, is even more astonishing. Consisting of over 14,700 coins and some 200 other gold and silver objects, it is one of the largest Roman treasures ever found in Britain; it is also the only one excavated in controlled archaeological conditions, thanks to the wisdom and prescience of its discoverer. The coins, which include 565 gold issues (itself the largest single group ever found in Britain of which reliable records exist), belong to the second half of the fourth century and to early in the fifth: the latest issue is of AD 407/8. How long after that the Hoxne treasure was buried we do not know, as Roman coinage did not reach the island after that date: but it may not have been long, because only two years later, in 410, came the official Roman withdrawal from Britain ordered by the emperor Honorius. This, then, was a hoard buried in chaotic and unstable times at the very end of Roman control in Britain.

The gold and silver objects at Hoxne did not include large pieces of silverware which must have been buried separately: instead we have the smaller items of a dinner service, including 78 silver spoons, 20 ladles, four exquisite silver pepper-pots (one taking the form of a female bust, probably an empress, another in the shape of an ibex), and a pair of elegant 'tooth-picks' in the form of an ibis bird. Only a prancing silver tigress, inlaid with *niello* (a black silver sulphide), which had become detached from a large silver jug or amphora, gives a hint of larger-scale vessels in the same ownership. Some of the spoons and other items have names inscribed on them, including Faustinus, Peregrinus, Silvicola (a woman's name) and Aurelius Ursicinus, the last occurring no less than ten times; but it would be rash to claim that Ursicinus owned the treasure, still less that we know anything about him. The gold jewellery comprises six necklaces, three rings, and 19 bracelets; the gold content is of the purest (94.7 per cent), higher than the modern maximum standard, 22-carat gold. The bracelets, all solid bangles, are outstanding; one matching pair is decorated with hunting scenes in low relief, others are in fine pierced work with intricate leaf or geometric patterns, and one incorporates an inscription, VTERE FELIX DOMINA IVLIANE, 'use this happily, lady Juliana'. The Hoxne treasure gives us a precious glimpse into the sumptuous life-style of the very wealthy in late Roman society, on a par (in terms of personal ornament and tableware) with anything known from the very heart of the Empire.

In an adjacent case is the stunning Mildenhall treasure, discovered by the plough around 1944 but kept secret by the farmer until 1946. Familiarity does not deaden the breathtaking impact on the viewer that this superlatively high quality silver tableware makes, of which the great circular dish 61 cm (2 ft) in diameter is the *pièce de résistance*. The photographic detail of it (Fig. 144) shows the central mask of Oceanus surrounded by nereids and tritons; the outer circle shows scenes of Bacchic revelry, with Bacchus himself, Pan,

144   Mildenhall, detail of the great silver dish (British Museum)

Silenus, Hercules, and maenads and satyrs. The dish is a
product of a Mediterranean workshop in the fourth century
AD; yet despite the pagan mythology which it and other items
in the treasure so emphatically display, it was found along
with silver spoons bearing the chi-rho Christian monogram.
This juxtaposition of pagan and Christian is not as surprising
as it may seem. Early Christians, especially before a new
Christian iconography had firmly established itself to replace
the old imagery, drew freely on pagan myths, especially those
that could be construed as having some relevance to
Christianity. Dionysiac (Bacchic) religion, a 'mystery' cult
like Christianity also believing in an after-life, need not,
therefore, have been anathema to the dish's Christian owner.
The old visual imagery embracing nearly 1,000 years of
Graeco-Roman paganism did not disappear overnight with the
advent of the new religion.

Also displayed here is the Water Newton treasure, found in
1975, another outstanding testimony of early Christianity in
Britain. This fourth-century hoard comprises 19 tiny votive
'leaf' plaques bearing the chi-rho monogram (the Christian
counterpart to the Barkway pagan votives noted above), and
nine silver vessels, one looking remarkably like some modern
communion chalices. This is the earliest known collection of
church plate from the Roman Empire, and the votive
inscriptions of the dedicators furnish us with the names of
members of an early Christian congregation in Britain –
Innocentia, Viventia, Publianus.

Finally, displayed at the opposite ends of one case, are two
rectangular late fourth-century silver dishes, each remarkable
in their different ways, and each found within a few years of
one other more than 250 years ago. Like the Mildenhall dish,
they are elaborately decorated with figured scenes, the
subjects of which are entirely pagan in content; they were
probably above all intended for show, conspicuous status
symbols of wealth and culture. One, bizarrely, is not even
Roman at all in its present form. The original dish (*lanx*) was
found at Risley Park in Derbyshire in 1729, and was broken
up into pieces for melting down. Curiously, however, casts
were made of the individual broken fragments before they
disappeared into the melting-pot, and a new silver tray was
made from the moulds of the various joining fragments. The

recast tray, 50 cm (1 ft 7 in) long, only came to light in 1991. It predominantly shows hunting scenes, a favourite pastime of late Roman gentry. A graffito on the base records that it was given by a bishop, a certain Exuperius, to the *ecclesia Bogiensis*, 'the church of Bogium', an unidentified place-name, possibly but not certainly in Britain (alternatively *Bogiensis* enshrines a personal name, 'Bogius' church', but this seems less likely). The neutral nature of the subject matter would have made the tray perfectly acceptable in the context of a Christian church. Defiantly pagan, on the other hand, is the superb *lanx* of the same size and approximate period as the Risley Park one, but of far superior craftsmanship. It was found in the river Tyne near Corbridge in 1734 or 1735, and shows Artemis (Diana), Athena (Minerva), Asteria (Leto's sister) and Leto (the mother of Artemis and Apollo) in front of a *tempietto* in which Apollo stands magisterially. The scene is probably meant to represent Delos, the far-off island in the Aegean sea, where Leto had given birth to Apollo and Artemis. Here in the dying days of Roman Britain, was a top-class piece of table-silver, redolent of the old pagan religion and values, in the possession of some unknown person (a high-ranking military officer?) on the very northern fringes of the Roman Empire. An object of such exquisite classical taste, however, is very much the exception, and emphatically not the rule, in the material culture of Roman Britain.

Its find-spot Corbridge lies, of course, in the immediate hinterland of our most famous and impressive Roman antiquity, the great Wall of Hadrian. But more remains of Roman Britain than a well known frontier-barrier and objects in museum showcases: several hundred monuments, differing immensely in character, can still be tracked down in these islands. Some of them may now be tucked away behind hedgerows or factory chimneys, others are lost on barren moorland, but all of them bear a living witness to nearly 400 years of Roman rule in Britain.

Gazetteer of visible remains not mentioned in the text

For an explanation of the symbols, see Introduction, pp. 5–6. Places listed here do not *appear in the index or on the maps at the beginning of each chapter, but information contained in the notes is indexed. I have taken account where possible of the county boundary changes in England in 1999, but not those which took place in Wales in 1996, where the 8 post-1974 counties have been replaced by 21 counties. The new boundaries (but not all the names) are, however, shown in the map on p. 300.*

Chapter 1

OS Grid ref.	1:50,000 map no.	Name	County	Description	Notes
TQ117330	187	Alfoldean	W Sussex	settlement *(e)*	1
TQ030175	197	Hardham	W Sussex	settlement *(e)*	1, 2
SU844261	197	Iping	W Sussex	settlement *(e)*	1
TQ404545	187	Titsey	Surrey	villa *(s)*	3
SU803039	197	Bosham	Sussex	building *(s)*	4
TQ052449	187	Farley Heath	Surrey	temple *(s)*	5
TR135424	189	Stowting	Kent	barrow *(e)*	
TR171520	179	Bishopsbourne	Kent	barrow *(e)*	
SU810402	186	Alice Holt	Hants	pottery kilns *(e)*	6

Notes
1 Three small road staging-posts, all displaying remains of earth ramparts.
2 Cut through by railway. Only south side and NE corner survive. Occupied AD 50–150.
3 Small building excavated in 1864, but now largely overgrown with nettles, and so likely to be of interest only to the most avid enthusiast. Parts of two rooms are visible, one with a hypocaust. This lies outside the area in Titsey Place open to the public in summer, and visits to the villa-site are therefore only possible by prior arrangement with the Agents, Strutt & Parker, 201, High Street, Lewes BN7 2NR (tel: 01273–47541). A small selection of finds from the villa and a nearby Roman temple are on display at the Clacket Lane service-station on the south (clockwise) side of the M25, which runs just south of the villa.

4 West wall of nave of Bosham Church is of Roman masonry with brick bonding-course. Base for Roman arch remains *in situ* below bases of Saxon chancel arch.

5 Foundations of a typical Romano-Celtic temple, dug in the nineteenth century in the usual fashion of the day, as this ditty by Martin Tupper *c.* 1848 amply demonstrates: Many a day/Have I wiled away/Upon hopeful Farley Heath/In its antique soil/Digging for spoil/Of possible treasure beneath.

6 Series of irregular mounds, mostly in the south end of the forest, covering sites of Roman kilns.

Chapter 2

OS Grid ref.	1:50,000 map no.	Name	County	Description	Notes
ST449015	193	Waddon Hill	Dorset	fort *(e)*	1
ST090270	181	Wiveliscombe	Somerset	fort *(e)*	2
ST007219	181	Clayhanger	Devon	fort *(e)*	3
SX034670	200	Nanstallon	Cornwall	fort *(e)*	4
SX662998	191	North Tawton	Devon	fort *(e)*	5
SS733072	191	Bury Barton	Devon	fort *(e)*	6
ST520226	183	Ilchester	Somerset	town *(e)*	7
SZ008999	195	Wimborne Minster	Dorset	building *(s)*	8
SU776631	175	Finchampstead	Berkshire	milestone *(s)*	9
SU420120	196	Bitterne	Hants	bath-house *(s)*	10

Notes

1 See p. 96 for context. Very slight earthworks.

2 Roman date not proven, but virtually certain.

3 Although located as recently as 1989, the rampart of this 2.7-acre (1.1-ha) fort is still (faintly) visible on the ground.

4 North, west and south sides incorporated in hedgerows; see *Britannia* iii (1972), 60 for detailed map.

5 In a field west of North Tawton station, on south side of railway. For detailed plan, see H Welfare and V Swan, *Roman Camps in England* (1995), 55, fig. 46.

6 Part of larger earthwork (?19 acres [8 ha]) visible on west side and at SW angle (immediately west and SW of farm, next to track). Later fort within, traceable on all sides except SW, where the farm has obliterated it. Fort probably occupied *c.* 55–75. Possibly the Roman NEMETOSTATIO.

7 Mound of rampart very faintly visible in fields east of village.

8 Tiny piece of tessellated floor is *in situ* on south side of the Minster's nave.

9 Uninscribed. In grounds of Banisters, a short distance from place of discovery.

10 Tiny baths (*c.* AD 175), with four rooms, converted into two-roomed structure later and demolished when the late Roman fort wall (clearly visible beyond; note change in ground-level) was built, probably *c.* 280/90. At left-hand end of Bitterne Manor House (flats), reached from Southampton by third turning on left off A3024 east of river-bridge. Private property: permission to view from the owner's agent (Mr Hunt), 91A Brookvale Road, Southampton.

Chapter 3

OS Grid ref.	1:50,000 map no.	Name	County	Description	Notes
SO494742	137	Leintwardine	Hereford	fort *(e)*	1
SO440428	161	Kenchester	Hereford	town *(e)*	2
SP045257	163	Spoonley Wood	Glos	villa *(s)*	3
ST645693	172	Keynsham	Somerset	villa *(s)*	4
ST656690	172	Somerdale	Somerset	villa *(s)*	5
SO577093	162	Scowles	Glos	iron mine	6
SO682119	162	Littledean	Glos	temple (?) *(s)*	7
SP274121	163	Widford	Oxon	mosaic	8
SP3011	164	Worsham Bottom	Oxon	villa *(s)*	9
ST526698	172	Gatcombe	Somerset	villa (?) *(s)*	10

Notes

1 Only on west side of village.

2 Almost totally ploughed out; best on NE near farm.

3 Difficult to find; walls mossy and nettle-grown; one mosaic (Victorian replica) visible. Permission to view from Charlton Abbots Manor.

4 Fragment of north wing of a courtyard villa (steps, water-tank, paved area, and two displaced gutters on the surface) visible near mortuary chapel in Keynsham cemetery. Figured mosaics from this villa are inaccessible in store in Keynsham Town Hall, pending establishment of a local museum.

5 Small villa untidily laid out at right of entrance to Cadbury's chocolate factory, transposed here in 1922 from its original position underneath the factory 300 m to north.

6 Open-cast rocky hollows, much overgrown with foliage, in the

location called Puzzlewood (badly signposted), 1 mile (1.6 km)
south of Coleford.

7 In the grounds of Littledean House (April–October 1100–1700),
up the slope behind the blue sign in the car-park. Now badly
overgrown and neglected (2001), this structure consists of, at the
lower level, a rectangular '*cella*' restored as a pool, together with
a surrounding ambulatory, and an upper area conjectured to be a
Romano-Celtic temple of square-within-a-square plan. Such a
double arrangement is unparalleled in Roman Britain. Much of
the visible masonry is modern and represents a 'tidying up' of
what was uncovered. While finds indicate some Roman activity
on the spot, it is by no means certain that the structure is Roman;
and both the restoration of the pool and the claim that the shrine
is in honour of Sabrina, goddess of the Severn (the river is not
even visible from the 'temple') are entirely fanciful.

8 Fragment *in situ* in floor of church.

9 Overgrown walls and one floor of red *tesserae* just visible in a
coppice.

10 Short section of late third-century defensive wall surrounding
what is probably a villa. Fork left on the farm drive and cross a
stream; the wall is at wooden railings in field on the right.

Chapter 4

OS Grid ref.	1:50,000 map no.	Name	County	Description	Notes
TM031082	168	Bradwell-on-Sea	Essex	fort *(s)*	1
TF782440	132	Brancaster	Norfolk	fort *(e)*	2
TL394554	154	Barton	Cambs	barrow *(e)*	3
TL456347	154	Langley	Essex	barrow *(e)*	4
TL372177	166	Youngsbury	Herts	barrow *(e)*	
TL899617	155	Eastlow Hill	Suffolk	barrow *(e)*	5
TQ840938	178	Hockley	Essex	barrow (?) *(e)*	6

Notes

1 Saxon Shore fort of OTHONA. One overgrown fragment of south
wall 1.20 m (4 ft) long and the same high; near cottage, to the right
of the fine seventh-century chapel, itself largely built of Roman
materials.

2 A slight hint of the fort platform is all that remains of Saxon Shore
fort of BRANODVNVM. The gullies to the east and west of it are
caused by natural erosion; the fort ditches are not now visible on
the surface.

3 At Lord's Bridge; 2.6 m (8 ft 6 in) high, probably *c*. AD 300 (?).
   When excavated it was found to contain a stone sarcophagus with
   a woman's body, 27 hobnails, bones of a chicken and a goose, and
   sheep's and pig's teeth.
4 Now largely ploughed away, on SW side of the NW–SE farm-track
   (not on its NE side, as wrongly shown on OS map).
5 On private land but visible from the road.
6 On south edge of Plumberow Wood, an earth mound 4 m (13 ft)
   high ('Plumberow Mount') and 25 m (82 ft) in diameter is
   assumed to be Romano-British; a coin of Domitian and Roman
   pottery was found in it in 1913.

Chapter 5

OS Grid ref.	1:50,000 map no.	Name	County	Description	Notes
SP043836	139	Metchley	W Midlands	fort *(e)*	1
SK181828	110	Brough-on-Noe	Derbys	fort *(e)*	2, 3
SO864886	139	Greensforge	Staffs	fort *(e)*	2
SO692783	138	Wall Town	Salop	fort *(e)*	2
SK700415	129	Castle Hill	Notts	town *(e)*	4
TA116012	113	Caistor	Lincs	town *(s)*	5
SP341598	151	Chesterton	Warwicks	town *(e)*	
SP693487	152	Towcester	Northants	town *(e)*	6
TL124985	142	Castor	Cambs	buildings *(s)*	7
SK982762	121	Riseholme	Lincs	barrow *(e)*	8
TL219747	142	Great Stukeley	Cambs	barrow *(e)*	9

Notes
1 See p. 259. NW corner of a vexillation fortress *c*. AD 45–55/65,
   behind Medical Faculty building, University of Birmingham.
   Reconstruction was attempted here many years ago but it was
   vandalized, and only an overgrown mound now remains visible. Of
   a smaller, late first-century fort, nothing is visible.
2 See p. 263.
3 NAVIO, occupied *c*. 75–120, and 165–350.
4 Part of north and east defences of MARGIDVNVM, visible as low
   mound, just north of roundabout.
5 Best fragment of late Roman defences (p. 297), 2.15 m (7 ft) high, is
   seen over railings on south side of churchyard, marked by a plaque,
   but (in 2000) very overgrown; part of a tower is visible in a yard
   reached between a gap in houses next to 6 Chapel Street; other

fragments in Grammar School grounds (Church Street) and in private cellar on the south corner of Bank Lane with Market Square.

6 Earth ramparts at NW corner of LACTODVRVM, in the field west of the police station; reached by the footpath to Greens Norton (signpost).

7 Two lumps of Roman walling project from the modern wall on Stocks Hill, opposite the church. Relaid mosaic in the dairy at Milton Hall. See p. 289.

8 2.75 m high, *c.* AD 80/100; a cremation pit with clay lamp and beaker, and bronze and glass fragments, was found inside.

9 Low and very overgrown. Note rise and fall of fence bordering the road.

Chapter 6

Chester:
The following visible fragments of the fortress, all on private property and only viewable by prior written arrangement, were not included in the text above: (i) 48, Eastgate Street (guard-chamber); (ii) 104, Watergate Street (furnace arch); (iii) 18, St Michael's Row (mosaic panel); (iv) 22, St Michael's Row (wall); (v) 28, Eastgate Street (column-base); (vi) under the car-park of 3–5, Shipgate Street, off Bridge Street (Roman mains culvert); (vii) garden of 5, Castle Place (a well in the official inn-cum-post-house [*mansio*], in the civilian settlement outside the fortress walls).

OS Grid ref.	1:50,000 map no.	Name	County	Description	Notes
SS796987	170	Blaen-cwm-Bach	West Glam	marching-camp *(e)*	1
ST002982	170	Twyn y Briddallt	Mid Glam	marching-camp *(e)*	2
ST059878	170	Pen-y-Coedcae	Mid Glam	marching-camp *(e)*	3
SO379007	171	Usk	Gwent	fort *(e)*	4
ST379917	171	Coed-y-Caerau	Gwent	fortlet *(e)*	5
SO169219	161	Pen-y-Gaer	Powys	fort *(e)*	6
SS607972	159	Mynydd Carn Goch	West Glam	2 practice camps *(e)*	
SN859107	160	Coelbren Gaer	West Glam	fort *(e)*	7
SN862102	160	Camnant	West Glam	marching-camp *(e)*	8
SN924164	160	Ystradfellte	Powys	marching-camp *(e)*	9
SN802263	160	Arosfa Gareg	Dyfed	marching-camp *(e)*	10
SN770352	146	Llandovery	Dyfed	fort *(e)*	
SN919507	147	Beulah	Powys	marching-camp *(e)*	11
SN647485	146	Pant-teg-Uchaf	Dyfed	practice camp *(e)*	12
SN644564	146	Llanio	Dyfed	bath-house *(s)*	13

OS Grid ref.	1:50,000 map no.	Name	County	Description	Notes
SO029920	128	Caersws	Powys	fort (e)	14
SO208989	128	Forden Gaer	Powys	fort (e)	
SH660557	115	Pen-y-Gwrhyd	Gwynedd	marching-camp (e)	15
SH787187	124	Brithdir	Gwynedd	signal station (e)	16
SO227435	148	Clyro	Powys	fort (e)	17
SN824818	136	Cae Gaer	Powys	fort (e)	18
SN828067	160	Hirfynydd	West Glam	fortlet (e)	
SN856935	136	Pen-y-Crogbren	Powys	fortlet (e)	
SH746572	115	Bryn-y-Gefeiliau	Gwynedd	building (e)	19
SH477454	123	Derwydd-bach	Gwynedd	marching-camp (e)	20
SH860278	124	Pont Rhyd Sarn	Gwynedd	practice camp (e)	
SN927699	136	Esgairperfedd	Powys	marching-camp (e)	21
SN985717	136	St Harmon	Powys	marching-camp (e)	22
SJ417637	117	Heronbridge	Cheshire	settlement (e)	
ST475912	171	Castle Tump	Gwent	building (s)	23
SS959699	170	Llantwit Major	South Glam	villa (e)	24

Notes
1 Best on west side (*titulus* survives) and near NE corner, due north of farm.
2 Most of outline traceable, with *claviculae* on NW and NE sides.
3 Only east end and angles are well preserved.
4 SE side of ʙᴠʀʀɪᴠᴍ, east of Court House.
5 Immediately NE of pre-Roman 'enclosure' marked on OS map.
6 Best preserved on north.
7 Whole fort visible as prominent banks, partly marked by field-boundaries.
8 Best on west side, and part of east, about 300 m south of 7.
9 Only a very low bank, best preserved near SE corner. Fire-breaks in the plantations are so positioned as to leave the ramparts free from trees.
10 Nearly whole circuit can be traced.
11 Most of north and west sides are traceable. A $\frac{1}{4}$ mile (400 m) to south is site of a Roman fort, partly covered by the farm (very prominent platform, but no real remains of ramparts).
12 Unfinished. North side is 0.60 m (2 ft) high. Another similar camp nearby (SN 641493) is now obscured by trees.
13 Remains of hypocausts, etc., clearly visible, but vandalized. On south side of a fort-site (invisible). Ask permission and directions from farm.
14 Best preserved on SW in road near station and level-crossing.
15 Very fragmentary condition, best seen on south side of A4086

200 m west of junction with A498, as road bends to left (west
rampart), and on east side of A498, also 200 m south of junction,
immediately beyond road-sign (south rampart and SE corner). See
P Crew and C Musson, *Snowdonia from the Air* (1996), 29 for
map and aerial photograph.

16 On summit of small hillock along the Roman road SE from
    Brithdir fortlet (the latter is not visible).
17 NE and SE sides of vexillation fortress (p. 301) covering 26 acres
    (11 ha), not occupied after *c.* AD 75.
18 See p. 339.
19 Prominent mounds with some stonework exposed; in annexe on
    west side of a fort (invisible).
20 Reed-covered, at best 0.30 m (1 ft) high: parts of NW and SW
    sides. A Roman fort and fortlet, now entirely quarried away,
    existed $\frac{1}{3}$ mile (500 m) to the east.
21 Most of the circuit is traceable.
22 Only south end, including *clavicula* at south gate, is visible.
23 On Ministry of Defence property and not accessible to the public.
24 Enclosure-banks, and mounds covering walls, of Roman villa.

Chapter 7

OS Grid ref.	1:50,000 map no.	Name	County	Description	Notes
SD925495	103	Elslack	N Yorks	fort *(e)*	
SD937902	98	Brough-by-Bainbridge	N Yorks	fort *(e)*	
SE578032	111	Doncaster	S Yorks	fort *(s)*	1
NY998104	92	Scargill Moor	Durham	shrines *(s)*	2
NY882112	92	Roper Castle	Cumbria	signal station *(e)*	3
NY829148	91	Punchbowl Inn	Cumbria	signal station *(e)*	4
NY844149	91	Johnson's Plain	Cumbria	signal station *(e)*	5
NY818147	91	Augill Bridge	Cumbria	signal station *(e)*	6
NY650238	91	Crackenthorpe	Cumbria	marching-camp *(e)*	7
SD913655	98	Malham Moor	N Yorks	marching-camp *(e)*	
NY494384	90	Old Penrith	Cumbria	fort *(e)*	
NX984211	89	Moresby	Cumbria	fort *(e)*	
NY203368	89	Caermote	Cumbria	fort *(e)*	8
NY110315	89	Papcastle	Cumbria	fort *(e)*	9
SD515908	97	Watercrook	Cumbria	fort *(e)*	9
NY609013	91	Low Borrowbridge	Cumbria	fort *(e)*	10
SE225991	99	Catterick	N Yorks	town *(s + e)*	11
SE672753	100	Hovingham	N Yorks	barrow *(e)*	12
NZ835151	94	Goldsborough	N Yorks	signal station *(e)*	13

Notes

1 Part of east wall of DANVM, in Church Street, uncovered in 1972, between church and multi-storey car-park 3.

2 See above, p. 406. The best approach is from Spanham farmhouse, $1\frac{1}{8}$ miles (1.8 km) to the east. Circular shrine is still very conspicuous, opposite footbridge over stream. Site of northern shrine is marked by a heap of stones.

3 See above, p. 407.

4 In pasture on crest of small hill beside inn.

5 Excavation in 1990 found a timber tower 4.25 m (14 ft) square surrounded by two ditches.

6 Possible Roman signal-tower, excavated 1975; two phases but no datable finds. The earthwork is partly cut by mounds covering a lead-mill flue and a chimney, remains of nineteenth-century industrial workings.

7 Very little remains now, but east angle survives as a bank nearly 1 m high on south side of Long Marton road, 150 m from its junction with A66. Full details in H Welfare and V Swan, *Roman Camps in England* (1995), 34-6.

8 Smaller fort inside NW corner of larger. Ramparts of both are grassy, rest of area full of reeds.

9 Only very faintly visible.

10 Well preserved remains of fort-platform, with ditches on west, beside the M6. An aqueduct-leat 550 m (1,800 ft) long brought water from Birk Knott to the west; it can be seen at SD 604006.

11 Stretch of east wall of CATARACTONIVM, excavated and restored in the nineteenth century. On south side of A6136, 100 m east of the bridge carrying the road over the A1, adjoining inside of racecourse track. In a lay-by on the west side of this road further south, a sign-board draws attention to a depression in the ground, site of a presumed amphitheatre.

12 Very well preserved, *c*. 3 m (10 ft) high. A villa with mosaics was found nearby in 1745 and is probably to be associated with it.

13 Now only a prominent mound; no stonework is visible. It measured 14.32 m (47 ft) square within an enclosure wall 34 m (111 ft) square.

Chapter 8

Numerous other Roman antiquities are visible on the Wall or in the Wall region, apart from the selection described above. They can be found with the help of the OS *Map of Hadrian's Wall* (HMSO, 2nd edn 1972), although there is very little to see at some of the sites marked on it as 'remains of'. The more recent edition of this map

(1989) is of much poorer quality and lacks the same clarity of detail. The numerous temporary camps in the area of the Wall, of which over 30 still have visible earthworks, can now be traced with much greater ease thanks to H Welfare and V Swan, *Roman Camps in England: the field archaeology* (1995). See Bibliography under 'Hadrian's Wall' for details; only one or two are briefly referred to in Ch. 8. The inscribed Roman quarry-face called Rock of Gelt near Bampton is not only very difficult to find, but is now virtually illegible. For it consult *RIB* (see App. 3: Abbreviations) I, 1007–16, where a large-scale map of its location can be found.

Chapter 9

OS Grid ref.	1:50,000 map no.	Name	County	Description	Notes
§1					
NT909009	80	North Yardhope	North'land	marching-camp *(e)*	1
NY818998	80	Bellshiel	North'land	marching-camp *(e)*	2
NT791096	80	Brownhart Law	Borders	fortlet *(e)*	3
NZ135885	81	Longshaws	North'land	fortlet *(e)*	4
NT425254	73	Oakwood	Borders	fort *(e)*	5
NT473547	66	Channelkirk	Borders	marching-camp *(e)*	6
NT555328	73	North Eildon	Borders	signal station*(e)*	7
NT344721	66	Inveresk	Lothian	bath-house *(s)*	8
NS731578	64	Bothwellhaugh	Strathclyde	fort *(e)*	9
NS910459	72	Cleghorn	Strathclyde	marching-camp *(e)*	10
NS928442	72	Castledykes	Strathclyde	fort *(e)*	11
NS944265	72	Wandel	Strathclyde	marching-camp *(e)*	12
NS994159	78	Little Clyde	Strathclyde	marching-camp *(e)*	13
NT030139	78	Redshaw Burn	Strathclyde	fortlet *(e)*	14
NS903049	78	Durisdeer	Dum & Gall	fortlet *(e)*	14
NY251991	79	Raeburnfoot	Dum & Gall	fort/fortlet *(e)*	14
NT303047	79	Craik Cross Hill	Dum & Gall	signal station *(e)*	14
NT092012	78	Tassiesholm	Dum & Gall	fort *(e)*	
NY389792	85	Gilnockie	Dum & Gall	marching-camp *(e)*	15
NY120818	78	Torwood	Dum & Gall	marching-camp *(e)*	16
NX968818	78	Carzield	Dum & Gall	fort *(e)*	17
NY566747	86	Bewcastle	Cumbria	fort *(e)*	18
NY579718	86	Gillalees	Cumbria	signal station *(e)*	19
NY595751	86	Barron's Pike	Cumbria	signal station *(e)*	20
§2					
NS761774	64	Westerwood	Strathclyde	fort *(e)*	5
NS678749	64	Auchendavy	Strathclyde	fort *(e)*	21

OS Grid ref.	1:50,000 map no.	Name	County	Description	Notes
§3					
NO171389	53	Black Hill	Tayside	signal station *(e)*	22
NN845108	58	Blackhill Wood	Perth & Kinross	signal station *(e)*	23
NS565998	57	Menteith	Central	marching-camp *(e)*	24
NJ655383	29	Glenmailen	Grampian	marching-camp *(e)*	25

In §2 above, only additional fort remains are listed; other visible pieces of Wall and Ditch can be found with the help of the OS *Map of the Antonine Wall*, 2nd edn HMSO 1975, and A Robertson (revised by L J F Keppie), *The Antonine Wall. A handbook to the surviving remains*, 5th edn 2001.

Notes
 1 Entire outline traceable of a nearly square camp, up to 1 m (3 ft) high, including three *tituli*; discovered in 1976, enclosing an area of 5 acres (2 ha). See p. 553.
 2 Much obscured by field-banks.
 3 Just north of the border fence.
 4 Rampart about 1.20 m (4 ft) high over the entire circuit.
 5 Very faint.
 6 Part of gigantic 165-acre (69-ha) camp, probably third-century.
 7 See above, p. 556.
 8 Four hypocaust *pilae* with a lump of concrete floor on top, probably re-erected in the nineteenth century as they are not set square within their heated room. Re-excavated and newly consolidated, 1987. Situated in the private garden of Inveresk House, immediately adjacent to the road to Musselburgh. It is part of the bath-house outside the Antonine fort (under St Michael's church); an Agricolan fort on a separate site 3 miles (4.8 km) south (Elginhaugh) was totally excavated before destruction in 1986.
 9 SE rampart 1.50 m (5 ft) high. Antonine. See now p. 560.
 10 Well preserved on NW and NE sides in Camp Wood with two *tituli* in NW side, but obscured by conifers and long grass.
 11 Faint except on east. Antonine, with Agricolan occupation below.
 12 140 m (450 ft) of east rampart and 30 m (100 ft) of south rampart visible. A fortlet lay immediately to the north but is now denuded and invisible.
 13 Best preserved near NW angle in the field beyond the farm.
 14 See above, p. 559.

15 Most of SE side of camp, including two *tituli*, is well preserved;
    partly in a wood.
16 Single surviving side is a field-boundary.
17 SE angle and part of south side only is visible. Antonine.
18 Outpost fort of Hadrian's Wall, built to a very unusual hexagonal
    plan, at first in the Hadrianic period in turf and timber, with
    defences revetted in stone in the mid second century, and further
    altered under Severus or later in the third century. Of the fort,
    only SW rampart survives as a bold mound; the lower bank in
    front of it is post-Roman. Castle sits on NE corner and contains
    many Roman stones.
19 Connected Bewcastle with Birdoswald on Hadrian's Wall.
20 Prominent ditch up to 1 m deep, 2 miles (3 km) east of Bewcastle.
21 The east ditches and rampart mound are faintly visible to the
    south of the modern road, as is the hollow of the Wall Ditch to
    the north of the fort.
22 Rampart and single ditch still clear. Flavian.
23 900 m north of Ardoch fort, much disturbed by rabbits, but the
    turf rampart survives up to 0.2 m (7 in) high, with a double ditch
    outside; excavation in 1997 found the post-holes of the square
    timber tower at the centre. Flavian. See Fig. 133 and p. 591.
24 Parts of two sides of an Agricolan camp, up to 0.3 m (1 ft) high,
    in rough moorland on the south side of Lake Menteith.
25 See p. 602; also faint traces of NE corner in pasture.

Further details of all these, and other, Scottish sites, with full details
of access, can be found in L J F Keppie, *Scotland's Roman Remains*,
2nd edition 1998.

Chapter 10

All the visible fragments of Roman London which are still *in situ*
have been mentioned in the text (as far as I know). The only
exception is a fragment of Basilica in 73 Cornhill, but for security
reasons it cannot be visited by members of the public.

In *Greater London*, a tiny piece of red tessellated floor belonging to a
Roman building in Greenwich Park (TQ 393774) has been preserved.
It is set in an enclosure in the north part of the park, 100 m from the
east wall, half-way between the Vanbrugh and Maze Hill Gates.
Further excavation took place here in 1977 and 1979 in advance of
tree-planting, and again in 1999, when a fragmentary inscription,
probably a religious dedication, was found, as were three other
fragments (*RIB* I, 37–9) in 1902. The floor belongs to a third-century
building, almost certainly belonging to a hill-top temple complex,
which replaced a predecessor erected *c*. 100.

Principal museums in Britain displaying Romano-British material

compiled by Matthew Symonds

A museum mentioned in the text is indicated by a page number in brackets; if the mention is more than a passing one, the number appears in bold type. References in the text usually also give opening hours, but these frequently change; telephone numbers of museums have therefore been added to enable readers to enquire about current times of opening. Readers should be reminded that although the museums listed below hold Romano-British material, that is no guarantee that any of it will necessarily be on display at any one time. Web site addresses have been supplied where they are known, but these are vulnerable to change (as of course are telephone numbers). If there is no official web site for a museum, an alternative web site which gives basic details including opening hours is cited instead where possible. Further details about each museum collection can be found in *Museums and Galleries in Great Britain and Ireland*, published annually by British Leisure Publications, or *Art Galleries and Museums of Britain*, KGP Publishing.

City and town museums

Aylesbury 01296–331441
   www.buckscc.gov.uk/museum/index.com
Bangor, Museum of Welsh Antiquities 01248–353368
Barnard Castle, Bowes Museum (pp. 400, 405–7) 01833–690606
   www.bowesmuseum.org.uk
Basingstoke 01256–465902
   www.hantsweb.gov.uk/museum/willis/reception.html
Battle 01424–775955
   www.1066country.com/battlemuseum/htm
Bedford, Museum 01234–353323
   www.kbnet.co.uk/bedford/town/museum.htm
Biggar, Moat Park Heritage Centre 01899–221050
   www.biggar-net.co.uk/museums/
Birmingham, City Museum and Art Gallery 0121–3031966
   www.bmag.org.uk
Bradford, City Art Gallery and Museum
   www.bradford.gov.uk/tourism/museums
Braintree, District Museum 01376–325266
Brecon, Brecknock Museum 01874–624121
Bridport 01308–422116

Brighton, Museum and Art Gallery 01273–290900
   www.brighton-hove.gov.uk/bhc/museums/brighton
Bristol, City Museum (pp. 158, 184–5) 0117–922–3571
   www.bristol-city.gov.uk/museums
Bromley (p. 91) 01689–873826
Bury St Edmunds, Moyse's Hall Museum 01284–757488
   www.stedmundsbury.gov.uk/moyses.htm
Buxton 01298–24658
Cambridge, University Museum of Archaeology and Ethnology
   (pp. 255, 406, 545) 01223–333516
   http://cumaa.archanth.cam.ac.uk
Canterbury, Roman Museum (pp. **62**, 79) 01227–785575
   **www.canterbury.gov.uk/outabout/leisure/museums/canterbury/
   roman_museum.html**
Canterbury Heritage Centre (p. 63) 01227–452747
   **www.canterbury.gov.uk/outabout/leisure/museums/canterbury/
   canterbury_heritage.html**
Cardiff, National Museum of Wales (pp. 334, 344, **355–6**)
   029–2039–7951
   www.nmgw.ac.uk/hmgc
Carlisle, Tullie House Museum (pp. 422, **531–2**) 01228–534781
   www.tulliehouse.co.uk
Carmarthen (p. 358) 01267–231691
   www.carmarthen-museum.org.uk
Castleford Public Library (Museum Room) 01977–305535
Chelmsford 01245–353066
   www.chelmsfordbc.gov.uk/museums/chelmsford.htm
Cheltenham 01242–237431
   www.cheltenhammuseum.org.uk/home/home.html
Chester, Dewa Roman Experience (p. **318**) 01244–343407
   **www.romans-in-britain.org.uk/ste_chester_dewa_roman_
   experience.htm**
Chester, Grosvenor Museum (p. **321**) 01244–321616
   www.chestercc.gov.uk/heritage/museum/home.html
Chichester, District Museum (p. **65**) 01243–784683
   www.chichester.gov.uk/museum
Cirencester, Corinium Museum (pp. **178**, 188) 01285–655611
   www.cotswold.gov.uk/museum.htm
Colchester, Castle (pp. **212–18**, 224, 228, 255) 01206–282931
   www.plus44.com/local/essex/csm.htm
Dartford, Borough Museum 01322–343555
   www.kent-museums.org.uk/kmpdartford.html
Derby, Museum and Art Gallery 01332–716659
   www.derby.gov.uk/museums
Devizes, Wiltshire Heritage Museum 01380–727369
   wanhs@wiltshireheritage.org.uk

Doncaster 01302–734293
   www.doncaster.gov.uk/leisure/document.asp?WSDOCID=583
Dorchester, Dorset County (pp. 102, 104, 107) 01305–262735
   www.dorset.museum.clara.net
Dover 01304–201066
   www.dover.gov.uk/museum
Dumfries 01387–253374
   www.dumfriesmuseum.demon.co.uk/dumfmuse.htm
Dundee, McManus Art Gallery and Museum 01382–434000
   www.dundeecity.gov.uk/a-z/m003.htm
Durham, Fulling Mill Museum of Archaeology (pp. **402**, 403, 509,
   545) 0191–374–3623
   www.dur.ac.uk/fulling.mill/FullingMill.html
Edinburgh, Huntly House Museum 0131–529–4143
Edinburgh, Museum of Scotland (pp. 555, **568–9**, 584, 598)
   0131–247–4422
   www.nms.ac.uk
Evesham 01386–446944
Exeter, Royal Albert (p. 111) 01392–665858
   www.exeter.gov.uk/tourism/museums/albert/albert.html
Falkirk, Callendar House 01324–503770
   www.falkirk.gov.uk/attract/pages/lom1m.htm
Folkestone, Gallery and Museum 01303–850123
   www.kent.gov.uk/e&l/artslib/MUSEUMS/Home.html
Glasgow, Art Gallery and Museum (p. 584) 0141–287–2609
   www.g3web.co.uk/glasgow_museums/art_gallery/index.htm
Glasgow, Hunterian Museum (pp. 566, **584**, 589, 598)
   0141–330–4221
   www.hunterian.gla.ac.uk/museum/museum_index.html
Gloucester, City Museum (pp. 171, 173, **175**) **01452-524131**
   www.mylife.gloucester.gov.uk/City%20Museum/museum.htm
Grantham (p. 297) 01476–568783
   www.lincolnshire.gov.uk/doc.asp?docid=7733catld=40
Guildford, Museum and Muniment Room 01483–444750
   **www.guildford.gov.uk/pages/leisure/culture/housegal/
   museummainpage.htm**
Halifax, Bankfield Museum and Art Gallery 01422–354823
   www.calderdale.gov.uk/ft_tourism/museums/bankfield.html
Harlow 01279–454959
   **www.hertsdirect.org/infoadvice/leisure/visits/htmus3y/locmus/
   58612?view=Herita**
Hereford, City Museum and Art Gallery 01952–882030
   www.westmidlandsarchives.org.uk/museums/html
Herne Bay 01227–367368
   www.canterbury.co.uk/en/guides/hernebay/places/museum.html

Hertford 01992–582686
   www.hertford.net/museum
Huddersfield, Tolson Memorial Museum 01484–223807
Hull, Hull and East Riding Museum (p. **430**) 01482–613902
   www.hullcc.gov.uk/museums
Ilchester 01935–841247
   www.southsomerset.gov.uk/Commune/ilchmusm.htm
Ilkley (p. **391**) 01943–600066
   www.ilkley.org/arts/fomh.htm
Ipswich, Museum 01473–213761
   www.ipswich.gov.uk/tourism/guide/museum.htm
Jedburgh, Abbey Museum 01835–863925
   www.historic-Scotland.gov.uk
Kendal 01539–721374
   www.kendalmuseum.org.uk
Kinneil House Museum, Bo'ness (pp. **571–2**) 01506–778530
   www.falkirkmuseums.demon.co.uk/museums/kinnmus.htm
Lancaster (p. 428) 01524–64637
Leeds, City Museum (p. 429) 0113–249–6453
   www.leeds.gov.uk/tourinfo/attract/museums/citymuse.html
Leicester, Jewry Wall Museum (p. **284**) 0116–247–3021
   www.leicestermuseums.ac.uk
Letchworth 01462–685647
   www.fleck.freeserve.co.uk/nhms/let/letmg.html
Lewes, Museum of Sussex Archaeology 01273–486290
   www.sussexpast.co.uk
Lincoln, Archaeology Centre (p. 271) 01522–545326
Littlehampton 01903–738100
   www.romansinsussex.co.uk/sussex/littlehampton.asp
Llandrindod Wells, Radnorshire Museum 01597–824513
Llandudno 01492–876517
   www.llandudno-tourism.co.uk/museum
London, British Museum (pp. 62, 84, 85, 88, 154, 235, 289, 313, 344,
   449, 510, 621, 625, 636, **641**) 020 76361555
   www.thebritishmuseum.ac.uk
London, Cuming Museum, Southwark (p. 632) 020–7701–1342
   www.londonse1.co.uk/attractions/cuming.html
London, Museum of London (pp. 611, 612, 618, 621, 622, 623, 630,
   631, **632**) 020–7600–3699 (desk)/020–7600–0807 (recorded
   information) **www.museumoflondon.org.uk**
Ludlow 01584–873857
   www.shropshire-cc.gov.uk/Museum
Luton 01582–546722
   www.luton.gov.uk/museums.htm
Maidstone, Museum and Art Gallery 01622–754497
   www.maidstone.museum.gov.uk

Malton (p. 388) 01653–695136
   **www.ryedale.co.uk/ryedale/social/maltonmuseum/
   maltonmuseum.html**
Manchester, City Art Gallery 0161–236–5244
   www.cityartgalleries.org.uk/live/city/navigation/frame.htm
Manchester, Manchester Museum 0161–275–2634
   http://museum.man.ac.uk
Margate 01843–231213
   www.ekmt.fsnet.co.uk
Maryport, Senhouse Roman Museum (p. **420**) 01900–816168
   www.senhousemuseum.co.uk
Melrose Abbey Museum (p. 558) 01896–822562
   www.historic-scotland.gov.uk
Melrose, Trimontium Museum, Ormiston Institute (p. **558**)
   01896–822651/822463
   www.trimontium.freeserve.co.uk
Middlesbrough, Dorman Museum 01642–311211
   www.24hourmuseum.org.uk/museum/NE000013.html
Newark-on-Trent 01636–655740
   **www.newark-sherwooddc.gov.uk/leisureservices/whatson/
   museums.htm**
Newbury 01635–30511
   **www.westberks.gov.uk/WestBerkshire/tourism.nsf/pages/
   musintro.html**
Newcastle upon Tyne, Museum of Antiquities (pp. 449, **466–9**, 485,
   519, 537, 545–6) 0191–222–7846/7849
   www.ncl.ac.uk/antiquities
Newport, Gwent (p. 370) 01633–840064
Newport, IOW, Carisbrooke Castle Museum 01983–523112
   www.carisbrookecastlemuseum.org.uk/index.htm
Northampton, Central Museum 01604–39415
   www.northampton.gov.uk/Museums/Northampton
Norwich, Castle Museum 01603–493625
   www.norfolk.gov.uk/tourism/museum
Nottingham, Castle Museum 0115–915–3700
   www.nottinghamcity.gov.uk/whatson/museums/castle.asp
Nottingham, University Museum 0115–951–4820
Nuneaton 01203–350720
   www.warwickshire.gov.uk/tourism/nbmuseum.htm
Ospringe, Maison Dieu (p. 93) 01795–533751
   www.faversham.org/history/dieu.html
Oxford, Ashmolean Museum (p. 125) 01865–278000
   www.ashmol.ox.ac.uk
Oxford, Museum of Oxford 01865–252761
   **www.oxford.gov.uk/oxford/leisurelist.nsf/pages/
   Museum+of+Oxford**

Perth 01738–632488
   www.museum@pkc.gov.uk
Peterborough, Museum & Art Gallery 01733–343329
   www.peterborougheritage.org.uk
Piddington Roman Villa Museum (opening 2002)
   www.members.aol.comunarcsoc/unashome.htm
Pontefract 01977–722740
   **www.wakefield.gov.uk/community/museumsarts/
   pomuseum.htm**
Poole, Waterfront Museum 01202–262600
   **www.romans-in-britain.org.uk/ste_poole_waterfront_
   museum.htm**
Reading, Museum and Art Gallery (p. **122**) 01189–399800
   www.museumofreading.org.uk
Ribchester (p. **392**) 01254–878261
   www.hotpots.com/RibbleValley/roman.htm
Rochester, Kent, Guildhall Museum 01634–848717
   www.kent-museums.org.uk/muscat.html
Rochester, Northumberland, Archaeological reconstruction centre
   'Brigantium' (p. **546**) 01830–520801
   www.brigantium.co.uk
Rotherham, Clifton Park Museum 01709–823635
   www.rotherham.gov.uk/pages/tourism/whatto/ccas/clifton.htm
Saffron Walden (p. 256) 01799–510333
   www.uttlesford.gov.uk/saffire/places/swmus.html
St Albans, Verulamium Museum (pp. 231, **233–5**) 01727–751810
   www.stalbansmuseums.org.uk
Salisbury, Salisbury and South Wiltshire Museum 01722–332151
   www.salisburymuseum.freeserve.co.uk
Scarborough, Rotunda Museum 01723–376941
   www.northyorkmoors-npa.gov.uk/explore/exp_hc_7.htm
Scunthorpe, Museum and Art Gallery 01724–843533
Selkirk, Halliwell's House 01750–20096
Sheffield, City Museum 0114–278–2600
   www.shef.ac.uk/city/musuems/citymus/html
Shrewsbury, Rowley's House Museum (p. 277) 01743–361196
   www.shrewsbury.museums.com/museums/shrews_museum
Skipton, Craven Museum 01756–706407
   www.cravendc.gov.uk/leisure/museums-craven.html
Southampton, God's House Tower Museum 02380–635904
   www.hants.gov.uk/leisure/navdef/godshouse
Stockport, Municipal Museum 0161–474–4460
   www.stockportmbc.gov.uk/Tourism/museum/default.asp
Stroud, District Museum 01452–770073
Sunderland, Museum and Art Gallery 0191–565–0723
   www.sunderland.com/vi/musgal.htm

Taunton, Castle Museum (pp. 97, **122**, 155) 01823–320201
   www.somerset.gov.uk/museums
Thetford, Ancient House Museum 01842–752599
   www.norfolk.gov.uk/tourism/museums/thetford.htm
Tunbridge Wells 01892–554171
   www.tunbridgewells.gov.uk/museum
Warrington 01925–442392
   www.warrington.gov.uk/Museum/museum_home.html
Warwick, Warwickshire County Museum 01926–412881
   www.cwn.org.uk/tourism/museums/warwickshire-museum
Wells (p. 155) 01749–673477
West Mersea, Mersea Museum (p. 255) 01206–385191
   www.mersea-island.com/about/Museum.htm
Whitby (p. 437) 01947–602908
   www.durain.demon.co.uk
Wimborne Minster, Priest's House Museum 01202–882533
Winchester, City Museum (p. **113**) 01962–848269
   www.winchester.gov.uk/heritage/heritage.htm
Winchester, The Brooks Experience (p. **113**) 01962–849030
Wookey Hole Caves, Museum 01749–672243
   www.wookey.co.uk
Worcester, City Museum and Art Gallery 01905–25371
Worthing, Museum and Art Gallery 01903–239999 x 2528 or
   01903–204229
   www.worthing.gov.uk
Yeovil 01935–424774
York, Yorkshire Museum (p. **376**) 01904–629745
   www.york.gov.uk

Site museums

Aldborough, Roman town [EH] (p. 428) 01423–322768
Baginton, Lunt Roman fort (p. 261) 01203–832381
   www.coventrymuseum.org.uk/Lunt
Bath, Roman Museum (pp. **161–6**) 01225–477791
   www.romanbaths.co.uk
Bignor Roman villa (p. 79) 01798–869259
   www.romansinsussex.co.uk/sussex/bignor_site.asp
Birdoswald Roman fort (p. 524) 016977–47602
   www.birdoswaldromanfort.org
Brading, Roman villa (p. **144**) 01983–406223
   www.brading.co.uk/romanvilla.htm
Caerleon, fortress baths (p. **302**) 01633–422518
   www.cadw.wales.gov.uk
Caerleon Legionary Museum (p. **311**) 01633–423134
   www.nmgw.ac.uk

Caernarfon, Segontium Museum (p. 347) 01286–675625
  www.cadw.wales.gov.uk
Carisbrooke Castle Museum (p. 149) 01983–523112
  www.carisbrookecastlemuseum.org.uk
Carvoran near Greenhead, Roman army museum (p. **519**)
  016977–47485
  www.vindolanda.com
Chedworth, Roman villa (p. 197) 01242–890256
  http://completely-cotswold.com/chedworth/info/villa/info.htm
Chesters, Roman fort [EH] (pp. **483**, 505, 519) 01434–681379
Corbridge Roman site [EH] (p. **475**) 01434–632349
Dover, Roman painted house (p. **48**) 01304–203279
  **www.romans-in-britain.org.uk/ste_dover_roman_painted_
  house.htm**
Fishbourne Roman palace (p. **72**) 01243–785859
  www.sussexpast.co.uk
Housesteads, Roman fort [EH] (p. **490**) 01434–344363
Lullingstone, Roman villa [EH] (p. **82**) 01322–863467
Newport, IoW, Roman villa (p. 147) 01983–529720/529963
  www.romans-in-britain.org.uk/ste_newport_roman_villa.htm
Orpington, Crofton Roman villa (p. **89**)
  01689–873826/0208–4624737
  **www.romans-in-britain.org.uk/ste_orpington_crofton_roman_
  villa.htm**
Richborough, Roman fort [EH] (p. **45**) 01304–612013
Rochbourne Roman villa (p. **130**) 01725–518541
  www.hants.gov.uk/museum/rockbourne
South Shields, Arbeia Roman fort (p. **449**) 0191–456–1369
  www.s-tyneside-mbc.gov.uk/tourism/arbeia.htm
Vindolanda (p. **510**) 01434–344277
  www.vindolanda.com
Wall Roman site [EH] (p. 295) 01543–480768
Wallsend, Segedunum Roman fort (p. **458**) 0191–295–5757
  www.hadrians-wall.org
Welwyn Roman baths (p. 252) 01707–271362
  www.hertsmuseums.org.uk/welwyn-roman-baths/index.htm
Wroxeter Roman city [EH] (p. **277**) 01743–761330

Details of all English Heritage sites [EH] can be found on
www.english-heritage.org.uk
Information about Hadrian's Wall can be accessed on
www.hadrians-wall.org
An unofficial but useful website is **www.romans-in-britain.org.uk**
Note also the directory **www.museums.co.uk** (not comprehensive).

Bibliography

This bibliography is intended for the reader who wants more information about a given site than the scope of this book allows. The list is not intended to be comprehensive; references to other works will be found in almost all the items listed below. A single asterisk in this appendix denotes a book suitable for the non-specialist reader; a double asterisk indicates a booklet or pamphlet, also intended for the general reader. The place of publication is London except where otherwise stated.

Abbreviations

AA	*Archaeologia Aeliana*
AntiqJ	*Antiquaries Journal*
ArchCamb	*Archaeologia Cambrensis*
ArchCant	*Archaeologia Cantiana*
ArchJ	*Archaeological Journal*
ASPROM	Association for the Study and Preservation of Roman Mosaics
BAR	British Archaeological Reports
BBCS	*Bulletin of the Board of Celtic Studies*
CA	*Current Archaeology*
CBA	Council for British Archaeology
CW	*Transactions of the Cumberland and Westmorland Antiquarian and Archaeological Society* (2nd series)
EH	English Heritage
HBMCE	Historic Buildings and Monuments Commission for England (*alias* English Heritage)
HMSO	Her Majesty's Stationery Office
ibid.	*ibidem* ('in the same place')
JBAA	*Journal of the British Archaeological Association*
JRA	*Journal of Roman Archaeology*
JRS	*Journal of Roman Studies*
OJA	*Oxford Journal of Archaeology*
PSAS	*Proceedings of the Society of Antiquaries of Scotland*
RCHM	Royal Commission on Historical Monuments
RCHME	Royal Commission on Historical Monuments of England
RIB	*The Roman Inscriptions of Britain I–II* (see 'Literary and Epigraphic Source Material' below)
TBGAS	*Transactions of the Bristol and Gloucestershire Archaeological Society*
VCH	Victoria County History

Guidebooks to Roman Britain

Many archaeological guidebooks are available which cover a much wider time-span than that attempted by the present book; the most recent is *T DARVILL, P STAMPER & J TIMBY, *England* (An Oxford Archaeological Guide), Oxford: Oxford University Press 2002. By contrast, the only comparatively recent guidebooks exclusively concerned with Roman Britain are *D E JOHNSTON (ed.), *Discovering Roman Britain*, 3rd edn, Aylesbury: Shire, 2002, with a more concise coverage than the present book; and *P OTTAWAY, *A Traveller's Guide to Roman Britain*, Routledge 1987, which contains fine, evocative photographs, but which is more a book for armchair reading than a practical handbook to use in the field. For German readers, there is also a selective guide (concentrating on industrial and 'economic' monuments, both Roman and medieval), by K GREWE, *Großbritannien. England–Schottland–Wales. Ein Führer zu bau- und technikgeschichtlichen Denkmälern aus der Antike und Mittelalter*, Stuttgart: Theiss 1999.

Brief Introductions

*T W POTTER, *Roman Britain*, British Museum Publications 1997
*P SALWAY, *Roman Britain. A Very Short Introduction*, Oxford: Oxford University Press 2000
*D SHOTTER, *Roman Britain*, Routledge 1998
*S HILL & S IRELAND, *Roman Britain*, Bristol: Bristol Classical Press 1996

General Works

S S FRERE, *Britannia*, Routledge, 3rd edn 1987; pbk edn, Pimlico 1991 (replaced now by the 4th edn, Folio Society 1999, but this is in limited circulation, being only available to members of the Society)
P SALWAY, *Roman Britain*, Oxford: Clarendon Press 1981
*P SALWAY, *The Oxford Illustrated History of Roman Britain*, Oxford: Oxford University Press 1993 (text without illustrations also available as *A History of Roman Britain*, 1997)
*P SALWAY, *The Roman Era* [Short Oxford History of the British Isles], Oxford: Oxford University Press 2002
*M TODD, *Roman Britain (55 BC–AD 400)*, 3rd edn, Oxford: Blackwell 1999
*J WACHER, *Roman Britain*, 2nd edn, Stroud: Sutton 1998
*T W POTTER & C JOHNS, *Roman Britain*, British Museum Publications 1992
*B JONES & D MATTINGLY, *An Atlas of Roman Britain*, Oxford: Blackwells 1990

M MILLETT, *The Romanization of Britain,* Cambridge: Cambridge University Press 1990

*M MILLETT, *The English Heritage Book of Roman Britain*, Batsford 1995

M TODD (ed.), *Research on Roman Britain 1960–89* [Britannia Monographs 11], Society for Promotion of Roman Studies 1989

R F J JONES (ed.), *Roman Britain: recent trends*, Sheffield: University of Sheffield 1991

S JAMES & M MILLETT (eds.), *Britons and Romans: advancing an archaeological agenda* [CBA Research Report 125], York: CBA 2001

R REECE, *My Roman Britain*, Cirencester: Cotswold Studies 1988

J WACHER, *A Portrait of Roman Britain*, Routledge 2000

*G DE LA BÉDOYÈRE, *The Golden Age of Roman Britain*, Stroud: Tempus 1999

*G DE LA BÉDOYÈRE, *Companion to Roman Britain*, Stroud: Tempus 1999

*L ALLASON-JONES, *Women in Roman Britain*, British Museum Publications 1989

*K & P DARK, *The Landscape of Roman Britain*, Stroud: Sutton Publishing 1997

*A S ESMONDE CLEARY, *The Ending of Roman Britain*, Batsford 1989/Routledge 2000

M E JONES, *The End of Roman Britain*, Ithaca, NY: Cornell University Press 1996

*N FAULKNER, *The Decline and Fall of Roman Britain*, Stroud: Tempus 2000

Literary and Epigraphic Source Material

*S IRELAND, *Roman Britain: a source book*, rev. edn Routledge 1996

K BRODERSEN, *Das römische Britannien: Spuren seiner Geschichte*, Darmstadt: Wissenschaftliche Buchgesellschaft 1998

*V A MAXFIELD & B DOBSON (eds.), *Inscriptions of Roman Britain*, 3rd edn, London Association of Classical Teachers 1995

R G COLLINGWOOD & R P WRIGHT, *The Roman Inscriptions of Britain* vol. I, 2nd edn, Stroud: Alan Sutton 1995

R GOODBURN & H WAUGH, *The Roman Inscriptions of Britain I: Epigraphic Indexes*, Stroud: Alan Sutton 1983

S S FRERE & R S O TOMLIN, *The Roman Inscriptions of Britain* vol. II, Fascicules 1–8 and Indices, Stroud: Alan Sutton 1990–5

A R BIRLEY, *The Fasti of Roman Britain*, Oxford: Clarendon Press 1981

M E RAYBOULD, *A Study of Inscribed Material from Roman Britain. An enquiry into some aspects of literacy in Romano-British society* [BAR British Series 281], Oxford: Archaeopress 1999

Bibliographical Sources

W BONSER, *A Romano-British Bibliography (55 BC–AD 449)*, Oxford: Blackwell 1964

Britannia. Consolidated index of volumes I–XXV 1970–94, Society for Promotion of Roman Studies 1995

Topography

Ordnance Survey Map of Roman Britain, HMSO, 4th edn 1978 (this is to be recommended in preference to the cartographic ugliness of the 5th edn, 1991)

Tabula Imperii Romani: Condate–Glevum–Londinium–Lutetia, Oxford University Press/British Academy 1983 (both this and the next item have comprehensive bibliographies in the gazetteer)

Tabula Imperii Romani: Britannia Septentrionalis, Oxford University Press/British Academy 1987

A L F RIVET & C SMITH, *The Place-Names of Roman Britain*, Batsford 1979

Invasion Period

*G WEBSTER, *The Roman Invasion of Britain*, Batsford 1980, rev. edn 1993

*G WEBSTER, *Rome against Caratacus*, Batsford 1981, rev. edn 1993

*G WEBSTER, *Boudica*, Batsford 1978, rev. edn 1993

*J PEDDLE, *Invasion: the Roman Conquest of Britain*, Stroud: Alan Sutton 1987

D BRAUND, *Ruling Roman Britain*, Routledge 1996

*M HENIG, *The Heirs of King Verica: culture and politics in Roman Britain*, Stroud: Tempus 2002

**P SEALEY, *The Boudiccan revolt against Rome*, Aylesbury: Shire 1997

S S FRERE & M FULFORD, 'The Roman invasion of AD 43', *Britannia* xxxii (2001), 45–55

The Archaeology of Roman Britain

General

R G COLLINGWOOD & I RICHMOND, *The Archaeology of Roman Britain*, Methuen, 2nd edn 1969 (out of date but still useful)

S S FRERE & J K ST JOSEPH, *Roman Britain from the Air*, Cambridge: Cambridge University Press 1983

Military

G WEBSTER, *The Roman Imperial Army of the First and Second Centuries AD*, Black, 3rd edn 1985

P A HOLDER, *The Roman Army in Britain*, Batsford 1982

D J BREEZE, *The Northern Frontiers of Roman Britain*, Batsford 1982

G DE LA BÉDOYÈRE, *Eagles over Britannia: the Roman Army in Britain*, Stroud: Tempus 2001

*R WILSON, *Roman Forts*, Bergstrom and Boyle/Constable 1980

**D J BREEZE, *Roman Forts*, Aylesbury: Shire 1983

A JOHNSON, *Roman Forts of the First and Second Centuries AD in Britain and the German Provinces*, Black 1983

*P BIDWELL, *English Heritage Book of Roman Forts in Britain*, Batsford 1997

P BIDWELL, R MIKET & B FORD (eds.), Portae cum turribus: *studies of Roman fort gates* [BAR British Series 206], Oxford: BAR 1988

D B CAMPBELL, '*Ballistaria* in first to mid-third century Britain: a re-appraisal', *Britannia* xv (1984), 75–84

C S SOMMER, *The Military* Vici *of Roman Britain*, Oxford: BAR 1984

H WELFARE & V SWAN (eds.), *Roman Camps in England: the field archaeology*, HMSO 1995

C M GILLIVER, *The Roman Art of War*, Stroud: Tempus 1999, 63–88 (on camps and camp defences)

A A R HENDERSON & L J F KEPPIE, '*Titulus* or *titulum*?', *Britannia* xviii (1987), 281–4

A RICHARDSON, 'The numerical basis of Roman camps', *OJA* 19 (2000), 425–37

D WOOLLISCROFT, *Roman Military Signalling*, Stroud: Tempus 2001

J S JOHNSON, *The Roman Forts of the Saxon Shore*, Elek, 2nd edn 1979

V MAXFIELD (ed.), *The Saxon Shore: a handbook produced on the occasion of the 15th International Congress of Roman frontier studies*, Exeter: Exeter University Press 1989

J COTTERILL, 'Saxon raiding and the role of late Roman coastal forts of Britain', *Britannia* 24 (1993), 227–39

P J CASEY, *Carausius and Allectus: the British usurpers*, Batsford 1994

D A WELSBY, *The Roman Military Defence of the British Province in its Later Phases*, Oxford: BAR 1982

Towns

J WACHER, *The Towns of Roman Britain*, 2nd edn, Batsford 1995

G WEBSTER (ed.), *Fortress into City: the consolidation of Roman Britain,* Batsford 1988

**J BENNETT, *Towns in Roman Britain*, 3rd edn, Aylesbury: Shire Publications 2002

*G DE LA BÉDOYÈRE, *The English Heritage Book of Roman Towns in Britain*, Batsford 1992

*P OTTAWAY, *Archaeology in British Towns: from the Emperor Claudius to the Black Death*, Routledge 1992, chs. 3 & 4

S GREEP (ed.), *Roman Towns: the Wheeler inheritance* [CBA Research Report 93], York: CBA 1993

H HURST (ed.), *The Coloniae of Roman Britain: new studies and a review* [Journal of Roman Archaeology Supplement series 36], Portsmouth, Rhode Island 1999

F GREW & B HOBLEY (eds.), *Roman Urban Topography in Britain and the Western Empire*, CBA Research Report 1985

J CRICKMORE, *Romano-British Urban Defences*, Oxford: BAR 1984

J MALONEY & B HOBLEY (eds.), *Roman Urban Defences in the West* [CBA Research Report 51], CBA 1983

S S FRERE, 'British urban defences in earthwork', *Britannia* xv (1984), 63–74

'Small Towns'

B C BURNHAM & J. WACHER, *The 'Small Towns' of Roman Britain*, Batsford 1990

A E BROWN (ed.), *Roman Small Towns in Eastern Britain and Beyond*, Oxford: Oxbow 1995

Villas and the countryside

A L F RIVET (ed.), *The Roman Villa in Britain*, Routledge 1969

M TODD (ed.), *Studies in the Romano-British Villa*, Leicester: Leicester University Press 1978

E SCOTT, *A Gazetteer of Roman Villas in Britain* [Leicester Archaeological Monographs 1], Leicester: University of Leicester 1993

*G. DE LA BÉDOYÈRE, *The English Heritage Book of Roman Villas and the Countryside*, Batsford 1993

K BRANIGAN & D MILES (eds.), *The Economies of Romano-British Villas*, Sheffield: University of Sheffield, n.d., but *c.* 1987

*R HINGLEY, *Rural Settlement in Roman Britain*, Seaby 1989

D MILES (ed.), *The Romano-British Countryside*, Oxford: BAR 1982

R M & D E FRIENDSHIP-TAYLOR (eds.), *From Round House to Villa*, Hackleton: Upper Nene Archaeological Society 1997

**D JOHNSTON, *Roman Villas*, rev. edn, Aylesbury: Shire 1983

*R HINGLEY, *Villages in Roman Britain*, new edn, Aylesbury: Shire 2000

M VAN DER VEEN, 'Charred grain assemblages from Roman-period corn driers in Britain', *ArchJ* cxlvi (1989), 302–19

Social aspects

J LIVERSIDGE, *Britain in the Roman Empire*, Routledge 1968

*A BIRLEY, *The People of Roman Britain*, Batsford 1979

*J ALCOCK, *English Heritage Book of Life in Roman Britain*, Batsford 1996

*T MCALEAVY, *Life in Roman Britain*, EH 1999

*J P ALCOCK, *Food in Roman Britain*, Stroud: Tempus 2001

A BURGERS, *The Water Supplies and Related Structures of Roman Britain* [BAR British Series 324], Oxford: BAR 2001

Roads

I D MARGARY, *Roman Roads in Britain*, Baker, rev. edn 1973

*D E JOHNSTON, *An Illustrated History of Roman Roads in Britain*, Bourne End: Spurbooks 1979

D E JOHNSTON (ed.), *The Viatores: Roman roads in the south-east Midlands*, Gollancz 1964

**R W BAGSHAWE, *Roman Roads*, Aylesbury: Shire 1979

*H LIVINGSTONE, *In the Footsteps of Caesar: walking Roman roads in Britain*, Shepperton: Dial House 1995

J P SEDGLEY, *Roman Milestones of Britain: their petrology and probable origin* [BAR British Series 18], Oxford: BAR 1975

H E H DAVIES, 'Designing Roman roads', *Britannia* xxix (1998), 1–16

Art, general

*J M C TOYNBEE, *Art in Roman Britain*, Phaidon 1962

J M C TOYNBEE, *Art in Britain under the Romans*, Oxford: Clarendon Press 1964

*M HENIG, *The Art of Roman Britain*, Batsford 1995

*J LAING, *Art and Society in Roman Britain*, Stroud: Alan Sutton 1997

Architecture

G. DE LA BÉDOYÈRE, *The Buildings of Roman Britain*, new edn, Stroud: Tempus 2001

P JOHNSON & I HAYNES (eds.), *Architecture in Roman Britain* [CBA Research Report 94], York: CBA 1996

**T ROOK, *Roman Baths in Britain*, Aylesbury: Shire 1992

D PERRING, *The Roman House in Britain*, Routledge 2002

S P ELLIS, 'Classical reception rooms in Romano-British houses', *Britannia* xxvi (1995), 163–78

S R COSH, 'Seasonal dining rooms in Romano-British houses', *Britannia* xxxii (2001), 219–42

Mosaics

*A RAINEY, *Mosaics in Roman Britain, a Gazetteer*, Newton Abbott: David and Charles 1973

D S NEAL, *Roman Mosaics in Britain* [Britannia Monographs 1], Society for Promotion of Roman Studies 1981

D S NEAL & S R COSH, *Roman Mosaics of Britain, Volume I. Northern Britain*, Illuminata for Society of Antiquaries 2002 (and three further volumes in preparation)

N A COOKSON, *Romano-British Mosaics* [BAR British Series 135], Oxford: BAR 1984

S SCOTT, *Art and Society in Fourth-Century Britain: villa mosaics in context*, Oxford: Oxford University Institute of Archaeology 2000

**P JOHNSON, *Romano-British Mosaics*, Aylesbury: Shire 1982

R STUPPERICH, 'A reconsideration of some fourth-century British mosaics', *Britannia* xi (1980), 289–301

R LING, 'Mosaics in Roman Britain: discoveries and research since 1945', *Britannia* xxviii (1997), 259–95

P WITTS, 'Mosaics and room function: the evidence from some fourth-century Romano-British villas', *Britannia* xxxi (2000), 291–324

Painting

**R LING, *Romano-British Wall Painting*, Aylesbury: Shire 1985

N DAVEY & R LING, *Wall-Painting in Roman Britain* [Britannia Monographs 3], Society for Promotion of Roman Studies 1982

Sculpture

E J PHILLIPS, *Corpus Signorum Imperii Romani Great Britain I.1. Corbridge. Hadrian's Wall east of the North Tyne*, Oxford: Oxford University Press for the British Academy 1977

B W CUNLIFFE & M G FULFORD, *Corpus Signorum Imperii Romani Great Britain I.2. Bath and the rest of Wessex*, Oxford: Oxford University Press for the British Academy 1982

S R TUFI, *Corpus Signorum Imperii Romani Great Britain I.3. Yorkshire*, Oxford: Oxford University Press for the British Academy 1983

L J F KEPPIE & B J ARNOLD, *Corpus Signorum Imperii Romani. Great Britain I.4. Scotland*, Oxford: Oxford University Press for the British Academy 1988

R J BREWER, *Corpus Signorum Imperii Romani Great Britain I.5. Wales*, Oxford: Oxford University Press for the British Academy 1988

J C COULSTON & E J PHILLIPS, *Corpus Signorum Imperii Romani Great Britain I.6. Hadrian's Wall west of the North Tyne, and Carlisle*, Oxford: Oxford University Press for the British Academy 1988

M HENIG, *Corpus Signorum Imperii Romani Great Britain I.7. Roman sculpture from the Cotswold Region with Devon and Cornwall*, Oxford: Oxford University Press for the British Academy 1993

J HUSKINSON, *Corpus Signorum Imperii Romani Great Britain I.8.*

Roman sculpture from Eastern England, Oxford: Oxford University Press for the British Academy 1994

V M HOPE, 'Words and pictures: the interpretation of Romano-British tombstones', *Britannia* xxviii (1997), 245–58

Small finds

*G DE LA BÉYODÈRE, *The Finds of Roman Britain,* Batsford 1989

P TYERS, *Roman Pottery in Britain*, Batsford 1996

**G DE LA BÉYODÈRE, *Pottery in Roman Britain*, Aylesbury: Shire 2000

*P WEBSTER, *Roman Samian Pottery in Britain* [CBA Practical Handbooks in Archaeology 13], York: CBA 1996

*J PRICE & S COTTAM, *Romano-British Glass Vessels: a handbook* [CBA Practical Handbooks in Archaeology 14], York: CBA 1998

**D ALLEN, *Roman Glass in Britain*, Aylesbury: Shire 1998

C JOHNS, *The Jewellery of Roman Britain*, University College London Press 1996

**P J CASEY, *Roman Coinage in Britain*, Aylesbury: Shire 1994

Religion

*M HENIG, *Religion in Roman Britain*, Batsford 1984

*M GREEN, *The Gods of the Celts*, Stroud: Alan Sutton 1986

*G WEBSTER, *The British Celts and their Gods under Rome*, Batsford 1986

*A WOODWARD, *The English Heritage Book of Shrines and Sacrifice*, Batsford 1992

W RODWELL (ed.), *Temples, Churches and Religion*, Oxford: BAR 1980

G L IRBY-MASSIE, *Military Religion in Roman Britain*, Leiden: Brill 1999

C THOMAS, *Christianity in Roman Britain to AD 500*, Batsford 1981

D WATTS, *Pagans and Christians in Roman Britain*, Routledge 1991

C F MAWER, *Evidence for Christianity in Roman Britain: the small finds* [BAR British Series 243], Oxford: Tempus Reparatum 1995

D WATTS, *Religion in Late Roman Britain: forces of change*, Routledge 1998

Burial

R PHILPOTT, *Burial Practices in Roman Britain: a survey of grave treatment and furnishing, AD 43–410* [BAR British Series 219], Oxford: BAR 1991

S BASSETT (ed.), *Death in Towns: urban responses to the dying and the dead, 100–1600*, Leicester: Leicester University Press 1992, 28–55

Chapter 1

General

*P DREWETT, D RUDDLING & M GARDINER, *The South-East to AD 1000*, Longmans 1988, 178–245

*A DETSICAS, *The Cantiaci*, Stroud: Alan Sutton 1983

*B CUNLIFFE, *The Regni*, Duckworth 1973

E W BLACK, *The Roman Villas of South-East England* [BAR British Series 171], Oxford: BAR 1987

S JOHNSON, *The Roman Forts of the Saxon Shore*, 2nd edn, Elek 1979

D BIRD, 'The Romano-British period in Surrey', in J & D G BIRD (eds.), *The Archaeology of Surrey to 1540*, Guildford: Surrey Archaeological Society 1987, 165–96

Roads (see also Ashdown Forest)

*A VINCENT, *Roman Roads of Sussex*, Midhurst: Middleton Press 2000

*A VINCENT, *Roman Roads of Surrey*, Midhurst: Middleton Press 2001

Richborough

**J S JOHNSON, *Richborough and Reculver, Kent*, EH 1987 (guidebook)

B CUNLIFFE (ed.), *Richborough V*, Society of Antiquaries Research Report 1968

Britannia i (1970), 240–8 (chronology); ii (1971), 225–31 (church); xix (1988), 411–12 (font)

A DETSICAS (ed.), *Collectanea Historica: essays in memory of Stuart Rigold*, Maidstone: Kent Archaeological Society 1981, 23–30 (construction details)

Reculver

**J S JOHNSON, *Richborough and Reculver, Kent*, EH 1987 (guidebook)

**B PHILP, *The Roman Fort at Reculver*, Dover: Kent Archaeological Rescue Unit, 8th. edn 1986

Lympne

S JOHNSON, *op. cit.* (see General), 53–6

Britannia xi (1980), 227–88; xvi (1985), 209–36

Dover

B PHILP, *The Excavation of the Roman Forts of the Classis Britannica at Dover 1970–1977*, Dover: Kent Archaeological Rescue Unit 1981

B PHILP, *The Roman House with Bacchic murals at Dover*, Dover: Kent Archaeological Rescue Unit 1989

**B PHILP, *The Roman Painted House at Dover*, Dover n.d.

ArchCant 114 (1994), 51–148 (*classis Britannica* fort excavations 'White Cliffs Experience')

ArchJ lxxxvi (1929), 29–46 (lighthouses)

Britannia xx (1989), 323–5 (new Shore-fort tower)

*J COAD, *English Heritage Book of Dover Castle*, Batsford 1995, 17–18 (lighthouses)

RIB II.2491.124 (graffito on tile)

Pevensey

**J GOODALL, *Pevensey Castle*, EH 1999 (guidebook)

Britannia xxvi (1995), 368 (1994 excavation)

Antiquity xlvii (1973), 138–40 (forgery of brick-stamps); lxix (1995), 1009–14 (dating)

Sussex Archaeological Collections 129 (1991), 250–1 (Roman name)

OJA 18 (1999), 95–117 (estimates of materials and labour)

Ashdown Forest

**I D MARGARY, *The London-Lewes Roman Road. A guide to the visible remains at Holtye and on Ashdown Forest*, Lewes: Sussex Archaeological Society n.d. [*c*. 1962]

Beauport Park

ArchJ cxxxi (1974), 171–99

Britannia x (1979), 139–56; xix (1988), 217–74

CA 77 (May 1981), 177–81

**G BRODRIBB, *The Roman Bath-house at Beauport Park*, Mountfield: Friends of Roman East Sussex 1995

Canterbury

***Ordnance Survey Historical Map and Guide: Roman and medieval Canterbury*, HMSO 1990

**A HARMSWORTH, *Roman Canterbury: a journey into the past*, Canterbury: Canterbury Archaeological Trust 1994 (principally for children)

*M LYLE, *English Heritage Book of Canterbury*, Batsford 1994, 26–42

S S FRERE, S STOW & P BENNETT, *Excavations on the Roman and Medieval Defences of Canterbury* (Archaeology of Canterbury vol. II), Maidstone: Canterbury Archaeological Trust 1982

Britannia i (1970), 83–113 (theatre); xvii (1986), 426; xviii (1987), 354–8; xix (1988), 481–4; xx (1989), 322–3; xxi (1990), 360–2; xxviii (1997), 451 (latest plan of Roman Canterbury); xxxii (2001), 382–3 (Riding Gate)

ArchCant cvii (1989), 117–54 (Riding Gate)

AntiqJ lxv (1985), 312–52 (silver treasure)

RIB II.2420.48 (inscribed spoon); 2433.19 (set-square); 2501.435 (chi-rho)

Rochester
**R ALLEN BROWN, *Rochester Castle* [EH Guide], HMSO 1969, 23–6
ArchCant lxxxiii (1968), 55–104; lxxxv (1970), 95–112; lxxxvii (1972), 121–57

Chichester
*A DOWN, *Roman Chichester*, Chichester: Phillimore 1988
Britannia x (1979), 227–54; xix (1988), 479; xxii (1991), 290
RIB I, 91 (Togidubnus inscription)

Fishbourne
**B CUNLIFFE, *Fishbourne Roman Palace. A Guide to the Site*, 3rd edn, Lewes: Sussex Archaeological Society 1994
*B CUNLIFFE, *Fishbourne, a Roman Palace and its Garden*, new edn, Stroud: Tempus 1998
B CUNLIFFE, *Excavations at Fishbourne 1961–9*, 2 vols., Society of Antiquaries 1971
B CUNLIFFE, A DOWN & D RUDKIN, *Excavations at Fishbourne 1969–88* [Chichester Excavations 9], Chichester: Chichester District Council 1996
J MANLEY & D RUDKIN, in N J HIGHAM (ed.), *Archaeology of the Roman Empire: a tribute to the life and works of Professor Barri Jones* [BAR International Series 940], Oxford: BAR 2001, 105–16 (1990s excavations)
CA 152 (April 1997), 314–17 (1990s excavations)
JRA 4 (1991), 160–9 (re-assessment by excavator); 6 (1993), 233–7 (suggested disassociation of proto-palace from Togidubnus)
Britannia xix (1988), 481 (west wing); xxi (1990), 360 (Medusa mosaic)
Sussex Archaeological Collections 135 (1997), 127–30 (Catuarus ring)

Bignor
**Bignor Roman Villa Guidebook*, Bignor n.d. [1988]
OJA ii (1983), 93–107
Sussex Archaeological Collections 133 (1995), 103–88 (excavations 1985–94)
Britannia xxvi (1995), 370; xxviii (1997), 447; xxix (1998), 428; xxxi (2000), 428; xxxii (2001), 377–9
Mosaic 28 (2001), 4–7 ('Terentius')

Lullingstone

**D S NEAL, *Lullingstone Roman Villa, North-West Kent*, EH 1991
(guidebook)

G W MEATES, *The Roman Villa at Lullingstone, Vol I: the site*,
Maidstone: Kent Archaeological Society 1979

G W MEATES, *The Roman Villa at Lullingstone, Vol II: the wall
paintings and finds*, Maidstone: Kent Archaeological Society 1987

C THOMAS, *Christian Celts: messages and images*, Stroud: Tempus
1998, 47–54 ('Avitus')

Orpington

B PHILP, *The Roman Villa Site at Orpington, Kent: excavations
(1988–9) and preservation (1991–2)*, Dover: Kent Archaeological
Rescue Unit 1996

**B PHILP, *The Crofton Roman Villa at Orpington*, Dover: Kent
Archaeological Rescue Unit 1992

S PALMER, *Excavation of the Roman and Saxon Site at Orpington*,
Bromley: London Borough of Bromley 1984

B PHILP & P KELLER, *The Roman Site at Fordcroft, Orpington*, Dover:
Kent Archaeological Rescue Unit 1995

CA 135 (August/September 1993), 106–9 (Crofton Road)

Archives of the Orpington District Archaeological Society 17.2
(1995), 20–46 (Fordcroft)

Keston

B PHILP, K PARFITT, J WILSON, M DUTTO & W WILLIAMS, *The Roman
Villa Site at Keston, Kent. First Report (Excavations 1968–1978)*,
Dover: Kent Archaeological Rescue Unit 1991 (villa)

B PHILP, K PARFITT, J WILSON & W WILLIAMS, *The Roman Villa Site at
Keston, Kent. Second Report (Excavations 1967 and 1979–80)*,
Dover: Kent Archaeological Rescue Unit 1999, 45–60 (mausolea)

Kent Archaeological Review 132 (1998), 39–41 (spina bifida)

Stone-by-Faversham and Ospringe

AntiqJ xlix (1969), 273–94; lvii (1977), 67–72; *ArchJ* cxxxviii
(1981), 118–45 (mausoleum)

D WATTS, *Christians and Pagans in Roman Britain*, Routledge 1991,
23, 118–19, 122 (for the 'Roman church' theory)

W WHITING, W HAWLEY & T MAY, *Report on the Excavation of the
Roman Cemetery at Ospringe, Kent*, Society of Antiquaries 1931

Practical Archaeology [Kent Archaeological Field School] 1 (1999),
8–9 ('fort')

ARA: Bulletin of the Association for Roman Archaeology 8 (Autumn
1999), 12–14 ('fort')

Kent Archaeological Review 129 (1997), 199–205 (Ospringe and
    Faversham)
Britannia xxxi (2000), 430 ('fort'); xxxii (2001), 384 (settlement)

Chapter 2

General
*M TODD, *The South West to AD 1000*, Longmans 1987, 189–235
*B CUNLIFFE, *Wessex to AD 1000*, Longmans 1993, 201–75
*B PUTNAM, *Discover Dorset: the Romans*, Wimborne Minster:
    Dovecote Press 2000
N M FIELD, *Dorset and the Second Legion*, Dorchester: Dorset Books
    1992
*M ASTON & I BURROW (eds.), *The Archaeology of Somerset: a review
    to 1500 AD*, Taunton: Somerset County Council 1982, 63–82
*L & R ADKINS, *A Field Guide to Somerset Archaeology*, Wimborne
    Minster: Dovecote Press 1992
*M ALSTON & R ISLES (eds.), *The Archaeology of Avon: a review from
    the Neolithic to the Middle Ages*, Bristol: Avon County Council
    1987
P ELLIS (ed.), *Roman Wiltshire and After: papers in honour of Ken
    Annable*, Devizes: Wiltshire Archaeological & Natural History
    Society 2001
*C WEATHERHILL, *Cornovia: ancient sites of Cornwall and Scilly*,
    Newmill, Penzance: Alison Hodge 1985
C THOMAS (ed.), *Rural Settlement in Roman Britain*, CBA 1966,
    43–67 and 74–98

Old Burrow & *Martinhoe*
Proceedings of the Devonshire Archaeological Society xxiv (1966),
    3–39

Hembury
Antiquity lviii (1984), 171–4

Hod Hill
I A RICHMOND, *Hod Hill II*, British Museum 1968
ArchJ cxiii (1966), 209–11 (summary)

Maiden Castle
**EH *Guide*, HMSO 1980
*N SHARPLES, *English Heritage Book of Maiden Castle*, Batsford
    1991, 116–31

N M SHARPLES, *Maiden Castle: excavation and field survey 1985–6*,
    HBMCE 1991, 99–102

J COULSTON, 'The archaeology of Roman conflict', in P W M FREEMAN
    & A POLLARD (eds.), *Fields of Conflict: progress and prospect in
    battlefield archaeology* [BAR International Series 958], Oxford:
    BAR 2001, 23–49 (Roman battlefield archaeology)

Jordon Hill
RCHM *Dorset* II, iii, HMSO 1970, 616–17
**E V TANNER, *Romano-Celtic Settlement on Jordon Hill near
    Weymouth, Dorset*, Preston: Parish of Preston and Sutton Poyntz
    1967

Dorchester
RCHM *Dorset* II, iii, HMSO 1970, 531–92
**B PUTNAM, *The Roman Town House at Dorchester*, Dorchester:
    Dorset County Council n.d. [2000]
***Roman Dorchester*, Dorchester: Dorset County Council 1999
Archaeologia cv (1976), 1–97 (amphitheatre)
ASPROM Newsletter 39, September 2001, 2 (Somerleigh Court)
C S GREEN, *Excavations at Poundbury Volume 1: the settlements*,
    Dorchester: Dorset Natural History and Archaeological Society
    1987, 49–51 (aqueduct)
CA 154 (September 1997), 364–9 (aqueduct)
*Proceedings of the Dorset Natural History and Archaeological
    Society* 120 (1998), 94–6 (aqueduct)

Exeter
*P BIDWELL, *Roman Exeter: fortress and town*, Exeter: Exeter City
    Council 1980
P BIDWELL, *The Legionary Bath-house and Basilica and Forum at
    Exeter*, Exeter: Exeter City Council and the University of Exeter
    1979
Britannia xix (1988), 472–3 (up-to-date fortress plan); xx (1989),
    313–14; xxi (1990), 348–50; xxii (1991), 281–2; xxv (1994), 286;
    xxvi (1995), 366–7; xxvii (1996), 435–6

Winchester
***Venta Belgarum: the Roman town of Winchester. Souvenir Guide*,
    Winchester: Winchester Museums Service 1997
J M ZANT, *The Brooks, Winchester, 1987–8. The Roman structural
    remains* [Winchester Museums Service Archaeology Report 2],
    Winchester 1993
Winchester Museums Service Newsletter 22 (1995), 4–9 (topography)

Proceedings of the Hampshire Field Club xxii (1962), 51–81 (city
    wall)
Britannia xx (1989), 316–19 (city wall; town-houses)

Silchester
*G C BOON, *Silchester, the Roman Town of Calleva,* Newton Abbott:
    David & Charles 1974
**M FULFORD, *Calleva Atrebatum: a guide to the Roman town at*
    Silchester, Silchester: Calleva Museum 1987
M FULFORD *ET AL.*, *Silchester: excavations on the defences 1974–80*
    [Britannia Monographs 5], Society for Promotion of Roman
    Studies 1984
M FULFORD, *The Silchester Amphitheatre: excavations of 1979–85*
    [Britannia Monographs 10], Society for Promotion of Roman
    Studies 1989
M FULFORD & J TIMBY, *Late Iron Age and Roman Silchester:*
    excavations on the site of the Forum-Basilica, 1977, 1980–86
    [Britannia Monographs 15], Society for Promotion of Roman
    Studies 2000
Archaeologia cv (1976), 277–302; *Britannia* xxv (1994), 119–26
    (church)
CA 161 (February 1999), 176–80; 177 (January 2002), 364–9 (Insula
    IX)
Britannia xxvii (1996), 387–8 (new plan); xxviii (1997), 87–168; xxxi
    (2000), 356–8 (both north gate); xxix (1998), 426–7; xxx (1999),
    369; xxxi (2000), 426–7; xxxii (2001), 373–4 (all Insula IX)
Medieval Archaeology 44 (2000), 1–23 (Ogham stone)
RIB I, 70 (Calleva stone); II, 2491.1 (Clementinus), 148 (*conticuere*
    omnes) and 159 (*satis*, 'enough')

Rockbourne
**D ALLEN, *Rockbourne Roman Villa. Guide*, revised edn,
    Winchester: Hampshire County Museums Service 1989
ArchJ cxl (1983), 129–50

Littlecote Park
***Littlecote Roman Villa, illustrated guide*, Swindon: Roman
    Research Marketing 1994
**B WALTERS & B PHILLIPS, *Archaeological Excavations in Littlecote*
    Park Wiltshire 1978. First Interim Report, Littlecote: Littlecote
    Estate 1979
**B WALTERS & B PHILLIPS, *Archaeological Excavations in Littlecote*
    Park Wiltshire 1981 & 82. Third Interim Report, Littlecote:
    Littlecote Roman Research Trust n.d. [*c.* 1983]
Britannia xii (1981), 1–5 (mosaic interpretation), 360; xiii (1982),

387–9; xiv (1983), 328–9; xv (1994), 332–3; xvi (1985), 308; xx
(1989), 315–17; xxi (1990), 353–4; xxiii (1992), 301

Bokerley Dyke & Soldier's Ring
H C BOWEN, *The Archaeology of Bokerley Dyke*, HMSO for RCHME
1990 (52–7 for Soldier's Ring)

Woodcuts & Rotherley
ArchJ civ (1947), 36–48

Berwick Down
C THOMAS (ed.), *op. cit.* (see General), 46–7

Meriden Down
RCHM *Dorset* III, ii, HMSO 1970, 298

Cerne Giant
P NEWMAN, *Lost Gods of Albion*, Robert Hale 1987, 68–97
R CASTLEDEAN, *The Cerne Giant*, Wincanton 1996
T DARVILL *ET AL.*, *The Cerne Giant: an antiquity on trial*, Oxford:
Oxbow 1999
Antiquité Classique xliv (1975), 570–80
AntiqJ lxxviii (1998), 463–71

Chysauster
**P M L CHRISTIE, *Chysauster and Carn Euny*, EH 1993 (guidebook)
ArchJ cxxx (1973), 238–40

Carn Euny
**P M L CHRISTIE, *Chysauster and Carn Euny*, EH 1993 (guidebook)
CA 44 (May 1974), 262–8

Scilly Isles
C THOMAS, *Exploration of a Drowned Landscape: archaeology and
history of the Isles of Scilly*, Batsford 1985, 163–5 (Nornour)
**S BUTCHER, *Nornour* (Isles of Scilly Museums Publication No. 7),
n.d.
Britannia xx (1989), 245–9 (shipwreck?)

Cornish milestones
RIB I, 2230–4
*C THOMAS, *English Heritage Book of Tintagel*, Batsford 1993, 13–14,
82–5

Isle of Wight
***Romans on the Wight*, Newport: Isle of Wight County Council
1992

*D J TOMALIN, *Roman Wight, a Guide Catalogue*, Newport: Isle of
    Wight County Council 1987

Brading
**D TOMALIN & R HANWORTH, *House for All Seasons: a guide to
    Brading Roman villa*, Brading: Oglander Roman Trust 1998
Britannia xxii (1991), 148–53; xxv (1994), 111–17 (mosaics)

Newport
AntiqJ ix (1929), 141–51 and 354–71
TOMALIN, *op. cit.* (see Isle of Wight), 13–18
**D J TOMALIN, *Newport Roman Villa*, Newport: Isle of Wight County
    Council, 2nd edn 1977
Britannia xix (1988), 477 (corn-drier)

Carisbrooke
C J YOUNG, in B HARTLEY & J S WACHER (eds)., *Rome and Her
    Northern Provinces: papers presented to Sheppard Frere*,
    Gloucester: Alan Sutton 1983, 290–301 (defences Saxon, not
    Roman)
C J YOUNG, *Excavations at Carisbrooke Castle, Isle of Wight,
    1921–1996* [Wessex Archaeology Report 18], Salisbury: Wessex
    Archaeology 2000, 10–19

Portchester
**S E RIGOLD, *Portchester Castle, Hampshire*, HMSO 1965
    (guidebook)
B CUNLIFFE, *Excavations at Portchester Castle, Vol I: Roman*, Society
    of Antiquaries 1975
A KING, in V A MAXFIELD & M J DOBSON, *Roman Frontier Studies 1989*,
    Exeter: University of Exeter Press, 108–10 (Bitterne)

Chapter 3

General
K BRANIGAN & P H FOWLER, *The Roman West Country*, Newton Abbot:
    David & Charles 1976
*K BRANIGAN, *The Roman Villa in South-West England*, Bradford-on-
    Avon: Moonraker 1976
RCHM *Gloucestershire I*, HMSO 1976, especially xxxiv–li
*A MCWHIRR, *Roman Gloucestershire*, Gloucester: Alan Sutton 1981
**M HEBDITCH & L GRINSELL, *Roman Sites in the Mendips, Cotswolds,
    Wye Valley and Bristol Region*, Bristol: Bristol Archaeological
    Research Group 1968

M HENIG & P BOOTH, *Roman Oxfordshire*, Stroud: Sutton Publishing 2000

Charterhouse
**J CAMPBELL, D ELKINGTON, P FOWLER & L GRINSELL, *The Mendip Hills in Prehistoric and Roman Times*, Bristol: Bristol Archaeological Research Group 1970
BRANIGAN & FOWLER, *op. cit.* (see General), 183–97
Proceedings of the University of Bristol Speleological Society xiii (1974), 327–47
Britannia xiii (1982), 113–23
Somerset Archaeology and Natural History 137 (1993), 59–67; 138 (1994), 75–9

Bath
**Ordnance Survey Historical Map and Guide: Roman and medieval Bath*, HMSO 1989
**B CUNLIFFE, *The Roman Baths: a view over 2000 years*, Bath: Bath Archaeological Trust 1993
*B CUNLIFFE, *Roman Bath Discovered*, 4th edn, Stroud: Tempus 2000
B CUNLIFFE, *Roman Bath*, Society of Antiquaries Research Report 1969
B CUNLIFFE & P DAVENPORT, *The Temple of Sulis Minerva at Bath*, 2 vols., Oxford University Committee for Archaeology 1988
Britannia vii (1976), 1–32 (western baths); x (1979), 101–7 (temple); xii (1981), 357 (defences); xxiv (1993), 254–5 (status); xxvii (1996), 358–60 (pediment head as Typheus)
M HENIG, in G R TSETSKHLADZE, A M SNODGRASS & A J N W PRAG (eds.), *Periplous: to Sir John Boardman from his pupils and friends*, Thames & Hudson 1999, 172–85 (temple dedicated by Togidubnus?)
OJA 18 (1999), 419–25 (star on pediment)

Gloucester
BRANIGAN & FOWLER, *op. cit.* (see General), 63–80
*C HEIGHWAY, *Gloucester: a history and guide*, Stroud: Alan Sutton 1985, 1–17
C HEIGHWAY, *The East and North Gates of Gloucester*, Bristol: Western Archaeological Trust 1983
**C HEIGHWAY, *The East Gate of Gloucester*, Gloucester: Gloucester City Museums and Gloucester Civic Trust 1980
H R HURST, *Kingsholm*, Cambridge: Gloucester Archaeological Publications 1985
H R HURST, *Gloucester: the Roman and later defences* (Gloucester Archaeological Report 2), Gloucester: Gloucester Archaeological Publications 1986

**J F RHODES, *Catalogue of Romano-British Sculptures in the Gloucester City Museum*, Gloucester: Gloucester City Museums 1964

TBGAS lxxxvi (1967), 5–15; xciii (1974), 15–100

Glevensis xiv (1980), 4–12

AntiqJ lv (1975), 338–45 (Bon Marché head)

Britannia vi (1975), 272–3; xvii (1986), 414, 429; xxi (1990), 345–6

Cirencester

N HOLBROOK, in T DARVILL & C GERRARD (eds.), *Cirencester: town and landscape*, Cirencester: Cotswold Archaeological Trust 1994, 57–86

J WACHER & A MCWHIRR, *Early Roman Occupation at Cirencester*, Cirencester: Cirencester Excavation Committee 1982

A MCWHIRR, L VINER & C WELLS, *Romano-British Cemeteries at Cirencester*, Cirencester: Cirencester Excavation Committee 1982

A MCWHIRR, *Houses in Roman Cirencester*, Cirencester: Cirencester Excavation Committee 1986

N HOLBROOK (ed.), *Cirencester Excavations V: Cirencester, the Roman town defences, public buildings and shops*, Cirencester: Cirencester Excavation Committee 1998

***Corinium Museum Cirencester, Exhibition Guide*, Cirencester: Cirencester Museum 1980

**D J VINER, *The Corinium Trail*, Cirencester: Cirencester Museum 1980

AntiqJ liii (1973), 191–218

TBGAS cvi (1988), 204–7 (quarry)

D S NEAL & S R COSH, in J R TIMBY, *Excavations at Kingscote and Wycomb, Gloucestershire*, Cirencester: Cotswold Archaeological Trust 1998, 77–9 (Kingscote mosaics)

RIB I, 103 (Jupiter inscription); II, 2447.20 (word square)

Sea Mills

TBGAS cv (1987), 15–108

King's Weston

**G C BOON, *King's Weston Roman Villa*, Bristol: Department of Archaeology, City Museum 1967 (guidebook)

TBGAS lxix (1950), 5–58; cxi (1993), 77–83

Bristol and Avon Archaeology 13 (1996), 47–51 (restoration)

Wadfield

JBAA i (1895), 242–50

TBGAS xc (1971), 124–8

RCHM, *Gloucestershire I* (see General), 121–3

Great Witcombe

D NEAL, in M R APTED, R GILYARD-BEER & A D SAUNDERS (eds.), *Ancient Monuments and their Interpretation*, Chichester: Phillimore 1977, 27–40

P LEACH, *Great Witcombe Roman Villa, Gloucestershire. A report on excavations by Ernest Greenfield, 1960–73* [BAR British Series 266], Oxford: Archaeopress 1998

Chedworth

*R GOODBURN, *The Roman Villa, Chedworth,* National Trust 1972, rev. edn 1981

TBGAS lxxviii (1959), 5–23

TBGAS ci (1983), 5–20 ('cult centre')

RCHM, *Gloucestershire I* (see General), 24–8

ARA: Bulletin of the Association for Roman Archaeology 9 (Summer 2000), 10–15 ('cult-centre' and new mosaics)

Britannia x (1979), 318–19; xvi (1985), 298; xviii (1987), 337–9; xix (1988), 465; xx (1989), 309–10; xxii (1991), 274; xxv (1994), 285; xxix (1998), 416–17; xxxii (2001), 369

Woodchester

RCHM, *Gloucestershire I* (see General), 132–4

Britannia xiii (1982), 197–228

**D J SMITH, *The Great Pavement and Roman Villa at Woodchester. Gloucestershire*, Woodchester: Woodchester Pavement Committee 1973

**J CULL, *Roman Woodchester: its villa and mosaic*, Andover: Pitkin Unichrome 2000

North Leigh

**D R WILSON & D SHERLOCK, *North Leigh Roman Villa, Oxfordshire* [EH Guide], HMSO 1980

Britannia xxx (1999), 199–245

Lydney

T V & R E M WHEELER, *The Prehistoric, Roman and Post-Roman Remains in Lydney Park*, Society of Antiquaries 1932

AntiqJ lxxix (1999), 81–143

RIB I, 305 (Blandinus); II, 2446.9 (oculist's stamp)

Littledean

Britannia xvi (1985), 299–300; xvii (1986), 410

Blackpool Bridge

*I D MARGARY, *Roman Roads in Britain*, Baker 1973, 332–3

*A W TROTTER, *The Dean Road*, Gloucester: Bellows 1936

*G SINDREY, *Roman Dean: the Forest of Dean in the Roman period*,
Lydney: Dean Archaeological Group 1990

Swainshill
Britannia xxiii (1992), 283–4; xxvii (1996), 418
ARA: Bulletin of the Association for Roman Archaeology 5 (Spring
1998), 5–6

Chapter 4

General
*R DUNNETT, *The Trinovantes*, Duckworth 1975
*K BRANIGAN, *The Catuvellauni*, Gloucester: Alan Sutton 1985
*R NIBLETT, *Roman Hertfordshire*, Stanbridge near Wimborne:
Dovecote Press 1995
*O BEDWIN (ed.), *The Archaeology of Essex*, Chelmsford: Essex
County Council 1996, 69–107
*S MARGESON, B AYERS & S HEYWOOD (eds.), *A Festival of Norfolk
Archaeology*, Norwich: Norfolk and Norwich Archaeological
Society 1996, 21–39
*I E MOORE with J PLOUVIEZ & S WEST, *The Archaeology of Roman
Suffolk*, Ipswich: Suffolk County Council 1988

Colchester
*P CRUMMY, *City of Victory*, Colchester: Colchester Archaeological
Trust 1997
**P CRUMMY, *In Search of Colchester's Past*, 2nd edn, Colchester:
Colchester Archaeological Trust 1984
**P CRUMMY, *Secrets of the Grave: the excavation of a Roman church
and two cemeteries in Colchester*, Colchester: Colchester
Archaeological Trust and Essex County Council, n.d. [*c.* 1990]
P CRUMMY, *Excavations at Lion Walk, Balkerne Lane, and
Middlesborough, Colchester, Essex* [Colchester Archaeological
Reports 3], Colchester: Colchester Archaeological Trust 1984
N & P CRUMMY & C CROSSAN, *Excavations of Roman and Later
Cemeteries, Churches and Monastic Sites in Colchester, 1971–88*
[Colchester Archaeological Reports 9], Colchester: Colchester
Archaeological Trust 1993
C F C HAWKES & P CRUMMY, *Camolodunum 2* [Colchester
Archaeological Reports 11], Colchester: Colchester Archaeological
Trust 1995
J FOSTER, *The Lexden Tumulus: a re-appraisal of an Iron Age burial
from Colchester, Essex* [BAR British Series 156], Oxford: BAR
1986
Britannia ii (1971), 27–47 (Gosbecks theatre); xxiv (1993), 1–6
(Temple of Claudius pre–54?); xxvi (1995), 11–27 (Temple of

Claudius post–54); xxviii (1997), 432–4; xxix (1998), 406–8
(Gosbecks, Stanway); xxx (1999), 57–89 ('child's' grave); *ibid.*
354 (Gosbecks, Stanway); xxxii (2001), 361–3 (general); *ibid.* 364
(Gosbecks)

CA 120 (June 1990), 406–8 (church); 132 (January 1993), 492–7
(Stanway)

ARA: Bulletin of the Association for Roman Archaeology 1 (Spring
1996), 6–7 (Gosbecks)

ArchJ clii (1995), 451–4 (arguing against church)

RIB II, 2503.119 (Memnon and Valentinus)

St Albans

**R NIBLETT, *Roman Verulamium*, St Albans: St Albans District
Council 2000

**K M KENYON & S S FRERE, *The Roman Theatre of Verulamium and
Adjacent Buildings*, n.d.

*R NIBLETT, *Verulamium. The Roman City of St Albans*, Stroud:
Tempus 2001

M HENIG & P LINDLEY, Alban and St Albans: Roman and medieval
architecture, art and archaeology [British Archaeological
Association Conference Transactions XXIV], Leeds: Maney 2001,
1–29

S S FRERE, *Verulamium Excavations* I, Society of Antiquaries 1972

S S FRERE, *Verulamium Excavations* II, Society of Antiquaries 1983

S S FRERE ET AL., *Verulamium Excavations* III, Oxford: Oxford
University Committee for Archaeology 1984

R NIBLETT, *The Excavation of a Ceremonial Site at Folly Lane,
Verulamium* [Britannia Monographs 14], Society for Promotion of
Roman Studies 1999

CA 101 (August 1986), 178–83; 130 (August 1992), 412–13 (both
Abbey); 132 (January 1993), 484–8 (Folly Lane)

Caistor St Edmund

Britannia ii (1971), 1–26 (public buildings); xx (1989), 300–1
(walls); xxvii (1996), 422 (amphitheatre)

J N L MYRES & B GREEN, *The Anglo-Saxon Cemeteries of Caistor by
Norwich and Markshall, Norfolk*, Society of Antiquaries 1973,
12–34

Caister-on-Sea

M J DARLING & D GURNEY, *Caister-on-Sea: excavations by Charles
Green 1951–5* [East Anglian Archaeology 60], Dereham: Norfolk
Museums Service 1993

Burgh Castle
**EH *Guide*, HMSO 1978
S JOHNSON, *Burgh Castle, Excavations by Charles Green 1958–61*
   [East Anglian Archaeology 20], Dereham: Norfolk Archaeological
   Unit 1983
Britannia xxvii (1996), 421–2

Car Dyke
AntiqJ xxix (1948), 145–63
Britannia x (1979), 183–96; xxix (1998), 402
Durobrivae vi (1978), 24–5

Welwyn
Hertfordshire Archaeology 9 (1983–6), 79–175

Bancroft
**B ZEEPVAT, *Roman Milton Keynes*, Milton Keynes: Milton Keynes
   Archaeology Unit & Aylesbury: Buckinghamshire County Council
   1991
R J WILLIAMS & R J ZEEPVAT, *Bancroft. A Late Bronze Age/Iron Age
   Settlement, Roman Villa and Temple-Mausoleum* [Buckinghamshire
   Archaeological Society Monograph Series 7], 2 vols., Aylesbury:
   Buckinghamshire Archaeological Society 1994

Harpenden
St Albans Architectural and Archaeological Society v (1937), 108–14
JBAA xxii (1959), 22–3
JRS xxviii (1938), 186 (summary and plan)

Mersea
VCH, *Essex* iii (1963), 159–61

Thornborough
Record of Buckinghamshire xvi (1953–60), 29–32; xx (1975), 3–56

Stevenage
Antiquity x (1963), 39

Bartlow
VCH, *Essex* iii (1963), 39–43

Chapter 5

General
*M TODD, *The Coritani*, new edn, Stroud: Alan Sutton 1991
J B WHITWELL, *The Coritani: some aspects of the Iron Age tribe and
   the Roman* civitas [BAR British Series 99], Oxford: BAR 1982

*J B WHITWELL, *Roman Lincolnshire* [History of Lincolnshire II], 2nd edn, Lincoln: History of Lincolnshire Committee 1992

*G WEBSTER, *The Cornovii*, new edn, Stroud: Alan Sutton 1991

P BOOTH, 'Warwickshire in the Roman period: a review of recent work', *Transactions of the Birmingham and Warwickshire Archaeological Society* c (1996), 25–57

R S O TOMLIN, *Transactions of the Leicestershire Archaeological and Historical Society* lviii (1982–3), 1–5 (for the name Corieltauvi rather than Coritani)

Baginton

Transactions of the Birmingham and Warwickshire Archaeological Society lxxxiii (1966–7), 65–129; lxxxv (1973), 7–92; lxxxvii (1975), 1–56

CA 4 (September 1967), 86–9; 24 (January 1971), 16–21; 28 (September 1971), 127–30; 44 (May 1974), 271–80; 63 (September 1978), 123–5

B HOBLEY, in P BIDWELL, R MIKET & B FORD (eds.), Portae cum turribus: *studies of Roman fort gates* [BAR British Series 206], Oxford: BAR 1988, 25–61

Echos du monde classique 8 (1989), 255–62 (recent work on west defences)

Britannia xxii (1991), 250; xxiii (1992), 284 (west defences)

Melandra Castle

R S CONWAY (ed.), *Melandra Castle*, Manchester: Manchester University Press 1906

Derbyshire Archaeological Journal lxxxiii (1963), 3–9 (fort); xci (1971), 57–118 (civilian settlement)

Britannia v (1974), 420; vi (1975), 244; vii (1976), 322–3; viii (1977), 387–8; ix (1978), 432; xvi (1985), 283; xx (1989), 286; xxii (1991), 245; xxvi (1995), 350; xxx (1999), 344 (baths)

Lincoln

WHITWELL, *op. cit.* (see General, first work cited), ch. 3

*M J JONES, *Lincoln. History and Guide*, Stroud: Alan Sutton 1993, 1–9

M J JONES ET AL., *The Defences of the Upper Roman Enclosure* [Archaeology of Lincoln 7/1], CBA 1980

C COLYER, B J J GILMOUR & M J JONES, *The Defences of the Lower City* [Archaeology of Lincoln 7/2], York: CBA 1999

M J JONES, in K PAINTER (ed.), *Churches Built in Ancient Times: recent studies in early Christian archaeology*, Society of Antiquaries 1994, 325–47 (early churches)

CA 26 (May 1971), 67–71; 83 (August 1982), 366–71; 129 (May/
    June 1992), 364–7, 376–9
AntiqJ lv (1975), 227–45; lix (1979), 84–7 (Saltergate)
Britannia v (1974), 422–4; vi (1975), 245; xi (1980), 61–72 (forum);
    xvi (1985), 284 (well); xxix (1998), 359–63 (St Peter-at-Gowts)
RIB I, 262 (tombstone)

Wroxeter
**R WHITE, *Wroxeter Roman City, Shropshire*, EH 1999 (guidebook)
*R WHITE & P BARKER, *Wroxeter: life and death of a Roman city*,
    Stroud: Tempus 1998
P BARKER *ET AL.*, *The Baths Basilica Wroxeter. Excavations 1966–90*
    [EH Archaeological Report 8], EH 1997
P ELLIS (ed.), *The Roman Baths and* Macellum *at Wroxeter:
    excavations by Graham Webster 1955–85* [EH Archaeological
    Report 9], EH 2000
AntiqJ xlvi (1966), 229–39 ('Old Work')
CA 157 (May 1998), 8–14 (geophysical survey)
RIB I, 288 (forum inscription)
AntJ xlviii (1968), 296–300 (Cunorix)

Leicester
K M KENYON, *Excavations at the Jewry Wall Site, Leicester*, Society of
    Antiquaries 1948
R BUCKLEY, J LUCAS *ET AL.*, *Leicester Town Defences: excavations
    1958–74* [Leicester Museums Publications 85], Leicester: Leicester
    Museums 1987
*Transactions of the Leicestershire Archaeological and Historical
    Society* xliv (1968–69), 1–10
**E BLANK, *A Guide to Leicestershire Archaeology*, Leicester:
    Leicester Museums 1970, 16–22
RIB II. 2491.3 and 150 (graffiti on tiles)

Water Newton
**J P WILD, *Romans in the Nene Valley*, Peterborough: Nene Valley
    Research Committee 1972
ArchJ cxxxi (1974), 140–70
Britannia xxxi (2000), 411

Orton Longueville
Durobrivae i (1973), 20–1; ii (1974), 4
Britannia vi (1975), 252
Northamptonshire Archaeology x (1975), 94–137

Wall

**P ELLIS, *Wall Roman Site, Staffordshire*, EH 1999 (guidebook)

J GOULD, *Letocetum. The rise and decline of a Roman posting station*, Walsall: privately printed by the author, 1998

Transactions of the Lichfield and South Staffordshire Archaeological and Historical Society v (1963–4), 1–47; viii (1966–7), 1–38; xi (1969–70), 7–31; xv (1973–4), 13–28; xxi (1979–80), 1–14

Britannia iii (1972), 316; vi (1975), 247; vii (1976), 328; viii (1977), 392; ix (1978), 435–6; xxviii (1997), 350–2; xxx (1999), 185–90

Great Casterton

P CORDER (ed.), *The Roman Town and Villa at Great Casterton*, Nottingham: University of Nottingham, 3 reports, 1951, 1954 and 1961

M TODD (ed.), *The Roman Fort at Great Casterton*, Nottingham: University of Nottingham 1968

Ancaster

M TODD, *The Roman Town at Ancaster: the excavations of 1955–1971*, Nottingham and Exeter: Universities of Nottingham and Exeter 1981

Britannia xxxii (2001), 297–9

Horncastle

Lincolnshire History and Archaeology xviii (1983), 47–88

Archaeology in Lincolnshire 1984–5, 56–8

Chapter 6

General

E NASH-WILLIAMS, *The Roman Frontier in Wales*, 2nd edn, revised by M G JARRETT, Cardiff: University of Wales 1969

*C J ARNOLD & J L DAVIES, *Roman and Early Medieval Wales*, Stroud: Sutton Publishing 2000

*W MANNING, *A Pocket Guide: Roman Wales*, Cardiff: University of Wales Press and Western Mail 2001

B C BURNHAM & J L DAVIES (eds.), *Conquest, Co-existence and Change: recent work in Roman Wales* [Trivium 25], Lampeter: St David's University College 1990

G SIMPSON, *Britons and the Roman Army*, Aldershot: Gregg 1964

E WADDELOVE, *Roman Roads of North Wales*, privately published by the author 1999

R W DAVIES, 'Roman Wales and Roman military practice camps', *ArchCamb* cxvii (1968), 103–18

Caerleon

**J K KNIGHT, *Caerleon Roman Fortress*, rev. edn, Cardiff: Cadw
    1994 (guidebook)

**R J BREWER, *Caerleon and the Roman Army. Roman Legionary
    Museum: a guide*, 2nd. edn, Cardiff: National Museum and
    Galleries of Wales 2000

**J D ZIENKIEWICZ, *Roman Gems from Caerleon*, Caerleon: Roman
    Legionary Museum 1987

*G C BOON, *The Legionary Fortress of Caerleon – Isca: a brief
    account*, Caerleon: Roman Legionary Museum 1987

J D ZIENKIEWICZ, *The Legionary Fortress Baths at Caerleon*, 2 vols.,
    Cardiff: National Museum of Wales and Cadw 1986

E EVANS *ET AL.*, *The Caerleon Canabae: excavations in the civil
    settlement* [Britannia Monographs 16], Society for Promotion of
    Roman Studies 2000

Britannia xxiv (1993), 27–140 (excavations beneath museum
    extension); xxv (1994), 250–1 (location of 'pipe' burial); xxv
    (1994), 310–12 (amphora *dipinto*)

RIB I, 316 (Diana), 322 (Mithras), 323 (curse-tablet), 331 (AD
    99/100), 334 (new barracks), 369 (Exuperatus)

Chester

**T J STRICKLAND, *Roman Chester*, Chester: Chester City Council
    1984

*P CARRINGTON (ed.), *English Heritage Book of Chester*, Batsford
    1994, 24–49

*D J P MASON, *Roman Chester: city of the eagles*, Stroud: Tempus
    2001

D F PETCH, in VCH, *History of Cheshire*, vol. I, University of London
    1987, 117–85

T J STRICKLAND & P J DAVEY, *New Evidence for Roman Chester*,
    Liverpool: University of Liverpool 1978

C LEQUESNE, *Excavations at Chester: the Roman and later Defences,
    Part 1*, Chester: Chester City Council 1999

Britannia xxvi (1995), 387–8 (inscribed tile); xxxii (2001), 347
    (amphitheatre)

Archaeologia cv (1976), 127–239 (amphitheatre)

CA 167 (March 2000), 405–13 ('elliptical' building)

Brecon Gaer

**Y *Gaer: Brecon Roman fort*, Terfyn, Glanwern: Atelier Productions
    1994 (guidebook)

ArchCamb cxx (1971), 91–101

RCAHM (Wales) *Brecknock: hill forts and Roman remains*, HMSO
    1986, 135–46

Gelligaer
**R J BREWER, *Gelligaer Roman fort*, Cardiff: National Museum of
　　Wales n.d. [*c.* 1980]
RCHM *Glamorgan* I.2, Cardiff: HMSO 1976, 95–8, 103
Britannia xxiv (1993), 249–54 (timber predecessor?)
RIB I, 397/8 (Trajanic building inscriptions)

Neath
RCHM *Glamorgan* I.2, Cardiff: HMSO 1976, 88–90
BBCS 39 (1992), 171–298
Britannia xv (1984), 269; xvi (1985), 256; xx (1989), 263; xxi
　　(1990), 306–7 (with plan); xxii (1991), 203–7, 210–11; xxiv
　　(1993), 247–9; xxv (1994), 250; xxvi (1995), 329; xxviii (1997),
　　401

Castell Collen
Studia Celtica 33 (1999), 33–90 (*vicus*)
RIB I, 414; *Britannia* xxxii (2001), 275–8 (Trajanic building
　　inscription?)
ArchCamb cxviii (1969), 124–34 (practice camps); cf. *Britannia* xxix
　　(1998), 341–53 (for the Chester group)

Y Pigwn
BBCS xxiii (1968–70), 100–3
RCAHM (Wales) *Brecknock* (see Brecon Gaer), 150–3
Britannia xxix (1998), 366–7 (practice camps)

Dolaucothi
**G B D JONES & P R LEWIS, *The Roman Gold Mines at Dolaucothi*,
　　Carmarthen: Carmarthen County Museum 1971
A E ANNELS & B C BURNHAM, *The Dolaucothi Gold Mines: geology
　　and mining history*, 2nd edn, Lampeter and Cardiff: University of
　　Wales 1986
AntiqJ xlix (1969), 244–72
Bonner Jahrbücher clxxi (1971), 288–300
Carmarthenshire Antiquary ix (1973), 3–27; x (1974), 3–16 (fort)
BBCS xix (1960), 71–84 (Cothi aqueduct); xxxi (1984), 304–13
Britannia xxi (1990), 304–6; xxii (1991), 203–7; *ibid.* 210–11; xxiv
　　(1993), 247–9; xxv (1994), 248 (Annell aqueduct); xxviii (1997),
　　325–36 (Carreg Pumsaint and mill); xxix (1998), 367; xxxi (2000),
　　372–3 (both on civilian settlement)
CA 119 (March 1990), 395–7 (fort)

Tomen-y-Mur
*P CREW & C MUSSON, *Snowdonia from the Air*, Penrhyndeudraeth:
　　Snowdonia National Park Authority and Aberystwyth: Royal

Commission on the Ancient Historical Monuments of Wales 1996, 26–8 and 30

ARNOLD & DAVIES, *op. cit.* (see General), 22, fig. 2.6

JRS lix (1969), 126–7 (Braich-ddu)

BBCS xviii (1958–60), 397–402 (Doldinnas)

Britannia xxviii (1997), 398–9 (Llyn Hiraethlyn)

Caerhun

Transactions of the Caernarvonshire Historical Society xxxv (1974), 7–13

Prestatyn

Britannia xvi (1985), 252–3; xvii (1986), 364

K BLOCKLEY, *Prestatyn 1984–5. An Iron Age Farmstead and Romano-British Industrial Settlement in North Wales* [BAR British Series 210], Oxford: BAR 1989

Caernarfon

**J L DAVIES, *Segontium Roman Fort*, Cardiff: Cadw 1990

P J CASEY & J L DAVIES, *Excavations at Segontium Roman Fort 1975–1979* [CBA Research Report 90], York: CBA 1993

RIB I, 429 (*actarius*), 430 (aqueduct), 436 (gold foil)

Caer Gybi

**L MACINNES, *Anglesey: a guide to ancient and historic sites on the Isle of Anglesey*, Cardiff: Cadw 1989 (guidebook)

Holyhead signal station

Britannia xii (1981), 314; xiii (1982), 328

Studien zu den Militärgrenzen Roms III [13. Internationaler Limeskongreß Aalen 1983], Stuttgart: Kommissionsverlag 1986, 58–9

Cardiff

RCHM *Glamorgan* I.2, Cardiff: HMSO 1976, 90–4

Morgannwg xxv (1981), 201–11 (early forts)

P V WEBSTER, in BURNHAM & DAVIES (see General), 35–9 (early forts)

Britannia x (1979), 273; xiii (1982), 331–2

Barry

Britannia xvi (1985), 57–125; xxii (1991), 225

Carmarthen

Carmarthenshire Antiquary v (1964–9), 2–5; vi (1970), 4–14, vii (1971), 58–63; xxviii (1992), 5–36

G C BOON (ed.), *Monographs and Collections relating to Excavations*

financed by HM Department of the Environment in Wales, Cardiff:
   Cambrian Archaeological Association 1978, especially 63–6
Britannia xxv (1994), 248–9

Caerwent
**R J BREWER, *Caerwent Roman Town*, 2nd edn, Cardiff: Cadw 1997
   (guidebook)
ArchCamb cxxxii (1983), 49–77 (with controversial dating of stone
   defences)
Britannia xiii (1982), 334; xiv (1983), 283–4; xv (1984), 270; xvi
   (1985), 259–60; xvii (1986), 369–70 (house and temple); xviii
   (1987), 307–9; xix (1988), 422–3; xx (1989), 264; xxi (1990),
   307–10; xxii (1991), 225–7; xxiii (1992), 258–9; xxiv (1993), 275;
   xxv (1994), 251–2; xxvi (1995), 330–1; xxvii (1996), 394–6
   (forum and basilica); xxix (1998), 370; xxx (1999), 322–3 (both,
   wall in car-park)
CA 174 (June 2001), 232–40 (1981–95 excavations)
ARA: Bulletin of the Association for Roman Archaeology 4 (1997), 12
   (wall in car-park)
RIB I, 310 (Ocelus), 311 (*civitas Silurum*)

Tre'r Ceiri
ArchJ cxvii (1960), 1–39
Britannia xxv (1994), 246

Holyhead Mountain, Caer Leb, Din Lligwy
**L MACINNES, *op. cit.* (see Caer Gybi above)
ArchCamb cxxxiii (1984), 64–82

Chapter 7

General
R M BUTLER (ed.), *Soldier and Civilian in Roman Yorkshire*, Leicester:
   Leicester University Press 1971
P R WILSON, R F J JONES & D M EVANS (eds.), *Settlement and Society in
   the Roman North*, Bradford: School of Archaeological Sciences,
   and Leeds: Yorkshire Archaeological Society 1984
*N HIGHAM, *The Northern Counties to AD 1000*, Longmans 1986,
   145–241
*H RAMM, *The Parisi*, Duckworth 1978
*N HIGHAM & G B D JONES, *The Carvetii*, Gloucester: Alan Sutton 1985
*B HARTLEY & R L FITTS, *The Brigantes*, Gloucester: Alan Sutton 1988
*D C A SHOTTER, *Romans and Britons in North-West England*,
   Lancaster: University of Lancaster 1993, new edn 1997
T WILMOTT & P WILSON (eds.), *The Late Roman Transition in the North*
   [BAR British Series 299], Oxford: Archaeopress 2000

R NEWMAN (ed.), *The Archaeology of Lancashire: present state and future priorities*, Lancaster: Lancaster University Archaeological Unit 1996, 75–9

*D SHOTTER & A WHITE, *The Romans in Lunesdale*, Lancaster: University of Lancaster, Centre for North-West Regional Studies 1995

**J H RUMSBY, *The Romans in East Yorkshire*, Derby: English Life Publications, 1980

J PRICE & P R WILSON (eds.), *Recent Research in Roman Yorkshire: studies in honour of Mary Kitson Clark* [BAR British Series 193], Oxford: BAR 1988

D A SPRATT (ed.), *Prehistoric and Roman Archaeology of North-East Yorkshire* [CBA Research Report 87], CBA 1993

I G SMITH, 'Some Roman place-names in Lancashire and Cumbria', *Britannia* xxviii (1997), 372–83 (controversial)

Roads (see also Wheeldale Moor)

*J SOUTHWORTH, *Walking the Roman Roads of Cumbria*, Robert Hale 1985

*M ALLAN, *The Roman Route Across the Northern Lake District*, Lancaster: University of Lancaster, Centre for North-West Regional Studies 1994

*P GRAYSTONE, *Walking Roman Roads in East Cumbria*, Lancaster: University of Lancaster, Centre for North-West Regional Studies 1994

*P GRAYSTONE, *Walking Roman Roads in the Fylde and the Ribble Valley*, Lancaster: University of Lancaster, Centre for North-West Regional Studies 1996

York

**Ordnance Survey Historical Map and Guide: Roman and Anglian York*, York: York Archaeological Trust and London: HMSO 1988

RCHM, *Roman York: Eburacum*, HMSO 1962

R M BUTLER (ed.), *op. cit.* (see General), 16–17, 45–53, 97–106, 179–92

P V ADDYMAN & V E BLACK (eds.), *Archaeological Papers from York Presented to M W Barley*, York: York Archaeological Trust 1984, 28–42

*P OTTAWAY, *The English Heritage Book of Roman York*, Batsford 1993

**J TOY, *York Minster: the story of the Foundations*, York: Dean and Chapter of York 1993

D PHILLIPS & B HEYWOOD, *Excavations at York Minster I: from Roman fortress to Norman cathedral*, Swindon: RCHME 1995

P OTTAWAY, *Excavations and Observations on the Defences and*

Adjacent Sites, 1971–90 [The Archaeology of York 3.3], York: CBA 1996

A B SUMPTER & S COLL, *Interval Tower SW5 and the SW Defences*, [Archaeology of York 3.2], CBA 1977, 57–95

*L ALLASON-JONES, *Roman Jet in the Yorkshire Museum*, York: The Yorkshire Museum 1996

RIB I, 665 (King's Square); 662–3 (Demetrios); 668 (inscription *in situ* at east angle); 712 (*aureficina*); 687 (Fortunata); 658 (Serapis); 721 (Ravenscar); *RIB* II, 2441.11 (bone plaque)

Stanwick

R E M WHEELER, *The Stanwick Fortifications, North Riding of Yorkshire* [Society of Antiquaries Research Report 17], Society of Antiquaries 1954

Britannia xvii (1986), 73–89; xx (1989), 277–8; xxi (1990), 324–5

Cawthorn

ArchJ lxxxix (1932), 17–78; cliv (1997), 260–7

Ryedale History 19 (1998–9), 6–13; 20 (2000–1), 5–8

Britannia xxxi (2000), 395; xxxii (2001), 339–40

Wheeldale Moor

*R H HAYES & J G RUTTER, *Wade's Causeway*, Scarborough: Scarborough & District Archaeological Society 1964

Malton

**L P WENHAM, *Derventio (Malton)*, Cameo Books 1974

Yorkshire Archaeological Journal 72 (2000), 7–15 (*vicus* house wall-plaster) Huddersfield: Cameo Books 1974

Castleshaw

F A BRUTON, *Excavation of the Roman Forts at Castleshaw. First and second interim reports*, Manchester: University Press 1908 and 1911

J WALKER (ed.), *Castleshaw: the archaeology of a Roman fortlet* [The Archaeology of Greater Manchester 4], Manchester: Greater Manchester Archaeological Unit 1989

Britannia xx (1989), 280–2; xxvii (1996), 413

CA 114 (April 1989), 235–9

Manchester

F A BRUTON (ed.), *The Roman Fort at Manchester*, Manchester: University Press 1909

G B D JONES & S GREALEY, *Roman Manchester*, Altrincham: Sherratt for Manchester Excavation Committee 1974

S BRYANT, M MORRIS & J S F WALKER, *Roman Manchester: a frontier settlement*, Manchester: Greater Manchester Archaeological Unit 1986

J WALKER, in P BIDWELL *ET AL.* (ed.), Portae cum turribus. *Studies in Roman fort gates* [BAR British Series 206], Oxford: BAR 1989, 83–111

Ilkley

**B R HARTLEY, *Roman Ilkley*, Ilkley: Ilkley Urban District Council 1987

Proceedings of the Leeds Philosophical & Literary Society xii (1966), 23–72

Britannia xiv (1983), 337; xxx (1999), 342

RIB I, 639 (Cornovian)

Blackstone Edge

I D MARGARY, *Roman Roads in Britain*, Baker 1973, 404 (assumed to be Roman)

Ribchester

*B J N EDWARDS, *The Romans at Ribchester: discovery and excavations*, Lancaster: University of Lancaster, Centre for North-West Regional Studies 2000

**B J N EDWARDS, *The Ribchester Hoard*, Preston: Lancashire County Books 1992

B J N EDWARDS & P V WEBSTER, *Ribchester Excavations. Parts 1–3*, Cardiff: University College Cardiff Department of Extramural Studies 1985–8

K BUXTON & C HOWARD-DAVIS, *Excavations at Roman Ribchetser 1980, 1989–90*, Lancaster: Lancaster University Archaeological Unit 2000

ArchJ cxxvii (1970), 277–9

Britannia xii (1981), 331; xxxi (2000), 399; xxxii (2001), 346

RIB I, 583 (Apollo Maponus), 587 (*templum*), 590 (Caracalla and Julia Domna)

Piercebridge

**P SCOTT, *Guide to the Visible Remains of Roman Piercebridge*, Durham: published by the author 1977

Transactions of the Archaeological Society of Durham and Northumberland vii (1936), 235–77; ix (1939–41), 43–68; (new series) i (1968), 27–44; vi (1982), 77–82

CA 40 (September 1973), 136–41

Britannia vi (1975), 234–5; x (1979), 285; xi (1980), 362 (all fort); xxx (1999), 111–32 (bridge)

Binchester

R E HOOPELL, *Vinovia, a Buried Roman City*, Whiting and Co. 1891

Transactions of the Archaeological Society of Durham and Northumberland xi (1958), 115–24; *ibid* (new series) ii (1970), 33–7

Britannia viii (1977), 379; ix (1978), 425–6; x (1979), 284; xi (1980), 361; xviii (1987), 318; xx (1989), 277; xxii (1991), 238; xxiii (1992), 314

R JONES, in W S HANSON & L J F KEPPIE (eds.), *Roman Frontier Studies 1979*, Oxford: BAR 1980, 233–54

I FERRIS & R JONES, in WILMOTT & WILSON, op. cit. (see General), 1–11

Lanchester

ArchJ cxi (1954), 220–1; cxlix (1992), 69–81 (geophysical survey)

Proceedings of the Society of Antiquaries of Newcastle upon Tyne, 4th series, iii (1927), 101–4

AA[5] 18 (1990), 63–77 (cemetery)

HARDING (ed.), *op. cit.* (see General), 214–16 (aqueducts)

RIB I, 1074 (Garmangabis), 1091–2 (AD 238/44)

Ebchester

AA xxxviii (1960), 193–229; xlii (1964), 173–85; *ibid.* (new series) iii (1975), 43–104

Britannia xvii (1986), 438

Arbeia Journal 1 (1992), 13–22

RIB I, 1101 (Breuci)

Greta Bridge

Britannia xxix (1998), 111–83

RIB I, 746 (AD 205/8)

Bowes

JRS lviii (1968), 179–81

Britannia ii (1971), 251 (fort); xix (1988), 491 (Scargill Moor); xx (1989), 277 (fort)

Yorkshire Archaeological Journal xlv (1973), 181–4 (aqueduct); xxxvi (1946), 383–6; xxxvii (1948), 107–16 (Scargill Moor)

Epigraphica 52 (1990), 63–76 (Scargill Moor)

RIB I, 730 (burnt bath-house), 732–3 (Scargill Moor), 740–1 (Bowes church)

Bowes Moor

I A RICHMOND, in W F GRIMES (ed.), *Aspects of Archaeology in Britain and Beyond*, Edwards 1951, 293–302

R A H FARRAR, in HANSON & KEPPIE, *op. cit.* (see Binchester), 211–31, at 220–4

D ROBINSON, *Archaeology on the Stainmore Pass: the result of archaeological investigations carried on in advance of the improvement of the A66 Trans-Pennine road*, Durham: Durham County Council/Barnard Castle: Bowes Museum 1993
CA 122 (November 1990), 62–6

Rey Cross
CW xxxiv (1934), 50–61

Maiden Castle
CW xxvii (1927), 170–7

Brough
CW lviii (1958), 31–56; lxxvii (1977), 14–47; *RIB* I, 757–8 (Brough Church)

Temple Sowerby
SEDGLEY, *op. cit.* (see Archaeology of Roman Britain: Roads), no. 79

Brougham
RCHM, *Westmorland*, HMSO 1936, 54
RIB I, 784–5 (tombstones)

Whitley Castle
S S FRERE & J K ST JOSEPH, *Roman Britain from the Air*, Cambridge: Cambridge University Press 1983, 119–20
Proc. Soc. Antiq. Newcastle i (1924), 249–55
AA[4] xxxvii (1959), 191–202
RIB I, 1198 (Nervii)

Troutbeck
CW lvi (1956), 28–36
H WELFARE & V SWAN, *Roman Camps in England: the field archaeology*, HMSO 1995, 44–50

Old Carlisle
CW li (1951), 16–39
ArchJ cxxxii (1975), 18, 24–5
RIB I, 893 and 905 (*ala Augusta*), 899 (*vikani*)

Maryport
M G JARRETT, *Maryport, a Roman Fort and its Garrison* [CW extra series], Kendal: Titus Wilson 1976
R J A WILSON (ed.), *Roman Maryport and its Setting*, Kendal: Trustees of the Senhouse Roman Museum 1997
****The Senhouse Roman Museum, Maryport: a guide to the Netherhall Collection*, Maryport: Senhouse Roman Museum 1999

Britannia xxxi (2000), 23–8; xxxii (2001), 337–9 (geophysics)
RIB I, 808–79 (inscriptions)

Swarthy Hill
CW^2 xcviii (1998), 61–106

Ravenglass
T W POTTER, *Romans in North West England* [Cumberland and
    Westmorland Research Series I] Kendal 1979, 1–138, especially
    48–50
CW lxxxv (1985), 81–5 (baths)
Bulletin of the John Rylands University Library 79 (1997), 3–41
    (diploma)

Hardknott
**D CHARLESWORTH, *Hardknott Roman Fort, Cumberland*, HMSO
    1972 (guide pamphlet)
**T GARLICK, *Hardknott Castle Roman Fort*, Dalesman: Clapham via
    Lancaster 1985
P BIDWELL, M SNAPE & A CROOM, *Hardknott Roman Fort, Cumbria*
    [CW Research Series 9], Kendal 1999

Ambleside
RCHM, *Westmorland*, HMSO 1936, 1–3
**T GARLICK, *Ambleside Roman Fort*, Clapham via Lancaster:
    Dalesman 1975
CW xciii (1993), 51–74 (*vicus*)
Britannia xxi (1990), 320; xxii (1991), 235 (granary); xxv (1994),
    261 (*vicus*)

Middleton
RIB I, 2283

Lancaster
G M LEATHER, *Lancaster Roman Bath House*, Lancaster: 'Contrebis'
    monograph 1979
*D SHOTTER & A WHITE, *The Roman Fort and Town of Lancaster*,
    Lancaster: University of Lancaster, Centre for North-West
    Regional Studies 1990
G B D JONES & D C A SHOTTER, *Roman Lancaster. Rescue Archaeology
    1970–5* [Brigantia Monographs 1], Manchester: University of
    Manchester 1992
Britannia xix (1988), 441–4

Aldborough
**C DOBINSON, *Aldborough Roman Town, North Yorkshire*, EH 1995
    (guidebook)
BUTLER (ed.), *op. cit.* (see General), 155–63
M C BISHOP, *Finds from Roman Aldborough* [Oxbow Monographs 65],
    Oxford: Oxbow 1996

Hull
**D J SMITH, *The Roman Mosaics from Rudston, Brantingham and
    Horkstow*, Hull: Hull Museums and Art Gallery 1976
I M STEAD, *Rudston Roman Villa*, Leeds: Yorkshire Archaeological
    Society 1980
RIB I, 707 (Brough-on-Humber theatre)

Beadlam
D S NEAL, *Excavations on the Roman Villa at Beadlam, Yorkshire*
    [Yorkshire Archaeological Report 2], Leeds: Yorkshire
    Archaeological Society 1996

Grassington
Antiquity ii (1928), 168–72

Ewe Close
CW xxxiii (1933), 201–26

Signal stations
**R G COLLINGWOOD, *The Roman Signal Station on Castle Hill*,
    Scarborough: Corporation of Scarborough 1925
**P OTTAWAY, *Romans on the Yorkshire Coast*, York: York
    Archaeological Trust, n.d. [*c.* 1995]
P OTTAWAY, in W GROENMAN-VAN WAATERINGE *ET AL.* (eds.), *Roman
    Frontier Studies 1995*, Oxford: Oxbow Books 1997, 135–41 (Filey)
ArchJ cliv (1997), 248 (Scarborough)
Scarborough Archaeological and Historical Society Transactions 33
    (1997), 6–13
RIB I, 721 (Ravenscar)

Chapter 8

General
**OS *Map of Hadrian's Wall*, 2nd edn HMSO 1972 (more handsome
    and more detailed than its successor, *Ordnance Survey Historical
    Map and Guide: Hadrian's Wall*, HMSO 1989)
**D J BREEZE, *Hadrian's Wall: a souvenir guide to the Roman Wall*,
    4th edn, EH 2001
*J COLLINGWOOD BRUCE, *Handbook to the Roman Wall*, 13th edn,

revised by C DANIELS, Newcastle upon Tyne: Harold Hill 1978 (14th edn, revised by D J BREEZE, is in preparation)

*D J BREEZE & B DOBSON, *Hadrian's Wall*, 4th edn, Harmondsworth: Penguin 2000

*S JOHNSON, *The English Heritage Book of Hadrian's Wall*, Batsford 1989

*D GREEN, *Discovering Hadrian's Wall*, Edinburgh: John Donald 1992

*G DE LA BÉDOYÈRE, *Hadrian's Wall: history and guide*, Stroud: Tempus 1998

*G B D JONES & D J WOOLLISCROFT, *Hadrian's Wall from the Air*, Stroud: Tempus 2001

*R EMBLETON & F GRAHAM, *Hadrian's Wall in the Days of the Romans*, Newcastle upon Tyne: Frank Graham 1984

*D SHOTTER, *The Roman Frontier in Britain*, Preston: Carnegie Publishing 1996

E BIRLEY, *Research on Hadrian's Wall*, Kendal: Titus Wilson 1961

C DANIELS (edn), *The Eleventh Pilgrimage of Hadrian's Wall 26 August–1 September 1989*, Carlisle: Cumberland and Westmorland Antiquarian and Archaeological Society and the Society of Antiquaries of Newcastle upon Tyne 1989

P BIDWELL (edn), *Hadrian's Wall 1989–1999*, Carlisle: Cumberland and Westmorland Antiquarian and Archaeological Society and the Society of Antiquaries of Newcastle upon Tyne 1999

D J A TAYLOR, *The Forts on Hadrian's Wall: a comparative analysis of the form and construction of some buildings* [BAR British Series 395], Oxford: Archaeopress 2000

J C MANN, *The Northern Frontier in Britain from Hadrian to Honorius*, Durham: University of Durham 1969 (ancient texts)

B R HARTLEY, 'Roman York and the northern military command', in R M BUTLER (edn), *Soldier and Civilian in Roman Yorkshire*, Leicester: University of Leicester Press 1971, 55–69

G B D JONES, 'The Solway Frontier: interim report, 1976–81', *Britannia* xiii (1982), 283–97

R L BELLHOUSE, *Roman Sites on the Cumberland Coast: a new schedule of coastal sites*, Carlisle: Cumberland and Westmorland Antiquarian and Archaeological Society 1989

N HODGSON, 'The Stanegate: a frontier rehabilitated', *Britannia* xxxi (2000), 11–22

D CHARLESWORTH, 'The turrets on Hadrian's Wall', in M R APTED, R GILYARD-BEER & A D SAUNDERS (eds.), *Ancient Monuments and their Interpretation*, Chichester: Phillimore 1977, 13–26

J G CROW, 'A review of current research on the turrets and curtain of Hadrian's Wall', *Britannia* xxii (1991), 51–63

M HASSALL, 'The date of the rebuilding of Hadrian's turf wall in stone', *Britannia* xv (1984), 242–4

B DOBSON, 'The function of Hadrian's Wall', *AA*[5] xiv (1986), 1–30

P R HILL & B DOBSON, 'The design of Hadrian's Wall and its implications', *AA*[5] xx (1992), 27–52

P T BIDWELL & M WATSON, 'Excavations on Hadrian's Wall at Denton, Newcastle upon Tyne, 1986–9', *AA*[5] xxiv (1996), 1–56, at 23–26 (fallen plaster rendering)

P R HILL, 'The stone turrets of Hadrian's Wall', *AA*[5] xxv (1997), 27–51

R KENDAL, 'Transport logistics associated with the building of Hadrian's Wall', *Britannia* xxvii (1996), 129–52

CA 164 (August 1999), 283–317 (Hadrian's Wall special issue)

The first and third works cited above give full details about how much of the Wall and its attendant structures are visible today, and should be consulted for all sites, although they are now badly out of date; but the two pilgrimage handbooks of 1989 and 1999 (edited by C DANIELS & P BIDWELL: see above) are indispensable for information on the latest research. For visible examples of temporary camps and practice camps in the Wall region, see H WELFARE & V SWAN, *Roman Camps in England*, HMSO 1995, 51–2, 74–5, 79–85, 90–2, 100–18, 120–3, 127–9 and 131–3. Below are listed some other items published (mostly) since 1978.

South Shields

**P BIDWELL, *The Roman Fort of Arbeia at South Shields*, Newcastle upon Tyne: Tyne and Wear Museums, revised edn 1996

J N DORE & J P GILLAM, *The Roman Fort at South Shields*, Newcastle upon Tyne: Society of Antiquaries of Newcastle upon Tyne 1979

R MIKET, *The Roman Fort at South Shields: excavation of the defences 1977–81*, Gateshead: Tyne and Wear County Council Museums 1983

P BIDWELL & S SPEAK, *Excavations at South Shields Roman Fort. Volume 1*, Newcastle upon Tyne: Society of Antiquaries of Newcastle upon Tyne with Tyne and Wear Museums 1994

Britannia xvii (1986), 332–3 (name); xviii (1987), 315; xix (1988), 431–3; xx (1989), 272–3; xxi (1990), 315; xxii (1991), 232; xxiii (1992), 267–9; xxv (1994), 264–5; xxvi (1995), 342–4; xxvii (1996), 408-10; xxviii (1997), 416 ; xxix (1998), 385; xxx (1999), 340; xxxi (2000), 385–9; xxxii (2001), 322–7

CA 133 (March/April 1993), 23–7

Arbeia Journal 6–7 (1997–8) [2001], 1–23 (possible shipwreck); *ibid.* 25–36 (1999/2000 excavations); *ibid.* 55–60 (ring-mail shirt)

RIB I, 1060 (aqueduct), 1064–5 (tombstones)

Wallsend

**w b griffiths, *Segedunum. Roman fort, baths and museum*, Newcastle upon Tyne: Tyne and Wear Museums 2000

Britannia vii (1976), 306–8; viii (1977), 371–2; ix (1978), 419; xi (1980), 355–8; xii (1981), 322; xiii (1982), 340–2; xiv (1983), 289; xv (1984), 277–8; xvi (1985), 268–70; xx (1989), 273; xxix (1998), 383–4; xxx (1999), 334–9; xxxi (2000), 389; xxxii (2001), 326

Newcastle upon Tyne

**l allason-jones, *A Guide to the Inscriptions and Sculptured Stones in the Museum of Antiquities of the University and the Society of Antiquaries of Newcastle-upon-Tyne*, Newcastle: Department of Archaeology 1989

RIB I, 1051 (Victory monument, *diffusis [barbaris] provincia [reciperatata]*); 1276 (High Rochester, Urbicus); 1284 (ditto, Mars and Hercules); 1280–1 (ditto, *ballistarium*); 1327–9 (Benwell, Antenociticus); 1340 (Benwell, *classis Britannica*); 1638 (MC 38); *RIB* II, 2415.55 (Anextiomarus)

Rudchester

AA[5] 19 (1991), 25–31 (field survey)

Haltonchesters

AA[5] xviii (1990), 55–62 (field survey); xxv (1997), 51–60; xxviii (2000), 37–46 (geophysical survey)

Britannia xxxii (2001), 328–9 (geophysical survey)

Corbridge

**j n dore, *Corbridge Roman Site, Northumberland*, EH 1989 (guidebook)

**m c bishop, *Corstopitum: an Edwardian excavation*, EH 1994 (historic photographs)

l allason-jones & m c bishop, *Excavations at Roman Corbridge: the hoard* [EH Archaeological Report 7], HBMC 1988

m c bishop & j n dore, *Corbridge. Excavations of the Roman fort and town 1947–80* [EH Archaeological Report 8], HBMC 1989

Chesters Bridge

p t bidwell & n holbrook, *Hadrian's Wall Bridges* [EH Archaeological Report 9], HBMCE 1989, 1–49

Britannia xxiii (1992), 269

Arbeia Journal I (1992), 40–4

Chesters
**J S JOHNSON, *Chesters Roman Fort, Northumberland*, EH 1990
    (guidebook)
AA[5] vii (1979), 114–26 (Hadrianic inscription)

Carrawburgh
**C DANIELS, *Mithras and his Temples on the Wall*, 3rd edn 1989,
    Newcastle: Museum of Antiquities at the University of Newcastle
    and Society of Antiquities of Newcastle upn Tyne
L ALLASON-JONES & B MCKAY, *Coventina's Well: a shrine on Hadrian's
    Wall*, Chesters: Trustees of the Clayton Collection 1985
RIB I, 1554–6 (*mithraeum*)

Sewingshields
AA[5] xii (1984), 33–147

Housesteads
**J CROW, *Housesteads Roman Fort, Northumberland*, EH 1989
    (guidebook)
*J CROW, *The English Heritage Book of Housesteads*, Batsford 1995

Barcombe quarry
Britannia vii (1976), 154 (wedge-marks)
J C COULSTON & E J PHILLIPS, *Corpus Signorum Imperii Romani Great
    Britain I.6. Hadrian's Wall West of the North Tyne, and Carlisle*,
    Oxford: Oxford University Press for the British Academy 1988,
    nos. 390 (boar) and 442 (phallus)

Vindolanda
**R BIRLEY, *Vindolanda*, Greenhead: Roman Army Museum
    Publications 1999 (guidebook)
*A BIRLEY, *Garrison Life at Vindolanda: a band of brothers*, Stroud:
    Tempus 2002
P T BIDWELL, *The Roman Fort of Vindolanda*, HBMCE 1985
R BIRLEY *ET AL.*, *Vindolanda Research Reports*, new series, 4 vols. to
    date, Hexham: Roman Army Museum Publications 1994–
R BIRLEY, J BLAKE & A BIRLEY, *1997 Excavations at Vindolanda. The*
    Praetorium *site*, Greenhead: Roman Army Museum Publications
    1998
R & A BIRLEY & J BLAKE, *1998 Excavations at Vindolanda. The*
    Praetorium *site*, Greenhead: Roman Army Museum Publications
    1999
A BIRLEY, *Vindolanda Military Bath-houses: excavations of 1970 and
    2000*, Greenhead: Roman Army Museum Publications 2001
**A BOWMAN, *The Roman Writing Tablets from Vindolanda*, British
    Museum Publications 1983

*A K BOWMAN, *Life and Letters on the Roman frontier*, British Museum Publications 1994

A K BOWMAN & J D THOMAS, *Vindolanda: the Latin writing tablets* [Britannia Monographs 4], Society for the Promotion of Roman Studies 1983

A K BOWMAN & J D THOMAS, *The Vindolanda Writing Tablets (Tabulae Vindolandenses II)*, British Museum Publications 1994

CA 153 (July 1997), 348–57; 178 (March 2002), 436–45

Britannia xxvii (1996), 299–328 (new writing tablets)

Britannia xviii (1987), 315–16; xix (1988), 434; xxiii (1992), 269–70; xxxi (2000), 390–1; xxxii (2001), 330

Peel Crag to Highshields Crags

*R WOODSIDE & J CROW, *Hadrian's Wall: an historic landscape*, National Trust 1999

CA 96 (April 1985), 16–19

Britannia xiv (1983), 290; xv (1984), 280; xvi (1985), 271; xvii (1986), 378–81; xviii (1987), 316–18; xix (1988), 434–6

Greatchesters

Britannia xxi (1990), 285–9 (aqueduct)

Carvoran

*R BIRLEY, *The Fort at the Rock: Magna and Carvoran on Hadrian's Wall*, Greenhead: Roman Army Museum Publications 1998

AA^5 xii (1984), 242–3 (Carvoran measure)

Britannia xxxi (2000), 391; xxxii (2001), 330–2

RIB I, 1778 (AD 136/8), 1783 (Jupiter of Baalbeck), 1792 (AD 163/6 and *dea Syria*); II, 2415.56 (*modius*)

Willowford Bridge

P T BIDWELL & N HOLBROOK, *Hadrian's Wall Bridges* [EH Archaeological Report 9], HBMCE 1989, 50–98

Birdoswald

**T WILMOTT, *Birdoswald Roman Fort: a history and souvenir guide*, Carlisle: Cumbria County Council 1995 (guidebook)

*T. WILMOTT, *Birdoswald Roman Fort: 1800 years on Hadrian's Wall*, Stroud: Tempus 2001

T WILMOTT, *Birdoswald. Excavations of a Roman fort on Hadrian's Wall and its successor settlements: 1987–92* [EH Archaeological Report 14], EH 1997

Britannia xxi (1990), 289–92 (Legio VI Victrix and the Wall near Birdoswald); xxx (1999), 91–110 (geophysical survey of fort); xxxi (2000), 391 (NW corner of fort, interior); xxxii (2001), 331–4 (geophysical survey of *vicus*)

Stanwix
Britannia xvi (1985), 271; xxix (1998), 382–3

Carlisle
ArchJ cxxxv (1978), 115–37
CA 68 (August 1979), 268–72; 86 (March 1983), 77–81; 101 (August
    1986), 171–7
Britannia xxiii (1992), 45–110 (first Flavian fort, annexe); xxvii
    (1996), 345–53 ('*mansio*' including Tullie House tank); xxix
    (1998), 31–84 (writing tablets)
RIB I, 986–7 (Cocidius, Bewcastle), 1935 (MC 50), 2059 (Bowness)

Chapter 9

General
G S MAXWELL, *The Romans in Scotland*, Edinburgh: James Thin, The
    Mercat Press 1989
*D BREEZE, *Roman Scotland: frontier country*, Batsford 1996
*L KEPPIE, *Scotland's Roman Remains*, 2nd edn, Edinburgh: John
    Donald 1998
**G MAXWELL, *A Gathering of Eagles: scenes from Roman Scotland*,
    Edinburgh: Canongate Books with Historic Scotland 1998
W S HANSON & D J BREEZE, 'The future of Roman Scotland', in W S
    HANSON & E A SLATER (eds.), *Scottish Archaeology: new
    perceptions*, Aberdeen: Aberdeen University Press 1991, 57–80

§1 Between the Walls

General
*J COLLINGWOOD BRUCE, *Handbook to the Roman Wall*, 13th edn, rev.
    by C DANIELS, Newcastle upon Tyne: Harold Hill 1978, 287–326
K A STEER, 'Roman and Native in Southern Scotland', *ArchJ* cxxi
    (1964), 164–7
**G JOBEY, *A Field Guide to Prehistoric Northumberland Part 2*,
    Newcastle upon Tyne: Frank Graham 1974 (lists with grid
    references and instructions on how to find the native settlements of
    Romano-British date still visible on the ground)

Waterfalls and *High House*
SEDGLEY, *op. cit.* (see Archaeology of Roman Britain: Roads), nos.
    106–7

Swine Hill to *Chew Green*
I A RICHMOND, 'The Romans in Redesdale', *Northumberland County
    History*, xv (1940), 63–159
H WELFARE & V SWAN, *Roman Camps in England: the field*

archaeology, HMSO 1995, 72–4, 75–9, 85–90, 92–5, 97–100, 123–7, 130–1 and 133–4
Britannia xxvii (1996), 408 (Dere Street sections)

Risingham
RIB I, 1234–5 (south gate, *principia*)

High Rochester
CA 164 (August 1999), 290–4 (recent work)
AA[5] xii (1984), 1–31 (cemetery)
RIB I, 1262 (*exploratores*); 1273 (Featherwood, now at Horsley); 1279 (AD 216)

Sills Burn South
Northern Archaeology 12 (1995), 39–43

South Yardhope
Britannia xiv (1983), 143–53

Pennymuir
RCHM (Scotland), *Roxburgh II*, HMSO 1956, 375–7

Woden Law
ibid. 169–72; *PSAS* cxii (1982), 277–84

Newstead
**w ELLIOTT, *The Trimontium Story*, 3rd edn, Melrose: The Trimontium Trust 1998
J CURLE, *A Roman Frontier Post and its People. The fort of Newstead*, Glasgow: Glasgow Univeristy Press 1911
PSAS 84 (1950), 1–38; cxxix (1999), 373–91 (north annexe); *ibid.* 393–8 (gems)
Britannia xix (1988), 431; xx (1989), 272; xxi (1990), 313–14; xxii (1991), 230; xxiii (1992), 267; xxv (1994), 260–1; xxvi (1995), 337–41; xxviii (1997), 412–14; xxix (1998), 381; xxx (1999), 332

Lyne
RCHM (Scotland), *Peebleshire I*, HMSO 1967, 172–5

Castle Greg
RCHM (Scotland), *Midlothian and West Lothian*, HMSO 1929, 140
Britannia xx (1989), 271

Bothwellhaugh
RCAHMS, *Lanarkshire*, Edinburgh: HMSO 1978, 119–21
Glasgow Archaeological Journal viii (1981), 46–94

Birrens

A S ROBERTSON, *Birrens (Blatobulgium)*, Edinburgh: Dumfries and
    Galloway Natural History and Antiquarian Society 1975
RIB I, 2110 (AD 157/8)

Burnswark
ArchJ cxv (1958), 234–6
Historia xxi (1972), 99–113
*Transactions of the Dumfriesshire and Galloway Natural History and
    Antiquarian Society* liii (1977–8), 57–104

§2 The Antonine Wall

**OS *Map of the Antonine Wall*, 2nd edn, HMSO 1975
G MACDONALD, *The Roman Wall in Scotland*, 2nd edn, Oxford:
    Clarendon Press 1934
W S HANSON & G S MAXWELL, *Rome's North West Frontier: the
    Antonine Wall*, Edinburgh: Edinburgh University Press 1983
*A S ROBERTSON, *The Antonine Wall*, 5th edn rev. by L J F KEPPIE,
    Glasgow: Glasgow Archaeological Society 2001
*D J BREEZE & B DOBSON, *Hadrian's Wall*, Harmondsworth: Penguin,
    4th edn 2000, 88–131
J P GILLAM, 'Possible changes in plan in the course of the construction
    of the Antonine Wall', *Scottish Archaeological Forum 7*,
    Edinburgh 1975, 51–6
L J F KEPPIE, 'The Antonine Wall 1960–1980', *Britannia* xiii (1982),
    91–111
N HODGSON, 'Were there two Antonine occupations of Scotland?',
    Britannia xxvi (1995), 29–49
D J WOOLLISCROFT, 'Signalling and the design of the Antonine Wall',
    Britannia xxvii (1996), 153–77
L J F KEPPIE, *Roman Inscribed and Sculptured Stones in the Hunterian
    Museum, University of Glasgow* [Britannia Monographs 13],
    Society for Promotion of Roman Studies 1998
**L J F KEPPIE, *Roman Distance Slabs from the Antonine Wall. A brief
    guide*, Glasgow: Hunterian Museum 1979

Kinneil
PSAS cxxvi (1996), 303–46

Cramond
Britannia v (1974), 163–224; viii (1977), 368; xxiii (1992), 264; xxix
    (1998), 380 (sculpture)
CA 59 (November 1977), 378–81; 155 (December 1997), 404–7
L J F KEPPIE & B J ARNOLD, *Corpus Signorum Imperii Romani Great
    Britain I.4, Scotland*, Oxford: Oxford University Press for the
    British Academy 1988, no. 65 (Eagle Rock)

Callendar Park
PSAS cxxv (1995), 577–600 (*lilia*, possible 'turret'?)

Bar Hill
A ROBERTSON, M SCOTT & L KEPPIE, *Bar Hill, a Roman Fort and its Finds*, Oxford: BAR 1975
Glasgow Archaeological Journal xii (1985), 49–81

Bearsden
**D J BREEZE, *The Roman Fort at Bearsden. 1973 excavations*, Edinburgh: Department of the Environment 1974
D J BREEZE, in D J BREEZE (ed.), *Studies in Scottish Antiquity Presented to Stewart Cruden*, Edinburgh: John Donald 1984, 32–68

§3 Romans in the Far North

General
O G S CRAWFORD, *The Topography of Roman Scotland North of the Antonine Wall*, Cambridge: Cambridge University Press 1949
R M OGILVIE & I A RICHMOND (eds.), *Tacitus' Agricola*, Oxford: Oxford University Press 1967, especially 52–76
J KENWORTHY (ed.), *Agricola's Campaigns in Scotland* (Scottish Archaeological Forum 12), Edinburgh: Edinburgh University Press 1981
*W S HANSON, *Agricola and the Conquest of the North*, Batsford 1987
G MAXWELL, *A Battle Lost: Romans and Caledonians at Mons Graupius*, Edinburgh: Edinburgh University Press 1990
J K ST JOSEPH, 'Air Reconnaissance in Britain 1965–8', *JRS* lix (1969), 113–19
J K ST JOSEPH, 'Air Reconnaissance in Britain 1969–72', *JRS* lxiii (1973), 228–33
J K ST JOSEPH, 'Air Reconnaissance in Britain 1973–6', *JRS* lxvii (1977), 143–5
J K ST JOSEPH, 'The camp at Durno and Mons Graupius', *Britannia* ix (1978), 271–88
A S HOBLEY, 'The numismatic evidence for the post-Agricolan abandonment of the Roman frontier in Scotland', *Britannia* xx (1989), 69–74

Ardoch
**D J BREEZE, *Ardoch Roman Fort, Braco near Dunblane: a guide*, Stirling: Rotary Club of Bridge of Allan & Dunblane 1983
D J BREEZE, in A O'CONNOR & P V CLARKE (eds.), *From the Stone Age to the 'Forty-Five. Studies presented to R B K Stevenson*, Edinburgh: John Donald 1983, 224–36
Britannia i (1970), 163–78; xxvi (1995), 332

Kaims Castle
ArchJ cxxi (1964), 196

Gask Ridge
Transactions of the Perthshire Society of Natural Science, special
    issue 1974, 14–29
D WOOLLISCROFT, in N J HIGHAM (ed.), *Archaeology of the Roman
    Empire: a tribute to the life and works of Professor Barri Jones*
    [BAR International Series 940], Oxford: Archaeopress 2001,
    85–93

Dunning
JRS lxiii (1973), 218–19; lxvii (1977), 140
Britannia i (1970), 274; xxvi (1995), 51–62
MAXWELL, *op. cit.* (see above, §3 General), 101–4

Inchtuthil
L F PITTS & J K ST JOSEPH, *Inchtuthil, the Roman Legionary Fortress*
    [Britannia Monographs 6], Society for Promotion of Roman
    Studies 1985
E A M SHIRLEY, *The Construction of the Roman Legionary Fortress at
    Inchtuthil* [BAR British Series 298], Oxford: Archaeopress 2000
*E A M SHIRLEY, *Building a Roman Legionary Fortress*, Stroud:
    Tempus 2001
Britannia xxvi (1985), 309–12; xxvi (1995), 309–12 (hospital); xxvii
    (1996), 111–28 (construction time); 397 (Cleaven Dyke Neolithic);
    xxx (1999), 297–9 (angle of pitch in roofs)

Kirkbuddo
CRAWFORD, *op. cit.* (see above, §3 General), 97–100

Raedykes
Ibid. 108–10
PSAS l (1916), 318–48

Normandykes
CRAWFORD, *op. cit.* (see above, §3 General), 110–12

Chapter Ten

General
R MERRIFIELD, *The Roman City of London*, Benn 1965
W F GRIMES, *The Excavation of Roman and Medieval London*,
    Routledge 1968
*A SORRELL, *Roman London*, Batsford 1969 (reconstruction-drawings)
*P MARSDEN, *Roman London*, Thames & Hudson 1980

J MORRIS, *Londinium: London in the Roman Empire*, Weidenfeld 1982

*R MERRIFIELD, *London, City of the Romans*, Batsford 1983

D PERRING, *Roman London*, Seaby 1991

C MALONEY, *The Upper Walbrook in the Roman Period* [Archaeology of Roman London 1], CBA and Museum of London 1990

D PERRING & S ROSKAMS, *Early Development of Roman London West of the Walbrook* [Archaeology of Roman London 2; CBA Research Report 70], CBA and Museum of London 1991

T WILLIAMS, *Public Buildings in the South-West Quarter of Roman London* [Archaeology of Roman London 3; CBA Research Report 88], CBA and Museum of London 1993

*G MILNE, *The English Heritage Book of Roman London*, Batsford 1995

J BIRD, M HASSALL & H SHELDON (eds.), *Interpreting Roman London*, Oxford: Oxbow 1996

B WATSON (ed.), *Roman London: recent archaeological work* [Journal of Roman Archaeology, Supplement Volume 24], Portsmouth, Rhode Island 1998

I HAYNES, H SHELDON & L HANNIGAN (eds.), *London Under Ground: the archaeology of a city*, Oxford: Oxbow 2000, 52–174

*J HALL & R MERRIFIELD, *Roman London*, HMSO and Museum of London 1986

**Londinium: a descriptive map and guide to Roman London*, 2nd edn, Ordnance Survey/HMSO 1988

**The London Wall Walk*, Museum of London 1985

CA 143 (June 1998), 44–56, 72–4 (various)

Origins
Transactions of the London and Middlesex Archaeological Society xxiv (1973), 1–73 (possible fort)

London Archaeologist 7.5 (1993), 122–6; *British Archaeology* 1 (February 1995), 7 (first London at Westminster – or Mayfair?)

Waterfront
*G MILNE (ed.), *The Port of Roman London*, Batsford 1985

Britannia xxi (1990), 99–183

Forum and Basilica
P MARSDEN, *The Roman Forum Site in London: discoveries before 1985*, HMSO 1987

G MILNE (ed.), *From Roman Basilica to Medieval Market: archaeology in action in the City of London*, HMSO 1992

Britannia xxi (1990), 53–97; xxiii (1992), 292

London Archaeologist 7.2 (1993), 31–6

'Palace'
CA 8 (May 1968), 215–19
Transactions of the London and Middlesex Archaeological Society
    xxvi (1975), 1–102
G MILNE, in BIRD *ET AL., op. cit.* (see above, General), 49–55

Baths and waterworks
CA 115 (June 1989), 244–5 (Huggin Hill)
Britannia xxi (1990), 342–4 (Huggin Hill); xxx (1999), 359–60
    (Botolph Lane)
Archaeology Matters 15 (September 2001), 7 (bucket and chain
    systems)

Amphitheatre
*N BATEMAN, *Gladiators at the Guildhall: the story of London's
    Roman amphitheatre and medieval Guildhall*, Museum of London
    Archaeology Service 2000
CA 137 (February/March 1994), 164–71
Britannia xxviii (1997), 51–85
NewsWARP 25 (1999), 19–22 (pine used)

Mithraeum
J SHEPHERD, *The Temple of Mithras, London. Excavations by W F
    Grimes and A Williams at the Walbrook* [EH Archaeological Report
    12], EH 1998
J M C TOYNBEE, *The Roman Art Treasures from the Temple of Mithras*
    [Special Paper 7], London and Middlesex Archaeological Society
    1986

Houses and shops
P ROWSOME, *Heart of the City: Roman medieval and modern London
    revealed by archaeology at 1, Poultry*, EH and Museum of London
    2000
London Archaeologist (Winter 1968), 3–5 (Lower Thames Street)
AntiqJ lvii (1977), 54–6 (Lower Thames Street)
Britannia xx (1989), 305 (Gutter Lane); xxii (1991), 271 (Lower
    Thames Street); xxxii (2001), 365–6 (Plantation Place)
ARA: Bulletin of the Association of Roman Archaeology 10 (February
    2001), 8–10 (Plantation Place)
Archaeology Matters 14 (May 2001), 2 (Gresham Street round
    houses)

Defences
J MALONEY, in J MALONEY & B HOBLEY (eds.), *Roman Urban Defences
    in the West* [CBA Research Report 51], CBA 1983, 96–117
CA 73 (August 1980), 55–60

Britannia xxii (1991), 265 (Houndsditch and Cooper's Row); xxx (1999), 358 (former GPO)

Cemeteries
J HALL, in BIRD *ET AL.*, *op. cit.* (see above, General), 57–84
B BARBER & D BOWSHER, *The Eastern Cemetery of Roman London* [MoLAS Monograph 4], Museum of London Archaeology Service 2000
Britannia xxxi (2000), 415 (Atlantic House)

Southark
****The Big Dig. Archaeology and the Jubilee Line extension*, Museum of London Archaeology, Service for the Jubilee Line Extension Project 1998
****Below Southwark: the archaeological story*, London Borough of Southwark for the Southwark and Lambeth Archaeological Excavation Committee 2000
A MACKINDER, *A Romano-British Cemetery on Watling Street* [MoLAS Archaeology Studies 4], Museum of London Archaeology Service 2000

Museum of London
Britannia xxii (1991), 159–72 (Southwark painting)
****C JONES, *Roman Mosaics*, Museum of London 1988
Mosaic 28 (2001), 11–12 (Gresham Street mosaic)
****H SWAIN & M ROBERTS, *The Spitalfields Roman*, Museum of London 1999
Minerva 7.4 (July/August 1996), 55–8 (new displays); 10.4 (July/August 1999), 25–8 (Spitalfields lady)
R S O TOMLIN, in BIRD ET AL, *op. cit.* (see above, General), 209–15 (sale of a Kentish wood)
RIB I, 17 (Marcianus); II, 2491.147 (Austalis); 2492.24 (fish-sauce)

British Museum
****Guide to the Antiquities of Roman Britain*, 3rd edn, Trustees of the British Museum 1964
****K S PAINTER, *The Mildenhall Treasure*, British Museum Publications 1977
****K S PAINTER, *The Water Newton Early Christian Silver*, British Museum Publications 1977
C JOHNS & T W POTTER, *The Thetford Treasure*, British Museum Publications 1983
****C JOHNS & R BLAND, *The Hoxne Treasure. An illustrated introduction*, British Museum Press 1993
A WOODWARD & P LEACH, *The Uley Shrines. Excavation of a ritual

complex on West Hill, Uley, 1977–9 [EH Archaeological Report
17], EH and British Museum Press 1993

R P J JACKSON & T W POTTER, *Excavations at Stonea Cambridgeshire
1980–85*, British Museum Press 1996

C JOHNS, *The Snettisham Roman Jeweller's Hoard*, British Museum
Press 1997

A KING, in P JOHNSON & I HAYNES, *Architecture in Roman Britain*
[CBA Research Report 94], York: CBA 1996, 56–69 (Meonstoke)

British Museum Magazine, Spring 2000, 22 (Hinton St Mary and coin
of Magnentius)

Archäologischer Anzeiger 1986, 571–81 (Birdoswald Hercules a
falsum?)

Britannia xxi (1990), 355 (Meonstoke); xxv (1994), 165–73 (Hoxne
treasure); xxvi (1995), 312–15 (Corbridge *lanx*); xxvi (1995), 323
(Thetford treasure); *ibid.* 391–3 (Hoxne treasure)

Minerva 2.6 (November/December 1991), 6–13 (Risley Park *lanx*)

RIB I, 12 (Classicianus), 812 (Maryport); 255, 258 (Lincoln soldiers)

L'Année Épigraphique 1922, 116 (Bordeaux)

Index